270

Contents

Introduction

London was – in the 19th century – a wonder of the world. The first city since ancient times to top a million inhabitants, an industrial powerhouse at the heart of the world's largest empire, it drew Monet from Paris to paint the smoggy Thames from the Savoy, while bad-boy poet Arthur Rimbaud saw in the city's vast railway stations cathedrals to modernity. Immigrants still feel London's pull today, bringing not wonder but their own energy and new ideas. You might feel it too, in our out-there nightlife, our food – once an international joke, now a rich stew of global influences and creativity – and our nation-defining cultural edifices, whether museums or theatres. London lives life at two paces. Where there is most money, things are more sedate, with the whisper of history audible in fine buildings and heritage sites that in places date to Roman times. Elsewhere, increasingly in the neighbourhoods beyond central London, the city is young, rich in variety and always hurrying after the next new thing. This guide takes you to the best of both Londons. We hope you enjoy our city.

Sky Garden p236

ABOUT THE GUIDE

This is one of a series of Time Out guidebooks to cities across the globe. Written by local experts, our guides are thoroughly researched and meticulously updated. They aim to be inspiring, irreverent, well-informed and trustworthy.

Time Out London is divided into five sections: Discover, Explore, Experience, Understand and Plan.

Discover introduces the city and provides inspiration for your visit.

Explore is the main sightseeing section of the guide and includes detailed listings and reviews for sights and museums; restaurants ⑩; pubs and bars ⑩; and shops ⑩, all organised by area with corresponding street maps for the key areas. To help navigation, each area of London has been assigned its own colour.

Experience covers the cultural life of the city in depth, including festivals, film, LGBT, music, nightlife, theatre and more.

Understand provides in-depth background information that places London in its historical and architectural context.

Plan offers practical visitor information, including accommodation options and details of public transport.

Hearts

We use hearts ♥ to pick out venues, sights and experiences in the city that we particularly recommend. The very best of these are featured in the Top 20 (*see p12*) and receive extended coverage in the guide.

Maps

A detachable fold-out map can be found on the inside back cover. There are also two overview maps (Greater London on *pp8-9*; Central London by area on *pp10-11*) and individual street maps for each of the key areas of the city. The venues featured in the guide have been given a grid reference so that you can find them easily on the maps and on the ground.

Prices

All our **restaurant listings** are marked with a pound symbol category from budget to blow-out (**£-££££**), indicating the price you should expect to pay for an average three-course meal for two (or the equivalent in a café or sharing plates venue) with drinks and service: **£** = under £60; **££** = £60-£100; **£££** = £100-£140; **££££** = over £140.

A similar system is used in our **Accommodation** chapter based on the hotel's standard prices for one night in a double room: **£** = under £130; **££** = £130-£250; **£££** = £250-£350; **££££** = over £350.

Discover

St Paul's Cathedral p224

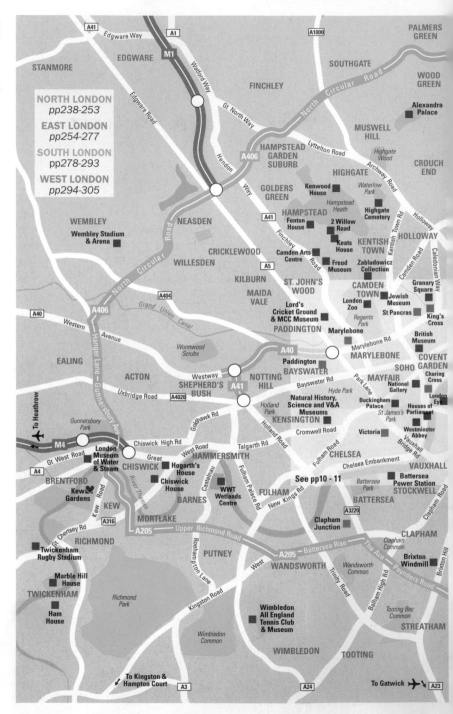

NORTH LONDON
pp238-253

EAST LONDON
pp254-277

SOUTH LONDON
pp278-293

WEST LONDON
pp294-305

A41
Edgware Way
A1
M1
A1000
PALMERS GREEN
STANMORE
EDGWARE
Watford Way
SOUTHGATE
WOOD GREEN
Gt North Way
North Circular Road
Alexandra Palace
FINCHLEY
Edgware Road
Hendon
MUSWELL HILL
Highgate Wood
CROUCH END
Lyttelton Road
Archway Road
HAMPSTEAD GARDEN SUBURB
A406
Way
HIGHGATE
HOLLOWAY
Kenwood House
Waterlow Park
Highgate Cemetery
Holloway
Kentish Town Rd
GOLDERS GREEN
Hampstead Heath
A41
HAMPSTEAD
Fenton House
2 Willow Road
Keats House
KENTISH TOWN
NEASDEN
Finchley Road
Camden Arts Centre
Freud Museum
Zabludowicz Collection
Camden Road
Caledonian Rd
WEMBLEY
CRICKLEWOOD
WILLESDEN
A5
CAMDEN TOWN
Jewish Museum
Granary Square
Wembley Stadium & Arena
KILBURN
ST. JOHN'S WOOD
London Zoo
St Pancras
King's Cross
A404
MAIDA VALE
Lord's Cricket Ground & MCC Museum
Regents Park
British Museum
North Circular Road
A406
Grand Union Canal
PADDINGTON
Marylebone
Marylebone Rd
A40
Western Avenue
Wormwood Scrubs
A40
Paddington
MARYLEBONE
COVENT GARDEN
EALING
ACTON
Westway
SHEPHERD'S BUSH
A41
NOTTING HILL
BAYSWATER
Bayswater Rd
Park Lane
SOHO
MAYFAIR
National Gallery
Charing Cross
Hanger Lane
Gunnersbury Ave
Uxbridge Road
A4020
Holland Park
Hyde Park
Buckingham Palace
Houses of Parliament
London Eye
Goldhawk Rd
Natural History, Science and V&A Museums
St James's Park
Westminster Abbey
To Heathrow
Gunnersbury Park
Chiswick High Rd
KENSINGTON
Cromwell Road
Victoria
Vauxhall Bridge Rd
M4
Gt West Road
London Museum of Water & Steam
Great
West Road
HAMMERSMITH
Talgarth Rd
CHELSEA
VAUXHALL
A4
CHISWICK
Hogarth's House
Castelnau
Fulham Palace Rd
Chelsea Embankment
STOCKWELL
BRENTFORD
Chiswick House
WWT Wetlands Centre
Fulham Rd
Battersea Park
Battersea Power Station
Kew Gardens
River Thames
BARNES
FULHAM
New Kings Rd
BATTERSEA
Clapham High St
KEW
Kew Road
MORTLAKE
A316
See pp10 - 11
A3220
Clapham Junction
CLAPHAM
Gt Chertsey Rd
A205
Upper Richmond Road
A205
Battersea Rise
Clapham Common
Brixton Windmill
RICHMOND
Roehampton Lane
WANDSWORTH
Wandsworth Common
The Ave
Poynders Road
Twickenham Rugby Stadium
PUTNEY
West
Trinity Road
Balham High Rd
Brixton Road
Marble Hill House
Kingston Road
Wimbledon All England Tennis Club & Museum
Tooting Bec Common
STREATHAM
TWICKENHAM
Ham House
Richmond Park
Wimbledon Common
WIMBLEDON
TOOTING
To Kingston & Hampton Court
A3
A24
To Gatwick
A23

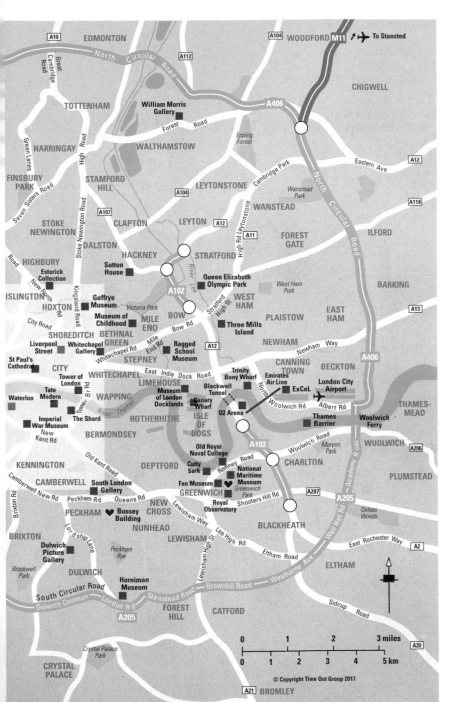

A10 EDMONTON

A104 WOODFORD M11 ✈ To Stansted

North Circular Road

Great Cambridge Road

A112

TOTTENHAM

William Morris Gallery

A406

CHIGWELL

Forest Road

Epping Forest

HARRINGAY

High Road

WALTHAMSTOW

Eastern Ave

A12

Green Lanes

FINSBURY PARK

STAMFORD HILL

A104

LEYTONSTONE

Cambridge Park

Wanstead Park

North Circular Road

A118

Seven Sisters Road

STOKE NEWINGTON

Stoke Newington Road

A107

CLAPTON

LEYTON

A12

WANSTEAD

ILFORD

DALSTON

HACKNEY

STRATFORD

A11

FOREST GATE

BARKING

HIGHBURY

Sutton House

River Lea

Queen Elizabeth Olympic Park

West Ham Park

EAST HAM

A13

Estorick Collection

New North Road

Kingsland Road

Geffrye Museum

A102

WEST HAM

ISLINGTON

HOXTON

Victoria Park

BOW

Stratford High St

PLAISTOW

City Road

Museum of Childhood

MILE END

Bow Rd

Three Mills Island

NEWHAM

Newham Way

A406

SHOREDITCH

BETHNAL GREEN

Mile End Rd

A12

Liverpool Street

Whitechapel Gallery

Ragged School Museum

CANNING TOWN

BECKTON

St Paul's Cathedral

CITY

Whitechapel Rd

STEPNEY

East India Dock Road

Trinity Buoy Wharf

Emirates Air Line

London City Airport

Tower of London

WHITECHAPEL

LIMEHOUSE

Blackwall Tunnel

ExCeL

Tate Modern

Tower Br Rd

WAPPING

Museum of London Docklands

North

Woolwich Rd

Albert Rd

THAMES-MEAD

Waterloo

River Thames

Canary Wharf

O2 Arena

Thames Barrier

Woolwich Ferry

Imperial War Museum

The Shard

ROTHERHITHE

ISLE OF DOGS

Woolwich Rd

Maryon Park

WOOLWICH

A206

New Kent Rd

BERMONDSEY

A102

CHARLTON

Old Kent Road

Old Royal Naval College

Ronney Road

PLUMSTEAD

KENNINGTON

DEPTFORD

Cutty Sark

National Maritime Museum

A207

A205

Academy Rd

Well Hall Rd

CAMBERWELL

South London Gallery

Peckham Rd

Queens Rd

Fan Museum

Greenwich Park

Oxleas Woods

Camberwell New Rd

Brixton Rd

PECKHAM

♥ Bussey Building

NEW CROSS

GREENWICH

Royal Observatory

Shooters Hill Rd

East Rochester Way

A2

Lord ship Lane

NUNHEAD

Lewisham Way

Lee High Rd

BLACKHEATH

ELTHAM

BRIXTON

Dulwich Picture Gallery

Peckham Rye

LEWISHAM

Lewisham High St

Eltham Road

Brockwell Park

DULWICH

Horniman Museum

South Circular Road

London Rd

Stanstead Road

Brownhill Road

Westhorne Ave

Sidcup Road

Dulwich Common

A205

FOREST HILL

CATFORD

Crystal Palace Park

CRYSTAL PALACE

0 1 2 3 miles

0 1 2 3 4 5 km

© Copyright Time Out Group 2017

A20

A21 BROMLEY

9

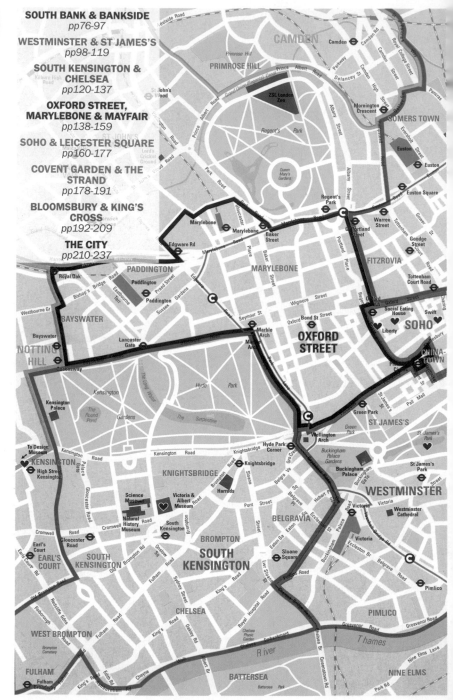

SOUTH BANK & BANKSIDE
pp76-97

WESTMINSTER & ST JAMES'S
pp98-119

SOUTH KENSINGTON & CHELSEA
pp120-137

OXFORD STREET, MARYLEBONE & MAYFAIR
pp138-159

SOHO & LEICESTER SQUARE
pp160-177

COVENT GARDEN & THE STRAND
pp178-191

BLOOMSBURY & KING'S CROSS
pp192-209

THE CITY
pp210-237

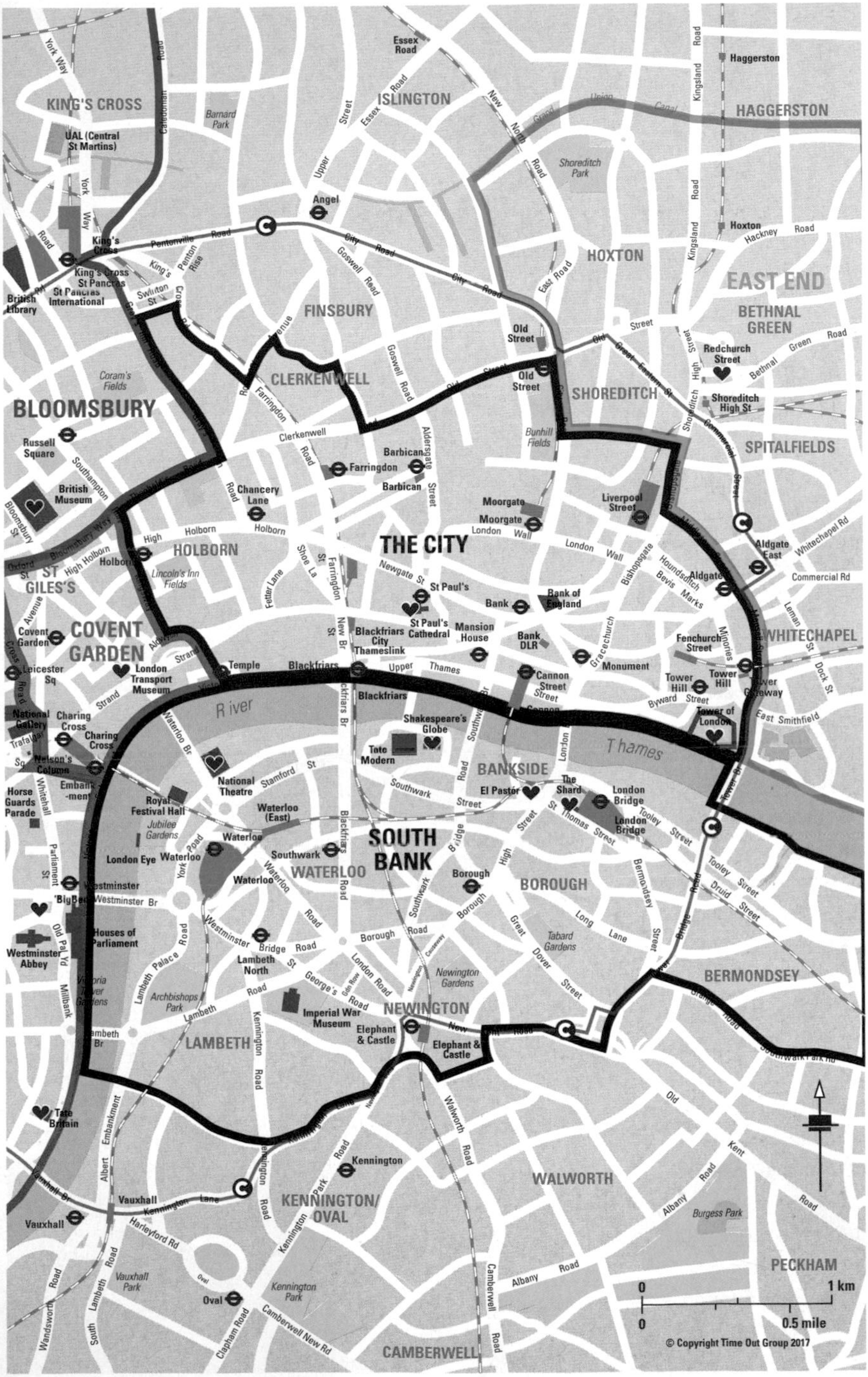

Top 20

From swish cocktails to historic sights, we count down the capital's finest

01

Design Museum *p302*

The loved but often neglected Design Museum finally has a home worthy of its sense of adventure: the former Commonwealth Institute is a dramatic, pioneering building that now houses a superb history of high- and low-brow design, as well as temporary exhibitions that will doubtless be eye-opening, silly, cerebral and fun by turns.

02

The Shard *p94*

A few years ago, we'd write features unlocking the secrets of where to go for the best views of London. Since 2000, when the still-excellent London Eye (*see p82*) opened, viewpoints have materialised in droves – the Walkie Talkie (*see p232*) and controversial extension to Tate Modern (*see p87*) only the more prominent recent additions. But the Shard remains closest to our hearts: it's so tall you almost feel you're on a different plane to the ant city below.

03

National Theatre *p362*

Under Nicholas Hytner, the National Theatre took the world by storm. It was the source of Spielberg's movie *War Horse*, as well as West End smash hit plays *The History Boys*, *One Man Two Guv'nors* and *The Curious Incident of the Dog in the Night-Time*. With Rufus Norris now in charge, it's a notch less populist – and has received some critical brickbats, largely unwarranted – but remains the must-do in this most theatrical city.

04

Social Eating House *p175*

Since he won a Michelin star soon after opening Pollen Street Social in 2011, chef Jason Atherton has opened at least one new London restaurant almost every year. Sosharu, Berners Tavern (*see p207*)… they're all great. But with food that's inventive without becoming too clever, served in a restaurant that always seems to buzz, Social Eating House is our never-fail favourite – and its Blind Pig cocktail bar a temptation in its own right.

05

London Transport Museum *p183*

We love the Museum of London (*see p228*), but for kids – and, more importantly, kids at heart – the thrill of climbing on and off the classic trains and buses at the Transport Museum never fades. That the museum offers a fine social history of the capital, told through its vital infrastructure, is merely a bonus.

06

06

Liberty *p152*

The capital is blessed with many brilliant department stores, from gloriously gaudy Harrods (*see p133*) to trailblazing Selfridges (*see p144*), but none is lovelier or more London than Liberty. Fashioned like a stately home, its jumbled rooms are charmingly old-fashioned – their beams used to belong to a Royal Navy ship – but full of cutting-edge international fashion and beauty brands.

07

Shakespeare's Globe *p360*

London's West End is a powerhouse of international theatre, but the best bargain is undoubtedly seeing one of Shakespeare's plays authentically staged at the Globe. It costs only £5 if you're prepared to stand as a 'groundling'. More expensive, but perhaps even more magical, are the candlelit plays (and period concerts) in the attached Sam Wanamaker Playhouse, a wood-panelled reconstruction of a Jacobean theatre.

08

St Paul's Cathedral *p224*

As architectural masterpieces go, St Paul's is at the frou-frou end of things, with its frothy Baroque exterior. But the grandeur of the interior is quite breathtaking – and no less so for Sir Christopher Wren's audacity in giving the authorities precisely the cathedral they didn't want.

08

09

British Museum *p198*

This is one of the world's greatest museums – and also one of its most popular. No wonder: it's a compendium of key artefacts from most of the significant cultures of the world, from Egyptian mummies and the Rosetta Stone to monumental Mesopotamian sculpture and even an Easter Island head. Every visit uncovers further revelations and, since entry is free, you can head back as often as you wish.

10

El Pastór *p91*

With artisan food markets now popping up in every London suburb, the star of Borough Market (*see p92*), the foodies' favourite™, has somewhat waned. But the tapas supremos Sam and Eddie Hart (Barrafina, *see p185*) knock it out of the park once more with their supremely busy no-booking taco restaurant here. And if the queue's too long, there are plenty of snacking options close at hand.

11

Tate Britain *p111*

Since its dramatic extension opened in 2016, Tate Modern (*see p87*) has been right back in the limelight. But as the architectural plaudits die down, we find ourselves drawn back to the original Tate: lovely premises, blockbuster shows every bit as good as those at its bombastic younger rival and the entire chronological span of British art since 1545 to walk through. It's not so busy, either.

12

Swift *p167*

Soho has long been London's risqué playground, but recently it has needed a bit of a nightlife kickstart: we reckon this cocktail bar is it. Glam-casual upstairs, darkly romantic downstairs, serving cocktails that range from aperitivi to reinvented classics, Edmund Weil and Roisin Stimpson (Nightjar; Oriole, *see p219*) have another huge hit on their hands.

13

Tower of London *p234*

Who doesn't love a castle? The beginnings of this one were built in 1078, when William the Conqueror wanted to point out he was the boss – not just of the city, though it was rebellious, but of the whole country. The Tower was witness to many of the key events in London's history and is now a fabulous showcase for the Crown Jewels, as well as home to the traditionally dressed 'Beefeaters' (Yeoman Warders) and their ravens.

14

Redchurch Street *p265*

In the heart of Shoreditch, this road – once as rough as a badger – has been properly swanked up. It's now London's most fashion-forward street, packed with beautiful shop after beautiful shop. Design-concept-shop-cum-cute-café? Here's Modern Society. Low-key, cool homewares store? There's Labour & Wait. It all makes for a great afternoon mooch.

15

St James's Park *p115*

One of the city's joys is its chain of incredibly central parks: you can walk from Kensington Gardens and Hyde Park through Green Park to St James's barely touching the tarmac. The last is our favourite. Why? It's the prettiest, with lovely lakes for waterfowl – not just ducks, but pelicans too – and has a delicious view of Buckingham Palace.

16

Maritime Greenwich *p282*

The grand colonnades of Wren's Old Royal Naval College (don't miss the restoration tours of the Painted Hall) draw you into historic Greenwich Park, a fine introduction to London's most expansive UNESCO World Heritage Site. It combines the National Maritime Museum, the Queen's House art gallery (reopened after 400th anniversary renovations), the gorgeous *Cutty Sark* sailing ship and, yes, the Prime Meridian.

17

Victoria & Albert Museum *p126*

Stroll into the V&A's main entrance –
that grand hall with its dramatic glass
chandelier – and the scale of this museum
of art and design, with its combination of
stately historical context and cutting-edge
modern design, is already apparent. It's
gallery after grand and gorgeous gallery,
with the reopened Weston Cast Court our
absolute favourite. The Science Museum
(*see p389*) and Natural History Museum
(*see p388*) are fabulous too – but the V&A is
unforgettable.

18

Bussey Building (CLF Art Café) *p341*

Once upon a time our snook was cocked
at the thought of Shoreditch warehouses
as the centre of all things cool – now
Peckham has taken their crown. Yep, if
you want to know what clubbing's about in
London just now, Bussey is where to be –
fun, creative and all mashed-up together.

19

Westminster *p106*

Eye-popping and of huge historic significance, the grand buildings around Parliament Square – collectively recognised as a UNESCO World Heritage Site – are mostly Victorian, but their core is ancient: at the heart of the Houses of Parliament is Westminster Hall, a medieval Great Hall, and almost every British monarch has been crowned in Westminster Abbey.

20

Royal Botanic Gardens (Kew Gardens) *p292*

Its origins reach back to 1759, when royal plant collector Queen Caroline began developing a garden, but Kew keeps up to date with temporary alfresco sculpture exhibitions and a focus on learning about plant habitats and the environment. But relax: this isn't a visit to the classroom, it's time well spent strolling in a huge and lovely garden, with greenhouses full of exquisite, exotic plants.

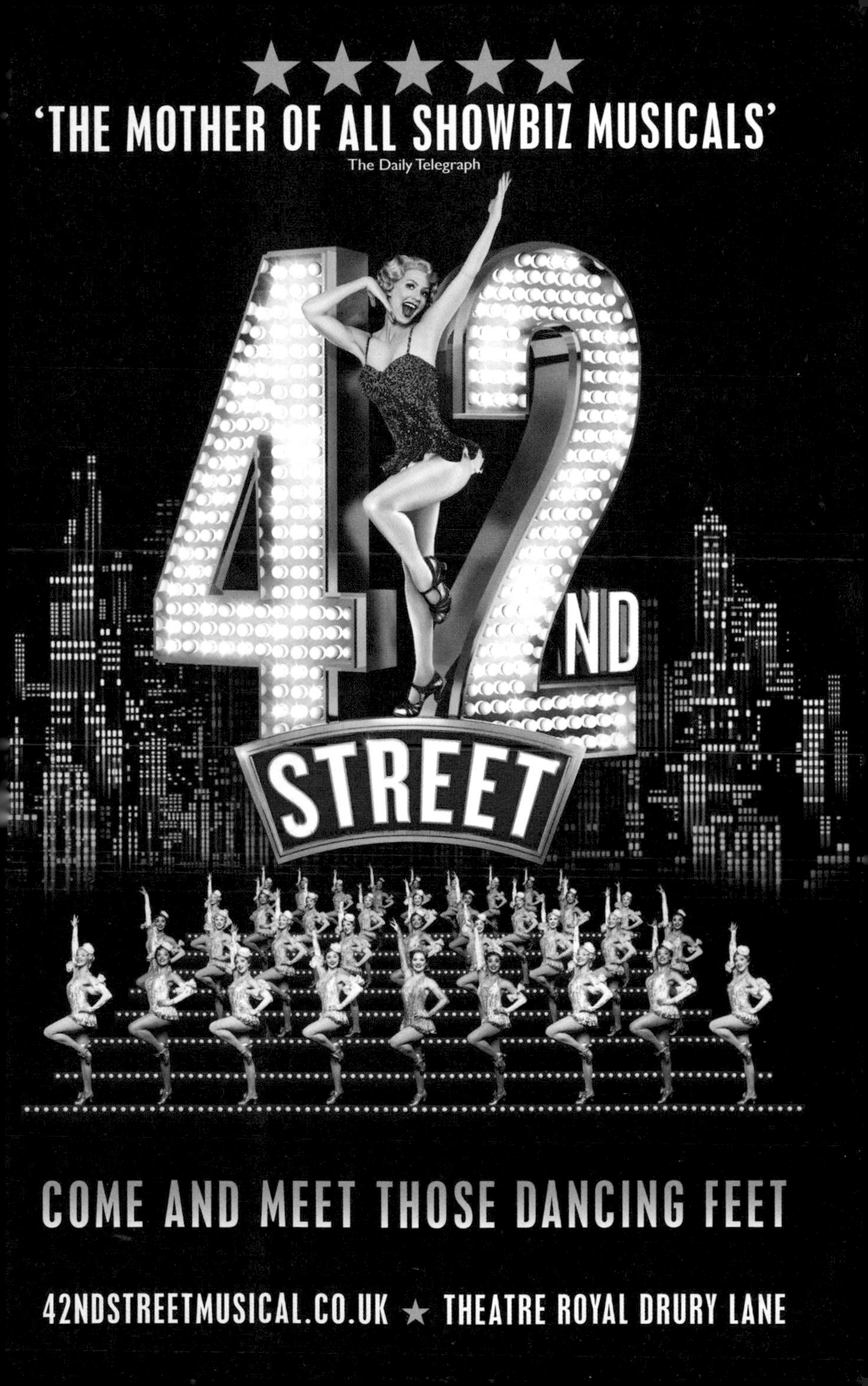
★★★★★
'THE MOTHER OF ALL SHOWBIZ MUSICALS'
The Daily Telegraph
42ND STREET
COME AND MEET THOSE DANCING FEET
42NDSTREETMUSICAL.CO.UK ★ THEATRE ROYAL DRURY LANE

Itineraries

Explore London's storied past in the daytime – enjoy the city's stellar present at night

Trafalgar Square

ESSENTIAL WEEKEND

Budget £200-£250 per person
Getting around walking, tube and Overground trains

▶ *Budgets include transport, meals and admission prices, but not accommodation and shopping.*

DAY 1

Morning

Today is a whistlestop walking tour of historic London. Get to Charing Cross or Leicester Square stations for 10am and start the day in **Trafalgar Square** (*see p102*). The centre of London is an impressive sight, especially when it isn't too full of tourists snapping pictures of themselves with the lions. Far beneath Nelson on his column, the Fourth Plinth bears contemporary art: check out David Shrigley's huge thumbs-up, *Really Good*, which will be replaced in 2018 by Michael Rakowitz's *The Invisible Enemy Should Not Exist* (*see p102*). The masterpieces of the **National Gallery** (*see p103*) – an encyclopaedia of Western art – are on the pedestrianised northern side of the square. But you've only got half an hour: at 10.45am you should head south down Whitehall,

keeping an eye out for the red-coated cavalryman on sentry duty. At 11am, the Horse Guards in shiny helmets and with shiny swords perform the daily **Changing of the Guard** ceremony (*see p311*; it's an hour earlier on Sunday). After the ceremonials, head through the parade ground into **St James's Park** (*see p115*) to see the pelicans and admire **Buckingham Palace** (*see p113*) at the end of the lake. Just out of the park's south-eastern corner is **Parliament Square** (*see p105*). This is a UNESCO World Heritage Site: admire Westminster Abbey, Parliament and the Queen Elizabeth Tower ('Big Ben' to most people). Then cross Westminster Bridge to County Hall and the London Eye and take a stroll east along the **South Bank** (*see p76*). This walk is modern London's biggest tourist cliché, but it's also great fun.

Lunch

By now you'll be famished and exhausted. Just beyond the merry-go-round and under Hungerford Bridge, the area around the **Southbank Centre** (*see p80*) is busy with places to eat, none of them particularly impressive but all perfectly acceptable.

Afternoon

Rejuvenated? Great. Go with the flow east past the **BFI Southbank repertory cinema** (*see p324*) and the **National Theatre** (*see p362*) to newly expanded **Tate Modern** (*see p87*) and Shakespeare's **Globe** (*see p86*), and finish your afternoon by walking across the Millennium Bridge for the slow climb up to 17th-century architectural masterpiece **St Paul's Cathedral** (*see p224*), right by St Paul's tube station. Last admission is 4pm, so you'll need to arrive by about 3.30pm to give yourself time.

St Paul's Cathedral from One New Change

Evening

Enough history. If you're cooked after all that walking, One New Change mall (*see p226*), neighbour of St Paul's to the east, has upmarket chain restaurants. But if you've still got a bit of puff, invest it in the 15-minute walk north into **Clerkenwell** (*see p216*) where there are infinitely superior eating options. Farringdon or Barbican tube stations are your best route back to your hotel.

DAY 2

Morning

We're not quite done with culture: are you ready for one of the world's finest museums? You betcha – arrive as close to 10am as you can to miss most of the crowds. The **British Museum** (*see p198*) is so full of treasures, you may not know where to begin: try turning left out of the middle of the covered courtyard for the extraordinary monumental antiquities, including the Parthenon Marbles. A morning will never be enough to do the museum justice, but that's all we're giving you today.

British Museum

Lunch

Wander south out of the museum to Covent Garden, where there are plenty of good eating options: **Great Queen Street** (*see p186*) is closest, but we recommend queuing for the superlative tapas at **Barrafina** (*see p185*) if you're after culinary fireworks.

Afternoon

Covent Garden Market (*see p180*) is catnip to tourists, but the fabulous **London Transport Museum** (*see p183*) is a better reason to linger. However, we'd take the chance to head north to the area around **Seven Dials**, which is crammed with boutiques (*see p189*). Take it at a stroll, though. We've got a big night planned.

Evening

If you're interested in how London has been changing, it's time to introduce yourself to **Peckham** (*see p286*), and from here it shouldn't take more than 40 minutes to get there. Head to Covent Garden tube, get the Piccadilly line west to Green Park, change to the Jubilee line east to Canada Water, and hop on the Overground for Clapham Junction getting off at Peckham Rye station. Peckham is currently London's coolest neighbourhood: eat at **Artusi** (*see p286*) then head to the **Bussey Building** (*see p341*) for some serious partying.

London Transport Museum

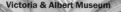
Victoria & Albert Museum

BUDGET BREAK

For the pound-conscious visitor
Budget £50-£70 per person
Getting around tube, walking

Good news, pound-stretchers! London, although expensive in most terms, is incredibly cheap for culture. Almost all of the key museums are free to enter, only charging to see their temporary exhibitions. The British Museum, both Tates and all three South Kensington museums are just the start, with many smaller collections (including the Soane, Wallace, Grant and Horniman) also eschewing an admission price. So you can have an extremely satisfying day in London for only as much as you pay for transport and food. To ensure your transport costs are as low as possible, get an Oyster card (£5 refundable deposit; *see p405*), or use the same contactless debit/ credit card for all your journeys. Your combined fares for the day will be capped at the price of a one-day travelcard for the zones you've travelled through (£7.70 for Zones 1-3).

Morning

Start at South Ken tube station, which is a short walk from one of London's – indeed, the world's – finest museums. The **Victoria & Albert Museum** (*see p126*) combines a palatial Victorian setting with collections that are a fascinating global history of art and design. Don't miss the stunning double-height Cast Courts, and we can never resist a cup of tea in the delightfully tiled Arts and Crafts style tea rooms – an affordable treat at £6-£8, including a cake, and not too packed if you go for elevenses rather than lunch or afternoon tea.

Lunch

Morning effectively filled with culture, walk ten minutes north into **Kensington Gardens** (*see p129*), the lovelier half of expansive Hyde Park. Mr Moneybags might be tempted to see **Kensington Palace** (*see p131*), but not us skinflints. Head instead to whatever's on at the **Serpentine Gallery** (*see p131*). Afterwards, head to the bridge but don't cross. Instead, turn right along the bank of the boating lake, past the Diana Princess of Wales Memorial Fountain, to grab a sandwich and a drink outside the Lido Café, then return and cross the bridge to the **Serpentine Sackler** for more contemporary art.

Kensington Gardens

Chiltern Street

Afternoon

Head to the north-east corner of the park, where you'll see Marble Arch (and pass the assorted soapbox crazies expounding their theories at Speakers' Corner, though they're mainly in attendance at weekends). You could sample the madness of Oxford Street by walking east along it, but we'd recommend saving your legs and getting the Central line one stop to Bond Street. Head north to the **Wallace Collection** (*see p148*), another free museum in another glorious setting, this time a grand 16th-century townhouse. It might be fun to window shop the boutiques of **Marylebone** (*see p145*), though you'll certainly bust the budget if you buy anything: Chiltern Street is one of London's trendiest.

Evening

When you've had enough of Marylebone, work out where you are: from the north, get the Bakerloo line from Baker Street to Piccadilly Circus; from the south, go back to Bond Street for the Central line to Tottenham Court Road. Either way, we're spending the night in **Soho**. Despite its reputation for naughtiness (you could still fritter away a fortune on dubious sexual pleasures, but you'd have to try quite hard to find the opportunities nowadays), Soho has become London's go-to place for cheap eats: almost everything in our selection of the city's best bargain eats (*see p48*) is here. Rather than bust the budget boozing, why not finish the evening with a film at the **Prince Charles** (*see p323*)? There might be a triple-bill all-nighter – after which, the Night Tube runs through Piccadilly Circus station, and the fare is still part of your capped travel for the day, even after midnight...

Shaftesbury Avenue

FAMILY DAY OUT

Keeping the kids amused
Budget £300-£400 for a family of four
Getting around tube, walking, boat. Allow plenty of time in your schedule for last-minute wee stops, getting lost and other child-rearing distractions.

Morning

The trick with many of London's greatest attractions is getting early – which can be a problem if you've multiple kids to corral, but it always pays off in reduced crowds. Get out at Tower Hill on the District and Circle lines and head down the steps to the **Tower** (*see p234*). There's lots to see and do here, with the experience enhanced by the presence of affable red-coated beefeaters (who are resident in the Tower: you can sometimes see their laundry hanging out to dry). Hustle to the Crown Jewels first thing, though. Queues build up rapidly to glide on the travelator past Her Majesty's baubles.

Lunch

The eating options around the Tower aren't terrific for kids, so grab sandwiches and cakes from the cluster of venues north-west of the Tower, and take them to the pier where you can eat during the 10-20-minute wait for next **Thames Clipper** to the London Eye. It's only a commuter service, but kids seem to love being on the water. Drinks are sold from the bar on board, but the available snacks are little more than crisps. Up to four under-11s travel for free with an accompanying adult, but only under-fives are free on the boat. For more details on child fares and photocards, *see p406*; for boat fares, *see p407*.

London Aquarium

Afternoon

While the **Shard** (*see p94*) provides the more eye-popping views, the constantly changing vista from the pods of the **London Eye** (*see p82*) can be more fun with the kids. Book your timeslot in advance for the cheapest tickets. When you're disgorged, you'll be confronted by the **London Aquarium**, **Shrek's Adventure** and the **London Dungeon** (for all, *see pp82-83*). They're all good, but you've already shelled out enough, so be ready to chivvy the little pesterers on to the **Southbank Centre** (*see p80*), possibly buying them off along the way with a run around the playground or a ride on the vintage merry-go-round. The buskers and living statues provide further distractions. If your luck's in, there'll be free child-focused entertainment in the foyer of the Royal Festival Hall; if there isn't, the combination of crowds and entertainers and ice-cream will keep the nippers happy.

Evening

The plan is to work your way steadily along the South Bank, with its fairy lights at night, as far as **Tate Modern** (*see p87*). Then you turn inland and head south to **Hixter Bankside** (16 Great Guildford Street, SE1 0HS, 7921 9508, www.hixrestaurants.co.uk/restaurant/hixter-bankside), where the open-plan layout feels relaxed, but the food is good enough to be a grown-up treat. Too ambitious? Not to worry: there are endless variations on pizza and burgers along the way. Head home from Waterloo (Northern, Bakerloo and Jubilee lines), if you don't get beyond the Southbank Centre, or Southwark (Jubilee line) from Hixter.

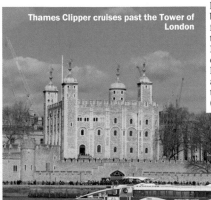
Thames Clipper cruises past the Tower of London

When to Visit

London by season

London doesn't really have an off-season, with interesting things going on all through the year (see *pp308-318* Events). The weather is never predictable, but nor is it particularly harsh – in winter you might even bless our polluted air, which keeps the temperature a degree or two higher than the surrounding countryside.

Spring
Our favourite time of year. This is a surprisingly green city, with blossoming cherry trees and crocuses, primroses and daffodils in the Royal Parks that ring central London. Spring often brings better weather than summer – and, outside the school holidays, fewer crowds. The Old Smoke can feel lively, pretty and far more cheerful than our fellow Brits would ever believe.

Summer
Summers can be rainy, but at the slightest sniff of fine weather Londoners are boozing at pavement tables like some fantasy of the south of France. The Tube becomes a sweaty hellhole, but suck it up: this is the season of al fresco cinema, music festivals in the parks and sipping Camparis with the trendsters on top of a multi-storey carpark in Peckham (see 286).

Autumn
Autumn has a good share of clear, crisp days, which often seem to fall kindly for Diwali and Bonfire Night fireworks. The kids are back at school after the summer holidays but it is rarely unpleasantly cold, so autumn is a great time of year for busy sightseeing.

Winter
There's plenty of fun to be had in the run-up to the big C, with roaring fires in trad pubs, the giant Christmas tree arriving in Trafalgar Square from Norway and the West End illuminations going up. Just don't count on seeing any snow. Christmas Day is pretty much the only time London closes down: there's no public transport and few attractions, shops or restaurants bother to open.

London Today

*Despite the rest of our nation, London remains defiantly
a global city*

It takes a lot to shake London's implacable sense of self. For some
20 years, Londoners believed their city to be the ideal future
model for the UK, a place the country admired and wanted
to emulate. Then came the 2016 EU referendum result, which
explicitly shunned cherished London values. This was followed
by the unexpectedly strong result for the anti-austerity, 'soft'
Brexit Labour party in a 2017 snap general election that was
supposed to be a coronation of Tory prime minister Theresa May,
with her pro-business, pro-austerity, 'no deal is better than a bad
deal' Brexit. Then there were terrorist and Islamophobic attacks
– on the Houses of Parliament, on revellers at London Bridge, on
worshippers at Finsbury Park mosque – and a horrific towerblock
fire. Confused, their confidence undermined, Londoners have
taken to celebrating what makes them different – things like
the landslide election in 2016 of a reassuringly centrist Muslim
Mayor. As the world turns towards isolationism, London too is
thinking increasingly of itself.

Norman Foster's City Hall

Mayor of London, Sadiq Khan

When Sadiq Khan emphatically won the election for London Mayor for Labour in May 2016, it felt like vindication of the city's largely open-minded liberal attitude. The divisive rhetoric of the right had been decisively rejected. The future looked positive.

Within weeks, Khan's electoral success felt like an anomaly. Within a year, it seemed unfathomable, so complex had been the overall cultural and political shifts across the country.

Khan had won on a modest left-wing platform, promising to address pollution, housing and extreme wage inequality, but also boasting he would be strongly 'pro-business'. There were no headline-grabbing initiatives to compare with Boris Johnson's promise to restore the Routemaster, the nostalgists' favourite red double-decker bus, or Ken Livingstone's creation of a Congestion Charge, but that was precisely what London wanted after those ego-driven predecessors.

Khan was no maverick. A solid Labour man, he exuded a quiet competence, making much of a humble background. He was the son of Pakistani immigrants; his dad, he reminded every interviewer, had been a bus driver, and he was raised in a south London council flat before studying law at a minor university. In a city of immigrants – around 40% of the population were born overseas, with many more second- or third-generation – this was normal.

The Mayor of London is responsible for an annual budget of £17 billion.

The other side of the tracks

His opponent, Conservative Zac Goldsmith, came from different stock. Born into a family of billionaires, he was raised in a Grade II-listed Georgian mansion and educated at Eton, before he was expelled and took a job as the editor of a magazine that, happily, was owned by his uncle.

Goldsmith was good-looking and charming. He also had a reputation for being an iconoclast with green credentials, essentially liberal in outlook, offering possible cross-party appeal. Which only made his election campaign the more shocking. Aided by the *Evening Standard*, London's right-wing daily newspaper, Goldsmith focused almost entirely on Khan's religion. He painted his opponent as an ally of Islamist terrorists, a closet extremist who would steal your gold and endanger the city. Evidence was scant: the problem was simply that Khan was a Muslim.

Khan dealt as phlegmatically with these hysterical accusations as he would do with the actual terrorist atrocities of 2017. By then, he was in office, having been rewarded with a huge majority. If there was a textbook for how not to run a campaign in London, Goldsmith had just written it. His humiliation was gold-plated in December 2016 when he fulfilled a promise to stand down as Conservative MP for Richmond Park to protest the government's decision to build a new runway at nearby Heathrow airport. He then stood again in the ensuing byelection as an anti-expansion independent, only to get thrashed by a Liberal Democrat party riding the wave of outrage from Richmond's genteelly furious pro-Europeans.

That's because, a month after Khan's election, London had voted overwhelmingly to Remain during an ugly EU referendum campaign. Outside traditional left-wing cities like Liverpool and London-lite cities such as Brighton, Manchester, Bristol and Oxford, the bulk of England had chosen to Leave, explicitly endorsing a campaign that leaned heavily on kneejerk anti-immigration rhetoric.

Londoners largely rejected that approach. That's partly because London is younger, more mobile and better educated than much of the rest of the country – even London's worst secondary schools obtain better results than the best schools in some parts of England – but the city is also a genuinely multiracial city, filled with numerous overlapping communities.

London is younger, more mobile and better educated than much of the rest of the country

London voted overwhelmingly to remain in the EU but found itself at odds with other parts of the country.

Even here, the picture is murky: Goldsmith's wafer-thin Tory victory over the Lib Dems in the 2017 snap election suggests pragmatism may have already trumped Londoners' Brexit anger.

Bust, boom and the housing ladder

London also voted Remain because the city had weathered the financial crash of 2008 better than the rest of the country. That's down to the resident financial sector, which was protected from the damage it had itself caused by the Bank of England and a desperate Labour government, and also because of a deranged property market, which went supernova after interest rates were cut to near nothing. Londoners might not have been particularly delighted by the super-rich profiting from the carelessness of the super-rich, nor that housing had become stupidly unaffordable, but the flow of money meant London continued to boom.

London's housing market continues to boom, but prices are unaffordable for those on low or average incomes.

It also left Khan with his biggest challenge. London's housing market is closed to first-time buyers. The population continues to rise, but the only housing built in any quantity is luxury flats for wealthy investors, and even these have dried up post-Brexit. There's little Khan can do to correct this other than strictly enforce regulations on the number of affordable housing units in new developments – and wait for the political consensus to finally accept state-built housing is a better use of money and land than any alternative.

Counter-intuitively, London has relatively low population density. It's essentially lots of two- and three-storey terraced houses interspersed with clusters of gargantuan glass towers. But transforming the entire cityscape into six-storey apartment blocks is a project beyond the Mayor's authority and ambition. Some breathing space would be found if developers built on the Green Belt – a protected ring of countryside that circles the city, acting as an artificial brake on endless sprawl – but this is

London is essentially lots of two- and three-storey terraced houses interspersed with clusters of gargantuan glass towers

politically controversial, and was explicitly ruled out by Khan during his election campaign.

Let's clear the air

Instead, he focused on air pollution. London's air is rank, more polluted than that of Beijing. At the start of 2017, London had exceeded its annual air pollution emission limits in some areas within five days. Climb a hill and look down on London and you can see the haze; blow your nose and you can see the snotty grey results in your handkerchief. So far, Khan has dabbled round the edges of the problem, introducing a charge for highly polluting vehicles entering the city centre from October 2017, but more imaginative solutions are required.

Island dwellers

The Mayor could also have an important voice on the two biggest issue in British politics: responses to terrorism and the outcome of Brexit. On the former, his reaction has been robust (beefing up policing) and collegiate (reaching out to all faith communities). Impeccable liberal politics. On the latter, all is to play for since the 2017 election. It's likely that London will suffer as a consequence of the referendum result, which, given that London is the biggest contributor to the country's tax income, could be devastating for the rest of the UK. The construction industry was one of the first to note a dwindling supply of foreign workers, while financial institutions are contemplating moving their headquarters to Frankfurt or Paris. Khan may have to spend the next few years making a lot of promises to CEOs who know desperation when they see it.

Otherwise, Khan's role is to be the most prominent political figurehead for the half of the population bewildered by the rhetoric surrounding Brexit and abandoned by a

Climb a hill and look down on London and you can see the haze; blow your nose and you can see the snotty grey results in your handkerchief

30 St Mary Axe (universally known as 'the Gherkin'; see p233) and the giant glass spike of the Shard (see p94) have become defining features of the London skyline.

Brexit-supporting Labour party that polled way above expectations in the 2017 election.

London was once seen as the 'Great Wen', a boil of poisonous pus bespoiling the verdant English countryside, but in the past 20 years had fashioned an image of itself as an open, outward-facing, multicultural city, more European than British.

That image – not entirely untrue, even if it is simplistic – was boosted by the fact almost every major institution is based in London, whether in politics, finance or the media. Londoners basked in this dominance, but it was increasingly resented by the rest of the country. Brexit – and, in part, the 2017 hung parliament – was an attack on the perceived 'metropolitan elite' of the privileged capital by people who saw London not so much as a boil, but as a bubble.

Khan responded with the 'London is open' slogan to show the world that London didn't plan to change. How the city can retain its cosmopolitan values in the face of Brexit is the big question.

Some have suggested London introduce its own visa system to ensure it can still attract much-needed migrant workers. Others have openly toyed with the idea of creating an independent London city-state: a petition to this effect was signed by 180,000 people. For some, this would recast London as a European version of Hong Kong or Singapore – ironically, exactly the sort of low-regulatory, low-tax haven envisaged for the whole country by some Brexiteers – while others seem to prefer the idea of a sort of walled medieval city designed to keep the Brexiting heathens out. Either way, the metaphor of London as an isolated cultural and economic island surrounded by post-apocalyptic wasteland has rarely had more traction.

Get real

None of which is to pretend that London is some sort of paradise. There is inequality

The metaphor of London as an isolated cultural and economic island surrounded by post-apocalyptic wasteland has rarely had more traction

caused by gig economy low wages, huge rents and a high cost of living – although the plummeting post-Brexit pound makes it great value for tourists from outside the UK.

But it's still a place that offers so much to enjoy and be proud of in terms of cultural and social opportunity. There is tremendous creativity in arts, fashion and music, even food. There's magnificent contemporary architecture and beautiful old parks. London has extraordinary diversity but also a united state-of-mind. It's that rare thing, a beautiful, (largely) clean, interesting city of great historical importance but also of genuine contemporary resonance.

But London is a city of competing interests. The story of the Tate Modern extension (*see p389*) is apposite. In 2016, the gallery celebrated its continuing success by opening a vast new tower, which included a top-floor public balcony. Visitors gleefully realised this allowed them to see straight into some nearby glass-fronted luxury flats. The overlooked residents lodged a legal complaint, insisting the view from the balcony be blocked, outraged that living in flats made of glass in central London meant other people could actually see them.

The Tate Modern extension is a hit with visitors but less popular with its well-heeled neighbours.

Living in a building site

Such glass towers have risen in huge waves across London, notably in the Nine Elms area between Chelsea Bridge and Vauxhall Bridge. This is the most intensive development area in Europe, almost all of it high-end residential aimed at wealthy investors. It includes the new US Embassy and the refurbished Battersea Power Station (*see p391*), a popular London landmark abandoned for decades, which is being developed by a Malaysian pension fund and will eventually be handed to Apple for offices. The power station will be surrounded luxury flats and swanky shops, bringing questionable benefit to London as a whole.

There is also a danger of over-build: with prices slowing, the power station's developers have already altered their affordable housing commitment. The horrific fire at Grenfell ⸺ower – a 24-storey block of social housing in west London – on 14 June 2017 only underlined London's inequalities. Many dozens of people were killed or injured, after a fire spread out of control due to cheap external cladding. Can even the pro-developer Tory government resist beefing up building regulations in the wake of such a tragedy?

An alternative to the Battersea Power Station redevelopment has been slowly taking shape in King's Cross over the past several years, filling dead industrial railway land with thriving shops, offices, parks and housing. As well as offices for Google and Facebook, King's Cross is now home to the Central St Martins art school and the Francis Crick Institute, a landmark medical research centre. The canal has been turned into an idyllic centrepiece. It's a flagship for what can and should be done across London.

The redevelopment of King's Cross and the Regent's Canal has transformed a formerly seedy area of the city.

King's Cross is the model for another major development on the site of the 2012 Olympic Park. Boris Johnson labelled this emerging arts cluster 'Olympicopolis' – a name as catchy as Johnson's bouffant hair was tameable – and it will eventually house an outpost of the V&A (*see p126*), a dance theatre run by Sadler's Wells (*see p368*) and the London College of Fashion. London's also getting a major piece of new infrastructure: the Crossrail east–west high-speed underground rail link (*see p407*) will begin partial operation in 2018.

Because of all this and so much more, London has felt like a building site for most of the decade. Londoners have grown tired of being shunted from one side of the road to another by blocked pavements, overshadowed by cranes and serenaded by pneumatic drills. But with so much in flux, no one would predict an end to disruption anytime soon.

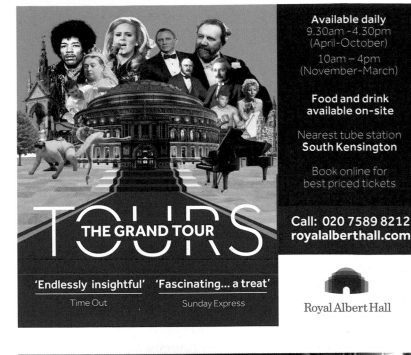

Eating

A great food city was born when London started to welcome the cuisine of every other nation

---

'Boiled beef and carrots,' sang Harry Champion, darling of the music hall, in 1909, 'that's the stuff for your derby kell, keeps you fit and keeps you well.' For decades that would indeed have been as good as stuff for your belly got in London. Not any more. It's still hard to point to any significant indigenous cuisine – eels, pie and mash, perhaps; afternoon tea and the hangover café fry-up in some ways; fish and chips if you ignore the fact it was invented elsewhere – but our restaurant culture has become a thing of joy, almost entirely through its voracious cosmopolitanism. Many cities claim you can eat your way round the world without setting foot outside their boundaries: well, in London it's true. We're so open to outside influences, in fact, we've even embraced British food, albeit in a rather modern form.

Modern British

For at least a decade we banged on about it – then, in 2009, Michelin caught on and gave **St John** (*p216*) a star. This modest whitewashed restaurant effectively reinvented British food. The idea was simple: take out-of-favour but flavour-packed cuts of meat and bits of animal (bone marrow, pig's trotters, hearts) and offer them in simple preparations that let the unique qualities of the ingredients shine – this was to become known as 'nose-to-tail' eating. For a period in the 2010s every new restaurant in London seemed to be claiming its 'modern British' culinary heritage, and indeed chefs from St John cropped up across London: the **Anchor & Hope** (*p85*), **Rochelle Canteen** (*p266*) and **Hereford Road** (*p298*) are notable. In truth, St John had struck upon a couple of key themes: localism (sourcing superb

The Barbary

ingredients from as close to home as possible, rather than flying them in from across the globe) and the newly casual gourmet diner, who was willing to pay for fine food but didn't relish the flim-flam of Mayfair haute-cuisine.

Of course, this stripped-back, blackboard menu approach doesn't disguise what's happening: serious cooking, often for top dollar. But there's still plenty of room in town for what visitors might consider 'British' without the 'modern' appendage: you might fancy fish and chips at **Poppies** (*p259*) or **Hook** (*p242*), for instance, or to indulge in the post-colonial excess of a leisurely afternoon tea (*see right*). There's also a handful of historic places serving what was, for a century, the staple diet of the London working man: eels, pie and mash. **M Manze** (*p94*) is our pick because it's relatively central, has classic utilitarian tiled premises and continues to serve eels – once cheap fodder yanked straight out of the Thames, now rare enough often to be too expensive for such establishments. A word of advice, though: unless you've sturdy Cockney genes, always avoid jellied in favour of stewed eels.

The world in one city

The reinvention of British cooking has long since slid off the cutting edge. With a new Levantine restaurant promised even on the out-of-towner vortex that is Leicester Square, it's safe to say London has hit peak Mediterranean. **The Barbary** (*p185*) and **Palomar** (*p177*) rapidly ascended the list of our favourite places to eat in London – not merely our favourite Mediterranean places – but **Ottolenghi** (*p252*), the pioneer, is also still well worth a visit.

In truth, Londoners experience cravings for wave after wave of global food. There was **Moro** (*p218*), with its fusion of North African and Spanish cooking. A few years ago came Peruvian, with **Ceviche Soho** (*p162*) still a

❤ Best of British

St John *p216*
The mod Brit pioneer: 'nose-to-tail' ingredients, in simple and excellent combinations.

Regency Café *p112*
Fry-up in a post-war art deco caff – save it for when your hangover really deserves one.

Hook Camden Town *p242*
Fish and chips, done with a bit of upmarket pizzazz.

M Manze *p94*
Proletarian cuisine, the way the Victorians knew it: pie or eels, mash, parsley sauce. Proper.

❤ Best afternoon tea

Diamond Jubilee Tea Salon at Fortnum & Mason *p117*
Cosseting staff go beyond the call of duty and the super-buttery scones are exceptional; £44 per person.

Foyer and Reading Room at Claridge's *p398*
This elegant art deco palace is where A-listers take tea, accompanied by a mollifying pianist; from £58 per person.

Wyld Tea at Dandelyan *p84*
Teeny sarnies and sweet treats matched with inventive booze from a cocktail maestro; from £55 per person.

Raw at La Suite West *p401*
A super-sleek, minimalist setting for a scrumptious vegan tea; from £29 per person.

top place to dine. Noodles had their moment: fast, casual, delicious bowls of goodness can be enjoyed at **Kanada-ya** (*p186*) or **Shoryu Ramen** (*p153*). Nordic cuisine and influences were everywhere for a while and remain very present: fine exponents include **Rök Smokehouse & Bar** (*p266*) and the very different **Snaps & Rye** (*p299*).

This is hardly a new phenomenon. You might choose to trace it back to curry's popularity in London following mass immigration from Bangladesh in the 1970s – with chicken tikka masala hailed as Britain's national dish by the 2000s. But before that there was Chinese (now ably represented in Chinatown by the likes of **Baiwei**, *p177*, and **Shuang Shuang**, *p177*, even the Taiwanese **Bao**, *p172*), Italian (check out **Bocca di Lupo**, *p168*), even French. We might have to head all the way back to the coffeehouses that flooded London from the Ottoman Empire during the 17th century, much to Charles II's consternation.

What's notable is how food arrives in London from abroad as cheap national cuisine, becomes dramatically popular, consolidates, and is then reinvented as a luxury. The plurality of pricey Italians in Chelsea and Mayfair is one example; the excellent **Gymkhana** (*p155*) might be another. But one does not replace the other: there are finally terrific, affordable curry options in the centre of town – **Tandoor Chop House** (*p187*) and its forebear **Dishoom** (*p185*) – as well as a growing number of decent options near (if not yet on) Brick Lane, which has for a long time failed to live up to its international fame: the long-standing **Tayyabs** (*p263*) and **Needoo Grill** (*p263*) have been joined by the excellent **Gunpowder** (*p260*).

Nordic cuisine and influences were everywhere for a while and remain very present

❤ **Best for a blowout**

Social Eating House *p175*
The finest establishment from one of London's finest chefs, Jason Atherton.

Roka *p209*
Beautifully presented raw and robata-grilled Asian deliciousness.

Chiltern Firehouse *p148*
Book before you travel to join the celebs enjoying Nuno Mendes's stellar cooking.

Hutong *p94*
Chinese with a view – from the Shard's 33rd floor.

It's good to share

Another trend that Londoners have made their own is well, what to call it? 'Small plates' if the cooking is contemporary, but then Spanish tapas and Chinese dim sum had nailed the idea of serving reduced portions of multiple dishes long before anyone thought the practice needed its own name. Our recent round-up of London's 100 best restaurants had **Barrafina** (*p185*) right at the top: not bad for a tapas joint set up by the British Hart brothers rather than Spaniards. There are lots of other superb tapas restaurants, not least **Ember Yard** (*p169*), but do try to eat at the Harts' Mexican taqueria **El Pastór** (*p91*) too. Then there's the enduring popularity of the *cicchetti* (Venetian bar snacks) served at Russell Norman's Polpo mini-chain (**Polpo Soho**, *p172*), and a Portuguese equivalent at Nuno Mendes' sweet little **Taberna do Mercado** (*p259*). For dim sum, try **Royal China** (*p132*) or the luxury offerings at **Yauatcha** (*p170*). The small plates concept proper is behind venues such as the **Shed** (*p303*), while Jason Atherton's superlative **Social Eating House** (*p175*) sells jars of pâté and nibbles to get diners dipping in and off to a suitably convivial start.

No bookings and other 'dirty' notions

Somewhere between place-making architects and green-lobby farmers' markets, street food found its foothold and began a city-wide takeover: the era of the 'dirty' burger – the one your doctor warned you not to eat – was upon us. There are now gatherings of stalls all over place: **King's Cross** (*p205*), Whitecross Street behind the **Barbican** (*p228*), the square at the back of the **Royal Festival Hall** (*p84*); check www.timeout.com for the latest openings and current stall listings. Again there has been a welcome gentrification in the genre: the brilliant, wickedly unhealthy burgers

❤ Best for small plates and sharing

Barrafina *p185*
Best tapas in London – better than many in Madrid – but be prepared to queue.

Polpo Soho *p172*
Venetian street food was the making of this terrific mini-chain.

Social Eating House *p175*
Kick off one of the finest meals in London with shareable jars and killer cocktails.

Royal China *p132*
Some of the best dim sum in London.

Shed *p303*
Anything the Spaniards can do… fine modern British tapas.

❤ Best for brunch

Wolseley *p116*
Grand setting, fine food – omelette Arnold Bennett, say.

Caravan King's Cross *p205*
Relaxed and boozy brunches on a fine modern square.

Dean Street Townhouse *p166*
Buzzy, with smooth service and four different styles of Bloody Mary.

Duck & Waffle *p236*
At the top of a skyscraper in the heart of the City.

Polpo

at **Bleecker** (*p112*) now have a permanent address, while **Bar Boulud** (*p132*) does a very upmarket take on the subject. **Burger & Lobster** (*p165*) is a slightly different tack on the same basic culinary navigation.

Street food is by no means all about high-cholesterol filth. Many stall-owners are able to trial an idea and make some money, without immediately taking on the heavy burden of renting a London restaurant space. **Som Saa** (*p259*) is an interesting case in point, having financed the transition through an insanely popular crowdfunding appeal; **Kricket** (*p172*) is another much-admired restaurant that found its feet as a stall. Oh, and when it comes to foodie markets, **Borough Market** (*p92*) is still the daddy for gourmet snacking, but the cognoscenti increasingly head a little further east to the less touristy **Maltby Street** (*p96*).

Taking a related – but rather different – approach to risk-free catering is the enduring trend for no-booking restaurants. The attraction for the restaurateur is obvious: no empty tables and the chance to generate a buzz. The attraction to the punter is, well, good food and a chance to experience a new culture of queuing... we mean to experience the flexibility of not booking in advance. Whatever our misgivings, many of these places are really worth the effort – see our best list, *right* – and, as a visitor free from the exigencies of a working life, you can always opt to visit at unconventional times and thereby avoid the worse of the lunch- and dinnertime queues.

Gastropubs and beautiful brasseries

Another kind of eaterie whose dominance of the London scene has waned, without it showing the remotest signs of disappearing, is the gastropub: restaurant-quality food, eaten in the relaxed atmosphere of a boozer that serves good beer and, generally, above-average wine. A few years ago every pub that

Borough Market

❤ Best walk-in restaurants

10 Greek Street *p162*
Modern British with Mediterranean touches – book at lunch if you will, or prepare to queue for dinner.

The Barbary *p185*
Entertainingly excellent Middle Eastern grub.

Burger & Lobster *p165*
The mini-chain that tells it like it is: lobster two ways or burger or head elsewhere.

Hoppers *p164*
Sri Lankan street food.

Padella *p90*
Excellent Italian at Borough Market.

Som Saa *p259*
Thai the way it should be.

MASALA ZONE

A REAL TASTE OF INDIA

BAYSWATER, 75 BISHOPS BRIDGE RD
COVENT GARDEN, 48 FLORAL ST
SELFRIDGES 4TH FL, 400 OXFORD ST
EARLS COURT, 147 EARLS COURT ROAD

CAMDEN, 25 PARKWAY
ISLINGTON, 80 UPPER ST
SOHO, 9 MARSHALL ST
MASALAZONE.COM

wasn't already a gastro was in the process of turning into one – now a lot of London pubs have realised that being a superb place for a drink is a perfectly solid ambition. Still, for a substantial – and often terrific, usually hearty – meal that doesn't demand you pull on a suit or cocktail dress, the gastropub is great: the **Harwood Arms** (*p136*) and the **Bull & Last** (*p250*) are established favourites, but foodie scholars could do worse than visit the **Eagle** (*p216*), widely celebrated as the originator of the genre back in the 1990s.

Taking on a similar role of providing noon till night dining – albeit with a more Continental flavour, generally higher price bracket and considerably greater interest in providing brunch and breakfast opportunities – are what we'll call the brasseries. The kings of London in this field are Chris Corbin and Jeremy King, who seem incapable of opening a dud: the **Wolseley** (*p116*), **Fischer's** (*p148*) and **Delaunay** (*p191*) are all great, combining a kind of Viennese glamour with very approachable menus. There are plenty of worthy competitors, though, among them **Dean Street Townhouse** (*p166*), which does some heavy lifting restoring the spirits of Soho's dissolute media workers, and **Bistrotheque** (*p270*), putting an idiosyncratic east London spin on the idea of all-day comfort food.

Things in bread and classic caffs

All of which leaves Londoners rotund but happy, lingering lovingly at every meal over the best food the world can offer. Not so much: dining al-desko on whatever can be grabbed from the nearest identikit sandwich chain is our familiar lot. The **Pret A Manger** (www.pret.com) and **Itsu** (www.itsu.com) chains are fine for grab-and-go lunches, while the supermarkets all have lunchtime sandwiches if you're starving, but when you can, check out a classic cafe for cheap, filling food, usually with

Bull & Last

❤ Best cheap eats

Bao *p172*
Fiery Taiwanese street food.

Herman ze German *p166*
Sausages. Yup, pretty much just that – top-quality imported German sausages.

Hoppers *p164*
Authentically wonderful Sri Lankan dishes.

Hummus Bros *p169*
Cheap and filling lunches – flatbread, houmous, topping, yum.

Roti Chai *p144*
Indian street food, served canteen style.

Good Egg *p272*
Persian and Iraqi dishes in a trendy small restaurant.

All of which leaves Londoners rotund but happy, lingering lovingly at every meal over the best food the world can offer

a bit of banter thrown in: neither the **Regency** (*p112*) nor **E Pellicci** (*p270*) are likely to trouble the Michelin adjudicators, but you won't regret paying either of them a visit.

Prices you'll like – and waiting that you won't

Dining in London can be expensive, and it certainly will be if you insist on dinner at posh City or Mayfair restaurants where the expense account rules. Remember: as a tourist, you're more flexible than the locals. Many of the swankiest venues offer exceptionally good value prix-fixe lunches, especially so if you're happy not to drink wine with your meal. Still too expensive? Most of the global food options we've discussed – not to mention the street food – are both tasty and inexpensive. If you're happy to experiment, you'll be able to eat extremely well without breaking the bank. There's bad news, though: that combination of good value and good quality? Often makes places busy. And the no-booking trend? Means queues. And the hot table you've promised yourself as a special treat? Make sure you book in advance. If something's great in London, somebody else knows about it and you're likely to have to wait – or book ahead. Again, make use of your flexibility: Londoners are time-constrained, but you can eat whenever you want to.

**In the know
Essentials**

Most restaurants accept credit cards (although American Express is least popular), but some of the cheaper places still only accept cash; if you're anywhere informal, like a street food stall, you should expect to use money rather than plastic. Service charges are frequently included in café and restaurant bills, but not always. Check: if such a charge hasn't been added, paying a tip of 10%-15% is usual. If you can, tip in cash: it's most likely to go directly to your server that way.

If you're happy to experiment, you'll be able to eat extremely well without breaking the bank

Berners Tavern, *p207*

Where to eat

The **South Bank** (*p76*), close to foodie-magnets Borough Market and Maltby Street, offers plenty of quality chain options strung along the riverside, but **Soho** (*p160*), just north of the Thames and less than half an hour's walk from the Southbank Centre, is probably the best place in London for eats, both cheap and chic: Herman ze German does a brisk trade not far from Jason Atherton's superb, upmarket Social Eating House and trend-setting 10 Greek Street, for example. East of Soho, **Covent Garden** (*p178*) remains a busy tourist trap, but some very decent eating options have emerged. Expense-account eats are concentrated in **Mayfair** (*p154*), where celebrity executive chefs thrive in the dining rooms of posh hotels. Further west, **Marylebone** (*p145*) is another foodie enclave, replete with top-notch delis and cafés, as well as terrific restaurants including Fischer's and the Chiltern Firehouse. **South Kensington and Chelsea** (*p120*) does expensive, special-occasion destinations, but runs to more affordable fare too at venues like Gallery Mess. **The City** (*p210*) remains relatively poor for evening and weekend eats, but **Clerkenwell** (*p216*), just beyond the old City walls, is a culinary hotspot: from the Modern Pantry to the Eagle, from St John to Moro, most London restaurant trends have kicked off here. However, the biggest change to London's dining geography over the last few years has been the growth of exciting options in the neighbourhoods, partly due to new restaurants struggling to meet steep rents in central London: try **Peckham** (*p286*), for instance, or any of the huge number of places in **east London** (*p254*).

Bao, *p172*

> The biggest change to London's dining geography over the last few years has been the growth of exciting options in the neighbourhoods

**In the know
Late lunch**

As you'll need to book a long way ahead for dinner at many of London's coolest restaurants, it is worth checking out lunchtimes, especially late lunches.

DINE OUT
LONDON

We've got the inside track on the city's hottest restaurants, so book with us and be ahead of the culinary curve.

 TIMEOUT.COM/ LONDON/RESTAURANTS

Drinking

Warm ale or chilled beer? Classic cocktails or crazy new confections? Pull up a bar stool – we've got it all here

It's the combination of rich traditions and a long history of bohemian revelry with a real taste for innovation that makes drinking in London such a pleasure these days. Any sense of rivalry with New York over which city is the world capital of booze is mostly a media confection: the truth is that London learnt the art of the bar from the Big Apple – and learnt that lesson surprisingly well – but we continue to own the pub. And recent years have proved the resilience of London's drinking scene: pubs are no longer shutting at the alarming rate that they did during the 2008/9 recession, while rising rents in central London have only encouraged a neighbourhood cocktail movement to thrive. You'll find a drinking culture with a conscience, too – with bars focused on sustainability and pubs supporting local brands and producers, especially with the current vogue for craft beer and small-batch gin. Above all, there's entertainment by the pint from spirited landlords, cocktail visionaries and the clued-up barflies who stand on the other side of the counter. When you're down the local, this city doesn't feel so sprawling after all.

Pub it and be damned

'The local' – the public house, with its colourful characters and cosy interior – remains the symbolic heart of boozing culture in the capital. Sure, the carcasses of street-corner pubs are littered around the city, often converted into luxury flats or chicken shops, but London's enduring love of the local is proved by a smattering of charming boozers saved by patrons who've campaigned for their protection from property developers. A drink in 'saved' pubs like the **Ivy House** (*see p287*) and **Elephant & Castle** (*see p86*) comes with a genuine sense of community.

Some pubs have stood the test of time without such a fight. Indeed, a handful of historic inns all claim to be the oldest pub in the capital. **Ye Olde Cheshire Cheese** (*see p220*), **Ye Olde Mitre** (*see p216*) and the **Prospect of Whitby** (*see p275*) are just a few of the pubs that have held licences since the 1600s. These creaking London legends are the best places to soak up a spot of history, warmed by the fire, ducking under low ceiling beams to fetch a pint

> A drink in 'saved' pubs like the Ivy House and Elephant & Castle comes with a genuine sense of community

Ye Olde Mitre

of lukewarm ale before settling in for a Sunday roast with all the trimmings.

Glasses full of creativity

London's front-running bars treat their craft with the same skill shown by the capital's best kitchens, some of them even using skills derived from so-called 'molecular gastronomy'. The cocktail scene never takes itself too seriously, though, offering a good time at most hours of the day and night. (Certainly, cocktail o'clock is no longer limited by traditional working hours and former licensing restrictions to 5.30pm.) You'll find quirkiness in presentation – witness drinks themed around childhood stories at **Blind Pig** (*see p175*) – or in the very setting: you can drink in an underground public toilet at **Ladies & Gentlemen** (*see p243*). Increasingly, there's wizardry to be found in the glasses of hotel bars: **Dandelyan** (*see p84*) is a leader, with cocktail maestro and founder Ryan Chetiyawardana fast becoming a household name (albeit under his pseudonym, Mr Lyan) thanks to drinks that incorporate madcap ideas, techniques and ingredients but never compromise on flavour. Tony Conigliaro is another well-established innovator: his key bar, **69 Colebrooke Row** (*see p252*), has a lab upstairs where he researches new confections, but his **Zetter Townhouse** (*see p219*) hotel bar is another winner. Wherever you end up, cocktails in the capital are more than ever about quality over quantity – even when they come with a good dose of fun.

Trending tipples

Whatever else you do, make sure you tap into London's craft beer 'revolution', another American import that we've taken to heart and made our own. Most pubs and bars (and even restaurants) these days will serve something interesting, from the keg or in a bottle,

❤ Best beer

BrewDog *p242*
Attitudinous beer pioneer.

Cask *p110*
No looker, but great ales.

Cock Tavern *p273*
Hackney's finest.

Lyric *p170*
Central location, 18 taps.

Waterloo Tap *p84*
A great selection and handy for the South Bank.

❤ Best cocktails

7 Tales *p219*
Asian-inspired alcohol.

69 Colebrooke Row *p252*
More mixmeister magic.

Connaught Bar *p156*
Pure Mayfair class.

Dandelyan *p84*
For Mr Lyan's inventive cocktails.

Satan's Whiskers *p270*
East London trendies and fabulous booze.

Swift *p167*
Glamorous new Soho bar.

Swift

usually hoppy and often brewed in London. It's a scene that's particularly active on the periphery, with grungy brewery taprooms and hip neighbourhood bottle shops where you can try and buy springing up on the outskirts of London, but there are plenty of poshed-up pubs in the centre of town that have dedicated themselves to the humble hop.

While grapes from around the world are well represented in a few wonderfully unstuffy new wine bars (try **Sager + Wilde**, *see p270*, or **Terroirs**, *see p187*), it's fair to say you won't find quite the same fervour for vino. More booze fanaticism is instead reserved for gin. 'Mother's ruin' first wreaked havoc on the capital in the 1700s, when home production made the spirit the crystal meth of the day and the government cracked down hard to protect public health. London's new gin craze is far more refined: the Chiswick-based distiller Sipsmith helped push through new laws for small-batch production in the UK, and local gin-making has since spread across town. You can sample it at source on a distillery tour or trail, or opt for one of the numerous bars claiming to stock the most varieties of gin in London – there's currently a bit of a war going on.

Strait-laced supping

Millennials have waved goodbye to by-numbers binge-drinking. Mocktails are now common on London bar menus, so locals no longer need to deploy the designated-driver excuse (which never really stood up anyway in the face of London transport). Indeed, in **Redemption** (6 Chepstow Road, Notting Hill, W2 5BH, 7313 9041, redemptionbar.co.uk) the city has a whole venue dedicated to alcohol-free drinking. You might also choose to hang out with fashion-forward types at one of London's late-night juice bars: **Ham's Yard Press Juice Bar** (6 Denman Street, Soho, W1D 7HD, 7287 2462, press-london.com) is one of the capital's

♥ Best pubs

Bradley's Spanish Bar *p209*
A cosy and unassuming little boozer, just off Oxford Street.

Coach & Horses *p166*
French House *p166*
A venerable pair of Soho classics.

Cross Keys *p187*
What's this? A genuinely good pub in touristy Covent Garden, you say?

Jerusalem Tavern *p219*
Former coffeehouse turned quintessence of London pub.

Ye Olde Mitre *p216*
A gem of an old pub down a blink-and-you'll-miss-it alley.

Sip fine wine in informal surroundings at Sager + Wilde.

Redemption proves that no alcohol doesn't have to mean no fun.

most 'slebby' hangouts... along with plenty of cold-pressed delights.

Of course, you needn't go completely vice-free. Coffee is as big as ever, thanks to the proliferation of masterful bean techniques – and, no doubt, to the fast pace of London life. You'll find on-site roasters, a plethora of brew technology and lab-style equipment, and beans sourced from far-flung places. Some coffee shops are well established on the caffeine scene – check out **Monmouth** (27 Monmouth Street, Covent Garden, WC2H 9EU, 7232 3010, www. monmouthcoffee.co.uk) – but don't ignore up-and-comers, from **Catalyst** to the **New Black** (10 Philpott Lane, the City, EC3M 8AA, www.thenewblack.coffee), which are using new methods in sleek Scandi-style surroundings.

The where and when of London drinking

Soho retains its reputation as the bohemian centre of the capital, for all that the razzle-dazzle naughtiness has now mostly been replaced by tech entrepreneurs and middle-aged media types. It still hosts character-filled pubs, but these have been joined by increasing numbers of chic cocktail bars. **Shoreditch** – its days as the epitome of cool receding fast as its denizens grow up – is still a lively part of town, packed with drinkers, but in-the-know boozers seem to have drifted north into **Hackney** or south to **Peckham** and **Brixton**, where fledgling and creative drinks scenes are beginning to flourish; here, you'll find cocktails at the £7-£8 mark as opposed to the £10-£12 prices of central London. If hell-raising hipsters aren't your bag, stick to **Mayfair**, **Covent Garden** or **west London**, where drinks are served with a side of sophistication, but heftier price tags exclude the hoi polloi.

Mondays are mostly a sober affair as Londoners recover from the weekend, but during the rest of the week there's enthusiastic after-work drinking; certainly, Thursday nights

❤ **Best outdoor venues**

Boundary *p399*
The rooftop bar at Conran's finest hotel is an east London must.

Earl of Essex *p253*
A purveyor of fine beer with a fine beer garden.

Frank's *p286*
Campari. Multistorey carpark. Peckham. Don't miss it.

Scottish Stores *p206*
Rare pub roof terrace in central London.

Sushisamba *p237*
Swish cocktails at the restaurant's Tree Bar on the 38th floor.

Sipsmith Distillery was in the vanguard of London's gin craze.

are every bit as big as Fridays for the post-work crowds. Pubs host relaxed, all-day drinking sessions as soon as the weekend hits, while a number of restaurants have adopted the trend for bottomless brunches (for the price of your food, the booze comes unlimited). It's the new Sunday lunch for London's weekend socialites.

In summer, locals go a bit drink crazy. They'll flock to rooftop bars – many making the pilgrimage to Peckham to visit **Frank's Café** (*see p286*), now a long-term seasonal highlight in a multistorey carpark – or to the riverside pubs of east London's Docklands or to the almost bucolic pubs that line the Thames in Hammersmith and Putney.

Although the Night Tube launched in London in 2016, many have questioned the need for a 24-hour tube service for London drinkers. The liberalisation of the licensing laws means that any pub or bar can apply to open late, but noise-nuisance restrictions mean most still close their doors around midnight, with only a handful of places (mostly in the periphery where neighbours are fewer or more tolerant) opening until 3am. In all cases, you'll have to be over 18 to be served alcohol (or even admitted to many venues at night), while many bars embrace a Challenge 21 policy – if you're fresh-faced, expect to have to show ID.

Monmouth Coffee Company

Pubs host relaxed, all-day drinking sessions as soon as the weekend hits, while a number of restaurants have adopted the trend for bottomless brunches

Frank's Café

Shopping

Fashion, flowers, food and famous labels

Bustling, street-smart, savvy – London is a city where creativity flourishes in every industry, none more so than fashion. The defining look of the city is experimental, just not necessarily avant-garde, with the late Alexander McQueen one perfect example: the critics' darling who created a viable commercial brand. Unlike the pristine, classical style of Paris, say, or the more nakedly commercial nous of New York, London is blessed with a fashion scene that thrives on invention. It is fed by a wealth of new talent arriving from the fashion colleges and across the planet, talent that's sustained by a busy mix of high-end boutiques, trashy chains, dignified department stores and anything-goes markets. Whatever else, it seems Londoners just won't stop shopping.

We Built This City, *p174*

It's the fashion

We'd argue London is currently the fashion capital of the world. So it should be no surprise that some of the world's finest fashion retailers are here, from small independents – like Soho's **Machine-A**, a tireless champion of the most exciting emerging designers – all the way up to the big department stores. Part of the secret is that the big guys who might be in danger of slowing down have learnt to collaborate with the little guys who are still quick on their feet.

Selfridges (*see p144*) is a fine example. Opened in 1909, it is one of a handful of central London department stores to have thrived ever since the Edwardian shopping boom – yet in 2017 it hosted a pop-up stocking exclusive clothes, gifts and accessories by Fashion East, a non-profit organisation founded explicitly to bring on new talent in the hipster homelands around Brick Lane.

A city of shoppers, London is a kind of petri dish – and we're not talking about germs. Big brands use the capital as a testing ground, so Londoners are exposed to all the latest initiatives and launches. After years of perfecting everything from the cut of the silk shirts to the scribbly font on the carrier bags, it was here that the H&M family launched the first branch of **& Other Stories** in 2013 – and it looks like the Swedish retail behemoth is at it again, choosing London as the place to open its first concept store, Arket.

❤ Best fashion shops

Browns Fashion *p157*
One of the capital's favourite fashion boutiques, credited with discovering Alexander McQueen, John Galliano and Christopher Kane.

Dover Street Market *p117*
London was the birthplace of Rei Kawakubo's pioneering store: exclusive fashion, affordable streetwear and an excellent café.

LN:CC *p274*
The 'Late Night Chameleon Cafe' in a Dalston warehouse has an interior straight out of the Death Star. Super-exclusive, super-expensive.

Machine-A *p170*
A platform for London's most exciting emerging designers. Come here to discover independent brands you've not yet heard of but will be incredibly happy to discover.

In the know
Opening hours

Shops are generally open 10am-6pm Monday to Saturday, with few closing on bank holidays (Christmas is the sole exception to that rule). Most don't open until around noon on Sundays, which gives you plenty of time to refuel for a day of pavement pounding with a good brunch (see *p45* Best brunches). In general the shops in central London close later on Thursday nights, with the Oxford Street stores staying open until 10pm.

Dover Street Market

It's not all about the high street, either: Japanese designer Rei Kawakubo of Comme des Garçons could have opened her ground-breaking concept store **Dover Street Market** in Tokyo's buzzy Ginza fashion district, but she placed it among the stuffy old cigars and suits of London's Mayfair.

Department stores and chain reactions

The sheer number of top-class designers creates fierce competition, so even the retail stalwarts have to remain fresh to survive. Selfridges is again the pioneer – for Christmas 2016 saw genderqueer performance gang **Sink the Pink** (*see p335*) putting on pantos in its basement – but even **Liberty** (*see p388*), which still trades William Morris pattern scarves from grand half-timbered premises like it's 1893, is in a constant state of reinvention, with refreshes to its beauty chamber, pop-ups from the likes of Tom Dixon and, most recently, hosting Maria Tash and her pretty piercings.

Elsewhere a high-street giant like **Topshop** (*see p145*) might rest on its laurels, complacent in its confidence that customers would always come through the doors. Not in London: the mammoth flagship store keeps things lively with a revolving roster of concessions, an in-store tattooist and a branch of Bleach hairdressers.

Only in London

While the city's particular strength is fashion, London has more to offer than posh frocks and directional sweatshirts. There's a wealth of niche shops, specialising in traditional umbrellas (**James Smith & Sons**, *see p188*), cheese (**Neal's Yard Dairy**, *see p188*) and gourmet teas (**Postcard Teas**, *see p157*) – even, in the mustachioed heartlands of east London, cacti (**Prick**, 492 Kingsland Road, E8 4AE, www.prickldn.com) and hand-carved wooden spoons (**Barn the Spoon**, 260 Hackney Road, E2 7SJ, barnthespoon.com).

LN:CC

Machine-A

In the know
Remember this

Not all souvenir shops are full of junk. Single-handedly rebuilding their tarnished reputation, **We Built this City** (see *p174*) is full of witty, cool and creative London-themed mementos. It's the kind of shop that can make a tea towel a pretty decent gift.

Market up

East London is also home to two of the city's best markets: **Columbia Road** (*see p270*) and **Broadway Market** (*see p272*). The source of their success is very different: Columbia Road kept true to its traditions, while Broadway Market underwent stunning reinvention in the 2000s. If you're really just after a stroll (and the jam-packed crowds are part of the fun), Columbia Road's the one: stop to smell the roses before investigating the dinky independent shops round the corner. Broadway Market is the nexus of dress-down catwalk and street eats, but it's still possible to pick up an intriguing little something from the accessory and apparel stalls, not to mention those selling something altogether more mouth-watering. For gifts to take back home, though, we say nip round the corner to Netil Market, a great little space dedicated to local designer-makers and the perfect spot to pick up locally made gifts.

♥ Best manicures

WAH Soho *p171*
Possibly the coolest hangout in the entire capital – and an attraction in itself – head here for its famous nail art.

Cheeky Holborn *p401*
Next door to the Hoxton Holborn, this is where to go at breakfast: get your nails done with a side of bee-pollen porridge – talk about multi-tasking.

Hula Nails *p229*
Pin-curled staff, super-kitsch decor and retro vibes at a Tiki-themed parlour.

Barber & Parlour *p265*
A multi-storey beauty and grooming gaff just off Redchurch Street; it offers top-notch manis, and has a cinema in its basement.

Columbia Road Market

Where To Spend It

London's shopping districts – the cheat sheet

Soho

The fear is that Soho will one day soon lose all its individuality to a developer-led invasion of faceless national brands. For the moment, it remains one of the most exciting places to shop in the city, with a slew of brilliant boutiques carrying independent labels: start with **OTHER/Shop** (*see p170*), now on Berwick Street, and Brewer Street's **Machine-A** (*see p170*), before taking on one-off international flagships, like contemporary Swedish sneaker brand **Axel Arigato** (*see p170*). And while nearby Carnaby Street may not be crawling with mods anymore, it has a healthy mix of one-off stores from international brands – notably London's only **Monki** (*see p174*).

Marylebone

Marylebone is a really lovely part of the city for a shopaholic wander. It has brilliant shops for contemporary design, but is also home to **Daunt** (*see p149*), with its stained-glass windows and titles arranged by country. Then there's cool, calm Chiltern Street, blessed with both pretty Victorian Gothic architecture and genuinely great independent shops, particularly for men: vintage Americana from **John Simons** (*see p150*) and a branch of trad British brand **Sunspel** (*see p265*).

Islington

With the design quarter Clerkenwell just down the road, Islington is well served by stylish little shops. Head down Camden Passage for teensy boutiques (**Annie's** vintage and wool shop **Loop** are favourites), dinky cafés and the bargain-filled antique stalls for which it's famous. Upper Street – the main thoroughfare – is mainly chain stores and mainstream restaurants (do check out the menswear at **Sefton**), but if you head down Essex Road there are a couple of nice surprises: **Molly Meg**, one of the sweetest kids' shops in London, and, just off the main road on Cross Street, a careful edit of brilliant brands and fine coffee at **Paper Mache Tiger**.

Shoreditch

It's hard these days to remember Shoreditch as a ropey part of town: this neighbourhood now attracts a mash-up of serious shoppers and people doing the Jack the Ripper walking tour. Nonetheless, it has managed to keep its individuality, with **Redchurch Street** (*see p265*) a shopping destination in its own right. It is also home to the apparently temporary **Boxpark** (actually resident since 2011), which hosts a changing roster of brands in its shipping containers. On Sundays, factor in time to visit the **Sunday Upmarket** in the Old Truman Brewery for vintage clothes, fashion, accessories and gifts from independent makers.

Covent Garden

Less stressful than busy Oxford Street, Covent Garden is full of chains (don't turn your nose up: there's a particularly good H&M with a separate beauty hall) but happily has a wealth of independent stores, too. It plays host to **Nigel Cabourn Army Gym** (*see p189*) – his only stand-alone retail concept outside Japan – and the **Vintage Showroom** (*see p189*), a famously good vintage store; the prettiest, daintiest jewellery from **Laura Lee** and, next door, quirky plastic accessories at **Tatty Devine**.

The two other key markets are at opposite ends of town. At the far end of the tourist-magnet South Bank, **Borough Market** (*see p92*) rejuvenated its noble history of food wholesaling with street eats and gourmet snacking – a reinvention that worked so well the cognoscenti now sniffily head a little further east of London Bridge to **Maltby Street** (*see p96*). Then, in west London, Notting Hill's **Portobello Road** (*see p300*) has stall after stall of vintage goodies – with admittedly few bargains, but great atmosphere. Up-and-coming designers come out in force on Fridays.

You're booked

The bookshop didn't die, it turns out. Like everywhere else, their survival in London comes down to creatively selected stock, helpful and informed sellers, fine events and, wherever possible, a café. At different ends of the spectrum, the **London Review Bookshop** (*see p202*) and **Foyles** (*see p164*) tick all these boxes. The former is a tiny place with stock that's all killer and no filler; the latter is a multi-storey book palace, pragmatically redeveloped a few years ago. To these can be added historic beauties, like **Daunt Marylebone** (*see p149*), specialists like comics emporium **Gosh!** (*see p170*), and the combination of both that is **Cecil Court** (*see p177*).

While we're being all old-fashioned... vinyl, eh? Bricks-and-mortar record-selling also survives, even thrives, when it knows its niche. In Soho, record shops keep on spinning near **Berwick Street** (*see p170*), while **Honest Jon's** (*see p299*) in Notting Hill and Brick Lane's **Rough Trade East** (*see p262*) are institutions – if, by institution, you mean something that's still full of life after decades doing what it does. Much like London itself.

In the know
Museum shops

In London, shopping opportunities crop up all the time. You might find yourself being all cultural at the **Barbican** (see p228), only to realise you're within grabbing distance of a carefully curated design, art and architecture gift shop. The same is true of **Tate Modern** (see p87), full of artist-designed exclusives; the new **Design Museum** (see p302), a trove of ingenious gadgets and sleek homeware; and the **V&A** (see p126), chock-a-block with bold jewellery and unusual gifts.

Honest Jon's

In the know
Practicalities

Don't forget your tote bag! If the store you're shopping in only has plastic bags, you will be charged 5p extra to use one. It isn't a lot of money and it goes to charity, but the scheme was introduced by the government to protect the environment by reducing the number of plastic bags being used, so best to come prepared.

If you're travelling from outside the EU you can claim back most of the VAT – the 20% 'value-added tax' that's included in the price of almost everything you buy – via a scheme called 'Tax Free Shopping' (see p415).

LONDON
LOOP

Gorgeous knitting & crochet supplies

Explore

Getting Started

Plan, pre-book and orientate yourself before you start exploring

The key to London's geography is that it is two cities, not one. The City is the area originally walled by the Romans, which, through its mercantile wealth and the weakness of English kings, secured considerable independence from Westminster. Westminster is where the monarchs and, latterly, Parliamentarians reside. Around these poles, the patchwork of districts grew up that are now central London.

For this guide, we first take a roughly clockwise journey through central London, starting with the district that has become over the last two decades its premier tourist area. A pleasant Thameside stroll takes throngs of visitors along the **South Bank** (*see p76*) past such key attractions as Tate Modern, Shakespeare's Globe and the Shard. Across the river lies **Westminster** (*see p98*), where you'll find Westminster Abbey, the Houses of Parliament and, overlooking delightful St James's Park, Buckingham Palace; to its north, Trafalgar Square is the official centre of London. **South Kensington and Chelsea** (*see p120*) is the land of plenty for cash-flash non-doms, but also boasts the immense cultural riches of the Natural History Museum, Science Museum and, our favourite, the V&A. We then explore

❤ Best viewpoints

Shard *p94*
Recognisable from across London and offering views of every bit of the city.

Duck & Waffle *p236*
The Gherkin's so close you could eat it from this 40th-floor restaurant.

Monument *p233*
Anything we can do... Wren already did. This 17th-century memorial to the Great Fire is a fine historic viewpoint.

Alexandra Palace *p343*
Come for the vista and stay for a gig or festival.

Sky Garden *p236*
Glorious at sunset – and admission is free with a pre-booked ticket.

London Eye *p82*
This Millenium big wheel is still a Thameside hit.

the West End – that part of London west of the City – from the shops of **Oxford Street & Marylebone** (*see p138*) via the restaurants and bars of formerly naughty **Soho** (*see p160*) – just north of **Leicester Square** – to the boutiques of **Covent Garden** (*see p178*), also home to the fine London Transport Museum. To the north, academic **Bloomsbury** (*see p192*) leads up to the revitalised **King's Cross** area (*see p203*), with the British Museum and British Library the major points of interest. Finally, we come to London's busy financial centre, the **City** (*see p210*), where you'll find St Paul's Cathedral, the Tower of London and the Museum of London, an essential stop to gain an understanding how London came to be.

Around these central areas is a doughnut of other sights you won't want to miss: Camden Market in **North London** (*see p242*); trendier-than-thou **East London** (*see p254*), where you'll find Spitalfields, Brick Lane and Shoreditch, with Dalston further north; **South London** (*see p278*), which combines the historic appeal of Greenwich and Kew Gardens with freshly funky Peckham; and **West London** (*see p294*), where Notting Hill is neighbour to the fabulous new Design Museum.

♥ Best London cliché

Buckingham Palace *p113*
Go on – try to make that Guardsman giggle.

Camden Market *p242*
Punks. With dyed, spiky hair and torn leather. You know, like it's still 1977.

Royal Academy of Arts *p158*
You could see the art – or grab a selfie in the classic red phonebox in the courtyard.

Stand on the left...
...and make the locals grumpy. When you're on a Tube escalator, you should stand on the *right* so that anyone who wants to can *walk* on the left. While you're at it, try hailing a black cab with its roof light off...

Trafalgar Square *p102*
See Nelson on his column, then catch an old-fashioned double decker bus (*see p74*).

In the know
Appy travels

Central London is easy to get around: if you're in doubt, get the nearest Tube from where you are to where you want to be. But, as more and more exciting things crop up in more peripheral neighbourhoods, you'll have to master 'multimodal' transport – in other words, travel like a Londoner using a mixture of the Tube, trains, buses and walking. The best advice? Download the free transport app **Citymapper** to your smartphone before arriving. Provide an address, point of interest or postcode and it lays out all your transport options, with connections, fares and time estimates for each. Want to find out what to do while you're out and about? Also download the digital edition of the free **Time Out magazine** to your phone or tablet to get our editors' selection of the best culture, food and fun each week. If you don't want to spend a fortune on roaming charges, Wi-Fi is available in hotels, major museums, several Tube stations and most cafés.

Getting around

London's a big city, but might not feel it. In the centre, many attractions are surprisingly close to each other: the **Transport for London walking distance map** (http://content.tfl.gov.uk/walking-tube-map.pdf) reveals, to cite only the best known example, that Covent Garden station is only five minutes' walk from Leicester Square station. It looks much further on the schematic Underground map. When you do need public transport, it offers good coverage of the city through a combination of underground trains (the Tube), surface trains (rail and Overground services), buses, cabs and taxis, even Thames boats and an official bike hire scheme; for details, *see pp404-409*.

Information and advice

There are tourist information centres in two of the focal sightseeing areas of London: the **City of London Information Centre** (7332 3456, www.cityoflondon.gov.uk) is next to St Paul's Cathedral (see *p224*) at the top of the slope down to the Millennium Bridge and across the Thames to Tate Modern (*see p87*), while the **Greenwich Tourist Information Centre** (0870 608 2000, www.visitgreenwich.org.uk) is in one of the halls of the historic Old Royal Naval College. An easy walk from Covent Garden, there's a further information point outside Holborn tube: the **Holborn Information Kiosk**

(closed weekends). **Travel Information Centres** at King's Cross, Euston, Liverpool Street and Victoria rail stations, and Piccadilly Circus tube (*see p150*) sell tickets for transport – and for some attractions.

Prices and discounts

There's good news for price-conscious visitors to London: admission to the permanent collections of almost all the key museums is absolutely free (they only charge for blockbuster temporary exhibitions). That means paid-for discount cards such as the **London Pass** (www.londonpass.com) only make sense if you're planning to do several of the eligible attractions: among them St Paul's (*see p224*), Westminster Abbey (*see p109*), the London Transport Museum (*see p183*), London Zoo (*see p245*), Kew Gardens (*see p292*) or any of the Historic Royal Palaces (including the Tower of London, *p234*). All our listings

---

**In the know
Rush hour**

Do try to avoid travelling at peak times. The Tube and buses can be extremely unpleasant at 7.30-9.30am and 4.30-6.30pm on weekdays, especially in the heat of summer – avoid the crush by travelling after 9.30am and you'll also pay less for your fare (which is then deemed 'off-peak').

give pricing information. For travel, by far the cheapest option is to use an **Oyster card** or **contactless credit/debit card** (*see p405*). And if you're partial to posh nosh, do check out the prix fixe lunches offered by most of London's swankier restaurants – especially in Mayfair. They aren't always cheap, but can be astonishingly good value for the quality.

Tours
On foot
For free, self-guided walking tours, head to **www.walklondon.org.uk** or the Greater London section of the Royal Geographical Society's **www.discoveringbritain.org**. Good choices for paid group tours include **And Did Those Feet** (www.chr.org.uk) and **Original London Walks** (www.walks. com). More idiosyncratic outings include London seen through its old maps (www. londontrails.wordpress.com), public conveniences (lootours.com), art scene (www.foxandsquirrel.com), fashion trends (www.urbangentry.com) and the radical history of the East End (www.eastendwalks. com). **Unseen Tours** (07514 266774, www. sockmobevents.org.uk) are noteworthy: they are led by homeless guides, who bring their own perspective to well-known landmarks and the quirkier nooks of the city.

By bicycle
The **London Bicycle Tour Company** (7928 6838, www.londonbicycle.com) runs a range of tours from the South Bank, while **Boris Bikes** can be an affordable option for self-starters (*see p409*).

By boat
Explore the River Thames by speedboat with **Thames RIB Experience** (3613 2356, www.thamesribexperience.com; £26.50-£55, £23.50-£39 reductions), by canoe with **London Kayak Tours** (0845 453 2002, www.londonkayaktours.co.uk, from £39) or take a more conventional hop-on, hop-off tour with **City Cruises** (7740 0400, www. citycruises.com; from £10, £5 reductions). There are narrowboat tours from Camden with **Jason's Trip Canal Boats** (www.jasons. co.uk; £9.50 single, £8.50 reductions; £14.50 return, £13.50 reductions; Apr-Nov).

By bus
Big Bus Company (7808 6753, bigbustours. com; from £31.50, £16.20 reductions, free under-5s) and **Original London Sightseeing Tour** (8877 1722, www. theoriginaltour.com; £32, £15-£29 reductions, free under-5s) both offer multiple hop-on, hop-off stops near the key central London sights, with the price of the ticket including a river cruise.

By car
Offering fun takes on London's motor-car culture are **Black Taxi Tours** of London (7935 9363, www.blacktaxitours.co.uk; £150 per cab) and **Small Car Big City** (7839 6737, smallcarbigcity.com; from £119 per car) in a groovy Mini Cooper.

By air
Money no object? Take an eye-popping aerial tour with **Adventure Balloons** (01252 844222, adventureballoons.co.uk; from £189; late Apr-mid Aug) or the **London Helicopter** (7887 2626, www. thelondonhelicopter.com; from £150).

Routemasters
London's original hop-on, hop-off double-decker bus

Trundling the streets since the 1950s, the hugely popular Routemaster bus, London's original hop-on, hop-off double-decker, was retired in 2005 – to howls of protest. Former mayor Boris Johnson vowed to resurrect the service – and did so with a fleet of handsomely designed red double-deckers, officially known as the New Routemaster (but routinely dubbed the 'Boris Bus'). The new fleet briefly offered the hop-on, hop-off service that was central to their design, but this proved pointlessly expensive and was quietly dropped, leaving the rear-access doors largely redundant. Found to be uncomfortably hot on the top deck in summer, the buses also used a hybrid engine technology that has been overtaken by cleaner, cheaper alternatives, so new mayor Sadiq Khan cancelled future orders in September 2016. Still, 195 more New Routemasters arrived in summer 2017, so they'll be running through London for a good while yet. But for a real nostalgia kick, you can still ride refurbished 1960-64 Routemasters for the same price as any other bus. A heritage service runs on route 15 (between Trafalgar Square and Tower Hill); head to stop F, on the Strand to the east of the square. Buses run every 15 minutes from around 9.30am; you must have a ticket or valid card before boarding (see p405).

South Bank & Bankside

An estimated 14 million people come this way each year, and it's easy to see why. Between the London Eye and Tower Bridge, the south bank of the Thames offers a two-mile procession of diverting arts and entertainment venues and events.

The area's modern-day life began in 1951 with the Festival of Britain, staged to boost morale in the wake of World War II. The Royal Festival Hall stands testament to the inclusive spirit of the project; it was later expanded into the Southbank Centre, alongside the BFI Southbank cinemas and the concrete ziggurat of the National Theatre.

The riverside really took off in the new millennium, with the arrival of the London Eye, the Millennium Bridge and Tate Modern, and the expansion of Borough Market, but it continues to thrive with the arrival of the Shard and Tate Modern's extraordinary new extension.

❤ Don't miss

1 The Shard *p94*
The bird's-eye view not every bird has the energy to flap up to.

2 El Pastór *p91*
Best of the new crop of restaurants at gourmet Borough Market.

3 Tate Modern *p87*
Power station turned burgeoning artistic powerhouse.

4 Dandelyan *p84*
Exhilarating new cocktails, right by the Thames.

5 Imperial War Museum *p84*
Conflict histories in refreshed displays.

London Eye

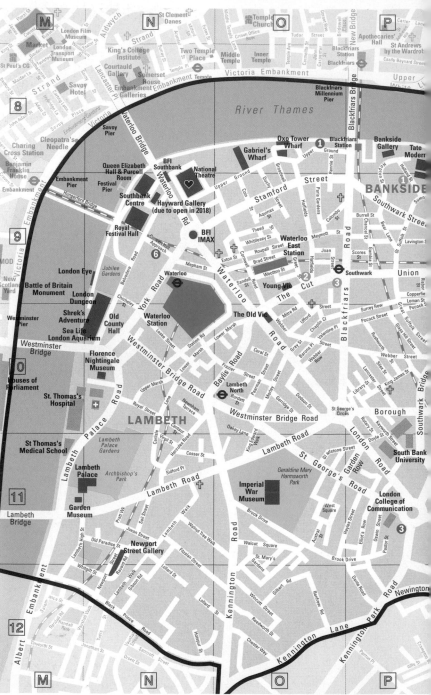

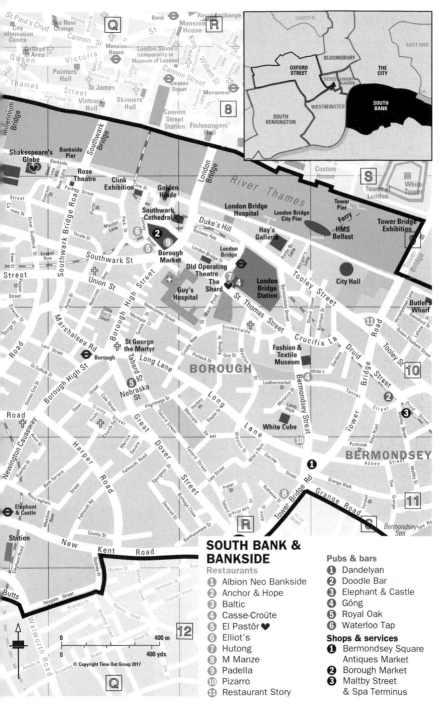

SOUTH BANK & BANKSIDE

Restaurants
1 Albion Neo Bankside
2 Anchor & Hope
3 Baltic
4 Casse-Croûte
5 El Pastór ♥
6 Elliot's
7 Hutong
8 M Manze
9 Padella
10 Pizarro
11 Restaurant Story

Pubs & bars
1 Dandelyan
2 Doodle Bar
3 Elephant & Castle
4 Gōng
5 Royal Oak
6 Waterloo Tap

Shops & services
1 Bermondsey Square Antiques Market
2 Borough Market
3 Maltby Street & Spa Terminus

SOUTH BANK

▶ *Embankment or Westminster tube, or Waterloo tube/rail.*

Thanks to the sharp turn the Thames makes around Waterloo, **Lambeth Bridge** lands you east of the river, not south, opposite the Tudor gatehouse of **Lambeth Palace**. Since the 12th century, it's been the official residence of the Archbishop of Canterbury. The palace is not normally open to the public, except on holidays. The church next door, St Mary at Lambeth, is now the **Garden Museum**, while worshippers of the cult of Damien Hirst do well to check out his ambitious new **Newport Street Gallery**. The benches along the river here are great for viewing the Houses of Parliament opposite, before things get crowded after **Westminster Bridge**, where London's major riverside tourist zone begins.

Next to the bridge is **County Hall**, once the seat of London government, now home to the **Sea Life London Aquarium** and the **London Dungeon**. In front of these attractions, in full view of the lovely **Jubilee Gardens**, the wheel of the **London Eye** rotates serenely.

When the **Southbank Centre** (*see p357*) was built in the 1950s and 1960s, the big concrete boxes that together contain the Royal Festival Hall (RFH), the Queen Elizabeth Hall (QEH), the Purcell Room and the Hayward Gallery were hailed as a daring statement of modern architecture. Along with the National Theatre, they comprise one of the largest and most popular arts districts in the world.

The centrepiece is Sir Leslie Martin's handsome **Royal Festival Hall** (1951), given a £91-million overhaul in 2007, which enhanced the acoustics and refurbished the seating of the main auditorium. The upper floors include an improved Poetry Library and event rooms, in which readings are delivered against the backdrop of the Eye and, on the far side of the river, Big Ben. Behind the hall, **Southbank Centre Square** hosts a food market every weekend, and there are cafés and chain restaurants all around.

Next door to the Royal Festival Hall, and just across from the building housing the QEH and the Purcell Room, the **Hayward Gallery** is a landmark of Brutalist architecture – all three venues are due to reopen at the end of the multi-million pound 'Let the Light In' refurbishment programme in 2018, with the Hayward leading the way in January.

Tucked under Waterloo Bridge is **BFI Southbank** (*see p324*); the UK's premier arthouse cinema, it's run by the British Film Institute. At the front is a second-hand book market – fun, but not brilliant for real finds. Due to its relative height and location just where the Thames bends from north–south to east–west, **Waterloo Bridge** provides some of the finest views of London, especially at dusk. It was designed by Sir Giles Gilbert Scott, the man behind Tate Modern, in 1942. East of the bridge is Denys Lasdun's terraced **National Theatre** (*see p362*), another Brutalist concrete structure, recently much improved.

Shaded by trees dotted with blue LEDs, the river path leads past a rare sandy patch of riverbed, busy with sand sculptors in warm weather, to **Gabriel's Wharf**, a collection of eateries and small independent shops that range from stylish to kitsch.

Next door, the deco tower of **Oxo Tower Wharf** was designed to circumvent advertising regulations for the stock-cube company that used to own the building. Saved by local action group Coin Street Community Builders, it now provides

♥ Time to eat & drink

Quick pasta fix
Padella *p90*

Borough Market bistro
Casse-Croûte *p93*

Party-time tacos
El Pastór *p91*

Michelin-starred innovations
Restaurant Story *p96*

A taste of old London town
M Manze *p94*

Thoroughly inventive cocktails
Dandelyan *p84*

Beer! Beer! Beer!
Waterloo Tap *p84*

Booze with a view
Gông *p96*

♥ Time to shop

The go-to for gourmets
Borough Market *p92*, Maltby Street *p96*

affordable housing, interesting designer shops and galleries, and restaurants (including a rooftop restaurant and bistro with more wonderful views). Next door, the **Mondrian** hotel (*see p399*) has brought a bit of buzz to this part of the South Bank – not least through the impressive ground-floor cocktail bar **Dandelyan**.

Sights & museums

Currently undergoing substantial refurbishment, the **Hayward Gallery** (Southbank Centre, Belvedere Road, SE1 8XX, 7960 4200, www.southbankcentre. co.uk) is set to reopen in January 2018. This versatile gallery has no permanent collection, but has always run a good programme of temporary exhibitions, among them Antony Gormley's fog-filled chamber for 'Blind Light', a rooftop rowing boat for group show 'Psycho Buildings' and Carsten Höller's roller-coaster slides.

Florence Nightingale Museum
*St Thomas' Hospital, 2 Lambeth Palace Road, SE1 7EW (7188 4400, www.florence-nightingale.co.uk). Westminster tube or Waterloo tube/rail. **Open** 10am-5pm daily. **Admission** £7.50; £4.80 reductions; £15 family; free under-5s. **Map** p78 N10.*

The nursing skills and campaigning zeal that made Nightingale a Victorian legend are honoured here. Reopened after refurbishment for the centenary of her death in 2010, the museum is now a chronological tour through a remarkable life via three key themes: family life, the Crimean War, health reformer. Among the period mementoes – clothing, furniture, books, letters and portraits – are Nightingale's lantern and stuffed pet owl, Athena.

Garden Museum
*Lambeth Palace Road, SE1 7LB (7401 8865, www.gardenmuseum.org.uk). Lambeth North tube or Waterloo tube/rail. **Open** 10.30am-5pm Mon-Fri, Sun; 10.30am-4pm Sat; check website for occasional closures. **Admission** Museum £10; £5-£8.50 reductions; free under-6s. Tower £3, free under-18s. **Map** p78 M11.*

Saved from demolition in the 1970s, the deconsecrated church of St Mary's is a fitting site for the world's first horticulture museum: it was the last resting place of intrepid plant hunter and gardener to Charles I, John Tradescant (c1570-1638). Recently reopened after a £7.5 million redevelopment, the museum's interior features seven galleries containing gardening memorabilia from 1600 to the modern day, including Britain's

Riverside at Southbank Centre

London Eye

oldest watering can and Harold Gilman's intriguing *Portrait of a Black Gardener*. The new courtyard extension contains a garden of rare plants, designed by Dan Pearson, and a café. You can climb the 14th-century tower and explore the Ark Gallery – based on the Tradescants' 17th-century cabinet of curiosities – as well as visiting temporary exhibitions. It's a quiet place for reflection, too.

The extension was built without foundations due to the 20,000 bodies buried on the site – some dating back to the Norman Conquest. During the works a vault containing no fewer than five lost archbishops was found. The stone sarcophagus containing the remains of William Bligh, the captain of the mutinous HMS *Bounty*, is also here.

London Dungeon

County Hall, Westminster Bridge Road, SE1 7PB (www.thedungeons.com/london). Westminster tube or Waterloo tube/rail. **Open** *10am-4pm Mon-Wed, Fri; 11am-5pm Thur; 10am-6pm Sat, Sun. School holidays varies.* **Admission** *£30; £24 reductions; free under-3s. Book online for 30% reductions.* **Map** *p78 N9.*

Visitors to this jokey celebration of torture, death and disease journey back in time to London's plague-ridden streets (rotting corpses, rats, vile boils, projectile vomiting) and meet some of the city's least savoury characters, from Guy Fawkes to Sweeney Todd. A cast of blood-splattered actors are joined by 'virtual' guests, such as Brian

Blessed as Henry VIII, as well as 18 different shows and 'surprises' – which could see you on the run from Jack the Ripper or getting lost in London's Victorian sewers. There are two thrill rides too: a turbulent boat trip down the Thames for execution, and a dark drop ride that plunges three storeys in the pitch black.

London Eye

Jubilee Gardens, SE1 7PB (www.londoneye. com). Westminster tube or Waterloo tube/ rail. **Open** *varies.* **Admission** *£24.95; £19.95 reductions; free under-3s. Ticket office in County Hall, next to London Eye. Book online for reductions.* **Map** *p78 N9.*

Here only since 2000, the Eye is nonetheless up there with Tower Bridge and 'Big Ben' among the capital's most postcard-friendly tourist assets. Assuming you choose a clear day, a 30-minute circuit on the Eye affords predictably great views of the city, with touchscreens in each of the 32 pods providing a guide to what you can see. Take a few snaps from the comfort of your pod and, there, your sightseeing's just about done – and the fact that the vista changes makes it a doughty competitor to the Shard (*see p94*). The Eye was the vision of husband-and-wife architect team Julia Barfield and David Marks, who entered a 1992 competition to design a structure for the millennium. Their giant wheel idea came second, but the winning entry is conspicuous by its absence. The Eye was planned as a temporary structure but its removal now seems unthinkable.

Newport Street Gallery

Newport Street, SE11 6AJ (3141 9320, www. newportstreetgallery.com/about). Vauxhall tube/rail or Lambeth North tube. **Open** *10am-6pm Tue-Sun.* **Admission** *free.* **Map** *p78 N11.*

Damien Hirst, the Young British Artist par excellence, isn't a man to do things by halves – unless, that is, taking half a street of listed warehouses and converting them into a huge gallery. Across two levels, six exhibition spaces and some 37,000sq ft of floor, his private collection of 3,000 works is displayed in temporary exhibitions: with holdings that include Picasso, Francis Bacon and Jeff Koons alongside YBA chums like Sarah Lucas and Gavin Turk, he's got plenty of art to choose from, but there's also taxidermy, indigenous art from the Pacific Northwest and anatomical models. The space was brilliantly reworked by Caruso St John (the architects won the 2017 Stirling Prize for their efforts) and has a fine restaurant run by the estimable Mark Hix.

Sea Life London Aquarium

County Hall, Westminster Bridge Road, SE1 7PB (www2.visitsealife.com/london). Westminster tube or Waterloo tube/rail. **Open** *10am-6pm Mon-Fri; 9.30am-7pm Sat, Sun. School holidays varies.* **Admission** *£25; £17.55 reductions; free under-3s. Book online for reductions.* **Map** *p78 N10.*

This is one of Europe's largest aquariums, and a huge hit with kids – perhaps too huge: it does get awfully crowded in the school holidays and at weekends. The inhabitants are grouped by geographical origin, beginning with the Atlantic, where blacktail bream swim alongside the Thames Embankment. The 'Rainforests of the World' exhibit has introduced poison arrow frogs, crocodiles and piranhas. The Ray Lagoon is still popular, though touching the friendly flatfish is no longer allowed (it's bad for their health). Starfish, crabs and anemones can be handled in special open rock pools instead, and the clown fish still draw crowds. There's a mesmerising Seahorse Temple, a tank full of turtles and enchanting Gentoo penguins. The centrepieces, though, are the massive Pacific and Indian Ocean tanks, with menacing sharks quietly circling fallen Easter Island statues.

Shrek's Adventure!

Riverside Building, County Hall, Westminster Bridge Road, SE1 7PB (www.shreksadventure. com/london). Westminster tube or Waterloo tube/rail. **Open** *10am-4pm Mon-Wed; Fri; 11am-5pm Thur; 10am-6pm Sat; 10am-5pm Sun.* **Admission** *£27.50; £22 reductions. Book online for 30% reductions.* **Map** *p78 N10.*

Opened in 2015, Shrek's Adventure! takes you on an immersive journey ('4D', in the jargon) through the worlds of the golden-hearted green ogre and other DreamWorks characters. It happens onboard a red double-decker bus, with Donkey as your driver to the Kingdom of Far, Far Away. Here you and your six- to 12-year-olds find yourselves part of the

story, solving clues, joining in the occasional singsong and generally doing silly things on a quest for that 'happy ever after' ending. With excellent set design and plenty of surprises, it's an engaging and amusing 75-minute trip into Shrek's off-kilter fairytale world.

Restaurants

Clustered around the **Royal Festival Hall**, you'll find plenty of chain restaurants (including Canteen, Feng Sushi, Giraffe, Pizza Express, Wahaca and Wagamama). There are also crêpe and pizza restaurants at **Gabriel's Wharf**, along the bank to the east, and good drinking and dining options in the **National Theatre** (*see p362*) and **BFI Southbank** (*see p324*).

Pubs & bars

A few floors up in the Royal Festival Hall building, the bar at **Skylon** (7654 7800, www.skylon-restaurant.co.uk) has one of the best river views in town, remaining relatively serene above the madness of the riverbank crowds.

♥ Dandelyan

Mondrian London, 20 Upper Ground, SE1 9PD (3747 1000, www.morganshotelgroup. com/mondrian). Blackfriars or Southwark tube. Open 4pm-1am Mon-Wed; noon-2am Thur-Sat; noon-12.30am Sun. Map p78 O8 ❶

The second bar opened by Ryan Chetiyawardana (aka bartender Mr Lyan) couldn't be more different from his first. Rather than occupying a converted Hoxton pub, Dandelyan has a prime spot off the lobby of the multimillion-pound Mondrian (*see p399*). The bar might be glamorous, luxurious and a bit formal, but the drinks show Chetiyawardana's invention and attention to detail are intact: the botanically themed drinks list includes ingredients such as 'chalk bitters', 'crystal peach nectar' and the archaic-sounding 'dandelion capillaire'. Everything is surprising without being show-off, and, importantly, it's all very drinkable.

♥ Waterloo Tap ££

Corner of Sutton Walk & Concert Hall Approach, SE1 8RL (3455 7436, www. waterlootap.com). Waterloo tube. Open noon-11pm Mon-Wed; noon-11.30pm Thur, Fri; 11am-11.30pm Sat; 11am-10pm Sun. Map p78 N9 ❻

Tucked away in a railway arch a short dash from Waterloo station, the Tap has bucked the trend towards the new breed of high-alcohol brews and stuck to its roots as a more traditional alehouse. You'll find no filament bulbs or scruffily chalked-up beer lists here. The 20-strong keg collection is

British-focused, with the north especially well represented (no surprise, given the original Tap is in Sheffield). If they're on, try something from Manchester's Cloudwater Brew Co, whose one-off, seasonal brews are never around for long.

WATERLOO & LAMBETH

▶ *Waterloo tube/rail or Lambeth North tube.*

Surprisingly, perhaps, there's plenty of interest around the stone-meets-glass rail terminus of London Waterloo. The most obvious attraction is the massive **BFI IMAX** (*see p322*), located in the middle of a roundabout at the southern end of Waterloo Bridge. The £20-million cinema makes use of a desolate space that, in the 1990s, was notorious for its 'Cardboard City' of homeless residents.

South, on the corner of Waterloo Road and the Cut, is the restored Victorian façade of the **Old Vic** theatre (*see p361*), which has settled comfortably into life after artistic director Kevin Spacey. Further down the Cut is the **Young Vic** (*see p367*), a hotbed of theatrical talent with a stylish balcony bar. Both bring a touch of West End glamour across the river.

Further south, into Lambeth, is the impressive – and steadily revamped – **Imperial War Museum**. The imposing premises were built in 1814 as a lunatic asylum (the Bethlehem Royal Hospital, aka Bedlam). After the inmates were moved out in 1930, the central block became the war museum, only to be damaged by air raids. Today, it provides a compelling and frequently hard-hitting history of armed conflict since World War I.

Sights & museums

♥ Imperial War Museum

Lambeth Road, SE1 6HZ (7416 5000, www. iwm.org.uk). Lambeth North tube or Elephant & Castle tube/rail. Open 10am-6pm daily. Admission free. Special exhibitions vary. Map p78 O11.

One of London's great museums – but probably the least famous of them – IWM London focuses on the military action of British and Commonwealth troops during the 20th century. One of the highlights, built to commemorate the 2014 centenary, is a state-of-the-art First World War gallery that takes a more considered, contemporary look at the conflict, examining the Home Front as much as the Western Front. Alongside huge set pieces like a walk-through trench is a heart-stopping collection of small, personal items and medical objects, including a magnet used to pull shrapnel from wounds. The Central Hall is an attention-grabbing repository of major artefacts: guns, tanks and aircraft hang from the ceiling (not least a Harrier GR9 that saw action in Afghanistan). Terraced galleries allow this section of the museum also to show a Snatch Land Rover from Iraq and an Argentine operating table from the Falklands.

The museum's tone darkens as you ascend. On the third floor, the Holocaust Exhibition (not recommended for under-14s) traces the history of European anti-Semitism and its nadir in the concentration camps. Upstairs, Crimes Against Humanity (unsuitable for under-16s) is a minimalist space in which a film exploring contemporary genocide and ethnic violence rolls relentlessly. At the top, a new gallery explores contemporary conflicts.

Restaurants

Anchor & Hope ££
36 The Cut, SE1 8LP (7928 9898, www. anchorandhopepub.co.uk). Southwark tube or Waterloo tube/rail. **Open** *5-11pm Mon; 11am-11pm Tue-Sat; 12.30-3.15pm Sun. Food served 6-10.30pm Mon; noon-2.30pm, 6-10.30pm Tue-Sat; 12.30-3.15pm Sun.* **Map** *p78 O9* ❷ *Gastropub*

Open for more than a decade, the Anchor & Hope is still a leading exponent of

using 'head-to-tail' ingredients (offal and unusual cuts of meat) in simple but artful combinations, served in a relaxed setting. Bookings aren't taken, so most evenings you'll join the waiting list for a table (45mins midweek is typical) and have to hover at the crammed bar. But the food is terrific: beautifully textured venison kofte, say, served on perkily dressed gem lettuce leaves; or rabbit served savagely red, with salty jus, fat chips and béarnaise sauce.

Baltic ££
74 Blackfriars Road, SE1 8HA (7928 1111, www.balticrestaurant.co.uk). Southwark tube. **Open** *5.30-11.15pm Mon; noon-3pm, 5.30-11.15pm Tue-Sat; noon-4.30pm, 5.30-10.30pm Sun.* **Map** *p78 O9* ❸ *Eastern European*

A modern take on Polish/central European classics is served in surroundings of understated glamour, with pared-down monochrome decor punctuated by a supersized chandelier dripping shards of golden amber. You'll struggle to find such enjoyable buckwheat blinis topped with smoked salmon or tender herring elsewhere. Home-style pleasures abound, such as rabbit braised in a fragrant broth flavoured with sweet prune and smoky bacon, served with little knobbly spätzle dumplings. Start with a classy clear vodka such as Zytnia (rye), then move on to one of Baltic's own tasty ginger or spicy orange varieties.

Imperial War Museum

Globe Theatre

BANKSIDE

▶ *Borough or Southwark tube, or Blackfriars or London Bridge tube/rail.*

In Shakespeare's day, the area known as Bankside was the centre of bawdy Southwark, neatly located just beyond the jurisdiction of the City fathers. As well as playhouses such as the Globe and the Rose, there were the famous 'stewes' (brothels) presided over by the bishops of Winchester, who made a tidy income from the fines they levied on the area's 'Winchester Geese' (or, in common parlance, prostitutes). There's less drinking, carousing and mischief-making here these days, but the area's cultural heritage remains alive thanks to the reconstructed **Shakespeare's Globe** and, pretty much next door to it, the recently dramatically extended **Tate Modern**, a former power station that's now a gallery.

Spanning the river in front of the Tate, the **Millennium Bridge** for pedestrians opened in 2000, when it became the first new Thames crossing in London since Tower Bridge (1894). Its early days were fraught with troubles: after just two days, the bridge was closed because of a pronounced wobble caused by the resonance of thousands of people crossing together, and didn't reopen until 2002. Its difficulties long behind it, the bridge is an elegant structure – a 'ribbon of steel' in the words of its conceptualists, architect Lord Foster and sculptor Anthony Caro. Cross it and you're at the foot of the stairs leading up to St Paul's Cathedral (*see p224*); to the west, the massively refurbished **Blackfriars** rail station not only has an entrance on the south bank of the river, but runs train platforms right across the river on the podiums of an earlier, incomplete version of **Blackfriars Bridge**.

Pubs & bars

Elephant & Castle

*119 Newington Causeway Road, South Bank, SE1 6BN (7403 8124, elephantandcastlepub. com). Elephant & Castle tube. **Open** noon-midnight Mon-Thur, Sun; noon-2am Fri, Sat. **Map** p78 P11* ③

Pub histories don't come much better than that of the Elephant and Castle. Back in the 18th century, the entire area was named after it. In 1991, DJ Matt 'Jam' Lamont's Sunday morning raves made it the birthplace of UK Garage. Then, in 2015, it lost its licence. Nearly suffering the ignominious fate of being turned into an estate agent, it was saved by the council, who gave it protected status as an asset of community value. It's now a trendy joint, with craft beer on tap.

Sights & museums

Bankside Gallery

*48 Hopton Street, SE1 9JH (7928 7521, www. banksidegallery.com). Blackfriars tube/rail or Southwark tube. **Open** (during exhibitions) 11am-6pm daily. **Admission** free; donations appreciated. **Map** p78 P8.*

In the shadow of Tate Modern, this tiny gallery is the home of the Royal Watercolour Society and the Royal Society of Painter-Printmakers. The gallery runs a changing programme of exhibitions, with many of the displayed works for sale.

Shakespeare's Globe

*21 New Globe Walk, SE1 9DT (7902 1400, www.shakespearesglobe.com). Blackfriars tube/rail or Southwark tube. **Open** Exhibition*

9am-5pm daily. Tours 9.30am-5pm daily (except during performances). **Admission** £16; £12.50-£14.50 reductions; £43 family; free under-5s. **Map** p78 P8.

The original Globe Theatre, where many of William Shakespeare's plays were first staged and which he co-owned, burned to the ground in 1613 during a performance of *Henry VIII*. Nearly 400 years later, it was rebuilt not far from its original site, using construction methods and materials based on as much historical detail as could be found.

A visit here isn't just a history lesson. The Globe is also a fully operating open-air theatre (*see p360*) and the productions are among the best in London. Each season (from 23 April – conventionally regarded as the Bard's birthday – into early October) includes several Shakespeare classics, performed by a company of established and upcoming actors, but works of other writers are also programmed.

The Globe also now offers performances in the Sam Wanamaker Playhouse – a candlelit indoor theatre alongside the Globe, which presents plays in a traditional and intimate Jacobean setting.

Even if you're not attending a play, you can do the Globe Exhibition and Tour: the tours run all year, even out of season (allow 90 minutes for the visit).

♥ Tate Modern

Bankside, SE1 9TG (7887 8888, www.tate.org. uk). Blackfriars tube/rail or Southwark tube. **Open** *10am-6pm Mon-Thur, Sun; 10am-10pm Fri, Sat.* **Admission** *free. Temporary exhibitions vary.* **Map** *p78 P8.*

Thanks to its industrial architecture, this powerhouse of modern art is awe-inspiring even before you enter. Built after World War II as Bankside Power Station, it was designed by Sir Giles Gilbert Scott, architect of Battersea Power Station. The power station shut in 1981; nearly 20 years later, it opened as an art museum, and has enjoyed spectacular popularity ever since. The gallery attracts five million visitors a year – twice as many as the original building was intended for, hence the ten-storey extension that rose from the power station's former fuel tanks to completion in 2016. Known first as the Switch House – then renamed the Blavatnik Building after major donor Len Blavatnik – this vast, partly folded tower has increased exhibition space by 60 per cent and features a top-floor viewing level, restaurant, and three new floors of galleries. It has allowed for a 'progressive rehang' of Tate Modern's permanent collection across both the Blavatnik Building and current Tate Modern building, with more room for lesser-known international art. The cavernous Turbine Hall, used to jaw-dropping

Tate Modern

effect for the massive Hyundai Commission installation each year, has become what the Tate is calling 'the street' that connects both buildings, with walkways at different points.

Beyond, the permanent collection draws from the Tate's many post-1900 international works, featuring heavy-hitters such as Matisse, Rothko and Beuys – but the grouping by theme rather than chronology can make it hard to pilot your way through, by contrast to the gallery's much-improved elder sibling, Tate Britain (*see p111*). Many visit for the very busy blockbuster shows – or the views from the extension platform, notwithstanding the overworked lifts – without spending much time on the permanent collection.

In the know
Tate-to-Tate

The polka-dotted Tate-to-Tate boat zooms to Tate Britain every 40 minutes, with a stop-off at the London Eye – a very enjoyable trip. Tickets are available at both Tates, on board, online or by phone (7887 8888; £8, £2.65-£5.35 reductions, free under-5s).

Restaurants
There are some handy chain restaurants (Pizza Express, The Real Greek, Tas Pide) on the river near the Globe Theatre, plus more (Tsuru, Leon) behind Tate Modern on Canvey Street. **Tate Modern Café: Level 2** is good for those with children.

Albion Neo Bankside ££
Pavilion B, Holland Street, SE1 9FU (3764 5550, www.albioncafes.com). Southwark tube. **Open** *11.30am-10pm Mon-Fri; 9am-11pm Sat; 9am-6pm Sun.* **Map** *p78 P9* ❶ *British*

This glass-walled eaterie just behind Tate Modern was the second of Terence Conran's poshed-up British cafés. A secluded outdoor terrace overlooks a beautifully landscaped garden of mature silver birches – perfect for summer dining. Breakfast runs from toast and Marmite to a full English or kidneys on sourdough. Later on, the menu expands to include fish and chips, pies, bread and butter pudding and classic afternoon teas.

BOROUGH

▶ *Borough or Southwark tube, or London Bridge tube/rail.*

On the east side of Southwark Bridge, you'll find the **Anchor Bankside** pub (34 Park Street, SE1 9EF, 7407 1577, www.taylor-walker. co.uk). Built in 1775 on the site of an even older inn, the Anchor has, at various points, been a brothel, a chapel and a ship's chandler. The outside terrace, across the pathway, offers fine river views – a fact lost on no one each summer, when it's invariably crammed with people.

All that's left of the Palace of Winchester, home of successive bishops, is the ruined rose window of the Great Hall on Clink Street. It stands next to the site of the bishops' former Clink prison, where thieves, prostitutes and debtors all served their sentences; it's now the **Clink Prison Museum** (1 Clink Street, SE1 9DG, 7403 0900, www.clink.co.uk). At the other end of Clink Street, St Mary Overie's dock contains a terrific full-scale replica of Sir Francis Drake's ship, the **Golden Hinde**.

The main landmark here is the Anglican **Southwark Cathedral**, formerly St Saviour's and before that the monastic church of St Mary Overie. Shakespeare's brother Edmund was buried in the graveyard; there's a monument to the playwright inside. Just south of the cathedral is **Borough Market**, a busy covered food market dating from the 13th century, although with its new glass-fronted premises you'd hardly think so. There's still plenty of Victorian ironwork to enjoy. This is London's 'foodiest' public food market; stalls are limited on Mondays and Tuesdays, but it is crammed with buyers and sellers for the rest of the week. It's surrounded by good places to eat and drink. Not far away, the **George** (77 Borough High Street, SE1 1NH, 7407 2056, www.george-southwark.co.uk) is London's last surviving galleried coaching inn. Owned by the National Trust, it hosted Charles Dickens, among many others.

Fans of gore should head to the interesting and thoroughly grisly **Old Operating Theatre, Museum & Herb Garret**, with its body parts and surgical implements.

Sights & museums

Golden Hinde
Pickfords Wharf, Clink Street, SE1 9DG (7403 0123, www.goldenhinde.com). London Bridge tube/rail. **Open** *9am-5.30pm daily.* **Admission** *£7; £5 reductions; £20 family; free under-3s.* **Map** *p78 Q9.*

This meticulous replica of Sir Francis Drake's 16th-century flagship is thoroughly seaworthy: the ship has even reprised the privateer's circumnavigatory voyage. You can visit by means of a self-guided tour, but if you've got kids it's much more fun to join in on a 'living history' experience (some overnight): participants dress in period clothes, eat Tudor fare and learn the skills of the Elizabethan seafarer; book well in advance. At weekends, the ship swarms with children dressed up as pirates for birthday dos.

Old Operating Theatre, Museum & Herb Garret
9A St Thomas' Street, SE1 9RY (7188 2679, oldoperatingtheatre.com). London Bridge

Golden Hinde

tube/rail. **Open** *10.30am-5pm daily.*
Admission *£6.50; £3.50-£5 reductions; £14 family.* **Map** *p78 R9.*

The tower that houses this reminder of the surgical practices of the past used to be part of the chapel of St Thomas' Hospital. Before moving there, operations took place in the wards. Visitors enter via a vertiginous spiral staircase to inspect a pre-anaesthetic operating theatre dating from 1822, with tiered viewing seats for students. The operating tools look more like torture implements.

Southwark Cathedral
London Bridge, SE1 9DA (7367 6700, www. cathedral.southwark.anglican.org). London Bridge tube/rail. **Open** *8am-6pm Mon-Fri; 8.30am-6pm Sat, Sun (closing times vary on religious holidays). Services 8am, 8.15am, 12.30pm, 12.45pm, 5.30pm Mon-Fri; 9am, 9.15am, 4pm Sat; 8.45am, 9am, 11am, 3pm, 6pm Sun.* **Admission** *free; suggested donation £4.* **Map** *p78 Q9.*

The oldest bits of this building date back more than 800 years. The retro-choir was the setting for several Protestant martyr trials during the reign of Mary Tudor. Inside, there are memorials to Shakespeare, John Harvard (benefactor of the American university) and Sam Wanamaker (the motivation and driving force behind the reconstruction of the Globe); Chaucer features in the stained glass. There are displays throughout the cathedral explaining its history. The courtyard is one of the area's prettiest places for a rest; there's also a café.

Restaurants

Borough Market, full of stalls selling all kinds of wonderful food, is a superb foraging place for street-food enthusiasts, as well as the home to one of London's finest restaurants, **El Pastór** (*seep91*).

Elliot's ££
12 Stoney Street, SE1 9AD (7403 7436, www. elliotscafe.com). London Bridge tube/ rail. **Open** *noon-3pm, 6-10pm Mon-Fri; noon-4pm, 6-10pm Sat.* **Map** *p78 Q9* ⑥
Brasserie

Light and airy, with stripped brick walls and a contemporary feel, Elliot's is a busy spot. The choices are to sit out front while watching the world going by, to perch at the bar or to take a seat in the bright back area. The seasonal menu is short but innovative, and the ingredients are carefully sourced. Smaller plates such as pickled mackerel with apple and rye cracker are listed alongside larger plates such as lox cheek, polenta horse radish and pickled walnut. Drinks include a selection of natural wines (orange wines are listed alongside the expected white, red and rosé).

❤ Padella ££
6 Southwark Street, SE1 1TQ (www.padella. co). London Bridge tube/rail. **Open** *noon-4pm, 5-10pm Mon-Sat; noon-5pm Sun.* **Map** *p78 Q9* ⑨ *Italian*

This sleek pasta bar, from the duo behind Islington's Trullo (*see p252*), is ideal for a classy express lunch. There's a changing mix

Southwark Cathedral

💙 El Pastór ££

7a Stoney Street, SE1 9AA (www. tacoselpastor.co.uk). London Bridge tube/ rail. **Open** *noon-3pm, 5-11pm Mon-Fri; noon-4pm, 6-11pm Sat.* **Map** *p78 Q9* **5** *Mexican*

Take two things to El Pastór: a mobile phone and this guide, so you can find yourself a local bar. It's a taco joint in a railway arch next to foodie magnet Borough Market (*see p92*) and it doesn't accept bookings. The wait can, at peak times, be up to two hours. But at least there's no standing in the rain: they take your number and text when your table is ready. Plus you're on holiday – go late, go early, don't go on Saturday, go and make us hard-working locals jealous.

Why all the fuss? Well, pedigree first of all. El Pastór comes from the Hart Brothers (Sam and Eddie with, for the first time, little bro James). The Harts have been opening enjoyable London restaurants for more than a decade: Fino in 2003, three Barrafinas – the first in Soho in 2007, the second (another of our favourite restaurants, *see p185*) in 2014, the third in 2015 – all of them serving great food in a great atmosphere.

The food here? To kick off, you might try a tuna tostada, a bowl of fresh guac and a prawn taco on a nicely firm corn tortilla. Or the strip of stonebass and some juicy chunks of chargrilled chicken. Don't miss the signature 24-hour marinated 'al pastór' pork – just the thought of which makes us smile. With the pork, make sure you get 'gringa' quesadilla: a dirty and delicious quarter slice of a large tortilla, served 'open-faced', with a messy tumble of meat, melted cheese,

coriander and salsa. Every bite brings sweet, salt, fire, squidge and crunch. And save space for the 'DIY' beef short rib, too. One of only two large plates on the menu, it easily feeds two as a main. What you get is a big hunk of flesh that officially arrives on the bone, though if you so much as suggestively wave your fork in its direction, the moist, tender meat instantly shouts 'Geronimo!' and leaps away.

In truth, the place is a high-class summary of London's current favourite things when it comes to food: the combination of dirty food (by which we mean naughty, high-fat meat, not anything insanitary) with international street snacks; the post-industrial archway setting where exposed brick and corrugated iron are all the decor you need; the sense that a restaurant visit should be a party. The Harts are working with ex A&R man Crispin Somerville: he and Sam were mates at Manchester Uni, and they later ran a Mexico City restaurant and club together. And they know how to throw a fiesta, with excellent, Latin-vibey music cranked up loud; staff who are smiley and obliging; and the lighting set to 'looking good, baby'.

But what makes eating here an essential London experience is that El Pastór brings together one of the best restaurant trends – carefully sourced ingredients served in simple, flavour-punch combinations – with one of the worst: whoever decided no-booking policies were cool? Oh, that's right. The Harts at Barrafina Frith Street back in 2007.

of classics and lesser-spotted varieties, such as *tagliarini* (skinny tagliatelle) or *pici cacio* (a kind of hand-rolled no-egg noodle from Siena), smothered in a simple yet moreish sauce of parmesan, butter and cracked black pepper. The eight-hour beef shin ragu served over pappardelle is a perennial favourite, while the smoked eel and cream tagliatelle – with just a hint of Sicilian lemon – is sublime. Dishes are small enough (and, at around £5-£9, cheap enough) to let you to order three between two.

Pubs & bars

Royal Oak

*44 Tabard Street, SE1 4JU (7357 7173, www. harveys.org.uk/pubs/the-royal-oak-london). Borough tube. **Open** 11am-11pm Mon-Sat; noon-9.30pm Sun. Food served noon-3pm, 5-10pm Mon-Fri; noon-4pm, 5-10pm Sat; noon-7.30pm Sun. **Map** p78 Q10* **5**

Perfectly treading the line between old-man boozer and cutesy retro watering hole, this Victorian corner pub's a lovely blend of the scruffy and the pretty. Selling mainly ales from Harvey's brewery in Sussex (which runs the pub), drinkers are largely men in their thirties and older. But the most important thing about this characterful boozer: it's curiously unbothered by the crowds you'll find in other Borough pubs, making it perfect for a quiet few pints.

Shops & services

❤ Borough Market

*8 Southwark Street, SE1 1TL (7407 1002, www. boroughmarket.org.uk). London Bridge tube/ rail. **Open** 10am-5pm Mon-Thur; 10am-6pm Fri; 8am-5pm Sat. **No cards**. **Map** p78 Q9* **2** *Market*

The food hound's favourite market is also London's oldest, dating back to the 13th century. It's the busiest, too, occupying a sprawling site near London Bridge. Gourmet goodies run the gamut, from fresh loaves and rare-breed meats, via fish, game, fruit and veg, to cakes and all manner of preserves, oils and teas; head out hungry to take advantage of the numerous free samples. A rail viaduct, vigorously campaigned against, is now in place, which means restored historic features have been returned and works disruption should be at an end. As if to celebrate, a Market Hall, facing on to Borough High Street, was opened: it acts as a kind of greenhouse for growing plants (including hops), as well as hosting workshops, tastings and foodie demonstrations. You can also nip in with your snack if the weather's poor.

> **In the know**
> **Timing is everything**
>
> Although Borough Market is open on Monday and Tuesday, those days are mainly for tradespeople, and there are fewer stalls open to the general public. Given that weekends are almost always mobbed, Wednesday and Thursday are normally the best days on which to visit.

Borough Market

LONDON BRIDGE TO TOWER BRIDGE

▶ *Bermondsey tube or London Bridge tube/rail.*

Nothing can compete with the colossal, 1,016-foot **Shard** development at London Bridge station (*see p94*) – it towers over the immediate area, and the London skyline from pretty much everywhere – but there are more modest discoveries to be made further to the east. Next to the Thames is **Hay's Galleria**. Once an enclosed dock, it's now dominated by a peculiar kinetic sculpture called *The Navigators*. Exiting on the riverside, you can walk east past the great grey hulk of **HMS Belfast** to Tower Bridge. Beyond the battleship you'll pass the pristine environs of the **More London** complex – sold off to Kuwaiti investors in a £1.7-billion property deal – part of which is **City Hall**, home of London's current government. There's a pleasant outside area called the Scoop, used for outdoor events, and a handful of chain cafés.

South of here, many of the historic houses on Bermondsey Street now host hip design studios or funky shops. This is also where you'll find the **Fashion & Textile Museum**, as well as Jay Jopling's largest **White Cube** art gallery (nos.144-152, 7930 5373, www.whitecube.com, 10am-6pm Tue-Sat, noon-6pm Sun). At the street's furthest end, the redevelopment of Bermondsey Square created an arthouse cinema and the Bermondsey Square Hotel (*see p401*), alongside a charming cemetery park, but old timers linger on: the classic eel and pie shop **M Manze** and a Friday **antiques market** – great for browsing, but get there early.

If the Borough Market crowds are getting too much for you on a Saturday, there is a winning cluster of food stalls around **Maltby Street**, **Druid Street** and nearby **Spa Terminus**, and on the redeveloped **Ropewalk**.

Back on the riverfront, a board announces when Tower Bridge is next due to be raised. The bridge is one of the lowest to span the Thames, hence its twin lifting sections (or bascules). The original steam-driven machinery can be seen at the **Tower Bridge Exhibition** (*see p236*). Further east, the former warehouses of **Butler's Wharf** are now mainly given over to dining: they are pleasant enough for watching the river if you're not particularly watching the pennies. The **Design Museum**, however, is long gone: it moved from here to Holland Park in 2016 (*see p302*).

Sights & museums

Fashion & Textile Museum
83 Bermondsey Street, SE1 3XF (7407 8664, www.ftmlondon.org). London Bridge tube/rail. **Open** *11am-6pm Tue, Wed, Fri, Sat; 11am-8pm Thur; 11am-5pm Sun.* **Admission** *£9.90; £6-£7.70 reductions; free under-12s.* **Map** *p78 R10.*

As flamboyant as its founder, fashion designer Zandra Rhodes, this pink and orange museum holds 3,000 of Rhodes's garments and her archive of paper designs, sketchbooks, silk screens and show videos. The varied and always interesting temporary exhibits explore the work of trend-setters or themes such as the development of underwear. A quirky shop sells wares by new designers.

HMS Belfast
The Queen's Walk, SE1 2JH (7940 6300, www.iwm.org.uk). London Bridge tube/rail. **Open** *Mar-Oct 10am-6pm daily. Nov-Feb 10am-5pm daily.* **Admission** *£14.50; £8-£12.80 reductions; free under-5s.* **Map** *p78 S9.*

This 11,500-ton 'Edinburgh' class large light cruiser is the last surviving big-gun World War II warship in Europe. It's also a floating branch of the Imperial War Museum, and is a popular if unlikely playground for children, who tear around its complex of gun turrets, bridge, decks and engine room. The *Belfast* was built in 1936, ran convoys to Russia, supported the Normandy Landings and helped UN forces in Korea before being decommissioned in 1963.

> **In the know**
> **Kapow!**
>
> Wondering where those big forward guns on **HMS Belfast** are pointing? Exploiting an effective range of a bit less than 12 miles, they'd put a shell through the plate-glass windows of a service station on the M1 motorway.

Restaurants

♥ Casse-Croûte £££
109 Bermondsey Street, SE1 3XB (7407 2140, cassecroute.co.uk). London Bridge tube/rail. **Open** *noon-10pm Mon-Sat; noon-4pm Sun.* **Map** *p78 R10* ❹ *French*

Romantically lit, with checked tablecloths and a tiny bar lined with digestifs, Casse-Croûte is a shot of warm, villagey France in Bermondsey. On the site of a former sandwich shop, Hervé Durochat's intimate bistro has space for just over 20 covers and feels genuinely familial. Best of all, the sensibly priced blackboard menu of boldly chosen French classics really delivers. From delicate shavings of calf's head in a tangy sauce *ravigote* to creamy mackerel fillets pepped up with a scoop of mustard ice-cream, dishes are fresh, simple and smartly executed.

Hutong ££££

The Shard, Level 33, 31 St Thomas Street, SE1 9RY (3011 3234, hutong.co.uk). London Bridge tube/rail. **Open** *noon-2.30pm, 6-10.30pm Mon-Fri; 11.30am-3.30pm, 6-10.30pm Sat, Sun.* **Map** *p78 R9* **7** *Chinese*

Like the original Hutong in Hong Kong, the Shard version is a glitzy place with amazing views, ersatz Old Beijing decor, and a Sichuan/northern Chinese menu. The traditionally fiery cuisine, big on chilli and sichuan pepper, has been toned down a little for the *gweilo* (foreigner) palate, but there's plenty to set the tastebuds alight. Delicate starters of chilled sliced scallops served with pomelo segments or octopus salad with hot and sour sauce, are followed by mouthwatering mains such as prawn wantons with *ma-la* ('numbing, spicy hot' sauce), a 'red lantern' of softshell crabs or Mongolian-style barbecue rack of lamb. It's not cheap but then this is the Shard, not Chinatown.

❤ M Manze £

87 Tower Bridge Road, SE1 4TW (7407 2985, www.manze.co.uk). Bus 1, 42, 188. **Open** *11am-2pm Mon; 10.30am-2pm Tue-Thur; 10am-2.30pm Fri; 10am-2.45pm Sat.* **Map** *p78 R11* **8** *Pie & mash*

One of the few remaining purveyors of the dirt-cheap traditional foodstuff of London's working classes. It's the oldest pie shop in town, established in 1902, with tiles, marble-topped tables and wooden benches – and is almost as beautiful as L Manze's on Walthamstow High Street, now Grade II-listed. Orders are simple: minced beef pies or, for braver souls, stewed eels with mashed potato and liquor (a thin parsley sauce).

Pizarro ££

194 Bermondsey Street, SE1 3TQ (7378 9455, www.pizarrorestaurant.com). Borough tube or London Bridge tube/rail. **Open** *noon-11pm Mon-Sat; noon-10pm Sun.* **Map** *p78 R11* **10** *Spanish*

José Pizarro's restaurant continues in the style set in his tapas-only bar, José, up the street (no.104, SE1 3UB, 7403 4902, joserestaurant.co.uk). Menus are more extensive here; the mostly traditional dishes are prepared with care and skill, using fine ingredients, and usually includes an expertly slow-braised beef stew. The space artfully

Top 20

❤ The Shard

32 London Bridge Street, SE1 9SG (0844 499 7111, www.theviewfromtheshard.com). London Bridge tube/rail. **Open** *10am-8.30pm daily.* **Admission** *£30.95; £21.95-£26.95 reductions; free under-4s. Book online for reductions.* **Map** *p78 R9.*

You can't miss the Shard – which is, after all, the point of the structure. Looking oddly similar to Saruman's tower in *The Lord of the Rings*, it shoots into the sky 'like a shard of glass' – to use the words of its architect, Renzo Piano, who doodled the idea for this vast edifice for its developer, Irving Sellar, on the back of a menu. In 2011, the Shard became the tallest building in the EU, but wasn't to reach its full height until 2012, when it topped out at 1,016ft. As is the fate of skyscrapers, the Shard's claims to be the tallest are relative: it's beaten in Moscow, the Arab Emirates and across South-east Asia.

But height isn't everything: it's the shape of this slim, slightly irregular pyramid that makes it noteworthy, an instantly recognisable centrepiece of views from pretty much everywhere in London – except, ironically, from the Victorian alleys at its foot, where the monstrous building plays peek-a-boo with visitors as they scurry around looking for a good snapshot.

Once you're inside, high-speed lifts whisk passengers up 72 floors to enjoy stunning 360°, 40-mile views, but the real joy of a visit is looking down: even seasoned London-watchers find peering down on the likes of the Tower of London from this extreme height oddly revelatory, like Google Earth in real-time.

If you've got a few quid in your pocket, a stay at the Shangri-La (*see p399*) gives you plenty of time to take it all in without the hoi polloi – and with the opportunity to swim in a rather narrow infinity pool on the 52nd floor. But you don't have to be resident to enjoy cocktails at Gŏng (also on the 52nd floor; *see p96*). Of the Shard's numerous eating options – a ground-floor deli (Láng) and four restaurants (Aqua Shard, Level 31; Oblix, Level 32; Hutong, Level 33; Ting, Level 35) – Hutong is our favourite (*see p94*).

► *If you're planning to take your time up there, note there are no toilets or refreshments on the viewing platforms.*

combines old-Spanish touches – tiles, warm wood, exposed brick – with a stripped-down 'New Bermondsey' look.

♥ Restaurant Story ££££
199 Tooley Street, SE1 2JX (7183 2117, www. restaurantstory.co.uk). London Bridge tube/ rail. Open 6.30-9pm Mon; noon-5pm, 6.30-9pm Tue-Sat. Map p78 S10 ⓫ *British*

Story, from starry young chef Tom Sellers, continues this area's rise to foodie heaven, having secured a Michelin star within months of opening. It's set in a sparse room – all the better to emphasise the view of the Shard through floor-to-ceiling windows, and, of course, the food: an enjoyable procession of modernist dishes layered with culinary puns (bread and dripping, for instance, features a lit candle made from dripping) and tastebud challenges (mackerel versus green strawberries).

Pubs & bars
This is one of the best bits of London in which to explore the extraordinary proliferation of craft breweries (*see p97* Bermondsey Beer Mile).

Doodle Bar
60 Druid Street, SE1 2EZ (7403 3222, www. thedoodlebar.com). Bermondsey tube. Open noon-11pm Thur; noon-midnight Fri, Sat; noon-6pm Sun. Map p78 S10 ❷

One of London's more original pop-up bars, Doodle now resides in an atmospheric Bermondsey railway arch. The concrete floor is high gloss, there's table football by the bar, and a street food van parks outside on weekends. But the real action is at the back: a narrow arch of a room with ping pong tables, where drinkers are encouraged to draw all over the walls. A well-curated wine list is accompanied by a handful of cocktails and the bar's own-brewed pale ale.

♥ Gōng
Level 52, The Shard, 31 St Thomas Street, SE1 9QU (7234 8208, www.gong-shangri-la.com). London Bridge tube/rail. Open noon-1am Mon-Sat; noon-midnight Sun. Map p78 R9 ❹

Take the express lift up the Shard to the 52nd floor to find London's highest bar. At this altitude, it's actually not so easy to pick out landmarks, but the views of the City are simply spectacular, especially if you book a two-hour slot across sunset. Be warned: you'll pay a premium for drinking in such an elevated location. Bermondsey Bubbles, for example, made with Jensen's gin, rose liqueur and champagne – is perfectly pleasant, but it doesn't leave much change from a £20 note.

There's usually a minimum £30 spend per person, but on Sunday, Monday or Tuesday (except bank holidays) you can enjoy the view for just the price of a bottle of beer or a glass of wine.

Shops & services
Bermondsey Square Antiques Market
Corner of Bermondsey Street & Long Lane, SE1 3UN (www.bermondseysquare.co.uk). Borough tube or London Bridge tube/rail. Open 6am-noon Fri. No cards. Map p78 R11 ❶ *Antiques*

Following the redevelopment of Bermondsey Square, the antiques market – which started in 1855 in north London – continues in an expanded space that now accommodates 200 stalls. Traditionally good for china and silverware, as well as furniture and glassware, there are now also food, fashion and crafts stalls. It's famous for being the spot where, back in the day, thieves could sell their goods with impunity: it's half car boot sale, half chic Parisian fleamarket. Get there early – lunchtime arrivals will be disappointed to find grouchy antiques sellers (well, they did start work at 4am) packing up.

♥ Maltby Street & Spa Terminus
Maltby Street, Ropewalk, SE1 3PA (www. maltby.st). Bermondsey or Southwark tube. Open 9am-4pm Sat; 11am-4pm Sun. Map p78 S10 ❸ *Food & drink*

Borough Market's trade has been challenged by former stallholders who have set up camp under the railway arches around Maltby Street and further south. Head here for delicious raclette from Kappacasein (Arch 1), craft beer from Kernel Brewery (Arch 11; *see p97* Bermondsey Beer Mile) and the city's finest custard doughnuts, courtesy of St John Bakery (Arch 72). Most producers are open on Saturday mornings, some on Sundays too – the website www.spa-terminus.co.uk has a useful map showing locations and opening hours.

> **In the know**
> **St John the fun**
>
> One of the highlights on Maltby Street is an outpost of St John (*see p219*). Long-established on Druid Street, the restaurant's bakery also runs a Saturday stall on Maltby Street and now there's also a restaurant in one of the railway arches (Ropewalk, 41 Maltby Street, SE1 3PA, 7553 9844, www. stjohngroup.uk.com, closed Mon & Tue) with a chalkboard menu that has plenty of options 'on toast'.

Bermondsey Beer Mile

Tap into London's craft ale scene

London has always been awash with beer – literally in 1814, when an exploding brewery on Tottenham Court Road created the London Beer Flood – but the current ubiquity of craft ale is remarkable. For a taster, explore Bermondsey's 'Beer Mile': half a dozen microbreweries occupying railway arches south of London Bridge. All open their tap rooms – the small bar attached to the brewery – every Saturday, allowing curious drinkers to savour some of London's tastiest brews in an intoxicating crawl. Start at South Bermondsey station and take a map (or make sure your smartphone's got juice) as the walk isn't straightforward, especially after a few pints.

The grandaddy of the scene is **Kernel** (Arch 11, Dockley Industrial Estate, SE16 3SF), which set up in the first wave of the London beer renaissance in 2007, but is now only open as a bottle shop. It was followed by **Partizan** (8 Almond Street, SE16 3LR), which used some of Kernel's old equipment, then **Brew By Numbers** (79 Enid Street, SE16 3RA), **Fourpure** (22 Trading Estate, Rotherhithe New Road, SE16 3LL) and **Anspach & Hobday** (118 Druid Street, SE1 2HH) – Anspach & Hobday also opens on Friday and Sunday, which are generally less busy than Saturday.

Collectively, they offer tasty evidence of the way London has embraced craft beer.

When Kernel began, there were less than half-a-dozen breweries in London; now they are in almost every neighbourhood. As drinking habits have been transformed, pubs that once served gassy lagers and tasteless bitters now compete to serve the widest range of new beers. As one Hackney landlord commented, 'You might not get more customers if you serve good beers, but you will definitely lose them if you don't.'

For once London was behind the curve. The microbrewery trend started in the United States in the 1980s, and parts of Scotland have had thriving scenes for years. But when it hit London, it hit big. That moment came with the 2008 recession, which lowered costs for new businesses. Craft ale tapped into a wider foodie trend that celebrated local produce and embraced more complex tastes, as found in IPAs ('India Pale Ale' – a light, hoppy, refreshing beer).

But London was also able to tap into a strong, lost tradition of brewing: IPAs, porters and several other varieties were created in London centuries ago, allowing canny current brewers to provide an experience that felt new and exciting, but was also deep in taste and rich in history.

Where better to enjoy that heady brew than under a railway arch in south-east London?

Westminster & St James's

The whole of the United Kingdom is ruled from this small portion of London. The monarchy has been in residence in Westminster since the 11th century, when Edward the Confessor moved west out of the walled City, and as the role of British kings and queens became increasingly ceremonial, Parliament was already here to take on the real business of government. It's a key destination for visitors as well, with the most significant area designated a UNESCO World Heritage Site back in 1987.

As well as being home to some of London's most impressive buildings – Westminster Abbey and the Houses of Parliament among them – it's also packed with culture: Tate Britain, the National Gallery and the National Portrait Gallery are all here. And for such an important part of London, it's surprisingly spacious. St James's Park is one of London's finest green spaces, Trafalgar Square is a tourist hotspot – and thanks to pedestrianisation along its northern edge, not an unpleasant one – while the Mall offers a regally broad approach route to Buckingham Palace.

❤ Don't miss

1 Tate Britain *p111*
The original Tate gallery, handsomely revamped.

2 St James's Park *p115*
Central London's prettiest park, replete with pelicans.

3 Westminster Abbey *p106 and p109*
Magnificent, sacred and packed to its reredos with history.

4 National Gallery *p103*
One masterpiece after another.

5 Fortnum & Mason *p117*
Historic department store with trad foodie treats.

Top of Nelson's Column, Trafalgar Square

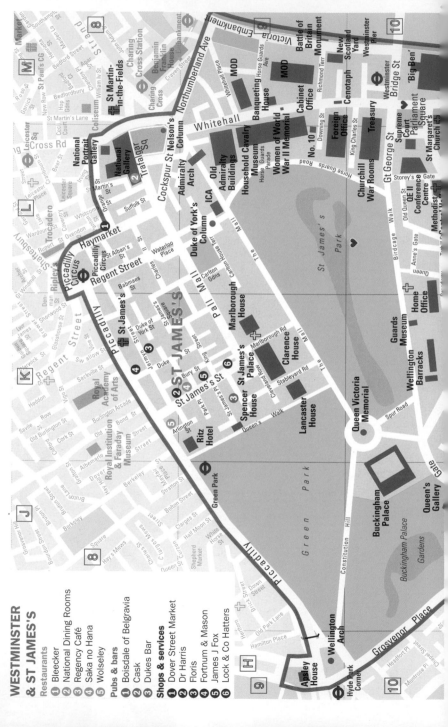

WESTMINSTER & ST JAMES'S

Restaurants
1. Bleecker
2. National Dining Rooms
3. Regency Café
4. Saka no Hana
5. Wolseley

Pubs & bars
1. Boisdale of Belgravia
2. Cask
3. Dukes Bar

Shops & services
1. Dover Street Market
2. Dr Harris
3. Floris
4. Fortnum & Mason
5. James J Fox
6. Lock & Co Hatters

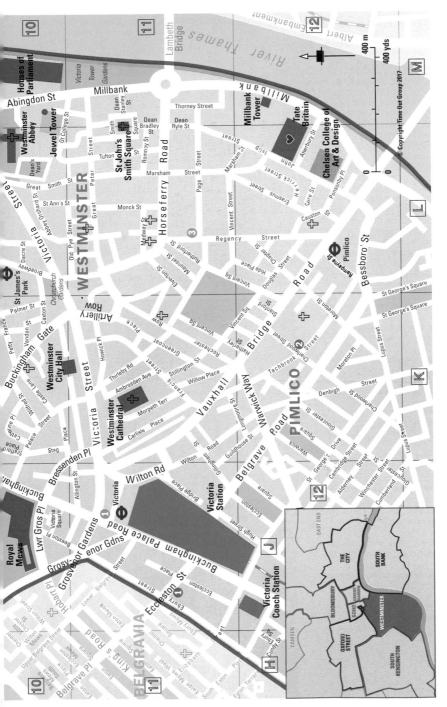

Houses of Parliament

Abingdon St

Westminster Abbey

Jewel Tower

Millbank

WESTMINSTER

St John's Smith Square

Thorney Street

Millbank Tower

Tate Britain

Chelsea College of Art & Design

Pimlico

St James's Park

Buckingham Gate

Westminster City Hall

Artillery Row

Westminster Cathedral

PIMLICO

St George's Square

Vauxhall

Bridge Road

Warwick Way

Bressenden Pl

Wilton Rd

Victoria

Victoria Station

Royal Mews

Buckingham Palace Road

Grosvenor Gardens

BELGRAVIA

Eccleston

King's Road

Victoria Coach Station

© Copyright Time Out Group 2017

400 m
400 yds

EAST END

THE CITY

SOUTH BANK

BLOOMSBURY

SOHO

CAMDEN

OXFORD STREET

WESTMINSTER

SOUTH KENSINGTON

TRAFALGAR SQUARE

▶*Leicester Square tube or Charing Cross tube/rail.*

I aid out in the 1820s by John Nash, ꟷ rafalgar Square is the heart of modern London. Tourists come in their thousands to pose for photographs in front of **Nelson's Column**. It was erected in 1840 to honour Vice Admiral Horatio Nelson, who died at the point of victory at the Battle of Trafalgar in 1805. The statue atop the 150-foot Corinthian column is foreshortened to appear in perfect proportion from the ground. The granite fountains were added in 1845; Sir Edwin Landseer's bronze lions joined them in 1867 – the metal has in places been worn very thin by tourists clambering over them. Stay off!

Once surrounded on all sides by busy roads, the square was improved markedly in 2003 by the pedestrianisation of the North Terrace, right in front of the **National Gallery**. A ban on feeding pigeons was another positive step. The square feels more like public space now, and is a focus for performance and celebration.

Around the perimeter are three plinths bearing statues of George IV and two Victorian military heroes, Henry Havelock and Sir Charles James Napier. The long-empty fourth plinth, which never received its planned martial statue, has been used since 1998 to display temporary, contemporary art. David Shrigley's huge thumbs-up, *Really Good*, will be followed in 2018 by Michael Rakowitz's *The Invisible Enemy Should Not Exist*.

Other points of interest around the square include an equestrian statue of Charles I dating from the 1630s. A dogged bunch of royalists gathers here every 31 January to mark Charles I's execution. Behind the statue, a plaque marks the original site of Edward I's **Eleanor Cross**, the official centre of London. (A Victorian replica of the cross is outside Charing Cross Station, *see p189*.) At the square's north-east corner is **St Martin-in-the-Fields**.

♥ Time to eat & drink

A beauty for brunch
Wolseley *p116*

Art deco café
Regency Café *p112*

Best burgers
Bleecker *p112*

Whisky a gogo
Boisdale of Belgravia *p112*

London's finest martini?
Dukes Bar *p117*

♥ Time to shop

Classic department store
Fortnum & Mason *p117*

New premises, same style
Dover Street Market *p117*

Sensational old-school scents
Floris *p117*

Trad titfers
Lock & Co Hatters *p118*

St Martin-in-the-Fields

Sights & museums

♥ National Gallery

Trafalgar Square, WC2N 5DN (7747 2885, www.nationalgallery.org.uk). Charing Cross tube/rail. **Open** *10am-6pm Mon-Thur, Sat, Sun; 10am-9pm Fri.* **Tours** *11.30am, 2.30pm Mon-Thur; 11.30am, 2.30pm, 7pm Fri; 11.30am, 2.30pm Sat, Sun.* **Admission** *free. Special exhibitions vary.* **Map** *p100 L8.*

Founded in 1824 to display 36 paintings, the National Gallery is now one of the world's great repositories for art. There are masterpieces from virtually every European school of art, from austere 13th-century religious paintings to the sensual delights of Titian, Caravaggio and Van Gogh. Dr Gabriele Finaldi, who became the gallery's director in 2015, has overseen major exhibitions such as 'Beyond Caravaggio' and 'Goya: The Portraits', which attracted record numbers of visitors.

The gallery itself is huge. Furthest to the left of the main entrance, the modern Sainsbury Wing extension contains the gallery's earliest works: Italian paintings by masters such as Giotto and Piero della Francesca, as well as the *Wilton Diptych*, one of the finest medieval pictures in the collection, showing Richard II with the Virgin and Child.

In the West Wing (left of the main entrance) are Italian Renaissance masterpieces by Correggio, Titian and Raphael. Straight ahead on entry, in the North Wing, are 17th-century Dutch, Flemish, Italian and Spanish Old Masters, including works such as Rembrandt's *A Woman Bathing in a Stream* and Caravaggio's *Supper at Emmaus*. Velázquez's *Rokeby Venus* is one of the artist's most famous paintings. Also in this wing are works by the great landscape artists Claude and Poussin. Turner insisted that his *Dido Building Carthage* and *Sun Rising Through Vapour* should hang alongside two Claudes here that particularly inspired him.

In the East Wing are some of the gallery's most popular paintings: you'll find works by the French Impressionists and Post-Impressionists, including Monet's *Water-Lilies*, one of Van Gogh's *Sunflowers* and Seurat's *Bathers at Asnières*. Don't miss Renoir's astonishingly lovely *The Skiff* (*La Yole*).

Downstairs, the opening of Gallery B – the first new gallery space in 26 years – transformed the ground floor in 2017 by connecting the once isolated Gallery A and main Ground Floor Galleries. 'Rubens and Rembrandt', a special display of paintings from the National Gallery's extensive collection of Dutch and Flemish art, kicked off the programme of free temporary exhibitions here.

You shouldn't plan to see everything in one visit, but free guided tours and audio guides help you make the best of your time.

National Portrait Gallery

St Martin's Place, WC2H 0HE (7306 0055, www.npg.org.uk). Leicester Square tube or Charing Cross tube/rail. **Open** *10am-6pm Mon-Wed, Sat, Sun; 10am-9pm Thur, Fri.* **Admission** *free. Special exhibitions vary.* **Map** *p100 L8.*

Portraits don't have to be stuffy. The NPG has everything from oil paintings of stiff-backed royals to photographs of soccer stars and gloriously unflattering political caricatures. On the ground floor, director Nicholas Cullinan (who joined in 2015) programmes interesting temporary exhibitions, not least a revealing pairing of cult Surrealist Claude Cahun with (no longer quite so) Young British Artist Gillian Wearing, alongside permanent galleries of contemporary portraiture in different media. Portraits of musicians, scientists, artists, philanthropists and celebrities are then arranged in chronological order from the top of the gallery to the bottom. On the second floor are the earliest works, portraits of Tudor and Stuart royals and notables, including Holbein's 'cartoon' of Henry VIII and the 'Ditchley Portrait' of his daughter, Elizabeth I, her pearly slippers placed firmly on a colourful map of England. On the same floor, the 18th-century collection features Georgian writers and artists, with one room devoted to the influential Kit-Cat Club of bewigged Whig (lcftish) intellectuals, the playwright Congreve and the poet Dryden among them. More famous names include Wren and Swift. The second floor also shows Regency greats, military men such as Wellington and Nelson, plus Byron, Wordsworth and other Romantics. The first floor is devoted to the Victorians (Dickens, Brunel, Darwin) and to 20th-century luminaries, such as TS Eliot and Ian McKellen.

St Martin-in-the-Fields

Trafalgar Square, WC2N 4JH (7766 1100, www.smitf.org). Leicester Square tube or Charing Cross tube/rail. **Open** *8.30am-1pm, 2-6pm Mon, Tue, Fri; 8.30am-1.15pm, 2-5pm Wed; 8.30am-1pm, 2-6pm Thur; 9.30am-6pm Sat; 3.30-5pm Sun. Brass Rubbing Centre 10am-6pm Mon-Wed; 10am-8pm Thur-Sat; 11.30am-5pm Sun.* **Admission** *free. Brass rubbing £4.50.* **Map** *p100 M8.*

There's been a church 'in the fields' between Westminster and the City since the 13th century, but the current one was built

in 1726 by James Gibbs, using a fusion of neoclassical and Baroque styles. The parish church for Buckingham Palace (note the royal box to the left of the gallery), St Martin's bright interior was restored a few years back, with Victorian furbelows removed and the addition of a brilliant altar window that shows the Cross, stylised as if rippling on water. Downstairs in the crypt are a fine café and the London Brass Rubbing Centre.

The lunchtime and evening concerts in the church (which rarely wander far from the embrace of Mozart and Bach) are often delightful, especially when candlelit.

Restaurants

Aside from all shine and no soul chains and tourist traps, there are few dining options. If you don't fancy the **National**, head ten minutes north to explore the multifarious dining opportunities in nearby **Soho** (*see pp160-177*).

National Dining Rooms ££
Sainsbury Wing, National Gallery, Trafalgar Square, WC2N 5DN (7747 2525, www. peytonandbyrne.co.uk). Charing Cross tube/rail. **Open** *Bakery 10am-5pm Mon-Thur, Sat, Sun; 10am-8pm Fri. Restaurant 10am-5.30pm Mon-Thur, Sat, Sun; 10am-8.30pm Fri.* **Map** *p100 L8* ❷ *British*

Ascend the stairs to Oliver Peyton's first-floor dining room – in the quieter Sainsbury Wing of the National Gallery – and enter a professionally run and peaceful place, where the views (over the square in one direction, of a vast Paula Rego mural in the other) are matched by good-quality food. No longer the bargain it once was, dishes are light, artfully presented and with clever additions.

WHITEHALL TO PARLIAMENT SQUARE

▶ *Westminster tube or Charing Cross tube/rail.*

The offices of the British government are lined along Whitehall, itself named after Henry VIII's magnificent palace, which burned to the ground in 1698. Walking south from Trafalgar Square, you pass the old Admiralty Offices and War Office, the Ministry of Defence, the Foreign Office and the Treasury, as well as the **Banqueting House**, one of the few buildings to survive the blaze. Also here is **Horse Guards**, headquarters of the Household Cavalry, the elite army unit that protects the Queen (*see p114* Household Cavalry Museum).

Either side of **Downing Street** – home to the prime minister (no.10) and chancellor (no.11), but closed to the public after IRA attacks in the 1980s – are significant war memorials. The millions who died in the service of the nation in World Wars I and II are commemorated by Sir Edwin Lutyens' dignified **Cenotaph**, focal point of Remembrance Day (*see p318*), while a separate memorial to the women of World War II, by sculptor John Mills, recalls the seven million women who contributed to the war effort. Just past the Cenotaph and hidden beneath government offices at the St James's Park end of King Charles Street, the claustrophobic **Churchill War Rooms** are where Britain's wartime prime minister planned the struggle.

The broad sweep of Whitehall is an apt introduction to the cluster of monuments of that make up the UNESCO World Heritage Site of Westminster (*see p106*).

Sights & museums
Banqueting House
Whitehall, SW1A 2ER (3166 6000, www.hrp. org.uk/banqueting-house). Westminster tube. **Open** *10am-5pm daily; phone to check.* **Admission** *£6; £5 reductions; free under-16s.* **Map** *p100 M9.*

This handsome Italianate mansion, which was designed by Inigo Jones and constructed in 1620, was the first true Renaissance building in London. The sole surviving part of the Tudor and Stuart kings' Whitehall Palace, the Banqueting House features a lavish painted ceiling by Rubens, glorifying James I, 'the wisest fool in Christendom'. Regrettably, James's successor, Charles I, did not rule so wisely. After losing the English Civil War to Cromwell's Roundheads, he was executed in front of Banqueting House in 1649 – the subject of a set of displays here.

Churchill War Rooms
Clive Steps, King Charles Street, SW1A 2AQ (7930 6961, www.iwm.org.uk). St James's Park or Westminster tube. **Open** *9.30am-6pm daily.* **Admission** *£17.25; £8.60-£13.80 reductions; free under-5s.* **Map** *p100 L10.*

Out of harm's way beneath Whitehall, this cramped and spartan bunker was where Winston Churchill planned the Allied victory in World War II, and the rooms powerfully bring to life the reality of a nation at war. The cabinet rooms were sealed on 16 August 1945, keeping the complex in a state of suspended animation: every pin stuck into the vast charts was placed there in the final days of the conflict. The humble quarters occupied by Churchill and his deputies give a tangible sense of wartime hardship, an

♥ Westminster

A short walk south of Trafalgar Square, on the bank of the Thames, is one of London's most dazzling sights – or several of them, to be precise. Laid out in 1868, the great space of Parliament Square is flanked by the **Houses of Parliament** (*see p108*), the neo-Gothic Middlesex **Guildhall** (since 2009 the UK's **Supreme Court**; *see p108*) and the twin spires of **Westminster Abbey** (*see p109*). Despite all the statues of British politicians (Disraeli, Churchill) and foreign dignitaries (Lincoln, Mandela and, since 2015, Gandhi), Parliament Square can seem little more than a glorified traffic island – especially when you're trying to cross the roads to have a closer look. But its symbolic value has been brought back into focus through court battles over its suitability as a site for political protest: initially against the occupation of Iraq in the 2000s; more recently over austerity and corruption. This is the beating heart of Westminster, inscribed as a UNESCO World Heritage Site in 1987. Any part of it alone would feature on most visitors' itineraries, but the combination – especially on a sunny day, when the yellow stone of Parliament is at its best – is an extraordinary historic and cultural nexus.

The centrepiece is an outrageous neo-Gothic fantasy, the seat of the British government. It is still formally known as the Palace of Westminster, though the only remaining parts of the medieval palace are Westminster Hall (which can be visited on one of the brilliant tours)

Houses of Parliament and Westminster Bridge

and the undervisited **Jewel Tower** (*see p108*). At the north end of the palace is the clocktower housing the huge 'Big Ben' bell that gives the clocktower its popular name; more than seven feet tall, the bell (itself formally known as the 'Great Bell') weighs over 13 tons. The tower was, in fact, renamed in 2012: rather than bowing to common usage, it became the Elizabeth Tower – in honour of the Queen's Diamond Jubilee. A spear-brandishing statue of Boadicea (the fierce British chieftain Boudica, misnamed by Classics-obsessed Victorians) aims her chariot at the heart of Parliament from the end of Westminster Bridge.

Take your time when exploring Westminster. A lot of the fun is to be had watching the place work: speculating about who's in that big black car with outriders, enjoying the spectacle as impatient men with serious briefcases thread through the slow-moving, shutter-snapping gaggles of tourists. You can even watch justice in action by dropping in on a session at the Supreme Court, which few Londoners seem to know even exists, let alone that it opens to visitors. But we're not the only people to recognise Westminster as one of London's glories, so arrive early to enjoy the Abbey in relative tranquillity, book ahead to get on a Parliament tour and do explore the 'lesser' sights. The Jewel Tower, especially, is unjustly neglected. For details of all of these attractions, see their listings elsewhere in this chapter.

effect reinforced by the wailing sirens and wartime speeches on the audio guide (free with admission).

Houses of Parliament

Parliament Square, SW1A 0AA (Commons information 7219 4272; Lords information 7219 3107; tickets 7219 4114, www.parliament. uk). Westminster tube. **Open** *(when in session) House of Commons Visitors' Gallery 2.30-10.30pm Mon; 11.30am-7.30pm Tue, Wed; 9.30am-5.30pm Thur; 9.30am-3pm Fri. House of Lords Visitors' Gallery 2.30-10pm Mon, Tue; 3-10pm Wed; 11am-7.30pm Thur; from 10am Fri.* **Tours** *9.15am-4.30pm Sat & summer recess; check website for details.* **Admission** *Visitors' galleries free.* **Tours** *£25.50; £11-£21 reductions; free under-5s.* **Map** *p100 M10.*

The British parliament has an extremely long history, with the first parliamentary session held in St Stephen's Chapel in 1275. The Palace of Westminster, however, only became the permanent seat of Parliament in 1532, when Henry VIII moved to a new des-res in Whitehall. The current Palace is a wonderful mish-mash of styles, dominated by Gothic buttresses, towers and arches. It looks much older than it is: the Parliament buildings were designed in 1860 by Charles Barry (ably assisted by Augustus Pugin) to replace the original building, which had been destroyed by fire in 1834. Now, the compound contains 1,000 rooms, 11 courtyards, eight bars and six restaurants, plus a small cafeteria for visitors. Of the original palace, only the Jewel Tower (see below) and, within the Parliament buildings, Westminster Hall, remain.

Visitors are welcome (subject to stringent security checks at St Stephen's Gate, the only public access point into Parliament) to observe the political debates in the House of Lords and House of Commons, but tickets must be arranged in advance through your embassy or MP, who can also arrange tours – even free trips up the 334 spiral steps of the Elizabeth Tower to hear 'Big Ben'. The experience of listening in on the Houses of Parliament in session is often soporific, but Prime Minister's Question Time at noon on Wednesday is often sparky: the PM has alternately to rebuff a barrage

of hostile questions from the opposition (and occasionally their own rebellious backbenchers) and massage value out of soft questions from loyal backbenchers eager to present the government in a good light.

Jewel Tower

Abingdon Street, SW1P 3JY (7222 2219, www. english-heritage.org.uk). Westminster tube. **Open** *Apr-Oct 10am-5pm daily. Nov-Mar 10am-4pm Sat, Sun.* **Admission** *£4.70; £2.80-£4.20 reductions; free under-5s.* **Map** *p100 M10.*

This easy-to-overlook little stone tower opposite Parliament was built in 1365 to house Edward III's treasure, complete with a moat that ran into the Thames. It is, with Westminster Hall, all that remains of the medieval Palace of Westminster. Over three storeys, joined by a spiral staircase, the tale is told: the Crown Jewels were evicted in 1512 (they are now displayed in the **Tower of London**, *see p234*) and the tower became an archive for parliamentary records, then, in the 19th-century, a testing site for standardised measurements. A fascinating and neglected piece of Westminster history.

St Margaret's Church

Parliament Square, SW1P 3PA (7654 4840, www.westminster-abbey.org/st-margarets-church). St James's Park or Westminster tube. **Open** *9.30am-3.30pm Mon-Fri; 9.30am-1.30pm Sat; 2-4.30pm Sun (times vary due to services). Services times vary; check website for details.* **Admission** *free.* **Map** *p100 M10.*

Tucked in next to the grandeur of Westminster Abbey, this little church was founded in the 12th century; since 1614, it's served as the official church of the House of Commons. The interior features some of the most impressive pre-Reformation stained glass in London. The east window (1509) commemorates the marriage of Henry VIII and Catherine of Aragon; others celebrate Britain's first printer, William Caxton (buried here in 1491), explorer Sir Walter Raleigh (executed in Old Palace Yard in 1618) and writer John Milton (1608-74), who married his second wife here in 1656.

Supreme Court

Parliament Square, SW1P 3BD (7960 1900, www.supremecourt.uk). St James's Park or Westminster tube. **Open** *9.30am-4.30pm Mon-Fri.* **Tours** *11am, 2pm, 3pm Fri.* **Admission** *free.* **Tours** *£7; £5 reductions; free under 16s.* **Map** *p100 L10.*

In 2005, Parliament made a momentous decision – not that anyone noticed. The right to adjudicate final appeals was taken from the House of Lords and given to a new,

In the know
'The mother of parliaments'

The best way to see the historic parliamentary buildings is to book on one of the revealing 90-minute guided tours (7219 4114, www.parliament.uk/visiting) on Saturday or during summer recess. Tours take in both Houses, Westminster Hall, the Queen's Robing Room and the Royal Gallery.

independent Supreme Court, which was duly opened by the Queen in 2009, directly opposite Parliament. Part of the notion was to open up higher processes of law to the public – in plain English, you can visit any time you like (through airport-style security gates) to see lawyers debate 'points of law of general public importance' in front of the country's most senior judges. Recent cases have included whether an MP can be tried in a magistrate's court for alleged criminal misconduct within Parliament, and how binding a prenuptial agreement should be. You can also look around the lovely Grade II*-listed, neo-Gothic premises, built for Middlesex County Council in 1913. There's even a café and souvenirs on sale.

▶ *The Supreme Court doesn't sit on Friday; visitors are still welcome but it isn't as interesting as when the court is in session.*

❤ Westminster Abbey

*20 Dean's Yard, SW1P 3PA (information 7222 5152, tours 7654 4834, www.westminster-abbey.org). St James's Park or Westminster tube. **Open** May-Aug 9.30am-3.30pm Mon, Tue, Thur-Sat; 9.30am-3.30pm, 4.30-6pm Wed. Sept-Apr 9.30am-3.30pm Mon, Thur, Fri; 2-3.30pm Tue; 9.30am-3.30pm, 4.30-6pm Wed; 9.30am-1.30pm Sat. Abbey Museum, Chapter House, College Gardens & **Tours** times vary; check website for details. **Admission** £20; £9-£17 reductions; £45 family; free under-5s. **Tours** £5. **Map** p100 L10.*

The cultural, historic and religious significance of Westminster Abbey is impossible to overstate, but also hard to remember as you're shepherded around, forced to elbow fellow tourists out of the way to read a plaque or see a tomb. The best plan is to get here as early in the day as you can – although it also quietens down towards closing time.

Edward the Confessor commissioned a church to St Peter on the site of a seventh-century version, but it was only consecrated on 28 December 1065, eight days before he died. William the Conqueror subsequently had himself crowned here on Christmas Day 1066 and, with just two exceptions, every English coronation since has taken place in the abbey.

Many royal, military and cultural notables are interred here. The most haunting memorial is the Grave of the Unknown Warrior, in the nave. Elaborate resting places in side chapels are taken up by the tombs of Elizabeth I and Mary Queen of Scots. In Innocents Corner lie the remains of two lads believed to be Edward V and his brother Richard (their bodies were found at the Tower of London), as well as two of James

Chapter House, Westminster Abbey

I's children. Poets' Corner is the final resting place of Chaucer, who was the first writer to be buried here. Few of the other writers who have stones here are buried in the abbey, but the remains of Dryden, Johnson, Browning and Tennyson are all present. Henry James, TS Eliot and Dylan Thomas have dedications – on the floor, fittingly for Thomas.

There are major changes afoot in the Abbey: the Triforium (a gallery set into the walls above the nave) is due to reopen in 2018 as the Queen's Diamond Jubilee Galleries, presenting treasures and historic oddities (not least the historic sequence of effigies of British monarchs, among them Edward II and Henry VII, wearing the robes they donned in life) to tell the long and complex history of this glorious place.

In the know
Saints alive

Westminster Abbey has many – almost too many – attractions, but when you're in the choir of the Henry VII Chapel, don't fail to look up: not only is the roof an exquisite example of pendant fan vaulting (a dull name for architecture of such intricacy), but you can admire an array of saints in niches along the walls, among them a bearded lady – St Wilgefortis.

Even when the abbey is at its most crowded, the 900-year-old **College Garden** – one of the oldest cultivated spaces in Britain, with some lovely mulberry trees – remains tranquil. Ask one of the staff to direct you there; they are very knowledgeable, so collaring the right person brings the abbey to life in a way the audioguide never can.

For snacks, there's a refectory-style restaurant – the **Cellarium Café & Terrace** (7222 0516, www.benugo.com/restaurants/cellarium-cafe-terrace) – next to the little souvenir shop.

Pubs & bars

While the **Red Lion** (48 Parliament Street, SW1A 2NH, 7930 5826, redlionwestminster.co.uk) is, by tradition, the politicians' favourite pub and the **Westminster Arms** (9-10 Storey Gate, SW1P 3AT, 7222 8520, www.westminsterarms.co.uk) has its own 'division bell' to summon drinkers back into the House to vote, most MPs nowadays prefer to drink in the privacy of Parliament's own taxpayer-subsidised bars. Opposite Big Ben, **Stephen's Tavern** (10 Bridge Street, SW1A 2JR, 7925 2286, ststephenstavern.co.uk), done out with dark woods, etched mirrors and Arts and Crafts-style wallpaper, is neither too touristy nor too busy.

MILLBANK

▶ *Pimlico or Westminster tube.*

Running south from Parliament along the river, Millbank leads eventually to **Tate Britain** (see *p111*). If you're walking that way (which is a good idea), look out on the left for **Victoria Tower Gardens**. Often overlooked, the gardens are a wonderful spot that is sometimes occupied by nothing more than its commemorative furniture: a distinguished statue of suffragette Emmeline Pankhurst, a fine cast of Rodin's *The Burghers of Calais* and a magnificent neo-Gothic folly/water fountain that celebrates the abolition of slavery. Less eye-catching is a small green plaque on the river wall dedicated to Peirson Frank, 'the man who saved London from drowning'. His covert rapid-response unit was responsible for mending the Thames wall during the Blitz: hit more than 120 times, it was never breached. The gardens have also been designated the site of a new £50 million National Holocaust Memorial – but given Brexit and government cuts, don't expect its arrival any time soon.

On the other side of the road, Dean Stanley Street leads to Smith Square, home

to the architecturally striking **St John's Smith Square** (*see p356*), built as a church in grand Baroque style and now a venue for classical music. Lord North Street, the Georgian terrace running north from here, has long been a favourite address of politicians; note the directions on the wall for wartime bomb shelters.

Across the river from Millbank is **Vauxhall Cross**, the oddly conspicuous HQ of the Secret Intelligence Service (SIS), commonly referred to by its old name, MI6. In case any enemies of the state were unaware of its location, the cream-and-green block appeared as itself in the 1999 James Bond film *The World is Not Enough* – reprising the role (and suffering impressively serious bomb damage) in 2012's *Skyfall*.

Pubs & bars

Cask

6 Charlwood Street, Pimlico, SW1V 6EE (7630 7225, www.caskpubandkitchen.com). Pimlico tube. **Open** *noon-11pm Mon-Sat; noon-10.30pm Sun. Food served noon-3pm, 5-10pm Mon-Fri; 12.30-9.30pm Sat, Sun.* **Map** *p100 K12* ❷

It's not much to look at – an awkward shape at the bottom of a newbuild block – but Cask has been blazing the trail for better beer for years. Its fridges and cellar are filled with an absurdly generous range of the finest brews from London, Britain and beyond, with something to satisfy the most ardent hophead or convert the most timid quaffer of fizzy yellow lager. Staff really know their stuff too – ask for a recommendation and you won't be disappointed.

VICTORIA

▶ *Pimlico tube or Victoria tube/rail.*

Victoria is chaotic. The rail station is a major hub for trains to southern seaside resorts and ferry terminals, while the nearby coach station is served by buses from all over Europe, and theatres dotted around the area add up to a kind of western outpost of the West End's Theatreland. But there's no real focus here, just one stand-out attraction: **Westminster Cathedral**. Not to be confused with Westminster Abbey (*see p386*), it is the headquarters of the Roman Catholic Church in England. South and east of Victoria Station are the Georgian terraces of Pimlico and Belgravia. Antiques stores and restaurants line Pimlico Road, and Tachbrook Street has some intriguing independent shops.

💗 Tate Britain

Millbank, SW1P 4RG (7887 8888, www.tate.
org.uk). Pimlico tube. **Open** *10am-6pm*
daily. Tours 11am, noon, 2pm, 3pm daily.
Admission *free. Special exhibitions vary.*
Map *p100 G5.*

Especially since the opening of its dramatic
Blavatnik extension in 2016, **Tate Modern**
(*see p87*) has been getting all the
attention. But (whisper it) we prefer the
original Tate Gallery – or Tate Britain,
as it's now known. This isn't nostalgia.
Tate Britain was handsomely refurbished
a few years ago, has a better organised
collection than its illustrious counterpart
and is much less busy – the lack of visitors
(relative lack, of course) wasn't much fun
for outgoing director Penelope Curtis, but
it sure makes viewing art more enjoyable.
Tate Modern is amazing. But as you queue
for the overburdened lifts to whizz up to
its controversial viewing platform (Tate
maps of the sights outside request a higher
suggested donation than those for the
collections within), you may find yourself
wondering if it's become more of a tourist
attraction than a place to love art.

While the international scope and themed
presentation of Tate Modern are laudable,
the effect for visitors can be disorientating
– some argue (outgoing director Nicholas
Serota acknowledged as much in the
Financial Times in 2010) that this
arrangement covered gaps in the collection
that might be cruelly exposed were it to be
displayed chronologically. No such anxieties
at Tate Britain, where a comprehensive

rehang in 2013 made the main floor into a
logical journey through the history of British
Art from Holbein in the 1540s, while key
artists are given more substantial treatment:
Blake and Henry Moore have their own
rooms, while JMW Turner occupies his own
extensive Clore Gallery.

Founded by sugar magnate Sir Henry
Tate, Tate Britain opened in a stately
riverside building in 1897 – built on the site
of the pentagonal Millbank Prison, which
held criminals destined for transportation
to Botany Bay – with a display of 245 British
paintings. Now, the collection is rather more
extensive. Constable, Millais, Whistler,
Hogarth and Bacon are all represented;
the blockbuster exhibitions – not least a
stunning Hockney retrospective in 2017 –
are increasingly excellent.

Tate Britain has also been surreptitiously
stealing a bit of the limelight back from
its starrier sibling with a long-term
redevelopment plan called the Millbank
Project. In an initial £45m tranche of
improvements, architects Caruso St John
improved the fabric of the oldest part of
the building, conserving original features,
upgrading the galleries, opening new spaces
to the public and adding a new café. Sturdier
floors meant that more sculpture could be
displayed, and the amount of natural light
was increased. The Millbank entrance is
lovely these days, with its stained glass and
striking spiral staircase; downstairs in the
restaurant, a new Alan Johnston ceiling
mural complements the restored 1926-27 Rex
Whistler wall mural *Pursuit of Rare Meats*.

Tate Britain Spiral Staircase

North of Victoria Street, towards Parliament Square, is **Christchurch Gardens**, burial site of Thomas ('Colonel') Blood, who stole the Crown Jewels in 1671. He was apprehended making his getaway but, amazingly, managed to talk his way into a full pardon. Also in the area is the former site of New Scotland Yard, sold to private investors for £370 million, with the Met moved to a new police headquarters on Victoria Embankment by the Ministry of Defence in 2016 – taking the name and famous revolving sign with them. The fabulous art deco former headquarters of London Underground at 55 Broadway is also now in private hands. Public outrage about Jacob Epstein's graphic nudes on the façade almost led to the resignation of the managing director in 1929; there was no such outrage at this more recent management decision.

Sights & museums

Westminster Cathedral

42 Francis Street, SW1P 1QW (7798 9055, www.westminstercathedral.org.uk). Victoria tube/rail. **Open** *6.30am-7pm Mon-Fri; 7.30am-7.30pm Sat; 7.30am-8pm Sun.* **Admission** *free; donations appreciated.* **Map** *p100 K11.*

With its domes, arches and soaring tower, the most important Catholic church in England looks surprisingly Byzantine. There's a reason: architect John Francis Bentley, who built it between 1895 and 1903, was heavily influenced by Hagia Sophia in Istanbul. Compared to the candy-cane exterior, the interior is surprisingly restrained (in fact, it's unfinished), but there are still some impressive marble columns and mosaics. Eric Gill's sculptures of the Stations of the Cross (1914-18) were dismissed as 'Babylonian' when they were first installed, but worshippers have come to love them. An upper gallery holds the 'Treasures of the Cathedral' exhibition, where you can see an impressive Arts and Crafts coronet, a Tudor chalice, holy relics and Bentley's amazing architectural model of his cathedral, complete with tiny hawks.

Restaurants

♥ Bleecker ££

205 Victoria Street, SW1E 5NE (www. bleeckerburger.co.uk). Victoria tube/rail. **Open** *11.30am-11pm Mon-Sat; 11.30am-10pm Sun.* **Map** *p100 J11* ❶ *Burgers*

The first bricks-and-mortar shop from this popular street-food burger outfit is pure filth... in the best possible way. Made with rare-breed, dry-aged beef, the burgers don't compromise on quality but there's nothing pretentious about them – they're just bun, cheese and killer pucks of meat. Serious carnivores will adore the award-winning 'Bleecker black': two pink patties sandwiching a slice of black pudding. But given the inevitable, crippling post-scoff food coma, be sure to come hungry and eat fast.

♥ Regency Café £

17-19 Regency Street, SW1P 4BY (7821 6596, regencycafe.co.uk). St James's Park tube or Victoria tube/rail. **Open** *7am-2.30pm, 4-7.15pm Mon-Fri; 7am-noon Sat.* **Map** *p100 L11* ❸ *Café*

Behind its black-tiled art deco exterior, this classic caff has been here since 1946. Customers sit on brown plastic chairs at Formica-topped tables, watched over by muscular boxers and Spurs stars of yore, whose photos hang on the tiled walls. Lasagne, omelettes, salads, every conceivable cooked breakfast and mugs of tannin-rich tea are meat and drink to the Regency. Still hungry? The improbably gigantic cinnamon-flavoured bread and butter pud will see you right for the rest of the week.

Pubs & bars

♥ Boisdale of Belgravia

15 Eccleston Street, SW1W 9LX (7730 6922, www.boisdale.co.uk). Victoria tube/rail. **Open** *noon-1am Mon-Fri; 6pm-1am Sat.* **Admission** *free before 10pm, then £12.* **Map** *p100 J11* ❶

There's nowhere quite like this posh, Scottish-themed enterprise, and that includes its sister branches in the City, Mayfair and Canary Wharf. If you're here to drink, there's a terrific choice of single malts. That said, the outstanding wine list is surprisingly affordable, with house selections starting at just over £20. Additional appeal comes from live jazz (six nights a week) and a heated cigar terrace. **Other locations** Swedeland Court, 202 Bishopsgate, the City, EC2M 4NR (7283 1763); Cabot Place, Canary Wharf, E14 4QT (7715 5818); 12 North Row, Mayfair, London, W1K 7DF (3873 8888).

In the know
View halloo

While we hesitate to recommend a sacred space merely for the secular pleasures it affords – ah, who are we kidding? Shin up the extraordinary 201ft-tall campanile (bell tower) at Westminster Cathedral for views that, while neither the highest or the most encompassing in London, offer a really impressive vista. Entry is £6 (£3 reductions).

ST JAMES'S

▶ *Green Park or Piccadilly Circus tube.*

One of London's most refined residential areas, St James's was laid out in the 1660s for royal and aristocratic families, some of whom still live here. It's a rewarding district, a sedate bustle of intriguing mews and grand squares. Bordered by Piccadilly, Haymarket, the Mall and Green Park, the district is centred on St James's Square.

Just south of the square, **Pall Mall** is lined with members-only gentlemen's clubs (in the old-fashioned sense of the word). Polished nameplates reveal such prestigious establishments as the **Reform Club** (nos.104-105), site of Phileas Fogg's famous bet in *Around the World in Eighty Days*, and the **Institute of Directors** (no.116). Around the corner on St James's Street, the **Carlton Club** (no.69) is the official club of the Conservative Party, founded in 1832; until the club's rules were finally changed in 2008, Lady Thatcher was the only woman to have been granted full membership. The world's oldest fine-art auctioneers, **Christie's** (7839 9060, www.christies.com), is on King Street.

At the south end of St James's Street, **St James's Palace** was built for Henry VIII in the 1530s. Extensively remodelled over the centuries, the red-brick palace is still the official address of the Royal Court, even though every monarch since 1837 has lived at Buckingham Palace. Here, Mary Tudor surrendered Calais, Elizabeth I led the campaign against the Spanish Armada, and Charles I was confined before his 1649 execution. The palace is home to the Princess Royal (the title given to the monarch's eldest daughter, currently Princess Anne); it's closed to the public, but you can attend Sunday services at its historic **Chapel Royal** (1st Sun of mth, Oct-Good Friday; 8.30am, 11.15am).

Adjacent to St James's Palace is **Clarence House**, former residence of the Queen Mother; a few streets north, delightful **Spencer House** is the ancestral home of the family of the late Princess Diana. Across Marlborough Road lies the pocket-sized **Queen's Chapel**, designed by Inigo Jones in the 1620s for Charles I's Catholic queen Henrietta Maria, at a time when Catholic places of worship were officially banned. The Queen's Chapel can only be visited for Sunday services (Easter-July; 8.30am, 11.15am).

To the south is the wonderful **St James's Park** (*see p115*), surely London's loveliest park. Along the park's northern boundary, **the Mall** connects Buckingham Palace with Trafalgar Square. It looks like a classic processional route, but the Mall was actually laid out as a pitch for Charles II to play 'pallemaille' (an early version of croquet imported from France) after the pitch at Pall Mall became too crowded. On the south side of the park, Wellington Barracks contains the **Guards Museum**; to the east, Horse Guards contains the **Household Cavalry Museum**.

Carlton House Terrace, on the north flank of the Mall, was the last project completed by John Nash before his death in 1835. Part of the terrace now houses the **ICA**. Just behind is the Duke of York column, commemorating Prince Frederick, Duke of York, who led the British Army against the French. He's the nursery rhyme's 'Grand old Duke of York', who marched his 10,000 men neither up nor down Cassel hill in Flanders.

Sights & museums

Buckingham Palace & Royal Mews
*The Mall, SW1A 1AA (Palace 0303 123 7300, Royal Mews 0303 123 7302, Queen's Gallery 0303 123 7301, www.royalcollection.org.uk). Green Park tube or Victoria tube/rail. **Open** admission times & prices vary. **Map** p100 J10.*

Although the nearby St James's Palace remains the official seat of the British court, every monarch since Victoria has used Buckingham Palace as their primary home. Originally known as Buckingham House, the present home of the British royals was constructed as a private house for the Duke of Buckingham in 1703, but George III liked it so much he purchased it for his German bride Charlotte in 1761. George IV decided to occupy the mansion himself after taking the throne in 1820 and John Nash was hired to convert it into a palace befitting a king. Construction was beset with problems, and Nash – whose expensive plans had always been disliked by Parliament – was dismissed in 1830. When Victoria came to the throne in 1837, the building was barely habitable. The

---

In the know
Long to reign over us

On the death in 2016 of King Bhumibol Adulyadej of Thailand, Queen Elizabeth II became the world's longest-reigning living monarch. Since becoming queen at the age of 25, succeeding her father King George VI, she has gone on to celebrate her Diamond Jubilee (60 years) in 2012, and smash the previous British record – held by her great-great-grandmother. Queen Victoria reigned for a paltry 63 years 216 days. Queen Elizabeth II's coronation was on 2 June 1953.

job of finishing the palace fell to the reliable but unimaginative Edward Blore ('Blore the Bore'). The neoclassical frontage now in place was the work of Aston Webb in 1913.

As the home of the Queen, the palace is usually closed to visitors, but you can view the interior for a brief period each year while the Windsors are away on their holidays; you'll be able to see the State Rooms, still used to entertain dignitaries and guests of state, and part of the garden. There's even a café – paper cups, sadly, but coloured a pretty blue-green and clearly marked with the palace crest for souvenir-hunters. At any time of year, you can visit the Queen's Gallery to see her personal collection of treasures, including paintings by Rubens and Rembrandt, Sèvres porcelain and the Diamond Diadem crown. Further along Buckingham Palace Road, the Royal Mews is a grand garage for the royal fleet of Rolls-Royces and home to the splendid royal carriages and the horses, individually named by the Queen, that pull them.

Clarence House
St James's Palace, The Mall, SW1 1BA (7766 7303, www.royalcollection.org.uk). Green Park tube. **Open** *Aug 10am-4.30pm Mon-Fri; 10am-5.30pm Sat, Sun. Closed Sept-July.* **Tours** *£10; £6 reductions; free under-5s.* **Map** *p100 K9.*

Currently the official residence of Prince Charles and the Duchess of Cornwall, this austere royal mansion was built between 1825 and 1827 for Prince William Henry, Duke of Clarence, who stayed on in the house after his coronation as King William IV. Designed by John Nash, the house has been much altered. Five receiving rooms and the late Queen Mother's British art collection are open to the public in August.

Guards Museum
Wellington Barracks, Birdcage Walk, SW1E 6HQ (7414 3428, www.theguardsmuseum. com). St James's Park tube. **Open** *10am-4pm daily.* **Admission** *£6; £2-£3 reductions; free under-16s.* **Map** *p100 K10.*

Just down the road from Horse Guards, this small museum tells the 350-year story of the Foot Guards, using flamboyant uniforms, period paintings, medals and intriguing memorabilia, such as the stuffed body of Jacob the Goose, the Guards' Victorian mascot, who was regrettably run over by a van in barracks. Appropriately, the shop is well stocked with toy soldiers of the British regiments.

Household Cavalry Museum
Horse Guards, Whitehall, SW1A 2AX (7930 3070, www.householdcavalrymuseum. co.uk). Westminster tube or Charing Cross tube/rail. **Open** *Apr-Oct 10am-6pm daily. Nov-Mar 10am-5pm daily.* **Admission** *£7; £5 reductions; £18 family; free under-5s.* **Map** *p100 L9.*

Household Cavalry is a fairly workaday name for the military peacocks who make up the Queen's official guard. They tell their stories through video diaries at this small but

---

In the know
On your guard

The Guards assemble on the parade ground at Wellington Barracks before marching on to the palace for Changing the Guard. The Cavalry assemble for their version of the ceremony on the parade ground outside the Household Cavalry Museum. *See p311 Changing the Guard.*

Horse Guards

❤ St James's Park

St James's Park tube. **Open** *5am-midnight daily.* **Map** *p100 L9.*

There's only one London park where you might spot a pelican swallow a pigeon. St James's Park, a 90-acre wedge of green between Westminster, Trafalgar Square and Buckingham Palace, is the oldest of eight royal parks – those parks that are Crown rather than municipal property. It is also one of London's finest, with narrow lanes meandering around a lake and gorgeous sculpted flower beds, a lakeside café, copious wildfowl and one of the most romantic views in the city. This comes from a bridge across the graceful central lake, which was created from a more formal canal by John Nash in the 1820s. Look east and, above the trees in the near distance, hover the spires, pinnacles and domes of Whitehall – with no square modern towers in sight, it looks like something from Prague or Disneyland; look west and, if the leaves are off the trees, you'll see **Buckingham Palace** (*see p113*).

The city is blessed with numerous parks, many formed from Crown or common land, some from land donated by wealthy philanthropists. **Regent's Park** (*see p244*), slightly north of the centre, is St James's closest rival, less genteel but every bit as much loved; further afield, Greenwich, Richmond, Brixton's Brockwell and east London's Victoria Park are all a rewarding wander. St James's is the finest of London's three central parks, more relaxed than **Hyde Park** (*see p129*), whose wide green spaces are ideal for sport, and more interesting than dull old **Green Park** (*see p118*). These three parks almost interlink, making a stroll east from Kensington Gardens to St James's a delight. St James's itself is the place for a wistful wander, or parking your posterior on a deckchair for a weekend summer concert at the bandstand. It's a peaceful place – except when it's used for ceremonial events like **Trooping the Colour** (*see p311*).

It's quite a transformation for a park, formed from a marshy field attached to a leper hospital, that later became a haunt of prostitutes. Henry VIII was the first to use the land for leisure, creating a bowling alley and ground for hunting. James I had more formal gardens laid out and imported a menagerie that included two crocodiles. In the 17th century, Charles II had it redesigned again, by the French landscape gardener from Versailles, adding a pair of pelicans that had been a gift from the Russian ambassador – pelicans have been resident ever since. In fact, wildlife has been a constant theme. Early occupants included deer, leopards and an elk, but by the 18th century the park was being used to graze cows – fresh milk could be bought here until 1905. Now, wildfowl are the draw, with 17 different species splashing about in the central lake. Those bag-jawed pelicans are fed between 2.30pm and 3pm daily.

entertaining museum, which also offers the chance to see medals, uniforms and shiny cuirasses (breastplates) up close. You also get a peek – and sniff – of the magnificent horses that parade just outside every day: the stables are separated from the main museum by no more than a screen of glass.

ICA (Institute of Contemporary Arts)

The Mall, SW1Y 5AH (7930 0493 information, 7930 3647 tickets, www.ica.org.uk). Piccadilly Circus tube or Charing Cross tube/ rail. **Open** *11am-11pm Tue-Sun. Galleries (during exhibitions) 11am-6pm Tue, Wed, Fri-Sun; 11am-9pm Thur.* **Admission** *free.* **Map** *p100 L9.*

Founded in 1947 by a collective of poets, artists and critics, the ICA moved to its current location on the Mall in 1968. Here it offers exhibitions, arthouse cinema, performance art, philosophical debates, art-themed club nights and anything else that might challenge convention – but 'convention' is so much harder to challenge now that everyone's doing it. Perhaps new director Stefan Kalmár – whose CV includes stints at New York's Artists Space and Munich's Bonner Kunstverein – will make it a must-visit for the culturati once more.

Spencer House

27 St James's Place, SW1A 1NR (7514 1958, www.spencerhouse.co.uk). Green Park tube. **Open** *Sep-Jul 10am-4.30pm Sun. Last tour 4.45pm.* **Admission** *£12; £10 reductions. Under-10s not allowed.* **Map** *p100 K9.*

One of the last surviving private residences in St James's, this handsome mansion was designed for John Spencer by John Vardy, but was completed in 1766 by Hellenophile architect James Stuart, hence the mock Greek flourishes. Lady Georgiana, the 18th-century socialite and beauty – played by Keira Knightley in *The Duchess* (2008) – lived here, but the Spencers left generations before their most famous scion, Diana, married into

the Windsor family. The palatial building has painstakingly restored interiors, and a wonderful garden, which is sometimes open to the general public.

Restaurants

In St James's Park, **St James's Café** (7925 2985, www.benugo.com/public-spaces/ st-james-s-park) is a good place to pick up some breakfast or lunchtime ciabatta. It's fairly low-key but the setting (overlooking the duck lake, with trees all around and the London Eye in the distance) is really wonderful.

Sake no Hana £££££

23 St James's Street, SW1A 1HA (7925 8988, sakenohana.com/london). Green Park tube. **Open** *noon-3pm, 6-11pm Mon-Thur; noon-3pm, 6-11.30pm Fri; noon-3.30pm, 6-11.30pm Sat.* **Map** *p100 K9* 4 *Japanese*

As you'd expect from the Hakkasan restaurant group, Sake No Hana is beautifully designed. That and the fine range of contemporary Japanese dishes and slick service make it popular place for business lunches and well-heeled families. For a filling meal, the 'Taste of Sake No Hana' (£29) consists of miso soup, a choice of sukiyaki, tempura or grilled dish, a handful of sushi and a dessert. There's also plenty for wine and saké buffs to get stuck into. Don't forget to glance upwards while you're dining: the sculptural wood slating above your head definitely deserves a look.

♥ Wolseley £££

160 Piccadilly, W1J 9EB (7499 6996, www. thewolseley.com). Green Park tube. **Open** *7am-midnight Mon-Fri; 8am-midnight Sat; 8am-11pm Sun.* **Map** *p100 K8* 5 *Brasserie*

A self-proclaimed 'café-restaurant in the grand European tradition', the Wolseley combines London heritage and Viennese grandeur. The kitchen is much celebrated for its breakfasts, and the scope of the main menu is admirable. From oysters, steak tartare or soufflé suisse, via wiener schnitzel or grilled halibut with wilted spinach and béarnaise, to Portuguese custard tart or apple strudel, there's something for everyone. On Sunday afternoons, three-tiered afternoon tea stands are in abundance. The Wolseley's owners, Chris Corbin and Jeremy King, run a number of London's favourite venues, including the **Delaunay** (*see p191*) and **Bar Américain** (*see p173*), and have opened their first hotel, the **Beaumont** (*see p398*).

Pubs & bars

❤ Dukes Bar
Dukes Hotel, 35 St James's Place, SW1A 1NY (7491 4840, www.dukeshotel.com/dukes-bar). Green Park tube. **Open** *2-11pm Mon-Sat; 4-10.30pm Sun.* **Map** *p100 K9* ❸

If you want to go out for a single cocktail, strong and expensive and very well made, go to Dukes. It's in a luxury hotel, but everyone gets the warmest of welcomes. There are three small rooms, all decorated in discreetly opulent style; you feel cocooned. The bar is famous for the theatre of its Martini-making – at the table, from a trolley, using vermouth made exclusively for them at the Sacred distillery in Highgate – but other drinks are just as good.

Shops & services

Heading west on Piccadilly, the shops become increasingly upmarket. **Jermyn Street**, dating back to 1664 when Charles II authorised Henry Jermyn to develop the area, has become a byword for bespoke gentlemen's clothing, with resident tailors including Turnbull & Asser, Hawes & Curtis and T M Lewin.

❤ Dover Street Market
18-22 Haymarket, SW1Y 4DG (7518 0680, www.doverstreetmarket.com). Green Park tube. **Open** *11am-7pm Mon-Sat; noon-6pm Sun.* **Map** *p100 L8* ❶ *Fashion*

Combining the energy of London's indoor markets with rarefied labels, Rei Kawakubo's ground-breaking multistorey store is a mecca for the fashion obsessed. Housing some of London's brightest stars – Grace Wales Bonner's wonderfully elegant menswear and Molly Goddard's dream dresses woven out of tulle – it's a real champion of the capital's pioneering fashion designers. All 14 of the Comme des Garçons collections are here, alongside exclusive lines from such designers as Lanvin and Azzedine Alaïa.

DR Harris
29 St James's Street, SW1A 1HB (7930 3915, www.drharris.co.uk). Green Park or Piccadilly Circus tube. **Open** *8.30am-6pm Mon-Fri; 9.30am-5pm Sat.* **Map** *p100 K9* ❷ *Health & beauty*

In a city overtaken by characterless chain pharmacies, the venerable DR Harris has remained unfazed – it's hung on tight to its identity since 1790 and demurely holds a royal warrant. A visit is much like stepping through a door into times past. Polished wooden cabinets are filled with bottles and jars with old-fashioned shaving brushes and manicure kits. Traditional it may be, but DR Harris appeals to modern sensibilities – none of the products are tested on animals, the use of palm oil is limited and nearly all packaging is recyclable.

❤ Floris
89 Jermyn Street, SW1Y 6JH (7747 3612, www.florislondon.com). Green Park tube. **Open** *9.30am-6pm Mon-Wed, Fri; 9.30am-7pm Thur; 10am-7pm Sat; 11.30am-5.30pm Sun.* **Map** *p100 K8* ❸ *Health & beauty*

Enterprising young Spaniard Juan Floris set up his fragrance shop in 1730 and it has been run by the same family ever since. One imagines not too much has changed. Everything is behind glass cabinets and oak-panelled counters in the manner of an old-fashioned apothecary, and smartly dressed men and women guide you through the selection process; much more civilised than a department store.

❤ Fortnum & Mason
181 Piccadilly, W1A 1ER (7734 8040, www.fortnumandmason.co.uk). Green Park or Piccadilly Circus tube. **Open** *10am-8pm Mon-Sat; noon-6pm Sun (11.30am for browsing).* **Map** *p100 K8* ❹ *Department store*

In business for over 300 years, Fortnum & Mason is as historic as it is inspiring. A sweeping spiral staircase soars through the four-storey building, while light floods down from a central glass dome. The iconic eau de nil blue and gold colour scheme with flashes of rose pink abounds on both the store design and the packaging of the fabulous ground-floor treats, such as chocolates, biscuits, teas and preserves. A food hall in the basement

has a good range of fresh produce; Fortnum's Bees honey comes from beehives on top of the building. There are various eateries, including an ice-cream parlour. The famous hampers start from £55 – though they rise to a whopping £1,000 for the most luxurious.

James J Fox
19 St James's Street, SW1A 1ES (7930 3787, www.jjfox.co.uk). Green Park tube. **Open** *9.30am-8pm Mon-Wed, Fri; 5.45pm Mon-Wed, Fri; 9.30am-8.45pm Thur; 9.30am-5pm Sat.* **Map** *p100 K9* ❺ *Cigars*

There are other cigar shops in London, but Fox is the grandest and most storied. Oscar Wilde died owing it money and the iconic image of Winston Churchill, with a cigar clenched between his teeth, is down to the fact he used to buy his Montecristos here. It's worth a visit just to see the clientele: a curious mixture of ageing Euro playboys, old Etonians and Mayfair gents. There's also a small museum.

❤ Lock & Co Hatters
6 St James's Street, SW1A 1EF (7930 8874, www.lockhatters.co.uk). Green Park tube. **Open** *9am-5.30pm Mon-Fri; 9.30am-5pm Sat.* **Map** *p100 K9* ❻ *Milliners*

Lock & Co is perhaps the most famous hat shop in the world. It is certainly one of the oldest, dating from 1759, and has been frequented by such names as Charlie Chaplin and Admiral Lord Nelson. But, history aside, it is simply very good. It has one of the most comprehensive selections of classic hats to be found anywhere in London: bowlers, top hats, homburgs, berets, panamas – all exquisitely made.

GREEN PARK & HYDE PARK CORNER

▶ *Green Park or Hyde Park Corner tube.*

The flat green expanse just beyond the Ritz on Piccadilly is **Green Park**; it's rather dull, except in spring, when the daffodils jolly things up.

Work your way along Piccadilly, following the northern edge of Green Park past the queue outside the **Hard Rock Café** (where the Vault's displays of memorabilia are free to visit and open every day; www.hardrock.com) to the Duke of Wellington's old home, **Apsley House**, opposite Wellington Arch. This is hectic **Hyde Park Corner**; Buckingham Palace (*see p113*) is just a short walk south-east, while Hyde Park and the upper-crust enclave of Belgravia are to the west. There is a collection of memorials

that are worth lingering over. The newest is the Bomber Command Memorial. Unveiled in 2012, it recognises the sacrifice of the 55,573 men of Bomber Command, killed between 1939 and 1945 as they pulverised Nazi-held Europe into submission. But we find Charles Sargeant Jagger's thoughtful tribute to the 49,076 men of the Royal Regiment of Artillery, slain between 1914 and 1919, to be more deeply moving. It's both vast – a huge Portland stone slab with giant gunners on three sides – and strangely muted, with a dead soldier lying peacefully in giant hobnail boots on the monument's north side.

Sights & museums
Apsley House
149 Piccadilly, W1J 7NT (7499 5676, www.english-heritage.org.uk). Hyde Park Corner tube. **Open** *Nov-Mar 10am-4pm Sat, Sun. Apr-Oct 11am-5pm Wed-Sun.* **Tours** *by*

arrangement. **Admission** £9.30; £5.60-£8.40 reductions; £24.20 family; free under-5s. Joint ticket with Wellington Arch £11.20; £6.70-£10.10 reductions; £29.10 family. **Map** p100 H9.

Called No.1 London because it was the first London building encountered on the road to the city from the village of Kensington, Apsley House was built by Robert Adam in the 1770s. The Duke of Wellington kept it as his London home for 35 years. Although his descendants still live here, several rooms are open to the public, providing a superb feel for the man and his era. Admire the extravagant porcelain dinnerware and plates or ask for a demonstration of the crafty mirrors in the scarlet and gilt picture gallery, where a fine Velázquez and a Correggio hang near Goya's portrait of the Iron Duke after he defeated the French in 1812. This was a last-minute edit: X-rays have revealed that Wellington's head was painted over that of Joseph Bonaparte, Napoleon's brother. In winter, the twilight tours at Apsley House are very atmospheric.

Wellington Arch

Hyde Park Corner, W1J 7JZ (7930 2726, www. english-heritage.org.uk). Hyde Park Corner tube. **Open** Apr-Oct 10am-6pm daily. Nov-Mar 10am-4pm daily. **Admission** £5; £3-£4.50 reductions; £13 family; free under-5s. Joint ticket with Apsley House £11.20; £6.70-£10.10 reductions; £29.10 family. **Map** p100 H9.

Built in the late 1820s to mark Britain's triumph over Napoleonic France, Decimus Burton's Wellington Arch was initially topped by an out-of-proportion equestrian statue of Wellington. However, Captain Adrian Jones's 38-ton bronze Peace Descending on the Quadriga of War has finished it with a flourish since 1912. The Arch has three floors, with an English Heritage bookshop and various displays, covering the history of the arch and the Blue Plaques scheme, and in the Quadriga Gallery providing space for excellent temporary exhibitions. There are great views from the balcony in winter (leafy trees obscure the sightlines in spring and summer).

Wellington Arch

South Kensington & Chelsea

There can be few cities in the world with a square mile so crammed with cultural highlights as you'll find in South Kensington: three of the world's greatest museums, a grand concert hall, university campuses and an expansive park. Neighbouring Knightsbridge, on the other hand, has no cultural pretensions: a certain type of Londoner comes here to spend, spend, spend – or hang around with the non-doms and hyperwealthy incomers who are spend, spend, spending in the designer shops and world-famous department stores. Chelsea, running between them and the river, has long since left its raffish youth behind – but there are pleasures to be found amid its red-brick gentility.

❤ Don't miss

1 Victoria & Albert Museum *p126*
A palace for global applied arts.

2 Chelsea Physic Garden *p135*
A place of botanical delight.

3 Science Museum *p125*
From maths to medicine: how the world works.

4 Harrods *p133*
Legendary department store.

5 Natural History Museum *p124*
Life on earth from prehistory to now.

121

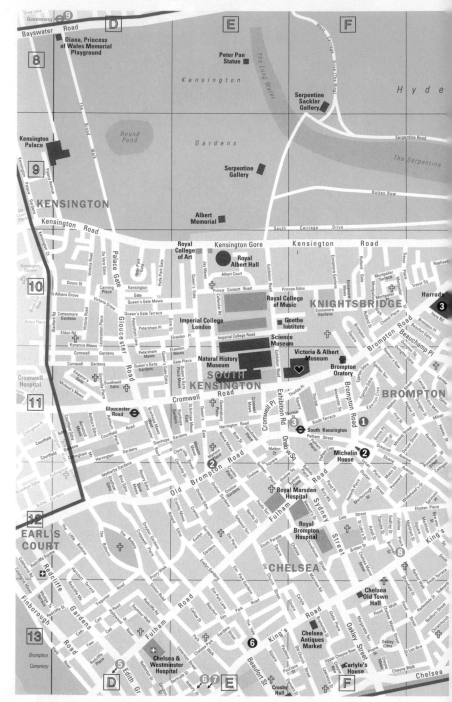

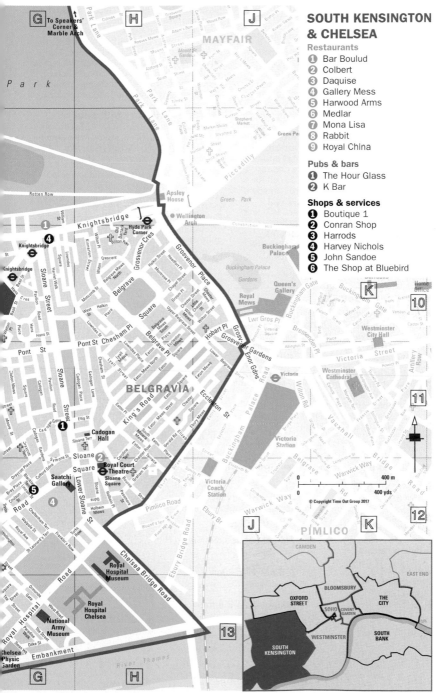

SOUTH KENSINGTON & CHELSEA

Restaurants
1. Bar Boulud
2. Colbert
3. Daquise
4. Gallery Mess
5. Harwood Arms
6. Medlar
7. Mona Lisa
8. Rabbit
9. Royal China

Pubs & bars
1. The Hour Glass
2. K Bar

Shops & services
1. Boutique 1
2. Conran Shop
3. Harrods
4. Harvey Nichols
5. John Sandoe
6. The Shop at Bluebird

SOUTH KENSINGTON

▶ *Gloucester Road or South Kensington tube.*

As far as cultural and academic institutions are concerned, this is the land of plenty. It was Prince Albert who oversaw the inception of its world-class museums, colleges and concert hall, using the profits of the 1851 Great Exhibition; the area was nicknamed 'Albertopolis' in his honour. You'll find the **Natural History Museum**, the **Science Museum** and the **Victoria & Albert Museum** (*see p126*), **Imperial College**, the **Royal College of Art** and the **Royal College of Music** (Prince Consort Road, 7591 4300, www.rcm.ac.uk; call for details of the musical instrument museum). The last forms a unity with the **Royal Albert Hall** (*see p355*), open since 1871 and variously used for boxing, motor shows, marathons, table-tennis tournaments, fascist rallies and rock concerts. Directly opposite is the endearingly pompous **Albert Memorial**.

Sights & museums
Albert Memorial
Kensington Gardens (0300 061 2000, www. royalparks.org.uk). South Kensington tube. **Tours** *Mar-Dec 2pm, 3pm 1st Sun of mth.* **Admission** *£8; £7 reductions.* **Map** *p122 E9.*

'I would rather not be made the prominent feature of such a monument,' was Prince Albert's reported response when the subject of his commemoration arose. Hard, then, to imagine what he would have made of this extraordinary thing, unveiled 15 years after

his death. Created by Sir George Gilbert Scott, it centres on a giant, gilded Albert holding a catalogue of the 1851 Great Exhibition, guarded on four corners by the continents of Africa, America, Asia and Europe. The pillars are crowned with bronze statues of the sciences, and the frieze at the base depicts major artists, architects and musicians. It's one of London's most dramatic monuments.

❤ Natural History Museum
Cromwell Road, SW7 5BD (7942 5000, www. nhm.ac.uk). South Kensington tube. **Open** *10am-5.50pm daily.* **Admission** *free. Special exhibitions vary.* **Tours** *free.* **Map** *p122 E11.*

Both a research institution and a fabulous museum, the NHM opened in Alfred Waterhouse's purpose-built, Romanesque palazzo on the Cromwell Road in 1881. Now joined by the splendid Darwin Centre extension, the original building still looks quite magnificent. The pale blue and terracotta façade just about prepares you for the natural wonders within.

The vast entrance hall previously home to the iconic *Diplodocus* skeleton is undergoing a transformation. While 'Dippy' is on tour, he will be replaced by another huge beast: a blue whale. Taking centre-stage in a new exhibition telling the tale of evolution and of human impact on the natural world, the 25m-long, 4.5-tonne skeleton will be suspended dramatically from the ceiling.

From the entrance hall, a left turn leads into the west wing, or Blue Zone, where queues form to see animatronic dinosaurs – especially the endlessly popular *T rex*. Here too, is the Mammals Hall, where you can stare out all manner of stuffed animals from a polar bear to a pygmy shrew. A display on

❤ Time to eat & drink
Brit with a twist
Rabbit *p137*

Meaty feasts
Bar Boulud *p132*

A Polish classic
Daquise *p129*

Caff snacks
Mona Lisa *p137*

❤ Time to shop
Great gifts
Natural History Museum, Science Museum and V&A shops, *p129*

Old-school bookselling
John Sandoe *p137*

Top-notch fashion
Boutique 1 *p137*

Shopping as theatre
Harrods *p133*

Fine design
The Shop at Bluebird *p137*

In the know
Clues to the queues

Especially in school holidays, there are often long queues at the main entrance of the Natural History Museum on Cromwell Road. Try the side entrance on Exhibition Road, instead: it is usually less busy and provides an impressive introduction to the collections as you ascend the escalator up into the Earth Galleries. Tickets to the dinosaur room can be booked online for free and allow you to enter at a specific time slot rather than queue.

biology features an illuminated, human-sized model of a foetus in the womb along with graphic diagrams of how it might have got there.

A right turn from the central hall leads past the Creepy Crawlies exhibition to the Green Zone. Stars include a cross-section through a giant sequoia tree and an amazing array of stuffed birds, including the chance to compare the egg of a hummingbird smaller than the nail on your little finger with that of an elephant bird (now extinct), almost football-sized.

Beyond is the Red Zone, where a *Stegosaurus* skeleton takes pride of place. Earth's Treasury is a mine of information on a variety of precious metals, gems and crystals; From the Beginning is a brave attempt to give the expanse of geological time a human perspective; Volcanoes and Earthquakes explores the immense energy and power of the natural world through dramatic film footage, interactive games and an earthquake simulator.

Many of the museum's 22 million insect and plant specimens are housed in the Darwin Centre, where they take up nearly 17 miles of shelving. With its eight-storey

Cocoon, this is also home to the museum's research scientists, who can be watched at work. But a great deal of this amazing institution is hidden from public view, given over to labs and specialised storage.

Outside, the delightful Wildlife Garden (Apr-Oct only) showcases a range of British lowland habitats, including a 'Bee Tree', a hollow tree trunk that opens to reveal a busy hive.

❤ Science Museum
Exhibition Road, SW7 2DD (7942 4000, www. sciencemuseum.org.uk). South Kensington tube. **Open** *10am-6pm daily.* **Admission** *free. Wonderlab £8; £6 reductions; £22.50 family. Special exhibitions vary.* **Map** *p122 E10.*

The Science Museum is a celebration of the wonders of technology in the service of our daily lives. On the ground floor, the shop – selling brilliant toys, not least because you can pretend they're educational – is part of the Energy Hall, which introduces the museum's collections with impressive 18th-century steam engines. In Exploring Space, rocket science and the lunar landings are illustrated by dramatically lit mock-ups

Natural History Museum Stegosaurus

♥ Victoria & Albert Museum

Cromwell Road, SW7 2RL (7942 2000, www.vam.ac.uk). South Kensington tube. **Open** *10am-5.45pm Mon-Thur, Sat, Sun; 10am-10pm Fri. Tours 10.30am, 12.30am, 1.30pm, 3.30pm daily.* **Admission** *free. Special exhibitions vary.* **Map** *p122 F11*

It comes to something when a museum can lay claim to having been opened as Queen Victoria's last public engagement. In 1899, the current premises of the V&A enjoyed that privilege. It has gone on to become one of the world's – let alone London's – most magnificent museums. It is a superb showcase for applied arts from around the globe, appreciably calmer than its tearaway cousins the **Science Museum** (*see p389*) and **Natural History Museum** (*see p388*) on the other side of Exhibition Road. All three South Ken museums would be must-visits in another city, but it is the sheer beauty of the V&A that keeps it closest to our heart.

The details? There are some 150 grand galleries over seven floors. They contain countless pieces of furniture, ceramics, sculpture, paintings, posters, jewellery, metalwork, glass, textiles and dress, spanning several centuries. You could run through the highlights for the rest of this guide, but key artefacts include the seven Raphael Cartoons, painted in 1515 as tapestry designs for the Sistine Chapel; the finest collection of Italian Renaissance sculpture outside Italy; the Ardabil carpet, the world's oldest and arguably most splendid floor covering, in the Jameel Gallery of Islamic Art; and

the Luck of Edenhall, a 13th-century glass beaker from Syria. The fashion galleries run from 18th-century court dress right up to contemporary chiffon numbers, while the architecture gallery has videos, models, plans and descriptions of various styles.

Over more than a decade, the V&A's ongoing FuturePlan transformation has been a revelation – more than 85 per cent of its public spaces have been restored and redesigned. The completely refurbished Medieval & Renaissance Galleries are stunning, but there are many other eye-catching new or redisplayed exhibits: they were preceded by the restored mosaic floors and beautiful stained glass of the 14th- to 17th-century sculpture rooms, just off the central John Madejski Garden, and followed by the Furniture Galleries – another immediate hit. The ambitious 'Europe 1600-1815' Galleries – centred around a stunning four-metre-long table fountain, painstakingly reconstructed from 18th-century fragments – collect European clothes, furnishings and other artefacts.

In the know
Monumental

Of all the wonders in the V&A, it was the magnificent Cast Courts we first fell in love with. Here you can ogle an 18ft-high plaster-cast of *David* and other monumental sculpture – faultless, full-scale facsimiles of Renaissance cathedral doorways and the like – in a painstakingly restored double-height gallery that dates to 1873. At least one of the copies here – of the late 15th-century Lubeck relief depicting Christ washing the feet of the Apostles – has outlasted its original.

Or there's the Toshiba Gallery of Japanese Art, exhibiting 550 works running from the sixth century AD to the first Sony Walkman and an origami outfit by Issey Miyake. On a smaller scale, the Ceramics Galleries have been renovated and supplemented with an eye-catching bridge; and the Theatre & Performance Galleries took over where Covent Garden's defunct Theatre Museum left off. Newer additions include the museum's 'Rapid Response Collection', which features examples of contemporary design and architecture reflecting important news events, while the major temporary exhibitions – Alexander McQueen, David Bowie – are frequently blockbuster sell-outs.

Summer 2017 saw the opening of a new entrance, directly into the heart of the museum from Exhibition Road, through the porcelain-tiled Sackler Courtyard to the purpose-built Sainsbury Gallery. It's a fitting introduction to a fabulous museum.

▶ *The V&A also runs the Museum of Childhood in Bethnal Green (see p269).*

Science Museum

and full-size models, before the museum gears up for its core collection in Making the Modern World. Introduced by Puffing Billy, the world's oldest steam locomotive (built in 1815), the gallery also contains Stephenson's Rocket. Also here are the Apollo 10 command module, classic cars and an absorbing collection of everyday technological marvels from 1750 up to the present.

In the main body of the museum, the second floor has a couple of the museum's newer additions. There's the Media Space, for excellent temporary exhibitions drawn from the museum's impressive photographic archive, and Information Age, the UK's first permanent gallery dedicated to the history of communications technology. It follows developments from the 19th-century establishment of an international telegraph network through broadcasting all the way up to the worldwide web. The stunning new Winton Gallery, designed by Zaha Hadid Architects using equations of airflow used in the aviation industry, reveals how mathematics has shaped the modern world. The centrepiece is a 1929 Handley Page aircraft designed as part of a competition to build safe aircraft. Other displays explore how maths is driven by real-world problems, from foetal monitoring and artificial intelligence to World War II code-breaking and astronomy. Here too is the Clockmakers' Museum, recently moved from the Guildhall and containing a John Harrison chronometer – he was the man who solved the problem of longitude.

The third floor is dedicated to flight, among other things, including the hands-on Launchpad Gallery, which has levers, pulleys, explosions and all manner of experiments for children (and their associated grown-ups). It is also home to Wonderlab: The Statoil Gallery (entry costs from £6). Opened in 2016, the exhibits are dedicated to communicating the properties and principles of the physical world by encouraging visitors to play with them. Fun mirrors help to explain geometry, plasma globes are effectively bottled lightning, and the chemistry bar is home to live experiments that let you get messy and spectacular with crystals, dry ice, bubble volcanoes and non-Newtonian fluids.

Beyond Making the Modern World, bathed in an eerie blue light, are the three floors of the Wellcome Wing, where the museum makes sure it stays on the cutting edge of science. On the ground floor, Antenna is a web-savvy look at breaking science stories, displaying video interviews and Q&As with real research scientists alongside the weird new objects they've been working on. Upstairs is the enjoyable and troubling Who Am I? gallery. A dozen silver pods surround

In the know
Kids' stuff

The Science Museum is great for kids – but everyone knows that, so be sure to arrive early if you don't like crowds and queues. Specifically child-friendly attractions include interactive experimental play in the Garden (basement; for three- to seven-year-olds), the Pattern Pod (ground floor; three- to eight-year-olds) and 'Engineer your Future' (Level 3; 11- to 16-year-olds), but the mathematics gallery (Level 2; over-11s), Wonderlab (Level 3; all ages) and Fly Zone flight simulators (Level 3; all ages) are usually a hit. There's a charge for Wonderlab and the simulators.

brightly lit cases of objects with engaging interactive displays – from a cartoon of ethical dilemmas that introduces you to your dorsolateral prefrontal cortex to a chance to find out what gender your brain is. Compelling objects include a jellyfish that's 'technically immortal', the statistically average British man (he's called Jose), a pound of human fat, displayed alongside a gastric band, and half of Charles Babbage's brain (good luck seeing the other half: it's in the Hunterian Museum, which is now closed until 2020).

Restaurants

♥ Daquise ££

*20 Thurloe Street, SW7 2LT (7589 6117, www. daquise.co.uk). South Kensington tube. **Open** noon-11pm daily. **Map** p122 F11* ❸ *Polish*

This much-loved grande dame of London Polish restaurants (established 1947) offers a home-from-home ambience with a stylish twist. In the shabby-chic, light and airy interior, enlivened with fresh flowers, robust, flavourful, no-nonsense traditional dishes are served with great charm. Classic cold starters of meltingly tender herring with cream, apple, onion and flax oil, or beetroot with subtly warming horseradish, are ladled directly from capacious earthenware bowls, while mains are assembled directly at the table from well-worn saucepans, borne by the chefs who lovingly prepared the dishes.

Pubs & bars

The Hour Glass

*279-283 Brompton Road, SW3 2DY (7581 2497, hourglasspub.co.uk). South Kensington tube. **Open** noon-11pm Mon-Sat; noon-1030pm Sun. **Map** p122 F11* ❶

In the posh-shop-big-museum nexus around South Kensington, this nice old pub has been scrubbed up by a couple of lads who own the nearby Brompton Food Market. The ground floor is a pleasant spot with plenty of standing, leaning and sitting room to enjoy an ale or a Cumberland scotch egg, while upstairs is a handsome dining room with sparkling glasses and crisp linen. Food is obviously a major part of the new venture, but it's still a great spot for a pint.

K Bar

*The Kensington, 109 -113 Queen's Gate, SW7 5LR (7589 6300, townhousekensington. com/k-bar). South Kensington tube. **Open** Bar 4-11pm Mon-Thur; 1-11pm Fri-Sun. Food served 6.30-10.30am Mon-Fri; 7-11am, noon-10.30pm Sat, Sun. **Map** p122 E11* ❷

Not just any old hotel bar, K Bar buzzes from early evening, with guests preparing for a night out, right through to the nightcap crowd. It's a relatively small area with large, comfy sofas lining the oak-panelled walls and a marble-topped bar adding an air of opulence. Table service is efficient and the competitively priced cocktails are expertly mixed; there's even menu of dessert drinks: bring a sweet tooth if you're trying the Crème Brûlée Martini.

Shops & services

The **V&A** has a superb gift shop, stuffed with stylish exhibition-related buys, the **Science Museum** has a lively range of geek-free science presents for kids and the **Natural History Museum** has cute cuddly dinosaurs.

Conran Shop

*Michelin House, 81 Fulham Road, SW3 6RD (7589 7401, www.conranshop.co.uk). South Kensington tube. **Open** 10am-6pm Mon, Tue, Fri; 10am-7pm Wed, Thur; 10am-6.30pm Sat; noon-6pm Sun. **Map** p122 F11* ❷ *Homewares*

Sir Terence Conran's flagship store in the Fulham Road's beautiful 1909 Michelin Building showcases furniture and design for every room in the house as well as the garden. In addition to design classics, such as the Eames DAR chair, there are plenty of portable accessories, gadgets, books, stationery and toiletries that make great gifts or souvenirs. There's another branch at 55 Marylebone High Street, W1U 5HS (7723 2223).

HYDE PARK & KENSINGTON GARDENS

▶ *Hyde Park Corner, Knightsbridge, Lancaster Gate or Queensway tube.*

At one and a half miles long and about a mile wide, **Hyde Park** (0300 061 2114, www.royalparks.org.uk) is one of the largest of London's Royal Parks. The land was appropriated in 1536 from the monks of Westminster Abbey by Henry VIII for hunting deer. Although opened to the public in the early 1600s, the parks were favoured only by the upper echelons of society. At the end of the 17th century, William III, averse to the dank air of Whitehall Palace, relocated to **Kensington Palace**. A corner of Hyde Park was sectioned off to make grounds for the palace and closed to the public, until King George II opened it on Sundays to those wearing formal dress. Nowadays, **Kensington Gardens** is delineated from Hyde Park only by the line of the Serpentine

In the know
Alternative play

The Diana Memorial Playground often has queues to get in. If you get bored, head to the south of the park and the Hyde Park Playground. Refurbished in 2014, it has a slide, nest swing and 'jungle area' for nature quests.

and the Long Water. Beside the Long Water is a bronze statue of **Peter Pan**, erected in 1912: it was in Kensington Gardens beside the Round Pond eight years earlier that playwright JM Barrie met Jack Llewelyn Davies, the boy who was the inspiration for Peter. The **Diana, Princess of Wales Memorial Playground** is a kids' favourite, as is Kathryn Gustafson's ring-shaped **Princess Diana Memorial Fountain**. Near the fountain, Simon Gudgeon's giant bird *Isis* was in 2009 the first sculpture added to the park for half a century. There are changing exhibitions of contemporary art at the **Serpentine Gallery**, which also has a Zaha Hadid-designed counterpart just across the bridge.

The **Serpentine** itself is London's oldest boating lake, home to ducks, coots, swans, tufty-headed grebes and, every summer, gently perspiring blokes rowing their children or lovers about. The lake is at the south end of Hyde Park, which isn't a beautiful park, but is of historic interest. The legalisation of public assembly in the park led to the establishment of **Speakers' Corner** in 1872 (close to Marble Arch tube), where political and religious ranters – sane and otherwise – still have the floor every Sunday afternoon. Marx, Lenin, Orwell and

the Pankhursts all spoke here. It has made the park a traditional destination for protest marches: notably the million opponents of the Iraq War in 2003; more recently, trades union protests against government austerity measures in 2012. There is also a moving memorial in the south-east corner of the park. On 7 July 2005, 52 people were killed by Islamist suicide bombers as they made their way to work. Their commemoration, set between the Lovers' Walk and busy Park Lane, consists of 52 ten-foot-tall, square steel columns, one for each fatality; each is marked with the date, time and location of that person's death.

The park perimeter is popular with skaters, as well as with bike- and horse-riders. If you're exploring on foot and the vast expanses defeat you, look out for the **Liberty Drives** (May-Oct). Driven by volunteers, these electric buggies, each with space for a wheelchair, pick up groups of sightseers and ferry them around; there's no fare, but offer a donation if you can.

Sights & museums
Diana, Princess of Wales Memorial Playground
Near Black Lion Gate, Broad Walk, Kensington Gardens, South Kensington, W8 2UH (0300 061 2000, www.royalparks. org.uk). Bayswater or Queensway tube. ***Open*** *Summer 10am-7.45pm daily. Winter 10am-dusk daily.* ***Admission*** *free; adults admitted only if accompanied by under-12s.* ***Map*** *p122 D8.*

Bring buckets and spades, if you can, to this superb playground: the focal attraction is a huge pirate ship, moored in a sea of sand.

Princess Diana Memorial Fountain

Magazine restaurant at the Serpentine Sackler Gallery

Other attractions include a tepee camp and a treehouse encampment with walkways, ladders, slides and 'tree phones'. Many of the playground's attractions appeal to the senses (scented shrubs, whispering willows and bamboo are planted throughout), and much equipment has been designed for use by children with special needs.

Kensington Palace

Kensington Gardens, W8 4PX (information 0844 482 7777, reservations 0844 482 7799 or 3166 6000, www.hrp.org.uk). High Street Kensington or Queensway tube. **Open** *Mar-Oct 10am-6pm daily. Nov-Feb 10am-4pm daily.* **Admission** *£19; £15 reductions; free under-16s. Book online for reductions.* **Map** *p122 D9.*

Sir Christopher Wren extended this Jacobean mansion to palatial proportions on the instructions of William III, initiating the palace's long love affair with royalty – which culminated with the floral memorials for one particular resident, Princess Diana, that were placed at the palace's gate after her fatal accident in 1997. Wren's work too was adapted, under George I, with the addition of intricate trompe l'oeil ceilings and staircases. Visitors can now follow a whimsical trail that focuses on four 'stories' of former residents – Diana, of course; William and Mary, and Mary's sister Queen Anne; Georges I and II; Queen Victoria – unearthing the facts through handily placed 'newspapers'. Artefacts include paintings by the likes of Tintoretto, contemporary art and fashion installations, and even Victoria's (tiny) wedding dress.

Serpentine & Serpentine Sackler galleries

Kensington Gardens, near Albert Memorial, W2 3XA (7402 6075, www.serpentinegalleries. org). Lancaster Gate or South Kensington tube. **Open** *10am-6pm Tue-Sun.* **Admission** *free; donations appreciated.* **Map** *p122 E9 & F8.*

The Serpentine Gallery – much-loved for its sometimes challenging exhibitions of contemporary art – originally had just the one secluded location in a small 1930s tea-house building south-west of the Long Water and Serpentine, into which were squeezed exhibition spaces and a bijou bookshop. Here, the rolling two-monthly programme of exhibitions features a mix of up-to-the-minute artists and edgy career retrospectives, but – perhaps symbolic of the gallery's limitations of space – every spring it also commissions a renowned architect, who's never before built in the UK, to build a temporary pavilion outside. The pavilion then hosts a packed programme of cultural events (June to September).

A permanent solution to the issue of space was found in 2013, when the gallery opened a

> ### In the know
> ### What Hadid did
>
> Zaha Hadid, who died in 2016, designed the very first Serpentine Pavilion back in 2000, but her singular architectural vision is now represented in London by the Serpentine Sackler Gallery, the Aquatics Centre in the Olympic Park (*see p276*) and, more recently, Mathematics: The Winton Gallery at the Science Museum (*see p125*).

second location, the Serpentine Sackler, just across the bridge from the original. Devoted to emerging art in all forms, the Sackler is a Grade II-listed, Palladian former gunpowder store, with a clean-lined restaurant over which the late architect Zaha Hadid cast a billowing white cape of a roof.

Restaurants

Royal China ££
13 Queensway, W2 4QJ (7221 2535, www. theroyalchina.co.uk). Bayswater or Queensway tube. Open noon-11pm Mon-Sat; 11am-10pm Sun. Map p122 D8 ➒ *Chinese*

Not far beyond the north side of the park, this stalwart of London's dim sum scene is always a pleasure to visit. Its perennial popularity ensures a lively atmosphere, and the authentic, perfectly prepared little dishes are head and shoulders above most of Chinatown's lazy offerings. The main menu features wonderfully light beef balls enlivened with strong accents of ginger and water chestnuts, while the delicious wun tun soup has light dumplings floating in a rich broth with an undertone of five-spice. Opt for dim sum and you can choose from the likes of crab and spinach steamed dumplings or prawn and chive packages in batter.

KNIGHTSBRIDGE

▶*Knightsbridge tube.*

Knightsbridge in the 11th century was a village celebrated for its taverns, highwaymen and the legend that two knights once fought to the death on the bridge spanning the Westbourne River (later dammed to form Hyde Park's Serpentine lake). In modern Knightsbridge, urban princesses would be too busy unsheathing the credit card to notice such a farrago. Voguish **Harvey Nichols** holds court at the top of Sloane Street, which leads down to **Sloane Square**. Expensive brands – Gucci, Prada, Chanel – dominate. East of Sloane Street is **Belgravia**, characterised by a cluster of embassies around **Belgrave**

Harrods

Square. Hidden behind the stucco-clad parades fronting the square are numerous mews, worth exploring for the pubs they conceal, notably the **Nag's Head** (53 Kinnerton Street, SW1X 8ED, 7235 1135).

For many tourists, Knightsbridge means one thing: **Harrods**. From its olive-green awning to its green-coated doormen, it's an instantly recognisable retail legend. Further along is the imposing **Brompton Oratory**.

Sights & museums

Brompton Oratory
Thurloe Place, Brompton Road, SW7 2RP (7808 0900, www.bromptonoratory.co.uk). South Kensington tube. Open 6.30am-8pm daily. Admission free; donations appreciated. Map p122 F11.

The second-biggest Catholic church in the country (after Westminster Cathedral; *see p112*) is formally the Church of the Immaculate Heart of Mary, but almost universally known as the Brompton Oratory. Completed in 1884, it feels older, partly because of the Baroque Italianate style but also because much of the decoration pre-dates the structure: Mazzuoli's 17th-century apostle statues, for example, are from Siena cathedral. During the Cold War, KGB agents used the Brompton Oratory as a dead-letter box. The church is popular with young, traditionally minded Catholics: the 11am Solemn Mass sung in Latin on Sundays is enchanting, as are Vespers, at 3.30pm; the website has details.

Restaurants

There's a branch of the popular – and self-explanatory – mini-chain **Burger & Lobster** (*see p165*) in **Harvey Nichols**.

❤ Bar Boulud £££
Mandarin Oriental Hyde Park, 66 Knightsbridge, SW1X 7LA (7201 3899, www. barboulud.com). Knightsbridge tube. Open noon-midnight Mon-Sat; noon-11pm Sun. Map p122 G10 ➊ *French*

Overseen by renowned chef Daniel Boulud, the restaurant has an eye-catching view of the open-plan kitchen, where chefs work in meditative calm. Charcuterie from Gilles Verot is a big draw, as are the elegant French brasserie options and finger-licking American staples. We've had burgers here and loved every bite – try a beef patty topped with pulled pork and green chilli mayonnaise – but other culinary gems might include a robust French onion soup, resplendent with caramelised onions and topped with molten gruyère.

Shops & services

♥ Harrods

87-135 Brompton Road, SW1X 7XL (7730 1234, www.harrods.com). Knightsbridge tube. **Open** *10am-9pm Mon-Sat; noon-6pm Sun (browsing from 11.30am).* **Map** *p122 G10* ❸ *Department store*

It might be unashamedly ostentatious, stuffed with tourists and in possession of the world's most vulgar statue (Dodi and Diana in bronze by the Egyptian escalators), but Harrods – London's most famous department store – is still spectacular. Serious shoppers browse the elegantly tiled and fragrant food halls on the ground floor or the wealth of exclusives in the beauty halls. But indulge the excesses too: Harrods has an art gallery, a stunning new interiors department and a kitchenware floor that hosts live cooking lessons from household names. Got kids? Head straight to Toy Kingdom on the third floor, with its enchanted forest, intergalactic science lab and bespoke sweets-maker. Elsewhere, Harrods excels at shoes – with a gargantuan footwear department stocking labels such as Ferragamo, Charlotte Olympia and Giuseppe Zanotti – and the Fashion Lab, on the fourth floor, is dedicated to young designer labels such as Zadig & Voltaire, Wildfox and the Kooples.

Harvey Nichols

109-125 Knightsbridge, SW1X 7RJ (7235 5000, www.harveynichols.com /store/ knightsbridge). Knightsbridge tube. **Open** *10am-8pm Mon-Sat; noon-6pm Sun (browsing from 11.30am).* **Map** *p122 G10* ❹ *Department store*

Once the watchword for luxury Knightsbridge shopping, Harvey Nicks lost ground to **Liberty** (*see p152*), **Selfridges** (*see p144*) and even Harrods, which were engaging better with their customers and seemed to get the idea of hosting dynamic shopping events. But it's beginning to fight back. Makeup junkies should head to the ground floor beauty space to pick up established brands like Charlotte Tilbury and Shu Uemura, or try something new with Beauty Bites – a lovely series of mini cosmetics, featuring up-and-coming brands. On the third floor, Sneaker Concept showcases high-fashion sports shoes. The clothing rails are full of top labels such as Alexander Wang, Balenciaga and Givenchy, and there's an excellent array of accessories and beauty buys from luxurious brands such as Tom Ford and COR (whose soap contains real silver). Finish off proceedings with lunch on the fifth floor, where the buzzy food department is located along with a branch of **Burger & Lobster** (*see p165*).

CHELSEA

▶ *Sloane Square tube then various buses.*

Chelsea is where London's wealthy classes play in cultural and geographical isolation. Originally a fishing hamlet, the area was a 'village of palaces' by the 16th century, home to the likes of Henry VIII's ill-fated advisor Sir Thomas More. Artists and poets (Whistler, Carlyle, Wilde) followed from the 1880s, before the fashionistas arrived with the opening of Mary Quant's Bazaar in 1955. Soon after, Chelsea had acquired a raffish reputation and was at the forefront of successive youth-culture revolutions. Synonymous with the Swinging Sixties and immortalised by punk, the dissipated phase of the **King's Road** is now a matter for historians as the street teems with pricey fashion houses and air-conditioned poodle parlours. Yet on a sunny day, it does make a vivid stroll. For one thing, you don't have to take yourself as seriously as the locals. And for another, the area is figuratively rich in historical associations, and literally so with the expensive red-brick houses that slumber down leafy mews and charming, cobbled side streets.

At the top (east end) of the King's Road is **Sloane Square**. It's named after Sir Hans Sloane, whose collections formed the basis of the British Museum (*see p198*). The shaded benches in the middle of the square provide a lovely counterpoint to the looming façades of Tiffany & Co and the enormous Peter Jones department store, in a 1930s building with excellent views from its top-floor café. A certain edginess is lent to proceedings by the **Royal Court Theatre** (*see p361*), which shocked the nation with its 1956 première of John Osborne's *Look Back in Anger*.

To escape the bustle and fumes, head to **Duke of York Square**, a pedestrianised enclave of boutiques and restaurants presided over by a statue of Sir Hans. In the summer, the cooling fountains attract hordes of children, their parents sitting to watch from the outdoor café tables or taking advantage of the Saturday food market. The square is also home to the mercilessly modern art of the **Saatchi Gallery**, housed in former military barracks.

The once-adventurous shops on the King's Road are now a mix of trendier-than-thou fashion houses and high-street chains. Wander **Cale Street** for some pleasing boutiques, or head for the **Chelsea Farmers' Market** on adjoining Sydney Street to find a clutter of artfully distressed rustic sheds housing restaurants and shops selling everything from cigars to garden products. Sydney Street leads to **St Luke's Church**, where Charles Dickens married Catherine Hogarth in 1836.

Towards the western end of the King's Road is **Bluebird**, a dramatic art deco former motor garage housing a café, a restaurant and the hip **Shop at Bluebird**, one of Chelsea's most notable remaining boutiques. A little further up the road, the **World's End** store (no.430) occupies what was once Vivienne Westwood's notorious leather- and fetishwear boutique Sex; a green-haired Johnny Rotten auditioned for the Sex Pistols here in 1975 by singing along to an Alice Cooper record on the shop's jukebox.

Running parallel to the King's Road, Chelsea's riverside has long been noted for its nurseries and gardens, lending a village air that befits a place of retirement for the former British soldiers living in the **Royal Hospital Chelsea**. In summer, the Chelsea Pensioners, as they're known, regularly don red coats and tricorn hats when venturing beyond the gates. The Royal Hospital's lovely gardens host the **Chelsea Flower Show** (*see p313*) each spring. Almost next door, the **National Army Museum** has reopened after major refurbishment.

West from the river end of Royal Hospital Road is **Cheyne Walk**. Its river-view benches remain good spots for a sit-down, but the tranquillity of the **Chelsea Physic Garden** – established on land bought by Sir Hans Sloane – is the real treat.

Further west on Cheyne Walk, the park benches of **Chelsea Embankment Gardens** face Albert Bridge, where signs still order troops to 'Break step when marching over this bridge'. In the small gardens, you'll find a statue of the great historian Thomas Carlyle – the 'sage of Chelsea', whose home is preserved (**Carlyle's House**). Nearby, a gold-faced statue of Sir Thomas More looks out over the river from the garden of **Chelsea Old Church**, where he once sang in the choir and may well be (partially) buried. Legend has it that the Thomas More Chapel, on the south side, contains More's headless body somewhere under the walls (his head, having been spiked on London Bridge, was 'rescued' and buried in a family vault in St Dunstan's church, Canterbury). Follow Old Church Street north and you'll find the **Chelsea Arts Club** (no.143), founded in

1871 by Whistler and now host to occasional public events, including classical recitals.

North of the western extremity of Cheyne Walk are **Brompton Cemetery** (suffragette Emmeline Pankhurst is buried here; *see p303*) and the home ground of London's first Champions League winners: Chelsea FC. Tickets for league games are hard to come by, but **Stamford Bridge** (Fulham Road, SW6 1HS, 0371 811 1955, www.chelseafc. com) does have the excellent **Chelsea Centenary Museum**.

Sights & museums

Carlyle's House
24 Cheyne Row, SW3 5HL (7352 7087, www. nationaltrust.org.uk/carlyles-house). Sloane Square tube or bus 11, 19, 22, 49, 170, 211, 319. **Open** *Mar-Oct 11am-5pm Wed-Sun. Closed Nov-Feb.* **Admission** *£6.50; £3.25 children; £16.25 family.* **No cards.** **Map** *p122 F13.*

Thomas Carlyle and his wife Jane moved to this four-storey, Queen Anne house in 1834. The house was inaugurated as a museum in 1896, 15 years after Carlyle's death, offering an intriguing snapshot of Victorian life. The writer's quest for quiet (details of his valiant attempts to soundproof the attic) strikes a chord today: he was plagued by the sound of revelry from Cremorne Pleasure Gardens.

Chelsea Centenary Museum
Stamford Bridge, Fulham Road, SW6 1HS (0371 811 1955, events.chelseafc.com/ room-item/museum). Fulham Broadway tube. **Open** *9.30am-5pm daily.* **Admission** *£11; £9-£10 reductions; free under-5s.* **Map** *p122 C14.*

Opened in 1877 as an athletics track (it was thought track and field had a more promising financial future than mere Association Football), Stamford Bridge was soon a football ground in search of a team. It became the home of the Blues in 1905; for its 100th anniversary the club celebrated with the opening of this fine museum. It provides a terrific social history of the game, helped along by the narrative of Chelsea's journey from music-hall joke to oil-money-funded Premier League titans. There are interactives, trophies – Chelsea are the only London club to have won the prestigious Champions League (in 2012) and the only British club to have won all the major European trophies (adding the Europa League, 2013; Cup Winners' Cup, 1971, 1998; and Super Cup, 1998) – and some ace memorabilia, including a photo of Raquel Welch in Chelsea strip making a valiant attempt to side-foot the ball.

In the know
Bigger and better

Plans for a new and expanded Stamford Bridge stadium, designed by Herzog & de Meuron and approved in 2017, are likely to affect the museum in due course; check the website for the latest news.

♥ Chelsea Physic Garden

66 Royal Hospital Road, SW3 4HS (7352 5646, www.chelseaphysicgarden.co.uk). Sloane Square tube or bus 11, 19, 22. **Open** *Apr-June, Sept, Oct 11am-5pm Mon, 11am-6pm Tue-Fri, Sun. July, Aug 11am-5pm Mon, 11am-6pm Tue, Thur, Fri, Sun; 11am-10pm Wed. Nov-Mar 11am-3pm Mon-Fri.* **Tours** *times vary; phone to check.* **Admission** *£9.50; £6.25 reductions; free under-5s.* **Tours** *free.* **Map** *p122 G13.*

Passing through these modest red-brick walls is like stepping into a secret garden: a place by the Thames but with its own microclimate, where rare plants from Britain and across the globe have been collected – and now thrive. Set up by apothecaries in 1673, Chelsea Physic Garden contains the world's oldest rock garden, created in 1773 from black Icelandic basalt imported by Joseph Banks (the most-famous plant hunter of all) and decorated with masonry from the Tower of London. Today the garden is also home to Britain's first garden of ethnobotany (the study of the botany of different ethnic groups and indigenous peoples), and a Garden of Medicinal Plants, tracing the chronology of plant remedies over almost an acre, from ancient Greek herbs to plants that are likely to be used in future medicine. The half-acre World Woodland Garden, which celebrates useful and medicinal plants from the Americas, Europe and East Asia, is home to more than 150 species of plant. Visitors can weave through it on a serpentine path or learn more about the collection from garden volunteers in one of the woodland clearings. There's also a shop where visitors can buy unusual plants, and a café serving very good homemade cakes.

National Army Museum

Royal Hospital Road, SW3 4HT (7730 0717, www.nam.ac.uk). Sloane Square tube or bus 170. **Open** *10am-5.30pm daily; until 8pm 1st Wed of the mth.* **Admission** *free.* **Map** *p122 G13.*

The National Army Museum reopened in 2017 after a three-year, £24m redesign – and a major rethink. A huge atrium has been carved out of the middle of the building, and the whole place is much lighter and less

Chelsea Physic Garden

gloomy, but the structural redevelopment isn't the biggest change. The museum now reflects evolving perceptions of the history of the British Army. As one graph on display reveals, there are fewer people serving in the regular army today than at any time in the last 200 years, yet its public profile has never been higher. To reflect this, the museum has five new galleries representing different aspects of the armed forces, with a much keener focus on social history and diversity. Some old-fashioned models of battles (notably Waterloo) and uniforms remain, of course, along with favourite exhibits such as Major Michael 'Bronco' Lane's frost-bitten fingertips and the skeleton of Napoleon's horse Marengo. In Play Base, under-eights can take on an assault course, climb aboard a command liaison vehicle or develop their fieldcraft skills.

Royal Hospital Chelsea

Royal Hospital Road, SW3 4HT (7881 5200, www.chelsea-pensioners.co.uk). Sloane Square tube or bus 11, 19, 22, 137, 170. **Open** *10am-4pm Mon-Fri.* **Admission** *free.* **Map** *p122 G13.*

Around 350 Chelsea Pensioners (retired soldiers) live at the Royal Hospital, founded in 1682 by Charles II for those 'broken by age or war' and designed by Sir Christopher Wren (with adjustments by Robert Adam and Sir John Soane). Retired soldiers are still eligible to apply for a final posting here if they're over 65 and in receipt of an Army or War Disability Pension for Army Service. The pensioners have their own club room, bowling green and gardens, and get tickets to Chelsea FC home games. The museum (same times) has more about their lives. The annual Chelsea Flower Show (*see p313*) is held in the grounds.

Saatchi Gallery

Duke of York's HQ, King's Road, SW3 4RY (7811 3070, www.saatchigallery.com). Sloane Square tube. **Open** *10am-6pm daily.* **Admission** *free.* **Map** *p122 G12.*

Charles Saatchi's gallery offers 50,000sq ft of space for temporary exhibitions. Given his fame as a promoter in the 1990s of what became known as the Young British Artists – Damien Hirst, Tracey Emin, Gavin Turk, Sarah Lucas et al – it will surprise many that the focus of exhibitions here has been internationalist in outlook, with China, Africa and India all featuring. Still, Richard Wilson's superb oil-sump installation *20:50* has survived from the Saatchi Gallery's previous incarnations and remains here as the only permanently displayed artwork.

Restaurants

Colbert £££

50-52 Sloane Square, SW1W 8AX (7730 2804, www.colbertchelsea.com). Sloane Square tube. **Open** *8am-11pm Mon-Thur; 8am-11.30pm Fri, Sat; 8am-10.30pm Sun.* **Map** *p122 H12* **2** *Brasserie*

Paying homage to Continental grand cafés with marble, linen napkins and mirrors aplenty, Colbert feels more casual and local than its siblings – the Wolseley (see *p116*), the Delaunay (see *p191*) and Bar Américain (see *p173*) – and the posters in the booth-lined bar area advertising performances by Olivier and Vivien Leigh at the Royal Court Theatre next door (see *p361*) lend a sense of history. It also trumps the others with pavement tables from which to admire the beautiful people. More importantly, it serves the best lunch in the area: perhaps a deliciously decadent smoked haddock florentine served on spinach, under a perfectly poached egg, in a buttery cream sauce; or a croque madame – perfectly fried brioche filled with melted comté cheese, jambon blanc and béchamel sauce, topped with a fried egg.

Gallery Mess ££

Saatchi Gallery, Duke of York's HQ, King's Road, SW3 4RY (7730 8135, www. saatchigallery.com/gallerymess). Sloane Square tube. **Open** *10am-11.30pm Mon-Sat; 10am-7pm Sun.* **Map** *p122 G12* **4** *Brasserie*

As befits its Chelsea location, this welcoming brasserie at the Saatchi art gallery is smarter than most, with white linen tablecloths, exposed brickwork and impressive bar all somewhat in thrall to the vaulted ceiling and expansive curtain of floor-to-ceiling arched windows. There's also a large outdoor terrace. Service is disarmingly friendly and mains offer comforting flavours and proportions. So you'll find cod and chips, steak sandwich, charcuterie and smoked fish platters, caesar salad and afternoon tea.

Harwood Arms £££

Corner of Walham Grove & Farm Lane, SW6 1QP (7386 1847, www.harwoodarms.com). Fulham Broadway tube. **Open** *Snacks served 5.30-11pm Mon; noon-11pm Tue-Thur; noon-midnight Fri, Sat. Lunch served noon-3pm Tue-Sun. Dinner served 6.15-9.30pm Mon-Sat; 6.15-9pm Sun.* **Map** *p122 C13* **5** *British*

It might look an upmarket pub, but the Harwood Arms is a serious restaurant with wine list to match. It showcases prime British produce through skilled, imaginative modern cooking. The mounted deer's head is a reminder that game and wild food are a speciality, with mains such as grilled haunch of Berkshire roe deer accompanied by beetroot, slivers of roast onion and pickled mushrooms. Expect fine dining, rather than pub portions, and you'll be more than happy. Be sure to book ahead.

Medlar £££

438 King's Road, SW10 0LJ (7349 1900, www. medlarrestaurant.co.uk). Fulham Broadway tube or bus 11, 22. **Open** *noon-3pm, 6.30-10.30pm Mon-Fri; noon-3pm, 6-10.30pm Sat; noon-3pm, 6-9.30pm Sun.* **Map** *p122 E13* ⑥ *Modern European*

The decor here is understated: a soothing grey-green colour scheme and unobtrusive artwork. The real artistry arrives on the plates, dishes of astounding excellence. Assemblies are complex and have lengthy names: crisp calf's brain with smoked duck breast, aïoli, pink fir potatoes and *tardivo* (raddichio), for example. But every ingredient justifies its place in entirely natural-seeming juxtapositions of flavour, texture and colour. And the execution is nearly flawless. Save room for wonderful (and relatively simple) puddings, such as cardamom custard with saffron oranges, pomegranate and langues de chat.

❤ Mona Lisa £

417 King's Road, SW10 0LR (7376 5447, monalisarestaurant.co.uk). Fulham Broadway tube or bus 11, 22. **Open** *6.30am-11pm Mon-Sat; 8.30am-5.30pm Sun.* **Map** *p122 E13* ⑦ *Italian/café*

Not much to look at, either inside or out, the Mona Lisa is hidden away at the 'wrong' end of the King's Road, just beyond World's End. But the bonhomie is infectious, and if you order the right thing, such as the meltingly tender calf's liver *alla salvia* (with butter and sage), served with old-school potatoes and veg, you won't give a fig about the decor. The menu ranges across breakfasts, sandwiches, burgers, omelettes, jacket potatoes and pastas to three-course blow-outs (at lunch, the latter is a real bargain).

❤ Rabbit £££

172 King's Road, SW3 4UP (3750 0172, www. rabbit-restaurant.com). Sloane Square tube. **Open** *6-11pm Mon; noon-midnight Tue-Sat; noon-6pm Sun.* **Map** *p122 F12* ⑧ *British*

More than a restaurant, Rabbit feels a bit like a theme bar that does food, right down to a 'stable door' entrance, outside which smokers linger. But to see it as a party venue does the cooking a disservice: the Gladwins dish up inventive mouthfuls of joy that warm you up for heavy, slow-cooked mains (perhaps pigs' cheeks with malt, stout, garlic and pennywort) and lighter, faster-cooked dishes (such as tempura duck liver). However, the

'British with a twist' ethos is best summed up by the desserts: try a Viennetta parfait made of Magnum ice-cream lollies, or an intriguing cep and white-chocolate bourbon. Rabbit's older sibling, The Shed (*see p303*) in Notting Hill is the Gladwin brothers' original 'wild' food eatery.

Shops & services

❤ Boutique 1

127/128 Sloane Street, SW1X 9AS (7118 0111, www.boutique1.com). Sloane Square tube. **Open** *10am-7pm Mon-Sat; noon-6pm Sun.* **Map** *p122 G12* ❶ *Fashion/accessories*

Selling the kind of clothes you'd consider going temporarily homeless for, since they cost a month's rent, Boutique 1 is the first European outpost of a swish Middle Eastern retailer. The stylish range of accessories, jewellery, shoes and beachwear are set out across two spacious floors, like a miniature department store. Even if you're not buying, come for swanky April's Café, the in-store eatery. With its low-hanging lighting, pale wooden furniture, scattered House of Hackney cushions and, through the windows, an urban garden, it's like being in the kitchen of your Scandi dreams.

❤ John Sandoe

10 Blacklands Terrace, SW3 2SR (7589 9473, www.johnsandoe.com). Sloane Square tube. **Open** *9.30am-6.30pm Mon-Sat; 11am-5pm Sun.* **Map** *p122 G12* ❺ *Books & music*

Tucked away on a side street, this 50-year-old independent has always looked just as a bookshop should, with stock literally packed to the rafters. The enthusiasm and knowledge of the staff can be taken as, forgive us, read – several have worked here for decades, their passion for books undimmed.

❤ The Shop at Bluebird

350 King's Road, SW3 5UU (7351 3873, www. theshopatbluebird.com). Sloane Square tube. **Open** *10am-7pm Mon-Sat; noon-6pm Sun.* **Map** *p122 E13* ❻ *Fashion/homewares*

Browsing the Shop at Bluebird is an unusually tranquil experience. The 10,000sq ft space, which began life as a garage back in the 1930s, has a white tiled floor and lots of natural light, tempting shoppers to roam calmly through its delightfully curated mix of fashion, beauty, homewares, books and music. The Shop was opened by John and Belle Robinson in 2005; it now has a reputation for tempting luxury brands and for discovering up-and-coming designers. There's an in-store spa, too.

Oxford Street, Marylebone & Mayfair

Oxford Street is working hard to stay top of London's shopping destinations, with a revamped roundabout at Marble Arch, wider pavements, the innovative pedestrian crossings at Oxford Circus, and an all-new 'eastern gateway' development near the shiny new Tottenham Court Road superstation, already partially open in anticipation of Crossrail's arrival in 2018.

North of London's busiest commercial artery are the luxury cafés and boutiques of Marylebone, bounded by Regent's Park at the furthest edge, with the Arab shisha cafés and juice bars of the Edgware Road to divide it from scruffy Paddington. South of Oxford Street, Mayfair oozes wealth, while to the south-east, neon-lit Piccadilly Circus is a bit of town every Londoner does their best to avoid.

❤ Don't miss

1 Liberty *p152*
A sweet combination of tradition and fashion.

2 Royal Academy of Arts *p158*
Impressive home to blockbuster shows.

3 Selfridges *p144*
London's leading department store.

4 The Connaught Bar *p156*
A place for civilised cocktailing.

5 Wallace Collection *p148*
A grand townhouse museum, full of art, armour and exquisite *objets*.

Burlington Arcade

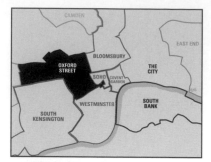

OXFORD STREET, MARYLEBONE & MAYFAIR

Restaurants

1. Bentley's Oyster Bar & Grill
2. Busaba Eathai
3. Chiltern Firehouse
4. Fischer's
5. Gymkhana
6. Kitty Fisher's
7. Providores & Tapa Room
8. Rasa W1
9. Roti Chai
10. Shoryu Ramen
11. Twist
12. Zoilo

Pubs & bars

1. The Connaught Bar
2. Mr Fogg's
3. Purl

Shops & services

1. Alexander McQueen
2. Alfie's Antiques Market
3. Berry Bros & Rudd
4. Browns
5. Burberry
6. Burlington Arcade
7. Cadenhead's Whisky Shop & Tasting Room
8. Collaborative Store
9. Daunt Books
10. Drake's
11. Gallery of Everything
12. Grays Antique Market & Grays in the Mews
13. Hamleys
14. J Crew
15. John, Bell & Croyden
16. John Simons
17. Karl Lagerfeld
18. KJ's Laundry
19. Liberty ❤
20. Paul Smith
21. Postcard Teas
22. Prism
23. Rigby & Peller
24. Selfridges
25. Smythson
26. Stella McCartney
27. Topshop/Topman
28. Waterstones Piccadilly

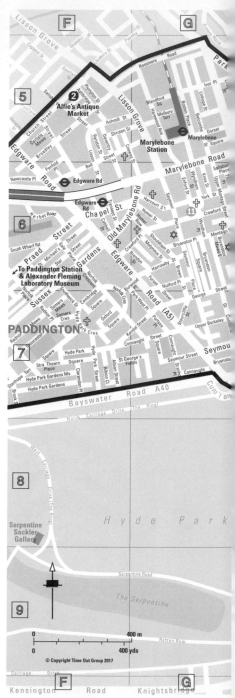

© Copyright Time Out Group 2017

OXFORD STREET, MARYLEBONE & MAYFAIR

Marble Arch

❤ Time to eat & drink

Fusion cooking pioneer
Providores & Tapa Room *p148*

Indian street food
Roti Chai *p144*

Viennese-style brasserie
Fischer's *p148*

Argentinian small plates
Zoilo *p149*

Modern European blow-out
Kitty Fisher's *p156*

Classic hotel cocktailing
Connaught Bar *p156*

Drinking in the world
Mr Fogg's *p156*

❤ Time to shop

Finest fashion department store
Selfridges *p144*

Where tradition meets style
Liberty *p152*

Curated fashion
Browns *p157*

Trendy threads for the teenage hordes
Topshop/Topman *p145*

Under-the-radar labels
Collaborative Store *p149*

Outsider art on celeb street
Gallery of Everything *p150*

Mall shopping the old-fashioned way
Burlington Arcade *p159*

OXFORD STREET

▶ *Bond Street, Marble Arch, Oxford Circus or Tottenham Court Road tube.*

Official estimates put the annual footfall at somewhere near 200 million people per year, but few Londoners love **Oxford Street**. A shopping district since the 19th century, it's unmanageably busy on weekends and in the run-up to Christmas. Even outside these times, it's rarely pretty, lined as it is with over-familiar chain stores and choked with bus traffic. The New West End Company (www.newwestend.com) has been charged with changing all that: Oxford Circus, Marble Arch and Regent Street are beginning to feel the benefits, with Tottenham Court Road next on the list.

The street gets smarter as you walk from east to west. The eastern end around Tottenham Court Road station is beginning to emerge from major redevelopment for Crossrail, which should be complete for service to begin running in 2018. Its lack of destination shops had already been solved by the opening of teen-magnet fashion flagship **Primark** (nos.14-28, 7580 5510, www.primark. com). The string of classy department stores – including **John Lewis** (nos.278-306, 7629 7711, www.johnlewis.com) and **Selfridges** – begins west of Oxford Circus, always chaotic with shoppers. Next stop along, Bond Street station, is also nearing the end of Crossrail disruption. Apart from the art deco splendour of Selfridges, architectural interest along Oxford Street is largely limited to Oxford Circus's four identical convex corners, constructed between 1913 and 1928. The crowds and rush of traffic hamper investigations, a problem the council addressed by widening pavements, removing street clutter and creating Tokyo Shibuya-style diagonal crossings, which actually work rather well.

At the western end of Oxford Street, stands **Marble Arch**, with its Carrara marble cladding and sculptures celebrating Nelson and Wellington. It was designed by John Nash in 1827 as the entrance to a rebuilt Buckingham Palace, but the arch was moved here in 1851, after – it is said – a fuming Queen Victoria found it to be too narrow for her coach. Now given a £2m revamp, it's been joined by renovated water fountains and gardens that contain an ongoing series of large-scale public sculpture commissions.

Oxford Street gained notoriety as the route by which condemned men were conveyed from Newgate Prison to the old Tyburn gallows, stopping only for a last pint at the **Angel** (61-62 St Giles High Street, 7240 2876), at the eastern end of the street, in the shadow of Centre Point. At the western end,

for over six centuries, crowds would gather to watch executions at Tyburn. Held in 1783, the final execution to be carried out here is marked by the most euphemistic circular plaque in London: around a humble cross, it says just 'The site of the Tyburn Tree'. This was the gallows that was London's main place of execution from 1388, silent witness to the death of highwayman Jack Sheppard (who drew crowds of 200,000) and the hanging of Cromwell's exhumed corpse.

North of Oxford Circus

▶ *Great Portland Street, Oxford Circus or Regent's Park tube.*

North of Oxford Circus runs **Langham Place**, notable for the Bath stone façade of John Nash's **All Souls Church** (Langham Place, 2 All Souls Place, 7580 3522, www. allsouls.org). Its bold combination of a Gothic spire and classical rotunda wasn't popular: in 1824, a year after it opened, the church was condemned in Parliament as 'deplorable and horrible'; a statue of Nash now stands outside, looking forlornly away.

Tucked to one side of the church you'll find the BBC's , an oddly asymmetrical art deco building, much extended by recent redevelopment. Over the road is the **Langham Hotel** (1C Portland Place, W1B 1JA, 7636 1000, www.langhamhotels.com), which opened in 1865 as Britain's first grand hotel and has been home at various points to Mark Twain, Napoleon III and Oscar Wilde.

North, Langham Place turns into **Portland Place**, designed by Robert and James Adam as the glory of 18th-century London. Its Georgian terraced houses are now mostly occupied by embassies and swanky offices. At no.66 is the **Royal Institute of British Architects** (RIBA). Parallel to Portland Place are **Harley Street**, famous for its high-cost dentists and doctors, and **Wimpole Street**, erstwhile home to the poet Elizabeth Barrett Browning (no.50), Sir Paul McCartney (no.57) and Sir Arthur Conan Doyle (2 Upper Wimpole Street).

In the know
Immodest protuberance

Prominent among the carvings on the original **BBC Broadcasting House** (see *p144*) is a 10ft-tall statue of Prospero and Ariel, the spirit of the air – or, in this case, the airwaves – from Shakespeare's *The Tempest*. When it was unveiled, the statue caused controversy due to the size of the airy sprite's manhood; artist Eric Gill was recalled and asked to make it more modest.

Sights & museums

BBC Broadcasting House

Portland Place, Upper Regent Street, W1A 1AA (0370 901 1227, www.bbc.co.uk/showsandtours/tours/bh_london). Oxford Circus tube. **Map** *p140 J6.*

Completed in 1932, this was Britain's first purpose-built broadcast centre; in 2013, it acquired a neighbour, New Broadcasting House. Tours are not currently offered to members of the public due to security concerns, but you can eat and drink in the café, which has views into the glass-sided newsroom. The Radio Theatre in the original BBC building is especially gorgeous; there you can join the audience for radio and TV shows, with ticketing information at www.bbc.co.uk/showsandtours/shows.

Restaurants

Busaba Eathai £

8-13 Bird Street, W1U 1BU (7518 8080, www.busaba.com/locations/busaba-st-christophers-place). Bond Street tube. **Open** *noon-11pm Mon-Thur; noon-11.30pm Fri, Sat; noon-10pm Sun.* **Map** *p140 H7* ② *Thai*

Busaba is a 16-strong chain – but it's not your average Thai joint. The dark, handsome interior combines dark wood, incense and dimly lit lanterns. With spacious shared tables, no reservations and brisk service, it remains a great spot for a casual meal with friends. Among the Thai classics, you'll find a few dishes that aren't often seen in London, such as *sen chan pad thai* (a pimped *pad thai* with crab originating from the Chanthaburi province of eastern Thailand).

♥ Roti Chai ££

3 Portman Mews South, W1H 6AY (7408 0101, www.rotichai.com). Marble Arch tube. **Open** *Dining room noon-10.30pm Mon-Sat; 12.30-9pm Sun. Street kitchen noon-10.30pm Mon-Sat; 12.30-9pm Sun.* **Map** *p140 H7* ⑨ *Pan-Indian*

The ground-floor 'street kitchen', with its utilitarian furniture and canteen vibe, is ideal for a swift midday feed – and the alert young staff keep things pacy. The menu is modelled on those of urban India's snack shacks, so you'll find food such as bhel pooris, chilli paneer and pani puri. Larger dishes include 'railway lamb curry' (tender meat and potato in a rich gravy spiced with star anise and cinnamon bark). In the basement, the evening-only 'dining room' is a darker, sexier (and pricier) space.

Shops & services

♥ Selfridges

400 Oxford Street, W1A 1AB (0800 123400, www.selfridges.com). Bond Street or Marble Arch tube. **Open** *9.30am-9pm Mon-Sat; noon-6pm Sun (browsing from 11.30am).* **Map** *p140 H7* ㉔ *Department store*

With its plethora of concession boutiques, store-wide themed events and collections from all the hottest brands, Selfridges is as dynamic as a department store could be. Although the store layout changes regularly, the useful floor plans make navigating the place easy-peasy. While the basement is chock-full of hip home accessories and stylish kitchen equipment, it's Selfridges' fashion floors that really get hearts racing. With a winning combination of new talent, hip and

Selfridges

edgy labels, high-street brands and luxury high-end designers, the store stays ahead of the pack. Highlights include the huge denim section, the extensive Shoe Galleries and, on the fifth floor, the 37,000sq ft Body Studio, a temple of top-notch activewear that aims to kit out people of all shapes and sizes. Level 4 hosts the predictably excellent Toy Shop. There are always new excitements in the food hall, ranging from great deli and bakery produce to classy packaged goods, while regularly changing pop-ups and special events keep customers on their toes.

❤ Topshop/Topman
36-38 Great Castle Street, W1W 8LG (7927 7644, www.topshop.com). Oxford Circus tube. **Open** *9.30am-9pm Mon-Sat; 10am-7pm Sun.* **Map** *p140 K7* **㉗** *Fashion*

Topshop has been the queen of the British high street for the past decade, and walking into the busy Oxford Street flagship of this massive chain, it's easy to see why. Spanning five huge floors, the place lays claim to being the world's largest fashion shop, and is always buzzing with fashion-forward teens and twentysomethings keen to get their hands on the next big trends. The store covers a huge range of styles and sizes, and includes free personal shoppers, boutique label concessions, capsule collections, a Cheeky nail salon, Hershesons Blow Dry Bar, Bleach London and Blink Brow Bar, as well as a café and sweet shop.

Topman is as on-the-ball and innovative as its big sister, stocking niche menswear labels such as Garbstore, and housing a trainer boutique, a suit section, and a new personal shopping suite, featuring consultation rooms, Xbox 360s and an exhibition space. Both shops are even more of a hive of activity than normal during London Fashion Week, when they host a series of special events.

MARYLEBONE & BAKER STREET

▶ *Baker Street, Bond Street, Marble Arch, Oxford Circus or Regent's Park tube.*

North of Oxford Street, the fashionable district known to its boosters as 'Marylebone Village' has become a magnet for moneyed Londoners, especially since the opening of André Balazs's **Chiltern Firehouse** effected the area's transformation from merely rich to actively fashionable. However, most visitors to the area head directly for the unfashionable but deathlessly popular waxworks of **Madame Tussauds**; there's also a small and oft-overlooked museum

at the neighbouring **Royal Academy of Music** (7873 7373, www.ram.ac.uk), while the northern end of Baker Street is unsurprisingly heavy on nods of respect to the world's favourite freelance detective at the **Sherlock Holmes Museum**. The Beatles painted 94 Baker Street with a psychedelic mural before opening it in December 1967 as the Apple Boutique, a clothing store run on such whimsical hippie principles that it had to close within six months due to financial losses. Fab Four pilgrims head to the **London Beatles Store** (no.231, 7935 4464, www.beatlesstorelondon.co.uk), where the ground-floor shop offers a predictable array of Beatles-branded accessories alongside some genuinely collectible items.

The area's beating heart for locals was always **Marylebone High Street**, which still teems with interesting shops – not least a hot drink and Gaultier collaboration at **Kusmi Tea** (no.15), Sicilian perfumier **Ortigia** (no.23) and the unapologetically British and thoroughly lovely **Daunt Books**. The name of the neighbourhood is a contraction of the church's earlier name, St Mary by the Bourne; the 'bourne' in question, Tyburn stream, still filters into the Thames near Pimlico, but its entire length is now covered. **St Marylebone Church** stands in its fourth incarnation at the northern end of the street. The

Sherlock Holmes Museum *p147*

church's garden hosts designer clothing and artisan food stalls at the **Cabbages & Frocks** market on Saturdays (www.cabbagesandfrocks.co.uk).

Lovely boutiques can be found on winding **Marylebone Lane**, among them **KJ's Laundry** and the self-explanatory **Button Queen** (no.76, 7935 1505, www.thebuttonqueen.co.uk), and the **Golden Eagle** (no.59, 7935 3228) hosts regular singalongs around its piano. There's fine food here, too, with smart, often upmarket eateries snuggling alongside delicatessens such as **La Fromagerie** (2-6 Moxon Street, W1U 4EW, 7935 0341, www.lafromagerie.co.uk) and century-old lunchroom **Paul Rothe & Son** (35 Marylebone Lane, 7935 6783). **Marylebone Farmers' Market** takes place in the Cramer Street car park every Sunday.

But if you're on trend and have money in your pocket, Marylebone's all about **Chiltern Street** these days. Eat at the **Chiltern Firehouse** if you can get a reservation, but on your way down the street, also note John Simons, Cadenhead's, Prism, the Gallery of Everything, that little sitar shop and – since you don't really have a reservation – the cool little **Monocle Café** (no.18, 7135 2040, cafe.monocle.com), the coffee shop of Tyler Brûlé's magazine.

Further south, the soaring neo-Gothic interior of the 19th-century **St James's Roman Catholic Church** (Spanish Place, 22 George Street, 7935 0943, www.sjrcc.org.uk) is lit dramatically by stained-glass windows; Vivien Leigh (née Hartley) married barrister Herbert Leigh Hunt here in 1932. Other cultural diversions include the **Wallace Collection** and the **Wigmore Hall** (*see p357*).

Part of the Romans' Watling Street from Dover to Wales, **Edgware Road** rules a definite north–south line marking the western edge of the West End. It's now the heart of the city's Middle East end: if you want to pick up your copy of *Al Hayat*, cash a cheque at the Bank of Kuwait or catch Egyptian football, head here.

That the name Paddington has been immortalised by a certain small, ursine Peruvian émigré (check out the 2014 film) is appropriate, given that the area has long been home to refugees and immigrants. It was a country village until an arm of the Grand Union Canal arrived in 1801, linking London to the Midlands, followed in the 1830s by the railway. **Paddington Station**, with its fine triple roof of iron and glass, was built in 1851 to the specifications of the great engineer Isambard Kingdom Brunel. (If you've a smartphone, there's interactive information available at Brunel's statue in the station.) Paddington's proximity to central London eventually drew in developers. To the east of the station, gleaming **Paddington Central** now provides a million square feet of office space, canalside apartments and restaurants. In St Mary's Hospital, the old-fashioned **Alexander Fleming Laboratory Museum** gives a sense of what the district used to be like.

Sights & museums

Alexander Fleming Laboratory Museum

St Mary's Hospital, Praed Street, W2 1NY (3312 6528, www.medicalmuseums.org). Paddington tube/rail. **Open** *10am-1pm Mon-Thur. By appt 2-5pm Mon-Thur; 10am-5pm Fri.* **Admission** *£4; £2 reductions; free under-5s.* **No cards.** **Map** *pull-out E6.*

Buzz in at the entrance on your left as you enter the hospital and head up the stairs to find this tiny, dusty, instrument-cluttered lab. Enthusiastic guides conjure up Professor Alexander Fleming who, in 1928, noticed that mould contamination had destroyed some Staphylococcus bacteria on a set-aside culture plate: he had discovered penicillin. The keen entrepreneurs across the street immediately began to advertise their pub's healthful properties, claiming the miracle fungus had blown into the lab from them. The video room has a documentary on Fleming's life and discovery.

Madame Tussauds

Marylebone Road, NW1 5LR (www.madametussauds.com/london). Baker Street tube. **Open** *varies.* **Admission** *£29; £24 reductions; free under-4s. Cheaper tickets available online in advance.* **Map** *p140 H5.*

Streams of humanity jostle excitedly here for the chance to take pictures of one another planting a smacker on a waxen visage of fame and fortune. Madame Tussaud brought her show to London in 1802, 32 years after it was founded in Paris, and it's been expanding ever since on these very premises since

In the know
Plan ahead

Popular exhibits at Madame Tussauds, such as Star Wars, will be extremely busy. The owners now issue only timed tickets, so book online in advance if you can (it's cheaper); if you can't, you'll probably have to queue for a time slot later that day – fill the time at the **Sherlock Holmes Museum** (see *opposite*).

1884. There are now some 300 figures in the collection: current movie A-listers who require no more than a first name (Angelina, Brad), as well as their illustrious forebears for whom the surname seems more fitting (Chaplin); a bevy of Royals (not least Wills and Kate), and sundry sports stars including Nadal, Bobby Moore and Mo Farah. Rihanna and One Direction can be found hanging out among the Music Megastars, while Dickens, Einstein and Madame Tussauds herself kick back in the Culture section. Proving they remain right on top of trends and current affairs, there's a section dedicated to YouTube stars Zoe and Alfie, as well as a Donald Trump alongside political luminaries such as Nelson Mandela, Martin Luther King and Barack Obama. What must they be thinking. If you're not already overheating, your palms will be sweating by the time you descend into the Chamber of Horrors in 'Scream', where only teens claim to enjoy the floor drops and scary special effects. Much more pleasant is the kitsch 'Spirit of London' ride, whisking you through 400 years of London life in a taxi pod.

Tussauds also hosts Marvel Super Heroes 4D, where interactives and waxworks of Iron Man, Spider-man and an 18-ft Hulk provide further photo ops, but the highlight is the nine-minute film in '4D' (as well as 3D projections, there are 'real' effects such as a shaking floor and smoke in the auditorium). There's a truly impressive Star Wars area, with expertly finished sets spread over two floors, so visitors can explore Yoda's swamp and the lava fields of Mustafar, where Anakin turns to the dark side. Waxworks show Luke Skywalker fighting

Darth Vader, Obi-Wan Kenobi and (teenage boys and their dads take note) a captive Princess Leia in Jabba's Throne Room. For an extra £5, you can visit the new Sherlock Holmes Experience, while the movie tie-ins continue with a King Kong-themed Skull Island Experience, complete with 18ft-tall animatronic gorilla head.

Sherlock Holmes Museum
221B Baker Street, NW1 6XE (7224 3688, www.sherlock-holmes.co.uk). Baker Street tube. **Open** *9.30am-6pm daily.* **Admission** *£15; £10 reductions.* **Map** *p140 G5.*

Founded in 1989 at what used to be no.239, the museum fought long and hard for the right to claim the address 221B Baker Street as its own. When you visit, you are likely to be greeted by an august person wearing a bowler hat and whiskers; this, you will deduce, is Dr Watson. And every lovingly recreated detail – murder weapons, Victoriana, waxwork tableaux of key scenes from Conan Doyle's stories – conspires to persuade visitors to suspend their disbelief and feel themselves travelling back in time to a preserved fragment of historical reality. Perhaps most interesting is a folder of letters

Sherlock Holmes Museum

upstairs in Mrs Hudson's room: they were all actually sent to Holmes by fans from all over the world, asking for help or offering their assistance as wannabe sleuths.

❤ Wallace Collection

Hertford House, Manchester Square, W1U 3BN (7563 9500, www.wallacecollection.org). Bond Street tube. **Open** *10am-5pm daily.* **Admission** *free.* **Map** *p140 H6.*

Built in 1776 and tucked away on a quiet square, this handsome house contains an exceptional collection of 18th-century French furniture, paintings and objets d'art, as well as an amazing array of medieval armour and weaponry taking up much of the ground floor. It all belonged to Sir Richard Wallace, who, as the illegitimate offspring of the fourth Marquess of Hertford, inherited in 1870 the treasures his father had amassed in the last 30 years of his life. Room after grand room contains Louis XIV and XV furnishings and Sèvres porcelain; the galleries are hung with paintings by Titian, Gainsborough and Reynolds, as well as Fragonard's *The Swing.*

Thoroughly refurbished, the Wallace is looking wonderful these days, especially upstairs, where the West Galleries display 19th-century and Venetian paintings (including a room of Canalettos) and the East Galleries are dedicated to Dutch paintings, among them a wonderful Rembrandt self-portrait hung directly opposite his less characterful painting of Titus, his son. At the back, the Great Gallery – following painstaking improvements to lighting and decor – is now the loveliest gallery room in London, with Franz Hals's *Laughing Cavalier*, Poussin's *A Dance to the Music of Time*, Velázquez's *The Lady with a Fan* and Rubens' *The Rainbow Landscape* shown to their very best advantage.

Restaurants

Chiltern Firehouse ££££

1 Chiltern Street, W1U 7PA (7073 7676, www.chilternfirehouse.com). Baker Street tube. **Open** *7-10.30am, noon-2.30pm, 5-10.30pm Mon-Wed; 7-10.30am, noon-3pm, 6-10.30pm Thur, Fri; 8-10am, 11am-3pm, 6-10.30pm Sat, Sun.* **Map** *p140 H6* ❸ *Modern European*

This lovely 1889 Grade II-listed Victorian Gothic fire brigade building has been rebuilt from the inside out to create London's buzziest hotel, but the discreetly gated garden is also the entrance to one of London's finest restaurants. The kitchen can do fiddly and pretty, exemplified by appetisers such as the tiny, slider-like 'doughnuts' filled with crab meat, but pretty is only part of the story. The restaurant's success is built on its reputation as a celeb-magnet but when that fades,

the flavour combinations and exemplary modern cooking techniques, as 'curated' by Portuguese superchef Nuno Mendes, will remain. The best seats are at the kitchen counter, from which you can watch the chefs work their magic.

❤ Fischer's £££

50 Marylebone High Street, W1U 5HN (7466 5501, www.fischers.co.uk). Baker Street or Regent's Park tube. **Open** *8am-11pm Mon-Sat; 8am-10.30pm Sun.* **Map** *p140 H5* ❹ *Austrian*

Chris Corbin and Jeremy King have made a habit of producing destination restaurants that don't feel stand-offish. This revival of the Mittel-European grand café is no exception. It's another celebrity hotspot – they love both Fischer's ageless elegance and its two-track booking system (fast-track for slebs; sidings for the hoi polloi) – but the prices here, in a setting where the monthly bill for wood polish might cause a Habsburg lip to tremble, are not as inflated as you'd expect. The main menu would be familiar to someone touring the Austro-Hungarian Empire in their charabanc, but there is fabulous sachertorte and strudel for those who can't manage a full meal.

❤ Providores & Tapa Room £££

109 Marylebone High Street, W1U 4RX (7935 6175, www.theprovidores.co.uk). Baker Street or Bond Street tube. **Open** *Providores noon-3pm, 6-10.30pm Mon-Fri; 10am-3pm, 6-10.30pm Sat; 10am-3pm, 6-10pm Sun. Tapa Room 8-11.30am, noon-10.30pm Mon-Fri; 9am-3pm, 4-10.30pm Sat; 9am-3pm, 4-10pm Sun.* **Map** *p140 H6* ❼ *Fusion*

Fusion cuisine is common in London these days, but Peter Gordon was one of the pioneers – and his flagship restaurant continues to shine. On the ground floor is the Tapa Room, a casual, buzzy space heaving with well-dressed locals knocking back top-quality coffee, New Zealand wines and an all-day menu of small plates. Upstairs is the more formal but still intimate Providores restaurant, where everything is ratcheted up a notch. The menu of small plates – roughly a sonnet in length and style – might include scallops with a bright salad and beurre noisette hollandaise or coconut laksa with a fish dumpling and quail's eggs.

Twist ££

42 Crawford Street, W1H 1JW (7723 3377, www.twistkitchen.co.uk). Edgware Road or Marylebone tube. **Open** *noon-3pm, 6-11pm Mon-Thur; noon-3pm, 6-11.30pm Fri; noon-3pm, 6pm-midnight Sat.* **Map** *p140 G6* ⓫ *Mediterranean*

It's not often you see an Italian chef embrace small plates, but that's precisely the twist Neapolitan Eduardo Tuccillo has put on the food at this charming little restaurant. Rather than stick to southern Italian dishes, he's mixed it up with Spanish and other Mediterranean influences. Top-flight ingredients are in evidence throughout, with perfectly made pasta slathered with a creamy mushroom sauce heady with truffle, or juicy prawns cooked *a la plancha* with chilli and garlic and served on a purée of Jerusalem artichoke. Dishes are on-trend without being pretentious, with an honest commitment throughout to quality cooking.

♥ Zoilo ££

9 Duke Street, W1U 3EG (7486 9699, zoilo. co.uk). Bond Street tube. **Open** *noon-2.30pm, 5.30-10.30pm Mon-Sat.* **Map** *p140 H7* ⑫ *Argentinian*

If the idea of deconstructed, small-plates Argentinian cooking seems a contradiction in terms, pull up a counter seat and prepare to be amazed. With few actual tables, most of the seating is around the ground-floor bar or the downstairs kitchen – it shouts 'watch us work, look how good we are!'. Diners can witness the creation of dazzling offerings like octopus cooked sous vide, fried *queso de chancho* ('head cheese'), or miniature steak, each rustled up with flair and a feel for authenticity. Desserts run from a traditional, ultra-sweet 'tres leches' milk cake to a tart passionfruit sorbet, and most of the all-Argentinian wine list is available by the glass or small carafe. Plates might be small, but when flavours are as compelling as these, you want as many different dishes as you can get.

Pubs & bars

Purl

50-54 Blandford Street, W1U 7HX (7935 0835, www.purl-london.com). Bond Street tube. **Open** *5-11.30pm Mon-Thur; 5pm-midnight Fri, Sat.* **Map** *p140 H6* ❸

Purl, one of London's first speakeasy-style bars, remains popular, which means that booking is advisable – though walk-ins will be seated if there's space. The layout of the bar, over a number of smallish spaces in a vaulted basement, gives the opportunity for genuine seclusion, if that's what you're looking for. And if you're interested in cutting-edge cocktail making, you're also in luck. Novel methods and unusual ingredients are used in many of the drinks, but the classics are always sound. And the music is chosen by someone who has very good taste in jazz.

Shops & services

Alfie's Antique Market

13-25 Church Street, NW8 8DT (7723 6066, www.alfiesantiques.com). Edgware Road tube or Marylebone tube/rail. **Open** *10am-6pm Tue-Sat.* **No cards. Map** *p140 F5* ❷ *Antiques*

Over almost four decades now, Alfie's three floors and basement have hosted at least a hundred dealers in vintage furniture and fashion, art, books, maps and the like behind the rather bold art deco façade. Alfie's has been an encouragement – and, in some cases, a stepping stone – for other dealers to set up businesses near here. But before you take on what is now the cluster of shops, many focused on 20th-century collectibles, at the east end of Church Street, repair to Alfie's pleasant rooftop café to revive flagging spirits.

Cadenhead's Whisky Shop & Tasting Room

26 Chiltern Street, W1U 7QF (7935 6999, www.whiskytastingroom.com). Baker Street tube. **Open** *10.30am-6.30pm Mon Thur; 11am-6.30pm Fri; 10.30am-6pm Sat.* **Map** *p140 H6* ❼ *Food & drink*

Cadenhead's is a survivor of a rare breed – the independent whisky bottler – and its shop is one of a kind, at least in London. Cadenhead's selects barrels from distilleries all over Scotland and bottles them without filtration or any other intervention.

♥ Collaborative Store

58 Blandford Street, W1U 7JB (7935 8123, www.instagram.com/the_collaborative_ store). Baker Street tube. **Open** *11am-7pm Mon-Sat; noon-6pm Sun.* **Map** *p140 H6* ❽ *Fashion*

Following a couple of great pop-ups, this concept store found a permanent place to call home. Only stocking independent designers and makers, it features plenty of under-the-radar brands. In the same space, you can pick up delicate, geometric jewellery from Clerkenwell's Miya Bonner, colourful furniture from Jennifer Newman and brilliant shoes from Ganor Dominic – all of them London-based. Every month the store also hosts workshops and pop-up events.

Daunt Books

83-84 Marylebone High Street, W1U 4QW (7224 2295, www.dauntbooks.co.uk). Baker Street tube. **Open** *9am-7.30pm Mon-Sat; 11am-6pm Sun.* **Map** *p140 H6* ❾ *Books & music*

This beautiful Edwardian shop's elegant three-level back room – complete with oak balconies, viridian-green walls and stained-glass window – houses a much-praised travel section featuring guidebooks, maps, language reference, travelogues and related fiction. Travel aside, Daunt is also a first-rate stop for literary fiction, biography, gardening and more, with a good range of author readings to boot. There are branches throughout the city, but this is by far the most handsome.

♥ Gallery of Everything

4 Chiltern Street, W1U 7PS (7486 8908, shop. musevery.com). Baker Street tube. **Open** *11am-6.30pm Tue-Sat; 2-6pm Sun.* **Map** *p140 H6* ⓫ *Art & merchandise*

It all started in a former dairy in Camden – or perhaps with Duchamp's urinal. The former was, in 2009, the site of the hugely popular Museum of Everything exhibition of outsider or non-academic or naïve or private or... well, of art you don't usually see in galleries. Further exhibitions followed, here and in other cities, all delivered with a winning pop sensibility and a shrewd eye for artistry and interest. This gallery-shop continues the good work – even if you're not in the hunt for original art, the excellent merchandise makes winningly idiosyncratic souvenirs.

John, Bell and Croyden

50-54 Wigmore Street, W1U 2AU (7935 5555, www.johnbellcroyden.co.uk). Bond Street tube. **Open** *8.30am-7pm Mon-Fri; 9.30am-7pm Sat; noon-6pm Sun.* **Map** *p140 J6* ⓯ *Pharmacy*

After two centuries of dishing out cures for Londoners' maladies, this venerable pharmacy has undergone a multimillion-pound revamp. Intriguing bits of antique paraphernalia are dotted among of-the-moment wellness fads – JB&C houses a royal prescription book, so you can gawp at Queen Victoria's beauty secrets (cold cream and Coraline toothpaste, FYI). The store is also home to a globetrotting selection of fancy brands, from French cult favourites (Embryolisse, La Roche Posay) to under-the-radar Antipodean suncare.

John Simons

46 Chiltern Street, W1U 7QR (3490 2729, www.johnsimons.co.uk). Baker Street tube. **Open** *11am-6pm Tue-Sat; noon-5pm Sun.* **Map** *p140 H6* ⓰ *Menswear*

The foundation of the Ivy League wardrobe is here: Harrington jackets, button-down shirts, knit ties, chinos and penny loafers – the kind of clothes you see on the cover of Blue Note albums. Lots of shops now sell this look, but John Simons is the correct and authentic version – we earnestly believe Miles came here just before the photoshoot for *Kind of Blue*.

KJ's Laundry

74 Marylebone Lane, W1U 2PW (7486 7855, www.kjslaundry.com). Bond Street tube. **Open** *10am-7pm Mon-Sat; 11am-5pm Sun.* **Map** *p140 J6* ⓲ *Fashion*

Since opening in 2006, proprietors Kate Allden and Jane Ellis have curated a delightful mix of both established and lesser-known designers from around the globe, with an emphasis on timeless elegance rather than cutting-edge style. Luxury knits, skinny jeans, floaty tops, cowboy boots and charm jewellery are all hardy perennials here.

Prism

54 Chiltern Street, W1U 7QX (7635 5407, prismlondon.com). Baker Street tube. **Open** *noon-6pm Mon-Wed; noon-7pm Thur; noon-6pm Fri; 10am-6pm Sat; noon-5pm Sun.* **Map** *p140 H6* ㉒ *Fashion*

Designer Anna Laub's clothing label was founded entirely according to her own wish list. After failing to find a bikini that fitted her body shape, she created a swimwear collection for the non-standard-sized woman, with 12 variations of the same bikini – including skimpy bottoms, '50s style pants and jumbo retro granny pants, which can be matched with triangle tops, bandeaux, bras and moulded cups. Everything in store is designed with the same particular eye, from the rubber-soled espadrilles to a beach bag that doubles as carry-on-luggage.

PICCADILLY CIRCUS & REGENT STREET

▶ *Oxford Circus or Piccadilly Circus tube.*

Busy **Piccadilly Circus** is an uneasy mix of the tawdry and the grand, a mix that has little to do with the vision of its architect. John Nash's 1820s design for the intersection of Regent Street and Piccadilly, two of the West End's most elegant streets, was a harmonious circle of curved frontages. But 60 years later, Shaftesbury Avenue muscled in and ruined it all. Still, a revamp of the traffic junction by the same design consultants who successfully remodelled Oxford Circus (here they ripped out a mile of railings to ease pedestrian access) has made it a bit more pleasant.

Alfred Gilbert's memorial fountain in honour of child-labour abolitionist Earl Shaftesbury was erected in 1893. It's properly known as the **Shaftesbury Memorial**, with the statue on top intended to show the Angel of Christian Charity, but critics and public alike recognised the likeness of **Eros** and their judgement has stuck.

Shaftesbury Memorial, Piccadilly Circus

The illuminated advertising panels around the intersection (www. piccadillylights.co.uk) appeared late in the 19th century and have been there ever since; a Coca-Cola ad has been here since 1955, making it the world's longest-running advertisement. Previously the lights have only been turned off during World War II, for Winston Churchill's funeral in 1965 and Princess Diana's funeral in 1997, but in January 2017 Piccadilly went dark for a major upgrade: Europe's largest single digital screen will be unveiled in the autumn.

Opposite the memorial, the **Trocadero Centre** (www.londontrocadero.com) has seen several ventures come and go, in a prime but tired location; many a London teenager ended a night begun in hope and promise with a deflated session on the video games that once bleeped and buzzed within. However, **Ripley's Believe It or Not!** is now well established – and will surely benefit if the massive budget hotel that has been mooted for the site over many years finally happens.

Connecting Piccadilly Circus to Oxford Circus to the north and Pall Mall to the south, **Regent Street** was designed by Nash in the early 1800s with the aims of improving access to Regent's Park and bumping up property values in Haymarket and Pall Mall. Much of Nash's architecture was destroyed in the early 20th century, but the street's broad curve retains some of the grandeur Nash intended for it.

Sights & museums

Ripley's Believe It or Not!

The London Pavilion, 1 Piccadilly Circus, W1J 0DA (3238 0022, ripleyslondon.com). Piccadilly Circus tube. **Open** *10am-midnight daily (last entry 10.30pm).* **Admission** *£27.95; £20.95 reductions; free under-4s. Book online 14 days in advance for 50% reductions.* **Map** *p140 L8.*

This 'odditorium' follows a formula more or less unchanged since Robert Ripley opened his first display at the Chicago World Fair in 1933: an assortment of 800 curiosities is displayed, ranging from the world's smallest road-safe car to da Vinci's *Last Supper* painted on a grain of rice – via the company's signature shrunken heads. There are strange works of art created from everyday objects (a portrait of Michelle Obama depicted in bottletops; Michael Jackson made out of sweets), exhibits that tell you about the curious traditions of obscure cultures, and a showcase of incredible human feats – the man who had his body reshaped so he looked like a lizard, the tallest man on earth, and so on. It's all brilliantly silly, offbeat fun.

❤ Liberty

Regent Street, W1B 5AH (7734 1234, www. liberty.co.uk). Oxford Circus tube. **Open** *10am-8pm Mon-Sat; noon-6pm Sun.* **Map** *p140 K7* ⓘ *Department store*

Founded in 1875, Liberty's present site was built in 1925 – its distinctive half-timbered frontage constructed from the remains of a couple of decommissioned warships, HMS *Hindustan* and HMS *Impregnable*. Which goes a good way to summarising the place: it's a superbly loveable mix of tradition and fashion. The store's interconnecting jumble of rooms, with the odd fireplace and cushioned window seat, have an intimate feel – as if you've strayed into a private room in a stately home. It's no accident: founder Arthur Lasenby Liberty wanted customers to feel as if they were exploring someone's home, keeping the shopping galleries small, albeit linked to three rather grand atriums.

Although Liberty trades well on its history, it has spent the last half decade squeezing innovation into its wood-panelled rooms. At the main entrance to the store is Wild at Heart's exuberant floral concession, and just off from here you'll find yourself in a room devoted to the store's own label. Fashion brands focus on high-end British designers, such as Vivienne Westwood and Christopher Kane. But despite being up with the latest fashions, Liberty still respects its dressmaking heritage with a range of cottons in the third-floor haberdashery department. Back in 2011 it expanded its men's floor, adding a huge tailoring and accessories chamber packed full of posh undies. The Paper Room soon followed on the ground floor, with micro-floral Liberty print stationery and gifts, and then the Dining Room opened – quirky cookware and gadgetry in a space modelled on the kitchen in *Downton Abbey*.

French publishing powerhouse Assouline opened its Literary Lounge on the ground floor, where you can flick through fashion, art and photography coffee-table books (which are, oddly, the size of coffee tables). The Beauty Hall then doubled in size – stocking cult brands such as Aesop, Le Labo and Byredo, and skincare from the much-celebrated Egyptian Magic at counters manned by an eerily beautiful staff – and three new treatment rooms were added.

For all its pomp and fizz, Liberty doesn't take itself too seriously – there's a genuine sense of whimsy in its approach to retail. Collaborations with brands such as Puma and Nike produce floral sneakers (that instantly sell out) and, via its Art Fabrics project, Liberty has worked with babydoll-dress fancier Grayson Perry and even Hello Kitty to create exclusive fabrics. Visitors can also have their moustache expertly trimmed and waxed at Murdock barbers or their barnacles plucked off by expert chiropodists in the Margaret Dabbs Sole Spa.

Restaurants

Bentley's Oyster Bar & Grill £££

11-15 Swallow Street, W1B 4DG (7734 4756, www.bentleys.org). Piccadilly Circus tube. **Open** *Oyster Bar 11.30am-11.30pm Mon-Sat; 11.30am-10.30pm Sun. Restaurant noon-3pm, 5.30-11pm Mon-Fri; 5.30-11pm Sat.* **Map** *p140 K8* ❶ *Fish & seafood*

Richard Corrigan first overhauled this grande dame of the capital's restaurant scene (established 1916) in 2005. The interior remains as polished as ever, with art deco windows, the original marble oyster bar and

wood panelling. Week nights in the more formal first-floor Grill restaurant have a restrained business-dinner vibe, but the downstairs oyster bar is pleasingly laid-back. Theatrics at the gleaming marble counter (part staff speedily shucking, part competitive knocking 'em back) provide entertaining distraction as you decide between menu classics and imaginative daily specials.

Shoryu Ramen £
9 Regent Street, SW1Y 4LR (no phone, www. shoryuramen.com). Piccadilly Circus tube. **Open** *11.15am-midnight Mon-Sat; 11.15am-10.30pm Sun.* **Map** *p140 L8* **⑩** *Japanese*

Shoryu pips its West End *tonkotsu* rivals when it comes to the texture and stock of its broth. As well as Hakata-style ramen (noodles in a rich, boiled-down, pork-bone broth), the other notable feature is speed. Both help to ease the hassle of no-bookings dining. Dracula *tonkotsu* – with caramelised garlic oil, balsamic vinegar and garlic chips – packs a flavoursome punch. Extra toppings such as bamboo shoots and boiled egg are to be expected, but *kaedama* (plain refill noodles) are a godsend for anyone sharing soup stock between small children. There's a varied choice of sides, sakés and sweets.

Shops & services

Burberry
121 Regent Street, W1B 4TB (7806 8904, www. burberry.com). Piccadilly Circus tube. **Open** *10am-8pm Mon-Sat; 11.30am-6pm Sun.* **Map** *p140 K8* **⑤** *Fashion*

The flagship store of the Burberry brand melds together the building's near-200 years of history with the attributes of hyper-modern retailing. Interactive mirrors react to micro-chipped products and respond with bespoke informative content. Welcoming assistants are armed with iPads, a 38sq ft TV live-streams shows, and acoustic performances are held on a hydraulic stage. But the gracious surroundings and an emphasis on natural light create a welcoming atmosphere. There's a beauty room here, as well as fashion and accessories.

Hamleys
188-196 Regent Street, W1B 5BT (0371 704 1977, www.hamleys.com). Oxford Circus tube. **Open** *10am-8pm Mon-Wed; 10am-9pm Thur, Fri; 9.30am-9pm Sat; noon-6pm Sun.* **Map** *p140 K7* **⑬** *Children*

Visiting Hamleys is certainly an experience – whether a good one or not will depend on your tolerance for noisy, over-excited children, especially during school holidays and the run-up to Christmas, when the store runs special kids' events. As you doubtless know, Hamleys is a ginormous toy shop, perhaps the most ginormous toy shop, with attractive displays of all this season's must-have toys across five crazed floors, and perky demonstrators ramping up the temptation levels.

J Crew

165 Regent Street, W1B 4AD (7292 1580, www.jcrew.com). Oxford Circus tube. **Open** *10am-8pm Mon-Sat; noon-6pm Sun.* **Map** *p140 K8* ⓮ *Fashion*

Established in 1983 as a catalogue label, J Crew has become one of America's most successful fashion brands. Happily the US export has brought with it American-style customer service: the staff are ultra-attentive and beam when they serve you. Go here for luxurious wardrobe basics for men, women and kids from cashmere knits to neat blazers.

Karl Lagerfeld

145-147 Regent Street, W1B 4JB (7439 8454, www.karl.com). Piccadilly Circus tube. **Open** *10am-8pm Mon-Wed, Fri, 10am-9pm Thur; noon-6pm Sun.* **Map** *p140 K8* ⓱ *Fashion*

Lagerfeld's first dedicated UK store is a temple to the man himself. Having cultivated an instantly recognisable appearance (slimline black tailoring, smoothly quiffed silver ponytail, black shades and superfluous fingerless gloves), the designer is set on flogging the hell out of it. In fact, the first thing that you see when you enter the store is a run of Karl robots and dolls. Behind them are neatly stacked Union Jack T-shirts emblazoned with Karl cameos, and trainers with a dogtooth-print that on closer inspection is a micro Karl motif.

MAYFAIR

▶ *Bond Street or Green Park tube.*

The gaiety suggested by the name of Mayfair, derived from a long-gone spring celebration, isn't matched by its atmosphere today. Even on Mayfair's busy shopping streets, you may feel out of place without the reassuring heft of a platinum card in your pocket. Nonetheless, there are many pleasures to enjoy if you fancy a stroll, not least the rapidly changing roster of blue-chip commercial art galleries.

The Grosvenor and Berkeley families bought the rolling green fields that would become Mayfair in the middle of the 17th century. In the 1700s, they developed the pastures into a posh new neighbourhood, focused on a series of landmark squares. The most famous of these, **Grosvenor Square** (1725-31), is dominated by the supremely inelegant US Embassy, due to close in 2017 for its move to Vauxhall. The embassy's only decorative touches are a fierce eagle and a mass of post-9/11 protective barricades. Out front, pride of place is taken by a statue of President Dwight Eisenhower, who stayed in nearby **Claridge's** (*see p398*) when in London; Roosevelt presides over the square itself, and its rather eloquent 9/11 memorial: 'Grief is the price we pay for love.' About the Ronald Reagan statue – complete with some of his oratorical greatest hits – the less said the better.

Brook Street has impressive musical credentials: GF Handel lived and died at no.25, and Jimi Hendrix roomed briefly next door at no.23, adjacent buildings that have been combined into **Handel & Hendrix in London**. For most visitors, however, this part of town is all about shopping. Connecting Brook Street with Oxford Street to the north, **South Molton Street** is home to the fabulous boutique-emporium **Browns** and the excellent **Grays Antique Market**, while **New Bond Street** is an A-Z of top-end, mainstream fashion houses.

Beyond New Bond Street, **Hanover Square** is another of the area's big squares, now a busy traffic chicane. Just to the south is **St George's Church**, built in the 1720s and once everyone's favourite place in which to be seen and to get married. Handel, who married nobody, attended services here. South of St George's, salubrious **Conduit Street** is where fashion shocker Vivienne Westwood (no.44) faces staid **Rigby & Peller**, corsetière to the Queen.

Running south off Conduit Street is the most famous Mayfair shopping street of all, **Savile Row**. Gieves & Hawkes (no.1) is a must-visit for anyone interested in the history of British menswear; at no.15, the estimable Henry Poole & Co has cut suits for clients including Napoleon III, Charles Dickens and 'Buffalo' Bill Cody. No.3 was the home of the Beatles' Apple Records and scene of their rooftop farewell concert, while the **Alexander McQueen** menswear shop is at no.9.

Two streets west, **Cork Street** was long the heart of the West End art scene – but Fitzrovia's Eastcastle Street these days mounts a pretty serious challenge. Still, **Flowers Central** (21 Cork Street, 7439 7766, www.flowersgalleries.com) is one of Mayfair's notable small galleries, facing off against heavy competition from major US art dealers: notably, the 10,000sq ft **David Zwirner** gallery (24 Grafton Street, 3538 3165, www.davidzwirner.com). **Pace** (6 Burlington Gardens, 3206 7600, www.

pacegallery.com), which shares premises at Burlington Gardens with the **Royal Academy** (*see p158*), also stages arresting shows. A couple of streets over is Albemarle Street, where you'll find the **Royal Institution**.

Just west of Albemarle Street, **44 Berkeley Square** is one of the original houses in this grand square. Built in the 1740s, it was described by architectural historian Nikolaus Pevsner as 'the finest terrace house of London'. Curzon Street, which runs off the south-west corner of Berkeley Square, was home to MI5, Britain's secret service, from 1945 until the '90s. It's also the northern boundary of **Shepherd Market**, named after a food market set up here by architect Edward Shepherd in the early 18th century and now a curious little enclave. From 1686, this was where the raucous May Fair was held, until it was shut down in the late 18th century due to 'drunkenness, fornication, gaming and lewdness'. You'll still manage the drunkenness easily enough at a couple of good pubs, but the flavour of the place is now captured by the presence of a tobacconist and a couple of leather-bag makers.

Sights & museums

Handel & Hendrix in London
25 Brook Street, W1K 4HB (7495 1685, handelhendrix.org). Bond Street tube. **Open** *11am-6pm Mon-Sat (last entry 5pm).* **Admission** *£10; £5 reductions; free under-5s.* **Map** *p140 J7.*

Separated by just a brick wall are the former homes of two of history's most innovative and influential musicians – George Frideric Handel (1685-1759) and Jimi Hendrix (1942-1970). George Frideric Handel moved to Britain from his native Germany aged 25 and settled in this house 12 years later, remaining here until his death in 1759. The house – where he composed his *Messiah, Music for the Royal Fireworks* and several operas – has been faithfully restored, with original and recreated furnishings, paintings and some of the composer's scores. The programme of events includes Thursday recitals on the museum's several period instruments, which – along with engaging staff – enliven what is otherwise a bit of a worthy experience. The Hendrix section of the museum couldn't be more different. The upstairs flat at no.23 where, in 1968, Jimi lived with one of his girlfriends has also been painstakingly restored, with his bedroom detailed down to the discarded fag butts. But here the life of the former occupant really comes through: in addition to the period bedroom, there's a

timeline room with a few artefacts and plenty of audio and film, and a brilliant, revealing annex where Jimi's record collection is itemised and explored. Yes, vinyl nerds, he did vibe on his illustrious former neighbour, buying both the *Messiah* and *Water Music* from HMV.

Royal Institution & Faraday Museum
21 Albemarle Street, W1S 4BS (7409 2992, www.rigb.org). Green Park tube. **Open** *9am-6pm Mon-Fri. Closes for events; phone ahead.* **Admission** *free.* **Map** *p140 K8.*

The Royal Institution was founded in 1799 for 'diffusing the knowledge... and application of science to the common purposes of life'; from behind its neoclassical façade, it's been at the forefront of London's scientific achievements ever since. In 2008, Sir Terry Farrell completed a £22m rebuild, hoping to improve accessibility and lure people in with more open frontage, a licensed café and spruced-up events. Instead, the RI found itself in a recession and saddled with major debt after reports in early 2013 that the premises would have to be sold, illustrious benefactors stepped in to help. So the RI continues to deliver its terrific rolling programme of talks and demonstrations. The Michael Faraday Laboratory, a replica of the great scientist's former workspace, is in the basement, alongside a working laboratory in which Royal Institution scientists can be observed researching their current projects. Some 1,000 of the RI's 7,000-odd scientific objects are on display, including the world's first electric transformer, a prototype Davy lamp and, from 1858, a print of the first transatlantic telegraph signal.

Restaurants

Gymkhana £££
42 Albemarle Street, W1S 4JH (3011 5900, www.gymkhanalondon.com). Green Park tube. **Open** *noon-2.30pm, 5.30-10.30pm Mon-Sat. Bar open until 1am.* **Map** *p140 K8* ⑤
Indian

Justly lauded, Gymkhana looks and feels like an Indian colonial club, with its retro ceiling fans, marble-topped tables and yesteryear photos of polo and cricket team triumphs. It serves a splendid spread of modern Indian dishes based on regional masalas and marinades: a starter of South Indian fried chicken wings, steeped in chilli batter, perhaps, followed by Goan pork vindaloo – slow-cooked chunks of suckling pig cheek, with a vinegary red chilli and garlic masala, spiced with sweet cinnamon and coriander.

♥ Kitty Fisher's ££££

10 Shepherd Market, W1J 7QF (3302 1661, www.kittyfishers.com). Green Park tube. **Open** *noon-2.30pm, 6.15-9.30pm Mon-Sat.* **Map** *p140 J9* ⑥ *Contemporary European*

Named after an 18th-century courtesan, known for her wit and extravagance, Kitty Fisher's will leave you with a big smile on your face – if you don't mind paying for the privilege. The signature dish is beef cut from a ten- to 12-year-old Galician milking cow, chargrilled and served with cheese-stuffed salad potatoes and blackened onion (£80, serves two). To cut your bill in half, stick to small plates (£6-£12.50) such as melted taleggio with London honey, wholegrain mustard and loads of shaved truffle, or whipped cod's roe on dainty soldiers. The basement dining room is intimate and hugely atmospheric, but tables do get booked up well in advance.

Rasa W1 £

6 Dering Street, W1S 1AD (7629 1346, www.rasarestaurants.com). Oxford Circus or Bond Street tube. **Open** *noon-3pm, 6-11pm Mon-Sat; 1-3pm, 6-9pm Sun.* **Map** *p140 J7* ⑧ *Indian*

The bright pink walls of this branch of the Rasa minichain are as bold as the flavours in their south Indian dishes – but a lot less tasteful. This Keralan joint offers the same wholesome and moorish basics as its Stoke Newington forebear – lentil daals and chewy coiled paratha – alongside more unusual dishes like *moru kachiathu*, a turmeric-infused, sweet-sour runny yoghurt dish made with mango and green banana. The eat-in or takeaway lunchboxes are sensational value for Mayfair at £6.

Pubs & bars

♥ The Connaught Bar

The Connaught, Carlos Place, W1K 2AL (7499 7070, www.the-connaught.co.uk). Bond Street or Green Park tube. **Open** *11am-1am Mon-Sat; 11am-midnight Sun.* **Map** *p140 J8* ①

Inside one of the more discreet of London's mega-expensive hotels, the Connaught Bar is all about old-school style and glamour. Designed by David Collins, its mirrors, low

---

In the know
Get barred

If the **Connaught Bar** (see *above*) is too lively for you, try the hotel's other drinking spot: the splendidly upholstered **Coburg** feels more like a country club.

---

lighting, silver leaf and tasteful palette will put you in mind of a deco steamship. Even if you can only stretch to a single drink, it's worth it, especially if you order a Martini – the trolley is wheeled up beside you and the drink mixed on top.

♥ Mr Fogg's

15 Bruton Lane, W1J 6JD (7036 0608, mr-foggs.com/residence). Green Park tube. **Open** *5.01pm-1.01am Mon-Wed; 4.01pm-2.01am; 2.01pm-2.01am Sat; 3.01pm-12.01am Sun.* **Map** *p140 J8* ②

For sheer spectacle, Mr Fogg's is hard to beat. The place is stuffed with the detritus left by the titular Victorian explorer: every wall is covered with hunting rifles, stuffed animals, weathered flags and maps – all imaginary souvenirs of course, but that doesn't make the profusion of clutter any less fun. With an interior like this, it would be easy for cocktails to take second place, but seriously knowledgeable bar staff make sure the drinks are punchy and altogether sensational.

Shops & services

This is a focal area for British designer showcases, with **Stella McCartney** and **Alexander McQueen** our top picks.

Alexander McQueen

4-5 Old Bond Street, W1S 4PD (7355 0088, www.alexandermcqueen.com). Green Park tube. **Open** *10.30am-6pm Mon-Wed, Fri, Sat; 10.30am-7pm Thur; noon-6pm Sun.* **Map** *p140 K8* ① *Fashion*

The late Alexander McQueen's collections are more wearable than ever. The UK's only store – where you can see the best of his designer womenswear – is a very posh contemporary space, full of baroque wood panels, marble and gilt mirrors. But – as with all things McQueen – in among the splendour something sinister must lurk. Look at the feet of chairs and tables and you'll see claws and hoofs. Gargoyles and skulls grimace and twist furtively from the flora and fauna of the moulded plaster panels. A real shopping experience.

Once you've checked out the flagship store, pay a visit to **Menswear** (9 Savile Row, W1S 3PF, 7494 8840), which has similarly macabre touches – as well as a bespoke tailoring workshop in the basement – and the diffusion line, **McQ** (14 Dover Street, W1S 4LW, 7318 2220).

Berry Bros & Rudd

3 St James's Street, SW1A 1EG (0800 280 2440, www.bbr.com). Green Park tube. **Open** *10am-9pm Mon-Fri; 10am-5pm Sat.* **Map** *p140 K9* ❸ *Food & drink*

Britain's oldest wine merchant has been trading in the same premises since 1698, and its heritage is reflected in its panelled sales and tasting rooms. Burgundy- and claret-lovers will drool at the hundreds of wines, but there are also decent selections from elsewhere in Europe and the New World.

♥ Browns

24-27 South Molton Street, W1K 5RD (7514 0016, www.brownsfashion.com). Bond Street tube. **Open** *10am-7pm Mon-Wed, Sat; 10am-8pm Thur, Fri; noon-6pm Sun.* **Map** *p140 J7* ❹ *Fashion*

The buying team at Browns are magicians, with an uncanny ability to pull in the most interesting, talking-point pieces of a designer's collection. Having been owned by Joan Burnstein and her family for the past four decades, Browns was acquired by fashion website Farfetch in 2015, with the aim of bringing technological innovation to its offerings. Among the 100-odd designers jostling for attention across five interconnecting shops are fashion heavyweights Chloé, Dries Van Noten and Balenciaga. You'll also find designs from rising stars, and shop exclusives are common. No.24 now houses Browns Focus, a younger and more casual look; while Labels for Less is loaded with last season's leftovers.

Drake's

3 Clifford Street, W1S 2LF (7734 2367, www. drakes-london.com). Green Park tube. **Open** *10am-6pm Mon-Fri; 11am-6pm Sat; noon-5pm Sun.* **Map** *p140 K8* ❿ *Menswear*

The subtle interplay between exuberance and understatement is what makes Drake's unique. Its parquet floors and soft white walls provide a neutral backdrop to showcase the Drake's look: classic British style, as it might be imagined by Italians. The place to release your inner gent.

Grays Antique Market & Grays in the Mews

58 Davies Street, W1K 5LP & 1-7 Davies Mews, W1K 5AB (7629 7034, www.graysantiques. com). Bond Street tube. **Open** *10am-6pm Mon-Fri; 11am-5pm Sat.* **Map** *p140 J7* ⓬ *Antiques*

Sibling of Alfie's (*see p149*), Grays gathers more than 200 dealers in a smart covered market building. They sell everything from antique furniture and rare books to vintage fashion and jewellery.

Paul Smith

9 Albemarle Street, W1S 4BL (7493 4565, www.paulsmith.co.uk). Green Park tube. **Open** *10am-6pm Mon-Wed; 10am-7pm Thur-Sat; noon-6pm Sun.* **Map** *p140 K8* ⓴ *Fashion*

The Paul Smith flagship is as big, glossy and imposing as an oligarch's art gallery, with the whimsical flourishes that made Smith Britain's most popular designer replaced by something on a much grander scale. There's that huge wrought-iron façade, which jars brilliantly with the Georgian elegance of the surrounding buildings, and white pillars within that spring from the parquet floor to showcase nostalgic record players and vintage radios. The full men's and women's collections are here, displayed on more wrought-iron and on chunks of reclaimed wood. Samples and previous season's stock are sold at discounts of up to 50% at the **Paul Smith Sale Shop** (23 Avery Row, W1X 9HB, 7493 1287).

Postcard Teas

9 Dering Street, W1S 1AG (7629 3654, www. postcardteas.com). Bond Street or Oxford Circus tube. **Open** *10.30am-6.30pm Mon-Fri; 11am-6.30pm Sat. Tastings £20; £15 reductions.* **Map** *p140 J7* ㉑ *Food & drink*

The range in this exquisite little shop is not huge, but it is selected with great care, and all teas are sourced from small cooperatives. There's a central table for those who want to try a pot; or book in for one of the tasting sessions held on Saturdays between 10am and 11am. Stunning tea-ware and accessories are also sold.

Rigby & Peller

22A Conduit Street, W1S 2XT (7491 2200, www.rigbyandpeller.co.uk). Oxford Circus tube. **Open** *9.30am-6pm Mon-Sat; 11am-5pm.* **Map** *p140 J7* ㉓ *Fashion*

Rigby & Peller make Elizabeth II's smalls – if it's good enough for Her Majesty, it's good enough for us. Established in 1939, the brand's royal warrant was granted in 1960. Book an appointment for the bespoke bra-making service or to be expertly fitted for ready-to-wear lingerie and swimwear. Premium brands such as Aubade, Lejaby, Huit and Simone Perele are also stocked, along with sports, bridal, mastectomy and maternity bras.

Smythson

40 New Bond Street, W1S 2DE (3535 8009, www.smythson.com). Bond Street tube. **Open** *9.30am-7pm Mon-Wed, Fri; 10am-8pm Thur; 10am-7pm Sat; noon-6pm Sun.* **Map** *p140 J7* ㉕ *Stationery*

Royal Academy of Arts

London's poshest stationers is a veritable paradise for paper-lovers. Established in 1887, Smythson made its name from selling extraordinarily desirable pigskin diaries, notebooks and personalised stationery – it has designed invitations and notelets for everyone from Stella McCartney to the Queen herself.

Stella McCartney

30 Bruton Street, W1J 6QR (7518 3100, www.stellamccartney.com). Bond Street or Green Park tube. **Open** *10am-7pm daily.* **Map** *p140 J8* ㉖ *Fashion*

It's hard not to adore Stella's flagship, all super-sleek in shiny black with the brand emblazoned on it in fuchsia. Her current collection presides over a main space decked out in lots of white marble with pops of pink: if you can't afford £1,000 for a chic tailored blazer or this year's 'It' bag, look to signature shades or some delicate jewellery. There's children's wear in a well-lit atrium towards the back, just before you get to the footwear shrine in a cosy back chamber. And there's a simply gigantic fitting room, where you have all the space you need to play dress up.

PICCADILLY

▶ *Green Park, Hyde Park Corner or Piccadilly Circus tube.*

Piccadilly's name is derived from the 'picadil', a type of suit collar that was in vogue during the 18th century. The first of the area's main buildings was built by tailor Robert Baker and, indicating the source of his wealth, nicknamed 'Piccadilly Hall'. A stroll through the handful of Regency shopping arcades confirms that the rag trade is still flourishing mere minutes away from Savile Row and Jermyn Street. At the renovated **Burlington Arcade**, the oldest and most famous of these arcades, 'beadles' – top-hatted security staff with fancy-pants braiding on their jackets – ensureBroadcasting there's no singing, whistling or hurrying in the arcade: such uncouth behaviour is prohibited by archaic by-laws. Formerly Burlington House (1665), the **Royal Academy of Arts** is next door to the arcade's entrance. It hosts several lavish, crowd-pleasing exhibitions each year.

To the west along Piccadilly, smartly uniformed doormen mark former car showroom turned restaurant, the **Wolseley** (*see p116*), and the expensive, exclusive **Ritz** (no.150, W1J 9BR, 7493 8181, www.theritzlondon.com).

Sights & museums

❤ Royal Academy of Arts

Burlington House, W1J 0BD (7300 8000, www.royalacademy.org.uk). Green Park or Piccadilly Circus tube. **Open** *10am-6pm daily (last admission 5.30pm).* **Admission** *free. Exhibitions vary.* **Map** *p140 K8.*

Britain's first art school was founded in 1768 and moved to the extravagantly Palladian Burlington House a century later, but it's now best known not for education but for exhibitions. Ticketed blockbusters are generally held in the Sackler Wing or the main galleries; shows in the John Madejski Fine Rooms are drawn from the RA's holdings, which range from Constable to Hockney, and are free. The biggest event here is the annual Summer Exhibition, which for more than two centuries has drawn from works entered by the public. The RA's restaurant, the Keeper's House, has a little courtyard 'garden'.

The RA has also expanded into a 19th-century building on a parallel street: 6 Burlington Gardens. Coveniently located directly behind the main location, it has been exhibiting unabashedly contemporary art, from Tracey Emin and David Hockney to lightworks by Mariko Mori. There's a Peyton & Byrne café here, and the Studio Shop.

As part of its 250th anniversary celebrations in 2018, the Royal Academy is undergoing major works to connect Burlington House and Burlington Gardens for the first time. New facilities will include additional spaces for exhibitions and displays, and a double-height lecture theatre.

St James's Piccadilly

197 Piccadilly, W1J 9LL (7734 4511, www. sjp.org.uk). Piccadilly Circus tube. **Open** *8am-6.30pm daily. Evening events times vary.* **Admission** *free.* **Map** *p140 K8.*

Consecrated in 1684, St James's is the only church Sir Christopher Wren built on an entirely new site. A calming building with few architectural airs or graces, it was almost destroyed in World War II, but painstakingly reconstructed. Grinling Gibbons, the woodcarver, created the delicate limewood garlanding around the sanctuary which thankfully survived the bombing and is one of the few real frills. Beneath a new tiled roof, the church stages regular classical concerts, provides a home for the William Blake Society (Blake was baptised here) and hosts markets in the churchyard: food on Monday, antiques on Tuesday, and arts and crafts from Wednesday to Saturday. There's a handy café in the basement with plenty of tables – and the church's hospitality extends to the homeless, who come to sleep in the pews. Blake would certainly approve.

Restaurants

Just across Piccadilly in St James's is one of the grandest brasseries to be found in London: the **Wolseley** (*see p116*).

Shops & services

The Royal Arcades are a throwback to shopping of the past – the **Burlington Arcade** is both the largest and grandest, but the **Piccadilly Arcade**, opposite it, and the **Royal Arcade**, at 28 Old Bond Street, are also worth a visit.

❤ Burlington Arcade

51 Piccadilly, W1J 0QJ (7493 1764, www. burlington-arcade.co.uk). Green Park tube. **Open** *9am-7.30pm Mon-Sat; 11am-6pm Sun.* **Map** *p140 K8* **❻** *Mall*

In 1819, Lord Cavendish commissioned Britain's very first shopping arcade. Nearly two centuries later, the Burlington is still one of London's most prestigious shopping

'streets', patrolled by 'beadles' decked out in top hats and tailcoats. Highlights include collections of classic watches at David Duggan, established British fragrance house Penhaligon's, and Sermoneta, selling Italian leather gloves in a range of bright colours. High-end food shops come in the form of Luponde Tea and Ladurée; head to the latter for exquisite Parisian macaroons. Burlington also houses a proper shoe-shine boy working with waxes and creams for just £6. This may not offer the best shopping in London, but it's certainly one of the best shopping experiences.

Waterstones Piccadilly

203-206 Piccadilly, W1J 9HD (7851 2400, www.waterstones.co.uk). Piccadilly Circus tube. **Open** *9am-10pm Mon-Sat; noon-6.30pm Sun.* **Map** *p140 K8* **㉘** *Books*

The flagship store of the chain is located in a handsome art deco former department store, where six floors are now stuffed with some 200,000 books, as well as two Café Ws (one on the lower ground-floor, one on the mezzanine) and, on the top floor, the 5th View Bar & Restaurant. The programme of readings, reading groups and workshops is lively and varied. London's only rival to **Foyles** (*see p164*).

Burlington Arcade

Soho & Leicester Square

For more than two centuries, poseurs, spivs, tarts, toffs, drunks and divas have gathered in Soho. But the district's time as the focus of all that's benevolently naughty – and a proportion of the truly wicked too – has gone. Prostitution has largely been cleared out; many of the area's music, film and advertising businesses have moved on, and even the once-thriving gay scene faces frequent venue closures. Instead, the sizeable residential community that remains is faced with an almost inconceivable number of bars, restaurants and shops. There are more chains among them than there used to be, but independents still dominate.

Just to the south of Soho, beyond London's bustling Chinatown, Leicester Square – known for cinemas and, for many years, drunk out-of-towners – is inching towards a classier reputation.

❤ Don't miss

1 Social Eating House *p175*
Not merely Jason Atherton's best restaurant, but one of the finest in London.

2 Swift *p167*
Wonderful cocktails in the heart of the West End.

3 Carnaby Street *p174*
Bringing West Soho back into fashion.

4 Algerian Coffee Stores *p168*
An aromatic piece of Soho history.

5 Foyles *p164*
The most impressive of London's large bookshops.

SOHO SQUARE & AROUND

▶ *Tottenham Court Road tube.*

Forming the area's northern gateway, Soho Square was laid out in 1681. It was initially called King's Square; a weather-beaten statue of Charles II stands in it. One of the square's benches is dedicated to singer Kirsty MacColl, in honour of her song named after the square.

Two classic Soho streets run south from the square. **Greek Street**, its name a nod to a church that once stood here, is lined with restaurants and bars, among them 50-year-old Hungarian eaterie the **Gay Hussar** (no.2, 7437 0973, gayhussar.co.uk) and the nearby **Pillars of Hercules** pub (no.7, 7437 1179), where the literati once enjoyed long, liquid lunches. Just by the Pillars, an arch leads to Manette Street and Charing Cross Road, where you'll find the bookshop **Foyles**. Back on Greek Street, no.49 was once Les Cousins, a folk venue (note the mosaic featuring a musical note); Casanova lived briefly at no.46.

Parallel to Greek Street is **Frith Street**, once home to Mozart (1764-65, no.20) and painter John Constable (1810-11, no.49). Humanist essayist William Hazlitt died in 1830 at no.6, now a discreet hotel named in his memory (no.6, 7434 1771, www. hazlittshotel.com). Further down the street are **Ronnie Scott's** (*see p350*), Britain's best-known jazz club, and, across from Ronnie's, the similarly mythologised 24-hour coffee haunt **Bar Italia** (no.22, 7437 4520).

Restaurants

♥ 10 Greek Street ££

10 Greek Street, W1D 4DH (7734 4677, www.10greekstreet.com). Tottenham Court Road tube. Open noon-2.30pm, 5.30-10.30pm Mon-Fri; noon-2.30pm, 5.30-10.45pm Wed-Sat. Lunch bookings taken; dinner walk-in only. Map p163 L7 ❶ *Modern European*

This small, unshowy restaurant has made a name for itself with a short but perfectly formed menu and an easygoing conviviality. Dishes are seasonal and the kitchen produces lots of interesting but ungimmicky combinations – such as a special of halibut fillet with yellow beans, chilli and garlic, on a vivid romesco sauce. It's good value too. Tables are closely packed, and in the evening it can get noisy; bookings are taken for lunch but not dinner.

♥ Ceviche ££

17 Frith Street, W1D 4RG (7292 2040, www. cevicheuk.com). Leicester Square tube. Open noon-11.30pm Mon-Sat; noon-10.15pm Sun. Map p163 L7 ❻ *Peruvian*

Ceviche showcases citrus-cured fish. It is available in half a dozen different forms, though the menu also includes everything from terrific chargrilled meat and fish skewers (*anticuchos*) to a simple but perfectly executed corn cake. Factor in the seating options (trendy at the steel counter-bar, more comfortable in the rear dining area), the charismatic, attentive staff and the party atmosphere, and it's no wonder this place has been such a huge hit.

♥ Time to eat & drink

Superb small plates
10 Greek Street *p162*

Exceptional foodie innovations
Social Eating House *p175*

Snack on sausages
Herman Ze German *p166*

Sri Lankan pancakes
Hoppers *p164*

Fiery Taiwanese finger food
Bao *p172*

Perfect Peruvian
Ceviche *p162*

London's best bar
Swift *p167*

Drink in the history
French House *p166*

Sup amid deco finery
Bar Américain *p173*

Coffee and campari
Bar Termini *p166*

Good pub, great location
The Lyric *p170*

♥ Time to shop

Manicure as masterpiece
WAH Nails *p171*

Biggest and best for books
Foyles *p164*

London fashion forward
Machine-A *p170*

Record shop with soul
Sounds of the Universe *p171*

Superstylish wardrobe staples
YMC *p174*

Book shops with atmosphere
Cecil Court *p177*

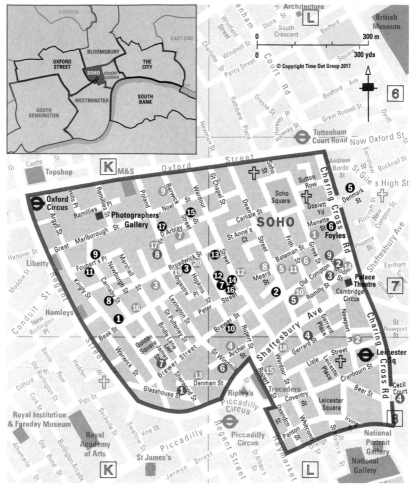

SOHO & LEICESTER SQUARE

SOHO & LEICESTER SQUARE

Restaurants

1. 10 Greek Street
2. Baiwei
3. Bao
4. Bocca di Lupo
5. Burger & Lobster
6. Ceviche
7. Copita
8. Dean Street Townhouse
9. Ember Yard
10. Herman Ze German
11. Hoppers
12. Hummus Bros
13. Kricket
14. La Bodega Negra
15. Palomar
16. Polpo Soho
17. Social Eating House ♥
18. Shuang Shuang
19. Temper
20. Yauatcha

Pubs & bars

1. Bar Américain
2. Bar Termini
3. Coach & Horses
4. Experimental Cocktail Bar
5. French House
6. The Lyric
7. Mark's Bar
8. Milk & Honey
9. Swift ♥

Shops & services

1. Albam
2. Algerian Coffee Stores
3. Axel Arigato
4. Cecil Court
5. Denmark Street
6. Foyles
7. Gosh!
8. Kingly Court
9. MAC Carnaby
10. Machine-A
11. Monki
12. OTHER/shop
13. Sounds of the Universe
14. Supreme
15. Universal Works
16. WAH Nails
17. YMC

163

Soho Square

❤ Hoppers £

*49 Frith Street, W1D 4SG (www.
hopperslondon.com). Tottenham Court Road
or Leicester Square tube.* **Open** *noon-2.30pm,
5.30-10.30pm Mon-Thur; noon-10.30pm Fri,
Sat. No reservations.* **Map** *p163 L7* ⑪ *Sri
Lankan*

For those not familiar with Sri Lankan
cuisine, a hopper is a bowl-shaped savoury
crepe, usually eaten at breakfast, and this
small stylish joint has them down to a T.
Decor is an effortless mix of old and new;
exposed brick meets wood panelling; pretty
patterned tiles meet carved-wood devil
masks. The menu, likewise, gives traditional
Sri Lankan street food a fashionable lift:
slender breaded and deep-fried mutton rolls
come with a ginger, garlic and chilli 'ketchup';
a dinky dish of roast bone marrow is treated
to a fiery 'dry' sauce, and the guinea fowl
curry is unapologetically spicy.

Shops & services

Denmark Street

Map *p163 L7* ⑤ *Musical instruments*

Just off the Charing Cross Road, Denmark
Street was in the 1960s the site of the
legendary recording studio Regent Sounds;
it is now a hub for music shops, principally
selling guitars, amps and FX pedals, but you'll
also find such esoterica as an early-music
specialist (no.11) that can supply all your
recorder and Baroque cello needs. There's an
upmarket Fernandez & Wells café (*see p191*) at
the far end of the short street, plus a swanky
burger joint halfway along; to the north,

Crossrail has done its disruptive work – many
fear subsequent redevelopment of Denmark
Street will shortly obliterate what's left of its
character.

❤ Foyles

*107 Charing Cross Road, WC2H 0EB (7437
5660, www.foyles.co.uk). Tottenham Court
Road tube.* **Open** *9.30am-9pm Mon-Sat;
noon-6pm Sun (browsing from 11.30am).*
Map *p163 L7* ⑥ *Books & music*

With 37,000sq ft of floorspace laid out around
an impressive central atrium, Foyles' eight
levels (four actual floors) are packed with
more than 200,000 books, as well as CDs
and a variety of more-or-less literary gifts.
Wherever you stand in this flagship store, you
can see every part of the building, and the
place is bathed in a gentle, contemplation-
inducing glow. The shop's focus is on the
social aspect of reading. A whole floor
is dedicated to events, from readings by
Michael Palin and Jarvis Cocker, to themed
book groups or literary tours, and there's a
space dedicated to contemporary art. The
swish café is run by Leafi, the people behind
the gallery cafés at the Whitechapel (*see p263*)
and the Courtauld (*see p191*).

In the know
See Siebe

While you're on Denmark Street, look out
for our favourite blue plaque in London: on
the south side of the street is a memorial to
Augustus Siebe. His claim to fame? Inventing
the diving helmet.

OLD COMPTON STREET & AROUND

▶ *Leicester Square or Tottenham Court Road tube.*

Linking Charing Cross Road to Wardour Street and crossed by Greek, Frith and Dean streets, Old Compton Street is London's gay catwalk. Tight T-shirts congregate around Balans, Comptons (for both, *see p331*) and the **Admiral Duncan** (no.54, 7437 5300, www.admiral-duncan.co.uk/soho). However, the street has an interesting history that dates back long before rainbow flags were hung above its doors: no.59 was formerly the 2i's Coffee Bar, the skiffle venue where stars and svengalis mingled in the late 1950s and early '60s.

Visit Old Compton Street in the morning for a sense of the mostly vanished immigrant Soho of old. Cheeses and cooked meats from **Camisa** (no.61, 7437 7610, www.icamisa.co.uk) and roasting beans from the **Algerian Coffee Stores** scent the air, as **Pâtisserie Valerie** (no.44, 7437 3466, www.patisserie-valerie.co.uk), first of a now significant national chain, does a brisk trade in croissants and cakes.

Valerie's traditional rival is the older **Maison Bertaux** (28 Greek Street, 7437 6007, www.maisonbertaux.com), an atmospheric holdover from the 19th century that sits near the southern end of Greek Street. At the corner of Greek and Romilly streets is the **Coach & Horses**, where irascible Soho flâneur Jeffrey Bernard held court for

decades. It's almost opposite the members' club **Soho House** (40 Greek Street, 7734 5188, www.sohohousegreekstreet.com; for **Dean Street Townhouse**, see *p166*; for **Shoreditch Rooms**, see *p401*), where media types and wannabes endeavour to channel the same vibe. Two streets along, Dean Street holds the **French House**; formerly the York Minster pub, it was de Gaulle's London base for French resistance in World War II and in later years became a favourite of painters Francis Bacon and Lucian Freud.

North of Old Compton Street on Dean Street sits the **Groucho Club** (no.45, 7439 4685, www.thegrouchoclub.com), a members-only media hangout that was founded in the mid 1980s and named in honour of the Groucho Marx quote about not wanting to join any club that would have him as a member. A few doors along, at no.28, the other famous Marx lived in a garret from 1850 to 1856; he would probably not have approved of the high-class, high-cost dinners served there now – at **Quo Vadis** (nos.26-29). To the north is the **Soho Theatre** (*see p366*), which programmes comedy, cabaret and new plays.

Restaurants

Burger & Lobster ££
36-38 Dean Street, W1D 4PS (7432 4800, www.burgerandlobster.com). Leicester Square tube. **Open** *noon-10.30pm Mon-Wed; noon-11pm Thur-Sat; noon-10pm Sun.* **Map** *p163 L7* ⑤ *American*

Foyles

The Soho branch of this sleek surf 'n' turf eaterie – which now has branches across town – offers a choice of, you've guessed it: burger or lobster. Meals start at £14, an all-in price that includes a huge carton of thin-cut fries and a side salad. For ultimate value, choose the lobster: steamed or grilled with just a lick of smoke. And if you're sensible enough to leave room for dessert, try one of the wicked desserts such as Snickers-in-a-tub pud: rich chocolate mousse layered on to a devilish peanut-studded salt caramel.

Dean Street Townhouse £££
69-71 Dean Street, W1D 3SE (7434 1775, www.deanstreettownhouse.com). Piccadilly Circus or Tottenham Court Road tube. **Open** *7am-midnight Mon-Thur; 7am-1am Fri; 8am-1am Sat; 8am-11pm Sun.* **Map** *p163 L7* ❽ *British*

All things to all people at all hours – whatever the Soho occasion, the chances are that Dean Street Townhouse will fit the bill. A leisurely breakfast, elevenses with the morning papers, a brisk business lunch, afternoon tea, pre-theatre snack, romantic dinner for two. Across a series of Georgian-era rooms, the restaurant buzzes from opening time until closing, which proves the simple, straightforward effectiveness of its menu of well-executed British classics.

❤ Herman Ze German £
33 Old Compton Street, W1D 5JU (7734 0431, www.hermanzegerman.co.uk). Leicester Square tube. **Open** *11am-11pm Mon-Wed; 11am-11.30pm Thur; 11am-midnight Fri, Sat; 11am-10.30pm Sun.* **Map** *p163 L7* ❿ *German*

Herman Ze German is a purveyor of German sausages, imported from a Schwarzwald (Black Forest) butcher called (we are not making this up) Fritz. They are *sehr gut*: the high-quality pork creates fat, juicy sausages. Our favourite – the bockwurst, made of smoked pork – has a delicate flavour, a springy middle and plenty of 'knack' when you bite into it. Just add ketchup and mustard for a cheap and delicious snack.

La Bodega Negra ££
9 Old Compton Street, W1D 5JF (7758 4100, www.labodeganegra.com). Leicester Square tube. **Open** *6pm-1am Mon-Sat; 6pm-midnight Sun.* **Map** *p163 L7* ⓮ *Mexican*

It's so dark and loud in this nightclub-like basement restaurant that you'll need a moment to adjust. The cooking is perhaps the least thrilling aspect of the place, though effort is put into presentation. Soft flour tacos with a tender beef filling are beautifully arranged on a wooden board. Factor in the

small portions and two-hour table limits and you might wonder what the fuss is all about. But that would be missing the point. You come here to see and be seen.

Pubs & bars
❤ Bar Termini
7 Old Compton Street, W1D 5JE (07860 945018, www.bar-termini.com). Leicester Square or Tottenham Court Road tube. **Open** *10am-11.30pm Mon-Thur; 10am-1am Fri, Sat; 11am-10.30pm Sun.* **Map** *p163 L7* ❷

Part of cocktail-maestro Tony Conigliaro's mini-empire (his drinks lab is at 69 Colebrooke Row; *see p252*), Bar Termini does two things: coffee and cocktails, in a room for 25, with seated service only, though you may stand if you order a single 'espresso al bar' (£1) – then drink and run in the Italian style. The coffee list has three signature brews, all of them classics but with a twist. The alcohol list has four negronis, a selection of *aperitivi*, four wines and one bottled beer. There are also baked goods by day, and charcuterie and cheese in the evening.

Coach & Horses
29 Greek Street, W1D 5DH (7437 5920). Leicester Square or Piccadilly Circus tube. **Open** *11am-11pm Mon-Thur; 11am-midnight Fri; 10am-midnight Sat; noon-10.30pm Sun. Food served 11am-10pm Mon-Sat; noon-10pm Sun.* **Map** *p163 K7* ❸

This Soho institution has mellowed since self-proclaimed 'London's rudest landlord' Norman Balon hung up his polishing cloth in 2006, but there's still plenty to make it stand out from the crowd. There are ten flavours of pickled eggs, for starters, and a 'secret' tea room upstairs. It's a curious mix of old-time standards and progressive ideas – you're unlikely to hear a rendition of 'My Old Man's A Dustman' while chomping on a tofu burger anywhere else.

❤ French House
49 Dean Street, W1D 5BG (7437 2799, www.frenchhousesoho.com). Leicester Square tube. **Open** *noon-11pm Mon-Sat; noon-10.30pm Sun. Food served noon-3.30pm daily.* **Map** *p163 L7* ❺

Through the door of this venerable establishment have passed many titanic

---

In the know
Daytime drinking

For visits to **Bar Termini** (*see above*) later than 5pm, you'll need to book. There's also a 60-minute time limit in the evenings.

❤ Swift

12 Old Compton Street, W1D 4TQ (7437 7820, www.barswift.com). Tottenham Court Road tube. **Open** *3pm-midnight Mon-Sat; 3-10.30pm Sun.* **Map** *p163 L7* **⑨**

What makes a great bar? Husband-and-wife team Edmund Weil and Rosie Stimpson should know. In 2010, they brought us **Nightjar** (*see p219*), which was such a huge success it now operates an online-only booking system and charges your credit card if you don't show up. And there are good reasons for its triumph: Nightjar is a gorgeous, low-lit room with comfortable seating, smooth table service and a long, playful cocktail list divided into historical eras (pre-Prohibition, post-war and so on) that is great for experimenting with new concoctions.

They didn't stop there. In 2015, they took on the Cock Tavern, under Smithfield Market, a pub formerly famous only for its pre-breakfast opening hours, and turned it into a theatrically glamorous jazz speakeasy called **Oriole** (*see p219*)– which was almost immediately block-booked, but whose feathers didn't tickle us quite so much.

Fast forward to 2017, though, and they hooked us again with Swift, which swooped into the former site of the celebrated, groundbreaking Lab Bar. It's no wonder that this place is a smasher: Weil and Stimpson have teamed up with folks who've worked in the equally wonderful **Milk & Honey** (*see p173*) and **Calloh Callay** (65 Rivington Street, Shoreditch, EC2A 3AY, 7739 4781, www.calloohcallaybar.com).

Swift is split in two: a buzzy, casual-yet-sparkling bar on the ground level and a dark lounge below. Upstairs, the look is faintly Italian, mirrored by a menu of affordable *aperitivi*. This includes an unmissable *sgroppino* – a thick and frothy prosecco-based drink with lemony sorbet floating on top. For snacks, you might order oysters, but we'd suggest diving into a Guinness welsh rarebit, heavy with pungent cheese and onion.

Pongy titbits notwithstanding, Swift makes a great date spot. If it's going well, take matters downstairs. The basement is lit for romantic trysts, the showy side of Oriole and Nightjar eschewed in favour of pared-back sophistication. Staff are attentive, guiding you through a menu of great originality that edges towards nightcaps: maybe the powerful Amber Cane, a manhattan reinvented with rum in place of the bourbon.

With their track record, Weil and Stimpson taking over the spot where London's cocktail-making reputation was cemented doesn't seem especially bold. Doing it in such a stripped-back way was the ballsy move – but, boy has it paid off.

❤ More mixmeisters

Ryan Chetiyawardana (Mr Lyan)
Dandelyan (*see p84*) and Super Lyan (*see p267*)

Tony Conigliaro
69 Colebrooke Row (*see p252*), Zetter Townhouse (*see p219*) and Bar Termini (*see p166*)

drinkers of the pre- and post-war eras. The venue's French heritage enticed de Gaulle to run a Resistance operation from upstairs – it's now a tiny restaurant. De Gaulle's image survives behind the bar, where beer is served in half-pints, and litre bottles of Breton cider are still plonked on the famed back alcove table.

Shops & services
♥ Algerian Coffee Stores
52 Old Compton Street, W1D 4PB (7437 2480, www.algcoffee.co.uk). Leicester Square tube. **Open** *9am-7pm Mon-Wed; 9am-9pm Thur, Fri; 9am-8pm Sat.* **Map** *p163 L7* **2** *Food & drink*

For more than 125 years, this unassuming little shop has been trading over the same wooden counter. The range of coffees is broad, with house blends sold alongside single-origin beans; some serious teas and brewing hardware are also available. If you're just passing, pick up an espresso or latte to go.

WARDOUR STREET & AROUND

▶*Leicester Square or Tottenham Court Road tube.*

Parallel to Dean Street, Wardour Street provides offices for film and TV production companies, but is also known for its rock history. No.100 was, for nearly three decades, the Marquee, where Led Zeppelin played their first London gig and Hendrix appeared four times. The latter's favourite Soho haunt was the nearby **Ship** pub (no.116), still with a sprinkling of music-themed knick-knacks. There's more music history at Trident Studios on nearby St Anne's Court: Lou Reed recorded *Transformer* here, and David Bowie cut both *Hunky Dory* and *The Rise and Fall of Ziggy Stardust* on the site.

When he was still known as David Jones, Bowie played a gig at the Jack of Clubs on **Brewer Street**, most recently the now also lamented Madame JoJo's. But this corner of Soho is most famous not for music but for its position at the heart of Soho's almost vanished but still notorious sex trade. The Raymond Revuebar opened on the neon alleyway of Walker's Court in 1958, swiftly becoming London's most famous strip club. It closed in 2004, became a series of short-lived gay clubs, then reopened as celebrity-infested, exclusive alt-cabaret club the **Box** (11-12 Walker's Court, W1F 0SD, www.theboxsoho.com), the London branch of a New York original.

North of here, **Berwick Street** clings on to its mix of old-school London raffishness and new-Soho style. The former comes courtesy of the fruit and veg market, and the egalitarian, old-fashioned and unceasingly popular **Blue Posts** pub (no.22, 7437 5008), where builders, post-production editors, restaurateurs and market traders gabble and glug as one beneath a portrait of Berwick Street-born star of stage and radio Jessie Matthews (1907-81). The fruit and veg have been here since 1778, but there's less fresh produce nowadays: instead stalls sell takeaway food – anything from a virtuous but vivid salad of couscous with charred vegetables to a juicy, dripping cheeseburger. Alongside the street eats, the likes of coffee bar **Flat White** (no.17, 7734 0370, flatwhitesoho.co.uk) and **Ember Yard** herald the area's likely future of upscale eating and drinking.

Restaurants
Bocca di Lupo ££
12 Archer Street, W1D 7BB (7734 2223, www.boccadilupo.com). Piccadilly Circus tube. **Open** *noon-3pm, 5.15-11pm Mon-Sat; noon-3pm, 5.15-9.30pm Sun.* **Map** *p163 L8* **4** *Italian*

The buzz is as important as the food at this popular restaurant. The menu is a slightly confusing mix of small and large plates to share: buttery brown shrimp on soft, silky white polenta, say, or a deep-fried mix of calamari, soft-shell crab and lemon. The radish, celeriac, pomegranate and pecorino salad with truffle dressing is a much-imitated Bocca di Lupo signature.

Copita £££
27 D'Arblay Street, W1F 8EP (7287 7797, www.copita.co.uk). Oxford Circus tube. **Open** *noon-11pm Mon-Sat. Food served noon-4.30pm, 5.30-10.30pm Mon-Fri; noon-10.30pm Sat.* **Map** *p163 K7* **7** *Tapas*

For an authentic taste of modern Spain, you can't go far wrong with Copita. Avoiding the standards of *patatas bravas* and *ensalada rusa*, the menu ventures admirably off the well-trodden tapas path with dishes such as sherry-braised pig cheeks, *empanadillas*

In the know
Ice, ice baby

The team behind Bocca di Lupo also runs **Gelupo**, the *gelateria* at no.7 (7287 5555, www.gelupo.com). Their blood-orange *granita* – dark, intense and made with only fruit and cane sugar – is one of our favourite desserts.

de carne, or sweet and smoky aubergine stew with tahini and mint. Each tapa should be accompanied by a little glass (*copita*) of Spanish wine or sherry from the well-informed list. Equally triumphant desserts include delicate rosemary ice-cream or lightly scented rosewater ice-cream with stewed strawberries. Like its sister restaurant, Barrica (*see p209*), the properly tapa-sized dishes mean you can get stuck into the menu without needing a crane to lift you out afterwards.

Ember Yard ££
60 Berwick Street, W1F 8SU (7439 8057, emberyard.co.uk). Oxford Circus or Tottenham Court Road tube. **Open** *noon-11pm Mon-Wed; noon-midnight Thur-Fri; 11am-midnight Sat; 11am-10pm Sun.* **Map** *p163 K7* ❾ *Tapas*

The fourth in a growing chain of new-style tapas bars, Ember Yard follows the winning template of its forebears – combining Italian and Spanish influences – but it places an even greater emphasis on the grill. The result is reminiscent of the fabulous charcoal-grill restaurants of the Basque country, especially if you're sitting near the glowing coals. Every flavour combination here is a winner, with the bar snacks among the best in Soho.

Hummus Bros £
88 Wardour Street, W1F 0TH (7734 1311, www.hbros.co.uk). Oxford Circus or Tottenham Court Road tube. **Open** *8.30am-10pm Mon-Fri; noon-10pm Sat, Sun.* **Map** *p163 L7* ⓬ *Café*

The humble chickpea paste is elevated to something altogether more delicious in the hands of Hummus Bros. Though the wraps aren't bad, go for the bowls of silky-smooth houmous sprinkled with paprika and olive oil. Mashed, cumin-scented fava beans is a good choice of topping, but our favourite is the chunky slow-cooked beef. Side dishes are heartily recommended, with deliciously smoky barbecued aubergine and zingy tabouleh particular highlights. Service is quick and casual.

Temper £££
25 Broadwick Street, W1F 0DF (3879 3834, temperrestaurant.com). Oxford Circus tube. **Open** *4-10.30pm Mon; noon-10.30pm Tue, Wed; noon-11pm Thur-Sat; noon-5pm Sun.* **Map** *p163 K7* ⓳ *Barbecue*

This Soho joint, from Scottish chef Neil Rankin, sources top-notch slabs of meat (think incredibly juicy pork or full-flavoured smoked goat) that are grilled or smoked over charcoal before being served up in small affordable portions. Flatbreads (basically a *roti* made with rendered animal fat and puffed up on the grill) come with eight exotic sprinkles and salsas (all homemade), while the rustic hand-pressed corn tacos are filled with the likes of melt-in-the-mouth soy-cured beef, or 'blowtorched' mackerel with

Temper

two kinds of citrus. Desserts, including the signature *kouign-amann* (a puff pastry 'cake') soaked in sweet-and-salty butterscotch and served with a *dulce de leche* ice-cream, are equally appealing.

Yauatcha ££££

15-17 Broadwick Street, W1F 0DL (7494 8888, www.yauatcha.com). Leicester Square, Piccadilly Circus or Tottenham Court Road tube. **Open** *noon-1pm Mon-Thur, Sun; noon-10.30pm Fri, Sat.* **Map** *p163 K7* 20 *Chinese*

Such acutely stylish venues rarely last, but after more than a decade Yauatcha can add longevity to its enviable list of attributes. The sensual basement of this Michelin-starred self-styled tea house has a nightclub vibe, with a long bar, spot-lit back tables and illuminated fish tank. Day-and-night dum sum offers exquisite combinations such as scallop and edamame crystal dumplings, while main courses hold interest with offerings of sea bass with shiitake and wolf berry. Exotic teas and East-West fusion desserts (yuzu brûlée tart) are further highlights, though grazing on exquisite snacks is undoubtedly the primary draw.

Pubs & bars

♥ The Lyric

37 Great Windmill Street, W1D 7LU (7434 0604, www.lyricsoho.co.uk). Piccadilly Circus tube. **Open** *11am-11.30pm Mon-Thur; 11am-midnight Sat, Sun; noon-10.30pm Sun. Food served noon-10pm daily.* **Map** *p163 L8* 6

Small, slightly shambolic and with a jovial share-a-table vibe, the Lyric is a longstanding favourite, not least because of its location near a fantastically crowded part of London where disappointing, pricey tourist traps are the norm. The Victorian pub's 18 taps pour out reliable pints, including Camden Hells and Brooklyn Lager, as well as more unusual guests – perhaps the hyper-citrussy High Wire Grapefruit brew from Magic Rock.

Shops & services

Berwick Street is really the heart of Soho, with its breezy street market (9am-6pm Mon-Sat), one of London's oldest. Dating back to 1778, it's seeing a bit of a revival with popular street-food stalls. The indie record shops that used to cluster here took a pasting in the noughties, but **Reckless Records** (no.30, 7437 4271, reckless.co.uk) and **Sister Ray** (no.75, 7734 3297, www.sisterray.co.uk) are now beneficiaries of the vinyl revival – along with nearby **Sounds of the Universe**.

Axel Arigato

19-23 Broadwick Street, W1F 0DF (7494 1728, axelarigato.com). Piccadilly Circus tube. **Open** *11am-7pm Mon-Wed; 11am-8pm Thur-Sat; noon-6pm Sun.* **Map** *p163 K7* 3 *Shoes*

After successfully building a fan base online, Swedish footwear brand Alex Arigato opened its flagship store in 2016. The handcrafted designer trainers are meticulously displayed on marbled pedestals and stone podiums, while the white colour scheme, concrete and mirrored surfaces of the shop's interior reflect its minimalist aesthetic. There are accessories and clothing too, as well as a selection of Japanese literature and objects that inspired the collection.

Gosh!

1 Berwick Street, W1F 0DR (7636 1011, www.goshlondon.com). Oxford Circus tube. **Open** *10.30am-7pm daily.* **Map** *p163 L7* 7 *Books & music*

There's nowhere better to bolster your comics collection. There's a huge selection of manga, but graphic novels take centre stage, from early classics such as Krazy Kat to Alan Moore's erotic Peter Pan adaptation *Lost Girls*. Classic children's books, of the This is London vein, are another strong point. First port of call? The central table, where you'll find new releases – sometimes even before official publication.

♥ Machine-A

13 Brewer Street, W1F 0RH (7734 4334, www.machine-a.com). Oxford Circus tube. **Open** *11am-7pm Mon-Wed; 11am-8pm Thur-Sat; noon-6pm Sun.* **Map** *p163 L7* 10 *Fashion*

Hats off (make it an Alex Mattsson baseball cap) to Machine-A for championing London's most exciting emerging designers at this Soho concept store. It's the natural habitat for the young, bold and brave, a small space full of pieces that practically sizzle with energy. Outside, the neon signage is a cheeky nod to its massage-parlour neighbours on Brewer Street.

OTHER/shop

3 Berwick Street, W1F 0DR (7734 6846, www.other-shop.com). Oxford Circus tube. **Open** *10.30am-6.30pm Mon-Sat; noon-5pm Sun.* **Map** *p163 L7* 12 *Fashion*

Founders of B Store, Matthew Murphy and Kirk Beattie, have more than a decade's experience of running an indie boutique. With a subtle industrial look, highlighter-yellow tiles and use of mixed materials to cover the walls – from exposed brick to reams of fabric – OTHER/shop specialises in wearable clothes for men and women with a creative twist. This applies to both its own range and guest labels including Peter Jensen and Christophe Lemaire.

💟 Sounds of the Universe
7 Broadwick Street, W1F 0DA (7734 3430, www.soundsoftheuniverse.com). Tottenham Court Road tube. **Open** *11am-7.30pm Mon-Sat; 11.30am-5.30pm Sun.* **Map** *p163 L7* ⓱ *Music*

SOTU's remit is broad. This is especially true on the ground floor (new vinyl and CDs), where grime and dubstep 12-inches jostle for space alongside new wave cosmic disco, electro-indie re-rubs and Nigerian compilations. The second-hand vinyl basement is big on soul, jazz, Brazilian and alt-rock.

Supreme
2-3 Peter Street, W1F 0AA (7437 0493, www.supremenewyork.com). Piccadilly or Leicester Square tube. **Open** *11am-7pm Mon-Sat; noon-6pm Sun.* **Map** *p163 L7* ⓮ *Fashion*

The London outpost of New York's legendary skate shop brings together the cult brand's skatewear, including apparel, accessories and decks. Ongoing collaborations with musicians, artists and designers ensures Supreme maintains the edgy style it originally made its name with back in 1994.

Universal Works
40 Berwick Street, W1F 8RX (3581 1501, www.universalworks.co.uk). Tottenham Court Road tube. **Open** *11am-7pm Mon-Sat; noon-5pm Sun.* **Map** *p163 K7* ⓯ *Menswear*

One of a number of newish men's brands that draw on Brit heritage in terms of design and craftsmanship, Universal Works has a street-orientated outlook on style. There's an aversion to flashiness, which lends individual pieces and the store that displays them a quiet, understated feel.

💟 WAH Nails
4 Peter Street, W1F 0DN (07983 261672, wah-london.com). Leicester Square tube. **Open** *10am-8pm Mon-Wed, Fri; 10am-10pm Thur; 11am-7pm Sat.* **Map** *p163 L7* ⓰ *Nail salon*

Any self-respecting nail-art fanatic will have heard of WAH, whose fanzine kicked off the nail art craze in London a few years ago. Its two-floor flagship salon offers the usual manicures, but also has room for a 'play and discover' area with immersive virtual-reality experiences, nail-printing and a product-testing zone. The futuristic space, complete with industrial concrete walls and cool cocktail bar, feels more like a club than a salon.

WEST SOHO

▶ *Piccadilly Circus or Oxford Circus tube.*

The area west of Berwick Street was rebranded 'West Soho' in a bid to give it some kind of upmarket identity – a foolish notion, but Brewer Street does have some interesting places, among them the **Vintage Magazine Store** (nos.39-43, 7439 8525), offering everything from retro robots to pre-war issues of *Vogue*. Star restaurant **Hix**, with its hip downstairs bar (Mark's Bar) is also here. On Great Windmill Street is the **Windmill Theatre** (nos.17-19), which gained fame in the 1930s and '40s for its 'revuedeville' shows with erotic 'tableaux' – naked women who remained stationary in order to stay within the law. The place is now a lap-dancing joint. North of Brewer Street is **Golden Square**. Developed in the 1670s, it became the political and ambassadorial district of the late 17th and early 18th centuries, and remains home to some of the area's grandest buildings (many now bases for media firms) and a purveyor of cinnamon buns: the **Nordic Bakery** (no.14A, 3230 1077, www.nordicbakery.com).

Just north of Golden Square is **Carnaby Street**, which became a fashion mecca shortly after John Stephen opened His Clothes here in 1956; Stephen, who went on to own more than a dozen fashion shops on the street, is now commemorated with a plaque at the corner with Beak Street. After thriving during the Swinging Sixties, Carnaby Street became a rather seamy commercialised backwater. However, along with nearby **Newburgh Street** and **Kingly Court**, it's revived, with the tourist traps and chain stores joined by a wealth of independent stores.

A little further north, just short of Oxford Street, is the **Photographers' Gallery**.

Sights & museums

Photographers' Gallery
16-18 Ramillies Street, W1F 7LW (7087 9300, www.thephotographersgallery.org. uk). Oxford Circus tube. **Open** *10am-6pm Mon-Wed, Fri, Sat; 10am-8pm Thur during exhibitions; 11am-6pm Sun.* **Admission** *£4; £2.50 reductions; free before noon. Temporary exhibitions vary.* **Map** *p163 K7.*

Given a handsome refit by Irish architects O'Donnell+ Tuomey, this old, brick corner building reopened in 2012 as the new home for London's only gallery dedicated solely to the photographic arts. The upper floors have two airy exhibition spaces, while a bookshop, print sales room and café (open from 9.30am Mon-Fri) are tucked into the ground floor and basement. The exhibitions are varied, and enhanced by quirky details such as the camera obscura in the third-floor Eranda Studio and a projection wall in the café.

Restaurants

Set in a grand art deco basement just off Piccadilly Circus, **Brasserie Zédel** is a huge, all-day French eaterie run by the team behind the **Wolseley** (*see p116*); good on its own terms, it's also home to the excellent **Bar Américain**.

❤ Bao £

53 Lexington Street, W1F 9AS (www. baolondon.com). Oxford Circus or Piccadilly Circus tube. **Open** *noon-3.30pm, 5.30-10pm Mon-Thur; noon-10.30pm Fri, Sat. No reservations.* **Map** *p163 K7* ❸ *Taiwanese*

This slick Taiwanese operation has successfully made the journey from market pop-up to permanent Soho establishment. The tantalising menu is fresh and innovative, based on Taiwanese street food dishes, with *xiao chi* (small eats) and of course *bao* (fluffy white steamed buns) stuffed with braised pork, soy-milk-marinated chicken, or even Horlicks ice-cream. What lifts this diner from merely great to sublime is the drinks list. Sakés, artisanal ciders, well-matched beers and hot oolong teas vie for attention

alongside creations such as foam tea – a chilled light oolong artistically topped with foamed cream. Arrive hungry, leave happy.

Kricket £££

12 Denman Street, W1D 7HH (7734 5612, www.kricket.co.uk). Piccadilly Circus tube. **Open** *noon-2.30pm, 5.30-10.30pm Mon-Sat.* **Map** *p163 K8* ⑬ *Indian*

A spin-off of a tiny but brilliant Brixton original, Kricket is stylish and sophisticated: exposed brick and sleek monogrammed barstools are dominated by an L-shaped counter, where you can dine looking over into a gleaming open kitchen. Just as good-looking is the menu. Indian-inspired small plates include delights such as tender kid goat *raan* dotted with pomegranate seeds; or perfectly creamy butter garlic crab with poppadoms perched on top for dipping. Comforting desserts, including delicately aromatic cardamom *kheer* rice pudding, should be accompanied by a glass or two of delicious spiced *masala chai* – with or without a shot of rum.

Polpo Soho ££

41 Beak Street, W1F 9SB (7734 4479, www. polpo.co.uk). Piccadilly Circus tube. **Open** *11.30am-11pm Mon-Sat; 11.30am-10pm Sun.* **Map** *p163 K7* ⑯ *Italian*

Bao

With peeling paint and battered wooden panelling, the decor may not look like much but you won't find better Venetian food anywhere in W1. Brown paper menus and chunky tumblers for wine glasses underline the sense of squatter chic, as does sharing small plates of unfussy food. These stretch from humble plates of olives to tasty crab *arancini*, sirloin steak and calf's liver, or spinach and egg *pizzette*.

Pubs & bars

💙 Bar Américain

Brasserie Zédel, 20 Sherwood Street, W1F 7ED (7734 4888, www.brasseriezedel. com). Piccadilly Circus tube. **Open** *4.30pm-midnight Mon-Wed; 4.30pm-1am Thur, Fri; 1pm-1am Sat; 4.30-11pm Sun.* **Map** *p163 K8* ❶

We love the simplicity of the cocktail list here: around 20 drinks, most of them tried and tested classics. Expertly rendered martinis, manhattans and daiquiris sit alongside such rarities as the martinez (a vermouth- and gin-based concoction that was the precursor of the martini) and inventive house specialities like the Lindy Hop (vodka, apple, lychee liqueur, orgeat and lemon). Fancy a quiet drink in the West End without having to pay through the nose? You can't do much better than the Américain's beautiful art deco interior.

Mark's Bar

Hix, 66-70 Brewer Street, W1F 9UP (7292 3518, www.marksbar.co.uk). Piccadilly Circus tube. **Open** *noon-1am Mon-Sat; noon-11.30pm Sun.* **Map** *p163 K8* ❼

The always busy basement cocktail bar at Mark Hix's restaurant is a first-rate establishment. Cocktails are king – especially the historical drinks, which manage to be both interesting and good, notably so with those on the Cocktail Explorer's Club list – but the gin and scotch lists also repay steady investigation. The bar 'snax' are terrific, and the place looks great, with its big, smoked mirrors.

Milk & Honey

61 Poland Street, W1F 7NU (7065 6800, www. mlkhny.com). Oxford Circus tube. **Open** *(non-members) 6-11pm Mon-Sat (2hrs max, last admission 9pm).* **Map** *p163 K7* ❽

This London outpost of the top-drawer Manhattan bar is a members' bar, but non-members can book the ground floor or basement bar up to 11pm. Reservation made, look for a tiny sign next to a buzzer on Poland Street, and proper cocktails made in a civilised but unstuffy atmosphere will be your reward. House rules state that the bar doesn't like noise, it doesn't like rowdy, it doesn't like poseurs or pickups; but then who does?

Shops & services

As famous as the King's Road back when the Sixties swung, **Carnaby Street** was, until a decade ago, more likely to sell you a postcard of the Queen snogging a punk rocker than a fishtail parka. But the noughties were kind and Carnaby is cool again, with **Kingly Court** a pioneer that brought in several hip boutiques.

Albam

23 Beak Street, W1F 9RS (3157 7000, www.albamclothing.com). Oxford Circus tube. **Open** *11am-7pm Mon-Sat; noon-5pm Sun.* **Map** *p163 K7* ❶ *Menswear*

With contemporary, pared-down British menswear having a bit of a renaissance, it's easy to forget who did it first and best. These days, big ticket items such as Shetland wool jumpers, floral printed cagoules and quilts abound, but Albam can still pull off a tapered chino, crisp shirt and a brilliant basic tee.

Kingly Court

Carnaby Street, opposite Broadwick Street, W1B 5PJ (7333 8118, www.carnaby.co.uk). Oxford Circus tube. **Open** *10am-7pm Mon-Sat; noon-6pm Sun.* **Map** *p163 K7* ❽ *Mall*

If you want to shop modern Carnaby Street, Kingly Court is the place to start – in fact, it's also the place that started the area's revival as a cool shopping destination. It's a three-tiered complex that contains a funky mix of established chains, independents, vintage and vintage-style boutiques. There's an increasing emphasis on food outlets, including cafés in the central courtyard.

MAC Carnaby

30 Great Marlborough Street, W1F 7JA (0370 192 5555, www.maccosmetics.co.uk). Oxford Circus tube. **Open** *10am-9pm Mon-Fri; 10am-8pm Sat; 10am-6pm Sun.* **Map** *p163 K7* ❾ *Cosmetics*

This impressive outpost of beauty heavyweight MAC features the brand's ever-popular collaborations and tongue-in-cheek limited edition lines – Haute

Dogs, for instance, whose lipsticks were inspired by pedigree pooches. There are also nine kaleidoscopic make-up stations, for quick drop-ins demos or longer, bookable lessons. Upstairs is dedicated to Mac's Pro line, beloved of make-up artists and drag queens alike. With an exhaustive selection of products, it's shopping nirvana for slap-happy amateurs and studious pros.

Monki

37 Carnaby Street , W1V 1PD (8018 7400, www.monki.com/gb). Oxford Circus tube. **Open** *10am-8pm Mon-Sat; noon-6pm Sun.* **Map** *p163 K7* ⓫ *Fashion*

Hailing from Sweden, Monki's aesthetic is a bold urban one featuring cute animal prints, oddly shaped sweater dresses and eccentric accessories – current hits include the animal-print backpacks, chunky leather ankle boots and cute woolly mittens emblazoned with big logos for less than a fiver.

♥ YMC

11 Poland Street, W1F 8QA (7494 1619, www.youmustcreate.com). Oxford Circus tube. **Open** *11am-7pm Mon-Sat; noon-5pm Sun.* **Map** *p163 K7* ⓱ *Fashion*

Impeccably designed staples are the forte of this London label. It's the place to head to for simple vest tops and T-shirts, stylish macs, tasteful knits and chino-style trousers, for both men and women.

CHINATOWN & LEICESTER SQUARE

▶ *Leicester Square tube.*

Shaftesbury Avenue is the very heart of Theatreland. The Victorians built seven grand theatres here, six of which still stand. The most impressive is the gorgeous **Palace Theatre** on Cambridge Circus, which opened in 1891 as the Royal English Opera House; when grand opera flopped, the theatre reopened as a music hall two years later. Appropriately, it's most famous for the musicals it has staged: *The Sound of Music* (1961) and *Jesus Christ Superstar* (1972) had their London premières here, and *Les Misérables* racked up 7,602 performances between 1985 and 2004. (The *Les Mis* juggernaut continues to rumble a few blocks west on Shaftesbury Avenue: there, the **Queen's Theatre** proudly proclaims it the world's longest-running musical; for our selection of the best of the West End, *see p364*.)

Marks & Co, the shop that was made famous by Helene Hanff's book 84 Charing

In the know
Something to remember us by

Tired of all the tourist tat? If you're after funky souvenirs, **We Built This City** (56B Carnaby Street, W1F 9QF, 3642 9650, www.webuilt-thiscity.com) is the place for you. It sells a selection of pieces by London artists inspired by the city around them from premises given a supercool graphic look, inside and out, by east London artist Camille Walala.

SOHO & LEICESTER SQUARE

💙 Social Eating House ££££

58 Poland Street, W1F 7NR (7993 3251, www.
socialeatinghouse.com). Oxford Circus tube.
Open *noon-2.30pm, 6-10.30pm Mon-Sat.*
Map *p163 K7* ⑰ *British*

It's not easy to maintain high standards while opening new restaurants, but chef-patron Jason Atherton has the golden touch. He started under Gordon Ramsay, under whose aegis he made Maze a Michelin-starred triumph. Just a year after leaving Ramsay in 2010, Atherton had opened his first solo restaurant, **Pollen Street Social**, and secured its first Michelin star. His style was now established: Atherton is known for witty reconstructions of familiar dishes. At Pollen Street, his 'quail brunch', for instance, comes as a bowl of 'cereal' (a savoury risotto with wild mushrooms), a slice of 'toast' (brioche, topped with a rich quail terrine) and a cup of 'tea' (quail stock and lapsang souchong, poured from a teapot at the table). And that's before the waiter opens the wooden box sitting next to you, which – hey, presto! – reveals two pieces of pine-smoked quail (breast and confit leg), which are gently placed on the risotto. It's culinary theatre of the best – and most delicious – kind.

That was 2011. Since then – in London alone – Atherton has opened eight great restaurants: in 2013, deluxe bistro **Little Social**, Pollen Street's more-casual sibling **Social Eating House** and hotel restaurant the **Berners Tavern**; in 2014, **City Social** (*see p237*); in 2015, **Social Wine & Tapas**; in 2016, **Temple & Sons** and **Sosharu** (for the bar, 7 Tales, *see p219*); in 2017, **Hai Cenato**. Unbelievably, they're all good. But Social Eating House is our favourite.

Key to Atherton's success had been delegation: at Social, he gave the chef role to his buddy and long-time head chef at Pollen Street Social, Paul Hood, whose dishes retain Pollen Street's playfulness. Try smoked duck 'ham', egg and chips, perhaps: the 'ham' is cured and smoked from duck breast on the premises, served with a breadcrumbed duck egg that's molten in the middle, but with an aroma of truffle oil. Or savour the umami in a roast cod main course that uses powdered Japanese *kombu* seaweed in a glaze, served with a creamy sauce of roasted cockles and just-in-season St George's mushrooms.

Presentation is a strong point of Hood's work, just as it is for his mentor, and the desserts show similar inventiveness, imagination and attention to detail.

A honey almond sponge, again inspired by the version at Pollen Street Social, comes nicely paired with a scoop of goat's curd ice-cream.

Even the premises are well thought through. The ground-floor dining room has a mirrored ceiling to create the sensation of space in a low room, while the smart cocktail bar upstairs, called the **Blind Pig**, has a separate entrance and is a destination in its own right (see below).

Most of the action is in the dining room, though, with a kitchen brigade who are clearly at the top of their game. In fact, if you visit the basement (where the duck smoker as well as the loos are housed), you can look straight through the glass-walled private dining room towards the kitchen, where you might see Hood at work with his team, weaving their magic with a spell-like calm.

In the know
Blind Pig

If you fancy getting straight to the booze, Social Eating House's excellent cocktail bar isn't immediately obvious at street level: look under the vintage 'Optician' sign and you'll find a doorknocker marked with a blindfolded hog. Once inside, you can get stuck into mighty fine cocktails with mighty silly names: who could resist a Slap 'n' Pickle (gin, brandy and pickle brine), Kindergarten Cup (incorporating 'Skittles-washed Ketel One'), or a Robin Hood, Quince of Thieves (brandy, quince liqueur, mead)?

SOHO & LEICESTER SQUARE

Chinatown

Cross Road, used to stand just opposite the Palace Theatre, on a road that was once a byword for bookselling. Barely any second-hand bookshops remain on Charing Cross Road, though some appealing new shops are opening in their stead; bibliophiles should keep on south towards Leicester Square, where **Cecil Court** continues to fight the good fight for readers. West of Charing Cross Road and south of Shaftesbury Avenue, officially just outside Soho, is London's **Chinatown**.

The Chinese are relative latecomers to this part of town. The city's original Chinatown was set around Limehouse in east London, but hysteria about Chinese opium dens and criminality led to 'slum clearances' in 1934 (interestingly, the surrounding slums were deemed to be in less urgent need of clearance). It wasn't until the 1950s that the Chinese put down roots here, attracted by the cheap rents along Gerrard and Lisle streets.

The ersatz oriental gates, stone lions and pagoda-topped phone boxes around Gerrard Street suggest a Chinese theme park, but this remains a close-knit residential and working enclave, a genuine focal point for London's Chinese community. The area is crammed with restaurants, Asian grocery stores, great bakeries and a host of small

shops selling iced-grass jelly, speciality teas and cheap air tickets to Beijing, but even here rising rents are pricing out some long-established family businesses.

South of Chinatown, **Leicester Square** was one of London's most exclusive addresses in the 17th century; in the 18th, it became home to the royal court of Prince George (later George II). Satirical painter William Hogarth had a studio here (1733-64), as did 18th-century artist Sir Joshua Reynolds – busts of both once resided in the small gardens at the heart of the square, along with a now vanished statue of Charlie Chaplin. They've been swept away in the fine refurbishment of the square, which has left just a statue of a wistful Shakespeare presiding over modish white 'ribbon' seating and the cut-price theatre-tickets booth, **tkts** (*see p359*).

For many years, locals left the square to the unimaginative tourists and drunk suburban kids that were its only denizens. But the arrival in 2011 of a couple of high-class hotels (for the **W**, *see p400*) and the reopening in 2012 of the Frank Matcham-designed, castle-like, red-brick **Hippodrome** (on the corner of Cranbourn Street and Charing Cross Road) as a high-rolling casino gave the area a bit of pull. Not all memories of the square's cheerfully tacky phase have gone, however: the Swiss glockenspiel has returned, with its 27 bells and mechanical mountain farmers chiming out the time on behalf of Switzerland Tourism.

Film premières are still regularly held in the monolithic **Odeon Leicester Square** (*see p323*), which once boasted the UK's largest screen and probably still has the UK's highest ticket prices; this is where the **London Film Festival** (*see p326*) kicks off every year. Get a price-conscious cinema fix just north of the square on Leicester Place, at the excellent **Prince Charles** rep cinema (*see p323*).

Restaurants

Baiwei ££
8 Little Newport Street, WC2H 7JJ (7494 3605). Leicester Square tube. **Open** *noon-11pm daily.* **Map** *p163 L8* ❷ *Chinese*

'One dish, one style; a hundred dishes, a hundred tastes.' Baiwei (which means 'a hundred flavours' in Chinese) exemplifies this Sichuanese culinary adage. Despite the Mao-era decor, it's a cosy place where authentic home-style cuisine is served with uncommonly friendly service. South-western dishes are typically robust, with an abundance of dried chillies, pepper and fragrant garlic and Baiwei's variations on Sichuan standards offer a pleasing contrast of flavours. Try the *gong bao* tofu (silky pieces of pan-fried egg tofu coated in lustrous sweet and sour sauce, then lavished with crunchy peanuts and dried chillies) or long beans mixed with lightly marinated fried minced pork.

Palomar ££
34 Rupert Street, W1D 6DN (7439 8777, thepalomar.co.uk). Leicester Square or Piccadilly Circus tube. **Open** *noon-2.30pm, 5.30-11pm Mon-Sat; noon-3.30pm, 6-9pm Sun.* **Map** *p163 L8* ❻ *Israeli*

Pulse-quickening dance music, free-flowing drink and vibrantly flavoured dishes are common in Israel's fashionable eateries, but rare in London's often po-faced Jewish restaurants. Palomar is set to buck the trend: run by Israeli-born nightclub entrepreneurs, it has become the West End's most unlikely hit. Many of its dishes are recognisably Sephardic. So you might start with Yemeni-style bread, *kubaneh* – a yeast bread served with rich tahini and tomato dips – and continue with Moroccan-style chermoula-stuffed sardines. Jew or Gentile doesn't matter: bring an appetite for fun as well as for food.

Shuang Shuang ££
64 Shaftesbury Avenue, W1D 6LU (7734 5416, www.shuangshuang.co.uk). Piccadilly Circus or Leicester Square tube. **Open** *noon-11pm Mon-Thur, Sun; noon-11.30pm Fri, Sat.* **Map** *p163 L8* ⓭ *Chinese*

Specialising in hotpot (an Asian version of a meat fondue, using broth to do the 'cooking'), Shuang Shuang requires concentration. Once you've picked from the mind-boggling array of raw ingredients whizzing round on the *kaiten* (sushi-bar conveyor belt), there's a choice of five broths and eight dipping sauces to decide on – or you can make your own. Each customer then cooks in their own personal bubbling cauldron, which should be turned up high then – once it's bubbling – low again. You'll be equipped with a timer and the friendly staff are on hand to advise. If that all sounds a bit complicated, fill up on snacks such as golden fritters of scallop and prawn with chilli and fresh herbs, or strips of deep-fried pig ear with heaps of cumin, salt and chilli.

Pubs & bars

Experimental Cocktail Club
13A Gerrard Street, W1D 5PS (7434 3559, www.chinatownecc.com). Leicester Square tube. **Open** *6pm-3am Mon-Sat; 6pm-midnight Sun.* **Admission** *£5 after 11pm.* **Map** *p163 L8* ❹

ECC is all elegant opulence, arranged over three floors of an old townhouse. Booking isn't essential (half of the capacity is kept for walk-ins) but is recommended (email only, between noon and 5pm). The cocktails are among London's best: sophisticated, complex and strong – try the Havana (cigar-infused bourbon, marsala wine, Bruichladdich Octomore single malt 'wash').

Shops & services

♥ Cecil Court
Between Charing Cross Road & St Martin's Lane, WC2N (www.cecilcourt.co.uk). Leicester Square tube. **Map** *p163 L8* ❹ *Books & music*

Quaint Cecil Court is known for its antiquarian book, map and print dealers, housed in premises that haven't changed in a hundred years. Notable residents include children's specialist Marchpane (no.16, 7836 8661); 40-year veteran David Drummond of Pleasures of Past Times (no.11, 7836 1142), with his playbills and Victoriana; and the mystical, spiritual and occult specialist Watkins Books (nos.19-21, 7836 2182).

Covent Garden & the Strand

Covent Garden has always been an index of the extremes of London life: on one hand, it used to be the capital's wholesale fruit and veg market; on the other, it has been home since the 1700s to the Royal Opera House, purveyor of that most refined of all the arts.

The masses now descend daily on the restored 19th-century market and its cobbled 'piazza' to peruse the increasingly high-end shops and gawp at the street entertainment, with even the most crowd-averse Londoner finding some aspects appealing: grudgingly the buskers; eagerly the London Transport Museum.

Down towards the Thames on the grubbily historic Strand, the Courtauld Gallery and the vast courtyard of Somerset House are further attractions.

❤ **Don't miss**

1 London Transport Museum *p183*
Fun for all the family, especially train and bus geeks.

2 J Sheekey *p187*
The fish restaurant that's always a star.

3 Vintage Showroom *p189*
An experience as much as a shop.

4 Courtauld Gallery *p191*
A delightfully creaky gallery with paintings by 20th-century masters.

COVENT GARDEN

▶ *Covent Garden or Leicester Square tube.*

Covent Garden was once the property of the medieval Abbey ('convent') of Westminster. After Henry VIII dissolved the monasteries, it passed to John Russell, first Earl of Bedford, in 1552; his family still owns land hereabouts. During the 16th and 17th centuries, they developed the area: the fourth Earl employed Inigo Jones to create the Italianate open square that remains the area's centrepiece.

A market was first documented here in 1640 and grew into London's pre-eminent fruit and vegetable wholesaler, employing over 1,000 porters; its success led to the opening of coffeehouses, theatres, gambling dens and brothels. A flower market was added (which has been, since 1980, the location of the London Transport Museum).

In the second half of the 20th century, it became obvious that the congested streets of central London were unsuitable for such market traffic and the decision was taken to move the traders out. In 1974, with the market gone, the threat of property development loomed for the empty stalls and offices. It was only through demonstrations that the area was saved. It's now a pleasant place for a stroll, especially if you catch it early before the crowds descend.

Covent Garden Piazza

Centred on Covent Garden Piazza, the area now offers a combination of gentrified shops, restaurants and cafés, supplemented by street artists and busking musicians in the lower courtyard. The majority of the entertainment takes place under the portico of **St Paul's Covent Garden**. Tourists favour the 180-year-old covered market, which combines upmarket chain stores with a collection of small, sometimes quirky but often rather twee independent shops. Its handsome architecture is best viewed from the terrace of the Amphitheatre Restaurant in the **Royal Opera House** (reopening spring 2018).

Since 2006, property investor Capco has consumed great chunks of prime real estate in Covent Garden, scooping up property on the Piazza, King Street, James Street, Long Acre and beyond – £780 million of it, to be exact. As a result, a slew of ho-hum shops have been replaced by high-street heavyweights and luxury brands. Fred Perry, Whistles, L'Artisan Parfumier, Kurt Geiger, Ralph Lauren's Rugby brand and Burberry Brit have all appeared. The world's largest **Apple Store** has also set up shop. Perhaps most tellingly, the West Cornwall Pasty Co became a Ladurée café, with waistcoated staff dispensing dainty orange-blossom macaroons where once they trowelled out pasties. Classy restaurateurs have also been lured in: Terroirs and Delaunay are near,

❤ Time to eat & drink

A tapas treat
Barrafina *p185*

Taiwanese street eats
Flesh & Buns *p185*

Middle East fun
The Barbary *p185*

Use your noodle
Kanada-Ya *p186*

Fish is the dish
J Sheekey *p187*

Punjabi grills
Tandoor Chop House *p187*

Steak place
Hawksmoor Seven Dials *p186*

Cocktails with class
Beaufort Bar at the Savoy *p191*

A proper pub
Cross Keys *p187*

Biodynamic wines
Terroirs *p187*

❤ Time to shop

Vintage-inspired fashion
Nigel Cabourn Army Gym *p189*

Beautiful brollies
James Smith & Sons *p188*

Chompable cheese
Neal's Yard Dairy *p188*

Naughty but nice
Coco de Mer *p188*

Marvellous menswear
Natural Selection *p188*

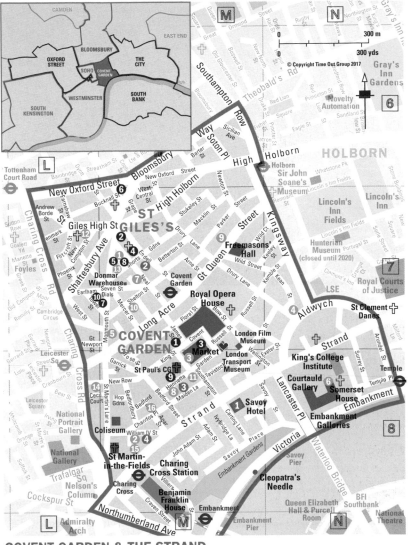

COVENT GARDEN & THE STRAND

Restaurants

1. The Barbary
2. Barrafina
3. Battersea Pie
4. Delaunay
5. Dishoom
6. Fernandez & Wells
7. Flesh & Buns
8. Frenchie
9. Great Queen Street
10. Hawksmoor Seven Dials
11. Ivy Market Grill
12. Kanada-ya
13. Native
14. J Sheekey
15. Tandoor Chop House
16. Wahaca

Pubs & bars

1. Beaufort Bar at the Savoy
2. Cross Keys
3. Dive Bar at Ape & Bird
4. Terroirs

Shops & services

1. Apple Store
2. Arthur Beale
3. Benjamin Pollock's Toy Shop
4. Blackout II
5. Coco de Mer
6. James Smith & Sons
7. Natural Selection
8. Neal's Yard Dairy
9. Nigel Cabourn Army Gym
10. Vintage Showroom

Covent Garden Market

while celeb-magnet the Ivy has opened a new restaurant, **Ivy Market Grill**, right on the piazza.

Change is barely evident elsewhere in Covent Garden. The **Apple Market**, in the North Hall, still has arts and crafts stalls from Tuesday to Sunday, and antiques on Monday. Across the road, the tackier **Jubilee Market** deals mostly in novelty T-shirts and other tat. And the always excellent **London Transport Museum** remains the stand-out attraction.

Elsewhere in Covent Garden

Outside Covent Garden Piazza, the area offers a mixed bag of entertainment, eateries and shops. Nearest the markets, most of the

In the know
Acton up

There's plenty to fill a morning in the London Transport Museum (see p183), but real transport geeks should get on a themed tour of the **Museum Depot** in Acton (most cost £8-£10; pre-book on 7565 7298 or at ticketfeed.ltmuseum.co.uk). This is where Transport for London stores all the stuff it can't display – more than 370,000 objects, ranging from minutiae all the way up to vehicles. The Depot also hosts two Open Weekends a year. It's heaven for the infrastructurally inclined.

more unusual shops have been superseded by a homogeneous mass of cafés, while big fashion chains – and the **St Martin's Courtyard mall** (www.stmartinscourtyard. co.uk) – have all but domesticated Long Acre. There are more interesting stores north of here on Neal Street and Monmouth Street; Earlham Street is also home to the **Donmar Warehouse** (see p364), a former banana-ripening depot that's now an intimate and groundbreaking theatre. On tiny Shorts Gardens next door is the **Neal's Yard Dairy**, purveyor of exceptional UK cheeses; down a passageway one door along is Neal's Yard itself, a pleasant courtyard with communal seating.

South of Long Acre and east of the Piazza, historical depravity was called to account at the former **Bow Street Magistrates Court**. Once home to the Bow Street Runners, the precursors of the Metropolitan Police, this was also where the Krays were famously tried and Oscar Wilde entered his plea when arrested for 'indecent acts' in 1895. It was snapped up by Qatari investors in 2016 and is set to become a £125million luxury hotel.

To the south, Wellington and Catherine streets mix restaurants and theatres, including the grand **Theatre Royal** (0844 412 4660, www.reallyusefultheatres. co.uk). Other diversions in and around Covent Garden include the museum at **Freemasons' Hall** (7395 9257, www. freemasonry.london.museum, call for details of tours), the eye-catchingly bombastic white stone building where Long

❤ London Transport Museum

Covent Garden Piazza, WC2E 7BB (7379 6344, www.ltmuseum.co.uk). Covent Garden tube. **Open** *10am-6pm Mon-Thur, Sat, Sun; 11am-6pm Fri.* **Admission** *£17.50; £15 reductions; free under-18s.* **Map** *p181 M7.*

Londoners and their transport, eh? There's no need to keep banging on about it, you might think. We beg to differ. Most Londoners spend more time commuting than they do having lunch, and their city's prodigious growth in Victorian times into the biggest, most flabbergastingly exciting and frankly unpleasant city the world had ever known was largely down to transport infrastructure, which supported an unprecedented population explosion.

It is this story that the London Transport Museum tells so well, tracing the city's transport history from the horse age to the present day. The museum also raises some interesting and important questions about the future of public transport in the city, even offering a fanciful imagining of London's travel network in the years ahead.

Engaging and inspiring, the Transport Museum's focus is on social history and design, which are illustrated by a superb array of preserved buses, trams and trains, backed up by some impressively solid temporary exhibitions. The collections are in broadly chronological order, beginning with the Victorian gallery, where a replica of Shillibeer's first horse-drawn bus service from 1829 takes pride of place. Along the way there is a Northern line simulator to drive, and train carriages and buses to jump on and climb up.

A new permanent gallery, London by Design, explores how, under the leadership of Frank Pick in the early 20th century, London Transport developed one of the most coherent brand identities in the world: that roundel, which now means tube station with no need for words, is down to him. The gallery also explores some of the network's enduring industrial design and arresting poster art from the likes of Abram Games, Graham Sutherland and Ivon Hitchens.

All in all, it's a great place for families, with younger children especially enjoying the small but terrific play zone, All Aboard, where they can repair a mini Tube train, make passenger announcements and operate the Emirates Air Line cable car – get there early if you don't want your gorgeous child overrun by everyone else's herberts.
▶ *For the Acton depot, see opposite.*

Royal Opera House

Acre becomes Great Queen Street; and the **Coliseum** (*see p357*), home of the English National Opera.

Sights & museums

London Film Museum
45 Wellington Street, WC2E 7BN (7836 4913, www.londonfilmmuseum.com). Covent Garden tube. **Open** *10am-6pm Mon-Fri, Sun; 10am-7pm Sat. Last entry 1hr before closing time.* **Admission** *£14.50; £9.50 reductions; £38 family; free under-5s. Tickets are available online in advance.* **Map** *p181 M7.*

'Bond In Motion', an exhibition of swanky vehicles from the James Bond films, has become a permanent feature at the London Film Museum's Covent Garden showroom. On display are cars, boats, motorbikes, sleds and jets including the Rolls-Royce Phantom III from *Goldfinger* (1964), the Aston Martin DB5 from *GoldenEye* (1995) and 'Wet Nellie' the underwater Lotus Esprit S1 from *The Spy Who Loved Me* (1977). The display also features action sequence boards, vehicle concept art, props and miniature models including the 1/3 scale model of AgustaWestland's AW101 helicopter, used during the filming of *Skyfall* (2012).

In the know
Cinema-bilia

The **London Film Museum** (see *above*) is stuffed with eye-catching props and memorabilia, but serious film buffs might prefer the **Cinema Museum** (see *p322*), whose collection spans a longer time period – all the way back to the 1890s – and includes projects, signage and other rarities.

Royal Opera House
Bow Street, WC2E 9DD (7304 4000, www. roh.org.uk). Covent Garden tube. **Open** *tours at 10.30am, 12.30pm, 2.30pm Mon-Sat.* **Admission** *tours £12; £11 reductions.* **Map** *p181 M7.*

The ROH was founded in 1732 by John Rich on the profits of his production of John Gay's *Beggar's Opera*; the current building, constructed roughly 150 years ago but extensively remodelled since, is the third on the site. Visitors can explore the massive eight-floor building as part of an organised tour, including the main auditorium, the costume workshops and sometimes even a rehearsal. Certain parts of the building are usually open to the general public – the glass-roofed Paul Hamlyn Hall, the Crush Bar (so named because in Victorian times the only thing served during intermission was orange and lemon crush) and the Amphitheatre Restaurant & Terrace, which has great views over the covered market – but until redevelopment work for the 'Open Up' project is complete (probably in spring 2018), entry is by tour or for those with valid performance tickets only. For music and ballet at the **Royal Opera House**, *see p358*.

St Paul's Covent Garden
Bedford Street, WC2E 9ED (7836 5221, www. actorschurch.org). Covent Garden tube. **Open** *8.30am-5pm Mon-Fri; 9am-1pm Sun (5pm when there is Evensong). Times vary Sat; phone for details.* **Services** *1.10pm Tue, Wed; 11am Sun. Choral Evensong 4pm 2nd Sun of mth.* **Admission** *free; donations appreciated.* **Map** *p181 M8.*

Known as the Actors' Church for its long association with Covent Garden's theatres, this pleasingly spare building was designed by Inigo Jones in 1631. A lovely limewood wreath by the 17th-century master carver Grinling Gibbons hangs inside the front door as a reminder that he and his wife are interred in the crypt. But most visitors come to see the memorial plaques: many thespians are commemorated here, among them Vivien Leigh, Charlie Chaplin and Hattie Jacques of *Carry On* fame.

Restaurants

♥ The Barbary ££
*16 Neal's Yard, WC2H 9DP (thebarbary. co.uk). Covent Garden tube. **Open** noon-3pm, 5-10pm Mon-Fri; noon-1pm Sat; noon-9.30pm Sun. No reservations. **Map** p181 M7* ❶ *North African*

The Barbary takes everything that's good about its sister restaurant Palomar (*see p177*) and reinvents it. Seating is on 24 stools arranged at a horseshoe-shaped counter bar. Down one wall, there's a standing counter, where they'll feed you snacks like deep-fried pastry 'cigars' filled with cod, lemon and Moroccan spices while you wait for a seat. And the food – inspired by the eponymous Barbary coast, which stretches from Morocco to Egypt – is heady with smoke and North African spices. The signature *naan e beber*, made to an ancient recipe, emerges from the fiercely hot tandoor deliciously fluffy and blistered. Main courses such as slow-braised octopus with oranges cooked over a coal-fired *robata* are impossibly tender; while *knafeh* (filo pastry filled with goat's cheese and pan-fried until it's crispy on the outside, chewy on the inside, and sprinkled with roasted pistachio nuts) is dessert heaven.

♥ Barrafina ££
*10 Adelaide Street, WC2N 4HZ (7440 1456, www.barrafina.co.uk). Charing Cross or Leicester Square tube. **Open** noon-3pm, 5-11pm Mon-Sat; 1-3.30pm, 5.30-10pm Sun. No reservations. **Map** p181 M8* ❷ *Tapas*

Like its predecessor in Soho, Barrafina Covent Garden takes no reservations, so arrive early – or late – if you don't want to queue at this perennially popular tapas restaurant. The menu is studded with tempting Mallorcan and Catalan dishes, but watch out if you're properly hungry: the bill adds up fast. Despite the fancy prices, remember that Barrafina is a modern Spanish tapas bar rather than a restaurant per se – that means that the list of sherries, cavas and other wines by the glass are as much a part of the appeal as the food, and perfect for experimenting with as you nibble. For the latest triumph from the same owners, *see p91*.

Battersea Pie £
*Lower ground floor, 28 The Market, WC2E 8RA (7240 9566, www.batterseapiestation. co.uk). Covent Garden tube. **Open** 11am-7pm Mon-Thur, Sun; 11am-8pm Fri, Sat. **Map** p181 M7* ❸ *British*

Serving proper British food at bargain prices, this pie-and-mash house is something of an anomaly in Covent Garden Market. Housed in one of the refurbished subterranean arches, it retains the traditional exterior and flagstone floor, but the fixtures and fittings are stylish and modern: bright white tiles, polished marble tables and a shiny counter. Besides traditional fillings such as steak and mushroom with stout are less expected versions, such as butternut squash and goat's cheese. Even for a counter-service place, this is a terrific little caff.

Dishoom ££
*12 Upper St Martin's Lane, WC2H 9FB (7420 9320, www.dishoom.com). Covent Garden or Leicester Square tube. **Open** 8am-11pm Mon-Thur; 8am-midnight Fri; 9am-midnight Sat; 9am-11pm Sun. **Map** p181 M7* ❺ *Pan-Indian*

A swish, self-styled 'Bombay café', Dishoom is filled with retro features: whirring ceiling fans, low-level lighting and vintage Bollywood posters. The place is crowded all day, from breakfast (for sausage naan rolls with chilli jam) to dinner (for the usual curries and tandoori grills). Quality can vary: *vada pau* (potato croquettes with sharp chutney in a fluffy Portuguese-style bun) and *bhel* (crunchy puffed rice with tangy tamarind chutney) are tasty; kebabs and curries are fairly standard renditions. There are also Dishooms on nearby Drury Lane, Soho's Dean Street and just off Granary Square in King's Cross.

♥ Flesh & Buns ££
*41 Earlham Street, WC2H 9LX (7632 9500, www.bonedaddies.com/flesh-and-buns). Covent Garden tube. **Open** noon-3pm, 5-10.30pm Mon, Tue; noon-3pm, 5-11pm Wed-Fri; noon-11pm Sat; noon-9.30pm Sun. **Map** p181 M7* ❼ *Taiwanese*

Flesh & Buns is hidden in a capacious basement, with industrial-chic decor and young, pierced and tattooed staff setting the tone. It serves hirata buns – a US take on Taiwanese street food – with a side order of rock music. Sweet, fluffy dough is folded, then steamed and brought to table. Diners then stuff these pockets with their choice of 'flesh'. Mustard miso and a few slices of subtly pickled apple make a foil for tender pulled pork; crisp-skinned grilled sea bass is served with fresh tomato salsa.

Frenchie £££

16 Henrietta Street, WC2E 8QH (7836 4422, www.frenchiecoventgarden.com). Covent Garden or Leicester Square tube. **Open** *noon-2.15pm, 5.30-10.30pm Mon-Fri; noon-2.15pm, 6-10.30pm Sat, Sun.* **Map** *p181 M8* ⑧ *French*

You'll have to be patient to secure a booking at Gregory Marchand's tiny Parisian-style bistro but, like its original French counterpart, it's worth the wait. Tucked away down a cobbled alley, Frenchie is all about impeccably composed modern European small plates – the menu might only list three ingredients but each dish is deceptively sophisticated. Playful starters include maple-sweetened bacon scones, still warm from the oven, or rich eggs mimosa with strands of black truffle. The signature pulled pig slider is a must-try, thanks to its house-smoked meat and lightly pickled, crunchy red cabbage. Be sure to pace yourself for a dazzling pud: the moist lemon polenta cake, served with silky ice-cream and morsels of honeycomb (for sweet) and dehydrated kalamata olives (for salt).

Great Queen Street ££

32 Great Queen Street, WC2B 5AA (7242 0622, www.greatqueenstreetrestaurant.co.uk). Covent Garden or Holborn tube. **Open** *Bar 5pm-midnight Tue-Sat. Restaurant noon-2.30pm, 5.30-10.30pm Mon-Sat; 1-3.30pm Sun.* **Map** *p181 M7* ⑨ *British*

The excellent location ensures Great Queen Street's popularity. The outdoor tables are almost never vacant, but walk-ins may find space at the bar, where the full menu is served. The menu changes daily, is produce-led and is predominantly British. There's minimal fussing with ingredients: a plump piece of bone-in smoked mackerel might be served with a dollop each of cooked gooseberries and horseradish; slow-cooked pork could arrive in a stew with a generous quantity of cockles.

❤ Hawksmoor Seven Dials £££

11 Langley Street,WC2H 9JG (7420 9390, thehawksmoor.com). Covent Garden tube. **Open** *noon-3pm, 5-10.30pm Mon-Thur; noon-3pm, 5-11pm Fri, Sat; noon-9.30pm Sun.* **Map** *p181 M7* ⑩ *Steakhouse*

The short main menu centres on steak (ribeye, T-bone, porterhouse, fillet, sirloin and more), at serious prices, plus the likes of grilled chicken, lobster with garlic butter, monkfish grilled over charcoal, and a meat-free choice for the odd misplaced vegetarian. A good kick-off is one of Hawksmoor's renowned cocktails.

Ivy Market Grill £££

1 Henrietta Street, WC2E 8PS (3301 0200, www.theivymarketgrill.com). Covent Garden tube. **Open** *8am-midnight Mon-Sat; 8am-11pm Sun.* **Map** *p181 M8* ⑪ *Modern European*

If you're after a culinary superstar, go elsewhere, but this is no mere cash-in on the celeb-courted **Ivy** (1-5 West Street, WC2H 9NQ, 7836 4751, www.the-ivy.co.uk) – and it's bang on the Piazza. The interior's lovely, in a classy, bourgeois brasserie, my-family-own-Dorset kind of way, and the menu's a good read too, with a pleasingly retro Continental feel to dishes that use mainly British ingredients. You aren't going to spot any A-listers round here, but we like the place: it's good-looking, with good service, opens late and serves breakfast, tea and all-day snacks.

❤ Kanada-Ya £

64 St Giles High Street, WC2H 8LE (7240 0232, www.kanada-ya.com). Tottenham Court Road tube. **Open** *noon-3pm, 5-10.30pm Mon-Fri; noon-3pm, 5-11pm Sat; noon-8.30pm Sun. No reservations.* **Map** *p181 L7* ⑫ *Japanese*

Small, brightly lit and minimal, this is not the place for a leisurely meal: there are always lengthy mealtime queues outside its doors. But there's a reason for Kanada-Ya's already-large fan base: exceptional ramen. If you don't eat pork, forget it; but those pork bones are simmered for 18 hours to create the smooth, rich, seriously savoury *tonkotsu* broth – one of the best in London. If you don't have much time, the wait at Ippudo, just opposite, is always more bearable than that at Kanada-ya.

Native ££

3 Neal's Yard, WC2H 9DP (3638 8214, www.eatnative.co.uk). Covent Garden tube. **Open** *12.30-2.30pm, 5.30-10pm Mon-Sat.* **Map** *p181 M7* ⑬ *British*

With sprigs of greens festooning whitewashed walls, fresh flowers on the tables and a menu inspired by wild British food, Native is an exciting restaurant with a free spirit. Venison features on the menu year-round, while, in season, ramson (wild garlic) pokes up like an unruly but delicious weed: in a fragrant broth of teeny palourde clams with pheasant and pig's trotter, perhaps. Other star turns included a trendy 'open' kebab of pink pigeon chunks beautifully offset by lightly pickled cabbage and a harissa-spiked sweet beetroot houmous. It's all delicately presented and reasonably priced, leaving you feeling calm and wholesome.

♥ J Sheekey £££
*28-32 St Martin's Court, WC2N 4AL (7240 2565, www.j-sheekey.co.uk). Leicester Square tube. **Open** noon-3pm, 5pm-midnight Mon-Fri; noon-3pm, 5.15pm-midnight Sat; noon-3.30pm, 5.30-10.30pm Sun. **Map** p181 L8* ⓮ *Fish & seafood*

After well over a century of service, Sheekey's status as a West End institution is assured. With its monochrome photos of stars of stage and screen, wooden panelling and cream crackle walls, and array of silver dishes atop thick white tablecloths, it oozes old-fashioned glamour. The menu runs from super-fresh oysters and shellfish via old-fashioned snacks (herring roe on toast) to upmarket classics (dover sole, lobster thermidor). The fish pie – a rich, comforting treat – is acclaimed, but we feel the shrimp and scallop burger merits similar status.

Adjoining Sheekey restaurant, J Sheekey Oyster Bar (nos.33-35, www.jsheekeyatlanticbar.co.uk) serves a similar menu – with an expanded range of oysters – to customers sitting at the counter.

♥ Tandoor Chop House ££
*8 Adelaide Street, WC2N 4HZ (3096 0359, tandoorchophouse.com). Charing Cross tube. **Open** 11.30am-11.30pm Mon-Fri; noon-11pm Sat; 1-10pm Sun. **Map** p181 M8* ⓯ *Indian*

This slightly less hectic, more refined mini-me version of the original branch of **Dishoom** (*see p185*) is by no means derivative. With cheerfully attentive service and a bustling Bombay vibe, it's a twist on what you'd get in an old-fashioned Brit 'chop house', only using Indo-Punjabi spices and swapping the grill for the tandoor. Plates are small and meant for sharing. Start with the pistachio-studded seekh kebab strewn with pomegranate seeds and coriander, or the 'beef dripping' keema naan. For mains, be sure to try the thickly marinated, fatty-edged lamb chops, all soot and spice, or the juice spice-rubbed rib-eye. But don't stop there: the malted kulfi ice cream is silky smooth and intense, served with chunks of caramelised banana and salted peanuts.

Wahaca £
*66 Chandos Place, WC2N 4HG (7240 1883, www.wahaca.co.uk). Covent Garden or Embankment tube. **Open** noon-11pm Mon-Sat; noon-10.30pm Sun. **Map** p181 M8* ⓰ *Mexican*

Thomasina Miers' Mexican 'market food' concept is a successful chain, now with a dozen branches across London. The restaurants share a cheery vibe, with young, efficient staff buzzing round bright interiors. The food is pleasant rather than especially memorable. Tortillas loom large – in soft, crisp, toasted and chip variations, and in flour and corn versions – though there are also a few grills (fish, steak or chicken served with green rice). The steak burrito is a particular favourite.

Pubs & bars

♥ Cross Keys
*31 Endell Street, WC2H 9BA (7836 5185, www.crosskeyscoventgarden.com). Covent Garden tube. **Open** 11am-11pm Mon-Sat; noon-10.30m Sun. **Map** p181 M7* ❷

Central London pubs with a local vibe are the rarest of things, but the Cross Keys is precisely that. With its canopy of copper implements, garish carpet and walls covered in vintage beeraphernalia, it feels like it hasn't changed for 30 years. Despite the local competition, it makes zero effort to appeal to tourists, which is ironic, since sipping a pint in the failing sunlight amid wafts from the nearby chippie is one of the most perfectly London experiences you'll get in the West End.

Dive Bar at Ape & Bird
*Basement, 142 Shaftesbury Avenue, WC2H 8HJ (7836 3119, www.polpo.co.uk). Leicester Square tube. **Open** 11.30am-11pm Mon-Sat; 11.30am-10pm Sun. **Map** p181 M8* ❸

Take the back entrance at the Ape & Bird restaurant and immediately head downstairs to enter a dusky, rustic cavern with bare concrete walls and a few flickering candles. This is where Soho and Covent Garden media types sip negronis until it's as dark outside as it is inside. Like the restaurant above (from the excellent Polpo minichain), Dive Bar is Venetian-inspired (Aperol, Campari and Cynar mixes dominate the cocktails) and it serves some of the best spritzers in town. A great hideaway in an area choked with touristy pubs.

♥ Terroirs
*5 William IV Street, WC2N 4DW (7036 0660, www.terroirswinebar.com). Charing Cross tube/rail. **Open** noon-11pm Mon-Sat. Food served noon-3pm, 5.30-11pm Mon-Sat. **Map** p181 M8* ❹

Terroirs – a wine bar with excellent food – is really two places under one roof. The always-crowded ground floor has a casual feel and a menu to match, focused on small plates for sharing. You can sample some of the same dishes in the atmospheric and surprisingly roomy basement, which feels more like a restaurant: the menu here, with its focus on rustic French dishes, seems designed to guide diners more towards a more traditional starter-main-dessert approach. The wine list is an encyclopaedia of organic and biodynamic bottles.

Shops & services

Apple Store

1-7 The Piazza, WC2E 8HB (7447 1400, www. apple.com/uk/retail). Covent Garden tube. **Open** *10am-8pm Mon-Sat; noon-6pm Sun.* **Map** *p181 M7* ❶ *Electronics & photography*

A temple to geekery, this is the world's biggest Apple Store, with separate rooms – set out over three storeys – devoted to each product line. The exposed brickwork, big old oak tables and stone floors make it an inviting place, and it's also the world's first Apple Store with a Start Up Room, where staff will help to set up your new iPad, iPhone, iPod or Mac, or transfer files from your old computer to your new one – all for free.

Arthur Beale

194 Shaftesbury Avenue, WC2H 8JP (7836 9034, www.arthurbeale.co.uk). Tottenham Court Road tube. **Open** *10am-7pm Mon-Wed, Fri, Sat; 10am-8pm Thur; 11am-5pm Sun.* **Map** *p181 M7* ❷ *Boat equipment*

There are some odd shops in London, but few beat the surprise factor of finding a yacht chandler in Shaftesbury Avenue. It may look old-fashioned but, for sailors, Arthur Beale's stock is as useful now as it ever was. On the ground floor you'll find everything from reels of rope, ship's bells, barometers and navigation lights to boating hardware such as cleats, fairleads and lacing hooks. Upstairs, there are books, boots and lifejackets.

Benjamin Pollock's Toy Shop

44 The Market, WC2E 8RF (7379 7866, www.pollocks-coventgarden.co.uk). Covent Garden tube. **Open** *10.30am-6pm Mon-Wed; 10.30am-6.30pm Thur-Sat; 11am-6pm Sun.* **Map** *p181 M8* ❸ *Children*

Best known for its Victorian-style cardboard toy theatres, Pollock's is also great for traditional toys such as knitted animals, china tea sets, masks, glove puppets, cards, spinning tops and fortune-telling fish.

Blackout II

52 Endell Street, WC2H 9AJ (7240 5006, www.blackout2.com). Covent Garden tube. **Open** *11am-7pm Mon-Fri; 11.30am-6.30pm Sat.* **Map** *p181 M7* ❹ *Vintage clothing*

There are dozens of good vintage stores in London, but this remains a firm favourite. Blackout II has been providing bright and beautiful frocks, handbags, shoes and all the trimmings for more than two-and-a-half decades. Here, you will find a wonderful array of dress-up clothes, from 1930s cocktail frocks to full-skirted '50s dresses and some slinky numbers that might have graced the sets of *Dynasty*. It's is a magpie's dream of costume jewellery, and also does clothing hire.

♥ Coco de Mer

23 Monmouth Street, WC2H 9DD (7836 8882, www.coco-de-mer.com). Covent Garden tube. **Open** *11am-7pm Mon-Sat; noon-6pm Sun.* **Map** *p181 M7* ❺ *Accessories*

London's most glamorous erotic emporium sells a variety of tasteful books, toys and lingerie, from glass dildos that double as objets d'art to a Marie Antoinette costume of crotchless culottes and corset. Trying on items can be fun as well: the peepshow-style velvet changing rooms allow your lover to peer through and watch you undress from a 'confession box' next door.

♥ James Smith & Sons

Hazelwood House, 53 New Oxford Street, WC1A 1BL (7836 4731, www.james-smith. co.uk). Holborn or Tottenham Court Road tube. **Open** *10am-5.45pm Mon-Fri; 10am-5.15pm Sat.* **Map** *p181 M7* ❻ *Accessories*

Nearly 190 years after it was established, this charming shop, with Victorian fittings still intact, is holding its own in the niche market of umbrellas and walking sticks. The stock here isn't the throwaway type of brolly that breaks at the first sign of a breeze. The lovingly crafted brollies – perhaps a classic City umbrella with a malacca cane handle at £175 – are built to last. A repair service is also offered.

♥ Natural Selection

46 Monmouth Street, WC2H 9LE (7240 3506, naturalselectionlondon.com). Covent Garden tube. **Open** *10.30am-7pm Mon-Sat; 11am-5pm Sun.* **Map** *p181 M7* ❼ *Menswear*

Originally a denim brand that took its name from Darwin's book *The Origin of Species by Means of Natural Selection*, Natural Selection has since branched out into a full ready-to-wear range of smart-casual essentials for men. Everything here is understated, but has a touch of sports luxe too. In the airy, stripped-back store, you can also get hold of a selection of fragrances, eyewear and accessories from brands like Thierry Lasry and No.288 footwear.

♥ Neal's Yard Dairy

17 Shorts Gardens, WC2H 9AT (7240 5700, www.nealsyarddairy.co.uk). Covent Garden tube. **Open** *10am-7pm Mon-Sat.* **Map** *p181 M7* ❽ *Food & drink*

Neal's Yard buys from small farms and creameries and matures the cheeses in its own cellars until they're ready to sell in peak condition. Names such as Stinking Bishop and Lincolnshire Poacher are as evocative as the aromas in the shop. It's best to walk in and ask what's good today: you'll be given tasters by the well-trained staff.

If you're gourmet shopping in **Borough Market** (*see p92*) , you'll find another branch of **Neal's Yard Dairy** (6 Park Street, Borough, SE1 9AB, 7367 0799, www. nealsyarddairy.co.uk).

♥ Nigel Cabourn Army Gym
28 Henrietta Street, WC2E 8NA (7240 1005, www.cabourn.com). Covent Garden tube. **Open** *11am-6.30pm Mon-Wed, Fri, Sat; 11am-7pm Thur; noon-5pm Sun.* **Map** *p181 M8* **❾** *Menswear*

This is the only Cabourn shop outside Japan, selling the hallowed designer's vintage-inspired collections, dreamed to life by consulting his vast personal archive of over 4,000 pieces. As the name might suggest, you're guaranteed to be able to get hold of some camo here, but there's also a solid amount of smart tailoring and shirting, all drawing on the best of British design.

♥ Vintage Showroom
14 Earlham Street, Seven Dials, WC2H 9LN (7836 3964, www.thevintageshowroom.com). Covent Garden tube. **Open** *varies.* **Map** *p181 L7* **❿** *Vintage menswear*

In the old FW Collins & Sons ironmongery, Roy Luckett and Doug Gunn show a tiny selection of their famous west London menswear archive, which they routinely loan out to big-name designers, denim brands and vintage obsessives. With stock sourced from around the world (Roy and Doug have some hair-raising stories of dealings with collectors and hoarders in obscure locations), it follows that the pair occasionally find it hard to part with an item, and they've been known to try to dissuade shoppers from buying the rarer pieces on display. But the shop has London's best men's vintage collection, with an emphasis on Americana (denim, sweats, a few choice tees) and classic military and British pieces.

THE STRAND, EMBANKMENT & ALDWYCH

▶*Embankment or Temple tube, or Charing Cross tube/rail.*

Until as recently as the 1860s, the Strand ran beside the Thames; indeed, it was originally the river's bridlepath. In the 14th century, it was lined with grand residences with gardens that ran down to the water. It wasn't

Cleopatra's Needle

until the 1870s that the Thames was pushed back with the creation of the Embankment and its adjacent gardens. By the time George Newnes's famed *Strand* magazine was introducing its readership to Sherlock Holmes (1891), the street boasted the Cecil Hotel (long since demolished), **Simpson's** (still going, under chef Gerry Rae), King's College and **Somerset House**. Prime Minister Benjamin Disraeli described it as 'perhaps the finest street in Europe'. While nobody would make such a claim today, there's still plenty to interest visitors.

In 1292, the body of Eleanor of Castile, consort to King Edward I, completed its funerary procession from Lincoln to the small hamlet of Charing, at the western end of what is now the Strand. The occasion was marked by the erection of the last of 12 elaborate crosses. A replica of the **Eleanor Cross** (originally set just south of nearby Trafalgar Square; *see p102*) was placed in 1865 on the forecourt of Charing Cross Station; it remains there today, looking like the spire of a sunken cathedral. Across the road, behind **St Martin-in-the-Fields** (*see p102*), is Maggi Hambling's weird memorial to a more recent queen, *A Conversation with Oscar Wilde*.

The Embankment itself can be reached down Villiers Street. Pass through the tube station to the point at which boat tours with on-board entertainment depart. Just to the east stands **Cleopatra's Needle**, an obelisk presented to the British nation by the viceroy of Egypt, Mohammed Ali, in 1820 but not set in place by the river for a further 59 years. The obelisk was originally erected around 1500 BC by the pharaoh Tuthmosis

Near the bottom of Carting Lane, one of the alleys down beside the **Savoy**, is an unusually fat lamp-post. This is, in fact, one of the last remaining sewage lamps in London: its light is powered by fumes from underground, funnelled up the post to be safely burnt off as fuel.

III at a site near modern-day Cairo, before being moved to Alexandria, Cleopatra's capital, in 10 BC. By this time, however, the great queen was 20 years dead.

Back on the Strand, the majestic **Savoy Hotel** (7836 4343, www.fairmont.com/savoy-london) was first opened in 1889, financed by profits from Richard D'Oyly Carte's productions of Gilbert and Sullivan's light operas at the neighbouring **Savoy Theatre**. The theatre, which pre-dates the hotel by eight years, was the first to use electric lights. Two grand hotels guard Aldwych, at the eastern end of the Strand: **One Aldwych** (7300 1000, www.onealdwych.com) and, directly opposite, **ME by Meliá London** (7395 3400, www.melia.com). This grand crescent dates only from 1905, but the name 'ald wic' (old settlement or market) has its origins in the tenth century. To the south is **Somerset House**. Almost in front of it is **St Mary-le-Strand** (7836 3126, www.stmarylestrand.org, 11am-4pm Mon-Fri, 10am-3pm Sun), James Gibbs's first public building, completed in 1717. On Strand Lane, reached via Surrey Street, is the so-called 'Roman' bath where Dickens took the waters – you have to peer through a dusty window.

On a traffic island just east of Aldwych is **St Clement Danes** (7242 8282, www.raf.mod.uk/stclementdanes). It's believed that a church was first built here by the Danish in the ninth century and dedicated to one of the many patron saints of mariners, but the current building is mainly Wren's handiwork. It's the principal church of the RAF. Just beyond the church are the **Royal Courts of Justice** and the original site of **Temple Bar** (for both, *see p222*).

Sights & museums

Benjamin Franklin House
36 Craven Street, WC2N 5NF (7925 1405, www.benjaminfranklinhouse.org). Charing Cross tube/rail. **Open** *box office 10.30am-5pm. Entry by tour only. Historical tours at noon, 1pm, 2pm, 3.15pm, 4.15pm Wed-Sun. Architectural tours at noon, 1pm, 2pm, 3.15pm, 4.15pm Mon.* **Admission** *£6-£8; free under-16s.* **Map** *p181 M8.*

This is the house where Franklin – scientist, diplomat, philosopher, inventor and Founding Father of the US – lived between 1757 and 1775. It isn't a museum in the conventional sense: there are few artefacts on display. Rather, it is explored through 45-minute 'historical experiences' (booking advised). These are led by an actress playing Franklin's landlady's daughter, Polly Hewson, using sound and visual projections on the plain walls of the house to conjure

As a rule, we're not the kind of travel guide that recommends cashpoints – but the lobby of the Law Courts branch of Lloyds bank (222 Strand, WC2R 1BB), just east of **St Clement Danes** (*see left*), is a thing of beauty – all richly coloured Doulton tiles and Victorian domestic-industrial loveliness. It opened as a restaurant in 1883, failed, failed again, and reopened as a Lloyds in 1895.

Somerset House

up the world in which Franklin lived. On Mondays, as an alternative to the Historical Experience tours, there are 20-minute Architectural tours.

♥ Courtauld Gallery
Somerset House, Strand, WC2R 0RN (7848 2777, www.courtauld.ac.uk/gallery). Temple tube. **Open** *10am-6pm daily.* **Admission** *£7; £6 reductions; students, unwaged & under-18s free.* **Map** *p181 N8.*

Located for the last two decades in the north wing of **Somerset House** (*see below*), the Courtauld has one of Britain's greatest collections of paintings, including several works of world importance. Although there are some outstanding early works (Cranach's *Adam & Eve*, for one), the collection's strongest suit is in Impressionism and Post-Impressionism. Popular masterpieces here include Manet's *A Bar at the Folies-Bergère*, but there are also superb works by Monet and Cézanne, important Gauguins, and some Van Goghs and Seurats. On the top floor, there's a selection of gorgeous Fauvist pieces and a lovely room of Kandinskys. Hidden downstairs, the little gallery café is delightful. Deposit bulky bags in the lockers downstairs.

Somerset House & the Embankment Galleries
Strand, WC2R 1LA (7845 4600, www. somersethouse.org.uk). Temple tube. **Open** *10am-6pm Mon, Tue, Sat, Sun (last entry to galleries 5pm); 11am-8pm Wed-Fri (last entry to galleries 7pm). Tours Tue, Thur, Sat.* **Admission** *Courtyard & terrace free. Embankment Galleries prices vary. Tours free; check website for details.* **Map** *p181 N8.*

The original Somerset House was a Tudor palace commissioned by the Duke of Somerset. In 1775, it was demolished to make way for the first purpose-built office block in the world. Architect Sir William Chambers spent the last 20 years of his life working on this neoclassical edifice overlooking the Thames, built to accommodate learned societies such as the Royal Academy and government departments. The taxmen are still here, but the rest of the building is open to the public. Attractions include the **Courtauld** (*see above*), the handsome fountain court and several eating options: from a terrace café and **Fernandez &**

Wells to Skye Gyngell's **Spring**, a pricey Italian restaurant. Several rooms around the courtyard are used to host lively art exhibitions. Downstairs on the Thames side of the building, the **Embankment Galleries** house exhibitions on a grander scale, and a Christmas market.

Restaurants
Delaunay £££
55 Aldwych, WC2B 4BB (7499 8558, www. thedelaunay.com). Covent Garden or Temple tube. **Open** *7am-midnight Mon-Fri; 8am-midnight Sat; 9am-11pm Sun.* **Map** *p181 N7* ❹ *Brasserie*

European grand cafés are the inspiration here, resulting in a striking interior of green leather banquette seating, dark wood, antique mirrors and a black-and-white marble floor. The menu runs from breakfast to dinner, taking in afternoon tea (try the Austrian-biased cakes, all made in-house). There's a dish of the day, soups, sandwiches, salads and egg dishes, plus savouries and crustacea. If the restaurant at Delaunay is full, try the no-bookings Counter café next door for cakes.

Fernandez & Wells £
East Wing, Somerset House, Strand, WC2R 1LA (7420 9408, www.fernandezandwells. com). Temple tube. **Open** *8am-10pm Mon, Tue; 8am-11pm Wed-Fri; 9am-10pm Sat; 9am-6pm Sun.* **Map** *p181 N8* ❻ *Café*

Four rooms in the east wing of Somerset House (*see left*) are set up for all-day grazing. Meat is central: the 'ham room' has carved slices of *lomito ibérico, jamón de lampiño*, or wild fennel Tuscan salami, while *morcilla* and the like arrive from an open grill. Breakfasts are simple but good. There's a scattering of Fernandez & Wells throughout the city.

Pubs & bars
♥ Beaufort Bar at the Savoy
The Savoy, 100 Strand, WC2R 0EW (7836 4343, www.fairmont.com/savoy-london). Charing Cross tube/rail or Embankment tube. **Open** *5pm-1am Mon-Sat.* **Map** *p181 M8* ❶

Set in London's most famous hotel, the ultra-suave Beaufort Bar is quite possibly the most attractive space to sip a drink in the city. Just off the busy lobby, it's a hideaway of supreme style and opulence, with jet-black walls, theatrical lighting and enough discreet touches of gold to remind you you're somewhere special. The drinks live up to the ambience, pushing the boundaries of mixology and incorporating fizz to great effect.

Bloomsbury & King's Cross

London's neighbourhoods north of Oxford Street are bookish and bohemian. Bloomsbury is best known as the home of the British Museum, but also has a handful of delightful small museums. To the west, Fitzrovia is a favourite source of stories for London nostalgists, but the days of post-war spivs and drunken poets have given way to an era of new-media offices. At least they keep the pubs lively and the quality of the restaurants high. To the north of Bloomsbury, the legendarily seedy King's Cross has gone the way of formerly raffish Fitzrovia, with the arrival of the British Library, the rebirth of St Pancras Station as an international rail hub and the emergence of the shiny new King's Cross Central district.

❤ Don't miss

1 British Museum *p198*
A treasure trove.

2 Wellcome Collection *p200*
Science made scintillating.

3 Roka *p209*
Treat yourself: robata grilled food and jewel-like sushi in a very glamorous location.

4 Novelty Automation *p199 and p201*
Coin-op giggles.

5 London Review Bookshop *p202*
Find yourself some inspiration.

HAJESTY QUEEN

British Museum

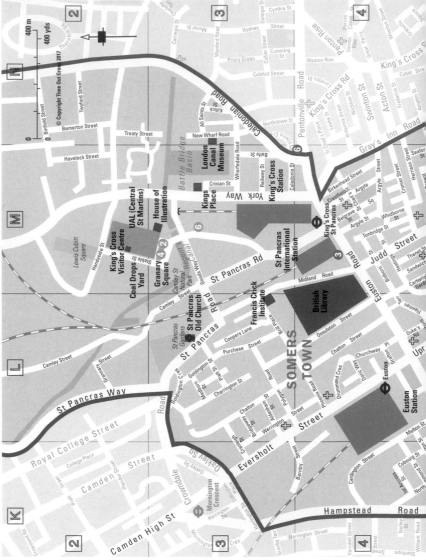

BLOOMSBURY & KING'S CROSS

Restaurants

1. Berners Tavern
2. Caravan King's Cross
3. Ethos
4. Grain Store
5. Honey & Co
6. Kerb
7. Koba
8. Lady Ottoline
9. Lantana
10. Lima London
11. Portland
12. Roka

Pubs & bars

1. All Star Lanes
2. Barrica
3. Booking Office
4. Bradley's Spanish Bar
5. Lamb
6. Scottish Stores

Shops & services

1. Blade Rubber Stamps
2. Heal's
3. Lewis Leathers
4. London Review Bookshop
5. Pentreath & Hall
6. Persephone Books

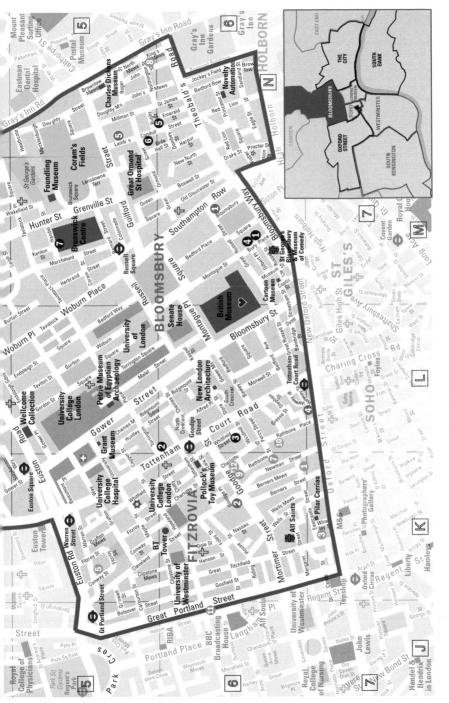

BLOOMSBURY

▶ *Euston Square, Holborn, Russell Square or Tottenham Court Road tube.*

Bloomsbury's florid name is, prosaically, taken from 'Blemondisberi' – the manor ('bury') of William Blemond, who acquired the area in the 13th century. It remained rural until the 1660s, when the fourth Earl of Southampton built **Bloomsbury Square** around his house. The Southamptons intermarried with the Russells, the Dukes of Bedford; together, they developed the area as one of London's first planned suburbs.

Over the next two centuries, the group built a series of grand squares. **Bedford Square** (1775-80) is London's only complete Georgian square (regrettably, its central garden is usually closed to the public); huge **Russell Square** has been restored as a public park with a popular café. To the east, the cantilevered postwar **Brunswick Centre** is full of shops, flats, restaurants and a cinema. The nearby streets, particularly Marchmont Street, are some of the more characterful in the West End.

Bloomsbury's charm is the sum of its parts, best experienced on a meander through its bookshops (many on Great Russell Street), pubs and squares. The blue plaques are a *Who's Who* of literary modernists – TS Eliot, Virginia Woolf, WB Yeats – with a few interlopers from more distant history: Edgar Allan Poe (83 Southampton Row), Anthony Trollope (6 Store Street) and, of course, Dickens (48 Doughty Street; now the **Charles Dickens Museum**).

On Bloomsbury's western border, Malet, Gordon and Gower streets are dominated by the **University of London**. The most notable building is Gower Street's University College, founded in 1826. Inside is the 'autoicon' of utilitarian philosopher and founder of the university, Jeremy Bentham: his preserved cadaver, fully clothed, sits in a glass-fronted cabinet. The university's main library is housed in towering Senate House on Malet Street, one of the city's most imposing examples of monumental art deco. It was the model for Orwell's Ministry of Truth in *1984* – but don't be scared to step inside: the lower floors and little café are open to the public.

South of the university sprawls the must-see **British Museum** (*see p198*). Running off Great Russell Street, where you'll find the museum's main entrance, are three attractive parallel streets (Coptic, Museum and Bury) and, nearby, the **Cartoon Museum**; also close by, Bloomsbury Way is home to Hawksmoor's restored **St George's Bloomsbury**. Across from here, Sicilian Avenue is an Italianate, pedestrian precinct of colonnaded shops – which has a smattering of places to eat and drink.

North-east of the British Museum, Lamb's Conduit Street is a convivial thoroughfare lined with interesting shops. At the north end of the street is **Coram's Fields**, a delightful children's park on the grounds of the former Thomas Coram's Foundling Hospital. Coram's legacy is commemorated in the **Foundling Museum**.

Sights & museums

Cartoon Museum
35 Little Russell Street, WC1A 2HH (7580 8155, www.cartoonmuseum.org). Tottenham Court Road tube. **Open** *10.30am-5.30pm Tue-Sun.* **Admission** *£7; £3-5 reductions; free under-18s.* **Map** *p194 M6.*

The best of British cartoon art is displayed on the ground floor of this former dairy. The displays start in the early 18th century, when high-society types back from the Grand Tour introduced the Italian practice of caricatura to polite company. From Hogarth, it moves through Britain's cartooning 'golden age' (1770-1830) to examples of wartime cartoons, ending up with modern satirists such as Gerald Scarfe and the wonderfully loopy Ralph Steadman. Upstairs is a celebration of

❤ Time to eat & drink

Best for brunch
Caravan King's Cross *p205*

Tasty and affordable lunches
Honey & Co *p208*

Vegetarian specialities
Grain Store *p205*

Culinary magic
Portland *p208*

For an Asian blow-out
Roka *p209*

Upmarket boozer – with a roof terrace
Scottish Stores *p206*

When atmosphere is everything
Bradley's Spanish Bar *p209*

❤ Time to shop

Bloomsbury's best bookstore
London Review Bookshop *p202*

Classic biker leathers
Lewis Leathers *p209*

Unusual souvenirs
Blade Rubber Stamps *p202*

UK comic art, with original 1921 Rupert Bear artwork by Mary Tourtel, Frank Hampson's Dan Dare, Leo Baxendale's Bash Street Kids and a painted Asterix cover by that well-known Briton, Albert Uderzo.

Charles Dickens Museum
48 Doughty Street, WC1N 2LX (7405 2127, www.dickensmuseum.com). Chancery Lane or Russell Square tube. Open 10am-5pm Tue-Sat. Tours by arrangement. Admission £9; £4-£6 reductions; free under-6s. Map p194 N5.

London is scattered with plaques marking addresses where Dickens lived, but this is the only one to have been preserved as a museum. He lived here from 1837 to 1840, writing *Nicholas Nickleby* and *Oliver Twist* while in residence. Ring the doorbell to gain access to four floors of Dickensiana, collected over the years from various former residences. Some rooms are arranged as they might have been when he lived here (especially atmospheric during the occasional candlelit openings); others deal with different aspects of his life, from struggling hack to famous performer. But the study has the key artefact: the chair and desk at which Dickens wrote *Great Expectations*, bought for the nation by the National Heritage Memorial Fund in 2015. Refurbishment has created a pleasant downstairs café and courtyard garden.

Coram's Fields
93 Guilford Street, WC1N 1DN (7837 6138, www.coramsfields.org). Russell Square tube. Open 9am-dusk daily. Admission free; adults admitted only if accompanied by under-16s. No cards. Map p194 M5.

This historic site dates to 1747, when Thomas Coram established the Foundling Hospital (now a museum; *see below*), but it only opened as a park in 1936. It is now probably the best playground in London – with the Diana, Princess of Wales Memorial Playground (*see p130*) its only real rival. It has sandpits, a small petting zoo, ride-on toys and several well-designed areas for different age groups, with the most challenging including a zip wire and some superb spiral slides.

Foundling Museum
40 Brunswick Square, WC1N 1AZ (7841 3600, www.foundlingmuseum.org.uk). Russell Square tube. Open 10am-5pm Tue-Sat; 11am-5pm Sun. Admission £8.25; £5.50 reductions; free under-16s. Map p194 M5.

This museum recalls the social history of the Foundling Hospital, set up in 1739 by shipwright and sailor Thomas Coram. Returning to England from America in 1720, Coram was appalled by the number of abandoned children he saw. Securing royal patronage, he persuaded Hogarth and Handel to become governors; it was Hogarth who made the building Britain's first public art gallery; works by artists as notable as Gainsborough and Reynolds are on display. The most heart-rending display is a tiny case of mementoes that were all mothers could leave the children they abandoned here.

Grant Museum of Zoology
University College London, Rockefeller Building, 21 University Street, WC1E 6DE (3108 2052, www.ucl.ac.uk/culture/grant-museum). Goodge Street tube. Open 1-5pm Mon-Sat. Admission free. Map p194 L5.

Now rehoused in a former Edwardian library belonging to University College, the Grant Museum retains the air of an avid Victorian collector's house, but visitors are engaged in dialogue about the distant evolutionary past via the most modern means available, including iPads and smartphones. The museum's 67,000 specimens include the remains of many rare and extinct creatures, including skeletons of the dodo and the zebra-like quagga (which lived in South Africa and was hunted out of existence in the 1880s), as well as pure oddities, not least the jar of moles. Don't miss the Micrarium – a kind of booth walled with little illuminated microscope slides.

Museum of Comedy
The Undercroft, St George's Church, Bloomsbury Way, WC1A 2SR (7534 1744, www.museumofcomedy.com). Holborn tube. Open noon-6pm Tue-Sun. Admission £5; £4 reductions; family £15. Map p194 M6.

The crypt below St George's Church in Bloomsbury is the unlikely location of the country's first museum dedicated to comedic artefacts. It's the brainchild of Martin Witts, owner of the Leicester Square Theatre. Over decades working alongside the heroes of British comedy, Witts has collected thousands of curiosities, including Tommy Cooper's magic props (all made by Cooper himself) and the Two Ronnies' glasses. These are on permanent display – along with temporary photographic exhibitions. Taking a charmingly old-school approach to interactivity, the museum has a portable TV on which you can watch, yes, videos of old comedy shows, as well as a record player for the collection of LPs. Attached to the museum, the Cooper Room is a 100-seat stand-up/theatre venue. And you can sup a lager (the comic's drink of choice) at the Comedians' Arms bar – itself an artefact, since the counter was recycled from Wilton's Music Hall (*see p366*).

❤ British Museum

*Great Russell Street, WC1B 3DG (7323
8299, www.britishmuseum.org). Russell
Square or Tottenham Court Road tube.*
Galleries *10am-5.30pm Mon-Thur, Sat,
Sun; 10am-8.30pm Fri.* ***Great Court*** *9am-
6pm Mon-Thur, Sat, Sun; 9am-8.30pm Fri.*
Multimedia guides *10am-4.30pm Thur,
Sat, Sun; 10am-7.30pm Fri.* ***Tours*** *Eye
Opener tours throughout the day. Highlights
tours (Fri-Sun, 90mins). See website
for details.* ***Admission*** *free; donations
appreciated. Temporary exhibitions vary.
Multimedia guides £6; £5.50 reductions.
Eye Opener tours free. Highlights tours £12.*
Map *p194 L6*

Officially the country's most popular tourist
attraction, with more than six million
visitors a year, the British Museum opened
in 1759. The first national museum to open to
the public anywhere in the world, it was free
to visit (and, since 2001, is so again) so that
'studious and curious persons' could pass
through its doors and look upon strange
objects collected from all over the globe.

It opened in Montagu House, which then
occupied this site, but the current building
is a neoclassical marvel built in 1847 by
Robert Smirke, one of the pioneers of the
Greek Revival style. In 2000, Lord Foster
added a glass roof to the Great Court, now
claimed to be 'the largest covered public
square in Europe' and a popular public
space ever since. This £100m landmark
surrounds the domed Reading Room, where
Marx, Lenin, Dickens, Darwin, Hardy and
Yeats once worked. (This was used by the
British Library until its move to purpose-
built quarters in King's Cross, *see p203*.) In
2014, the museum added a new building to
its western corner, containing the Sainsbury
Exhibitions Gallery, dedicated to the
museum's fabulous, sell-out blockbuster
shows, starting with *Vikings: Life and
Legend*. Previous exhibitions included a rare
visit from China's Terracotta Army and an
eye-opening tour of Ice Age art.

In the museum proper, star exhibits
include ancient Egyptian artefacts –
the Rosetta Stone on the ground floor,
mummies upstairs – and Greek antiquities,
including the marble friezes from the
Parthenon known as the Elgin Marbles.
Room 41 displays Anglo-Saxon artefacts,
including the famous Sutton Hoo treasure.
Also upstairs, the Celts gallery has

Assyrian lion hunt reliefs

Lindow Man, killed in 300 BC and so well preserved in peat you can see his beard, while the ground-floor Wellcome Gallery of Ethnography holds an Easter Island statue and regalia collected during Captain Cook's travels. The King's Library provides a calming home to a permanent exhibition entitled 'Enlightenment: Discovering the World in the 18th Century', a 5,000-piece collection devoted to the extraordinary formative period of the museum. The remit covers archaeology, science and the natural world; the objects displayed range from Indonesian puppets to a beautiful orrery (a mechanical solar system model).

You won't be able to see everything in one day, so buy a souvenir guide and pick out the show-stoppers, concentrate on a particular area or plan on making several visits. Highlights tours focus on specific aspects of the huge collection.

In the know
In translation

The Rosetta Stone (Room 1) is almost always invisible behind a crowd – head to the King's Library in the opposite wing and you can scrutinise a perfect replica at your leisure.

♥ Best overlooked artefacts

Marble horse *Room 21*
A fourth-century BC statue from the Mausoleum at Halikarnassos.

Assyrian lion hunt reliefs *Room 10a*
Created for the palace at Nineveh (in modern-day Iraq) in the mid seventh century BC.

Egyptian prosthetic toe *Room 63*
Made from wood and dating from the sixth century BC.

Helmet and crushed skull *Room 56*
From the ancient Mesopotamian city of Ur, c.2,500 BC.

Three human figurines *Room 59*
From Bab edh-Dhra, near the Dead Sea, c.3,000 BC.

♥ Novelty Automation
*1A Princeton Street, WC1R 4AX (novelty-automation.com). Chancery Lane or Holborn tube. **Open** Term time 11am-6pm Mon-Wed, Fri-Sat; noon-8pm Thur. School holidays daily; hours vary. **Admission** free; tokens £1 each. **Map** p194 N6.*

See p201 Silliness as an Art Form.

Petrie Museum of Egyptian Archaeology
*University College London, Malet Place, WC1E 6BT (7679 2884, www.ucl.ac.uk/culture/petrie-museum). Warren Street tube. **Open** 1-5pm Tue-Sat. **Admission** free; donations appreciated. **Map** p194 L5.*

The Petrie Museum of Egyptian Archaeology – set up in 1892 by eccentric traveller and diarist Amelia Edwards – is named after Flinders Petrie, tireless excavator of ancient Egypt. Where the British Museum's Egyptology collection is strong on the big stuff, the Petrie is an extraordinary selection of minutiae (amulets, pottery fragments, tools, weapons, weights and measures, stone vessels, jewellery), which provide an insight into how people lived and died in the Nile Valley. Highlights include colourful tiles, carvings and frescoes from heretic pharaoh Akhenaten's capital Tell el Amarna. The museum also has the world's largest collection of mummy portraits from the Roman period (first to second centuries AD). Computers offer 3D views of select objects from the 80,000-strong collection.

St George's Bloomsbury
*Bloomsbury Way, WC1A 2SA (7242 1979, www.stgeorgesbloomsbury.org.uk). Holborn or Tottenham Court Road tube. **Open** vary. Services 9am Tue, Thur; 9am, 1.10pm Wed, Fri; 10.30am Sun. **Admission** free. **Map** p194 N6.*

Consecrated in 1730, St George's is a grand and disturbing Nicholas Hawksmoor church, with an offset, stepped spire that was inspired by Pliny the Elder's account of the Mausoleum at Halicarnassus. Highlights include the mahogany reredos and sculptures of lions and unicorns clawing at the base of the steeple. The opening hours are erratic, but on Sundays, the church always remains open for visitors after the regular service. Do head down to the Undercroft for a compelling (and free) little exhibition on the building of the church above (as well as the Museum of Comedy, *see p197*), and check online for details of concerts.

Stairwell at the Wellcome Collection

💙 Wellcome Collection

183 Euston Road, NW1 2BE (7611 2222, www. wellcomecollection.org). Euston Square tube or Euston tube/Overground. **Open** *Galleries 10am-6pm Tue, Wed, Fri, Sat; 10am-10pm Thur; 11am-6pm Sun. Library 10am-6pm Mon-Wed, Fri; 10am-8pm Thur; 10am-4pm Sat.* **Admission** *free.* **Map** *p194 L5.*

Wellcome Collection is a free museum and library for the 'incurably curious'. Celebrating its tenth birthday in 2017, this gathering of international and medical oddities (Napoleon's toothbrush, Victorian amulets, Polynesian medical aids) is complemented by brilliant temporary exhibitions ('Bedlam' explored mental health and asylums; 'The Institute of Sexology' was all about bumping uglies) that explore art, health and what it means to be human. Over its first decade, the museum has grown to attract far more visitors than the original premises could cope with, so the ground-floor exhibition gallery, shop and café-restaurant, and well-displayed historic collection (Medicine Man) and science-themed contemporary art gallery (Medicine Now) upstairs have been enhanced by a typically ingenious adaptation. Connected to the lower floors with a showpiece spiral staircase, space has been found upstairs for a new restaurant, an extra gallery and the handsome Reading Room. The latter has a slightly studious air and a mezzanine stuffed with medical and scientific books, but it's a public space too, manned by explainers and librarians who can introduce you to historic artwork (some of it in boxes that must be opened with protective white gloves) and extraordinary artefacts (a dentist's workstation, a Smoky Sue Smokes for Two pregnancy doll). Fascinating interactives include the 'Virtual Autopsy' table – effectively a giant tablet where you can swipe

cuts through 3D cadavers – and a replica of Freud's couch. Now with two temporary exhibition spaces and a compelling year-round programme of live events, Wellcome Collection is livelier than ever.

Restaurants

Lady Ottoline £££

11A Northington Street, WC1N 2JF (7831 0008, www.theladyottoline.com). Chancery Lane or Russell Square tube. **Open** *noon-11pm Mon-Sat; noon-5pm Sun. Food served until 10.30pm Mon-Fri; noon-4pm, 6-10pm Sat; until 4pm Sun.* **Map** *p194 N5* ⑧ *Gastropub*

One of a minichain of upmarket gastropubs, all of which have a commitment to drink as well as food, with space for drinkers and a selection that runs from cocktails and real ales to a thoughtful wine list. Food is served in the ground-floor bar at the Lady Ottoline, but for a more sedate meal, it's best to dine in the pleasant first-floor room. The menu is a bit more adventurous than at most gastropubs – witness creamy rabbit pie with pomegranate salad.

Pubs & bars

Check out the fine cask beers at the historic **Museum Tavern** (49 Great Russell Street, 7242 8987), opposite the British Museum. It actually pre-existed the museum as the Dog & Duck, but changed its name to cash in on the new institution in the 1760s.

All Star Lanes

Victoria House, Bloomsbury Place, WC1B 4DA (7025 2676, www.allstarlanes.co.uk). Holborn tube. **Open** *Bar 3-11.30pm Mon-Wed; 3pm-midnight Thur; noon-2am Fri;*

Silliness as an Art Form

Put a coin in the slot and enter Tim Hunkin's world of crazy

Want a divorce? Fancy a cheap holiday? Need to launder money or lose weight? All these things and many others can be achieved for the modest outlay of a pound (sometimes two) at the nutty slot machines of **Novelty Automation** (see p199).

These lovingly crafted moving sculptures are almost all the work of Tim Hunkin, a cartoonist who fell in love with coin-in-the-slot machines. There are one or two by other exponents of this most idiosyncratic of arts: for instance, Paul Spooner's funny and alarming device The Dream, which sees a couple's sleep disturbed by something nasty in the woodshed.

Visitors to London with long memories and a long-established taste for quirky attractions may remember Cabaret Mechanical Theatre, which resided on the lower level of Covent Garden's Apple Market from 1984 to 2000. Some of its exhibits then found a home in the arcade on Southwold Pier in Suffolk, while others travelled the world, and a selection of these lovely handmade jokes operated by

cogs and levers has returned to London. Now, in a small shabby space behind a Bloomsbury shopfront, people of all ages are shown a good time. When some brave soul has a go at Test Your Nerve – a slot machine that invites you to place your hand beneath the jowls of a huge, red-eyed dog and keep it there while the horrible hound growls and drools – the entire place erupts.

The antidote to that experience is Microbreak: strap yourself into a battered easy chair on a wobbly platform and 'enjoy all the benefits of a holiday with none of the downsides' – you even get a hot blast of sun, courtesy of the lamp on top of the telly in front of you.

Nerves steadied, you might be ready to juggle nuclear waste with the 'remote manipulator arm' in My-Nuke, or to offer yourself to the Autofrisk machine, which invites visitors to have themselves patted down by a pair of disembodied hands in heavy-duty rubber gloves. Where else can you get fun of that calibre for a quid?

*11am-2am Sat; 1am-10.30pm Sun. Kitchen closes 1hr earlier. **Map** p194 M6* ❶

Of Bloomsbury's two subterranean bowling dens, this is the one with aspirations. Walk past the lanes and smart, diner-style seating, and you'll find yourself in a comfortable, subdued side bar with chilled glasses, classy red furnishings, an unusual mix of bottled lagers and some impressive cocktails. There's an American menu and, at weekends, DJs. **Bloomsbury Bowling Lanes** (basement of Tavistock Hotel, Bedford Way, WC1H 9EU, 7183 1979, www.bloomsburybowling.com) offers a pints-and-worn-carpets take on the same game – as well as gigs and private karaoke booths.

Lamb
*94 Lamb's Conduit Street, WC1N 3LZ (7405 0713, www.thelamblondon.com). Holborn or Russell Square tube. **Open** 11am-11pm Mon-Wed; 11am-midnight Thur-Sat; noon-10.30pm Sun. Food served noon-9.30pm daily. **Map** p194 N5* ❺

The standard range of Young's beers is dispensed from a central horseshoe bar in this 300-year-old pub, around which are ringed original etched-glass snob screens, used to prevent Victorian gentlemen from being seen when liaising with 'women of dubious distinction'. A sunken back area gives access to a convenient square of summer patio.

Shops & services

❤ Blade Rubber Stamps
*12 Bury Place, WC1A 2JL (7831 4123, www.bladerubberstamps.co.uk). Holborn or Tottenham Court Road tube. **Open** 10.30am-6pm Mon-Sat; 11.30am-4.30pm Sun. **Map** p194 M6* ❶

Blade Rubber Stamps is a shrine to wooden-handled rubber stamps. Neatly stacked shelves display arty stamps depicting chandeliers, cityscapes, images of Henry VIII, London buses, *Alice in Wonderland* characters, cutesy puppies and telephone boxes. Handy potential purchases include homework stamps ('check spelling', 'keep trying') and adorable love-letter writing kits. Unmounted sheets of rubber stamps, ink pads in every shade, glitters, glues, stencils, stickers, sticks of sealing wax, and a range of magazines and books complete the stock.

❤ London Review Bookshop
*14 Bury Place, WC1A 2JL (7269 9030, www.lrbshop.co.uk). Holborn or Tottenham Court Road tube. **Open** 10am-6.30pm Mon-Sat; noon-6pm Sun. **Map** p194 M6* ❹ *Books & music*

From the inviting and stimulating presentation to the quality of the books selected, this is an inspiring bookshop. Politics, current affairs and history are well represented on the ground floor; downstairs, audio books lead on to exciting poetry and philosophy sections, everything you'd expect from a shop owned by the purveyor of long-form critical writing that is the *London Review of Books*. Browse through your purchases in the adjoining London Review Cakeshop.

Pentreath & Hall
*17 Rugby Street, WC1N 3QT (7430 2526, www.pentreath-hall.com). Holborn tube. **Open** 11am-6pm Mon-Sat. **Map** p194 N5* ❺ *Homewares*

This petite store looks like the drawing room of a smart country house scaled to the size of a Shoreditch studio flat, scattered with beautifully made decorative artefacts and accessories such as watercolours above the mantelpiece, vintage maps and fine chinaware mugs. Alongside design and architecture books (Ben Pentreath is an architect), there's a notable range of découpage plates and trays from Bridie Hall (the designer is a joint owner of the shop) with designs from archival natural history and geographical sources.

Persephone Books
*59 Lamb's Conduit Street, WC1N 3NB (7242 9292, www.persephonebooks.co.uk). Russell Square tube. **Open** 10am-6pm Mon-Fri; noon-5pm Sat. **Map** p194 N5* ❻ *Books*

Persephone Books independently publishes the works of 20th-century women writers (and a few men) in beautifully rendered publications. Pick from a range that includes Diana Athill's *Midsummer Night in the Warehouse*, a classic memoir about a failed love affair, or Virginia Woolf's *A Writer's Diary*. The shop itself spills over into the Persephone office at the back (or is it the other way around?), giving the store a slightly ramshackle, writer's room feel, with herbal tea and upscale literary chit-chat always seeming to be on the table.

Skoob
*Unit 66, The Brunswick Centre, WC1N 1AE (7278 8760, www.skoob.com). Russell Square tube. **Open** 10.30am-8pm Mon-Sat; 10.30am-6pm Sun. **Map** p194 M5* ❼ *Books & music*

A back-to-basics basement beloved of students from the nearby University of London, Skoob showcases some 50,000 titles covering virtually every subject, from philosophy and biography to politics and the occult. Prices are reasonable, but the organisational dial is set to browse rather than strict alphabetical efficiency.

KING'S CROSS & ST PANCRAS

▶ *King's Cross St Pancras tube/rail.*

North-east of Bloomsbury, King's Cross is becoming a major European transport hub, thanks to a £500m makeover of the area. The renovated and restored **St Pancras International** was the key arrival, but neighbouring **King's Cross station** has since benefited with a handsomely restored 1851 façade overlooking a public square, nicely balancing the splendidly restored **Great Northern Hotel** (*see p400*), plus an expanded station concourse with snazzy cascading roof, much-improved restaurants and cafés, and – yes – a sawn-in-half luggage trolley that symbolises Harry Potter's **Platform 9¾**. If joining the queue for a photo-op doesn't satisfy your cravings, there are plenty of souvenirs in the **Harry Potter Shop** (7803 0500, www. harrypotterplatform934.com).

It's the area to the north that holds our attention, however. **King's Cross Central** is impressive in stats alone: 67 acres, 20 'historic structures' being refurbed, 'up to 2,000 homes and serviced apartments', 'up to 500,000sq ft of retail space', 20 new streets, three new bridges, ten new parks and squares, and 400 trees planted. The concept behind the numbers is interesting too. The developers have tried to create from scratch a 'mixed-use' development – one with the virtues of multiplicity and

resilience normally found in communities that have grown up over time. To this end, they are paying careful attention to the area's industrial heritage, to attracting a mix of residents, and to the kind of events that might draw in visitors. So, heading north-east from the station, King's Boulevard leads directly to the fine **Granary Square**, where the University of the Arts London is the most important new resident. (There's also a rather sci-fi illuminated tunnel connecting the new offices beside King's Boulevard to King's Cross station itself.) The whole area seems more cohesive and populous than it did, with the **Kings Place** arts complex (*see p390*), **London Canal Museum** and **St Pancras Old Church** no longer feeling as though they are isolated in a wasteland.

Sights & museums

British Library
96 Euston Road, NW1 2DB (01937 546060, www.bl.uk). Euston or King's Cross St Pancras tube/rail. **Open** *9.30am-8pm Mon-Thur; 9.30am-6pm Fri; 9.30am-5pm Sat; 11am-5pm Sun.* **Admission** *free; donations appreciated.* **Map** *p194 L4.*

'One of the ugliest buildings in the world,' opined a Parliamentary committee on the opening of the new British Library in 1997. But don't judge a book by its cover: the interior is a model of cool, spacious functionality, the collection is unmatched (150 million items and counting), and the

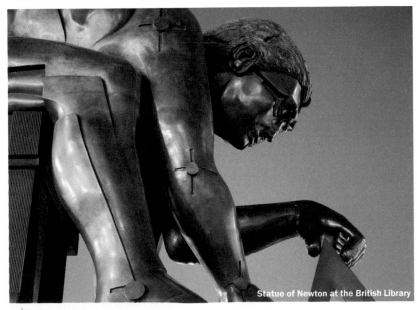
Statue of Newton at the British Library

reading rooms (open only to cardholders) are so popular that regular users complain that they can't find a seat. The focal point of the building is the King's Library, a six-storey glass-walled tower housing George III's collection, but the library's main treasures are on permanent display in the John Ritblat Gallery: the Lindisfarne Gospels, a Diamond Sutra from AD 868, original Beatles lyrics. There is also a great programme of temporary exhibitions and associated events: the Folio Society Gallery, a floor up from the entrance, is free and hosts focused little shows based around key artefacts, while the engaging blockbuster shows to the left are ticketed but cover meaty themes such as sci-fi, Gothic literature, the 800th anniversary of Magna Carta and the English language itself.

Camley Street Natural Park
12 Camley Street, N1C 4PW (7833 2311, www. wildlondon.org.uk /reserves/camley-street-natural-park). King's Cross St Pancras tube/ rail. Open 10am-5pm daily (closes at 4pm in winter). Admission free. Map p194 M3.

A small but thriving green space on the site of a former coal yard, Camley Street is near the heart of the renovated King's Cross. London Wildlife Trust's flagship reserve, it hosts pond-dipping and nature-watching sessions for children, and its wood-cabin visitor centre is used by the Wildlife Watch Club.

Francis Crick Institute
1 Midland Road, NW1 1AT (3796 0000, www. crick.ac.uk). King's Cross St Pancras tube/ rail. Open 10am-8pm Wed; 10am-3pm Thur; 10am-5pm Fri, Sat. Admission free. Map p194 L3.

Come out of the eastern exit from St Pancras and, just north of the British Library (*see p203*), you'll see a 46ft-tall sculpture of different triangles in weathered steel: this is *Paradigm*, by Conrad Shawcross. It marks the entrance to the Crick, an altar to biomedical research, where a crack team of around 1,500 scientists are dedicated to gaining a better understanding of disease. Completed in 2016, the building opened an exhibition space in 2017 where members of the public can learn about the cutting-edge work going on next door and the future of human health. A busy events programme includes 'Meet the Scientist' evenings.

Granary Square
www.kingscross.co.uk/granary-square. King's Cross St Pancras tube/rail. Map p194 M3.

Filled with choreographed fountains (1,080 water spouts, operating 8am-8pm daily, and lit in many colours at night), the square's terracing down to the canal is already populated most sunny days. No wonder:

there's a ready supply of students from UAL Central Saint Martins college of art, which in 2011 moved into the building behind – a sensitively and impressively converted, Grade II-listed 1850s industrial building. Fronting on to the square are two restaurants and a café, with the **House of Illustration** (*see below*) tucked around the corner, and Coal Drops Yard and Lewis Cubitt Square beginning to open up the industrial land beyond it.

House of Illustration
2 Granary Square, N1C 4BH (3696 2020, www.houseofillustration.org.uk). King's Cross St Pancras tube/rail. Open 10am-6pm Tue-Sun. Admission £7.50; £4-£5 reductions; family £18; free under-5s. Map p194 M3.

The world's first gallery dedicated to the art of illustration has demonstrations, talks, debates and hands-on workshops covering all aspects of illustration, from children's books and scabrous cartoons to advertising and animation, as well as a regular programme of temporary exhibitions, usually dedicated to a single illustrator: Quentin Blake, for instance, or EH Shepard, who drew the captivating pictures for *Winnie-the-Pooh*.

London Canal Museum
12-13 New Wharf Road, off Wharfdale Road, N1 9RT (7713 0836, www.canalmuseum.org. uk). King's Cross St Pancras tube/rail. Open 10am-4.30pm Tue-Sun (until 7.30pm 1st Thur of mth). Admission £5; £2.50-£4 reductions; family £12; free under-4s. Map p194 N3.

Housed on two floors of a former 19th-century ice warehouse, the London Canal Museum has a barge cabin to sit in and models of boats, but the displays on the history of the ice trade (photos and videos about ice-importer Carlo Gatti) are perhaps the most interesting. The canalside walk (download a free MP3 audio tour from the museum website) from Camden Town to the museum is lovely, and in summer don't miss the tours – organised by the museum – that explore dank Islington Tunnel, an otherwise inaccessible Victorian canal feature.

St Pancras International
Euston Road, N1C 4QP (7843 7688, www. stpancras.com). King's Cross St Pancras tube/ rail. Open 24hrs daily. Admission free. Map p194 M4.

The redeveloped St Pancras station has become a destination in more ways than the obvious, now containing large sculptures, the self-proclaimed 'longest champagne bar in Europe', high-end boutiques – even a gastropub and farmers' market. But the new additions are mere window-dressing for the stunning original structures: famously,

George Gilbert Scott's grandiloquent red-brick exterior (much of which is now the **St Pancras Renaissance hotel**), but even more impressively William Barlow's Victorian glass-and-iron roof to the train shed, a single span that is airy and light, as though he wished to create some kind of cathedral to 19th-century industry and transport.

St Pancras Old Church & St Pancras Gardens

Pancras Road, NW1 1UL (7419 6679, www.posp.co.uk/st-pancras-old-church). Mornington Crescent tube or King's Cross St Pancras tube/rail. **Open** *Church & gardens 9am-dusk. Services times vary; check website for details.* **Admission** *free.* **Map** *p194 L3.*

St Pancras Old Church has been ruined and rebuilt many times. The current structure is handsome, but it's the churchyard that delights. Among those buried here are writer William Godwin and his wife, Mary Wollstonecraft; over their grave, their daughter Mary Godwin (author of *Frankenstein*) declared her love for poet and future husband Percy Bysshe Shelley. Also here is the last resting place of Sir John Soane, one of only two Grade I-listed tombs (the other is that of Karl Marx, in Highgate Cemetery; *see p250*). Designed for his wife, the tomb's dome influenced Gilbert Scott's design for the classic red British phone box.

Restaurants

The new area behind King's Cross station is shaping up to be something of a gastronomic destination, with a handful of restaurants (there's a **Dishoom**, see *p185*, round the corner from Granary Square if **Caravan** and **Grain Store** are too busy) and healthy street-food scene.

**In the know
Ticking the Cross**

For information about the area's ongoing development and some neat merchandise, visit the **King's Cross Visitor Centre** (Western Transit Shed, 11 Stable Street, N1C 4AB, 3479 1795, www.kingscross. co.uk/visitor-centre, 10am-5pm Mon-Fri; 10am-4pm Sat).

❤ Caravan King's Cross ££

Granary Building, 1 Granary Square, N1C 4AA (7101 7661, www.caravankingscross. co.uk). King's Cross St Pancras tube/rail. **Open** *8am-10.30pm Mon-Fri; 10am-10.30pm Sat; 10am-4pm Sun.* **Map** *p194 M3* ②
Global

This is an altogether bigger, more urbane operation than the original Caravan on Exmouth Market. The ethos is the same, however: welcoming staff and a menu of what they call 'well-travelled food'. Most are small plates – deep-fried duck egg with baba ganoush, chorizo oil and crispy shallots, say, or grits, collard greens and brown shrimp butter – plus a few large plates and (at King's Cross only) a handful of first-class pizzas. Recent favourites include a naughty-but-nice crispy fried chicken with jerk mayo and pawpaw salsa. The setting, overlooking the fountains of Granary Square, is another plus, and there's a good range of drinks, including cocktails.

❤ Grain Store £££

Granary Square, 1-3 Stable Street, N1C 4AB (7324 4466, www.grainstore. com). King's Cross St Pancras tube/rail. **Open** *noon-2.30pm, 5.45-10.30pm Mon-Fri; 10am-10.30pm, 6-10.30pm Sat; 10.30am-3.30pm Sun.* **Map** *p194 M3* ④
Modern European

St Pancras International

Grain Store, right next to Caravan, is a rather different proposition. The restaurant is run by Bruno Loubet, whose cooking is grounded in the classical traditions of south-west France, but not bound by them. The menu is a pick 'n' mix of fine ingredients and cuisines – a dish such as sticky pork belly with a corn and quinoa tamale is typical – but throughout there are consistency of style and imaginative, successful flavour pairings that are recognisably Loubet. There's a bar, too, with excellent cocktails conceived by barmeister Tony Conigliaro – try the bellini, made not with peach purée but with celeriac purée.

Kerb £

King's Boulevard, NC1 (www.kerbfood.com/kings-cross). King's Cross St Pancras tube/rail. **Open** *noon-2pm Wed-Fri.* **Map** *p194 M3* ⑥ *Street food*

Street food collective Kerb pitches up in various sites across London – and has led a peripatetic existence around King's Cross over the last several years. Now back in King's Boulevard, where it all began, half a dozen traders dish up some seriously tasty food to hundreds of hungry passers-by. The stalls rotate, so there's always something new to try, whether Sri Lankan *kothu roti* or barbecue ribs, houmous salads or black pudding rolls. The website has details of who's selling what on any particular day.

Pubs & bars
Booking Office

St Pancras Renaissance Hotel, Euston Road, NW1 2AR (7841 3566, www.stpancraslondon.com). King's Cross St Pancras tube/rail. **Open** *6.30am-midnight Mon-Wed; 6.30am-1am Thur, Fri; 7am-1am Sat; 7am-midnight Sun.* **Map** *p194 M4* ❸

Sit indoors at this smart cocktail bar and you'll gaze at Sir George Gilbert Scott's lofty interior, a stirring example of the Victorian architect's interpretation of Gothic revival. Outside, under spacious canopies, you'll have a nearly ceiling-level view of St Pancras International station. The cocktail list gives prominent place to traditional punches, served in mugs, but the list is a long one. Martinis are well made, and the Victorian Gimlet (vodka, lime juice and seasonal fresh fruit juice) is a wonderful and refreshing potion. Warning: the free bar snacks – coated peanuts – are dangerously addictive.

❤ Scottish Stores

2-4 Caledonian Road, N1 9DT (3384 6497, www.thescottishstores.co.uk). King's Cross St Pancras tube/rail. **Open** *8am-11pm Mon-Wed; 8am-midnight Thur-Sat.* **Map** *p194 M4* ⑥

Transformed from a seedy strip club into a handsome wood-panelled pub, the Scottish Stores is a reflection of the area's transformation from grotty to gleaming over the last decade or so. Run by a good old-fashioned gentleman, it specialises in interesting beers, such as the Basqueland Brewing Project IPA, as well as some more traditional draught options, all of which can be enjoyed out on the roof terrace – quite a find in this area.

FITZROVIA

▶ *Goodge Street or Tottenham Court Road tube.*

Squeezed in between Tottenham Court Road, Oxford Street, Great Portland Street and Euston Road, Fitzrovia isn't as famous as Bloomsbury, but its history is just as rich. The origins of the name are hazy: some

St Pancras Old Church & St Pancras Gardens *p205*

believe it comes from **Fitzroy Square**, named after Henry Fitzroy (son of Charles II); others insist it's due to the famous **Fitzroy Tavern** (16A Charlotte Street, 7580 3714), focal venue for London bohemia of the 1930s and '40s and a favourite with the likes of Dylan Thomas and George Orwell. Fitzrovia also had its share of artists: James McNeill Whistler lived at 8 Fitzroy Square, later taken over by British Impressionist Walter Sickert, while Roger Fry's Omega Workshops, blurring the distinction between fine and decorative arts, had its studio at no.33. Fitzrovia's raffish image is largely a thing of the past (media offices are in the ascendance these days) but the steady arrival of new galleries – notably the likes of **Pilar Corrias** along Eastcastle Street – has given the district back some of its artiness, even if local rents mean it will never again be home to the dissolute.

The district's icon is the **BT Tower**, completed in 1964 as the Post Office Tower. Its revolving restaurant and observation deck featured in any film that wanted to prove how much London was swinging (*Bedazzled* is just one example). The restaurant is now reserved for corporate functions, but Charlotte Street and neighbouring byways have plenty of good options for food and drink.

Sights & museums

All Saints

7 Margaret Street, W1W 8JG (7636 1788, www.allsaintsmargaretstreet.org.uk). Oxford Circus tube. **Open** *7am-7pm daily. Services 7.30am, 8am, 1.10pm, 6pm, 6.30pm Mon-Fri; 7.30am, noon, 6pm, 6.30pm Sat; 8am, 10.20am, 11am, 5.15pm, 6pm Sun.* **Admission** *free.* **Map** *p194 K6.*

Providing respite from the tumult of Oxford Street, this 1850s church was designed by William Butterfield, one of the great exponents of the Victorian Gothic revival. The church looks as if it has been lowered on to its tiny site, so tight is the fit; its lofty spire is the second-highest in London. Behind the polychromatic brick façade, the lavish interior is one of the capital's finest, with luxurious marble, flamboyant tile work and glittering stones built into its pillars.

Pilar Corrias

54 Eastcastle Street, W1W 8EF (7323 7000, www.pilarcorrias.com). Oxford Circus tube. **Open** *10am-6pm Mon-Fri; 11am-6pm Sat.* **Admission** *free.* **Map** *p194 K7.*

Formerly a director at the pioneering Lisson and Haunch of Venison galleries, Corrias opened this 3,800sq ft, Rem Koolhaas-designed gallery in 2008. It was one of the

first of an influx of private galleries to the area – several coming to Eastcastle Street from the art-saturated East End.

Pollock's Toy Museum

1 Scala Street, W1T 2HL (7636 3452, www. pollockstoys.com). Goodge Street tube. **Open** *10am-5pm Mon-Sat.* **Admission** *£6; £3-£5 reductions; free under-3s.* **Map** *p194 K6.*

Named after Victorian toy theatre printer Benjamin Pollock, this place is in turns beguiling and creepy, a nostalgia-fest of old board games, tin trains, porcelain dolls and gollies. It is fascinating for adults but less so for children: describing a pile of painted woodblocks in a cardboard box as a 'Build a skyscraper' kit may make them feel lucky to be going home to *Minecraft*. Having said that, the Pollock's Toy Museum shop is good for wind-up toys and other funny little gifts for children.

Restaurants

Berners Tavern £££

10 Berners Street, W1T 3NP (7908 7979, www.bernerstavern.com). Oxford Circus or Tottenham Court Road tube. **Open** *7-10.30am, noon-midnight Mon-Fri; 9am-4pm, 5pm-midnight Sat, Sun.* **Map** *p194 K6* ❶ *Modern European*

The huge lobby bar of the London Edition hotel (*see p400*) looks fabulous, but the vast dining room, with its ornate plasterwork ceiling and lively bar area, looks even better. Food is playful and appealing: tender pork belly with capers, golden raisins and apple coleslaw, and cod with fennel and cider sauce, are sublime. Any caveats? Sometimes dizzy service; frequent upselling of extras; and lighting so low it's hard to read the menu. But Berners Tavern is glamtastic. Wear your best threads, and book ahead for a preliminary cocktail in the candle-lit Punch Room bar (7908 7949, www.editionhotels.com/london) – at the back of the hotel.

Ethos £

48 Eastcastle Street, W1W 8DX (3581 1538, ethosfoods.com). Oxford Circus or Tottenham Court Road tube. **Open** *8am-10.30pm Mon-Fri; 11.30am-10pm Sat; 10am-5pm Sun.* **Map** *p194 K7* ❸ *Vegetarian*

Ethos is a vegetarian, self-serve buffet, where you pay for your food by its weight. It opens early in the day with a short breakfast menu (avocado on toast, fruit salad, granola, porridge), then rolls on through to lunch and dinner with dishes with a pretty broad global range. Although it's most popular as a midday spot, the drinks list (three beers and a dozen wines) and the rarity of affordable vegetarian eateries in the West End mean it's also a good dinner destination.

❤ Honey & Co £
25A Warren Street, W1T 5LZ (7388 6175, www. honeyandco.co.uk). Warren Street tube. **Open** *8am-10.30pm Mon-Fri; 9.30am-10.30pm Sat.* **Map** *p194 K5* ⑤
Middle Eastern

A bijou delight, with small tables and chairs packed closely together. The kitchen is run by an accomplished Israeli husband-and-wife team. This pedigree shines in a daily-changing menu that draws influences from across the Middle East. The meze selection includes fabulously spongy, oily bread, sumac-spiked tahini, smoky taramasalata, crisp courgette croquettes with *labneh*, pan-fried feta and a bright salad with lemon and radishes. A main might be a whole baby chicken with lemon and a chilli and walnut *muhamara* paste. It's imaginative home-style cooking, and service is charming.

Koba ££
11 Rathbone Street, W1T 1NA (7580 8825, www.kobalondon.com). Goodge Street or Tottenham Court Road tube. **Open** *noon-2.45pm, 5.30-10.45pm Mon-Sat; noon-2.45pm, 5.30-10pm Sun.* **Map** *p194 K6* ⑦
Korean

Koba is one of the strongest players on the West End Korean scene. Barbecue meats such as beef *kalbi* or *bulgogi* are well marinated, and grilled at the table by efficient staff.

Roka

Barbecued squid is fresh as a daisy, with just the right amount of tongue-tingling heat in the vibrant red sauce. Stews make a sound choice too, with umami-rich stocks and accompanying bowls of pearly rice. Service is polished but not too formal, and the dark, modern, east Asian meets industrial, interior is slick. Drinks include Korean beers, *soju* and a short wine list.

Lantana £
13 Charlotte Place, W1T 1SN (7637 3347, www. lantanacafe.co.uk). Goodge Street tube. **Open** *8am-6pm Mon-Fri (kitchen closes 3.30pm); 9am-5pm Sat, Sun (kitchen closes 4pm).* **Map** *p194 K6* ⑨ *Café*

Lantana is a lively spot. Its look – wooden tables, mismatched chairs, small pieces of art on white walls – is now commonplace, but the staff pride themselves on their coffee-making and baking skills, and rightly so. The flat whites are super-smooth and go well with a moist raspberry friand or an Aussie 'cherry ripe' cake slice. The breakfast and brunch menu includes the likes of maple French toast with streaky bacon, grilled banana and candied pecans. Savoury dishes can be ordered with a glass of wine. The kiosk next door sells some dishes as takeaways.

Lima London ££
31 Rathbone Place, W1T 1JH (3002 2640, www.limalondongroup.com/fitzrovia). Tottenham Court Road tube. **Open** *5.30-10.45pm Mon; noon-2.30pm, 5.30-10.45pm Tue-Sat; 5-9pm Sun.* **Map** *p194 L6* ⑩
Peruvian

Part of the 'Peruvian wave' of restaurants that hit the capital back in 2012, Lima London pitched itself squarely at the high end. The modish rear dining room mixes the hum of low-level beats with polite chatter. Well-drilled staff bring out a medley of carefully crafted small plates, the likes of sea bream ceviche flecked with hot *aji limo* chilli and pieces of roasted corn, and thick wedges of suckling pig – part dense meat, part salty, crispy crackling – matched by a rough corn mash spiked with two kinds of peppers.

❤ Portland £££
113 Great Portland Street, W1W 6QQ (7436 3261, portlandrestaurant.co.uk). Oxford Circus tube. **Open** *noon-2.30pm, 6-10pm Mon-Sat.* **Map** *p194 K6* ⑪ *Contemporary European*

It is rare to go to a restaurant and be astonished, but nothing prepared us for this bold, powerful, surprising food: chef Merlin Labron-Johnson was cooking like a wizard. For this level of cooking, the menu is great value, offering small plates at £5-£7. Favourite dishes include pig's head croquettes, aged mimolet cheese and granola, or pickled shiitake mushrooms. Desserts – such as 'chocolate bar, peanut butter praline, peanut ice-cream' – are skilfully executed and the wine list is short but imaginative. It's a small, bare-wood, no-frills kind of place, but it's very attractive and the flavours are sensational.

♥ Roka ££££
37 Charlotte Street, W1T 1RR (7580 6464, www.rokarestaurant.com). Goodge Street or Tottenham Court Road tube. **Open** *noon-3.30pm, 5.30-11.30pm Mon-Fri; 12.30-4pm, 5.30-11.30pm Sat; 12.30-4pm, 5.30-10.30pm Sun.* **Map** *p194 K6* ⑫ *Japanese*

Roka gets top marks for glitz and glamour. Much of the action takes place at the central robata grill, where a repertoire of contemporary *izakaya*-inspired food is created in full view. The 13-course tasting menu is popular with first-time diners, taking them on a spin of the best Roka has to offer: elegant dishes such as hand-made *kimchi*, sashimi and sticky skewers of *tebasaki* (chicken wings) are finished off with a trio of desserts, featuring delights such as Pocky-style chocolate and sesame biscuit sticks. It isn't cheap, but each dish is impeccable.

Pubs & bars

Barrica
62 Goodge Street, W1T 4NE (7436 9448, www.barrica.co.uk). Goodge Street or Tottenham Court Road tube. **Open** *noon-3pm, 5.30-10.30pm Mon-Fri; noon-10.30pm Sat.* **Map** *p194 K6* ②

With its canary-yellow walls, rich wood and marble, Barrica is a little taste of laidback Spain in the busy West End. The speciality? Sherry. A selection of 16, to be precise: from the intensely sweet to the bone-dry and salty. There are also around 30 Spanish wines, selected by the bar's oenophile owner. It's not just about the impressive alcohol offerings, though: be sure to try a few dishes off the brilliant tapas menu too.

♥ Bradley's Spanish Bar
42-44 Hanway Street, W1T 1UT (7636 0359, www.bradleysspanishbar.com). Tottenham Court Road tube. **Open** *noon-11.30pm Mon-Thur; noon-midnight Fri, Sat; 1-10.30pm Sun.* **Map** *p194 L7* ④

There's something of the Barcelona dive bar about this place, with San Miguel or Cruzcampo on draught, but Bradley's isn't really very Spanish. In fact, it's not even a bar. Bradley's is definitely a pub, and with its jumble sale decor and tattered furniture, it sure puts the 'shabby' in 'shabby chic'. But don't be put off: Londoners love Bradley's

for its low-key and unpretentious vibe and shoppers and foreign exchange students fill the cramped two-floor space. After all, there's a good jukebox (playing vinyl, retro fans) and a good atmosphere – what more could anyone want?

Shops & services

The electronics shops that congregated at the south end of Tottenham Court Road have pretty much vanished, but the arrival back in 2015 of the first Google Shop, a 'shop in a shop' at **Currys PC World** (nos.145-149), caused a bit of a cyberstir. In truth, the rebirth of little-loved Tottenham Court Road tube as a Crossrail station is driving a minor revival north of the previously scruffy end of Oxford Street.

Heal's
196 Tottenham Court Road, W1T 7LQ (7636 1666, www.heals.co.uk). Goodge Street tube. **Open** *10am-7pm Mon-Wed, Fri, Sat; 10am-8pm Thur; noon-6pm Sun.* **Map** *p194 L6* ❷ *Homewares*

Heal's may be the grand old dame of interiors stores, on this site since 1840, but its commitment to sourcing new designers is impressive. Established names such as Orla Kiely, Clarissa Hulse and LSA are also well represented among the mirrors, rugs, bed linen, clocks, cushions, art and photography. The ground floor has a cornucopia of kitchenware and gift items, plus a terrific lighting department with such delights as Tom Dixon's Beat pendant shades. Most of the furniture is upstairs, and for mid-century modernist fans, there's a great selection of vintage Danish makes.

♥ Lewis Leathers
Mottram House, 3-5 Whitfield Street, W1T 2SA (7636 4314, www.lewisleathers.com). Tottenham Court Road tube. **Open** *11am-6pm Mon-Sat.* **Map** *p194 L6* ❸ *Fashion*

It's the heritage leather biker brand that boasts Cara Delevigne and Kate Moss as customers. Established in 1892, the history of Lewis Leathers is plastered on the wall in nostalgic posters from TT racer days of the 1920s through to the '70s. Here, you can pick and choose from a wide range of leather goods, whether it's a classic racer jacket, trousers, a studded belt or some seriously sleek heeled boots. The shop also stocks a variety of denim, T-shirts, sneakers, goggles and even books, including its current issue of Nick Clements' *Men's File Archive*. Of course, quality leather like this costs (jackets retail at upwards of £600).

The City

The City's current fame merely as the financial heart of London does no justice to its 2,000-year history. Here – on top of a much more ancient ritual landscape – the Romans founded the city they called Londinium, building a bridge to the west of today's London Bridge. They left a forum-basilica, an amphitheatre, public baths and the defensive wall that still defines what we now call the Square Mile (an area, in fact, of 1.21 square miles).

Although the City has just over 9,000 residents, 330,000 people arrive each weekday to work as bankers, lawyers and traders, taking over 85 million square feet of office space. Tourists come, too, to see St Paul's Cathedral, the Tower of London and the Museum of London. There is much else besides: no area of London offers quite so much in so small a space. Roman ruins? Medieval churches? Iconic 21st-century towers? You've come to the right place.

To understand the City properly, visit on a weekday when the great economic machine is running at full tilt and the commuter is king. Despite efforts by the City authorities to improve the district's prospects as a weekend leisure destination, many of the streets still fall eerily quiet on Saturday and Sunday. If you do visit at the weekend, try the Cheapside shops

THE CITY

Heron Tower *p232*

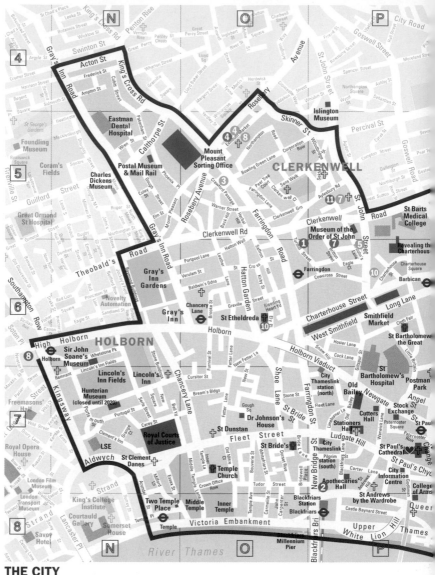

THE CITY

Restaurants
1. City Càphê
2. Duck & Waffle
3. Eagle
4. Exmouth Market
5. Foxlow
6. Look Mum No Hands
7. Modern Pantry
8. Moro
9. Pull'd
10. St John
11. Sweetings

Pubs & bars
1. 7 Tales
2. Black Friar
3. Black Rock
4. Café Kick
5. City Social Bar
6. Draft House
7. Jerusalem Tavern
7. Princess Louise
8. Sushisamba
9. Ye Olde Mitre
10. Zetter Townhouse

Shops & services
1. F Flittner
2. Hula Nails
3. One New Change
4. Royal Exchange

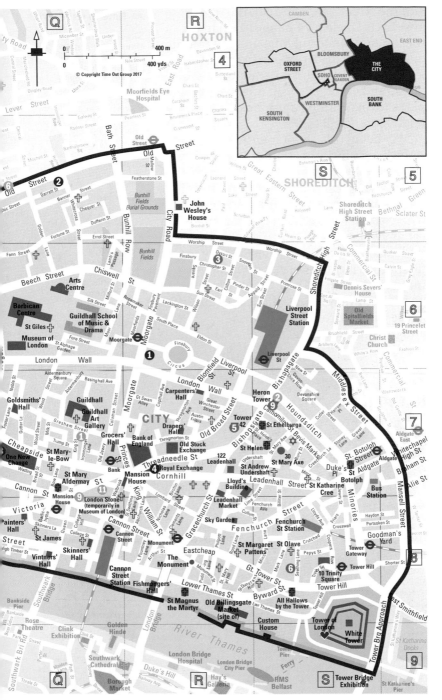

and the street's anchor mall, the rather antiseptic One New Change; drop in on the always wonderful Museum of London; or just do as a discerning minority of locals do – potter about the place's odd nooks and crannies, from unexpected parks to disregarded churches, in relative tranquillity.

We begin this chapter with a couple of rather more lived-in adjuncts to the City proper: Holborn, where London-connoisseurs can wander some of the city's finest small museums, and Clerkenwell, where you'll find some of the best places to eat anywhere in London. They are underscored by historic Fleet Street, famous for its now-absent newspaper industry, to the south of which you can ponder powdered wigs and legal quiddities in the calm surrounds of Temple and the Inns of Court.

♥ Time to eat & drink

Sky-high breakfasts
Duck & Waffle *p236*

Fabulous fusion
Modern Pantry *p218*

Meaty treats
Foxlow *p218*

Food that's Moorish
Moro *p218*

Modern British
St John *p219*

Highly inventive cocktails
Zetter Townhouse
Clerkenwell *p219*

Cheap beer in Victorian splendour
Princess Louise *p216*

Asian-influenced confections
7 Tales *p219*

In the atmosphere
Jerusalem Tavern *p219*

Whisky from an oak
Black Rock *p229*

THE CITY

HOLBORN

▶ *Holborn tube.*

A sharp left turn out of Holborn tube on to Kingsway and then another left leads to the unexpectedly lovely **Lincoln's Inn Fields**. Surely London's largest square (indeed, it's more of a park), it's blessed with gnarled oaks casting dappled shade over a tired bandstand. On the south side of the square, the neoclassical façade of the Royal College of Surgeons hides the **Hunterian Museum** (35-43 Lincoln's Inn Fields, WC2A 3PE (7869 6560, www.rcseng.ac.uk/museums), a fascinating collection of grisly artefacts including half of Charles Babbage's brain and Churchill's dentures, sadly closed for redevelopment until 2020. Facing it from the north is the equally curious **Sir John Soane's Museum**.

East of the square lies **Lincoln's Inn** (7405 1393, www.lincolnsinn.org.uk), one of the city's four Inns of Court. Its grounds are open to the public, with an odd mix of Gothic, Tudor and Palladian buildings. On nearby Portsmouth Street lies the **Old Curiosity Shop** (nos.13-14, WC2A 2ES,

7405 9891, www.the-old-curiosity-shop. com), its timbers apparently known to Dickens, but now selling decidedly modern shoes. Nearby, Gray's Inn Road runs north alongside the sculpted gardens at **Gray's Inn** (7458 7800, www.graysinn.org.uk). Known as the Walks, they date to 1606 and are open noon-2.30pm weekdays.

Opened in 1876 on Chancery Lane as a series of strongrooms in which the upper classes could secure their valuables, the

**In the know
Get the gen**

Newcomers to the City are advised to head straight to **St Paul's** (see *p224*), not just for the beauty of the architecture, but because the spiky-roofed **City of London Information Centre** (7332 3456, www.cityoflondon. gov.uk) is there, on the river side of the cathedral. Open daily (9.30am-5.30pm Mon-Sat; 10am-4pm Sun), it has information on sights, events, walks and talks, as well as offering tours with specialist guides, and has free Wi-Fi.

London Silver Vaults (7242 3844, www.thesilvervaults.com) are now a hive of dealers buying, selling and repairing silverware. There are also glittering displays on **Hatton Garden**, the city's jewellery and diamond centre – which suffered a dramatic heist in 2015. It's no distance to walk but a million miles in nature from the Cockney fruit stalls and sock merchants of the market on **Leather Lane** (10am-2pm Mon-Fri).

Further on is **Ely Place**, its postcode absent from the street sign as a result of it not falling under the jurisdiction of the City of London; instead, it is a private road with its own beadles to police it. The church garden of ancient **St Etheldreda** produced strawberries so delicious that they made the pages of Shakespeare's *Richard III*; a celebratory Strawberrie Fayre is still held on the street each June. The 16th-century **Ye Olde Mitre** is one of the city's most atmospheric pubs, hidden down a barely marked alley.

Sights & museums

St Etheldreda

14 Ely Place, EC1N 6RY (7405 1061, www.stetheldreda.com). Chancery Lane tube. **Open** *8am-5pm Mon-Sat; 8am-12.30pm Sun.* **Admission** *free; donations appreciated.* **Map** *p212 C3.*

Dedicated to the saintly seventh-century Queen of Northumbria, this is Britain's oldest Catholic church and London's only surviving example of 13th-century Gothic architecture; it was saved from the Great Fire by a change in the wind. The crypt is darkly atmospheric, untouched by traffic noise, and the stained

glass (actually from the 1960s) is stunning. It's a peaceful place.

❤ Sir John Soane's Museum

13 Lincoln's Inn Fields, WC2A 3BP (7405 2107, www.soane.org). Holborn tube. **Open** *10am-5pm Tue-Sat; also 6-9pm 1st Tue of mth. Tours 11am, noon Tue, Sat; noon Thur, Fri.* **Admission** *free; donations appreciated. Tours £10.* **Map** *p212 A4.*

When he wasn't designing notable buildings (among them the original Bank of England), Sir John Soane (1753-1837) obsessively collected art, furniture and architectural ornamentation. In the 19th century, he turned his house into a museum to which, he said, 'amateurs and students' should have access. The result is this perfectly amazing place.

The modest rooms were modified by Soane with ingenious devices to channel and direct daylight, and to expand space, including walls that fold out to display paintings by Canaletto, Turner and Hogarth. The Tivoli Recess – the city's first gallery of contemporary sculpture, with a stained-glass window and plaster sunbursts – has been restored, and further stained glass illuminates a bust of Shakespeare. The Breakfast Room has a beautiful domed ceiling, inset with convex mirrors, while the Monument Court contains a sarcophagus of alabaster, so fine that it's almost translucent, that was carved for the pharaoh Seti I (1291-78 BC) and discovered in the Valley of the Kings. There are also numerous examples of Soane's eccentricity, not least the cell for his imaginary monk 'Padre Giovanni'.

The museum recently completed a £7 million project to restore previously unseen

Sir John Soane's Museum

THE CITY

parts of the building and to create a new shop, exhibition gallery and flexible space for displays and events. The second floor contains the Model Room, open for the first time since 1850. It holds Britain's largest collection of historical architectural models.

Formerly a treasured secret of the cognoscenti, the museum now welcomes 93,000 people a year: arrive early and expect to queue – but you won't regret it.

Restaurants

Leather Lane has daytime street food and good coffee bars: **Department of Coffee & Social Affairs** (nos.14-16, EC1N 7SU, www.departmentofcoffee.com) and **Prufrock Coffee** (nos.23-25, EC1N 7TE, 7242 0467, www.prufrockcoffee.com), while **Catalyst** is on parallel Gray's Inn Road (no.48, WC1X 8LT, www.catalyst.cafe).

Pubs & bars

♥ Princess Louise

208-209 High Holborn, WC1V 7BW (7405 8816, princesslouisepub.co.uk). Holborn tube. Open 11am-11pm Mon-Fri; noon-11pm Sat; noon-6.45pm Sun. Food served noon-2.30pm, 6-8.30pm Mon-Thur; noon-2.30pm Fri. Map p212 C3 ❼

With its magnificent Victorian interior restored to its former glory by the Sam Smith's Brewery, the old Louise oozes charm. The ground-floor saloon is spectacularly ornate with etched glass, mirrors, buffed wood panelling and a warren of Victorian frosted-glass booths, each with direct access to the bar. An open fire completes the atmosphere. While the pub is busiest at weekends, a preponderance of stools and bright lighting give the Princess a post-work rather than pre-night-out vibe.

Ye Olde Mitre

1 Ely Court, EC1N 6SJ (7405 4751, www.yeoldemitreholborn.co.uk). Farringdon tube/rail. Open 11am-11pm Mon-Fri. Food served 11.30am-9.30pm Mon-Fri. Map p212 C3 ❾

Largely due to its location – down a barely marked alley between Hatton Garden's jewellers and Ely Place – this little traditional pub, the foundation of which dates to 1546, is a favourite of 'secret London' lists. There's always a good range of ales on offer at the tiny central bar, but people come for the atmosphere: lots of cosy dark wood and some overlooked curiosities, such as the tree in the front bar. It's a cherry tree that Good Queen Bess is said to have danced around, but now supports a corner of the bar.

CLERKENWELL & FARRINGDON

▶*Farringdon tube/rail.*

Few places encapsulate London's capacity for reinvention quite like Clerkenwell, an erstwhile religious centre that takes its name from the parish clerks who once performed Biblical mystery plays on its streets. The most lasting holy legacy is that of the 11th-century knights of the Order of St John; the remains of their priory can still be seen at St John's Gate, a crenellated gatehouse that dates from 1504 and is home to the **Museum of the Order of St John**. For a little peace and quiet, stroll by the Charterhouse in Charterhouse Square. This Carthusian monastery, founded in 1370, is now Anglican almshouses which retain the original 14th-century chapel and a 17th-century library. In 2017 it opened to the public for the first time, as **Revealing the Charterhouse**.

By the 17th century, Clerkenwell was a fashionable locale, but the Industrial Revolution soon buried it under warehouses and factories. Printing houses were established, and the district gained a reputation as a safe haven for radicals, from 15th-century Lollards to 19th-century Chartists. In 1903, Lenin is believed to have met Stalin for a drink in what is now the **Crown Tavern** (43 Clerkenwell Green, EC1R 0EG, 7253 4973, www.thecrowntavernec1. co.uk), one year after moving the publication of the newspaper *Iskra* to no.37A (now the **Marx Memorial Library**; 7253 1485, www.marx-memorial-library.org).

Industrial dereliction and decay were the theme until property development in the 1980s and '90s turned Clerkenwell into a desirable area to live in and visit. The process was aided by a slew of artfully distressed gastropubs (following the lead of the **Eagle**), and the food stalls, fashion boutiques, restaurants and bars along the colourful strip of **Exmouth Market**. Now, the area is one of London's dining powerhouses, with **St John** the acknowledged pioneer of the new British cuisine – reviving the taste for unfavoured cuts of meat and offal under the catchy motto of 'nose-to-tail eating'.

Sights & museums

Islington Museum

245 St John Street, beneath Finsbury Library, EC1V 4NB (7527 2837, www.islington.gov.uk). Angel tube. **Open** *10am-5pm Mon, Tue, Thur-Sat.* **Admission** *free.* **Map** *p212 C1.*

The museum covers local history and the political and ethical credentials of the borough, exemplified by local residents such as reformist preacher John Wesley, playwright Joe Orton and eminent feminist Mary Wollstonecraft.

Museum of the Order of St John

St John's Gate, St John's Lane, EC1M 4DA (7324 4005, www.museumstjohn.org. uk). Farringdon tube/rail. **Open** *Oct-June 10am-5pm Mon-Sat. July-Sept 10am-5pm mon-Sat. Tours 11am, 2.30pm Tue, Fri, Sat.* **Admission** *free. Suggested donation £5; £4 reductions. Tours free.* **Map** *p212 D2.*

Now best known for its ambulance service, the Order of St John's roots lie in Christian medical practices from the Crusades of the 11th to 13th centuries. Artefacts related to the Order of Hospitaller Knights, from Jerusalem, Malta and the Ottoman Empire, are displayed (among them Caravaggio's *The Cardsharps*); there's a separate collection relating to the ambulance service. A major refurbishment has reorganised the galleries in the Tudor gatehouse and, across St John's Square, opened to the public the Priory Church (10.30am-12.30pm, 2-4pm, by prior arrangement), its secluded garden and the pleasingly gloomy 12th-century crypt.

Postal Museum & Mail Rail

Phoenix Place, WC1X 0DA (www. postalmuseum.org). Russell Square tube or Farringdon tube/rail. **Open** *10am-5pm daily.* **Admission** *£16; £8 reductions (incl donation). Family play area (45min session) £5; £3.75 with Mail Rail ticket.* **Map** *p212 N5.*

Used to shuttle post across London, the Mail Rail opened in 1927 as one of the earliest driverless electric railways. Closed in 2003, it was mothballed for more than a decade. But now some of its disused tunnels have been revived as part of the new Postal Museum, where you can find out about what was effectively the first social network: the Royal Mail. Exhibits – many of them interactive – display such rare artefacts as a priceless sheet of Penny Black stamps and the original 1966 plastercast of the Queen, which remains on our stamps to this day. But the highlight for visitors will inevitably be hitching a subterranean ride on the refurbished Mail Rail. The whole museum is due to open in summer 2017.

Revealing the Charterhouse

Charterhouse Square, EC1M 6AN (3818 8873, www.thecharterhouse.org). Barbican tube. **Open** *11am-4.45pm Tue-Sun. 55min Standard tour 11.30am, 1.45pm, 2.45pm; 2hr Brother's tour 2.15pm Tue, Thur, Sat.* **Admission** *free. Tours £10-15.* **Map** *p212 P6.*

This tiny museum documents the history of the Charterhouse from the Black Death to the present day – or, more accurately, from the present day to the Black Death, since the chronology runs backwards, from details of the lives of some of the Brothers who still live in these almshouses, past some neat artefacts – not least a sacred statue recut into the shape of a brick that was built into a wall after the 16th-century Dissolution of the Monasteries – to the touchingly displayed skeleton of a victim of that most deadly mid 13th-century plague. Be sure to drop into the chapel (past a plaque dedicated the author William Thackeray), where an old wooden door – half burnt away – records how close the Charterhouse came to destruction in the Blitz. The tours last an hour (two hours if you opt for one led by a Brother) and are well worth the money: not only do you hear the whole history of the place, but you get access to private areas of the Charterhouse – such as the Great Hall and the solitary monks' cells, complete with hatch by the main door where food came in and, er, rubbish came out.

Restaurants

Eagle ££

159 Farringdon Road, EC1R 3AL (7837 1353, www.theeaglefarringdon.co.uk). Farringdon tube/rail. **Open** *noon-11pm Mon-Sat; noon-5pm Sun. Food served noon-3pm, 6.30-10.30pm Mon-Fri; 12.30-3.30pm, 6.30-10.30pm Sat; 12.30-4pm Sun.* **Map** *p212 B2* ❹ *Gastropub*

Widely credited with launching the revolutionary notion of serving restaurant-quality food in a boozer when it opened in its current form in 1991, the Eagle has long since passed into both legend and middle age. But this high-ceilinged corner room remains a cut above the gastropub competition. Globetrotting mains are chalked twice daily above the bar/open kitchen. You can just drink but few do, aware they're missing the big-flavoured likes of moreish tomato and bread soup; daisy-fresh scallops, pan-fried and served on toast with chorizo; and succulent leg of lamb with jansson's temptation (a potato gratin-style Swedish dish).

Exmouth Market £
Exmouth Market, EC1R 4QE (www.exmouth-market.com). Farringdon tube/rail. **Open** *noon-3pm Mon-Fri.* **Map** *p212 C2* ⑤ *Street food*

On weekdays the stalls here serve takeaway food in sufficient variety to satisfy carnivores, omnivorous and even vegetarians. Regular attendees include Spinach & Agushi, with their Ghanaian stews, Pasean pastas, Mac & Cheese, Meat Head BBQ, Spanish dishes from La Cochinita, and Freebird burritos.

❤ Foxlow ££
69-73 St John Street, EC1M 4AN (7014 8070, www.foxlow.co.uk). Farringdon tube/rail. **Open** *noon-3pm, 5.30-10.30pm Mon-Fri; 11am-3.30pm, 5.30-10pm Sat; 11am-3.30pm Sun.* **Map** *p212 D2* ⑥ *International*

Will Beckett and Huw Gott, the duo behind the very popular Hawksmoor steakhouses (*see p186*), scored again at Foxlow. It has a cosily masculine vibe (warm woods, low lighting, comfy retro-themed furniture) and a compact menu of meaty dishes to comfort and soothe, plus impeccably sourced steaks. 'Smokehouse rillettes' sees a smoky mound of beef, turkey, pork and lardo knocked into shape by a tart jumble of cucumber, pickles and capers. The youthful staff are an absolute marvel, with

Spinach & Agushi on Exmouth Market

bags of personality, beaming smiles and a nothing's-too-much-trouble attitude.

Look Mum No Hands £
49 Old Street, EC1V 9HX (7253 1025, www.lookmumnohands.com). Barbican tube or Old Street tube/rail. **Open** *7.30am-10pm Mon-Fri; 8.30am-10pm Sat; 9am-10pm Sun. Food served noon-9pm Mon-Fri; 2.30-9pm Sat, Sun.* **Map** *p212 E2* ⑦ *Café*

Look Mum is a cycle-friendly café-bar with cycle parking in a courtyard, a small workshop and plenty of space to hang out, snack, use the Wi-Fi and – in the evenings – drink bottled beer or well-priced wine. Live afternoon screenings of cycle races take place in the big main room. The food is simple: expect cured meat platters, baked tarts, pastries and cakes.

❤ Modern Pantry £££
47-48 St John's Square, EC1V 4JJ (7553 9210, www.themodernpantry.co.uk). Farringdon tube/rail. **Open** *Café 8-11am, noon-10pm Mon; 8-11am, noon-10.30pm Tue-Fri; 9am-4pm, 6-10.30pm Sat; 10am-4pm, 6-10pm Sun. Restaurant noon-3pm, 6-10.30pm Tue-Fri; 9am-4pm, 6-10.30pm Sat; 10am-4pm Sun.* **Map** *p212 D2* ⑧ *International*

Chef Anna Hansen creates enticing fusion dishes that make the most of unusual ingredients sourced from around the globe. Antipodean and Asian flavours (yuzu, tamarind) pop up frequently, alongside plenty of seasonal British fare (wild garlic, purple sprouting broccoli); the combinations can seem bewildering on the page, but rarely falter in execution, and the signature dish of sugar-cured prawn omelette with chilli, coriander and spring onion is always a winner. The stylish ground-floor café is quite feminine in feel, with soothing white and grey paintwork, white furniture and burnished copper light fittings; there's a more formal restaurant upstairs.

❤ Moro ££
34-36 Exmouth Market, EC1R 4QE (7833 8336, www.moro.co.uk). Farringdon tube/rail or bus 19, 38, 341. **Open** *Restaurant noon-2.30pm, 6-10.30pm Mon-Sat; 12.30-2.45pm Sun. Tapas available noon-3.30pm, 4.30-10.30pm Mon-Sat from the bar.* **Map** *p212 C2* ⑨ *North African/Spanish*

Back in 1997, in a former supermarket on Exmouth Market, Sam(antha) and Sam Clarks set the benchmark for a distinctly British style of Mediterranean cooking that puts a North African twist on Iberian food. Their restaurant (and beautifully produced cookbooks) is still in London's culinary front rank some 20 years later. Moro provides a spectacular showcase for modern Spanish and Portuguese wines, and vibrantly fresh food that throws out surprising and pleasurable flavours at every turn.

Next door to Moro is its offshoot Morito (no.32, EC1R 4QE, 7278 7007, www.morito. co.uk), a fine no-bookings tapas bar.

❤ St John £££
26 St John Street, EC1M 4AY (7251 0848, www.stjohngroup.uk.com). Barbican tube or Farringdon tube/rail. Open Restaurant noon-3pm, 6-11pm Mon-Fri; 6-11pm Sat; 12.30-4pm Sun. Bar 11am-11pm Mon-Fri; 6-11pm Sat; noon-5pm Sun. Map p212 D3 ⑪ *British*

Fergus Henderson and Trevor Gulliver's restaurant has been praised to the skies for reacquainting the British with the full possibilities of native produce, and especially anything gutsy and offal-ish. Perhaps as influential, however, has been its almost defiantly casual style. The mezzanine dining room in the former Smithfield smokehouse has bare white walls, battered floorboards and tables lined up canteen-style. St John's cooking is famously full-on, but also sophisticated, concocting flavours that are delicate as well as rich, as in black cuttlefish and onions, with a deep-flavoured ink-based sauce with a hint of mint. The airy bar here is a great place for a drink and a no-fuss snack.

Pubs & bars

Clerkenwell has a compelling claim to being the birthplace of the now ubiquitous gastropub: the **Eagle** (*see p217*), which kicked things off, is a perfectly decent place for a drink too. Meanwhile, Brit cuisine pioneer **St John** (*see above*) is a good option for a relaxed glass of wine, while for cocktails book ahead to visit **Oriole** (East Poultry Avenue, Central Markets, EC1A 9LH, 3457 8099, www.oriolebar.com), showy little sister of **Nightjar** (129 City Road, Hoxton, EC1V 1JB, 7253 4101, www.barnightjar.com) and elder sibling to **Swift** (*see p167*).

❤ 7 Tales
Soshuru, 64 Turnmill Street, EC1M 5RR (3805 2304, sosharulondon.com/seventales-board). Farringdon tube/rail. Open noon-2.15pm, 5.30-10pm Mon-Thur; noon-2.15pm, 5.30-10.30pm Fri, Sat. Map p212 O6 ①

In the basement of Jason Atherton's restaurant (for more on Atherton, *see p175*), 7 Tales is a wonderfully cool cocktail bar with a playful tone. In homage to Tokyo, the walls are plastered with black-and-white images of the city's street signage, picked out in the glow from a cheeky neon sign that says 'drink sake stay soba'. It's not pure silliness,

though – the creative cocktails are absolutely flawless, the music selection is slick-as-hell hip hop and staff are just plain charming.

Café Kick
43 Exmouth Market, EC1R 4QL (7837 8077, www.cafekick.co.uk). Angel tube or Farringdon tube/rail. Open 11am-11pm Mon-Thur; 11am-midnight Fri, Sat; noon-10.30pm Sun. Food served noon-3pm Mon-Fri; noon-10pm Sat, Sun. Map p212 C1 ③

Clerkenwell's most likeable bar is this table football gem. The soccer paraphernalia is authentic, retro-cool and mainly Latin (you'll find a Zenit St Petersburg scarf amid the St Etienne and Lusitanian gear); bar staff, beers and bites give the impression you could be in Lisbon. A modest open kitchen ('we don't microwave or deep-fry') dishes out tapas, sandwiches and charcuterie platters. The **Bar Kick** on Shoreditch High Street (at no.127) is a bit more of a barn, but also good fun.

❤ Jerusalem Tavern
55 Britton Street, EC1M 5UQ (7490 4281, www.stpetersbrewery.co.uk/london-pub). Farringdon tube/rail. Open 11am-11pm Mon-Fri. Map p212 P6 ⑥

Despite the carefully scuffed wooden floors, peeling paint and tables that look like they've had centuries-worth of pints spilled on them, the Jerusalem Tavern has actually only been a pub since 1990 – it was originally a coffeehouse. Still, the place feels embedded in the history of the area, notwithstanding nods to modernity from the poshed-up bar snacks, taxidermy cabinets and beer from the excellent St Peter's Brewery in Suffolk that includes premium-strength IPAs and whisky-accented ale. Crowds frequently spill out onto the side streets.

❤ Zetter Townhouse Clerkenwell
49-50 St John's Square, EC1V 4JJ (7324 4545, www.thezettertownhouse.com). Farringdon tube/rail. Open 7am-midnight Mon-Wed, Sun; 7am-1am Thur-Sat. Map p212 D2 ⑩

The decor at Townhouse embodies a 'more is more' philosophy: every square inch of surface area is occupied by something lovely. The result: one of the most beautiful bars in London. The cocktail list is high quality, devised by Tony Conigliaro, the man behind the brilliant 69 Colebrooke Row (*see p252*), among others. Even though Conigliaro is known as a techno-wizard, the original drinks here are fairly simple and restrained, as well as being typically wonderful. Among the house cocktails, check out the Köln Martini, Lime Blossom Fizz and the White Mrytle Kir. Service is friendly and helpful.

FLEET STREET

▶ *Temple tube or Blackfriars tube/rail.*

Without Fleet Street, the daily newspaper might never have been invented. Named after the vanished River Fleet, Fleet Street was a major artery for the delivery of goods into the City, including the first printing press, which was installed behind **St Bride's Church** in 1500 by William Caxton's assistant, Wynkyn de Worde, who also set up a bookstall in the churchyard of St Paul's. London's first daily newspaper, the *Daily Courant*, rolled off the presses in 1702; in 1712, Fleet Street saw the first of innumerable libel cases when the *Courant* leaked the details of a private parliamentary debate.

By the end of World War II, half a dozen offices were churning out scoops and scandals between Strand and Farringdon Road. Most of the newspapers moved away after Rupert Murdoch won his war with the print unions in the 1980s; the last of the news agencies, Reuters, finally followed suit in 2005. Until recently, the only periodical published anywhere near Fleet Street was a comic, the much-loved *Beano*, but in 2009 left-wing weekly the *New Statesman* moved into offices around the corner on Carmelite Street. Relics from the media days remain: the Portland-stone **Reuters building** (no.85), the Egyptian-influenced **Daily Telegraph building** (no.135) and the sleek, black **Daily Express building** (no.120), designed by Owen Williams in the 1930s and arguably the finest art deco building in London. Tucked away on an alley behind St Bride's Church is the **St Bride Foundation** (7353 3331, www.sbf.org.uk), dedicated to printing and typography. There's an interesting programme of events and courses, a library and temporary exhibitions that show off the Foundation's collections,

which include rare works by Eric Gill and maquettes for Kinnear and Calvert's distinctive road signs.

At the top of Fleet Street itself is the church of **St Dunstan-in-the-West** (7405 1929, www.stdunstaninthewest.org), where the poet John Donne was rector in the 17th century. The church was rebuilt in the 1830s, but the eye-catching clock dates from 1671. The clock's chimes are beaten by clockwork giants who are said to represent Gog and Magog, tutelary spirits of the City. Next door, no.186 is the house where Sweeney Todd, the 'demon barber of Fleet Street', reputedly murdered his customers before selling their bodies to a local pie shop. The legend, sadly, is a porky pie: Todd was invented by the editors of a Victorian penny dreadful in 1846 and propelled to fame rather later by a stage play.

Fleet Street was always known for its pubs; half the newspaper editorials in London were composed over liquid lunches, but there were also more literary imbibers. If you walk down Fleet Street, you'll see **Ye Olde Cheshire Cheese** (no.145, 7353 6170), a favourite of Dickens and Yeats. In its heyday, it hosted the bibulous literary salons of Dr Samuel Johnson, who lived nearby at 17 Gough Square (**Dr Johnson's House**). It also had a famous drinking parrot, the death of which prompted hundreds of newspaper obituaries. At no.66, the **Tipperary** (7583 6470) is the oldest Irish pub outside Ireland: it sold the first pint of Guinness on the British mainland in the 1700s. Just south of Fleet Street, near Blackfriars station, is the **Black Friar**, a lovely, art nouveau meets Arts and Crafts pub. **Blackfriars Bridge** – designed by Thomas Cubitt and dating from 1869 – is a handsome beast, with its red-and-white painted ironwork, and now runs alongside London's first cross-river railway station: needing to extend Blackfriars' platforms to accommodate longer trains, the designer simply ran them right across the Thames. Now commuters can peer along the Thames without bothering to leave the station.

Sights & museums

Dr Johnson's House

17 Gough Square, off Fleet Street, EC4A 3DE (7353 3745, www.drjohnsonshouse.org). Chancery Lane tube or Blackfriars tube/rail. **Open** *May-Sept 11am-5.30pm Mon-Sat. Oct-Apr 11am-5pm Mon-Sat. Tours by arrangement; groups of 10 or more only.* **Admission** *£6; £2.50-£5 reductions; £12 family; free under-5s. Tours £5. No cards.* **Map** *p212 C4.*

In the know
No piss take

One of many bits of Victorian arcana that Lee Jackson's fine sanitary history, *Dirty Old London*, revealed to us was the 'urine deflector'. Before public conveniences, to stop men relieving themselves in dark corners, sloping shelves were built into walls that would deposit any urine on the would-be urinator's shoes. We were delighted to discover one remains, in the wall of the Bank of England (see p229) no less, near the corner of Lothbury and Bartholomew Lane. But Jackson himself found the finest array: a row on Clifford's Inn Passage, off Chancery Lane. ·

Famed as the author of one of the first – as well as the most significant – unquestionably the wittiest – dictionaries of the English language, Dr Samuel Johnson (1709-84) also wrote poems, essays, literary criticism, a novel and an early travelogue, an acerbic account of a tour of the Western Isles with his biographer James Boswell. You can tour the stately Georgian townhouse where he came up with his inspired definitions – 'to make dictionaries is dull work' was his definition of the word 'dull' while 'oats' is a 'grain, which in England is generally given to horses, but in Scotland supports the people'.

St Bride's Church

Fleet Street, EC4Y 8AU (7427 0133, www. stbrides.com). Temple tube. **Open** *8am-6pm Mon-Fri; 10am-6.30pm Sun. Times vary Sat; phone to check. Tours 2.15pm Tue.* **Admission** *free. Tours £6.* **Map** *p212 C4.*

Hidden down an alley south of Fleet Street, St Bride's is known as the journalists' church: in the north aisle, a shrine is dedicated to hacks killed in action. Down in the crypt, a surprisingly interesting little museum displays fragments of the churches that have existed on this site since the sixth century, as well as some portions of Roman tessellated floor, which you can view using a pair of angled mirrors.

In the know
Feline good

A neat statue of Johnson's cat Hodge sits contentedly in the square outside **Dr Johnson's House** (*see left*).

Pubs & bars

Black Friar

174 Queen Victoria Street, EC4V 4EG (7236 5474, www.nicholsonspubs.co.uk). Blackfriars tube/rail. **Open** *9am-11pm Mon-Sat; noon-10.30pm Sun.* **Map** *p212 C5* ❶

Built in 1875 on the site of a medieval Dominican friary, the Black Friar had its interior completely remodelled in the Arts and Crafts style. It is now part of the Nicholson's stable – the group runs most of the trad pubs in the City, serving moderate food but decent real ales – so you'll come here for the intricate friezes and carved slogans ('Industry is Ale', 'Haste is Slow') of the main saloon bar. You're basically sinking an ale in the middle of a stunning work of art. Admittedly, there's a far more prosaic bar adjoining it, but this remains one of London's most interesting pub interiors.

Birth of a tradition

An 18th-century Fleet Street pâtissier, William Rich, was famous for tiered wedding cakes, which he modelled on the lovely Wren-designed spire of **St Bride's** (*see above*) – the template for bride cakes ever since, as the tour guides never tire of explaining. Intriguingly, the church's marital connections might run much deeper than that. It's likely that the holy well that gave the original church its location had been a site of pagan worship – including the blessing of relationships.

St Bride's Church

TEMPLE & THE INNS OF COURT

▶ *Temple tube.*

At its eastern end, the arterial Strand becomes Fleet Street at **Temple Bar**, the City's ancient western boundary and once the site of Wren's great gateway (which was removed to Hertfordshire but is now in Paternoster Square beside St Paul's). A newer, narrower, but still impressive wyvern-topped monument marks the original spot. The area has long been linked to the law, and here stands the splendid neo-Gothic **Royal Courts of Justice**. On the other side of the road, stretching almost to the Thames, are the several courtyards that make up **Middle Temple** (7427 4800, www. middletemple.org.uk) and **Inner Temple** (7797 8250, www.innertemple.org.uk), two of the Inns of Court that provided training and lodging for London's medieval lawyers. Anybody may visit the grounds, but access to the grand, collegiate buildings is for lawyers and barristers only.

Middle Temple was the HQ of the Knights Templar, a religious order of warrior monks founded in the 12th century to protect pilgrims to the Holy Land. The Templars built the original **Temple Church** in 1185, but fell foul of Philip IV of France, who pressured the pope into suppressing their order.

At Temple Bar, the sweet Strand branch of **Twinings** (no.216, 7353 3511, www.twinings. co.uk) is London's oldest tea shop (dating to 1717), with some interesting memorabilia in the rear. Almost due south of Temple Bar, alongside Middle Temple, is the immensely popular and generally fabulous **Two Temple Place**.

Sights & museums

Royal Courts of Justice
Strand, WC2A 2LL (7947 6000, www. theroyalcourtsofjustice.com). Temple tube. **Open** *9.30am-4.30pm Mon-Fri.* **Admission** *free. Tours £13; £10 reductions; under 15s free.* **Map** *p212 B4.*

Two of the highest civil courts in the land sit in these imposing buildings: the High Court and the Appeals Court. Visitors are welcome to observe the process of law in any of the 88 courtrooms, but very little happens in August and September.

Temple Church
Off Fleet Street, EC4Y 7BB (7353 3470, www. templechurch.com). Chancery Lane or Temple tube. **Open** *varies.* **Admission** *£5; £3 reductions; free under 16s.* **Map** *p212 B5.*

Inspired by Jerusalem's Church of the Holy Sepulchre, the Temple Church was the chapel of the Knights Templar. The rounded apse contains the worn gravestones of several Crusader knights, but the church was refurbished by Wren and the Victorians, and was damaged in the Blitz. Not that that puts off the wild speculations of fans of Dan Brown's *The Da Vinci Code*. There are organ recitals most Wednesdays at 1.15pm.

Two Temple Place
2 Temple Place, WC2R 3BD (7836 3715, www. twotempleplace.org). Temple tube. **Open** *Exhibitions late Jan-mid Apr 10am-4.30pm Mon, Thur-Sat; 10am-9pm Wed; 11am-4.30pm Sun. Private tours only mid Apr-late Jan.* **Admission** *free. Tours free but must be booked in advance.* **Map** *p212 B5.*

The pale Portland-stone exterior and oriel windows here are handsome – but the interior is extraordinary. You get a hint about what's to come before you open the door: look right and there's a cherub holding an old-fashioned telephone to his ear. Built as an estate office in 1895 to the close specifications of William Waldorf Astor, Two Temple Place now opens to the public for three months a year with immensely popular exhibitions of 'publicly-owned art from around the UK', arranged by an up-and-coming curator. Ring the bell and you're warmly welcomed by volunteers into a house with decor that combines sublime, extravagant craftsmanship with a thorough lack of interest in coherence: above porphyry tiles, the Three Musketeers adorn the banisters of a staircase; intricately carved literary characters crowd the first floor, mixing Shakespeare with Fenimore Cooper; the medieval-style Great Hall, with lovely stained glass, crams together 54 random busts – Voltaire, Marlborough and Anne Boleyn enjoying the company of Mary Queen of Scots.

ST PAUL'S & AROUND

▶ *St Paul's tube.*

The towering dome of **St Paul's Cathedral** is, excluding the 'Big Ben' clocktower, probably the definitive symbol of traditional London and an architectural two fingers to the Nazi bombers that pounded the city in 1940 and 1941. North of the cathedral is the redeveloped **Paternoster Square**, a modern plaza incorporating a sundial that rarely tells the time. The name harks back to the days when priests from St Paul's walked the streets chanting the Lord's Prayer (*Pater noster*, Latin for 'Our Father').

Also of interest is Wren's statue-covered **Temple Bar**. It once stood at the intersection of Fleet Street and Strand, marking the boundary between the City of London and neighbouring Westminster; during the Middle Ages, the monarch was allowed to pass through the Temple Bar into the City only with the approval of the Lord Mayor of London. The archway was dismantled as part of a Victorian road-widening programme in 1878 and became a garden ornament for a country estate in Hertfordshire, before being installed in its current location, as the gateway between St Paul's and Paternoster Square, in 2004. The gold-topped pillar in the centre of the square looks as if it commemorates something important, but it's just an air vent for the Underground.

South of St Paul's, steps cascade down to the **Millennium Bridge**, which spans the river to Tate Modern (*see p87*) and now offers the main gateway to the City for tourists. The grand **St Lawrence Jewry Memorial Fountain** is another peripatetic monument: kept in storage since the 1970s after it was removed from the church (*see p230*), it was placed here in 2011. The structure dates to 1866. The stairs take you close to the 17th-century **College of Arms** (130 Queen Victoria Street, EC4V 4BT, 7248 2762, www.college-of-arms.gov.uk), official seat of British heraldry. Originally created to identify competing knights at medieval jousting tournaments, coats of arms soon became an integral part of family identity for the landed gentry of Britain. Scriveners still work here to create beautiful heraldic certificates, but only the Earl Marshal's Court is open to the general public.

East of the cathedral is the huge **One New Change** shopping mall and office development. Designed by French architect Jean Nouvel, its most interesting aspects are a gash that gives views straight through the building to St Paul's and, for a fine roof-level panorama, the sixth-floor public terrace and bar-restaurant. Meekly hidden among the alleys behind it, you'll find narrow Bow Lane. At one end sits **St Mary-le-Bow** (7248 5139, www.stmarylebow.co.uk; closed Sat, Sun), built by Wren between 1671 and 1680. The church bells; peals once defined anyone born within earshot as a true Cockney. At the other end of Bow Lane is **St Mary Aldermary** (7248 9902, www.moot.uk.net; closed Sat). With a pin-straight spire designed by Wren's office, this was the only Gothic church by him to survive World War II. Inside, there's a fabulous moulded plaster ceiling and original wooden sword rest (London parishioners carried arms until the late 19th century).

There are more Wren creations south of St Paul's. On Garlick Hill, named for the medieval garlic market, is **St James Garlickhythe** (7236 1719, www.stjamesgarlickhythe.org.uk, open 11am-3pm Thur, and at other times for services). The official church of London's vintners and joiners, it was built by Wren in 1682. Hidden in the tower are the naturally mummified remains of a young man, nicknamed Jimmy Garlick, discovered in the vaults in 1855. The church was hit by bombs in both World Wars, and partly ruined by a falling crane in 1991, but the interior has been convincingly restored. On Queen Victoria Street, **St Nicholas Cole Abbey** was the first church rebuilt after the Great Fire.

Built on the site of the infamous Newgate Prison to the north-west of the cathedral is

Old Bailey *p224*

the **Old Bailey**. A remnant of the prison's east wall can be seen in Amen Corner.

Sights & museums

Old Bailey (Central Criminal Court)
Corner of Newgate Street & Old Bailey, EC4M 7EH (7192 2739, www.cityoflondon. gov.uk). St Paul's tube. **Open** *Public gallery 9.55am-12.40pm, 1.55-3.40pm Mon-Fri. Reduced court sitting Aug.* **Admission** *free. No under-14s; 14-16s only if accompanied by adults.* **Map** *p212 D4.*

A gilded statue of blind (meaning impartial) justice stands atop London's most famous criminal court. The current building was completed in 1907; the site itself has hosted some of the most famous trials in British history, including that of Oscar Wilde. Anyone is welcome to attend a trial, but bags, cameras, dictaphones, mobile phones and food are banned (and no storage facilities are provided).

> **In the know**
> **Get me out of here!**
>
> A blocked-up door in **St Sepulchre Without**, opposite the Old Bailey, is the visible remains of a priest tunnel into the court; the Newgate Execution Bell is also kept in the church.

Restaurants

Gordon Ramsay's brasserie **Bread Street Kitchen** (10 Bread Street, EC4M 9AJ, 3030 4050, www.gordonramsayrestaurants. com) is the best of several eating options in One New Change.

Pull'd £
61 Cannon Street, EC4N 5AA (3752 0326, www.howtopull.co.uk). Mansion House tube. **Open** *7am-3.30pm Mon; 7am-9pm Tue-Fri.* **Map** *p212 E5* ⑩ *American*

Pull'd cram a lot of stuff in their bread or rice: flavourful leaves, high-grade tomato salad, grated cheese, tasty coleslaw made with red cabbage... as a base for slow-cooked pork, beef or chicken. Top off with your choice of sauces, including a sprightly salsa verde and a better-than-average barbecue sauce. The place mainly operates as a takeaway, but you can also pull up a stool to the counters.

Sweetings ££££
39 Queen Victoria Street, EC4N 4SA (7248 3062, www.sweetingsrestaurant.co.uk). Mansion House tube. **Open** *11.30am-3pm Mon-Fri.* **Map** *p212 E5* ⑫ *Fish & seafood*

♥ St Paul's Cathedral

St Paul's Churchyard, EC4M 8AD (7246 8348, www.stpauls.co.uk). St Paul's tube. **Open** *8.30am-4.30pm Mon-Sat. Galleries, crypt & ambulatory 9.30am-4.15pm Mon-Sat. Special events may cause closure; check before visiting. Tours of cathedral & crypt 10am, 11am, 1pm, 2pm Mon-Sat.* **Admission** *Cathedral, crypt & gallery (incl tour) £18; £8-£16 reductions; £44 family; free under-6s. Book online for reductions.* **Map** *p212 D4.*

St Paul's Cathedral hasn't been lucky through most of its history, but it has been at the centre of some of London's most momentous events. The first cathedral to St Paul was built on this site in 604, but fell to Viking marauders. Its Norman replacement, a magnificent Gothic structure with a 490ft spire (taller than any London building until the 1960s), burned in the Great Fire – its spire having already collapsed many years before. The current church was commissioned in 1673 from Sir Christopher

THE CITY

Wren, as the centrepiece of London's resurgence from the ashes, and though modern buildings now encroach on the cathedral from all sides, the passing of three centuries has done nothing to diminish the appeal of the master architect's finest work.

After £40m-worth of restoration removed most of the Victorian grime from the outside walls, the extravagant main façade looks as brilliant today as it must have when the last stone was placed in 1708. The vast open spaces of the interior contain memorials to national heroes such as Wellington and Lawrence of Arabia. The statue of John Donne, metaphysical poet and former Dean of St Paul's, is often overlooked, but it's the only monument to have been saved from Old St Paul's. There are also more modern works, including a Henry Moore sculpture and Bill Viola's video installation *Martyrs (Earth, Air, Fire, Water)*. The Whispering Gallery, inside the dome, is reached by 259 steps from the main hall; the acoustics here are so good

that a whisper can be bounced clearly to the other side of the dome. Steps continue up to first the Stone Gallery (119 tighter, steeper steps), with its high external balustrades, then outside to the Golden Gallery (152 steps), with its giddying views.

Before leaving St Paul's, head down to the maze-like crypt (through a door whose frame is decorated with skull and crossbones), which contains a shop and café, and memorials to such dignitaries as Alexander Fleming, William Blake and Admiral Lord Nelson, whose grand tomb (purloined from Wolsey by Henry VIII but never used by him) is right beneath the centre of the dome. To one side is the small, plain tombstone of Christopher Wren himself, inscribed by his son with the epitaph, 'Reader, if you seek a monument, look around you'; at their request, Millais and Turner were buried near him.

In the know
Triforium tours

As well as tours of the main cathedral and self-guided audio tours (which are free), you can join special tours of the Triforium, visiting the library and Wren's 'Great Model' – the ruinously expensive prop he used to sell his design to the church commissioners – at 11.30am and 2pm on Monday and Tuesday and at 2pm on Friday (pre-book on 7246 8357, £8 on top of general ticket price). On the tour you'll see the exquisite Dean's Staircase – one of the loveliest features in the whole church. Each step rests elegantly on the previous one, with such perfect balance that no central support is required, giving the curves an airiness that is quite enchanting.

Things don't change much at this enduring City classic, and that's the way everyone likes it. The walls remain covered with photos of old sports teams, and many of the staff have been here for years. Lobster and crab bisques preface a choice of fish and seafood dishes that read and taste like upmarket versions of a pub-side stall – smoked fish, whitebait, trout and so forth. Top-quality fish are then served fried, grilled or poached to order. The handful of more elaborate dishes includes an excellent fish pie.

Shops & services

One New Change

New Change Road, EC4M 9AF (7002 8900, www.onenewchange.com). Mansion House or St Paul's tube or Bank tube/DLR. **Open** *10am-6pm Mon-Wed, Sat; 10am-8pm Thur, Fri; noon-6pm Sun; check website for opening hours of individual shops.* **Map** *p212 E4* ❸ *Mall*

This sprawling Jean Nouvel-designed development is opposite the east end of St Paul's Cathedral, and features a warren of high-street retailers, office buildings and restaurants (Jamie Oliver's Barbecoa, Wahaca, Ramsay's Bread Street Kitchen). Nicknamed the 'stealth building' due to its dark, low-slung design, the place is unsurprisingly popular with City workers on lunchbreaks or post-work spending sprees among predictable chain stores. Take the glass elevator up to the top floor, though, and you'll be rewarded with an unexpected view – St Paul's, yes, but on a level with its roof rather than above or below it. Enjoy it for free, or accompanied by a pricey drink or tapas.

NORTH TO SMITHFIELD

▶ *Barbican or St Paul's tube.*

North of St Paul's Cathedral on Foster Lane is **St Vedast-alias-Foster** (7606 3998, www. vedast.org.uk), another finely proportioned Wren church, restored after World War II using spare trim from other churches in the area. Further west on Little Britain (named after the Duke of Brittany) is **St Bartholomew-the-Great**, founded along with **St Bartholomew's Hospital** in the 12th century. Popularly known as Bart's, the hospital treated air-raid casualties throughout World War II; shrapnel damage from German bombs is still visible on the exterior walls. Scottish nationalists now come here to lay flowers at the monument to William Wallace, executed in front of the church on the orders of Edward I in 1305.

Just beyond Bart's is the fine ironwork of **Smithfield Market**. The market had been under almost constant threat of redevelopment, usually with promises to maintain historic façades, but now seems to have landed itself a rather wonderful future tenant: the Museum of London (*see p228*), funding permitting, will move here in 2021. Smithfield's provides a colourful, not to say visceral, link to an age when the quality of British beef was a symbol of national virility and good humour. Meat has been traded here for a millennium; the current market, designed by Horace Jones, opened in 1868, though it's since been altered (in part thanks to World War II bombs). At weekends, one former cold storage warehouse opposite the market opens as the indefatigable superclub **Fabric** (*see p339*).

St Bartholomew-the-Great

THE CITY

Sights & museums

Museum of St Bartholomew's Hospital

North Wing, St Bartholomew's Hospital, West Smithfield, EC1A 7BE (bartshealth. nhs.uk/bartsmuseum). Barbican tube or Farringdon tube/rail. **Open** *10am-4pm Tue-Fri.* **Admission** *free; donations appreciated. Tours £7; £6 reductions; children free.* **Map** *p212 D4.*

Be glad you're living in the 21st century. Many of the displays in this small museum inside St Bart's Hospital relate to the days before anaesthetics, when surgery and carpentry were kindred occupations. Every Friday at 2pm, visitors can take a guided tour of the museum that takes in the Hogarth paintings in the Great Hall, the little church of St Bartholomew-the-Less, neighbouring St Bartholomew-the-Great and Smithfield.

In the know
Skulls and specimens

Also in the hospital grounds, **Barts Pathology Museum** (3rd floor, Robin Brook Centre, 7882 5555, www.qmul.ac.uk/ bartspathology) has a riveting collection of 5,000 human specimens (including the skull of PM Spencer Perceval's assassin, who was killed in 1812). The need for tight regulations of the collection means it can only open infrequently to the public.

St Bartholomew-the-Great

West Smithfield, EC1A 9DS (7600 0440, www.greatstbarts.com). Barbican tube or Farringdon tube/rail. **Open** *8.30am-5pm Mon-Fri (until 4pm Nov-Feb); 10.30am-4pm Sat; 8.30am-8pm Sun.* **Admission** *£5; £4.50 reductions; £12 family; free under-7s.* **Map** *p212 D4.*

This atmospheric medieval church was built over the remains of the 12th-century priory hospital of St Bartholomew, founded by Prior Rahere, a former courtier of Henry I. The church was chopped about during Henry VIII's reign and the interior is now firmly Elizabethan, although it also contains donated works of modern art. You may recognise the main hall from *Shakespeare in Love* or *Four Weddings and a Funeral*. If you need refreshment, the church has a bar-café in the 15th-century cloister, serving coffee, monastery beers and home-made weekday lunches.

MUSEUM OF LONDON & THE BARBICAN

▶ *Barbican tube or Moorgate tube/rail.*

From Bart's, the road known as **London Wall** runs east to Bishopsgate, following the approximate route of the old Roman wall. Tower blocks have sprung up here like daisies, but the odd lump of weathered stonework can still be seen poking up between the office blocks, marking the path of the old City wall. You can patrol the remaining stretches of the wall, with panels (some barely legible) pointing out highlights all the way to the Tower of London. Also of interest is peaceful **Postman's Park**, next to one of the exit staircases from the **Museum of London**, which itself is due to relocate to the Smithfield Market.

The area north of London Wall was reduced to rubble by German bombs in World War II. In 1958, the City of London and London County Council clubbed together to buy the land for the construction of 'a genuine residential neighbourhood, with schools, shops, open spaces and amenities'. What Londoners got was the **Barbican**, a vast concrete estate of 2,000 flats that feels a bit like a university campus after the students have gone home. Casual visitors may get the eerie feeling they have been miniaturised and transported into a giant architect's model, but design enthusiasts will recognise the Barbican – with its landmark saw-toothed towers – as a prime example of 1970s Brutalism, softened a little by time and rectangular ponds of friendly resident ducks. Learn to love the place by taking one of the regular, 90-minute architectural tours of the complex (www. barbican.org.uk/education, £12.50, £10 reductions) – which will also help you to navigate its famously confusing layout.

The main attraction here is the Barbican arts complex, with its library, cinema, theatre and concert hall – each reviewed in the appropriate chapters – plus the **Barbican Art Gallery** and **Conservatory** (open 11am-5pm Sun), a steamy greenhouse full of tropical plants, exotic fish and twittering birds. Marooned amid the towers is the only pre-war building in the vicinity: the restored 16th-century church of **St Giles Cripplegate** (7638 1997, www. stgilescripplegate.com; Mon-Thu, Sun), where Oliver Cromwell was married and John Milton buried.

North-east of the Barbican on City Road are **John Wesley's House** and **Bunhill Fields**, the nonconformist cemetery where William Blake, the preacher John Bunyan and novelist Daniel Defoe are buried.

Sights & museums

Barbican Art Gallery

Barbican Centre, Silk Street, EC2Y 8DS (7638 8891, www.barbican.org.uk/artgallery). Barbican tube or Moorgate tube/rail. **Open** *10am-6pm Mon-Wed, Sat, Sun; 10am-9pm Thur, Fri. Last entry 1hr before closing.* **Admission** *varies.* **Map** *p212 D4.*

The art gallery on the third floor at the Barbican Centre isn't quite as 'out there' as it would like you to think, but the exhibitions on architecture, fashion, design and pop culture are usually diverting at the very least – and accompanied by interesting programmes of events. On the ground floor, the Curve is a second – long, thin and, yes, curved – gallery that commissions large-scale installations. They're free, and can be superb.

John Wesley's House & the Museum of Methodism

Wesley's Chapel, 49 City Road, EC1Y 1AU (7253 2262, www.wesleyschapel.org. uk). Moorgate or Old Street tube/rail. **Open** *10am-4pm Mon-Wed, Fri, Sat; 10am-12.45pm, 1.30-4pm Thur; after the service until 1.45pm Sun. Tours available; groups of 6 or more phone ahead.* **Admission** *free; donations appreciated.* **Map** *p212 D4.*

John Wesley (1703-91), the founder of Methodism, was a man of legendary self-discipline. You can see the minister's nightcap, preaching gown and personal experimental electric-shock machine on a tour of his austere home on City Road. The adjacent chapel has a small museum on the history of Methodism and fine memorials of dour, sideburn-sporting preachers. Downstairs (to the right) are some of the finest public toilets in London, built in 1899 with original fittings by Sir Thomas Crapper.

♥ Museum of London

150 London Wall, EC2Y 5HN (7001 9844, www.museumoflondon.org.uk). Barbican or St Paul's tube. **Open** *10am-6pm daily.* **Admission** *free; suggested donation £5.* **Map** *p212 D4.*

One of the original settlements established by the Romans after their first invasion in 43AD, Londinium – as it was known then – has survived war, plague and fire to become the bustling metropolis it is today. This journey, from ancient marshland to one of the greatest cities on earth, is documented through a mind-boggling array of exhibits alongside innovative interactive displays.

On the entrance floor, the social history of London is told in chronological displays that begin with 'London Before London', where artefacts include flint axes from 300,000 BC, found near Piccadilly, and the bones of an aurochs, an extinct type of wild cattle. 'Roman London' includes an impressive reconstructed dining room complete with mosaic floor. Windows overlook a sizeable fragment of the City wall, whose Roman foundations have clearly been built on many times over the centuries. Sound effects and audio-visual displays illustrate the medieval, Elizabethan and Jacobean city, with particular focus on the plague and the Great Fire, which marked 400-year anniversaries in 2016.

Downstairs, the lower-ground-floor gallery tells the story of the city from 1666 to the present day. This newer space features everything from an unexploded World War II bomb, suspended in a room where the understated and very moving testimony of ordinary Blitz survivors is screened, to clothes by the late Alexander McQueen and the impressive golden Lord Mayor's coach (it dates from 1757). There are displays and brilliant interactives on poverty (an actual debtor's cell has been reconstructed, complete with graffiti), finance, shopping and 20th-century fashion, including a recreated Georgian pleasure garden, with mannequins that sport Philip Treacy masks and hats. Some displays are grand flourishes – the suspended installation that chatters London-related web trivia in the Sackler Hall, a printing press gushing changing news-sheets, a grand gallery space for Thomas Heatherwick's delicate flower 'Cauldron' from the 2012 Olympics – others ingeniously solve problems: games to engage the kids, glass cases in the floors to maximise display space.

The museum's biggest obstacle had always been its location: the entrance is two floors above street level, and hidden behind a dark and rather featureless brick wall. With visitor numbers higher than ever, the museum is set to move half a mile from its current location to take up residence in the abandoned Victorian market at Smithfield – the architects' design (by Stanton Williams and Asif Khan) has already been selected for a putative grand opening in 2021.

Postman's Park

*Entrances from St Martin's Le-Grand, Aldersgate Street or King Edward Street. St Paul's tube. **Open** 8am-7pm (or dusk) daily. **Map** p212 D4.*

A soothing little park in itself, Postman's Park is best known for the Watts Memorial to Heroic Sacrifice: a wall of ceramic plaques, established in 1900, each of which commemorates a heroic but doomed act of bravery. Most date to Victorian times – pantomime artiste Sarah Smith, for example, who received 'terrible injuries when attempting in her inflammable dress to extinguish the flames which had engulfed her companion (1863)' – but the first new plaque for 70 years was added in 2009. It was dedicated to 30-year-old Leigh Pitt, who died while saving a child from drowning.

Restaurants

Dining options in the **Barbican** aren't inspiring, although the café-bar in the new Beech Street cinema screens (*see p389*) is appealing, as is a French-style chain brasserie **Côte** (57 Whitecross Street, EC1Y 8AA, 7628 5724, http://cote-restaurants. co.uk) next door. The **Chiswell Street Dining Rooms** (56 Chiswell Street, EC1Y 4SA, 7614 0177, www.chiswellstreetdining. com) is an upscale alternative nearby. But, for a slap-up lunch on the go there are some cheap-and-cheerful offerings at the energetic food market (11am-5pm Mon-Fri) on Whitecross Street.

Pubs & bars

♥ Black Rock

*9 Christopher Street, EC2A 2BS (7247 4580, http://blackrock.bar). Liverpool Street tube/rail. **Open** 5pm-midnight Mon-Thur; 5pm-2am Fri, Sat. **Map** p212 D4 ❷*

Tucked away in the maze-like streets behind Liverpool Street station, this dimly lit subterranean whisky lounge is the place for connoisseurs to blow a hole in their bank accounts. One side of the room is lined with cabinets filled with over 250 bottles, while down the middle a table made from half of an English oak tree has two booze-filled channels hewn in the wood. Choose from the Cherry River – bourbon and morello with spices – or the Table Whisky, an ever-evolving house blend.

Shops & services

F Flittner

*86 Moorgate, EC2M 6SE (7606 4750, www. fflittner.com). Moorgate tube/rail. **Open***

*8am-6pm Mon-Wed, Fri; 8am-6.30pm Thur. **Map** p212 F4 ❶ Health & beauty*

In business since 1904, Flittner seems not to have noticed that the 21st century has begun. Hidden behind beautifully frosted doors (marked 'Saloon') is a simple, handsome room, done out with an array of classic barber's furniture that's older than your gran. Within these hushed confines, up to six black coat-clad barbers deliver straightforward haircuts (dry cuts £18-£20, wet cuts £25-£30) and shaves (£25 with hot towels).

Hula Nails

*203-205 Whitecross Street, EC1Y 8QP (7253 4453, www.hulanails.com). Old Street tube/ rail. **Open** 11am-7.30pm Mon, Tue, Thur, Fri; 11am-9pm Wed; 11am-6pm Sat. **Map** p212 D4 ❷ Health & beauty*

Hula's boudoir-style beauty rooms are gloriously decked out in Hawaian wall coverings, with plush velvet sofas and burlesque flourishes (airbrush tans are dried off with a feathery fan, while beauticians have a distinctly burlesque air about them). The salon specialises in luxurious grooming rather than skincare – customers come here for chocolate lycon waxes that leave a trace of glitter on the skin, and super-longlasting bio-gel manicures, rather than facials and massages. Nail treatments take place in the window of the parlour, so you can gossip as you watch the media types go by.

BANK & AROUND

▶ *Mansion House tube or Bank tube/DLR.*

Above Bank station, seven streets come together to mark the symbolic heart of the Square Mile, ringed by some of the most important buildings in the City. Constructed from Portland stone, the Bank of England, the Royal Exchange and Mansion House form a stirring monument to the power of money: most decisions about the British economy are still made within this small precinct. Few places in London have quite the same sense of pomp and circumstance.

Easily the most dramatic building is the **Bank of England**, founded in 1694 to fund William III's war against the French. It's a fortress, with no accessible windows and just one public entrance (leading to the **Bank of England Museum**). The outer walls were designed in 1788 by Sir John Soane, whose own museum can be seen in Holborn (**Sir John Soane's Museum**, *see p215*). Millions have been stolen from its depots elsewhere in London, but the bank itself has never been robbed. Today, it's responsible for printing the nation's banknotes and setting the base interest rate. On the south side of the junction is the Lord Mayor of London's official residence, **Mansion House** (7626 2500, www.cityoflondon.gov.uk), an imposing neoclassical building constructed by George Dance in 1753; there are tours at 2pm on Tuesday. It's the only private residence in the country to have its own court and prison cells for unruly guests. Just behind Mansion House is the superbly elegant church of **St Stephen Walbrook** (7626 9000, www.ststephenwalbrook.net; 10am-4pm Mon, Tue, Thur; 11am-3pm Wed; 10am-3.30pm Fri), built by Wren in 1672. Its gleaming domed, coffered ceiling was borrowed from Wren's original design for St Paul's; other features include an incongruous modernist altar, sculpted by Sir Henry Moore and cruelly dubbed 'the camembert'. The Samaritans were founded here in the 1950s.

To the east of Mansion House is the **Royal Exchange**, flanked by statues of James Henry Greathead, who invented the machine that cut the tunnels for the London Underground, and Paul Reuter, who founded the Reuters news agency here in 1851. In 1972, the exchange shifted to offices on Threadneedle Street, thence to Paternoster Square in 2004, where it remains.

The period grandeur is undermined by the monstrosity on the west side of the junction, **No.1 Poultry**. The name fits: it's a turkey. A short walk down Queen Victoria Street is the Roman **Temple of Mithras** – discovered by accident in the 1950s, the little temple was a media sensation. Duly opened to the public, just a few scrubby courses of old brick remained, and no longer on the original site. Things have moved on since then: Museum of London Archaeology have re-excavated the site, and a better restoration of the Temple will reopen in due course – back where it was found, a site that is in the process of becoming the new headquarters of Bloomberg, the financial news and media company.

Further south, a left on to **Cannon Street** leads to the traditional site of the **London Stone**, a dull chunk of oolitic limestone with an interesting history – and fascinating mythology. Perhaps a Roman milestone, it was mentioned by both Shakespeare and William Blake. The removal of the stone is said to presage the fall of London – and it *has* been removed for redevelopment of its former home at no.111 and is currently on display in the Museum of London. Roughly opposite the address is the late Wren church of **St Michael Paternoster Royal** (7248 5202, 9am-5pm Mon-Fri), the final resting place of Richard 'Dick' Whittington. Later transformed into a rags-to-riches pantomime

hero, the real Dick Whittington was a wealthy merchant elected Lord Mayor of London four times between 1397 and 1420. The role of Dick Whittington's cat is less clear – many now believe that 'cat' was actually slang for a ship – but an excavation to find Whittington's tomb in 1949 did uncover a mummified medieval moggy. The happy pair are shown in the stained-glass windows.

Returning to Bank, stroll north along Prince's Street, beside the Bank of England's blind wall. Look right along Lothbury to find **St Margaret Lothbury** (7726 4878, www.stml.org.uk, 7.15am-5.15pm Mon-Fri). The grand screen dividing the choir from the nave was designed by Wren himself; other works here by his favourite woodcarver, Grinling Gibbons, were recovered from various churches damaged in World War II. Lothbury also features a beautiful neo-Venetian building, now apartments, built by 19th-century architect Augustus Pugin, who worked with Charles Barry on the Houses of Parliament.

South-east of Bank on Lombard Street is Hawksmoor's striking, twin-spired church of **St Mary Woolnoth** (7726 4878, 7.15am-5.15pm Mon-Fri), squeezed in between what were 17th-century banking houses. Only their gilded signboards now remain, a hanging heritage artfully maintained by the City's planners.

Further east on Lombard Street is Wren's **St Edmund the King** (7621 1391, www.spiritualitycentre.org, open by arrangement), which now houses a centre for modern spirituality. Other significant churches in the area include Wren's handsome red-brick **St Mary Abchurch**, off Abchurch Lane, and **St Clement**, on Clement's Lane, immortalised in the nursery rhyme 'Oranges and Lemons'. Over on Cornhill are two more Wren churches: **St Peter-upon-Cornhill**, mentioned by Dickens in *Our Mutual Friend*, and **St Michael Cornhill**, which contains a bizarre statue of a pelican feeding its young with pieces of its own body – a medieval symbol for the Eucharist, it was sculpted by someone who had plainly never seen a pelican.

North-west of the Bank of England is the **Guildhall**, the City of London headquarters. 'Guildhall' can either describe the original banqueting hall or the cluster of buildings around it, of which the **Guildhall Art Gallery** and the church of **St Lawrence Jewry** (7600 9478, www.stlawrencejewry.org.uk, 8am-1pm Mon-Thur), opposite the hall, are also open to the public. St Lawrence is another restored Wren, with an impressive gilt ceiling. Within, you can hear the renowned Klais organ at lunchtime organ recitals (usually from 1pm Tue).

Glance north along Wood Street to see the isolated tower of **St Alban**, built by Wren in 1685 but ruined in World War II and now an eccentric private home. At the end of the street is **St Anne & St Agnes**, laid out in the form of a Greek cross, and now home to a music charity.

Sights & museums

Bank of England Museum
*Entrance on Bartholomew Lane, EC2R 8AH (7601 5545, www.bankofengland.co.uk/ museum). Bank tube/DLR. **Open** 10am-5pm Mon-Fri. **Admission** free. **Map** p212 F4.*

Housed inside the former Stock Offices of the Bank of England (there's a full-size recreation of Sir John Soane's Bank Stock Office from 1693), this surprisingly lively museum explores the history of the national bank. As well as ancient coins and original artwork for British banknotes, the museum offers a rare chance to lift nearly 30lbs of gold bar (you reach into a secure box, closely monitored by CCTV) and displays Kenneth Grahame's resignation letter – the *Wind in the Willows* author worked here for thre decades.

Guildhall
*Gresham Street, EC2V 7HH (7332 1313, www. guildhall.cityoflondon.gov.uk). St Paul's tube or Bank tube/DLR. **Open** 10am-5pm Mon-Sat; noon-4pm Sun. Great Hall closes for functions; phone ahead. **Admission** free. **Map** p212 E4.*

The City of London and its progenitors have been holding grand ceremonial dinners in this hall for eight centuries. Memorials to national heroes line the walls, shields of the 100 livery companies grace the ceiling, and every Lord Mayor since 1189 gets a namecheck on the windows. Many famous trials have taken place here, including the treason trial of 16-year-old Lady Jane Grey, 'the nine days' queen', in 1553. Above the internal entrance to the Guildhall are statues of Gog and Magog, mythical giants who are said to protect the City. (They originate in the medieval legend of an exiled Trojan who wrestled a giant Briton, Gogmagog, whose name over time was split into a pair of giants.) The current statues replaced 18th-century forebears that were destroyed in the Blitz.

Guildhall Art Gallery
*Guildhall Yard, off Gresham Street, EC2V 5AE (7332 3700, www.cityoflondon.org. uk). St Paul's tube or Bank tube/DLR. **Open** 10am-5pm Mon-Sat; noon-4pm Sun. **Admission** free. Temporary exhibitions vary. **Map** p212 E4.*

The City of London's gallery had always a favourite of ours – even before a comprehensive rehang to celebrate the gallery's 15th anniversary in 2014. Upstairs, dull portraits of royalty and long-gone mayors were replaced by the entertaining and informative thematic display of the Victorian Collection. Here, you'll find lushly romantic and superbly camp Pre-Raphaelite works by Frederic Leighton, Dante Gabriel Rossetti and John Everett Millais; you wouldn't mess with Clytemnestra, as painted by John Collier in 1832. A few steps down from the entrance, a mezzanine gallery holds sun-filled abstracts by Matthew Smith; continuing to the Undercroft you'll find various London-themed pieces, some of historical and sociological more than artistic merit, but fascinating nonetheless. There are also neat heritage displays of Roman artefacts and medieval charters that explain the background to Dick Whittington, Gog and Magog and various other topics. Still towering over the temporary exhibition spaces on this floor is John Singleton Copley's *Defeat of the Floating Batteries at Gibraltar*, all two storeys of it.
▶ *Across the courtyard, beside the library, the **City of London Police Museum** (7332 1868, www.cityoflondon.police.uk, closed Sun) opened in 2017. It's free, and a thoroughly diverting account of seeking Jack the Ripper and fighting cybercrime and terrorism.*

Restaurants

City Càphê £
*17 Ironmonger Lane, EC2V 8EY (www. citycaphe.com). Bank tube/DLR. **Open** 11.30am-4.30pm Mon-Fri. **Map** p212 E4* ②
Vietnamese

Long before you see this charming Vietnamese café, you'll smell enticing aromas wafting down the street. At lunchtime, you can expect to see a queue at the door; staff are calmly efficient, so don't baulk at the length –

THE CITY

it disappears in next to no time. The menu is easy to follow and most options are available with beef, pork, chicken or tofu. Seating in the bright, modern interior is limited, so City Càphê is not the place for a long lunch, but it's perfect for a quick bite or a tasty takeaway.

Shops & services

Royal Exchange

Bank, EC3V 3LR (7283 8935, www. theroyalexchange.co.uk). Bank tube/ DLR. **Open** *Shops 10am-6pm Mon-Fri. Restaurants 8am-11pm Mon-Fri. Check individual outlets for details.* **Map** *p212 F5* ❹ *Mall*

This Parthenon-like building is the former home of the London Stock Exchange, founded by ace financier Sir Thomas Gresham back in 1565 to facilitate the newly invented trade in stocks and shares with Antwerp. Destroyed by the Great Fire, and again in 1838, the current premises date to 1844, when they were opened by Queen Victoria, but stopped trading in 1939. The Exchange reopened in 2001 as a rather upmarket mall, with a grand champagne bar and expensive fashion and gift shops – if your desire for a fancy fountain pen or flash watch subsides, it's still worth a look to see City dwellers in repose.

In the know
Hop to it

The gilded grasshopper hanging over 68 Lombard Street is the heraldic emblem of Sir Thomas Gresham, founder of the Royal Exchange (see p232).

MONUMENT & THE TOWER OF LONDON

▶ *Aldgate, Monument or Tower Hill tube, Liverpool Street tube/Overground/rail, or Tower Gateway DLR.*

From Bank, King William Street runs south-east towards London Bridge, passing the small square containing the **Monument**. South on Lower Thames Street is the moody-looking church of **St Magnus the Martyr**; nearby are several relics from the days when this area was a busy port, including the old Customs House and **Billingsgate Market**, London's main fish market until 1982 (when it moved to east London).

North of the Monument along Gracechurch Street is the atmospheric **Leadenhall Market**, constructed in 1881

by Horace Jones (who also built the market at Smithfield; *see p226*). The vaulted roof was restored to its original Victorian finery in 1991, and City workers come here in droves to lunch at the pubs, cafés and restaurants, including the historic **Lamb Tavern**. Fantasy fans may recognise the market as Diagon Alley in *Harry Potter & the Philosopher's Stone*.

Behind the market is Lord Rogers' high-tech **Lloyd's of London** building, constructed in 1986, with all its ducts, vents, stairwells and lift shafts on the outside, like an oil rig dumped in the heart of the City. Rogers has a new building, 122 Leadenhall (the **Cheesegrater**) – the second-tallest building in the City – directly opposite. The original Lloyd's Register of Shipping, decorated with evocative bas-reliefs of sea monsters and nautical scenes, is on Fenchurch Street, where the next in the sequence of distinctive new City skyscrapers emerged: Rafael Viñoly's 20 Fenchurch Street (www.20fenchurchstreet. co.uk), nicknamed the **Walkie Talkie** due to its distinctive top-heavy shape, and now providing wonderful views from the **Sky Garden**. South of Fenchurch Street, on Eastcheap (derived from the Old English *ceap*, meaning 'barter'), is Wren's **St Margaret Pattens**, with an original 17th-century interior.

Several more of the City's tallest buildings are nearby. To the north, the ugly and rather dated **Tower 42** (25 Old Broad Street) was the tallest building in Britain when it was built until the construction of One Canada Square in Docklands in 1990. And topping out at 755 feet (including a radio mast), **Heron Tower** (110 Bishopsgate, www. herontower.com) became the City's tallest building at the end of 2009. Its 46 storeys include bar-restaurants, complete with outdoor terraces and reached by an external, glass-sided lift. A rival, 945-foot monster called the **Pinnacle** was begun on Bishopsgate – having stalled, it looks like it will be reborn under a new design. Also on Bishopsgate, behind Tower 42, is **Gibson Hall**, the ostentatious former offices of the National Provincial Bank of England.

A block south, St Mary Axe is an insignificant street named after a vanished church that is said to have contained an axe

In the know
Big, bigger, biggest

The tallest skyscraper in the City, **Heron Tower** is only the third tallest building in Greater London after **One Canada Square** (see p389) and, of course, the **Shard** (see p94).

used by Attila the Hun to behead English virgins. It is now known for Lord Foster's **30 St Mary Axe**, arguably London's finest modern building. The building is known as '**the Gherkin**', for reasons that are obvious. On curved stone benches either side of 30 St Mary Axe are inscribed the 20 lines of Scottish poet Ian Hamilton Finlay's 'Arcadian Dream Garden', a curious counterpart to Lord Foster's building. Nearby are two medieval churches that survived the Great Fire: **St Helen's Bishopsgate** and **St Andrew Undershaft**. The latter, right at the foot of the Cheesegrater, contains a Hobbit-sized statue of John Stow, who wrote London's first guidebook, the *Survey of London*, in 1598. The quill his effigy holds is replaced by the Lord Mayor every three years (next in 2017).

The north end of St Mary Axe intersects with two interesting streets. The more northerly, **Houndsditch**, is where Londoners threw dead dogs and other rubbish in medieval times – the ditch ran outside the London Wall, dividing the City from the East End. The southerly one is Bevis Marks, home to the superbly preserved **Bevis Marks Synagogue** (7621 1188, www.sephardi.org.uk/bevis-marks; 10.30am-2pm Mon, Wed, Thur; 10.30am-1pm Tue, Fri; 10.30am-12.30pm Sun; admission £5, £2.50-£4 reduction; tours 11.15am Wed, Fri; 10.45am Sun), founded in 1701 by Sephardic Jews fleeing the Spanish Inquisition. Services are still held in Portuguese as well as Hebrew.

South along Bevis Marks are **St Botolph's-without-Aldgate** and the tiny stone church of **St Katharine Cree** (7488 4318, www. sanctuaryinthecity.net; 9.30am-4pm Mon-Fri) on Leadenhall Street, one of only eight churches to survive the Great Fire. Inside is a memorial to Sir Nicholas Throckmorton, Queen Elizabeth I's ambassador to France, who was imprisoned for treason on numerous occasions, despite – or perhaps because of – his friendship with the temperamental queen.

Further south, towards the Tower of London, streets and alleys have evocative names: Crutched Friars, Savage Gardens, Pepys Street and the like. The famous diarist lived in nearby Seething Lane and observed the Great Fire of London from **All Hallows by the Tower**. Pepys is buried in the church of **St Olave** (7488 4318, www. sanctuaryinthecity.net; 9am-5pm Mon-Fri) on Hart Street, nicknamed 'St Ghastly Grim' by Dickens due to the skulls above the entrance.

Marking the eastern edge of the City, the **Tower of London** was the palace of the medieval kings and queens of England. Home to the Crown Jewels and the Royal Armoury, it's one of Britain's best-loved tourist attractions and, accordingly, is mobbed by visitors seven days a week. Overlooking the Tower from the north, beside the tube station, **Trinity Square Gardens** contain a humbling memorial to the tens of thousands of merchant seamen killed in the two World Wars, as well as a set of four plaques commemorating more than 125 Catholics who were executed at the Tower Hill scaffold between 1381 and 1747. Across the road is the small square in which London's druids celebrate each spring equinox with an elaborate ceremony. Just beyond is one of the City's finest Edwardian buildings: the former **Port of London HQ** at 10 Trinity Square, with a huge neoclassical façade and gigantic statues symbolising Commerce, Navigation, Export, Produce and Father Thames. It's now a luxury hotel, run by Four Seasons. Next door is **Trinity House**, the home of the General Lighthouse Authority, founded by Henry VIII for the upkeep of shipping beacons along the river.

At the south-east corner of the Tower is **Tower Bridge**, built in 1894 and still London's most distinctive bridge. Used as a navigation aid by German bombers, it escaped the firestorm of the Blitz. East across Bridge Approach is **St Katharine Docks**, the first London docks to be formally closed. The restaurants around the marina, slightly hidden behind modern office blocks, offer more dignified dining than those around the Tower.

Sights & museums

All Hallows by the Tower
Byward Street, EC3R 5BJ (7481 2928, www. ahbtt.org.uk). Tower Hill tube or Tower Gateway DLR. **Open** *8am-5pm Mon-Fri; 10am-5pm Sat, Sun. Tours Apr-Oct 2-4pm most weekdays; donation requested.* **Admission** *free; donations appreciated.* **Map** *p212 G6.*

Often described as London's oldest church, All Hallows is built on the foundations of a seventh-century Saxon church. Much of what survives today was reconstructed after World War II, but several Saxon details can be seen in the main hall, where the Knights Templar were tried by Edward II in 1314. The undercroft contains a museum with Roman and Saxon relics and a Crusader altar. William Penn, the founder of Pennsylvania, was baptised here in 1644.

Monument
Monument Street, EC3R 8AH (7626 2717, www.themonument.info). Monument tube. **Open** *Apr-Sept 9.30am-6pm daily. Oct-Mar 9.30am-5.30pm daily.* **Admission**

❤ Tower of London

Tower Hill, EC3N 4AB (3166 6000, www. hrp.org.uk /tower-of-london). Tower Hill tube or Tower Gateway DLR. **Open** *Mar-Oct 10am-5.30pm Mon, Sun; 9am-5.30pm Tue-Sat. Nov-Feb 10am-4.30pm Mon, Sun; 9am-4.30pm Tue-Sat.* **Admission** *£25; £12-£19.50 reductions; £45-63 family; free under-5s. Book online for reductions.* **Map** *p212 H6.*

If you haven't been to the Tower of London before, you should go now. Despite the exhausting crowds and long climbs up barely accessible, narrow stairways, this is one of Britain's finest historical attractions. Who wouldn't be fascinated by a close-up look at the crown of Queen Victoria or the armour (and prodigious codpiece) of King Henry VIII? Or, indeed, a castle that's barely an arrow-shot away from the financial heart of Britain? The buildings of the Tower span 900 years of – mostly violent – history, and the bastions and battlements house a series of interactive displays on the lives of British monarchs, and the often excruciatingly painful deaths of traitors. There's easily enough to do here to fill a whole day, which makes the steep entry price pretty good value, and it's worth joining one of the highly recommended and entertaining free tours led by the Yeoman Warders (or Beefeaters).

Make the Crown Jewels your first stop. Beyond satisfyingly solid vault doors, you get to glide along a set of travelators (each branded with the Queen's official 'EIIR' badge) past such treasures of state as the Monarch's Sceptre, mounted with the Cullinan I diamond, and the Imperial State Crown, which is worn by the Queen each year for the opening of Parliament.

The other big draw is the Royal Armoury in the central White Tower, with its swords, armour, poleaxes, morning stars (spiky

In the know
Palatial comfort

In the Thameside wall of the Tower is the unexpectedly beautiful Medieval Palace, with its reconstructed bedroom and throne room, as well as spectacularly complex stained glass in the private chapel. On a hot day, the whole palace is deliciously cool – welcome respite when you've been struggling round with the throng on a hot summer's day.

THE CITY

maces) and other gruesome tools for separating human beings from their body parts. The reassembled Line of Kings, a collection of arms and armour (some belonging to monarchs), life-sized wooden horses and the carved heads of kings, is eccentric pro-monarchy propaganda that dates from the Restoration. Kids are entertained by swordsmanship games, coin-minting activities and even a child-sized longbow. The garderobes (medieval toilets) also seem to appeal.

Back outside, Tower Green – where executions of prisoners of noble birth were carried out (the last execution, of World War II German spy Joseph Jakobs, was in 1941) – is marked by a stiff glass pillow, sculpted by poet/artist Brian Catling. Overlooking the green, Beauchamp Tower, dating from 1280, has an upper floor full of intriguing graffiti by the prisoners who were held here. The Tower only ceased functioning as a prison in 1952 and over the years counted Anne Boleyn, Rudolf Hess and the Krays among its inmates.

Towards the entrance, the 13th-century Bloody Tower is another must-see that gets overwhelmed by numbers later in the day. The ground floor is a reconstruction of Sir Walter Raleigh's study, the upper floor details the fate of the Princes in the Tower.

In the know
Gem of an Idea

It's best to visit the Crown Jewels as early in the day as you possibly can: if you wait until you've pottered around a few other things, the queues are usually immense.

£4.50; £2.30-£3 reductions; free under-5s. **Map** p212 G6.

One of 17th-century London's most important landmarks, the Monument is a magnificent Portland stone column, topped by a landmark golden orb with more than 30,000 fiery leaves of gold – it looks decidedly like the head of a thistle. The Monument was designed by Sir Christopher Wren and his (often overlooked) associate Robert Hooke as a memorial to the Great Fire. The world's tallest free-standing stone column, it measures 202ft from the ground to the tip of its golden flames, exactly the distance east to Farriner's bakery in Pudding Lane, where the fire is supposed to have begun on 2 September 1666. The viewing platform is surrounded by a lightweight mesh cage, but the views are great – you have to walk 311 steps up the internal spiral staircase to enjoy them, though. At least, everyone who makes it to the top gets a certificate.

St Botolph's-without-Aldgate
Aldgate High Street, EC3N 1AB (7283 1670, www.stbotolphs.org.uk). Aldgate tube. **Open** *9am-3pm Mon-Fri. Eucharist 1.05pm Tue, Thur; 10.30am Sun.* **Admission** *free; donations appreciated.* **Map** *p212 G6.*

The oldest of three churches of St Botolph in the City, this handsome monument was built at the gates of Roman London as a homage to and to ask the intercession of the patron saint of travellers. The building was reconstructed by George Dance in 1744 and a beautiful ornamental ceiling was added in the 19th century by John Francis Bentley, who also created Westminster Cathedral.

St Ethelburga Centre for Reconciliation & Peace
78 Bishopsgate, EC2N 4AG (7496 1610, www.stethelburgas.org). Bank tube/DLR or Liverpool Street tube/rail. **Open** *11am-3pm 1st & 3rd Mon of the mth, or by prior arrangement.* **Admission** *free; donations appreciated.* **Map** *p212 G6.*

Built around 1390, the tiny church of St Ethelburga was reduced to rubble by an IRA bomb in 1993 and rebuilt as a centre for peace and reconciliation. Behind the chapel is a Bedouin tent where events are held to promote dialogue between the faiths (phone or check the website for details), an increasingly heated issue in modern Britain.

St Helen's Bishopsgate
Great St Helen's, off Bishopsgate, EC3A 6AT (7283 2231, www.st-helens.org.uk). Bank tube/DLR or Liverpool Street tube/rail. **Open** *9.30am-12.30pm Mon-Fri; afternoons by appt.* **Admission** *free.* **Map** *p212 G6.*

St Mary Woolnoth (see p230) is another star, along with **St Magnus Martyr** (see below), of TS Eliot's *The Waste Land*: keeping 'the hours/With a dead sound on the final stroke of nine'.

Founded in 1210, St Helen's Bishopsgate is actually two churches knocked into one, which explains its unusual shape. The church survived the Great Fire and the Blitz, only to be partly wrecked by IRA bombs in 1992 and 1993. The hugely impressive 16th- and 17th-century memorials inside include the grave of Thomas Gresham, founder of the Royal Exchange (see p232).

St Magnus the Martyr

Lower Thames Street, EC3R 6DN (7626 4481, www.stmagnusmartyr.org.uk). Monument tube. **Open** *10am-4pm Tue-Fri. Mass 12.30pm Tue-Fri; 11am Sun.* **Admission** *free; donations appreciated.* **Map** *p212 G6.*

Downhill from the Monument, this looming Wren church marked the entrance to the original London Bridge. There's a scale model of the old bridge inside the church, and the porch has a timber from the original version. There's also a statue of axe-wielding St Magnus, the 12th-century Earl of Orkney. The church is mentioned at one of the climaxes of TS Eliot's *The Waste Land*: 'Where the walls/Of Magnus Martyr hold/Inexplicable splendour of Ionian white and gold.'

♥ Sky Garden

20 Fenchurch Street (entrance via Philpot Lane), EC3M 8AF (7337 2344, http:// skygarden.london). Monument tube. **Open** *10am-6pm Mon-Fri; 11am-9pm Sat, Sun. Advance booking required.* **Admission** *free. Photo ID required.* **Map** *p212 G6.*

The distinctive but not widely admired skyscraper, 20 Fenchurch Street, has a major calling card. The airport-style security in the unprepossessing lobby gives no hint of

Visitors must book a 90-minute timeslot on the **Sky Garden** (see above) website at least three days in advance. If no slots are available, try booking a table at the **Sky Pod Bar** (cocktails there cost around a tenner) or at one of the two restaurants (the **Darwin Brasserie** is cheaper than the **Fenchurch Restaurant**): all three also give access to the viewing floors.

the splendid experience in store upstairs. You're funnelled into a lift that zips 35 floors up the building everybody knows as the 'Walkie Talkie', which you walk out of to be knocked sideways by the soaring space on the top floors. Flanked by flights of steps rising through lush, leafy plants to a series of terraces, this vast open-air piazza commands outstanding views of the capital. There are irritations: the health-and-safety glass screens deny you the sense of intimacy with the city outside the Sky Garden – a feeling emphasised by the guards refusing to let you stick your camera up over the parapet. But this is a space that changes with the light, with the rewards becoming richer as darkness falls. If you're lucky enough to get a decent sunset, it's truly spectacular, with the detailed panorama transformed into an impressionistic night scene before your eyes. Bring a memory card for your camera, and in winter a warm coat.

Tower Bridge Exhibition

Tower Bridge Road, SE1 2UP (7403 3761, www. towerbridge.org.uk). Tower Hill tube or Tower Gateway DLR. **Open** *Apr-Sept 10am-5.30pm daily. Oct-Mar 9.30am-5pm daily.* **Admission** *£9; £3.90-£6.30 reductions; £14.10-£22.50 family; free under-5s.* **Map** *p212 G6.*

Opened in 1894, this is the 'London Bridge' that wasn't sold to America. Originally powered by steam, the drawbridge is now opened by electric rams when big ships need to venture upstream (check when the bridge is next due to be raised on the bridge's website or follow the Twitter feed). An entertaining exhibition on its history is displayed in the old steamrooms and the west walkway, which provides a crow's-nest view along the Thames. Since 2014, when glass panels were placed in the walkways, you've also been able to look directly down past your own feet at the river below – assuming you're not prone to vertigo.

Restaurants

♥ Duck & Waffle £££

Floor 40, Heron Tower, 110 Bishopsgate, EC2N 4AY (3640 7310, http://duckandwaffle. com). Liverpool Street tube/rail. **Open** *24hrs daily. Food served 6-11am, 11.30am-4pm, 5-11pm, 11.30pm-5am Mon-Fri; 6am-4pm, 5-11pm, 11.30pm-5am Sat, Sun.* **Map** *p212 G4* ❸ *Modern European*

There's a dedicated entrance in Heron Tower from which a glass lift whizzes you up to Duck & Waffle on the 40th floor, or its glitzier sibling Sushisamba (see p237) below. The views are stunning – if you're pointed the right way and, preferably, sitting at a window table (many of which are for couples). Food is an on-trend mix of pricey small plates, raw offerings (oysters, ceviche) and a few main courses (including the namesake duck confit and waffle), as well as sensational barbecue-spiced crispy pigs' ears. Service wavers between keen and offhand, and the acoustics are terrible. But Duck & Waffle is open 24/7 – even though the menu is limited between midnight and 5am, all-night dining is pretty much unheard of in London.

Pubs & bars

City Social Bar
Tower 42, 25 Old Broad Street, EC2N 1HQ (7877 7703, http://citysociallondon.com). Liverpool Street tube/Overground/rail. **Open** *noon-late Mon-Fri; 4pm-late Sat.* **Map** *p212 G4* ➍

Chef-about-town Jason Atherton (*see p175*) took over what had been a pretty run-of-the-mill City restaurant on the 24th floor of what used to be the NatWest Tower – and made it pretty terrific. It is mighty expensive, however, so we recommend the attached bar, which anyone can just show up to – having negotiated two lots of security, an escalator and at least one lift. Still, the bar food and drink is of a far higher standard than you might expect. The cocktails are great, with just enough invention to make them worth the lofty prices: the Oh My Gourd!, for example, comprises pumpkin-infused Tapatio Blanco tequila, lychee, lime, agave – and a pumpkin crisp. Bar snacks aren't so decently priced, but are characteristically Atherton: a 'ploughman's basket' (£15) came with cheese, bread and things in little jars, picnic-style on a checked cloth.

Draft House
14-15 Seething Lane, EC3N 4AX (7626 3360, www.drafthouse.co.uk). Tower Hill tube or Tower Gateway DLR. **Open** *noon-11pm Mon-Wed, Fri, Sat; noon-midnight Thur.* **Map** *p212 G5* ➎

Pretty much the archetypal 'beer bars', members of the Draft House chain focus on serving a brilliant range of superb beers, simple but relaxed surroundings, and eats that don't deviate far from the sausage/burger/hot dog booze-fodder axis. In addition to its handy location, this branch has a big screen for sporting events – which it shows with great verve and much audience advice to the players.

Sushisamba
Floors 38 & 39, Heron Tower, 110 Bishopsgate, EC2N 4AY (3640 7330, www.sushisamba.

Sky Garden

com). Liverpool Street tube/rail. **Open** *11.30am-1.30am Mon, Tue, Sun; 11.30am-2am Wed-Sat.* **Map** *p212 G4* ➑

Duck & Waffle (*see opposite*) is a floor higher and has 24-hour opening, but Sushisamba's two small bars and outdoor roof terrace bar have the edge for views; tell the door staff you don't have a meal reservation but are going to the bar, then take the lift to the 39th floor to avoid another volley of questions, and walk on in. The few cocktails are a little unimaginative – try the saké list instead. But this is a classic destination bar: views, a blinged-up crowd, and relatively easy access. If you do want to eat, the restaurant serves a fusion of Japanese, Brazilian and Peruvian cuisines, with a highlight being the sushi. That's not an eye-opener these days, but then your eyes are bound to be elsewhere.

In the know
The high life

Not long ago finding places where people could eat or drink in London with good views was surprisingly hard – and when you got up there, the quality wasn't always good. Nowadays, you're spoilt for choice in the City alone. There's open-all-hours **Duck & Waffle** and fine-dining at **Sushisamba** in Heron Tower; Jason Atherton's excellent **City Social** in Tower 42; and, perhaps more for the view than the nibbles, the Darwin Brasserie, Fenchurch Seafood and the Sky Pod Bar in the Walkie Talkie.

THE CITY

North London

North London's list of famous former residents gives a good idea of the scope of the area – from Amy Winehouse and Noel Gallagher to Karl Marx, John Keats and Charles Dickens, a huge variety of people have been drawn to its mix of pretty, sleepy retreats and buzzing, creative party zones. First stop is normally Camden Town, with its markets, indie pubs and general alternative vibe, but there's further joy to be found in the leafy squares of Islington. Further to the north, Hampstead and Highgate offer genteel village life and a glorious public space: Hampstead Heath.

❤ Don't miss

1 ZSL London Zoo *p245*
If you don't love this zoo, then you haven't seen the penguins yet.

2 69 Colebrooke Row *p252*
Drink beneath the laboratory of a cocktail magician.

3 Kenwood House/Iveagh Bequest *p249*
See a Rembrandt, have a café lunch and head out onto the Heath.

4 Salut! *p252*
The finest modern European food, at a price you'll like.

5 Camden Market *p242*
Heaven for teens, hell for grown-ups, an experience for everyone.

CAMDEN & AROUND

▶ *Camden Town tube, Chalk Farm tube or Camden Road Overground.*

Despite the pressures of gentrification, Camden refuses to leave behind entirely its grungy history as the cradle of British rock music. Against a backdrop of social deprivation, venues such as the **Electric Ballroom** (184 Camden High Street – but seemingly always under threat of redevelopment) and **Dingwalls** (Middle Yard, Camden Lock, NW1 8AB, 01920 823098, www.dingwalls.com) provided a platform for musical rebels. By the 1990s, the Creation label was based in nearby Primrose Hill (*see p244*), unleashing My Bloody Valentine and the Jesus & Mary Chain on the world, before making it big with Oasis. The Gallagher brothers were often seen trading insults with Blur at the **Good Mixer** (30 Inverness Street, 7916 7929, www.thegoodmixer.com). The music still plays at the **Roundhouse** (*see p345*) in the north, **Koko** (*see p343*) to the south, and any number of pubs and clubs between.

Before the Victorian expansion of London, this was no more than a watering stop on the highway to Hampstead, with two notorious taverns – the Mother Black Cap and Mother Red Cap – frequented by highwaymen and brigands. (The latter is now the **World's End/Underworld**.) After the gaps between the pubs were filled in with terraced houses, the borough became a magnet for Irish and Greek railway workers, many of them working in the engine turning-house that is now the Roundhouse. The area's squalor had a powerful negative influence on the young Charles Dickens, who lived briefly on Bayham Street – you can see a blue plaque that commemorates his residence there.

From the 1960s, things started to pick up, helped by an influx of students, lured by low rents and the growing arts scene that nurtured punk, then indie, then Britpop – and now any number of short-lived indie-electro and alt-folk hybrids, whose young protagonists will all tell you with great fervour about the Camden they knew before it went upmarket.

Parts of Camden still have a rough quality, but the hardcore rebellion of the rock 'n' roll years has been replaced by a more laid-back carnival vibe, as young shoppers join the international parade of counterculture costumes. Tourists travel here in their thousands for the sprawling mayhem of **Camden Market**, which stretches north from the tube along boutique-lined Camden High Street and Chalk Farm Road.

But there are unmistakable signs of gentrification: not least **Shaka Zulu** (Stables Market, Chalk Farm Road, NS1 8AB, 3376 9911, www.shaka-zulu.com), a hugely over-the-top Zulu-themed bar-restaurant, right beneath **Gilgamesh** (7428 4922, www. gilgameshbar.com), a hugely over-the-top Sumerian-themed bar-restaurant. Drop in to **Proud** (*see p342*) if you want to reset your cultural compass.

Cutting through the market is **Regent's Canal**, which opened in 1820 to provide a link between east and west London for horse-drawn narrowboats loaded with coal. The canal towpath is a convenient walking route west to **Regent's Park** and **ZSL London Zoo**, or east to Islington.

Camden's single avowed 'sight' is west of Camden Town – the excellent **Jewish Museum** – but it remains a good bit of town for rough-and-ready gigs. As well as Koko and the Roundhouse, there are plenty of pub stages where this year's hopefuls try to get spotted: try **Camden Assembly** (*see p346*), **Underworld** (*see p347*) and the **Dublin Castle** (94 Parkway, 7485 1773), where Madness and, later, Blur were launched. The **Jazz Café** (*see p348*) and the **Blues Kitchen** (*see p348*) offer a different vibe.

North-east of Camden, scruffy **Kentish Town** (*see p243*) used to be where you came for gigs at the **Forum** (*see p345*), but it has quietly become a great place for eating and drinking too – and it's just a tube stop or bus ride from the craziness of the market.

In the know
Canal pleasures

No longer of much industrial value, the Victorian Regent's Canal is instead used by the jolly tour boats of the **London Waterbus Company** (7482 2550, www. londonwaterbus.co.uk) and **Walker's Quay** (7485 6210, www.walkersquay.com), which make very pleasant runs between Camden Lock and Little Venice in the warmer months. Alternatively, it's an enjoyable half-hour walk east then south from Camden Lock on the Regent's Canal to Granary Square (see p390), passing the sweet little **Camley Street Natural Park** (see p204) on the opposite bank. Keep going – you'd need to allow a couple of hours – and you'll eventually reach the Thames at the **Limehouse marina**).

Sights & museums
Jewish Museum
*Raymond Burton House, 129-131 Albert Street, NW1 7NB (7284 7384, www.jewishmuseum. org.uk). Camden Town tube. **Open** 10am-5pm Mon-Thur, Sat, Sun; 10am-2pm Fri.*

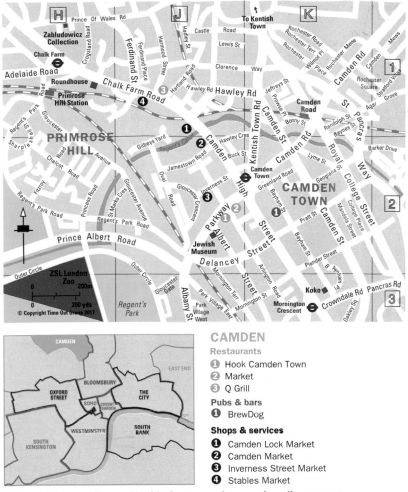

CAMDEN

Restaurants
1. Hook Camden Town
2. Market
3. Q Grill

Pubs & bars
1. BrewDog

Shops & services
1. Camden Lock Market
2. Camden Market
3. Inverness Street Market
4. Stables Market

▶ *Some of the areas discussed in this chapter are shown on the pull-out map at the back of this guide.*

❤ Time to eat & drink

Pub brunch
Bull & Last *p250*

All-day eats
Ottolenghi *p252*

Affordable haute cuisine
Salut! *p252*

Excellent Italian
Trullo *p252*

Creative cocktails
69 Colebrooke Row *p252*

Beer in a fine Georgian pub
Earl of Essex *p253*

❤ Time to shop

Hot home accessories
Aria *p253*

Heaven for teens
Camden Market *p242*

Arts, crafts and everything between
Cass Art *p253*

NORTH LONDON

Admission *£7.50; £3.50-£6.50 reductions; free under-5s.* **Map** *p241 J2.*

This museum is a brilliant exploration of Jewish life in Britain since 1066, combining fun interactives – you can wield the iron in a tailor's sweatshop, sniff chicken soup, pose for a wedding photo or take part in some Yiddish theatre – with serious history. There's a powerful Holocaust section, using the testimony of a single survivor, Leon Greenman, to bring tight focus to the unimaginable horror of it all. Opposite, a beautiful room of religious artefacts, including a 17th-century synagogue ark and silver Torah ornaments, does an elegant job of introducing Jewish ritual. Access is free to the downstairs café, located beside an ancient ritual bath, and to the shop.

Restaurants

Hook Camden Town £

63-65 Parkway, NW1 7PP (3808 5112, www. hookrestaurants.com). Camden Town tube. **Open** *noon-3pm, 5-10pm Mon-Thur; noon-10.30pm Fri, Sat; noon-9pm Sun.* **Map** *p241 J2* ❶ *Fish & chips*

Hook will make you feel as if you're at the seaside. The simple, maritime-themed furnishings are reminiscent of a beach hut. The walls are painted blue like sea and sky. And, as on any seaside visit, you'll be eating fish and chips. The menu changes daily: Hook gets some fish from Cornish day boats. Other fish are farmed, and Hook isn't afraid to use lesser-known species such as ling. Fish is served tempura as well as breaded, and there are some lovely home-made sauces alongside the usual tartare.

Market ££

43 Parkway, NW1 7PN (7267 9700, www. marketrestaurant.co.uk). Camden Town tube. **Open** *noon-2.30pm, 6-10.30pm Mon-Fri; 11am-3pm, 6-10.30pm Sat; 11am-3pm Sun.* **Map** *p241 J2* ❷ *British*

One of the best venues to eat in the area. 'Simple things, done well' is a phrase that could apply to the whole operation. The narrow space has been denuded back to its structural brick; specials are chalked on a blackboard. The proudly British and mainly meaty food is straightforward and effective too, such as a signature pie – chicken and leek, say – or the 'modern British' standard of onglet and chips.

Q Grill £££

29-33 Chalk Farm Road, NW1 8AJ (7267 2678, http://q-bbq.co.uk). Camden Town or Chalk Farm tube. **Open** *11am-11.30pm Mon-*

Thur; 11am-midnight Fri; 9am-midnight Sat; 10am-11pm Sun. **Map** *p241 J1* ❸ *American*

Q updates American classics with skill and intelligence. The large, high-ceilinged room is edgy and sexy – dark walls, rusty girders and vintage wooden butchers' paraphernalia – with loud rock as the soundtrack, but make no mistake: Q is a slick operation. The polished, attentive service never misses a beat, even when the kitchen is on the point of combustion. Children's menu is £5.50.

Pubs & bars

The **Lock Tavern** (*see p340*) and **Proud** (*see p342*) are good Camden DJ bars, while the **Blues Kitchen** (see *p348*) and scuzzy indie-den the **Dublin Castle** (*see p240*) supply live music.

BrewDog

113 Bayham Street, NW1 0AG (7284 4626, www.brewdog.com). Camden Town tube or Camden Road Overground. **Open** *noon-11.30pm Mon-Thur; noon-midnight Fri, Sat; noon-10.30pm Sun.* **Map** *p241 K2* ❶

The Scottish craft brewery's Camden outpost – its other branches include Shoreditch and Clerkenwell – is an initiation into the exciting world of craft beer, but never feels intimidating. The drinks list features BrewDog's own beers on keg draught (alongside select guests), while fridges hold a selection of bottles from other microbreweries, mainly from the US.

Shops & services

❤ Camden Market

Camden Lock Market *Camden Lock Place, off Chalk Farm Road, NW1 8AF (7485 7963, www. camdenlockmarket.com).* **Open** *10am-6pm daily (note: there are fewer stalls Mon-Fri).* **Map** *p241 J1* ❶

Camden (Buck Street) Market *Camden High Street, NW1 (www.camdenmarket.com).* **Open** *9.30am-5.30pm daily.* **Map** *p241 J2* ❷

Inverness Street Market *Inverness Street, NW1 7HJ (www.camdenlock.net/inverness).* **Open** *8.30am-5pm daily.* **Map** *p241 J2* ❸

Stables Market *off Chalk Farm Road, opposite Hartland Road, NW1 8AH (7485 5511).* **Open** *10.30am-6pm Mon-Fri (reduced stalls); 10am-6pm Sat, Sun.* **Map** *p241 J1* ❹

All Camden Town or Chalk Farm tube

Camden's sprawling collection of markets is a smörgåsbord of street culture. Wander past loitering goths and punks to join the throng of tourists, locals and random celebs fighting it out at the vast and varied selection of shops

Side Dish

Some of Camden's best eating is – in unheralded Kentish Town

Until recently, Kentish Town was just a cheap place to live with a gig venue attached. Now it isn't a very cheap place to live, with a gig venue attached and a surprising concentration of restaurants and bars. The arrival of **Dirty Burger** (79 Highgate Road, NW5 1TL, 3310 2010, www.eatdirtyburger. com), a little shack made of corrugated iron that just happens to be run by members' club Soho House, may have been the tipping point. It's all salvaged wood and rusty chairs, with barely room for 20 diners and a menu that offers only cheeseburgers, fries, onion fries, a tiny breakfast menu and drinks – but what deliciously naughty burgers they are.

The foodies' noses twitched – and brought them here. They found plenty to enjoy. Keeping to the fast food theme, **E Mono** (287 Kentish Town Road, NW5 2JS, 7485 9779) is for kebabs that feel like they're worth a coronary and the **Arancini Factory** (115 Kentish Town Road, NW1 8PB, 3583 2242, www. arancinibrothers.com) serves Sicilian-style deep-fried risotto balls in various formats.

Forget the foodies, what about the hipsters? They'll be needing coffee – and craft beer. For the former: the **Fields Beneath** (52A Prince of Wales Road, NW5 3LN, 7424 8838) is tiny, but has a real neighbourhood feel. For the latter? **Camden Town Brewery** is actually based in Kentish Town and you can pop in to its brewery tap (55-59 Wilkin Street Mews, NW5 3NN, 7485 1671, www.camdentownbrewery.com).

Now we've had a couple of pints, another recommendation: go to the loo. Not any loo, but the public toilet that now operates as a bar, **Ladies & Gentlemen** (2 Highgate Road, NW5 1NR, www.ladiesandgents.co). There are a few seats at the bar, but mostly it's table service – delivered with a smile and loads of enthusiasm. The cocktails are generally £8-£9 and mix the classics with the new. Or try basement bar **Knowhere Special** (296 Kentish Town Road, NW5 2TG, www.knowherespecial.com). It has low lighting, great music, and a resident jack russell named Otto.

But, of course, no tale of overnight transformation stands up to much scrutiny, as a visit to the **Pineapple** (51 Leverton Street, NW5 2NX, 7284 4631, www.facebook.com/ ThePineapplePub) will reveal. It's a very good, very normal, backstreet boozer. It dates to the mid 19th century, and you can feel the history in the weathered wood of the joyously unmodernised main bar. There's also a conservatory at the back, and outdoor tables. But what really makes it stand out is that when the pub was threatened with redevelopment into flats in 2002, locals started a campaign to save it – and got the place listed by English Heritage in just eight days: in the words of the citation, it is 'an unusually exuberant example of a mid-Victorian pub...'. Substitute 'neighbourhood' for 'pub' and you might be talking about Kentish Town itself.

Camden Town Brewery

and stalls. Saturdays are not for the faint-hearted or the middle-aged – crowds craving lava lamps, skull rings, fashion, interiors, music and vintage swarm about. Teenagers are likely to be in seventh heaven. Camden Market proper (on the junction with Buck Street) is the place for cheapo jeans, T-shirts and accessories, and the same goes for Canal Market. Down the road, a multimillion-pound redevelopment project is in the midst of transforming the once boho Stables Market into something a little more sterile. However, vintage threads can still be found here alongside crafts, antiques and the now-sprawling Proud gallery and bar. Next door, the pleasant, waterside Camden Lock Market suffered a terrible fire in summer 2017 – when it's back up and running, you'll be able to find everything from corsets and children's clothes to Japanese tableware and multicultural street food.

In the know
Avoid or enjoy?

Weekdays are much quieter in Camden – which can be the difference between pleasure and torment for anyone above voting age. For variety, atmosphere and brownie points from your teenaged children, the weekends are obligatory.

Planet Bazaar in Camden's Stable Market

REGENT'S PARK & PRIMROSE HILL

▶ *Regent's Park or Chalk Farm tube..*

Regent's Park (open 5am-dusk daily) is one of London's most delightful open spaces. Originally a hunting ground for Henry VIII, it remained a royals-only retreat long after it was formally designed by John Nash in 1811; only in 1845 did it open to the public. Attractions run from the animal noises and odours of **ZSL London Zoo** to the fragrant blooms of roses in **Queen Mary's Garden** and the enchanting **Open Air Theatre** (*see p361*); rowing-boat hire, lovely waterfowl lakes, ice-cream stands and the **Espresso Bar** (7935 5729, open 8am-4pm daily) complete the picture. West of Regent's Park rises the golden dome of the **London Central Mosque** (www.iccuk.org); exit to the south and you're in Marylebone (*see p145*).

With a postcard-worthy view of the city's skyline, steep little **Primrose Hill**, to the north of Regent's Park, is just as attractive as the celebrities who frequent the gastropubs and quaint cafés along **Regent's Park Road** and **Gloucester Avenue**. It's all rather spacious and slow-moving after the crowds in Camden proper, although the restaurants fill up fast. Try upmarket Greek bistro **Lemonia** (89 Regent's Park Road, 7586 7454, www.lemonia.co.uk). For a gastropub feed, head to Gloucester Avenue: both the **Engineer** (no. 65, 7483 1890, www.theengineerprimrosehill.co.uk) and **Lansdowne** (no. 90, 7483 0409, www.thelansdownepub.co.uk) are here. On a clear day, the walk up the hill is a delight, with fabulous views back over London.

Sights & museums

Zabludowicz Collection
176 Prince of Wales Road, NW5 3PT (7428 8940, www.zabludowiczcollection.com). Chalk Farm tube or Kentish Town West Overground. **Open** *noon-6pm Thur-Sun.* **Admission** *free.* **Map** *p241 H1.*

In the know
Secret garden

On the Inner Circle of Regent's Park there's an unremarkable gate – push through it and you'll find yourself in **St John's Lodge Gardens**. The lodge was bought for a staggering sum by a relation of the Sultan of Brunei in the 1990s, but its garden – built in 1889 as a place 'fit for meditation' – is open to the public.

ZSL London Zoo

This former Methodist chapel – a remarkable neoclassical building that makes a superb setting for art exhibitions – holds three shows a year, enabling artists to create experimental new work and curators to build exhibitions around the Collection's global emerging art in all media.

💜 ZSL London Zoo

Regent's Park, NW1 4RY (7722 3333, www.zsl.org/london-zoo). Baker Street or Camden Town tube then bus 274, C2. ***Open*** *daily, times vary; check website for details.* ***Admission*** *£29.75; £22-£26.80 reductions; free under-3s. Book online for reductions.* ***Map*** *p241 H3*

London Zoo has been open in one form or another since 1826. Spread over 36 acres and containing more than 600 species, it cares for many of the endangered variety – part of the entry price (pretty steep at nearly £30 in peak season) goes towards the ZSL's projects around the world. Regular events include 'animals in action' and keeper talks. Exhibits are entertaining: look out, for example, for the re-creation of a kitchen overrun with large cockroaches. In the fabulous 'In with the Lemurs' exhibit, you get to walk through jungle habitat with the long-tailed primates leaping over your head. Other major attractions are 'Tiger Territory', where Sumatran tigers can be watched through floor-to-ceiling windows, and 'Gorilla Kingdom'. The relaunched 'Rainforest Life' biodome and the 'Meet the Monkeys' attractions allow visitors to walk through enclosures that recreate the natural habitat of, respectively, tree anteaters and sloths, and black-capped Bolivian squirrel monkeys. Personal encounters of the avian kind can be had in the Victorian Blackburn Pavilion – as well as at Penguin Beach, where the black-and-white favourites are plainly visible as they swim underwater; responses to the snakes and crocodiles in the reptile house tend to involve a good proportion of shudders. Bring a picnic and you could easily spend the day here.

ST JOHN'S WOOD

▶ *St John's Wood tube.*

The woodland that gives St John's Wood its name was part of the great Middlesex Forest, before the land was claimed by the Knights of St John of Jerusalem. Areas of forest were cleared for private villas in the mid-19th century, but the district has retained its green and pleasant glow – proximity

---

In the know
Abbey Roads

It's funny for locals – but not so much for tourists: in 2012, a new station appeared on the map, called Abbey Road. Unfortunately for Beatles fans, it's on the DLR extension in east London (near the Olympic Park), completely the wrong side of town for the famous St John's Wood studio and its zebra crossing. Don't be fooled!

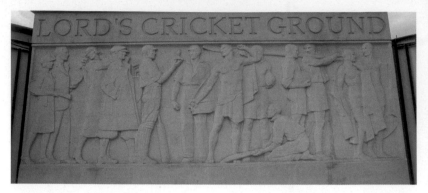

to the western edge of Regent's Park helps. Some uncharacteristically sensitive redevelopment during the 1950s has left the area smart and eminently desirable to those with the money: £2 million is considered a bargain for a modest semi. The expensive tastes of the locals are reflected in the posh boutiques along the High Street. The main tourist attraction is **Lord's** cricket ground, but a steady stream of music fans pay tribute to the Beatles on the zebra crossing in front of **Abbey Road Studios** (3 Abbey Road, NW8 9AY, 7266 7000, www.abbeyroad.com). The studio, founded in 1931 by Sir Edward Elgar, is still used to record albums and film scores, including soundtracks to the *Lord of the Rings* trilogy, *Star Wars* prequels and *Harry Potter* films. Up the Finchley Road from St John's Wood is Swiss Cottage, worth a visit for the modernist library designed by Sir Basil Spence in the early '60s.

Sights & museums

Lord's Tour & MCC Museum

St John's Wood Road, St John's Wood, NW8 8QN (7616 8500, www.lords.org). St John's Wood tube. Entry to museum as part of the tour; times vary. **Tickets** *£20; £12-15 reductions; £49 family; free under-5s.* **Map** *pull out F4.*

Lord's is more than just a cricket ground. As the headquarters of the Marylebone Cricket Club (MCC), it is the official guardian of the sport's rules – and, consequently, a portion of the nation's heart – and celebrated its bicentenary (on the current site) in 2014. Opened in 1953, the museum's highlight is the unfeasibly tiny urn containing the Ashes: this coveted trophy, battled over since 1882/83, never leaves Lord's, so it will still be here no matter what happens when we take on Australia again down under in 2017/18. There's also memorabilia celebrating legends of the game (Jack Hobbs, Don Bradman, Shane Warne and, above all, WG Grace) and

plenty of pleasing oddities, not least a stuffed sparrow mounted on the cricket ball that killed it on 3 July 1936.

Restaurants

Singapore Garden £££

83 Fairfax Road, NW6 4DY (7624 8233, www. singaporegarden.co.uk). Swiss Cottage tube. **Open** *noon-2pm, 6-10pm Mon-Thur; noon-2pm, 6-10.30pm Fri, Sat; noon-4pm, 6-10pm Sun. Singaporean & Malay*

In a capital city that represents the cuisine of nearly every nation in the world, from Iceland to India, Nepal to New Zealand, it's surprisingly difficult to find Singaporean and Malay food. But at this Swiss Cottage stalwart you can feast not only on Malaysian dishes, but on specialities from the Singapore Straits – an island melting-pot whose majority Chinese population and shared history (and border) with Malaysia makes for some very interesting happenings on your plate. Skip the everyday Cantonese stuff in favour of Straits classics: mouthwatering sambals, curries and noodles. It's hawker-style food, but served in a stylish, restaurant setting.

Tamada ££

122 Boundary Road, NW8 0RH (7372 2882, www.tamada.co.uk). Kilburn Park or St John's Wood tube, or Kilburn High Road Overground. **Open** *6-11pm Tue-Fri; 1-3.30pm, 6-11pm Sat; 1-3.30pm, 6-9pm Sun. Georgian*

Those unfamiliar with Georgian cuisine will find themselves pleasantly surprised at this understated neighbourhood restaurant. A crossroads between East and West, delicately spiced plates such as *kuchmachi* (tender cubes of pork heart, liver and lung in a rich, mildly spicy gravy spiked with tangy pomegranate seeds) or *lobio* (a red bean vegetarian stew the consistency of porridge, boosted by coriander, served with pickled green tomatoes and gherkins) offer a highly satisfying meal.

WE'LL TELL YOU WHERE TO GO

Wherever you're exploring, we've got
the insider insight on the world's best
destinations.

TIMEOUT.COM/
LONDON/TRAVEL

HAMPSTEAD

▶ *Hampstead tube, or Gospel Oak or Hampstead Heath Overground.*

It may have been absorbed into London during the city's great Victorian expansion, but hilltop Hampstead still feels like a Home Counties village. It has long been a favoured roost for literary and artistic types: Keats and Constable lived here in the 19th century, and sculptors Barbara Hepworth and Henry Moore took up residence in the 1930s. However, the area is now popular with City workers, who are among the only people able to afford what is some of London's priciest property.

The undisputed highlight of the district is **Hampstead Heath**, the vast and in places wonderfully overgrown tract of countryside between Hampstead village and Highgate that is said to have inspired CS Lewis's Narnia. The heath covers 791 acres of woodland, playing fields, swimming ponds and meadows of tall grass that attract picnickers and couples in search of privacy.

The south end of the heath is where you'll find dinky Hampstead village, all genteel shops and cafés, restaurants and lovely pubs such as the **Holly Bush**. While you're there, tour the gorgeous sunken gardens and antique collection at **Fenton House** or gaze at the stars from the **Hampstead Scientific Society Observatory** (Lower Terrace, www.hampsteadscience.ac.uk/astro), open on clear Friday and Saturday evenings and Sunday lunchtimes from mid September to mid April. A stroll along nearby Judges Walk reveals a line of horse chestnuts and limes virtually unchanged since they appeared in a Constable painting in 1820. Constable was buried nearby at **St John-at-Hampstead Church** (7794 5808, www.hampsteadparishchurch.org.uk), as was the comedian Peter Cook. At the top of Hampstead, North End Way divides the main heath from the wooded West Heath, one of London's oldest gay cruising areas (but perfectly family-friendly by day).

You can swim here too, in bucolic majesty. **Hampstead Heath Swimming Ponds** (www.cityoflondon.gov.uk/hampstead; £2, £1 reductions) are the only places in the UK to offer life-guarded open-water public swimming all year round. Competent swimmers aged eight and above are allowed in, but remember there's no shallow end – you just jump straight in.

East of Hampstead tube, a maze of postcard-pretty residential streets shelters **Burgh House** (New End Square, 7431 0144, www.burghhouse.org.uk), a Queen Anne house with a small local-history museum and gallery. Also in the area are **2 Willow Road**, architect Ernö Goldfinger's self-designed 1930s residence, and **40 Well Walk**, Constable's home for the last ten years of his life. Downhill towards Hampstead Heath Overground station is **Keats House**.

Further west, and marginally closer to Finchley Road tube, is the **Freud Museum**, while the contemporary art exhibitions of **Camden Arts Centre** are almost opposite Finchley Road & Frognal Overground station.

Sights & museums

2 Willow Road

2 Willow Road, NW3 1TH (7435 6166, www.nationaltrust.org.uk/2-willow-road). Hampstead tube or Hampstead Heath Overground. **Open** *Mar-Oct 11am-5pm Wed-Sun. Tours 11am, noon, 1pm, 2pm.* **Admission** *by guided tour only £6.50; £3.25 reductions; £16.25 family; free under-5s. Joint ticket with Fenton House £11, £5.50 reductions.*

A surprising addition to the National Trust's collection of historic houses, this small modernist building was designed by Hungarian-born architect Ernö Goldfinger. The house was made to be flexible, with ingenious movable partitions and folding doors. Home to the architect and his wife until their deaths, it contains a fine, idiosyncratic collection of art by the likes of Max Ernst and Henry Moore. Goldfinger also designed Notting Hill's Trellick Tower. Ian Fleming despised the architect and named a James Bond villain after Goldfinger.

Camden Arts Centre

Arkwright Road, NW3 6DG (7472 5500, www.camdenartscentre.org). Finchley Road tube or Finchley Road & Frognal Overground. **Open** *10am-6pm Tue, Thur-Sun; 10am-9pm Wed.* **Admission** *free.*

Under director Jenni Lomax, this 50-year-old gallery eclipses larger, younger venues. The annual artist-curated shows – sculpture, automata, film works – have been among the most memorable in recent history. The Centre also hosts a comprehensive programme of talks, events and workshops, and boasts a

NORTH LONDON

Kenwood House

good bookshop and a great café, which opens on to a surprisingly tranquil garden.

Fenton House
3 Hampstead Grove, NW3 6RT (7435 3471, www.nationaltrust.org.uk). Hampstead tube. **Open** *Mar-Oct 11am-5pm Wed-Sun. Closed Nov-Feb.* **Admission** *House & gardens £7.70; £3.80 reductions; £19 family; free under-5s. Gardens £2. Joint ticket with 2 Willow Road £11, £5.50 reductions.*

Set in a gorgeous garden, with a 300-year-old apple orchard, this manor house is notable for its 17th- and 18th-century harpsichords, virginals and spinets, which are still played at lunchtime and evening concerts (usually Wed; phone for details). Also on display are European and Chinese porcelain, Chippendale furniture and some artful and intricate 17th-century needlework.

Freud Museum
20 Maresfield Gardens, NW3 5SX (7435 2002, www.freud.org.uk). Finchley Road tube. **Open** *noon-5pm Wed-Sun.* **Admission** *£8; £4-£6 reductions; free under-12s.*

Driven from Vienna by the Nazis, Sigmund Freud lived in this quiet house in north London with his wife Martha and daughter Anna until his death in 1939. Now a museum with temporary exhibitions, the house displays Freud's antiques, art and therapy tools, including his famous couch. Unusually, the building has two blue plaques, one for Sigmund and another for Anna, a pioneer in child psychiatry.

Keats House
10 Keats Grove, NW3 2RR (7332 3868, www.cityoflondon.gov.uk/things-to-do/keats-house). Hampstead tube, Hampstead Heath Overground or bus 24, 46, 168. **Open** *11am-5pm Wed-Sun.* **Admission** *£6.50; £3.25-5.50 reductions; free under-18s.*

Keats House was the Romantic poet's last British home before tuberculosis forced him to Italy and death at the age of only 25. A leaflet guides you through each room, starting from the rear, as well as providing context for Keats's life and that of his less famous friend and patron, Charles Brown. Painstaking renovation has ensured the decorative scheme is entirely accurate, down to pale pink walls in Keats's humble bedroom. The garden, in which he wrote 'Ode to a Nightingale', is particularly pleasant.

♥ Kenwood House/Iveagh Bequest
Hampstead Lane, NW3 7JR (8348 1286, www.english-heritage.org.uk). Hampstead tube, or Golders Green tube then bus 210. **Open** *10am-4pm daily.* **Admission** *free.*

Set in lovely grounds at the top of Hampstead Heath, Kenwood House is every inch the country manor house. Built in 1616, the mansion was remodelled in the 18th century for William Murray, who made the pivotal court ruling in 1772 that made it illegal to own slaves in England. The house was purchased by brewing magnate Edward Guinness, who was kind enough to donate his art collection to the nation in 1927. After extensive, splendid renovations, it reopened in 2014. The interiors have been returned to a state that enhances such highlights of the collection as Vermeer's *The Guitar Player*, Gainsborough's *Countess Howe*, and one of Rembrandt's finest self-portraits (dating to c1663). There's a terrific kids' room with games and activities too.

Restaurants

♥ Bull & Last ££

168 Highgate Road, NW5 1QS (7267 3641, www.thebullandlast.co.uk). Kentish Town tube/rail then bus 214, C2, or Gospel Oak Overground then bus C11. **Open** *Bar noon-11pm Mon-Thur; noon-midnight Fri, Sat; noon-10.30pm Sun. Restaurant breakfast 9-11am Sat, Sun; other hours vary.* Gastropub

For a place with such a good reputation for its food, the Bull & Last is refreshingly pubby: heavy wooden furniture, velvet drapes, stuffed animals and old prints decorate both the bar and the upstairs dining room. The latter is a calmer and cooler place to eat than the ground-floor bar, and allows diners to focus on dishes such as pig's cheek with watermelon pickle, basil and sesame. There are (big) roasts at weekends, a changing selection of beers and ciders from small breweries and a decent wine list.

Pubs & bars

Holly Bush

22 Hollymount, NW3 6SG (7435 2892, www.hollybushhampstead.co.uk). Hampstead tube or Hampstead Heath Overground. **Open** *noon-11pm Mon-Sat; noon-10.30pm Sun. Food served noon-4.30pm, 6-10pm Mon-Sat; noon-8pm Sun.*

As the trend for gutting old pubs claims yet more Hampstead boozers, this place's cachet increases. Located on a quiet hilltop backstreet, this Grade II-listed building was originally built as a house in the 1790s and used as the Assembly Rooms in the 1800s, before becoming a pub in 1928. A higgledy-piggledy air remains, with three low-ceilinged bar areas and one bar counter at which decent pints are poured. Sound food and a good choice of wines by the glass are further draws.

HIGHGATE

▶*Archway or Highgate tube.*

Taking its name from the tollgate that once stood on the High Street, Highgate is inexorably linked with London's medieval mayor, Richard 'Dick' Whittington. As the story goes, the disheartened Whittington, having failed to make his fortune, fled the City as far as Highgate Hill, but turned

back when he heard the Bow bells peal out 'Turn again, Whittington, thrice Mayor of London'. Today, the area is best known for the atmospheric grounds of **Highgate Cemetery**. Adjoining the cemetery is pretty **Waterlow Park**, created by low-cost housing pioneer Sir Sydney Waterlow in 1889, with ponds, a mini-aviary, tennis courts, and a cute garden café in 16th-century **Lauderdale House** (8348 8716, www.lauderdalehouse.co.uk), former home of Charles II's mistress, Nell Gwynn. North of Highgate tube, shady **Highgate Woods** are preserved as a conservation area, with a nature trail, an adventure playground and a café that hosts live jazz during the summer. It is a surviving remnant of the vast Middlesex Forest that once spread in every direction.

Sights & museums

Highgate Cemetery

Swains Lane, N6 6PJ (8340 1834, www.highgate-cemetery.org). Archway tube. **Open** *East Cemetery Mar-Oct 10am-5pm Mon-Fri; 11am-5pm Sat, Sun. Nov-Feb 10am-4pm Mon-Fri; 11am-4pm Sat, Sun. Tours 2pm Sat. West Cemetery by tour only, check website for times.* **Admission** *£4; free under-18s. Tours East Cemetery £8, £4 reductions. West Cemetery £12; £6 reductions.*

The final resting place of some very famous Londoners, Highgate Cemetery is a wonderfully overgrown maze of ivy-cloaked Victorian tombs and time-shattered urns. Visitors can wander at their own pace through

In the know
Visiting times

Highgate Cemetery closes during burials, so call ahead before you visit – even if you're only planning a mooch round the East Cemetery.

NORTH LONDON

Highgate Cemetery

the East Cemetery, with its memorials to Karl Marx, George Eliot and Douglas Adams, but the most atmospheric part of the cemetery is the foliage-shrouded West Cemetery, laid out in 1839. Only accessible on an organised tour (book ahead, dress respectfully and arrive 30 minutes early), the shady paths wind past gloomy catacombs, grand Victorian pharaonic tombs, and the graves of notables such as poet Christina Rossetti, scientist Michael Faraday and poisoned Russian dissident Alexander Litvinenko.

Pubs & bars

Bull

13 North Hill, N6 4AB (8341 0510, www. thebullhighgate.co.uk). Highgate tube. **Open** *noon-11pm Mon-Thur, Sun; noon-midnight Fri; 10am-midnight Sat. Food served until 10pm Mon-Sat; until 9pm Sun.*

First impressions would suggest the Bull is just another suburban gastropub, but note the enamelled beer memorabilia on the walls and garlands of hop flowers: this pub holds beer in extremely high esteem. You might catch a glimpse of the Willy Wonka tubing and brass vats of the brewing equipment, and the beer taps reveal almost nothing recognisable from the average high-street chain pub. Five of the pumps dispense the fine products of the London Brewing Company, made on the premises, and keg fonts advertise the likes of Sierra Nevada Torpedo and Veltins Pils.

ISLINGTON

▶ *Angel tube or Highbury & Islington tube/ Overground.*

Islington started life as a country village beside one of Henry VIII's expansive hunting reserves. It soon became an important livestock market, supplying the Smithfield meat yards, before being enveloped into Greater London. The 19th century brought industrial development along the Regent's Canal and later industrial decay, but locals kept up their spirits at the area's music halls, launchpads for such working-class heroes as Marie Lloyd, George Formby and Norman Wisdom. From the 1960s, there was an influx of arts and media types, who gentrified the Georgian squares and Victorian terraces, and opened cafés, restaurants and boutiques around Upper Street and Essex Road. It is now a suburban bower of the *Guardian*-reading middle classes.

Close to Angel station on Upper Street, the **Camden Passage** antique market bustles with browsing activity on Wednesdays and Saturdays. The music halls have long gone, but locals still take advantage of the celluloid offerings at the **Screen on the Green** (*see p325* Everyman & Screen Cinemas) and the stage productions at the **Almeida** theatre (*see p364*).

North of Angel, Regency-era Canonbury Square was once home to George Orwell (no. 27) and Evelyn Waugh (no. 17A). One of the handsome townhouses now contains the **Estorick Collection of Modern Italian Art**. Nearby, on Compton Terrace, the Grade I-listed gothic masterpiece **Union Chapel** (*see p350*) is still a working church, but also a help centre for London's homeless and a superb music venue. Just beyond the end of Upper Street is **Highbury Fields**, where 200,000 Londoners fled in 1666 to escape the Great Fire. The surrounding district is best known as the home of Arsenal Football Club, who abandoned the charming Highbury Stadium in 2006 for the gleaming 60,000-seat behemoth that is the **Emirates Stadium** (Hornsey Road, N7 7AJ). Fans can either take a fine self-guided audio tour of the stadium or check out the memorabilia at the **Arsenal Museum** (7619 5000, www. arsenal.com). Dedicated football fans will enjoy walking a couple of blocks east to Avenell Road, where Archibald Leitch's palatial East Stand has been preserved as offices; on parallel Highbury Hill, a single painted house marks the entrance to the vanished West Stand.

Sights & museums

Estorick Collection of Modern Italian Art

39A Canonbury Square, N1 2AN (7704 9522, www.estorickcollection.com). Highbury & Islington tube/Overground or bus 271. **Open** *11am-6pm Wed-Sat; noon-5pm Sun.* **Admission** *£6.50; £4.50 reductions; free under-16s, students.*

Originally owned by American political scientist and writer Eric Estorick, this is a wonderful repository of early 20th-century Italian art – substantially renovated for its reopening in 2017. It is one of the world's foremost collections of futurism, Italy's brash and confrontational contribution to international modernism. The galleries are full of movement, machines and colour, while the temporary exhibits meet the futurist commitment to fascism full on. There is also a shop and café.

Restaurants

Oldroyd ££

344 Upper Street, N1 0PD (8617 9010, www. oldroydlondon.com). Angel tube. **Open** *noon-11pm Mon-Thur; noon-11.30pm Sat; 11am-10pm Sun.* **Map** *pull-out P3. Modern European*

The first solo restaurant from Tom Oldroyd (former chef-director at Polpo, *see p172*) is a small place with big ambition. If you've eaten at Polpo, you won't be surprised by the high-impact flavourings and combinations, but here the menu draws on France and Spain as well as Italy. The tiny open-air kitchen offers a diminutive selection of stunning nibbles from £4 (radishes with smoked cod's roe, for instance) to £11 (paella of squid, rabbit and broad beans), with select wines to match. There's hardly enough room to swing a cat, but it's a tasty menu by a renowned chef at very reasonably prices.

♥ Ottolenghi ££

287 Upper Street, N1 2TZ (7288 1454, www. ottolenghi.co.uk). Angel tube or Highbury & Islington tube/Overground. **Open** *8am-10.30pm Mon-Sat; 9am-7pm Sun. Café*

Hit cookbooks have made this flagship branch of the burgeoning Ottolenghi empire a point of pilgrimage for foodies the world over. French toast made from brioche and served with crème fraîche and a thin berry and muscat compote makes a heady start to the day. Or there's welsh rarebit, scrambled eggs with smoked salmon or a lively chorizo-spiked take on baked beans served with sourdough, fried egg and black pudding. In the evening (when bookings are taken), the cool white interior works a double shift as a smart and comparatively pricey restaurant serving elegant fusion dishes for sharing.

♥ Salut! ££

412 Essex Road, N1 3PJ (3441 8808, salut-london.co.uk). Essex Road rail. **Open** *6-11pm Mon-Wed; noon-3pm, 6-10pm Thur-Sat; noon-3pm, 6-10pm Sun. Modern European*

Salut offers a relaxed take on modern European haute cuisine. The menu is understated but everything on it demonstrates exquisite attention to detail: on one recent visit, king crab and watercress came with unexpected crab roe foam and micro herb pesto; the 'selection of onions' with a juicy pork belly was three colourful piles of alliums that were in turn pickled, caramelised and charred to perfection; poached pear was perfectly complemented by fermented berries, rich fruit jelly, hazelnut crumble and white chocolate foam. These beautiful plates of food taste as good as they look – without breaking the bank.

Smokehouse ££

63-69 Canonbury Road, N1 2DG (7354 1144, www.smokehouseislington.co.uk). Highbury & Islington tube/Overground. **Open** *6-10pm Mon-Fri; noon-4pm, 6-10pm Sat; noon-9pm Sun. Barbecue*

Chef Neil Rankin has become London's high priest of barbecue. Trendy though the menu seems – it includes French bistro dishes, carefully sourced British produce and even Korean flavours – the mutton chops come from the grill, not the barman's cheeks, and they come fatty and full-flavoured. Mullet is smoked, cut into translucent slivers and served with white pickled clams, radishes and sea purslane. Pit-roasted corn on the cob, slathered with buttery smoked béarnaise sauce, shows that a barbecue expert doesn't just cook flesh.

♥ Trullo ££

300-302 St Paul's Road, N1 2LH (7226 2733, www.trullorestaurant.com). Highbury & Islington tube/Overground. **Open** *12.30-2.45pm, 6-10pm Mon-Sat; 12.30-3pm Sun. Italian*

While evenings are still busy-to-frantic in this two-floored contemporary trattoria, lunchtime finds Trullo calm and the cooking relaxed and assured. Grills and roasts from the carte might include Black Hampshire pork chop and cod with cannellini beans and mussels, while pappardelle with beef shin ragù has been a staple since Trullo's early days and remains a silky, substantial delight.

Pubs & bars

The **Old Queen's Head** (*see p342*) is a boisterous and lively pub.

♥ 69 Colebrooke Row

69 Colebrooke Row, N1 8AA (07540 528 593, www.69colebrookerow.com). Angel tube. **Open** *5pm-midnight Mon-Wed, Sun; 5pm-1am Thur; 5pm-2am Fri, Sat.*

It's not easy to get a seat in the flagship of bar supremo Tony Conigliaro without booking. Punters come for the outstanding cocktails – some of which may push the boundaries of what can be put in a glass, but they always maintain the drinkability of the classics. Take the Terroir, for instance, which lists as its ingredients 'distilled clay, flint and lichen', and tastes wonderfully like a chilled, earthy, minerally vodka. It's made in Conigliaro's upstairs laboratory, which also produces bespoke cocktail ingredients such as Guinness reduction, paprika bitters, rhubarb cordial and pine-infused gin. There's a subtle jazz-age vibe in the small, tight, low-lit room and – on certain nights – a pianist belts out swinging standards.

Craft Beer Company

55 White Lion Street, N1 9PP (7278 0318, www.thecraftbeerco.com/islington). Angel tube. **Open** *4-11pm Mon-Thur; noon-1am Fri, Sat; noon-10.30pm Sun. Food served 5-10pm Mon-Thur; noon-3pm, 5-10pm Fri; noon-4pm, 4.30-10pm Sun.* **Map** *pull-out O3* **10**

Each of London's five Craft Beer Co pubs has dozens of taps, but this Islington outpost is the only one that could also be labelled cosy. A comfortable pub with an excellent beer list is a dangerous proposition. You could certainly spend many happy hours (and rather a lot of money – the list is long but not cheap) finding a new favourite pint with the help of the knowledgeable, friendly bar staff. Outdoor tables and a covered yard offer the beer buffs who flock here the option of a little daylight, too.

♥ Earl of Essex

25 Danbury Street, N1 8LE (7424 5828, www.earlofessex.net). Angel tube. **Open** *noon-11.30pm Mon-Thur; noon-midnight Fri, Sat; noon-11pm Sun.*

The first thing you notice on entering this backstreet Georgian pub is the beautiful island bar-bak with a 1960s 'Watney Red Barrel' sign; the second is the vast list of beers on offer. There are 11 on keg, five on cask, plus a couple of quality ciders. The range covers Britain (including a pouring from the on-site Earl's Brewery), Europe and the USA. Staff are happy to offer tastings and know their stuff. On the menu, dishes are all listed with beer recommendations. Whether you really need a suggested beer match for a fishfinger sandwich is a matter of opinion, but it's a nice touch.

Shops & services

Islington isn't the shopping area it once was – many of the boutiques have been replaced by chains – but Upper Street still rewards

a stroll and Camden Passage is full of little cafés and boutiques, not least crafters' favourite wool shop Loop at no.15 (www.loopknittingshop.com).

♥ Aria

Barnsbury Hall, Barnsbury Street, N1 1PN (7704 1999, www.ariashop.co.uk). Angel tube or Highbury & Islington tube/Overground. **Open** *10am-6.30pm Mon-Sat; noon-5pm Sun. Homewares*

Housed in an impressive Victorian-era former concert hall, Aria is one of London's best design destinations. As well as mid-range contemporary designed kitchenware, clocks and lighting by Alessi, Marimekko and Kartell, there are quirkier international treasures, including vintage Indian trestle market tables and Finnish folklore cushions from Klaus Haapaniemi.

♥ Cass Art

66-67 Colebrooke Row, N1 8AB (7619 2601, www.cassart.co.uk). Angel tube. **Open** *10am-7pm Mon-Wed, Fri, Sat; 10am-8pm Thur; 11.30am-5.30pm Sun, open for browsing from 11am. Art supplies*

This cavernous store, hidden down a back street by Tony Conigliaro's cocktail bar *(see p252)*, houses a dazzling array of art materials. Everything is here, from sable brushes and oil paints to Winsor & Newton inks and artists' mannequins. You'll find all you need for crafting too, with full accessories for screen printing, calligraphy and découpage. It's absolutely brilliant for kids, with stickers, origami and paper-doll sets from hip French brand Djeco, art toys like Etch-a-Sketch and more felt-tip pens and glitter pots than you can shake a glue stick at.

twentytwentyone

274-275 Upper Street, N1 2UA (7288 1996, www.twentytwentyone.com). Angel tube or Highbury & Islington tube/Overground. **Open** *10am-6pm Mon-Sat; 11am-5pm Sun. Homewares*

There's a definite Scandi-slant to furniture store twentytwentyone. Set over two spacious floors, its sleek lines, muted colours and clean outlines display minimalistic furniture, accessories and ceramics at their most appealing. We love the functionality of the Lonneberga Wood stacking beds, which will transform a study into a guest room, and the off-kilter angles of Martino Gamper's colourful Arnold Circus stool. The El Baúl golf-ball-like storage box is perfect for hiding kids' toys somewhere chic. You can also find the world's most stylish smoke alarm here – a tactile pastel ingot that simply sticks to the ceiling.

East London

Browse Instagram today, and it's hard to believe how recently east London was notorious for slums and cursed with the city's smelliest and most unpleasant industries. Jack the Ripper stalked through Whitechapel; the presence of the docks – the sanitised remains of which can be enjoyably explored at Wapping and Limehouse – later attracted some of the most brutal bombing during the Blitz. How things change. East London now comprises much of what is most vibrant about the capital: Spitalfields and Brick Lane, Shoreditch and Hoxton, Dalston and Hackney are all must-visits, while the Olympic Park and Docklands also have plenty of interest.

❤ **Don't miss**

1 Redchurch Street *p265*
London's best shopping street. Period.

2 Geffrye Museum *p264*
Bijou and beautiful – a fascinating museum of interior design.

3 Super Lyan *p267*
From the pioneer of a new wave of London cocktail bars.

4 Broadway Market *p273*
Shop and people-watch by the canal in Hackney.

5 Columbia Road Market *p270*
Sunday flower power and a street packed with independent shops.

EAST LONDON

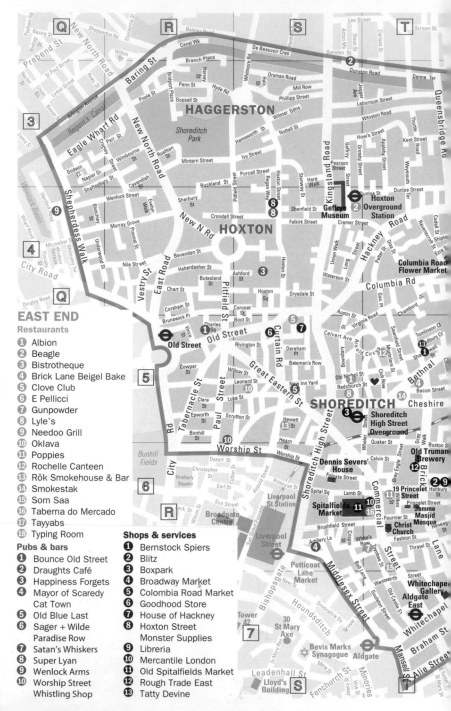

EAST END

Restaurants
1. Albion
2. Beagle
3. Bistrotheque
4. Brick Lane Beigel Bake
5. Clove Club
6. E Pellicci
7. Gunpowder
8. Lyle's
9. Needoo Grill
10. Oklava
11. Poppies
12. Rochelle Canteen
13. Rök Smokehouse & Bar
14. Smokestak
15. Som Saa
16. Taberna do Mercado
17. Tayyabs
18. Typing Room

Pubs & bars
1. Bounce Old Street
2. Draughts Café
3. Happiness Forgets
4. Mayor of Scaredy Cat Town
5. Old Blue Last
6. Sager + Wilde Paradise Row
7. Satan's Whiskers
8. Super Lyan
9. Wenlock Arms
10. Worship Street Whistling Shop

Shops & services
1. Bernstock Spiers
2. Blitz
3. Boxpark
4. Broadway Market
5. Colombia Road Market
6. Goodhood Store
7. House of Hackney
8. Hoxton Street Monster Supplies
9. Libreria
10. Mercantile London
11. Old Spitalfields Market
12. Rough Trade East
13. Tatty Devine

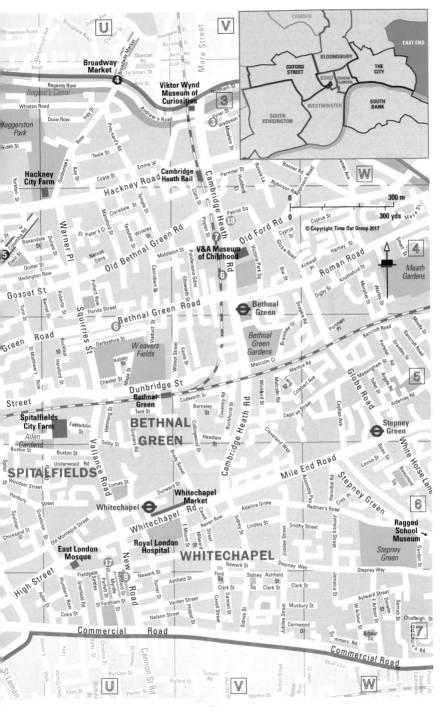

SPITALFIELDS

▶ *Aldgate East tube or Liverpool Street tube/rail.*

Approach this area from Liverpool Street Station, up Brushfield Street, and you'll know you're on the right track when the magnificent spiky spire of **Christ Church Spitalfields** comes into view. The area's other signature sight, **Spitalfields Market**, has upmarket stalls and restaurants, gathered underneath a vaulted Victorian roof, now alongside a rather sterile redeveloped square and office blocks.

Outside, along Brushfield Street, the shops might look as if they're from Dickens' day, but most are recent inventions: the charming grocery shop **A Gold** (no.42, 7247 2487, www.agoldshop.com) was lovingly restored in the noughties and the deli **Verde & Co** (no.40, 7247 1924, www.verdeandco. co.uk) was inspired by local food shops found in – whisper it – France. Settle any anxieties about gentrification by heading a few streets south: on Sundays, the salt-of-the-earth **Petticoat Lane Market** hawks knickers and cheap electronics around Middlesex Street.

A block north of Spitalfields Market is **Dennis Severs' House**, while across from the market, on the east side of Commercial Street and in the shadow of Christ Church, the **Ten Bells** (84 Commercial Street, 7247 7532, www.tenbells.com) is where one of Jack the Ripper's victims drank her last gin. On the next corner, Sandra Esqulant's **Golden Heart** pub (no.110, 7247 2158) has hosted every Young British Artist of note, ever since the day Gilbert & George decided to pop in on their new local.

The streets between here and Brick Lane to the east are dourly impressive, lined with tall, shuttered Huguenot houses; **19 Princelet Street** (7247 5352, www.19princeletstreet.org.uk) opens to the public a few times a year as the Museum of Immigration and Diversity. This unrestored 18th-century house was home first to French silk merchants and later to Polish Jews who built a synagogue in the garden; its spare exhibition now serves as a symbol of the many changes this area has witnessed.

Sights & museums

Christ Church Spitalfields
Commercial Street, E1 6LY (7377 6793, www. spitalfieldsvenue.org/church-life). Liverpool Street tube/rail or Shoreditch High Street Overground. **Open** *10am-4pm Mon-Fri; 1-4pm Sun.* **Admission** *free.* **Map** *p256 T6.*

Built in 1729 by architect Nicholas Hawksmoor, this splendid church has in recent years been restored to its original state (tasteless alterations had been made to the building following a lightning strike in the 19th century). Most tourists get no further than cowering before the wonderfully overbearing spire, but the revived interior is impressive too, its pristine whiteness in marked contrast to its architect's dark reputation. The formidable 1735 Richard Bridge organ is almost as old as the church. Regular concerts are held here, notably during the annual Spitalfields Music Festival (*see p318*).

Dennis Severs' House
18 Folgate Street, E1 6BX (7247 4013, www.dennissevershouse.co.uk). Liverpool

❤ Time to eat & drink

Full English breakfast
E Pellicci *p270*

Quality brunch
Good Egg *p272*

Fiery Thai
Som Saa *p259*

Nordic grills and pickles
Rök Smokehouse and Bar *p266*

Small plates and knock-out wine
Legs *p272*

Cocktails to savour
Super Lyan *p267*, Satan's Whiskers *p270*

Brilliant riverside boozer
Grapes *p275*

Wonderful wine
Sager + Wilde Paradise Row *p270*

Beer, beer, beer
Wenlock Arms *p267*

Great drinks, excellent service
Happiness Forgets *p267*

❤ Time to shop

London's best boutiques
Redchurch Street *p265*

Hip, home-grown interiors
House of Hackney *p268*

Clothes that don't try too hard
Hub *p274*

Old-school, tech-lite bookshop
Libreria *p261*

Hip recordings
Rough Trade East *p262*

Amazing Perspex jewellery
Tatty Devine *p262*

Street tube/rail or Shoreditch High Street Overground. **Open** *noon-2pm, 5-9pm Mon; 5-9pm Wed, Fri; noon-4pm Sun.* **Admission** *daytime visits £10; £5 reductions; evening visits £15-£50.* **Map** *p256 S6.*

The ten rooms of this original Huguenot house have been decked out to recreate vivid snapshots of daily life in Spitalfields between 1724 and 1914. A tour through the compelling 'still-life drama', as American creator Dennis Severs dubbed it, takes you through the cellar, kitchen, dining room, smoking room and upstairs to the bedrooms. With hearth and candles burning, smells lingering and objects scattered apparently haphazardly, it feels as though the inhabitants have deserted the building only moments before you arrived.

Restaurants

Gunpowder ££
11 Whites Row, E1 7NF (7426 0542, www. gunpowderlondon.com). Aldgate East tube or Liverpool Street tube/rail. **Open** *noon-3pm, 5.30-10.30pm Mon-Sat.* **Map** *p256 T6* **⑦**
Indian

Despite its 'Curry Mile' reputation, it's still surprisingly hard to find a good Indian restaurant in the Brick Lane area. This tiny family-run restaurant – with a kitchen headed by Nirmal Save, once a chef at Mayfair's storied Tamarind – aims to bring quality small-plate eating to Indian food, ditching stomach-bursting breads and creamy sauces for delights such as *rasam ke bomb*, chilli cheese toast and Chettinad pulled duck served with homemade

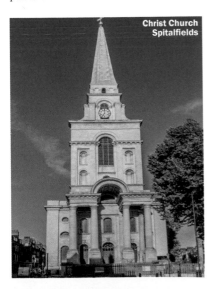
Christ Church
Spitalfields

oothappam. The place oozes passion without a hint of pretension; at weekends it positively buzzes.

Poppies £
6-8 Hanbury Street, E1 6QR (7247 0892, www.poppiesfishandchips.co.uk). Liverpool Street tube/rail or Shoreditch High Street Overground. **Open** *11am-11pm Mon-Thur; 11am-11.30pm Fri, Sat; 11am-10.30pm Sun.* **Map** *p256 T6* **⑪** *Fish & chips*

Poppies' pick and mix assortment of shiny British kitsch – including a jukebox, mini red telephone box and a monochrome photo of heart-throb Cliff Richard – makes it look like a simulation of a fish and chip shop. But the food on the plate is excellent, and offered grilled as well as fried. Extending beyond the staples of cod and haddock, the menu encompasses mackerel, seafood platters and jellied eels. The bill, however, gives the game away – Poppies is a cut above the average chippie.

♥ Som Saa £££
43a Commercial Street, E1 6BD (7324 7790, www.somsaa.com). Shoreditch High Street Overground. **Open** *6-10.30pm daily.* **Map** *p256 T6* **⑮** *Thai*

Taking up this permanent site last year after a monstrously successful crowdfunding campaign, Som Saa isn't somewhere you come for a cheeky green curry and a plate of pad thai – this is authentic, red-hot food from Thailand's north-eastern provinces. Take the deep-fried seabass with Isaan (north-eastern) herbs, for instance. The delicate flesh comes loose easily, leaving a cartoon fish skeleton and crunchy roasted-rice-battered skin, herbs (mint, coriander, Thai basil), mandolin-thin shallots and a puddle of sweet-sour-salt-fire sauce. The effect is thrilling: like setting off ooh-aahh fireworks of taste and texture.

Taberna do Mercado £££
Old Spitalfields Market, 107b Commercial Street, E1 6EW (7375 0649, www. tabernamercado.co.uk). **Open** *noon-9.30pm Mon-Sat; noon-8pm Sun.* **Map** *p256 T6* **⑯** *Portuguese*

When the chef of the paparazzi-swarmed Chiltern Firehouse (*see p148*) set up his own restaurant, London's gourmets took notice. Especially since Nuno Mendes decided to go back to his Lisbon roots, applying his fancy culinary techniques and latest ideas to classic dishes. The wittiest example is the 'house tinned fish': prawns cooked sous-vide to mimic the pasteurisation effect of the canning process, then immersed in prawn-flavoured olive oil, with a tangy kick from Goan balchao tomato, and served in a tin with toasted sourdough. You might try meaty sandwiches, something from the grill or one of half a dozen traditional puddings. The wine list is affordable; the room is spacious and bright, with a large terrace in the covered market; and the staff seem genuinely passionate about what they do.

Note: no bookings are taken for dinner; lunch reservations are by email only (lunch@tabernamercado.co.uk).

Pubs & bars

Mayor of Scaredy Cat Town
12-16 Artillery Lane, E1 7LS (7078 9639, www. themayorofscaredycattown.com). Liverpool Street tube/rail or Shoreditch High Street Overground. **Open** *5pm-midnight Mon-Thur; 3pm-midnight Fri; noon-midnight Sat; noon-10.30pm Sun.* **Map** *p256 S6* ❹

Part of the trend for 'secret' speakeasies, this one is a basement bar beneath the Breakfast Club. The entrance is the one that looks like a big Smeg fridge door. Go inside and you'll find a quirky, dimly lit cocktail bar clad in exposed brick and wood: it's all a bit like a cabin from *Twin Peaks*. The drinks menu makes an amusing mockery of more self-conscious 'underground' venues. The cocktails– classics and house specials – are well crafted on the whole.

Shops & services

Mercantile London
17 Lamb Street, E1 6EA (7377 8926, www. themercantilelondon.com). Shoreditch High Street Overground. **Open** *11am-7pm Mon-Sat; 10am-6pm Sun.* **Map** *p256 T6* ❿ *Fashion*

This boutique, full of independent labels (not to mention an in-store dog called Robert), is enough to restore your faith in the future of London retail. Founder Debra McCann has a good eye for striking fashion that ordinary women will covet, so labels err on the side of tasteful rather than daft – think high-waisted jeans, batwing silk blouses and cool ankle boots at sensible prices (£70-£100 for a silk top, £150 for well-made leather boots).

Old Spitalfields Market
Brushfield Street, E1 6AA (www. oldspitalfieldsmarket.com). Liverpool Street tube/rail or Shoreditch High Street Overground. **Open** *10am-5pm Mon-Fri, Sun; 11am-5pm Sat.* **Map** *p256 S6* ⓫ *Market*

Operating from these premises since 1887, the market at Spitalfields had since 1682 sold fruit and veg wholesale. When that function moved out to Leyton in 1991, battles began over redevelopment of a site toothsomely placed next to the vast wealth of the City. Fortunately, the most aesthetic part of the market was saved, where you'll find fashion, crafts and plenty to eat. The cooler (and cheaper) purchases are found around Brick Lane, but it's still a pleasant venue.

BRICK LANE

▶ *Aldgate East tube or Shoreditch High Street Overground.*

Join the crowds flowing east from Spitalfields Market along Hanbury Street at the weekend, and the direction you turn at the end determines which Brick Lane you see. Turn right and you'll know you're in 'Banglatown', the name adopted by the ward back in 2002: until you hit the bland modern offices beside the kitsch Banglatown arch, it's almost all Bangladeshi cafés, curry houses, grocery stores, money-transfer services and sari shops – plus the **Pride of Spitalfields** (3 Heneage Street, 7247 8933), an old-style East End boozer serving ale to all-comers. Between Fournier Street and Princelet Street, **Jamme Masjid Mosque** is a key symbol of Brick Lane's hybridity. It began as a Huguenot chapel, became a synagogue and was converted, in 1976, into a mosque – in other words, immigrant communities have been layering their experiences on this street at least since 1572, when the St Bartholomew's Day Massacre forced many French Huguenots into exile.

If you turned left when you hit Brick Lane, you'll find yourself in a land of boho gentrification. On Sunday, there's a lively street market, complemented by the trendier UpMarket and Backyard Market (for arts and crafts), which are both held in the **Old Truman Brewery** (nos.91-95). Here, pedestrianised Dray Walk, full of hip independent businesses, is crowded every day. As you head north on Brick Lane, you'll find bars, cafés and vintage fashion shops.

Sights & museums

Spitalfields City Farm
Buxton Street, E1 5AR (7247 8762, www. spitalfieldscityfarm.org). Shoreditch High Street Overground. **Open** *Oct-Mar 10am-4pm Tue-Sun; Apr-Sept 10am-4.30pm Tue-Sun.* **Admission** *free.* **Map** *p256 U5.*

A taste of the countryside in the scruffy city, this is a welcoming and brilliantly maintained green spot. Friendly residents up for a pat include Bayleaf the donkey and a loveable pair of hairy hogs. The farm shop sells homegrown produce – the range of veg grown is remarkable for the location – but for tourists the café is a more likely destination. There's always something going on, from laid-back weekend festivals to the kids' Wild Club.

Restaurants

Brick Lane Beigel Bake £
159 Brick Lane, E1 6SB (7729 0616). Shoreditch High Street Overground. **Open** *24hrs daily.* **Map** *p256 T5* ➍ *Jewish*

This little East End institution rolls out perfect bagels (egg, cream cheese, salt beef, at seriously low prices), good bread and moreish cakes. Even at 3am, fresh-baked goods are pulled from the ovens at the back; no wonder the queue for bagels trails out the door when the local bars and clubs close. Note: this is essentially a takeaway operation – don't expect to be able to linger.

Smokestak £
35 Sclater Street, E1 6LB (3873 1733, smokestak.co.uk). Liverpool Street tube/rail or Shoreditch High Street Overground. **Open** *noon-3pm, 5.30-11pm Mon-Fri; noon-11pm Sat; noon-9.30pm Sun.* **Map** *p256 T5* ⓮ *Street food*

Having built a cult following for its smokehouse meats, Smokestak did the decent thing, opening up a restaurant proper: this semi-industrial space with a hum of throbbing beats. There's a man-tastic, meat-lovin' vibe, the place full of bearded blokes in their 30s supping craft beers and cocktails. Beef brisket is the signature dish, coming as a single hunk of flesh or, shredded, in a bun. Smoked overnight, for 12-14 hours, over English oak, it's moist, smoky, sweet and salty

– and priced at a fiver. That's scandalously good value for London. The sticky toffee pud is insanely good, but may push you over the edge. Come here hungry – we mean *caveman* hungry – and be sure to order plenty of the citrussy fennel and celery slaw as palate-cleansing yin to all that meaty yang.

Shops & services

Bernstock Speirs
234 Brick Lane, E2 7EB (7739 7385, www. bernstockspeirs.com). Shoreditch High Street Overground. **Open** *10am-6pm Mon-Fri; 11am-6pm Sat; 11am-5pm Sun.* **Map** *p256 T5* ➊ *Accessories*

Paul Bernstock and Thelma Speirs's unconventional hats for men and women have a loyal following, being both wearable and fashion-forward. Past ranges have included collaborations with Peter Jensen and Emma Cook.

Blitz
55-59 Hanbury Street, E1 5JP (7377 8828, www.blitzlondon.co.uk). Shoreditch High Street Overground. **Open** *11am-7pm Mon-Sat; noon-6pm Sun.* **Map** *p256 T6* ➋ *Fashion*

The team from Blitz have transformed this old furniture factory into a vintage department store. There's a furniture selection from Broadway Market's the Dog & Wardrobe, an accessories floor, a book collection and rails and rails of neatly presented fashion. Buyers Jan Skinners and John Howlin look to nearby Brick Lane for inspiration, which means the selection is all killer and no filler – and cleaned, steamed and folded before it hits the shop floor.

❤ Libreria
65 Hanbury Street. E1 5JP (libreria.io). Shoreditch High Street Overground. **Open** *11am-6pm Tue, Wed; 11am-9pm Thur-Sat; noon-6pm Sun.* **Map** *p256 T6* ➒ *Books*

This tech-free bookshop is so into printed words on physical pages that using your mobile phone is banned. 'Techpreneur' – and

Rough Trade East

former special advisor to David Cameron – Rohan Silva founded the analogue bookshop as a reaction against digital distractions. The shelves were designed by Slade School artists, their contents arranged to maximise the possibility of chance book discoveries, and there are a whisky bar for events and a risograph printing press downstairs.

♥ Rough Trade East
*Dray Walk, Old Truman Brewery, 91 Brick Lane, E1 6QL (7392 7788, www.roughtrade. com). Shoreditch High Street Overground. **Open** 9am-9pm Mon-Thur; 9am-8pm Fri; 10am-8pm Sat; 11am-7pm Sun. **Map** p256 T6* **12** *Music*

The indie music label Rough Trade – perhaps most famous for signing the Smiths in the early 1980s – set up this 5,000sq ft record store, café and gig space in the noughties when the death of music shops in the face of internet price-cutting was widely accepted as inevitable. Perversely, Rough Trade instead offered a physical space where music-lovers could browse a dizzying range of vinyl and CDs, spanning punk, indie, dub, soul, electronica and more, providing them with 16 listening posts and a stage for live sets. Now its triumph seems like it was always certain.

♥ Tatty Devine
*236 Brick Lane, E2 7EB (7739 9191, www. tattydevine.com). Shoreditch High Street Overground. **Open** 10am-6.30pm Mon-Fri; 11am-6pm Sat; 10am-5pm Sun. **Map** p256 T5* **13** *Jewellery*

Shoreditch pioneers Tatty Devine (AKA art-school pals Harriet Vine and Rosie Wolfenden) began making and selling their distinctive perspex jewellery from this bijou boutique in 2001. Since then, they've opened a store in Covent Garden and a concession in Selfridges (*see p144*), collaborated with everyone from Ashish to Rob Ryan, and seen their designs sold in over 200 shops worldwide. As well as now-classic perspex pieces such as the anchor and dinosaur necklaces and volume-control brooch, you'll find rings, cufflinks and earrings in enamel, wood and silver.

WHITECHAPEL

▶*Aldgate East tube or Whitechapel tube/ Overground.*

Not one of London's prettier thoroughfares, busy but anonymous Whitechapel Road sets the tone for this area. One bright spot is **Whitechapel Gallery**, west from the foot of Brick Lane, while a little to the east, the **Whitechapel Bell Foundry** (nos.32 & 34) made its last bell on 22 March 2017, having been in business in these premises since 1738, during which time it produced Philadelphia's Liberty Bell and 'Big Ben' (*see p106*). At Whitechapel's foremost place of worship, it isn't bells but a muezzin that summons the faithful each Friday: the **East London Mosque**, founded elsewhere in 1910 and now the focal point for the largest Muslim community in Britain, can accommodate 10,000 worshippers. Behind is Fieldgate Street and the dark mass of **Tower House**, a former doss house whose 700 rooms have, inevitably, been redeveloped into flats. Joseph Stalin and George Orwell (researching his book *Down and Out in Paris and London*) kipped here for pennies.

East again is the frontage of the Royal London Hospital – the hospital itself is now in the vast blue tower block looming over it from behind – and in the alleys to the south, a small crypt on Newark Street holds the **Royal London Hospital Archives & Museum** (7377 7608, bartshealth.nhs.uk, 10am-5pm Mon-Fri by appointment only). Inside are reproduction letters from Jack the Ripper (including the notorious missive 'From Hell', delivered with an enclosed portion of human kidney) and information on Joseph Merrick, the 'Elephant Man', rescued by Royal London surgeon Sir Frederick Treves. Behind the hospital is the high-tech **Centre of the Cell** (4 Newark Street, 7882 2562, www.centreofthecell. org), which gives visitors a lively, interactive insight into cell biology in a purpose-built pod, suspended over labs investigating cancer and tuberculosis.

Sights & museums
Whitechapel Gallery
77-82 Whitechapel High Street, E1 7QX (7522 7888, www.whitechapelgallery.org). Aldgate East tube. Open 10am-6pm Tue, Wed, Fri-Sun; 11am-9pm Thur. Admission free. Temporary exhibitions vary. Map p256 T7.

This East End stalwart, a perennial favourite of avant-garde aficionados and art students, continues to build on a stellar reputation as a contemporary art pioneer that began with exhibitions of Picasso – *Guernica* was shown here in 1939 – Jackson Pollock, Mark Rothko and Frida Kahlo. The Grade II-listed building underwent a 21st-century refurb that saw it expand into the similarly historic former library next door – rather brilliantly, the architects left the two buildings stylistically distinct rather than trying to smooth out their differences. As well as nearly tripling its exhibition space, the Whitechapel gave itself a research centre and archives, plus a café/bar. With no permanent collection, there's a rolling programme of temporary shows, but an increasing number of artists have contributed permanently to the fabric of the building: a few years back, Rachel Whiteread added gold vine leaves to the gallery's frontage.

Restaurants
Needoo Grill £
85-87 New Road, E1 1HH (7247 0648, www. needoogrill.co.uk). Whitechapel tube/ Overground. Open noon-11.30pm daily. Map p256 U7 ⑨ *Pakistani*

This squashed space doesn't suffer from the same problem of endless queues as its rival Tayyabs, though you will usually have a wait. Bright red walls, leather benches and blaring flatscreen TVs are the order of the day, yet with curries this good, the decor just fades into the background. What you get are succulent karahi dishes and specials that include nihari (lamb on the bone) and a very passable biriani. Service is swift and friendly.

Tayyabs £
83-89 Fieldgate Street, E1 1JU (7247 6400, www.tayyabs.co.uk). Aldgate East tube or Whitechapel tube/Overground. Open noon-11.30pm daily. Map p256 U6 ⑰ *Pakistani*

Tayyabs is a full-on, hectic, loud, in-and-out sort of place, and if you come here without booking, expect to wait up to an hour for a table. But we recommend this Punjabi stalwart because of the cheapness and boldness of the food. Fiery grilled lamb chops are a must. The rest of the menu is all about rich dhals and masala channa; unctuous, slow-cooked lamb curries; and good versions of North Indian staples – spice-rubbed tikka, hot, buttery breads and juicy kebabs. The corkage-free bring-your-own-bottle policy doesn't do its popularity any harm.

SHOREDITCH & HOXTON

▶ *Old Street tube/rail, or Hoxton or Shoreditch High Street Overground.*

The story is familiar: in the 1980s, impecunious artists moved into the derelict warehouses in the triangle formed by Old Street, Shoreditch High Street and Great Eastern Street, and quickly turned it into the place to be. At which point, rising rents drove the artists out. They've been replaced by the tech-hip denizens of 'silicon roundabout' – a tongue-in-cheek name for the area around Old Street roundabout that became a focus for digital start-ups, the beginning of **East London Tech City** (www. techcityuk.com).

Nightlife permeates the area (linking conveniently to Brick Lane), with centres on Curtain Road, the lower end of Kingsland Road and around Hoxton Square. But the nature of the scene has changed dramatically: growing up in some people's eyes, losing its edge for others. New hotels and smart shops are opening, and cocktail bars are more prevalent than bug-eyed rave holes. There's culture of yet another type to come – or, more accurately, return – since the remains of the **Curtain Theatre** were found behind a pub on Plough Yard, south of Great Eastern Street. The Curtain, which opened in 1577, is intimately connected to Shakespeare's early career, probably hosting the première of *Romeo and Juliet*. A 250-seat outdoor auditorium (managed by the Globe; *see p360*) and a Shakespeare museum and display of the archaeology – beneath

Geffrye Museum

a 40-storey apartment block – are due for completion in 2019.

At present, apart from seemingly countless galleries – Wharf Road neighbours **Parasol Unit** (no.14, N1 7RW, 7490 7373, www.parasol-unit.org) and **Victoria Miro** (no.16, N1 7RW, 7336 8109, www.victoria-miro.com) and not-for-profit pioneer **Raven Row** (56 Artillery Lane, E1 7LS, 7377 4300, www.ravenrow.org) are notable – the area's sole bona fide tourist attraction is the exquisite **Geffrye Museum**, a short walk north up Kingsland Road. The surrounding area is dense with good, cheap Vietnamese restaurants (with **Mien Tay** and **Sông Quê** our favourites).

To the east, it's a short walk towards Bethnal Green and **Columbia Road flower market**.

Sights & museums

♥ Geffrye Museum
136 Kingsland Road, E2 8EA (7739 9893, www.geffrye-museum.org.uk). Hoxton Overground. Open 10am-5pm Tue-Sun. Almshouse tours 1st Sat, 1st & 3rd Tue, Wed of mth. Admission free; donations appreciated. Almshouse tours £4; free under-16s. Map p256 S4.

Housed in a set of 18th-century almshouses, the Geffrye Museum has for more than a century offered a vivid physical history of the English interior. Displaying original furniture, paintings, textiles and decorative arts, the museum recreates a sequence of typical middle-class living rooms from 1600 to the present. It's an oddly interesting way to take in domestic history, with any number of intriguing details to catch your eye – from

a bell jar of stuffed birds to a particular decorative flourish on a chair. There's an airy restaurant overlooking the lovely gardens, which include a walled plot for herbs and a chronological series in different historical styles.

Restaurants

Albion ££
2-4 Boundary Street, E2 7DD (7729 1051, www.albioncaff.co.uk). Shoreditch High Street Overground. Open 8am-11pm Mon-Thur, Sun; 8am-1am Fri-Sat. Map p256 S5 ❶ *British*

Albion may describe itself as a 'caff', but no greasy spoon was ever designed and owned by Terence Conran. But, in spirit at least, it is a kind of café for 21st-century Shoreditch – a place where locals can drop in for a casual breakfast, lunch or dinner, or a cup of tea and a slice of cake. Menu descriptions suggest dishes wouldn't seem out of place in your average caff too – ham and mustard sandwich, devilled kidneys, sausage and mash, fish and chips – but they're all prepared with good-quality ingredients and great care. Albion is on the ground-floor

In the know
Unlocking the Geffrye

The **Geffrye Museum** (*see left*) has an ambitious expansion plan in place, which – final funding efforts permitting – will close the place in early 2018 for major redevelopments that are not due for completion until late 2019. Visit while you still can!

❤ Redchurch Street

Map p256 S5.

For the cognoscenti, this is London's best shopping street. As late as the 2000s it was an almost entirely anonymous – even rather grim – cut-through from the north end of Brick Lane to Shoreditch High Street, but this part of London was changing unimaginably fast.

First had come the artists and bug-eyed clubbers, who loved the low rents and space provided by post-industrial semi-dereliction, as well as the freedom they found here from the restrictions that suburban neighbours impose on late-night living. The oft-parodied, tiresomely self-conscious hipster was to follow – and a much-missed restaurant, Les Trois Garçons, which took over a corner pub on Redchurch Street, filled the gap between these generations, providing fine dining in a thoroughly idiosyncratic style, amid flamboyant decor that combined rococo chandeliers and taxidermy.

As Shoreditch went mainstream, Les Trois Garçons morphed into a interiors shop – then departed for Marylebone. But smart, individualistic fashion and homewares shops had by now found their feet on Redchurch Street – in the lee of London's financial powerhouse, the City – a sweet spot between disposable incomes and urban cool. It helped when Terence Conran opened his superb **Boundary** hotel (*see p399*) here; **Soho House** soon followed round the corner on Ebor Street (*see p401*). Some saw the death of Shoreditch and high-tailed it north into Dalston, where the party continues; but many welcomed an impressive growth in civilised, imaginative, independent-minded shopping – driven by art and fashion.

While the artists are long gone from Shoreditch and the clubbers now outnumbered by hen parties, Redchurch Street calmly goes about its business. **Caravan**, at no.3, was one of the first of the new breed of shops here, opened by stylist and author Emily Chalmers in 2008 to offer eccentric vintage-style homewares and gifts. Aussie botanical beauty shop **Aesop** (no.5A) and classic menswear brand **Sunspel** (no.7) anchor one end of the street. Further up are fancy chocolates at **Mast Brothers** (nos.19-29), high-quality, eminently wearable clothes at **Modern Society** (no.33), the darkly lit headquarters of fashion store **Hostem** (nos.41-43), and vintage-style up-dos and manicures at **Painted Lady** (no.65). **Labour & Wait** (no.85) sells aesthetically pleasing mops, bread bins and other simply designed essentials, and there are Finnish folk-arty interiors at **Klaus Haapaniemi & Co** (no.81) and cutting-edge design at concept store **Monologue London** (no.93).

There's the sweet boutique cinema **Electric Shoreditch**, beneath multi-storey beauty and grooming emporium **Barber & Parlour** (nos.64-66), and plenty of refuelling options: **Albion** (no.45; *see p264*), the **Owl & Pussycat** gastropub (no.34) and New Zealand-born **Allpress Espresso Bar** (no.58).

EAST LONDON

of Conran's swanky boutique hotel, the Boundary (see p399).

Beagle ££
397-400 Geffrye Street, E2 8HZ (7613 2967, www.beaglelondon.co.uk). Hoxton Overground. Open Café/Bar 7am-midnight Mon-Fri; 8am-midnight Sat, Sun. Restaurant 6-10.30pm Mon-Fri; 10am-3pm, 6-10.30pm Sat; 10am-12.45pm, 1-4pm Sun. Map p256 S4 ❷ *British*

Beagle is a smart all-rounder in the railway arches beneath Hoxton station. There's a bar, serving sophisticated cocktails, leading into a dining area with open kitchen. A back-to-basics British ethos governs the food. Grilled cuttlefish comes with new potatoes and a salsa-like coriander pesto. Pigeon terrine, made in-house, is well textured and has a slightly gamey flavour.

Clove Club ££££
Shoreditch Town Hall, 380 Old Street, EC1V 9LT (7729 6496, www.thecloveclub.com). Old Street tube/rail or Shoreditch High Street Overground. Open 6-9.30pm Mon; noon-2.30pm, 6-9.30pm Tue-Sat. Map p256 S5 ❺ *Modern European*

It can sometimes be hard to know if a restaurant is trying to make food that you will savour and enjoy, or simply creating dishes for Instagram. Taking no chances, Clove Club does both. Its daily changing menu – a no-choice list of nine courses – is economically worded in describing a succession of small plates, seasonal and championing British produce, yet oddly esoteric. The best dishes tend to be the ones that aren't trying too hard to impress: perhaps a dish of Ruby Red beef, ramson and potato, which came as a generous piece of slow-cooked beef, very tender and moist; the ramson (wild garlic) was barely discernable, but it helped tick the 'seasonal' and 'wild' boxes.

Lyle's £££
Tea Building, 56 Shoreditch High Street, E1 6JJ (3011 5911, lyleslondon.com). Shoreditch High Street Overground. Open 8am-11pm Mon-Fri; noon-11pm Sat. Food served noon-2.30pm, 6-10pm Mon-Sat. Map p256 S5 ❽ *British*

Dinner at Lyle's is a long, leisurely affair. You can book and stay as long as you like, as there's no turning tables. The pricing is fair: the no-choice menu costs £49, which gets you four small courses (plus bread, petits fours and filtered tap water), served in a drawn-out procession. The chef is James Lowe, one of the most talented cooks in town; the sweet staff know their food, and the semi-industrial setting (polished concrete floors, exposed

girders, whitewashed brick walls) makes for a thoroughly relaxing setting. Set aside two and a half hours or so – then settle in and enjoy your meal.

Oklava ££
74 Luke Street, EC2A 4PY (7729 3032, oklava. co.uk). Old Street tube/rail. Open noon-3pm, 5.30-10pm Tue-Fri; 5.30-10pm Sat; noon-4pm Sun. Map p256 S5 ❿ *Turkish*

The streets east of Old Street are paved with cheap kebab shops, but Oklava isn't that kind of Turkish. The look is contemporary chic, with an open kitchen and sleek designer furnishings. As for the cooking, Selin Kiazim has gone back to her Turkish-Cypriot roots in a modish, creative way, showing off skills learnt at Providores (see p148). Plates are small, made for sharing, and bursting with flavour: mostly bold and southern-Med-meets-Middle-Eastern, but with dashes and splashes from other parts of the planet. On our last visit service was exceptional, the ambience vibrant, and prices very reasonable.

Rochelle Canteen ££
Rochelle School, Arnold Circus, E2 7ES (7729 5677, www.arnoldandhenderson.com). Shoreditch High Street Overground. Open 9-11.30am, noon-3pm Mon-Fri. Tea served 3-4.30pm Mon-Fri. Map p256 T5 ⓬ *British*

Eating at Melanie Arnold and Margot Henderson's daytime-only spot remains a distinctive treat: entry is via a buzzer on a tiny door in the wall of an old Victorian school, now a hub of creative studios. Inside, a handful of outdoor tables and a former bike shed converted into an airy, modern space act as the canteen for those creatives – and lucky outsiders in the know. The short but enticing menu might include pea soup with bantam egg and mint; grilled quails and green sauce; rabbit rillettes; and a pork chop with mustard and chard. Newcomers to the Shoreditch dining scene can come and go, but Rochelle Canteen stands firm, and stands out.

♥ Rök Smokehouse and Bar
26 Curtain Road, EC2A 3NY (7377 2152, roklondon.co.uk). Old Street tube/rail or Shoreditch High Street Overground. Open 5-11pm Mon-Thur; 5pm-1am Fri, Sat. Map p256 S5 ⓭ *Modern European*

Habitually filled with pristine 30-year-olds, not a beard hair out of place, the narrow, low-lit dining room has white walls, dark-wood tables, a small open kitchen with a custom-made charcoal grill, and jars of homemade pickles adorning the bar. The food, with its powerfully flavoured meat cures, pickles and jams, is vaguely Nordic, but centres on British produce, with the odd wild-card southern European ingredient: witness the single scallop, served sizzling in the chilli-hot oil from Italian 'nduja sausage, or the pot of juicy mussels steamed in east-London wheat beer ('It's Cockney marinière,' joked our waiter). Although meat – including two huge fennel-cured lamb chops, cooked sous-vide then finished over the coals – is the star, the sides are equally impressive. In fact, our only bugbear is the teeny size of the tables for two.

Pubs & bars

Late-night hangout **Charlie Wright's International Bar** (*see p348*) and the multitasking **Book Club** (*see p340*) are at least as much about drinking as the events they host.

Bounce Old Street

*241 Old Street, EC1V 9EY (3657 6525, www. bouncepingpong.com). Old Street tube/rail. **Open** 4-11pm Mon, Tue, Thur; 4pm-midnight Wed; 4pm-1am Fri, Sat; 1-10.30pm Sun. **Map** p256 R5* **①**

Whether you're a ping-pong pro or whiff whaff wally, there's fun to be had here, the second of two vast bars dedicated to table tennis. Like its Holborn predecessor, Bounce Old Street buzzes with fun as balls land everywhere but the table and glow under the UV lights. There's an open-plan restaurant serving traditional Italian pizzas along a 25ft counter, and suave cocktails at the bar. Neither of which are likely to improve your game.

❤ Happiness Forgets

*8-9 Hoxton Square, N1 6NU (7613 0325, www. happinessforgets.com). Old Street tube/rail or Shoreditch High Street Overground. **Open** 5-11pm daily. **Map** p256 S4* **③**

From the moment you walk in, the staff will know how to make you happy. The short list of original cocktails is unfailingly good: lots of nice twists on classic ideas but never departing from the essential cocktail principles of balance, harmony and drinkability. Star turns: Mr McRae, Perfect Storm and Tokyo Collins. But the classics are brilliantly handled too, the food is fabulous and so is the service. This is a very special place but not very large: booking is a good idea.

Old Blue Last

*38 Great Eastern Street, EC2A 3ES (www. theoldbluelast.com). Old Street tube/rail or Shoreditch High Street Overground. **Open** noon-midnight Mon-Wed, Fri, Sat; noon-1am Thur. **Map** p256 S5* **⑤**

Despite being at the heart of the Shoreditch party scene, the Old Blue Last defies

preconceptions. Absent are the clichéd bare lightbulbs and brick walls, and, while London- and US-made craft beers are available, low-brow big-brand brews like Heineken and Grolsch get prime representation. Furniture is minimal, something you'll be thankful for from 7pm onwards, when nearby digital drones flock in to decompress over pints. Its enduring popularity – and reputation for first-class live music – keep the Old Blue Last noteworthy among the East End newcomers.

❤ Super Lyan

*155 Hoxton Street, N1 6PJ (3011 1153, www. superlyan.com). Hoxton Overground. **Open** 5-11.45pm Tue; 5pm-midnight Wed, Thur, Sun; 5pm-1am Fri, Sat. **Map** p256 S4* **⑧**

Comparing Super Lyan to your local boozer is like comparing Heston Blumenthal's Fat Duck to a greasy spoon. The latest venture from mixologist Ryan Chetiyawardana ('Mr Lyan') is in the basement of his former experimental cocktail bar White Lyan, which gained a reputation for eschewing the usual cocktail components (such as ice, citrus, sugar and fruit) and distilling its own spirits. Following in its footsteps, Super Lyan will focus on classic cocktails using unconventional ingredients and intriguing techniques. The secluded setting – plain dark walls, dim lighting and worn leather upholstery – is deliberately low-key so all attention is focused on the main event: the artistry of the cocktails.

❤ Wenlock Arms

*26 Wenlock Road, N1 7TA (7608 3406, www. wenlockarms.com). Old Street tube/rail. **Open** 3-11pm Mon-Thur, Sun; noon-1am Fri, Sat; noon-11pm Sun. **Map** p256 Q4* **⑨**

On an unremarkable backstreet, this old pub was the tap for a nearby brewery, and poured its first pint in 1836; it closed with its parent brewery in the 1960s, then reopened in 1994, whereupon it won awards for the quality of its real ale and plaudits for the toastiness of its real fire. Having fought off threats of redevelopment and spruced itself up with a new paint job, new furniture and even more

In the know
Mixmeister

When it opened in 2013, White Lyan was a genuine pioneer in a new London cocktail movement. Since then cocktailian Ryan Chetiyawardana and his team have gone on to open the very different but also excellent **Dandelyan** (see p84) and recently relaunched White Lyan as **Super Lyan** (see above).

beer fonts, the Wenlock is the quintessence of all that is good about pubs – minimal decor, minimal food (salt-beef sandwiches, own-made scratchings) and a great range of ace beer.

Worship Street Whistling Shop

63 Worship Street, EC2A 2DU (7247 0015, www.whistlingshop.com). Old Street tube/rail. **Open** *5pm-midnight Mon, Tue; 5pm-1am Wed, Thur; 5pm-2am Fri, Sat.* **Map** *p256 R5* **❿**

This cellar cocktail bar is decked out in what seems to be a speakeasy/Victorian mash-up (dark wood and lots of eccentric decorative touches). It makes much of its experimental techniques; if your curiosity is tickled by the sound of 'enzymes, acids, proteins and hydrocolloids', you're all set. The list is mercifully short, and classics are well handled. There's an extensive selection of spirits, including the bar's own barrel-aged ones. Staff are skilled, friendly and eager to please.

Shops & services

Once a shabby cut-through, **Redchurch Street** (*see p265*) has gone on to become a strong contender for London's best shopping street.

Boxpark

2-10 Bethnal Green Road, E1 6GY (7033 2899, www.boxpark.co.uk). Shoreditch High Street Overground. **Open** *11am-7pm Mon-Wed, Fri, Sat; 11am-8pm Thur; noon-6pm Sun.* **Map** *p256 S5* **❸** *Mall*

Refitted shipping containers plonked underneath the elevated Shoreditch High Street Overground station make up this contemporary 'shopping mall'. Installed in 2011, the units of Boxpark are full of high-street labels (Puma, Nike), but also contain an impressive array of independents, usually some street food and an endless stream of pop-ups. The food stalls are open daily from 8am to 11pm (10am to 10pm on Sunday).

Goodhood Store

151 Curtain Road, EC2A 3QE (7729 3600, www.goodhood.co.uk). Old Street tube/ rail. **Open** *10.30am-6.30pm Mon-Fri; 10.30am-7pm Sat; noon-6pm Sun.* **Map** *p256 S5* **❻** *Fashion*

A first stop for East End trendies, Goodhood is owned by streetwear obsessives Kyle and Jo. Japanese independent labels are well represented, while other covetable brands include Pendleton, Norse Projects and Wood Wood.

♥ House of Hackney

131 Shoreditch High Street, E1 6JE (7739 3901, www.houseofhackney.com). Old Street tube/ rail or Shoreditch High Street Overground. **Open** *10am-7pm Mon-Sat; 11am-5pm Sun.* **Map** *p256 S5* **❼** *Homewares*

House of Hackney has the makings of a new Liberty (*see p152*): buy your future design classics now, we say. This is one of the most gorgeous retail establishments to land in London in years – bedecked in the deliberately over-the-top juxtapositions of print-on-print-on-print that have made the brand's name, and with the entrance

House of Hackney

full of flowers. Upstairs, you'll find rolls of gorgeous paper, fabric, trays, mugs, fashion and collaborative designs with brands such as Puma; downstairs are generously proportioned sofas and plump armchairs in more-is-more combinations of print and texture.

Hoxton Street Monster Supplies
*159 Hoxton Street, N1 6PJ (7729 4159, www. monstersupplies.org). Hoxton Overground. **Open** 1-5pm Thur, Fri; 11am-5pm Sat. **Map** p256 S4* ❽ *Children*

Purveyor of quality goods for monsters of every kind, this curious little shop stocks jars of Thickest Human Snot and pots of Salt Made From Tears of Anger – oddly reminiscent of lemon curd and of smoked sea salt. Follow the creepy music past a pinboard plastered with notices for missing brains and gravestone engravers, and you'll find a wall of cabinets piled high with Milk Tooth chocolate bars, Witches' Brew tea and Tinned Fear (a can of stories courtesy of Zadie Smith, Joe Dunthorne and Meg Rosoff). Proceeds support the Ministry of Stories' creative writing and mentoring centre for local children. Mind the invisible cat on your way out.

BETHNAL GREEN

▶ *Bethnal Green tube/Overground, Cambridge Heath Overground or Mile End tube.*

Once a gracious suburb of spacious townhouses, by the mid 19th century Bethnal Green was one of the city's poorest neighbourhoods. As in neighbouring Hoxton, an upturn in fortunes over the last couple of decades was in part occasioned by Bethnal Green's adoption as home by a new generation of artists, with the **Maureen Paley** gallery (21 Herald Street, E2 6JT, 7729 4112, www.maureenpaley.com) having set up here in 1984, but the new Bethnal Green is typified by the arrival of the ambitious Town Hall Hotel and its **Typing Room** restaurant. Then take a seat at **E Pellicci**, the exemplary traditional London caff, for a taste of the old Bethnal Green.

The **V&A Museum of Childhood** is close to Bethnal Green tube station, but the area's other main attraction is a bit of a walk away (almost in Shoreditch). Nonetheless, a visit to the weekly **Columbia Road flower market** is a lovely way to fritter away a Sunday morning. A microcosmic retail community has grown up around the market: try **Treacle** (nos.110-112, 7729 0538) for groovy crockery and cupcakes; **Angela**

Flanders (no.96, 7739 7555) for perfume; and **Marcos & Trump** (no.145, 7739 9008) for vintage fashion.

Sights & museums
Ragged School Museum
*46-50 Copperfield Road, E3 4RR (8980 6405, www.raggedschoolmuseum.org.uk). Mile End tube. **Open** 10am-5pm Wed, Thur; 2-5pm 1st Sun of mth. Tours by appt. **Admission** free; donations appreciated. **Map** p256 W6.*

Ragged schools were an early experiment in public education: they provided tuition, food and clothes for destitute children. This one was the largest in London, and Dr Barnardo himself taught here. It's now a sweet local museum that contains complete mock-ups of a ragged classroom and Edwardian kitchen, with displays on vanished local history.

V&A Museum of Childhood
*Cambridge Heath Road, E2 9PA (8983 5200, www.vam.ac.uk/moc). Bethnal Green tube/Overground or Cambridge Heath Overground. **Open** 10am-5.45pm daily. **Admission** free; donations appreciated. **Map** p256 V4.*

Home to one of the world's finest collections of children's toys, dolls' houses, games and costumes, the Museum of Childhood is part of the Victoria & Albert Museum (see p126). It has been amassing childhood-related objects since 1872 and continues to do so, with *Incredibles* figures complementing bonkers 1970s puppets, Barbie dolls and Victorian praxinoscopes. The museum has lots of hands-on stuff for kids dotted about the many cases of historic artefacts, including dressing-up boxes and soft play areas, though the cases themselves might be of more interest to nostalgic adults than their spawn. Regular small exhibitions are held upstairs, while the café in the central space helps to revive flagging spirits.

Viktor Wynd Museum of Curiosities
*11 Mare Street, E8 4RP (7998 3617, www. thelasttuesdaysociety.org). Bethnal Green tube/Overground. **Open** noon-11pm Wed-Sun. **Admission** £5. **Map** p256 V3.*

This oddity is both on the art circuit and determinedly off any beaten track. Peek through the windows and you'll see a world in which velvet-cloaked Victorians might reside. Entering the shop, which is also the spiritual home of the esoterically minded Last Tuesday Society, reveals a wunderkammer of shells, skulls, taxidermy specimens and assorted weirdness and tat, from a two-headed lamb to McDonald's Happy Meal toys and condoms used by the Rolling Stones.

Art gets a designated space in the first-floor gallery, where the shows tend towards the eerily surreal. There's a cocktail bar and café if you need bracing up again; admission includes the price of a cup of tea.

Restaurants

Bistrotheque ££

23-27 Wadeson Street, E2 9DR (8983 7900, www.bistrotheque.com). Bethnal Green tube/Overground. Open 6-10.30pm Mon-Thur; 6-11pm Fri; 11am-4pm, 6-11pm Sat; 11am-4pm, 6-10.30pm Sun. Bar 5.30pm-midnight Mon-Fri; 11am-midnight Sat; 11am-11pm Sun. Map p256 V3 ❸
French

Head to the first floor of this East End trendsetter for the light, white restaurant and big oval bar (where walk-ins can eat and good cocktails are mixed). Although the hipster count is high, the service is friendly, and there's a level of professionalism that's missing from many local restaurants. The kitchen is capable of highs – we've had a stellar duck confit with puy lentils and mushrooms – but a steady B-plus is more usual; the generous prix fixe costs £25 for three good-sized courses. The menu (and short wine list) is more French-leaning than truly Gallic and the popular weekend brunch adds the likes of US-style pancakes with bacon and maple syrup. Less welcome at brunch are the 90-minute dining slots.

❤ E Pellicci £

332 Bethnal Green Road, E2 0AG (7739 4873, epellicci.com). Bethnal Green tube/Overground or bus 8. Open 7am-4pm Mon-Sat. No cards. Map p256 U5 ❻ *Café*

You go to Pellicci's as much for the atmosphere as for the food, although the food is more than edible. Opened in 1900, and still in the hands of the same family, this Bethnal Green landmark has chrome and Vitrolite outside, wood panelling with deco marquetry, Formica tabletops and stained glass within – it earned the café a Grade II-listing in 2005. Fry-ups are first rate, and the fish and chips, daily grills and Italian specials aren't half bad.

Typing Room £££

Town Hall Hotel, Patriot Square, E2 9NF (7871 0461, www.typingroom.com). Bethnal Green tube/Overground or Cambridge Heath Overground. Open 6-10pm Tue, Wed; noon-2.30pm, 6-10pm Thur; noon-2.30pm, 6-10.30pm Fri, Sat. Map p256 V4 ❽
Modern European

This room – once using for mayoral correspondence, now part of Bethnal Green's Town Hall Hotel – is blessed by the culinary gifts of Lee Westcott, protégé of Jason Atherton, the man behind Social Eating House (*see p175*) and many other of London's finest restaurants. Westcott's menu follows several 'modernist' food trends – not least New Nordic: a bit of dehydration here, some smoking there, plus sprigs, twigs and petals – to produce dishes that are so intricate and exquisite it is almost a pity to eat them. Service is warm and professional and the setting quietly stylish.

Pubs & bars

❤ Sager + Wilde Paradise Row

250 Paradise Row, E2 9LE (7613 0478, www.sagerandwilde.com). Bethnal Green tube/Overground. Open 6pm-midnight Tue-Fri; noon-midnight Sat, Sun. Map p256 V4 ❻

This bar-restaurant lies in a railway arch, low lit in the evenings, with a cathedral-like vaulted ceiling the colour of Carrara marble and a spacious courtyard which faces the traffic-free street. The wine list is intimidatingly vast, but, thankfully, the staff know it well and adroitly help you navigate it. Abundant beverages aside, the food is excellent, having enlisted the talents of Sebastian Myers (formerly of Chiltern Firehouse, *see p148*) to produce British dishes with European flourishes.

❤ Satan's Whiskers

343 Cambridge Heath Road, E2 9RA (7739 8362). Bethnal Green tube/Overground or Cambridge Heath Overground. Open 5pm-midnight daily. Map p256 V4 ❼

Satan's Whiskers might sound like a Captain Haddock curse, but it refers to a classic cocktail containing gin, orange and vermouth topped with Grand Marnier and orange bitters. It's a staple on the otherwise daily changing menu here, along with seductive alternatives – this tiny bar was set up by three bartenders, and they really know their stuff. Leather booths, an illuminated ice box and taxidermy for decor all add to the atmosphere.

Shops & services

❤ Columbia Road Market

Columbia Road, E2 7RG (www.columbiaroad.info). Hoxton Overground or Bethnal Green tube/Overground. Open 8am-3.30pm Sun. Map p256 T4 ❺ *Market*

On Sunday mornings, this unassuming East End street is transformed into a delightful swathe of fabulous plant life and the air is fragrant with blooms and the shouts of old-school Cockney stallholders (most offering

Columbia Road Market

deals for 'a fiver'). But a visit here isn't only about flowers and pot plants: alongside the market is a growing number of shops selling everything from pottery and arty prints to cupcakes and perfume; don't miss **Ryantown's** delicate paper cut-outs at no.126 (7613 1510 robryanstudio.com/ryantown). Refuel at **Jones Dairy** (23 Ezra Street, 7739 5372, www.jonesdairy.co.uk).

DALSTON & HACKNEY

▶ *Dalston Junction, Dalston Kingsland, Hackney Central or London Fields Overground.*

Occupying the area around the junction of Balls Pond Road and Kingsland Road, scruffy **Dalston** may be summed up these days by African-flavoured Ridley Road market: routinely praised by hipsters for its authentic cultural mix, it's still 'real' enough that stallholders were caught selling 'illicit' meat in 2012. No such problems at the delicious Turkish *ocakbaşı* (grill restaurants) along Stoke Newington Road, although the throngs of hipsters OMGing over sharing plates and the latest 'dirty' food pop-up are the current zeitgeist. In truth, even as the brand managers descend, Dalston remains a cool and lively part of London. All tribes play together happily enough at the appealingly urban **Dalston Jazz Bar** (4 Bradbury Street, 7254 9728, www.dalstonjazzclubrestaurant.co.uk), the brilliant **Vortex Jazz Club** (*see p350*) and **Café Oto** (*see p338*). Also nearby is

an appealing 'micropark', the delightfully urban **Dalston Eastern Curve Garden** (13 Dalston Lane, E8 3DF, dalstongarden.org).

Neighbouring **Stoke Newington** is the richer cousin of Dalston and poorer cousin of Islington. At weekends, pretty **Clissold Park** (www.clissoldpark.com) is overrun with picnickers and mums pushing prams. Most visitors head here for bijou **Church Street**. This curvy road is lined with second-hand bookshops, cute boutiques and kids' stores, and superior cafés and restaurants – Keralan vegetarian restaurant **Rasa** (no.55, 7249 0344, www.rasarestaurants.com) was the pioneer in what is now a bit of a foodie hotbed. Another local highlight is **Abney Park Cemetery** (www.abney-park.org), a wonderfully wild, overgrown Victorian boneyard and nature reserve.

North of Bethnal Green and east of Stoke Newington, **Hackney Central** has few blockbuster sights, but has been one of London's fastest gentrifying areas – doubtless soon to be overtaken by Peckham (*see p286*). Its administrative centre is Town Hall Square on Mare Street, where you'll find a century-old music hall, the **Hackney Empire** (291 Mare Street, E8 1EJ, 8985 2424, www.hackneyempire. co.uk); an art deco town hall; and the fine little **Hackney Museum** (1 Reading Lane, E8 1GQ, 8356 3500, www.hackney.gov. uk/cm-museum.htm) in the 21st-century library. Opposite, an ambitious failed music venue has become a terrific cinema (**Hackney Picturehouse**; *see p325*). Within walking distance to the east is the historic **Sutton House**.

In the southern part of Hackney, the area of **London Fields** demonstrates the area's changing demographics. Once a failing fruit and veg market, **Broadway Market** is now brimming with young urbanites and trendy families. From here, you can walk east – dodging cyclists and joggers – along the Regent's Canal to **Victoria Park**. Opened in 1845 to give the impoverished working classes access to green space, this sprawling, 290-acre oasis was designed by Sir James Pennethorne, a pupil of John Nash; its elegant landscaping (with rose garden and waterfowl lake) is indeed reminiscent of Nash's Regent's Park (*see p240*). There's also a terrific lakeside café. At the eastern end of the park, across a nasty dual carriageway, is the mish-mash of artist-colonised post-industrial buildings that makes up **Hackney Wick**.

Sights & museums

Sutton House & Breaker's Yard

2-4 Homerton High Street, E9 6JQ (8986 2264, www.nationaltrust.org.uk/sutton-house). Hackney Central Overground. **Open** *times vary; check website for details. Closed Jan.* **Admission** *£5.40; £2.70 reductions; £13.60 family; free under-5s.*

The oldest house in east London, red-brick Sutton House is owned by the National Trust and was built in 1535 for Henry VIII's first secretary of state, Sir Ralph Sadleir. It has been sensitively restored, retaining the authentic original decor: you'll be able to see a Tudor kitchen, Jacobean and Georgian interiors, an Edwardian chapel, medieval foundations in the cellar and 1980s graffiti up under the roof. Sutton House also has one London's oldest loos (a 16th-century garderobe, boarded up in the 1700s) and, in the Breaker's Yard, a crisply contemporary community garden whose highlight is the Grange – chopped-up caravans rebuilt into a parody stately home.

Restaurants

♥ Good Egg £

93 Stoke Newington Church Street, N16 0AS (thegoodeggn16.com). Stoke Newington rail. **Open** *9am-4pm Mon; 9am-11pm Tue-Fri; 10am-11pm Sat, Sun. Middle Eastern*

From the slatted bench that runs round one wall, it's interesting to sit and contemplate what an efficient job the owners have done with a small space – it's compact but not packed, stylish but not slavishly so, with an open kitchen, bar, high stools and central service stations all fitted in. The 'plates' here are Middle Eastern-influenced, a real trend

at the moment, but convincing: perhaps an Iraqi pitta with fried aubergine, chopped egg and mango pickle inside airy bread, or keenly priced spicy and crunchy *za'atar* fried chicken. There are also bigger dishes like Persian smoked brisket or whole roast cauliflower with tahini and pomegranate. The Good Egg is open all day (except Monday evenings), with tempting breakfasts ensuring this little space is full morning to night.

Jidori ££

89 Kingsland High Street, E8 2PB (7686 5634, www.jidori.co.uk). Dalston Kingsland Overground. **Open** *6-11pm Mon, Tue; noon-3pm, 6-11pm Wed-Thur; noon-3pm, 6pm-midnight Fri; 6pm-midnight Sat. Japanese*

The *izakaya* – a kind of Japanese pub, but with better food and worse beer – serves almost anything chicken-related, grilled on a stick: juicy hearts, intestines, skin. Essentially there to mop up the saké, they just happen to be really great bar snacks. At Brett Redman's yakitori restaurant each skewer is great and they're all very different: perhaps the wing with shiso and lemon – crisp, pleasantly sweet and a little sharp – or the moreish *tsukune* skewers – packed full of chives and served with a raw egg to dip the meat into. There's a nice selection of craft beer – local and Japanese – plus a well-curated cocktail menu.

♥ Legs ££

120-122 Morning Lane, E9 6LH (3441 8765, www.legsrestaurant.com). Hackney Central Overground. **Open** *5-11pm Wed-Fri; 10am-11pm Sat; 10am-4pm Sun. British*

So much more than a neighbourhood wine bar, Legs is a terrific place to eat, with a compact menu of small plates, each more brilliant than the last. Sit at one of the four 'kitchen bar' stools, and ask for advice on the short but appealing wine list – chef and owner Magnus Reid's laid-back appearance belies the extent of his expertise and enthusiasm – then watch him work. Every dish is a delightful tumble of texture and taste: superficially simple but using bold, bright combinations that elevate them well past the ordinary. And the staff, when they're not poking fun at each other's music on the shared playlist, fizz with passion for the food and a genuine love for their customers.

Pubs & bars

Cock Tavern

*315 Mare Street, E8 1EJ (no phone, www. thecocktavern.co.uk). Hackney Central Overground. **Open** noon-11pm Mon-Thur; noon-1pm Fri, Sat; noon-10.30pm Sun.*

The Cock is the sort of place you walk into and think: this is a bloody good pub. It's dark, uncomplicated and resonant with merry conversation. Put simply, it's a room for grown-ups to stand in and drink beer. It's timelessly classic – aside from the Victorian beards on the bar staff, it could be any era since 1920. It's usually rammed, which is mainly down to the fabulous beer and cider: the pub cellar is home to the Howling Hops microbrewery, whose output is mostly drunk on the premises, while plenty of guest beers pop up on the 22 taps. A bartop cabinet displays scotch eggs and pork pies, and there's a jar of pickled eggs.

Draughts Café

*337 Acton Mews, E8 4EA (www. draughtslondon.com). Haggerston Overground. **Open** 10am-4pm, 6-11pm Mon-Fri; 10am-midnight Sat; 10am-11pm Sun. **Map** p256 S2* ②

If the phrase 'Let's play Seven Wonders' appeals more than making a DJ request, Draughts is for you. This bar-café has a library of more than 500 board games, from Articulate and Cranium to newer (and more complex) classics Carcassonne and Pandemic. Admission is £5 per person, which buys you unlimited play and, crucially, the help of a 'game guru', who'll offer guidance on rules and which game would suit your party. Food, craft beer, ale, cider and wine are available.

Shops & services

❤ Broadway Market

*Broadway Market, E8 4QL (www. broadwaymarket.co.uk). London Fields Overground or bus 394. **Open** 9am-5pm Sat. **Map** p256 U3* ④ *Market*

The coolest and most ridiculous of east London's young trendies can be found at this endearing market, where fruit-and-veg sellers trade alongside vintage clothes 'specialists'. It's as busy as a beehive, but the slew of

cafés, pubs, restaurants and boutiques along the street – plus the market itself, plus the nearby Netil Market for further streetfood, plus Saturday's School Yard Market, plus the overspill of drunks and slumming may-do-wells on London Fields when there's even a whiff of sunshine – is a fine education in new London.

Hackney Walk

*Morning Lane, E9 6LH (7287 9601, www. hackneywalk.com). Hackney Central or Homerton Overground. **Open** 10am-6pm Mon-Sat; 11am-5pm Sun. Fashion*

Is there a more unlikely part of town for a fashion nexus? From Hackney Central station, you stroll past junkyards, a supermarket, tower blocks and takeaways. But thanks to a £2m fund to regenerate the area, Hackney's Morning Lane has become the home of London's first luxury retail outlet. The developer (Manhattan Loft Corporation, which was behind the rebirth of St Pancras International) capitalised on footfall to the nearby Burberry factory outlet (29-31 Chatham Place, E9 6LP, 8328 4287) by renting neighbouring property to Aquascutum (7-8 Ram Place, E9 6LT, 3096 1863, www.aquascutum.com) and, in a converted pub, Pringle (90 Morning Lane, E9 6NA, 8533 1158, pringlescotland.com); there are monster bargains to be had at all three. Other brands currently here might include Nike, Anya Hindmarch, Gieves & Hawkes and Nicole Farhi. The converted Victorian railway arches opposite the old Burberry factory provide space for discount outlets of designer brands, workshops and pop-up spaces for up-and-coming local designers.

EAST LONDON

273

♥ Hub

*49 & 88 Stoke Newington Church Street, N16 0AR (no.49: 7524 4494, no.88: 7275 8160, www.hubshop.co.uk). Stoke Newington Overground. **Open** 10.30am-6pm Mon-Sat; 11am-5pm Sun. Fashion*

With its edited selection of mid-market heritage and emerging labels, Stoke Newington boutique Hub is the ideal place to cultivate that casual, not-trying-too-hard look. At no.49, ladies snap up Sessùn coats, Petit Bateau shirts, jeans by Dr Denim and holdalls by Great Plains from a decidedly un-feminine shop, while gents stock up on Barbour jackets, Herschel backpacks and Wolsey hats at no.88.

Kristina Records

*44 Stoke Newington Road, N16 7XJ (7254 2130, www.kristinarecords.com). Dalston Kingsland Overground. **Open** noon-8pm Mon, Wed-Fri; noon-7pm Sat; noon-6pm Sun. Music*

Kristina is a living, breathing experience for living, breathing music fans, with a clean and uncluttered layout that makes shopping for vinyl the kind of pleasure that websites can never replicate. For the dedicated dance-music fan, the racks of new house and techno are a goldmine, while expertly chosen soul and jazz oldies are also represented.

LN-CC

*18-24 Shacklewell Lane, E8 2EZ (3174 0744, www.ln-cc.com). Dalston Kingsland Overground. **Open** 10am-6pm Mon-Sat. Fashion, books & music*

'Late Night Chameleon Club' is as mysterious as its name suggests. Accessed by appointment via a basement-level door in an unlikely Shacklewell warehouse building, the store is a Tim Burton-like wonderland rendered in natural wood with a secret dancefloor, tree house, listening library and London's most unique edit of super-rare fashion. Ostensibly a showroom for internet boutique LN-CC.com, the space is a gallery for upscale design, selling super-posh brands such as Rick Owens, Givenchy, Lanvin and any number of hard-to-pronounce rarities. With vinyl, art books and eyewear, and stock in different themed zones, LN-CC is a shop like no other.

WALTHAMSTOW

▶ *Walthamstow Central tube/rail.*

Once felt to be on the fringes of civilisation, Walthamstow is now a trendy and desirable suburb. The pubs and shops of quaint

Walthamstow Village, a few minutes' walk east of the tube station, are centred on ancient St Mary's Church and the neat little **Vestry House Museum** (Vestry Road, E17 9NH, 8496 4391, www.walthamforest.gov.uk; closed Mon, Tue), which contains one of the world's first motor cars. Further north, near the junction of Hoe Street and Forest Road, is peaceful Lloyd Park; the grand Georgian house at its entrance is home to the **William Morris Gallery** – the Arts and Crafts master was a Walthamstow boy.

William Morris Gallery

*Forest Road, E17 4PP (8496 4390, www. wmgallery.org.uk). Walthamstow Central tube. **Open** 10am-5pm Wed-Sun. **Admission** free.*

The 18th-century Water House was William Morris's family home, with the artist, socialist and source of all that flowery wallpaper living here between 1848 and 1856. It features permanent displays of printed and woven fabrics, rugs and painted tiles by Morris and other members of the Arts and Crafts movement, as well as humble domestic objects including Morris's coffee cup and the satchel he used when distributing his radical pamphlets. There's a great café too.

DOCKLANDS

London's docks were fundamental to the prosperity of the British Empire. Between 1802 and 1921, ten separate docks were built between Tower Bridge in the west and Woolwich in the east, employing tens of thousands of people. Yet by the 1960s, the shipping industry was changing irrevocably. The new 'container' system of cargo demanded larger, deep-draught ships, as a result of which the work moved out to Tilbury, whence lorries drove the containers into the city. By 1980, the London docks had closed.

The London Docklands Development Corporation (LDDC), founded in 1981, spent £790m of public money on redevelopment, only for a country-wide property slump in the early 1990s to leave the shiny new high-rise offices and luxury flats unoccupied. Nowadays, though, focal **Canary Wharf** is a booming rival to the City, supporting an estimated 90,000 workers. It is at the heart of the **Isle of Dogs** peninsula, the origin of whose name – first recorded in 1588 – remains uncertain; one theory claims Henry VIII kept his hunting dogs here. In the 19th century, a huge system of docks and locks transformed what had been just drained marshland, with the West India Docks cutting right across the peninsula, so the Isle of Dogs finally lived up to the island part of its name.

Almost all the interest for visitors is to be found in the vicinity of Cesar Pelli's **One Canada Square**, which was the country's tallest habitable building from 1991 to 2012, when it was topped by the Shard (*see p94*). Once dramatic, the building now almost disappears amid similarly sized office-block clones. Shopping options are limited to the mall beneath the towers (www.mycanarywharf.com), but you'll find a crisp garden behind Canary Wharf tube station and a selection of upmarket chain restaurants. Across a floating bridge over the basin to the north, the brilliant **Museum of London Docklands** is flanked by a pub and a couple of bar-restaurants.

For atmospheric riverside, head to the section between the City and Docklands proper. Just a few stops from where the Docklands Light Railway starts at Bank station is Shadwell, from where you can walk south to **Wapping**. In 1598, London chronicler John Stowe described Wapping High Street as 'a filthy strait passage, with alleys of small tenements or cottages, inhabited by sailors' victuallers'. This can still be imagined as you walk along it now, flanked by tall Victorian warehouses. The historic **Town of Ramsgate** pub (no.62, 7481 8000), dating from 1545, helps. Here, 'hanging judge' George Jeffreys was captured in 1688, trying to escape to Europe in disguise as a woman. Privateer Captain William Kidd was executed in 1701 at Execution Dock, near Wapping New Stairs; the bodies of pirates were hanged from a gibbet until seven tides had washed over them. Further east, the touristy but appealing **Prospect of Whitby** (57 Wapping Wall, 7481 1095) dates from 1520 and counted Pepys and Dickens among its regulars. It has a riverside terrace and balcony outside, and a handsome pewter bar counter and flagstone floor within.

In the know
Historic vistas and rural delights

It's well worth heading south on the DLR to Island Gardens station at the tip of the Isle of Dogs. From narrow **Island Gardens** park, there's a famous view of Greenwich (see p280) – and the entrance to the Victorian pedestrian tunnel. Nearby to the north, at **Mudchute Park & Farm** (Pier Street, 7515 5901, www.mudchute.org), a complete farmyard of animals ruminate in front of the skyscrapers.

In the know
Wild for swimming

For a bracing dip in a spectacular setting, the **Royal Victoria Dock** (www.londonroyaldocksows.co.uk) offers weekend swimming sessions. There are lifeguards and all swimmers are issued with a safety tag in case they find themselves in metaphorical as well as literal deep water.

Sights & museums

Museum of London Docklands
No.1 Warehouse, West India Quay, Hertsmere Road, E14 4AL (7001 9844, www. museumoflondon.org.uk/museum-london-docklands). Canary Wharf tube/DLR or West India Quay DLR. **Open** *10am-6pm daily.* **Admission** *free. Temporary exhibitions vary.*

Housed in a 19th-century warehouse (itself a Grade I-listed building), this museum explores the complex history of London's docklands and the river over two millennia. Displays spreading over three storeys take you from the arrival of the Romans all the way to the docks' 1980s closure and the area's subsequent redevelopment. The Docklands at War section is very moving, while a haunting new permanent exhibition sheds light on the dark side of London's rise as a centre for finance and commerce, exploring its involvement in the slave trade. You can also walk through full-scale mock-ups of a quayside and a dingy riverfront alley. Temporary exhibitions are set up on the ground floor, where you'll also find a café and a docks-themed play area. Just like its elder sibling, the Museum of London (*see p228*), the MoLD has a great programme of special events.

Restaurants

Docklands is short of destination restaurants – but long on upmarket chains, with **Carluccio's** (www.carluccios.com) and **Jamie's Italian** (www.jamieoliver. com/italian) among many decent options at Canary Wharf.

Pubs & bars

♥ Grapes
76 Narrow Street, E14 8BP (7987 4396, www. thegrapes.co.uk). Limehouse or Westferry DLR. **Open** *noon-11pm Mon-Sat; noon-10.30pm Sun. Food served noon-9.30pm daily.*

If you're trying to evoke the feel of the Thames docks before their Disneyfication into Docklands, these narrow, ivy-covered

and etched-glass 1720 riverside premises
in Limehouse are a good place to start: the
downstairs is all wood panels and nautical
jetsam; upstairs is plainer, but it's easier to
find seats for Sunday lunch. Expect good
ales and a half-dozen wines of each colour by
glass and bottle.

OLYMPIC PARK & LEA VALLEY

▶ *Stratford tube/DLR/Overground.*

The Olympic Park, scene of the 2012 Games,
is a square mile of the Lower Lea Valley
in east London. That sporting summer,
which exceeded most predictions and won
over many critics, is long gone but the
contentious business of 'legacy' remains:
arguments over what benefits have been
brought to Londoners by the £8.77 billion
that was spent on the Games may continue
for generations. The physical legacy, at least,
is clear: the **Queen Elizabeth Olympic Park**
(www.queenelizabetholympicpark.co.uk),
as it was renamed, comprises immaculate
parklands to the north, laced by a network
of paths and waterways. By the Timber
Lodge café and facilities, the Tumbling
Bay Playground is especially good for kids,
and this is where you'll find the Lee Valley
VeloPark. The 7,500-seat Copper Box Arena
has provided a flexible indoor venue for
sport (notably boxing) and concerts. In the
southern part of the park are the handsome
Zaha Hadid-designed Aquatics Centre
(www.londonaquaticscentre.org) which is
open to the public, further children's play
areas, walking trails and a couple of dozen
public artworks, not least the landmark
ArcelorMittal Orbit. The **Olympic
Stadium** is the home ground of West Ham
Football Club, which took up residence
for the 2016/17 season, but it continues to
host other major sporting events: it was the
principal venue for the 2015 Rugby World
Cup, and in 2017 both the IAAF World
Championships and IPC World Athletics
Championships will be here. There are
ambitious plans to create an 'Olympicopolis'
by 2018 – a cultural hub involving the V&A
(see p126), University College London,

Sadler's Wells (*see p368*) and even the
Smithsonian – planned to rival South Ken's
'Albertopolis'. The main entrance to the
park is from Stratford town centre, just
to the east, which has the **Discover** (*see
p277*) story centre and a massive Westfield
shopping mall.

For a good vantage point on the park,
head to the **Common Greenway Café**
(9am-5pm daily) in the brightly painted,
recycled shipping containers of the **View
Tube** (The Greenway Marshgate Lane, E15
2PJ, theviewtube.co.uk) or, if you've a chunk
of time on your hands, stroll south along the
River Lea to **Three Mills Island**, which has
an impressive new playground.

If you make it all the way down the Lea
to the Thames, you'll find **Trinity Buoy
Wharf**, while the impressively vast **Royal
Docks** lie further to the east – it's best to get
the DLR to Royal Victoria or Royal Albert
stations for them. As well as the ExCeL
conference centre, you'll find the black and
pointy **Crystal** exhibition space and the
Emirates Air Line cable car, which takes
travellers high over the river to the **O2** (*see
p344*) on the far bank. Down by the river,
the **Thames Barrier Park** opened in 2001 as
London's first new park in half a century. It
has a lush sunken garden of waggly hedges
and offers perhaps the best land views
of the Thames Barrier (*see p293*). If you
don't fancy walking, enter the park from
Pontoon Dock DLR.

Unless you're checking in at **London
City Airport** (*see p413*), keep on the DLR
as far as King George V to get a free ferry
(every 15mins daily; *see p293*) that chugs
pedestrians and cars across the river, or
stay in your carriage as the DLR passes
under the river all the way to its final stop at
Woolwich Arsenal.

Sights & museums

ArcelorMittal Orbit
*3 Thornton Street, Queen Elizabeth Olympic
Park, Stratford, E20 2AD (0333 800 8099,
arcelormittalorbit.com). Stratford tube/
DLR/Overground/rail. **Open** check website
for details. **Admission** £11.50; £5.50-£8.50*

EAST LONDON

reductions; £32 family. With slide £15; £10-£12 reductions; £46 family.

Perhaps the most dramatic structure in the Olympic Park, the Orbit overlooks the Stadium. Designed by sculptor Anish Kapoor and engineer Cecil Balmond, it is red, 374ft tall and not much loved by locals. The peripheral location – compared to both Shard (*see p94*) and Eye (*see p82*) – meant the view was always interesting rather than must-see, but the addition of a spiral slide by Belgian artist Carsten Höller in 2016 changed the whole nature of the attraction. You can still visit for the view, but most will choose to pay a bit more to fly down the world's longest and tallest tunnel slide – taking a dozen turns around the Orbit in the 40 seconds it takes to zoom through the structure. Note: the slide is for over-sevens only, with a minimum height of 1.3m.

Crystal
*Royal Victoria Dock, 1 Siemens Brothers Way, E16 1GB (7055 6400, www.thecrystal. org). Royal Victoria DLR. **Open** 10am-5pm Tue-Sun. **Admission** £8; £5 reductions. Tour £10; £6 reductions.*

The Crystal attempts to explain in an engaging fashion how cities work, and how they might meet the challenges of global warming, population growth, ageing and the shortage of key resources, especially water. The two floors of interactives are slick and fun: beat the computer at face recognition, or plan the transport for different cities. There's a good café (open from 8.30am Mon-Fri, 10am Sat, Sun).

Discover Children's Story Centre
*383-387 High Street, Stratford, E15 4QZ (8536 5555, www.discover.org.uk). Stratford tube/DLR/Overground/rail. **Open** 10am-5pm daily. **Admission** £6.50; £5.50 reductions; free under-2s; £22 family.*

The UK's first creative-learning centre offers all sorts of imaginative exploration, while downstairs houses temporary interactive exhibitions. The garden is good fun too.

Emirates Air Line
North terminal *27 Western Gateway, E16 4FA. Royal Victoria DLR.*

South terminal *Edmund Halley Way, SE10 0FR (www.tfl.gov.uk/modes/emirates-air-line). North Greenwich tube.*

Open *Apr-Sept 7am-9pm Mon-Fri; 8am-9pm Sat; 9am-9pm Sun. Oct-Mar 7am-8pm Mon-Fri; 8am-8pm Sat; 9am-8pm Sun.* **Tickets** *£4.50 single; £2.30 reductions, free under-5s.*

Arguments for a cable car across the Thames as a solution to any of London's many transport problems are, at best, moot, but its value as a tourist thrill is huge. The comfy pods zoom 295ft up elegant stanchions at a gratifying pace. Suddenly there are brilliant views of the expanses of water that make up the Royal Docks, the ships on the Thames, Docklands and the Thames Barrier. Good fun and good value – but note that the cable car may not run in high winds.

Three Mills Island
Three Mills Lane, E3 3DU (0300 003 0610, www.visitleevalley.org.uk). Bromley-by-Bow tube.

Just south of the Olympic Park, this island on the River Lea takes its name from the three mills that ground flour and gunpowder here. The House Mill, built in 1776, is the oldest and largest tidal mill in Britain and can be visited by tour (8980 4626, www. housemill.org.uk, £3, £1.50 reductions, free under-16s; May-Oct 11am-3.30pm Sun; Mar, Apr, Dec 10am-3.30pm 1st Sun of mth). Even when that's closed, the island provides pleasant walks that can feel surprisingly rural – and the new Wild Kingdom children's playground is a joy.

Trinity Buoy Wharf
64 Orchard Place, E14 0JW (7515 7153, www. trinitybuoywharf.com).

Where the River Lea flows into the Thames at Bow Creek, Trinity Buoy Wharf is pure incongruity. Built in the early 1800s, it was a depot and repair yard for shipping buoys, and it was here, in the 1860s, that James Douglass – later designer of the fourth Eddystone Lighthouse – built London's only lighthouse. Open every weekend from 11am to 4pm (5pm in summer), the lighthouse is the perfect setting for the haunting *Longplayer* sound installation (longplayer.org). Here too, floating on a raft to preserve it, is *SS Robin* (www.ssrobin.org), a steamship so rare it is included (with the *Cutty Sark, see p280,* and HMS *Belfast, see p93*) in the National Historic Fleet.

In the know
Cable car card entry

Tickets for the Emirates Air Line *(see left)* are cheaper if you use an Oyster card or the contactless card you've been using for public transport, and you'll avoid queuing at the ticket desk.

South London

South London was once best known for its lack of public transport and the late-night cabbies' refrain: 'I don't go south of the river, mate.' Of course, the bus network meant it was always perfectly navigable to those in the know, but the expansion of the Overground network of light rail links (effectively the Tube, but using surface trains) has opened south London up to the uninitiated, with some parts – notably Peckham – rivalling east London for hipster cred. There are superb historic attractions, not least Greenwich and the Royal Botanic Gardens, Kew, both of which are UNESCO World Heritage sites, and Hampton Court Palace, which might as well be. And several of the less prestigious institutions are equally fascinating, with Dulwich Picture Gallery and the Horniman Museum notable. We explore in an arc through south London's key areas, from east to west.

♥ Don't miss

1 Maritime Greenwich *p282*
Beautiful buildings, fascinating history.

2 Royal Botanic Gardens, Kew *p292*
A park like no other.

3 Horniman Museum *p291*
Taxidermy, anthropology and some brilliant jellyfish.

4 Artusi *p286*
Peckham's finest restaurant.

5 Hampton Court Palace *p291*
Ravishing in red brick.

IAM NOVA PROGENIES CŒLO

Painted Hall, Old Royal Naval College

GREENWICH & GREENWICH PENINSULA

▶ *North Greenwich tube for Greenwich Peninsula. Cutty Sark DLR or Greenwich DLR/rail for Maritime Greenwich.*

When it was the Millennium Dome, the **O2 Arena** (*see p344*) was universally derided. A couple of decades on, it's a lauded entertainment complex and rather popular landmark. You can get very close to it, too: buy a ticket for **Up at the O2** (www.theo2.co.uk/upattheo2) and you can walk right over the top, safely attached to a security line. The Dome's arrival on the **Greenwich Peninsula** eventually triggered redevelopment of what had been an area of semi-industrial dereliction. Its eastern environs are now a mass of new buildings (www.greenwichpeninsula.co.uk), with a handful of attractions around Peninsula Square: the **Now Gallery** (Peninsula Square, SE10 0ES, nowgallery.co.uk), pricey **Craft London** bar-restaurant (8465 5910, craft-london.co.uk), the **Meantime Beer Box** bar (www.meantimebeerbox.com) and the **Peninsula Garden**, designed by Tom Dixon's studio. The planted jetty **Farmopolis** has joined the already well-established **Greenwich Peninsula Ecology Park** (www.tcv.org.uk/greenwichpeninsula) and spinal **Central Park**. A rather elegant (but, for public-transport purposes, almost entirely unused) cable car, the **Emirates Air Line** (*see p277*), runs from the east flank of the peninsula right across the Thames.

The west flank of the peninsula winds slowly into **Greenwich**, with the riverside walk – opposite the Isle of Dogs and the aggressively bland office blocks of **Canary Wharf** (*see p274*) – affording broad, flat, bracing views and some impressive works of public art: *Slice of Reality*, a rusting ship cut in half by Richard Wilson, sits near Alex Chinneck's 2014 sculpture *A Bullet from a Shooting Star*, a 115-foot-tall electricity pylon turned upside-down.

Riverside Greenwich is an irresistible mixture of maritime, royal and horological history, a combination that earned it recognition as a UNESCO World Heritage Site in 1997 (*see p282*) and, to celebrate the Golden Jubilee, a Royal Borough in 2012. Indeed, royalty has haunted Greenwich since 1300, when Edward I stayed here. Henry VIII was born in Greenwich Palace; the palace was built on land that was later taken over by Wren's Royal Naval Hospital, now the **Old Royal Naval College**. The college is now a very handy first port of call. Its Pepys Building not only contains the **Greenwich Tourist Information Centre** (0870 608 2000, www.visitgreenwich.org.uk), but is also the home of **Discover Greenwich**, which provides a great overview of the area's numerous attractions. Just opposite, shoppers swarm to **Greenwich Market**, a handsome 19th-century building sheltering a mixture of shops and stalls.

Near the DLR stop is Greenwich Pier; every 15 minutes (peak times), the popular and speedy **Thames Clipper boats** (7001 2200, www.thamesclippers.com) shuttle passengers to and from central London. This is where you'll find the **Cutty Sark**, as well as a domed structure that is the entrance to a Victorian pedestrian tunnel that emerges on the far side of the Thames in Island Gardens. The tunnel is rather dingy, due to incomplete repair work, but it's still fun to walk beneath the river.

At the north end of Greenwich Park are the **Queen's House** and **National Maritime Museum**, beyond which it's a ten-minute walk (or shorter shuttle-bus trip) south up the park's dramatically steep slopes to the **Royal Observatory**, offering superb views out over the Royal Naval College to Canary Wharf. At night, the bright green Meridian Line Laser illuminates the path of the Prime Meridian across the London sky.

Sights & museums

Cutty Sark
King William Walk, SE10 9HT (8312 6565, www.rmg.co.uk/cuttysark). Cutty Sark DLR. Open 10am-5pm daily. Admission £13.50; £7-£11.50 reductions; free under-5s. Map p281 Ab13.

Built in Scotland in 1869, this tea clipper was the quickest in the business when she was launched in 1870 – renovation after the *Cutty Sark* went up in flames in 2007 was rather slower. But you can visit her once more (by timed tickets) in her permanent berth in a purpose-built dry dock beside the Thames. The ship is now raised three metres off the ground and surrounded by a dramatic glass 'skirt', which allows visitors to admire the hull from underneath for the first time – while sipping a cup of tea from the museum café, should they desire. Critics objected that the glazed canopy obscures the elegant lines of the *Cutty Sark*'s hull – as well as raising fears about the stresses that are being put on the elderly ship – but the visitor experience is much improved, with interactives giving context to a story of reckless, high-speed trade in tea, wine, spirits, beer, coal, jute, wool and castor oil. The sailing clippers were gradually put out of business by steamships: by 1922, the *Cutty Sark* was the last of her breed afloat. The space beneath the ship

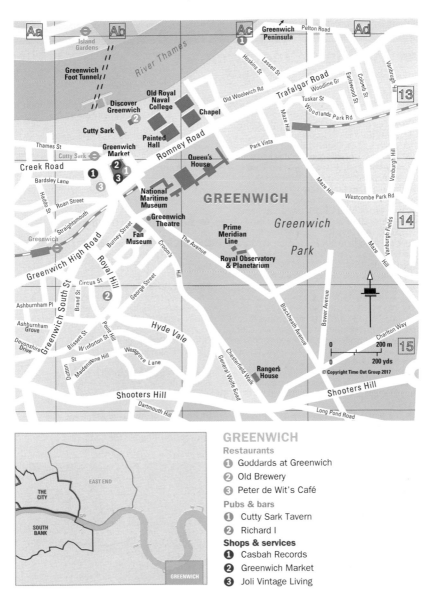

GREENWICH

Restaurants
1. Goddards at Greenwich
2. Old Brewery
3. Peter de Wit's Café

Pubs & bars
1. Cutty Sark Tavern
2. Richard I

Shops & services
1. Casbah Records
2. Greenwich Market
3. Joli Vintage Living

▶ *Some of the areas discussed in this chapter are shown on the pull-out map at the back of this guide.*

❤ **Time to eat**

Simply superb cooking
Artusi *p286*

'Natural' wine and fine small plates
Naughty Piglets *p288*

Thai street food
Begging Bowl *p287*

❤ **Time to shop**

Arcade shopping, south London style
Brixton Village *p289*

SOUTH LONDON

♥ Maritime Greenwich

If you're coming to Greenwich, allow yourself two luxuries. First, give yourself a whole day to explore. The Royal Museums Greenwich alone comprise four major attractions – the world's biggest nautical history museum, the **National Maritime Museum** (*see p283*); tea clipper the **Cutty Sark** (*see p280*); modest architectural pioneer the **Queen's House** (*see p386*), and, plonked on the Meridian, the **Royal Observatory** (*see p284*). On top of that, you'll want time to explore Wren's **Old Royal Naval Hospital** (*see p283*) and Greenwich Park itself. Second, treat yourself to a boat trip along the Thames to get here (for Thames Clippers, *see p407*). Seeing the vistas change as you approach this most historic area of London is an unparalleled joy – redolent of the long period when the city was utterly dependent on its river. The Thames was Britain's arterial connection to the world, whether in the form of Tudor explorers setting sail to unknown lands and unimaginable wealth with their monarch's blessing still in their ears, or during the Victorian era, when industrial-scale exploitation of Britain's panoply of colonies meant the river was always choked with vessels and the docks opposite Greenwich on the Isle of Dogs were full of cargo ships and lighters unloading them.

Inscribed by UNESCO as a World Heritage Site in 1997, Maritime Greenwich should – once you've set foot on land – be approached only one way: through the **Old Royal Naval College**. Walk south between the grand colonnades by Sir Christopher Wren (1632-1723). These were deliberately placed to frame the Queen's House – begun by Inigo Jones (1573-1652) in 1616, the first building in Britain to be designed on Classical principles. You cannot fail to be impressed, perhaps a little daunted, by the ambition of the hospital's late 17th-century architecture.

UNESCO applauded the coherence of the site, the way that its various layers of history played off each other. This continues south into **Greenwich Park**, laid out by André Le Nôtre (1613-1700), who created the gardens at Versailles as the chief gardener of French King Louis XIV. Among the park's ancient trees, a towering slope is topped by the **Royal Observatory** – a collaboration between Wren and the less well-known but extremely significant scientist and polymath, Robert Hooke (1635-1703), which also marks the work of astronomer John Flamsteed (1646-1719), who predicted solar eclipses and laid the groundwork for later advances in navigation.

It was here that the British Empire was born, here that England made the Enlightenment her tool, and here that you can spend happy hours finding out about it all – or just having a boozy picnic on the grass surrounded by extraordinary buildings.

♥ Best Baroque buildings

Christ Church Spitalfields *p258*
Unforgettable due to Nicholas Hawksmoor's doom-laden spike of a spire.

The Monument *p233*
The least architecturally interesting structure on this list – but it has a fascinating history and wonderful views of the City.

Old Royal Naval College *p283*
Just for those breathtaking colonnades.

St John's Smith Square *p356*
Thomas Archer's four corner towers exemplify Baroque inventiveness.

St Paul's Cathedral *p224*
Wren's masterpiece – and surely the finest Baroque building in the country.

displays another lost tradition: an exhibit of more than 80 figureheads, including Florence Nightingale, William Wilberforce, Hiawatha and Sir Lancelot.

Discover Greenwich & the Old Royal Naval College

*2 Cutty Sark Gardens, SE10 9NN (8269 4799, www.rmg.co.uk/cutty-sark). Cutty Sark DLR or Greenwich DLR/rail. **Open** 10am-5pm daily. Grounds 8am-11pm daily. **Admission** free. Tours free. **Map** p281 Ab13.*

The block of the Old Royal Naval College nearest to the *Cutty Sark* is now the excellent Discover Greenwich. It's full of focused, informative exhibits on architecture and the building techniques of the surrounding buildings, the life of Greenwich pensioners, Tudor royalty and so forth, delivered with a real sense of fun: while grown-ups read about coade stone or scagliola (popular fake-stone building materials), for example, children can build their own chapel with soft bricks or try on a knight's helmet. There's also a well-stocked shop and a Tourist Information Centre.

It's a perfect introduction to the superb collection of buildings that make up the Naval College. Designed by Wren in 1694, with Hawksmoor and Vanbrugh helping to complete the project, it was originally a hospital for the relief and support of seamen and their dependants, with pensioners living here from 1705 to 1869, when the complex became the Royal Naval College. The Navy left in 1998, and the neoclassical buildings now house part of the University of Greenwich and Trinity College of Music. The public are allowed into the impressive rococo chapel, where there are free organ recitals, and the **Painted Hall** (*see below*), a tribute to William and Mary that took Sir James Thornhill 19 years to complete. Nelson lay in state in the Painted Hall for three days in 1806, before being taken, in grand river procession, to St Paul's Cathedral for his funeral.

In the know
Painted Hall ceiling tours

Rather brilliantly making a virtue of the necessity of renovating Sir James Thornhill's triumphalist ceiling painting (1707-1726) in the Painted Hall of the **Old Royal Naval College**, hour-long 'tours' are being offered. You walk up 60ft of scaffolding stairs to admire his work from closer than you'll ever again manage. Book in advance at ornc.digitickets.co.uk or call 8269 4799; tickets cost £10 (£5 reductions).

Fan Museum

*12 Crooms Hill, SE10 8ER (8305 1441, www.thefanmuseum.org.uk). Cutty Sark DLR or Greenwich DLR/rail. **Open** 11am-5pm Tue-Sat; noon-5pm Sun. **Admission** £4; £3 reductions; £10 family; free under-7s. **Map** p281 Ab14.*

The world's most important collection of hand-held fans is displayed in a pair of Georgian townhouses. There are about 3,500 fans, including some beauties in the Hélène Alexander collection, but not all are on display at any one time. For details of fan-making workshops and exhibitions, see the website. There's also a lovely orangery serving afternoon tea.

National Maritime Museum

*Park Row, SE10 9NF (8858 4422, information 8312 6565, www.rmg.co.uk/national-maritime-museum). Cutty Sark DLR or Greenwich DLR/rail. **Open** 10am-5pm daily. **Admission** free; donations appreciated. Temporary exhibitions vary; check website for details. **Map** p281 Ab14.*

The world's largest maritime museum contains a huge store of creatively organised maritime art, cartography, models, interactives and regalia. The ground level has galleries covering maritime London, the titanic battle of Dreadnought battleships at Jutland in 1916 and Turner's painting *The Battle of Trafalgar*. You can then weave through to the Sammy Ofer extension, centred on 'Voyagers: Britons and the Sea' – a collection of 200 artefacts, accompanied by an audio-visual installation called the Wave. The Compass Lounge (with free Wi-Fi) allows you to explore the collection using computers, and you'll find the ticket desk, café and shop here, as well as access downstairs to the temporary gallery that is building a reputation for compellingly varied exhibitions (Samuel Pepys, Yinka Shonibare and pioneering American landscape photographer Ansel Adams have all featured) and outside directly into the park.

'The Atlantic: Slavery, Trade, Empires', on Floor 1, recounts the disturbing history of the transport of people and goods between Britain, Africa and the Americas during the 17th to 19th centuries, including a drawing of precisely how slaves were packed into the gunwales of a translatlantic sailing ship, while 'Traders' looks at the East India Company and 'The Great Map' is a large interactive floor map of the oceans.

Floor 2 holds the interactives: 'The Bridge' has a ship simulator, 'All Hands' lets six- to 12-year-olds load cargo (under-eights can enjoy 'Ahoy!' on the ground floor), and you can try your hand as a ship's gunner. But here too is one of the centrepieces of the museum: 'Nelson, Navy, Nation' recalls the seaborne battles of the 18th century, and the glamour and gore of life as a naval officer at the time. The key artefact is Nelson's Trafalgar uniform, blood-stained and with fatal bullet-hole, accompanied by a 3D reconstruction of him, as if laid in his coffin.

The museum recently received £12.6m in funding to create four permanent galleries in the East Wing, an area previously closed to visitors. The 'Endeavour Galleries', due to open in 2018, will look at exploration through the ages, with displays on the Pacific and polar regions, Tudor and Stuart sailors, and, enticingly, 'sea things'.

Queen's House

*Romney Road, SE10 9NF (8858 4422, www. rmg.co.uk/queens-house). Cutty Sark DLR or Greenwich DLR/rail. **Open** 10am-5pm daily. **Admission** free. **Map** p281 Ac14.*

Celebrating its 400th anniversary in 2017, Queen's House has reopened after extensive refurbishment, complete with gold-leaf artistry from Turner Prize winner Richard Wright on the ceiling of the Great Hall. Formerly the summer villa of Charles I's queen, Henrietta Maria, the house was completed in 1638 by Inigo Jones, the first Palladian building in the country. As well as the stunning 1635 marble floor, look for Britain's first centrally unsupported spiral stair (much more beautiful than that makes it sound), fine painted woodwork and ceilings, and the proportions of the Great Hall – it is a perfect cube. The art collection of the National Maritime Museum is held here, with displays including portraits of famous maritime figures, works by Hogarth and Gainsborough, some arresting 20th-century wartime art, and William Hodges' exotic paintings from the voyages of Captain Cook. As part of the refurbishment, Orazio Gentileschi's royal-commissioned painting *Joseph and Potiphar's Wife* has been put on show here for the first time since 1650.

Ranger's House

*Chesterfield Walk, SE10 8QX (8294 2548, www.english-heritage.org.uk). Blackheath rail, Cutty Sark DLR or bus 53. **Open** Apr-Sept guided tours only. Tours 11am, 2pm Sun-Wed. Oct-Mar closed. Tickets £7.60; £4.60-£6.80 reductions; free under-5s. **Map** p281 Ac15.*

The house of the 'Ranger of Greenwich Park' (a post held by George III's niece, Princess Sophia Matilda, from 1815) now contains the treasure amassed by Julius Wernher, a German who made his considerable fortune trading in South African diamonds. His booty – medieval and Renaissance art, jewellery, bronzes, tapestries, furniture, porcelain,

paintings – is displayed through a dozen lovely rooms in this red-brick Georgian villa, built in 1723, the back garden of which hosts the fragrant Greenwich Park rose collection.

Royal Observatory & Planetarium

*Blackheath Avenue, Greenwich Park, SE10 8XJ (8312 6565, www.rmg.co.uk/royal-observatory). Cutty Sark DLR or Greenwich DLR/rail. **Open** 10am-5pm daily. **Admission** £9.50; £5 reductions; £20 family; free under-5s. **Map** p281 Ac14.*

The northern section of this two-halved attraction chronicles Greenwich's horological connection. Flamsteed House, the observatory built in 1675 on the orders of Charles II, contains the apartments of Sir John Flamsteed and other Astronomers Royal, as well as instruments used in timekeeping since the 14th century. John Harrison's four timekeepers, used to crack the problem of longitude, are here, while the onion dome houses the country's largest (28-in) refracting telescope – it was completed in 1893. The courtyard is where tourists gather for their Prime Meridian Line photo-opportunity, and you must pay for entry to this whole section of the attraction.

The south site houses the **Astronomy Centre** (free admission), which is also home to the Peter Harrison Planetarium and the Astronomy & Time Galleries, where daily and weekend star shows cost £5.50-£7.50. The 120-seat planetarium's architecture cleverly reflects its astronomical position: the semi-submerged cone tilts at 51.5 degrees, the latitude of Greenwich, pointing to the north star, and its reflective disc is aligned with the celestial equator.

Restaurants

On the upper floor of the Sammy Ofer extension of the National Maritime Museum *(see p283)*, the **Parkside Café & Terrace** offers fine park views, whether you essay solid British eats with cocktails, or cakes and a cuppa.

Goddards at Greenwich £

*22 King William Walk, SE10 9HU (8305 9612, www.goddardsatgreenwich.co.uk). Greenwich rail/DLR or Cutty Sark DLR. **Map** p281 Ab14* ❶ *Pie & mash*

A family business since the 1890s, Goddards opened a shiny new shop in 2012. The location means it's a tourist favourite, but that doesn't put the locals off – it's justly one of London's most popular pie shops. The mash and liquor (parsley sauce) are practically perfect, though the pies can be dry and a bit dense. The huge range of fillings now available – steak and ale, lamb and rosemary – rather overshadow the traditional minced beef.

Old Brewery £££
Pepys Building, Old Royal Naval College, SE10 9LW (3437 2222, www.oldbrewerygreenwich. com). Cutty Sark DLR. **Open** *10am-11pm Mon-Sat; 10am-10.30pm Sun. Food served 10am-10pm daily.* **Map** *pp281 Ab13* ❷
British

The flagship of the Greenwich-based Meantime Brewery: by day, it's a café; by night, a restaurant. There's a small bar, with tables outside in a large walled courtyard – a lovely spot in which to test the 50-strong beer list – but most of the action is in the vast, high-ceilinged main space. Dishes, such as Barnsley lamb chop and black-pudding hash, come with matching beers.

Peter de Wit's Café £
21 Greenwich Church Street, SE10 9BJ (8305 0048, www.peterdewitscafe.co.uk). Cutty Sark DLR. **Open** *11am-6pm Thur, Fri; 9am-6pm Sat, Sun.* **Map** *p281 Ab14* ❸ *Café*

The olde-worlde frontage isn't cynically engineered to pull in tourists: this café is in one of Greenwich's oldest buildings, part of which was around when King Henry VIII was a nipper. More importantly, the main dishes – fried breakfasts, classic sandwiches, daily quiches – are made from carefully sourced local ingredients, with the able support of Aeropress coffee from small-batch roasters, plenty of gluten-free teatime treats, and Meantime lager. The interiors are resolutely modern, with bright-blue chairs, white walls, and chalkboard menus, but history nerds can wander through to the pretty courtyard and marvel at the back of the building, which dates to medieval times.

Pubs & bars

As well as the rather civilised **Old Brewery** (*see above*), Meantime also runs a proper pub that's pretty handy for the attractions: the **Greenwich Union** (56 Royal Hill, SE10 8RT, 8692 6258, www.greenwichunion.com).

Cutty Sark Tavern
4-6 Ballast Quay, SE10 9PD (8858 3146, www. cuttysarkse10.co.uk). Cutty Sark DLR. **Open** *11.30am-11pm Mon-Sat; noon-10.30pm Sun. Food served noon-10pm Mon-Sat; noon-9pm Sun.* **Map** *p281 Ac13* ❶

Were it a couple of miles inland, the Cutty Sark would be a charming but unremarkable pub, with better-than-average grub and a decent, if unadventurous, selection of ales and wine. But add the mighty Thames and it becomes three floors of bow-fronted

Georgian magic, with the top-level room in particular giving fantastic river views up- and downstream. Secure a window seat, or a table on the cobbled street outside, and imagine yourself in a scene from *Our Mutual Friend*.

Richard I
52-54 Royal Hill, SE10 8RT (8692 2996, www. richardthefirst.co.uk). Greenwich rail/DLR. **Open** *noon-11pm Mon-Sat; noon-10.30pm Sun. Greenwich rail/DLR.* **Map** *p281 Ab15* ❷

This two-bar Young's pub adjoining the Greenwich Union is not far from its centenary. For many years it resisted the urge to update, but now it's had a major refurbishment and all the trends are firmly ensconced: modern-style pub grub that includes mac 'n' cheese two ways alongside the Sunday roasts; craft beer in bottles alongside a good range of cask ales; and a well-chosen wine list. There are lots of tables in the garden and conservatory too.

Shops & services

Casbah Records
320-322 Creek Road, SE10 9SW (8858 1964, www.casbahrecords.co.uk). Cutty Sark DLR. **Open** *11.30am-6pm Mon; 10.30am-6pm Tue-Fri; 10.30am-6.30pm Sat, Sun.* **Map** *p281 Ab14* ❶ *Music*

After 20 years of trading as a Greenwich Market stall, Casbah Records found a more permanent base. The emphasis is on edgy girl groups, garage, psych and '60s soul, but the store also stocks a variety of classic rock, indie and electronica, along with books, DVDs, prints and vintage comics.

Greenwich Market
King William Walk, SE10 9HZ (8269 5096, www.greenwichmarketlondon.com). Cutty Sark DLR. **Open** *10am-5.30pm daily.* **Map** *pp281 Ab14* ❷ *Market*

Greenwich Market can trace its origins to 1737 – although the current covered building dates only to the 19th century. On Thursdays and Fridays, up to 120 stalls are dominated by

In the know
A taste for it

In the unimaginable days before every railway arch in the city was a microbrewery (that was 1999, nostalgia fans), Alastair Hook set up Meantime Brewery in Greenwich, with the simple aim of bringing quality beer back to London. This pioneer has a fine brewery tap, the **Tasting Rooms** (Blackwall Lane, SE10 0AR, 3384 0582, www.meantimebrewing.com/tasting-rooms).

antiques and classic 20th-century pieces; the weekends are for the craftier end of things. There is also a cluster of shops dedicated to art, fashion and jewellery. If you're flagging, there is plenty of street food.

Joli Vintage Living
8 Nelson Road, SE10 9JB (3417 5790). Cutty Sark DLR. Open 11am-6pm Mon-Fri; 10am-6pm Sat, Sun. Map p281 Ab14 ❸ *Vintage*

Just off Church Street, this quirky boutique sells quality retro clothes, chic furniture and eye-popping costume jewellery.

PECKHAM

▶ *Peckham Rye or Denmark Hill Overground/rail.*

Now routinely dubbed 'the new Dalston' (because everywhere obviously has to be the new somewhere else), Peckham's appearance as a happening neighbourhood is news to precisely no one in London – even the *Sunday Times* had caught on by spring 2017. But don't let that put you off.

London's finest club, the **Bussey Building** (see *p341*), and an illustrious multistorey car park (*see below*) are both on focal Rye Lane, as is the excellent **PeckhamPlex** cinema (see *p327*). Most of the businesses here are run or frequented by members of the largest overseas Nigerian community – this is the beating heart of Little Lagos. It was very different in the late 18th and early 19th centuries: this was then the Oxford Street of south London, with moneyed Victorians flocking in horse-drawn cabs and carriages to department stores Jones & Higgins and Holdron's. At the northern end, Peckham Square is being redeveloped, with the new **Peckham Platform** gallery (www.peckhamplatform.com) to join Will Allsop's striking, award-winning **Peckham Library** (122 Peckham Hill Street, E15 5JR), while due south of Rye Lane is **Peckham**

Rye, where as a child poet-visionary William Blake saw his angels in the 1760s; it's now a prettily laid-out park with well-kept gardens – including a restored Japanese garden created in 1908. To the west, Bellenden Road could be called Peckham Village (it probably already is by the estate agents), with its fancy dining spots, boutiques selling gifts and homewares, and indie grocery shops. Further west is fertile ground for the arts: here you'll find the excellent **South London Gallery**, next door to the **Camberwell College of Arts** (45-65 Peckham Road, 7514 6302, www.arts.ac.uk/camberwell/), where Pink Floyd's Syd Barrett and film director Mike Leigh were once students.

Sights & museums
South London Gallery
65-67 Peckham Road, SE5 8UH (7703 6120, www.southlondongallery.org). Oval tube then bus 436, or Elephant & Castle tube/rail then bus 12, 171. Open 11am-6pm Tue, Thur-Sun; 10am-9pm Wed. Admission free; temporary exhibitions vary.

In 1891, William Rossiter opened the pioneering South London Fine Art Gallery. A century later, renamed the South London Gallery, it found new renown as the site of the first exhibition of *Everyone I Have Ever Slept With 1963-1995*, Tracy Emin's infamous tent. A beacon for Brit Art in the 1990s, the gallery remains one of London's leading contemporary art venues. A £1.8m extension swallowed up the three-storey townhouse next door in order to add two extra exhibition spaces, a resident artist's flat and, in an atrium, the No.67 restaurant.

Restaurants
♥ Artusi ££
161 Bellenden Road, SE15 4DH (3302 8200, artusi.co.uk). Peckham Rye Overground/ rail. Open 6-10.30pm Mon; noon-2.30pm, 6-10.30pm Tue-Sat; 12.30-8pm Sun. Italian

This Peckham restaurant is so cutting-edge, so minimal, that there's not even a name above the door. Chef Jack Beer's menu – only to be found on a chalkboard by the entrance – is confidently simple. Starters range from safe options such as ricotta and tomato salad, or prosciutto and mortadella, to more adventurous: seared ox heart with olives, perhaps, or pig's head with salsa verde. Precision cooking is evident in mains such as just-cooked whole lemon sole with roasted garlic and monk's beard. It's an unpretentiously low-key place with charming and knowledgeable staff, interesting drinks and excellent food.

♥ Begging Bowl ££

*168 Bellenden Road, SE15 4BW (7635 2627, www.thebeggingbowl.co.uk). Peckham Rye Overground/rail. **Open** noon-2.30pm, 6-10pm Mon-Sat; noon-3pm, 6-9.30pm Sun. Thai*

Instead of the familiar Thai fare, chef Jane Alty offers street food. Colour-coded by price, and designed for sharing tapas-style, the dishes focus on more unusual ingredients such as a rich but mellow curry featuring firm-fleshed yam bean root. Seasonal Western ingredients are also given some Thai treatment, to produce dishes like trout in sour orange curry, or fennel and chicory with a relish of minced pork, prawn, coconut and yellow bean. The dining room has a contemporary feel, with big windows and colourful, painted reclaimed wood lining one wall, and there's a decent list of wines and cocktails.

Peckham Refreshment Rooms ££

*12-16 Blenheim Grove, SE15 4QL (7639 1106, peckhamrefreshment.com). Peckham Rye Overground/rail. **Open** 11am-3pm, 6-10.30pm Mon-Fri; 10am-3pm, 6-10.30pm Sat. Modern European*

This small-plates restaurant just steps from the station entrance has proved such a hit with Peckham's burgeoning media set that it has expanded into the adjoining premises and now boasts a proper dining room alongside its more informal communal tables. The main menu features nicely put-together dishes each showcasing two or three high-quality ingredients. The only downer is the rough-and-ready fittings, which make for terrible acoustics.

Persepolis £

*28-30 Peckham High Street, SE15 5DT (7693 8007, foratasteofpersia.co.uk). Peckham Rye Overground/rail. **Open** 10.35am-9pm daily. Persian*

This little café inside a Persian delicatessen is a fun place serving fun food – colourful, crowded and charmingly bonkers. A handful of chairs and tables have been shoehorned between shelves stuffed with shisha pipes, embossed glassware, musical instruments, spices and specialist foodstuffs. They provide the setting for a liberal vegetarian interpretation of Iranian and Levantine dishes. Meze and wraps form the bedrock, with seasonally inspired fillings such as quince, halloumi and caramelised celeriac.

Pubs & bars

Four Quarters

*187 Rye Lane, SE15 4TP (3754 7622, www.facebook.com/fourquartersbar). Peckham Rye Overground/rail. **Open** 5.30pm-1am Mon-Wed; 5.30pm-1.30am Thur; 5pm-2am Fri; 1pm-2am Sat; 3.30-11pm Sun.*

A dedicated classic and retro arcade games bar, the Four Quarters is where to go if you want to brush up on your 'Street Fighter II' skills or play 'Pac Man' until your eyes go square. It's primarily a bar, but also opens as a café in the afternoons. There's a good selection of craft beers to choose from, alongside the usual favourites, and hearty pub food is served. To utilise the stacks of old arcade games, there are regular gaming tournaments, plus one-off events and film screenings.

Ivy House

*40 Stuart Road, SE15 3BE (7277 8233, www.ivyhousenunhead.com). Brockley Overground or Nunhead rail. **Open** noon-11pm Mon-Thur; noon-midnight Fri, Sat; noon-10.30pm Sun.*

In 2012, the owners gave their tenants one week's notice to ship out after selling the Ivy House to developers. Instead of going quietly, the tenants set about raising £1m to buy the pub and turn it into a cooperative. Nowadays friendly, committed staff welcome locals of all ages for a mates-rates pint of locally brewed ale, carefully sourced pub food (including generous Sunday roasts), and events ranging from live music to yoga classes, knitting circles and kids' dance lessons. It's all housed in a Grade-II listed building, with original beams, wall-to-wall wood panelling, leaded windows and an open fire.

Shops & services

Review

*131 Bellenden Road, SE15 4QY (www.reviewbookshop.co.uk). Peckham Rye Overground/rail. **Open** 10am-6pm Wed, Fri, Sat; noon-7pm Thur; 11am-5pm Sun. Books*

Review is the brainchild of Roz Simpson, founder of the Peckham Literary Festival (held in the shop each November) and author Evie Wyld. It's a tiny shop that's intelligently curated, with mags and 'zines, as well as non-book purchases, and it's famously dog-friendly (the website even has a dog-themed reading list). The events programme is particularly strong.

VAUXHALL & BRIXTON

▶ *Brixton or Vauxhall tube/rail.*

Vauxhall's heyday was in the 18th century when the infamous Pleasure Gardens, built back in 1661, reached the height of their popularity: a mingling of wealthy and not-so-wealthy, with everyone getting into trouble on 'lovers' walks'. When the Gardens closed in 1859, the area became reasonably respectable – all that remains is **Spring Garden**, behind popular gay haunt the **Royal Vauxhall Tavern** (aka RVT; *see p334*); there are a number of other, mostly gay clubs nearby with terrifyingly late opening hours. Down on the river is the cream and emerald ziggurat designed by Terry Farrell for the Secret Intelligence Service (formerly MI6).

To the south is Brixton, a lively hub of clubs and music. The town centre has been enjoying significant redevelopment, with **Windrush Square** completed at the end of Coldharbour Lane in 2010. The square's name is significant: HMT *Windrush* was the boat that brought West Indian immigrants from Jamaica in 1948. They were hardly welcomed, but managed to make Brixton a thriving community. As late as the 1980s, tensions were still strong, as the Clash song *Guns of Brixton* famously illustrates. The rage of the persecuted black community, still finding itself isolated and under suspicion decades after arriving, is better expressed by dub poet Linton Kwesi Johnson – try *Sonny's Lettah (Anti-Sus Poem)* for starters. The riots of 1981 and 1985 around Railton Road and Coldharbour Lane left the district scarred for years.

Now, most visitors come to Brixton for **Brixton Village**, two covered arcades that date to the 1920s and '30s and have been – with Market Row – Grade II listed, but Pop Brixton has muscled in on the act too. The district's main roads are modern and filled with chain stores, but there's also some attractive architecture – check out the **Ritzy Cinema** (Brixton Oval, Coldharbour Lane, SW2 1JG, 0871 902 5739, www.picturehouses. co.uk), dating to 1911. Brixton's best-known street, **Electric Avenue**, got its name when, in 1880, it became one of the first shopping streets to get electric lights.

Minutes south of Brixton's hectic centre, flanked by Tulse Hill and Dulwich Road, **Brockwell Park** (www.brockwellpark.com) is one of London's most underrated green spaces. Landscaped in the early 19th century for a wealthy glass-maker, the park contains his Georgian country house – now a café – an open-air swimming pool, bowling green, walled rose garden and miniature railway. Each July, there's an enjoyable country fair. If that doesn't seem bucolic enough, visit **Brixton Windmill** just off Brixton Hill a little further west.

Sights & museums

Brixton Windmill

Windmill Gardens, off Blenheim Gardens, SW2 5BZ (www.brixtonwindmill.org). Brixton tube/rail. **Open** *Tours Mar-Oct, usually 2nd weekend of the mth; see website for details. Book in advance. Nov-Feb closed.* **Admission** *free.*

Built in 1816 and in service until 1934, Brixton Windmill was operated by the Ashby family for the whole of its working life. The four-storey brick tower mill has been restored with lottery funding and there are about 25 open days a year when visitors can take a short or long guided tour for a fascinating glimpse into a lost London industry. The tours get booked up quickly: there isn't much room in the windmill, so numbers are limited to three adults or two adults and two children at a time.

Restaurants

Brixton Village (*see p289*) has numerous food options – from naughty street food to more salubrious international dishes.

Franco Manca £

Unit 4, Market Row, Electric Lane, SW9 8LD (7738 3021, www.francomanca.co.uk). Brixton tube/rail. **Open** *noon-5pm Mon; noon-11pm Tue-Fri; 11.30am-11pm Sat; 11.30am-10.30pm Sun. Pizza*

With its top-notch, UK-sourced (when possible) ingredients, speedy and friendly service, and rapid turnover, the original Brixton branch of Franco Manca remains, for our money, the best pizza joint in London. Here, you can sate a craving for genuine, Neapolitan-style pizza, with a flavourful slow-rise sourdough crust and a variety of traditional and innovative toppings.

♥ Naughty Piglets ££

28 Brixton Water Lane, SW2 1PE (7274 7796, www.naughtypiglets.co.uk). Brixton tube/rail. **Open** *6-10pm Tue, Wed; noon-2.30pm, 6-10pm Thur; noon-3pm, 6-10pm Fri, Sat; noon-3pm Sun. Contemporary European*

Run by husband-and-wife team Joe Sharatt and Margaux Aubry, Naughty Piglets is a 'natural' wine bar with a perfectly matched small-plate menu. Left to ferment naturally with little intervention, the wines are distinctly different in character (tasting something like a dry cider) and go particularly well with steamed mussels or clams. As well as seafood, the brief

Black and proud

Gathered over a quarter of a century, the **Black Cultural Archives** (www.bcaheritage. org.uk) finally found a permanent home. Britain's first black cultural centre opened in 2014 in the Grade II-listed Raleigh Hall on Brixton's Windrush Square, running a busy programme of events and exhibitions.

blackboard menu includes French classics such as fatty duck rillettes or more unusual options like BBQ Korean pork belly.

Pop Brixton £
49 Brixton Station Road, SW9 8PQ (3879 8410, www.popbrixton.org). Brixton tube/ rail. Street food

Pop Brixton is community initiative in the heart of Brixton, run in partnership with Lambeth Council, which uses a jumble of shipping containers to showcase young businesses. It covers over 4500sq feet and features over 50 traders – all of whom are independent, the majority local. The site has four bars and 16 street-food stalls and sit-down restaurants, not least the highly rated Indian joint **Kricket** (for the West End branch, *see p172*). There's also a large greenhouse space for communal dining and a programme of music and entertainment. Pop Brixton is currently (until at least autumn 2018) open all year round, open air in summer, but weather-proofed for winter.

Pubs & bars
Crown & Anchor
*246 Brixton Road, SW9 6AQ (7737 0060, www.crownandanchorbrixton.co.uk). Stockwell tube or Brixton tube/rail. **Open** 4.30pm-midnight Mon-Thur; 4.30pm-1am Fri; noon-1am Sat; noon-11pm Sun. Food served 5-10pm Mon-Fri; noon-10pm Sat; noon-8pm Sun.*

The most exciting feature of this pub, after a back-to-basics restoration, is the lengthy bar with its endless fonts: seven cask ales, 14 keg beers and ciders. It's a friendly place, devoted to great beer.

Shops & services
Bookmongers
*439 Coldharbour Lane, SW9 8LN (7738 4225, www.bookmongers.com). Brixton tube/rail. **Open** 10.30am-6.30pm Mon-Sat; 11am-4pm Sun. Books*

This Brixton institution is everything you could want from a second-hand bookshop.

Run by American-born Patrick Kelly, who opened the shop more than 20 years ago, it's developed a devoted following. Its stock is inspiring and well-organised, if slightly overflowing, and the resident dog adds to the charm.

❤ Brixton Village
*Corner of Coldharbour Lane & Brixton Station Road, SW9 8PR (brixtonmarket.net/ brixton-village). Brixton tube/rail. **Open** 8am-6pm Mon; 8am-11.30pm Tue-Sun. Check website individual shops. Mall*

Once almost forgotten, Granville Arcade has found a new lease of life. It opened in 1937, when it was proclaimed 'London's Largest Emporium', and in the 1960s became a Caribbean market. But by the 1990s, many of the arcade's units were unoccupied and its old art deco avenues were falling into a dilapidated state. In 2009, Lambeth Council called in urban-regeneration agency Space Makers, which launched a competition for local entrepreneurs to apply for a unit. It then awarded the best initiatives a place on site, and renamed the space Brixton Village, in line with its eclectic, locally minded new contents – from bijou bakeries and vintage boutiques to international eateries and fledgling fashion labels. Highlights here include **Margot Waggoner's Leftovers** (unit 71), with its Marseille lace and vintage sailor dresses, and **Binkie and Tabitha's Circus** (unit 70), which juxtaposes retro glassware with an assortment of socialist literature, but many people come just to eat: at **Casa Morita**, at **Fish, Wings & Tings**, at **KaoSarn**…

BATTERSEA & AROUND

▶ *Battersea Park or Clapham Junction rail.*

Battersea started life as an island in the Thames, but it was reclaimed when the marshes were drained. Huguenots settled here from the 16th century and, prior to the Industrial Revolution, the area was mostly farmland. The river is mostly dominated by Sir Giles Gilbert Scott's four-chimneyed **Battersea Power Station** (www. batterseapowerstation.co.uk), which can be seen close up from all trains leaving Victoria Station. Images of this iconic building have graced album covers (notably Pink Floyd's *Animals*) and films (among them Ian McKellen's *Richard III* and Michael Radford's *1984*), and its instantly recognisable silhouette pops up repeatedly as you move around the capital. Work started on what was to become the largest brick-built structure in Europe in 1929, and the power station was in operation through to the early 1980s. Too impressive to be destroyed, its future continues to be the subject of intense public debate. The current redevelopment masterplan by Uruguayan architect Rafael Viñoly, driven by the provision of luxury flats sold off-plan overseas, is linked to the provision of a Northern line tube extension (which should open in 2020). The developers took down the badly weather-damaged chimneys in 2014, but has now rebuilt them.

Overlooking the river, a little further west, **Battersea Park** (www.batterseapark.org) has beautiful lakes (one with a fine Barbara Hepworth sculpture) and gardens. Much of the park was relandscaped in 2004 according to the original 19th-century plans, albeit with some modern additions left in place: the **Russell Page Garden**, designed for the 1951 Festival of Britain; a **Peace Pagoda** built by a Buddhist sect in 1985 to commemorate Hiroshima Day; the **Pump House Gallery** (8871 7572, pumphousegallery.org.uk), and the **Children's Zoo**. The park extends to the Thames; from the wide and lovely riverside walk you can see both the elaborate Albert Bridge and the simpler Battersea Bridge, rebuilt between 1886 and 1890 by sewer engineer Joseph Bazalgette.

Battersea Park Children's Zoo

Battersea Park, Chelsea Embankment, SW11 4NJ (www.batterseaparkzoo.co.uk). Battersea Park rail. **Open** *Wummer 10am-5.30pm daily. Winter 10am-4.30pm daily.* **Admission** *£9.50, £7.50 reductions.*

A charming little zoo run by a family who also run wildlife parks in Derbyshire and an otter

and owl sanctuary in the New Forest. Living alongside the usual rabbits, goats, sheep and chickens are more exotic (some endangered) species such as meerkats, lemurs, Asian short-clawed otters, a Vietnamese pot-bellied pig, monkeys, emus, tortoises and talking mynah birds. In the meerkats' enclosure children can make their way down a tunnel to pop out on a level with the creatures. The zoo also has indoor and outdoor play areas, picnic tables, a coffee shop and nappy-changing facilities.

OTHER ATTRACTIONS

Scattered around south London are many standalone attractions that are certainly worth a visit in their own right.

Dulwich Picture Gallery

Gallery Road, Dulwich, SE21 7AD (8693 5254, www.dulwichpicturegallery.org. uk). North Dulwich or West Dulwich rail. **Open** *10am-5pm Tue-Sun. Tours 3pm Sat, Sun.* **Admission** *£7; free-£6 reductions; free under-18s. Special exhibitions vary. Tours free.*

This bijou attraction was designed by Sir John Soane in 1811 as the first purpose-built gallery in the UK but celebrated its bicentenary as a public gallery in 2017. It's a beautiful space that shows off Soane's ingenuity with lighting effects. The gallery displays a small but outstanding collection of work by Old Masters, offering a fine introduction to the Baroque era through works by Rembrandt, Rubens, Poussin and Gainsborough, and the temporary shows are often fantastic. Nice café-restaurant too.

Eltham Palace & Gardens

Court Yard, SE9 5QE (8294 2548, www. english-heritage.org.uk). Eltham or Mottingham rail. **Open** *10am-5pm Mon-Thur, Sun.* **Admission** *£14.40; £13 reductions; £8.60 5-15s; £37.40 family.*

Just half an hour from central London, Eltham Palace is a cut-and-shut job: a medieval hall with a fabulous 1930s mansion attached. Henry VIII lived here as a boy, but when millionaire couple Stephen and Virginia Courtauld were looking for a country house within easy reach of London, the derelict palace – its Great Hall was being used as a barn – fitted the bill. They commissioned a state-of-the-art residence filled with mod cons: en suite bathrooms (at a time when only posh hotels offered such luxury); underfloor heating; piped music; and a centralised vacuuming system that hooked up with every room – it occasionally backfired, smothering the maids with dust.

In the know
Vintage shopping

London used to be brilliant for vintage shopping, with people spinning yarns about that amazing Etro find they picked up for a fiver. You can still get quality vintage from the **Vintage Showroom** (see p189) in Covent Garden, a great store with famously knowledgeable staff. If you like your bargains closer to the basement, Brick Lane's **Beyond Retro** (110-112 Cheshire Street, E2 6EJ, 7613 3636, www.beyondretro. com) and **Rokit** (107 Brick Lane, E1 6SE, 7247 3777, www.rokit.co.uk) are piled high with clobber that's cool but unlikely to be pedigree. In fact, savvy shoppers know that the real gems are in the capital's charity shops: the proximity of **Trinity Hospice** (40 Northcote Road, SW11 1NZ, 7924 2927, www.royaltrinityhospice.london) and **Fara** (70 Chatham Road, SW11 6HG, 8973 0910, www.faracharityshops.org) to the affluent Londoners of Battersea and Clapham make them excellent hunting grounds for discarded delights.

You approach the building via the oldest medieval bridge in the country, crossing the moat just like the film stars, explorers, politicians and royalty whom the Courtaulds entertained in their fabulous party palace. The huge, lavish reception rooms, along with Virginia and Stephen's separate bedrooms, bathrooms and sitting rooms, were all opened to the public in 1999, but the latest restoration has spruced up the gardens too: Stephen, a keen gardener, had his prize-winning orchids evacuated to Kew at the start of World War II. In the games room, you're at liberty to play snooker billiards on the original table. There is a children's playground and a restaurant in the glasshouse.

❤ Hampton Court Palace

East Molesey, Surrey, KT8 9AU (0844 482 7777, www.hrp.org.uk). Hampton Court rail, or riverboat from Westminster or Richmond to Hampton Court Pier (Apr-Oct). **Open** *Palace Apr-Oct 10am-6pm daily. Nov-Mar 10am-4.30pm daily. Grounds dawn-dusk daily.* **Admission** *Palace, courtyard, cloister & maze Apr-Oct £17.50; £8.75-£14.50 reductions; £43.80 family; free under-5s. Nov-Mar £16.50; £8.25-£14 reductions; £42.50 family; free under-5s. Maze only £4.50; £2.50 reductions. Gardens only £5.20; £4.80 reductions; free under-15s.*

This spectacular palace, once owned by Henry VIII, is just a half-hour journey from central London – but will take you back 500 years through history. It was built in 1514 by Cardinal Wolsey, the high-flying Lord Chancellor, but Henry liked it so much he seized it for himself in 1528. For the next 200 years it was a focal point of English history: Elizabeth I was imprisoned in a tower by her jealous and fearful elder sister Mary I; Shakespeare gave his first performance to James I in 1603; and, after the Civil War, Oliver Cromwell was so besotted by the building he ditched his puritanical principles and moved in to enjoy its luxuries.

Centuries later, the rosy walls of the palace still dazzle. Its vast size can be daunting, so it's a good idea to take advantage of the guided tours. If you do decide to go it alone, start with Henry VIII's State Apartments, which include the Great Hall, noted for its beautiful stained-glass windows and elaborate religious tapestries; in the Haunted Gallery, the ghost of Catherine Howard – Henry's fifth wife, executed for adultery in 1542 – can reputedly be heard shrieking. The King's Apartments, added in 1689 by Wren, are notable for a splendid mural of Alexander the Great, painted by Antonio Verrio. The Queen's Apartments and Georgian Rooms feature similarly elaborate paintings, chandeliers and tapestries, while the new Cumberland Art Gallery –

Hampton Court Palace

in beautifully restored Georgian rooms – shows works from the Royal Collection by Holbein, Rembrandt and Caravaggio. The Tudor Kitchens are great fun, with their giant cauldrons, fake pies and blood-spattered walls.

More extraordinary sights await outside, where the exquisitely landscaped gardens offer topiary, Thames views, a reconstruction of a 16th-century heraldic garden and the famous Hampton Court maze.

❤ Horniman Museum

100 London Road, Forest Hill, SE23 3PQ (8699 1872, www.horniman.ac.uk). Forest Hill rail. **Open** *10.30am-5.30pm daily.* **Admission** *free; donations appreciated. Temporary exhibitions vary. Aquarium £4; £2 reductions; £9 family; free under-3s.*

The Horniman is an eccentric-looking art nouveau building with extensive gardens. The Natural History Gallery is dominated by an ancient walrus (overstuffed by Victorian taxidermists, who thought they ought to get

❤ Royal Botanic Gardens (Kew Gardens)

Kew, Richmond, Surrey, TW9 3AB (8332 5655, www.kew.org). Kew Gardens tube/ Overground, Kew Bridge rail or riverboat to Kew Pier. **Open** *from 9.30am; check website for closing times.* **Admission** *£15; £14 reductions; free under-17s.*

Kew's lush, landscaped beauty represents the pinnacle of our national gardening obsession. From the early 1700s until 1840, when the gardens were given to the nation, these were the grounds for two fine royal residences – the White House and Richmond Lodge. Early resident Queen Caroline, wife of George II, was very fond of exotic plants brought back by botanists voyaging to far-flung parts of the world, and these formed the basis for the collection. Then, in 1759, the renowned 'Capability' Brown was employed by George III to improve on the work of his predecessors here, William Kent and Charles Bridgeman. Thus began the shape of the extraordinary garden that today attracts hundreds of thousands of visitors each year – and was made a UNESCO World Heritage Site in 2003. Covering half a square mile, Kew feels surprisingly big – you'll want to pick up a map at the ticket office as well as following the handy signs.

Head straight for the 19th-century greenhouses, filled to the roof with plants – some of which have been here as long as the enormous glass structures themselves. Although the Temperate House will be closed until at least 2018 for much-needed restoration work, the sultry Palm House remains open, with its tropical palms, bamboo, tamarind, fig and mango trees, as well as fragrant hibiscus and frangipani.

Also worth seeking out are the Princess of Wales Conservatory, divided into ten climate zones; the Marine Display, downstairs from the Palm House (it isn't always open, but when it is you can see the delightful seahorses); and the lovely, quiet indoor pond of the Waterlily House (closed in winter). At the southern end of the gardens, there's a Chinese Pagoda dating to 1762.

Kew doesn't just do history. There's art, too, with sculptures like Henry Moore's *Reclining Mother and Child* in stunning settings that change with the light of each season, and the exquisite Victorian botanical drawings found in the Marianne North Gallery. The Xstrata Treetop Walkway was one hugely popular addition

to the gardens, allowing visitors to take a completely different kind of woodland walk – 60ft up in the leaf canopy. Another is *The Hive*, a 55ft-high, 40 tonne installation by Wolfgang Buttress in a wildflower meadow. First erected at the 2015 Milan Expo, it's a massive lattice within which visitors can stand, lie or sit as thousands of LEDs flicker and an orchestral arrangement plays, triggered by the activity of bees in a nearby hive.

❤More great gardens

Chelsea Physic Garden *p135*
London's finest secret garden.

Chiswick House Gardens *p304*
William Kent's 'natural' approach to landscape in the 18th century was revolutionary.

Garden Museum *p81*
Reopened in 2017.

Hampstead Heath *p248*
The whole heath is lovely, but the Pergola and Hill Gardens, overlooking the West Heath, especially so.

Hampton Court Palace *p291*
Versailles on Thames.

Palm House

the wrinkles out of the animal's skin) and ringed by glass cabinets containing pickled animals, stuffed birds and insect models. Other galleries include African Worlds and the Centenary Gallery, which focuses on world cultures. The Music Gallery contains hundreds of instruments: their sounds can be unleashed via touch-screen tables. The museum's popular showpiece Aquarium is a series of tanks and rock pools covering seven distinct aquatic ecosystems.

Strawberry Hill
*268 Waldegrave Road, Twickenham, Middx, TW1 4ST (8744 1241, www. strawberryhillhouse.org.uk). Richmond tube/ Overground/rail then bus R68, or Strawberry Hill rail. **Open** House hours vary; check website for details. Garden 10am-5.30pm daily. Tours 10am Wed, 10.30am Sat. **Admission** House £12.50; £6.25 reductions; free under-16s. Garden and tours free.*

Antiquarian Horace Walpole, who created the Gothic novel with his book *The Castle of Otranto*, had already laid the groundwork for the Gothic Revival of Victorian times as early as the 1700s. Pre-booked tickets, at 20-minute intervals, allow you to explore the crepuscular nooks and crannies of his 'play-thing house', this 'little Gothic castle', including – since 2015 – the study in which he wrote *Otranto*.

Thames Barrier
*1 Unity Way, Woolwich, SE18 5NJ (8305 4188, www.environment-agency.gov.uk/ thamesbarrier). Woolwich Dockyard rail, or North Greenwich tube then bus 472. **Open** 10.30am-5pm Thur-Sun. **Admission** Information Centre £4; £2.50-£3.50 reductions; free under-5s.*

This adjustable dam has been variously called a triumph of modern engineering and the eighth wonder of the world – more prosaically, it's saved London from being flooded approaching 100 times since it was built in 1982 for an eye-watering £535m. The shiny silver fins, lined up across Woolwich Reach, are an impressive sight. The Barrier is in regular use for maintenance purposes; check the website for a current timetable. To learn more, look around the information centre, where you'll find an account of the 1953 flood that led to the barrier's construction, displays on Thames wildlife and a pleasant café.

Twickenham Rugby Stadium
*Whitton Road, Twickenham, Middx, TW2 7BA (8892 8877, www.englandrugby. com/twickenham/world-rugby-museum). Hounslow East tube then bus 281, or Twickenham rail. **Open** Museum 10am-5pm Tue-Sat; 11am-5pm Sun. Tours times*

vary. **Admission** £20; £12-15 reductions; free under-5s.

Parts of Twickenham Stadium, the home of English rugby union, are currently under redevelopment, though it hasn't affected matches. You can still take a guided tour, too, · poking around the England dressing room, the players' tunnel and the Royal Box. The World Rugby Museum – with memorabilia charting the game's development from the late 19th century and a scrum machine – should reopen some time in 2018.

Wimbledon Lawn Tennis Museum
*Museum Building, All England Lawn Tennis Club, Church Road, Wimbledon, SW19 5AE (8946 6131, www.wimbledon.com/museum). Southfields tube. **Open** 10am-5pm daily; ticket holders only during championships. **Admission** (incl tour) £25; £15-£21 reductions; free under-5s.*

Highlights at this popular museum on the history of tennis include a 200° cinema screen that allows you to find out what it's like to play on Centre Court, and a recreation of a 1980s men's dressing room, complete with a 'ghost' of John McEnroe. Visitors can also enjoy a behind-the-scenes tour.

WWT Wetland Centre
*Queen Elizabeth's Walk, Barnes, SW13 9WT (8409 4400, www.wwt.org.uk). Hammersmith tube then bus 283, Barnes rail. **Open** Mar-Oct 9.30am-5.30pm daily. Nov-Feb 9.30am-4.30pm daily. **Admission** £12.26; £6.75-£9.17 reductions; free under-4s.*

The 43-acre Wetland Centre is only four miles from central London, but feels a world away. Quiet ponds, rushes, rustling reeds and wildflower gardens all teem with bird life – some 150 species. There are over 300 varieties of butterfly, 20 types of dragonfly and four species of bat. You can explore water-recycling in the Rain Garden or try the interactive section: pilot a submerged camera around a pond, learn the life-cycle of a dragonfly or make waves in a digital pool.

In the know
River crossings

Connoisseurs of urban infrastructure will enjoy a trip on the workmanlike **Woolwich Ferry** (8853 9400), a pair of lumpen diesel-driven boats that cart pedestrians (for free) and cars across the river every ten minutes daily. You might also fancy a walk through the 1640-foot-long **Woolwich Foot Tunnel**, which dives underneath the Thames between Grade II-listed red-brick entrance towers, built in 1912.

West London

For a fading cadre of right-wing politicians and a certain kind of celeb, Notting Hill is the coolest address in London, with Portobello Market surrounded by some of the most expensive addresses in west London. As in so many parts of London, any patina of funkiness is down to previous generations of residents – poor working class and immigrants mostly – who made the place in their own image. The huge Notting Hill Carnival gives the best flavour of this community. More high-end, elegant housing is found to the south in Holland Park and Kensington, where there are said to be more millionaires per square mile than in any other part of Europe. Apart from rubbernecking the rich, visitors should come here for the ambitious new Design Museum and delightful park. Further afield, you'll find the surprising cluster of sights around Chiswick – and, an arch on the far horizon, Wembley.

❤ **Don't miss**

1 Design Museum *p302*
A classic reborn in stunning listed premises.

2 Portobello Road Market *p300*
Big, busy and lots of fun.

3 Holland Park *p301*
One of London's finest parks.

4 Nama *p298*
Vegan dishes that look as good as they taste.

5 Leighton House *p301*
An eccentric Victorian gem.

WEST LONDON

NOTTING HILL

▶ *Ladbroke Grove, Notting Hill Gate or Westbourne Park tube*

Head north up Queensway from Kensington Gardens, then west along **Westbourne Grove**, and the road gets posher the further you go; cross Chepstow Road and you're in upmarket **Notting Hill**. Fashionable restaurants and bars exploit the lingering street cred of the fast-disappearing black and working-class communities. **Notting Hill Gate** isn't a pretty street, but the leafy avenues to the south are; so is **Pembridge Road**, to the north, leading to the boutique-filled streets of Westbourne Grove and Ledbury Road, and to **Portobello Road** and its renowned market.

Halfway down the road, **Blenheim Crescent** has a couple of independent booksellers, but the Travel Bookshop (nos.13-15), on which the movie *Notting Hill* focused its attention, has gone. Under the Westway, that elevated section of the M40 motorway linking London with Oxford, is the small but busy **Portobello Green Market**.

North of the Westway, Portobello's vitality fizzles out. It sparks back to life at **Golborne Road**, the heartland of London's North African community. Here, too, is a fine Portuguese café-deli, the **Lisboa Pâtisserie** (no.57, 8968 5242). At the north-eastern end of the road stands **Trellick Tower**, an architecturally significant, like-it-or-loathe-it piece of Ernö Goldfinger modernism. At its western end, Golborne Road connects with Ladbroke Grove, which can be followed north to **Kensal Green Cemetery**.

Sights & museums

Kensal Green Cemetery
Harrow Road, Kensal Green, W10 4RA (8969 0152, www.kensalgreencemetery.com). Kensal Green tube/Overground. **Open** *Apr-Sept 9am-6pm Mon-Sat; 10am-6pm Sun. Oct-Mar 9am-5pm Mon-Sat; 10am-5pm Sun.* **Tours** *(meet at the Anglican chapel) Mar-Oct 2pm Sun. Nov-Feb 2pm 1st & 3rd Sun of mth.* **Admission** *free. Tours £7; £5 reductions.* **No cards.**

Behind a neoclassical gate is a green oasis of the dead. It's the resting place of the Duke of Sussex, sixth son of George III, and his sister, Princess Sophia; also buried here are Wilkie Collins, Anthony Trollope and William Makepeace Thackeray.

Museum of Brands, Packaging & Advertising
111-117 Lancaster Road, W11 1QT (7243 9611, www.museumofbrands.com). Notting Hill Gate tube. **Open** *10am-6pm Tue-Sat; 11am-5pm Sun.* **Admission** *£9; £5-£7 reductions; £24 family; free under-7s.* **Map** *p297 A6.*

In 2015, the Museum of Brands found itself a glam new home: it's still in Notting Hill, but now has extra space for its seemingly endless collection of wrappers, posters, toys, boxes and general collectibles. The main part of the display is the 'time tunnel', a winding corridor of dark cabinets stuffed with colourful curios arranged chronologically. With the arrival of each new decade an information panel helps to put the changing designs and new fashions into context. A separate gallery functions as a sort of shrine to a few favourite brands: one cabinet holds every iteration of can and bottle

❤ Time to eat

Start the day like a Dane
Snaps & Rye *p299*

High-class and hospitable
Ledbury *p298*

Sushi without soy
Yashin *p303*

Modern European with ace desserts
108 Garage *p298*

Vegan eats that don't dress down
Nama *p298*

❤ Time to shop

Come for the atmosphere – not for bargains
Portobello Market *p300*

Next year's fashion, today
Couverture & the Garbstore *p299*

Record store that's the pulse of west London
Honest Jon's *p299*

Curated fashion and homewares
Merchant Archive *p300*

Like what you saw? Buy it from the shop!
Design Museum *p302*

Portobello Road Market

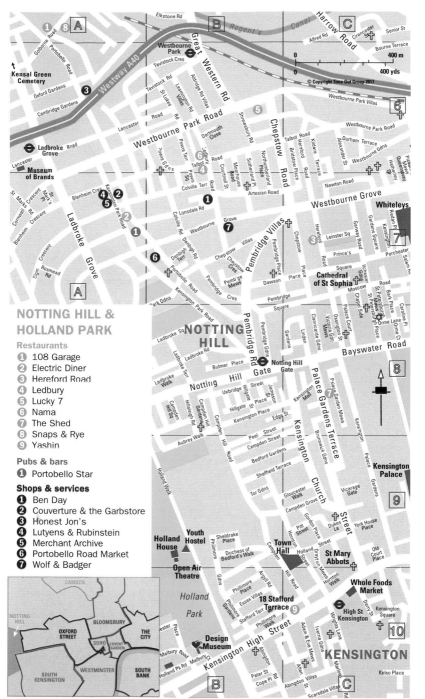

NOTTING HILL &
HOLLAND PARK

Restaurants
1. 108 Garage
2. Electric Diner
3. Hereford Road
4. Ledbury
5. Lucky 7
6. Nama
7. The Shed
8. Snaps & Rye
9. Yashin

Pubs & bars
1. Portobello Star

Shops & services
1. Ben Day
2. Couverture & the Garbstore
3. Honest Jon's
4. Lutyens & Rubinstein
5. Merchant Archive
6. Portobello Road Market
7. Wolf & Badger

WEST LONDON

produced by Guinness, another is packed with Kellogg's cereal boxes. We'd prefer a bit more analysis of the social trends that created all these designs – but as a nostalgia-stuffed tribute to the many, many things we buy, the museum is unparalleled.

Restaurants

♥ 108 Garage ££

108 Golborne Road, W10 5PS (8969 3769, www.108garage.com). Ladbroke Grove tube. **Open** *noon-2.45pm, 6-9.45pm Tue-Sun.* **Map** *p297 A5* ❶ *Modern European*

This garage conversion is a rather lovely spot, its dining room a handsome mix of dark mid-century furniture, bare bricks, corrugated iron and great washes of copper. The food is meticulous, from the near-liquid chicken-liver parfait to the lightly seared veal sweetbread atop charred cabbage. Best of all are the desserts: sweet potato ice-cream on a bed of popcorn and zingy sheep's yoghurt; or dense chocolate *crémeux* with artichoke ice-cream perched on a mound of toasted wild rice.

Electric Diner ££

191 Portobello Road, W11 2ED (7908 9696, www.electricdiner.com). Ladbroke Grove tube. **Open** *8am-midnight Mon-Wed; 8am-1am Thur-Sat; 8am-11pm Sun.* **Map** *p297 A7* ❷ *American*

The unfinished brick and concrete walls, low lighting, French grey-painted plank ceiling, red leather banquettes and lively open kitchen evoke a sort of chic US railway car diner. The hip vibe extends to the menu, which features artery-unfriendly American classics: cheeseburgers, hot dogs, milkshakes. Each dish is well thought out and uses good ingredients: French fries are thin and crispy, and even a simple Bibb lettuce and avocado salad was enlivened with chives and tarragon.

Hereford Road ££

3 Hereford Road, W2 4AB (7727 1144, www.herefordroad.org). Bayswater tube. **Open** *noon-3pm, 6-10.30pm Mon-Sat; noon-4pm, 6-10pm Sun.* **Map** *p297 C7* ❸ *British*

This restaurant makes its intentions clear: the first thing you see upon entering the long, narrow space is the kitchen; if it were any more open, you'd be eating off the chefs' laps. Sit and wonder how the restaurant can manage to serve two marvellous courses for £13.50 at lunch as you tuck into hearty dishes such as devilled duck livers with shallots, brill with roasted cauliflower, or onglet and chips. The slightly fancier à la carte menu includes the likes of pot roast rabbit, turnips and bacon.

♥ Ledbury £££

127 Ledbury Road, W11 2AQ (7792 9090, www.theledbury.com). Westbourne Park tube. **Open** *6.30-9.45pm Mon, Tue; noon-2pm, 6.30-9.45pm Wed-Sun.* **Map** *p297 B6* ❹ 0 *French*

Few haute establishments have the hospitable hum of the Ledbury, and even fewer boast two Michelin stars. But this former pub remains top-tier for gustatory good times. British ingredients – smoked eel, Cumbrian lamb – line up alongside delicacies such as Tokyo turnips, Bresse chicken and black truffle, but it's chef Brett Graham's clever contemporary treatment of them that sets the place apart. Ledbury signatures are consistently thrilling – particularly the flame-grilled mackerel with pickled cucumber, celtic mustard and shiso; and, well, all the desserts.

Lucky 7 £

127 Westbourne Park Road, W2 5QL (7727 6771, www.lucky7london.co.uk). Royal Oak or Westbourne Park tube. **Open** *noon-11pm Mon-Thur; 9am-11.30pm Fri; 9am-11.30pm Sat; 9am-10.30pm Sun.* **Map** *p297 B6* ❺ *American*

Lucky 7's American-retro decor is a smile from floor to ceiling, with outsized, wildly kitsch figurines stealing the show. The menu is 90% breakfast, burgers and outlandishly rich desserts, with craft beer, some cocktails and many shakes to ease it down. The place's only drawback is size – seating capacity is just a couple of dozen – which, combined with the no-bookings policy, means you'll often have to queue. But quality is high enough to merit a wait.

♥ Nama ££

110 Talbot Road, W11 1JR (7313 4638, namafoods.com). Westbourne Park tube. **Open** *noon-10pm Tue, Wed; noon-11pm Thur; 9am-11pm Fri, Sat; 9am-6pm Sun.* **Map** *p297 B6* ❻ *Vegan*

Against an austerely stylish backdrop (stark white walls, high ceilings, throbbing beats) that's more art gallery than restaurant, Nama isn't the cuddliest vegan eaterie – the staff and diners are far too cool for hugging trees. But what it lacks in warmth, it makes up for in frighteningly good cooking. 'Rice' is fashioned from tiny grated *kohlrabi* (a sweet cabbage). In the must-order 'sushi', this is combined with tiny pieces of cashew (for richness) as well as cucumber, avocado and sesame (for authentic flavours); in the Thai coconut curry, it's sprinkled with black sesame seeds and served with a creamy yellow-curry sauce and folds of mandolin-thin pickled fennel.

❤ Snaps & Rye £

93 Golborne Road, W10 5NL (8964 3004, www.snapsandrye.com). Westbourne Park tube. **Open** *8am-6pm Tue, Wed; 8am-11pm Thur-Sat; 10am-5pm Sun. Food served 8am-3pm Tue, Wed; 8am-3pm, 6.30-9.30pm Thur-Sat; 10am-3pm, 6.30-9pm Sun.* **Map** *p297 A5* ❽ *Danish*

Snaps (alcohol infusions) & Rye (the accompanying food) embodies all that's best about Scandinavian design: simple and functional, but every detail designed or chosen with aesthetic pleasure in mind. The owners have also taken great pains to make their food, prepared by British chef Tania Steytler, as good as it can possibly be. While Denmark's famous open-faced sandwiches (smørrebrød) are simple in concept, Steytler raises them to great heights through the use of superb ingredients, masterly cooking skills and attention to detail. Other options are meatballs, herring, cured salmon and apple cake. Feeling the cold but don't fancy snaps? Try cocio, a Nordic hot chocolate.

Pubs & bars

Portobello Star

171 Portobello Road, W11 2DY (3588 7800, www.portobellostarbar.co.uk). Ladbroke Grove or Notting Hill Gate tube. **Open** *11am-11.30pm Mon-Thur, Sun; 11am-12.30am Fri, Sat.* **Map** *p297 A7* ❶

This 'cocktail tavern' deftly blends discerning bar and traditional boozer. The well-stocked bar is manned by friendly staff thoroughly educated in the art of adult refreshment. Mixologist Jake Burger's impeccable, approachable directory of drinks is the last word on sophisticated intoxication. Ginger Pig pies are on hand to soak up the alcohol.

Shops & services

Ben Day

3 Lonsdale Road, W11 2BY (3417 3873, www. benday.co.uk). Ladbroke Grove or Notting Hill Gate tube. **Open** *11am-6pm Tue-Sat; 11am-5pm Sun.* **Map** *p297 B7* ❶ *Jewellery*

Everything here is handmade in the studio below the shop and, although you can buy off the shelf, bespoke is what Ben Day does best. Love the green chrysoprase cocktail ring but have your heart set on purple? No problem: 30 years of sourcing rare stones ensures there's no one better placed to track it down. Best of all, whether you're a jewellery novice or a gem collector with a sky's-the-limit budget, Day's discretion, enthusiasm and down-to-earth manner make shopping here a pleasure.

❤ Couverture & the Garbstore

188 Kensington Park Road, W11 2ES (7229 2178, www.couvertureandthegarbstore.com). Ladbroke Grove tube. **Open** *10am-6pm Mon-Sat; noon-5pm Sun.* **Map** *p297 A7* ❷ *Fashion/homewares*

Cult shop Couverture & the Garbstore sticks it to The Man with an under-the-radar collection of independent labels and up-and-coming designer fashion ('when it sells out, you're out of luck' is the theme). On the lower level of this slick three-storey boutique is designer Ian Paley's menswear label, the Garbstore. The ground and upper levels house Emily Dyson's much-admired lifestyle concept Couverture, where you'll find an enticing array of homewares and beautiful women's and children's fashion.

❤ Honest Jon's

278 Portobello Road, W10 5TE (8969 9822, www.honestjons.com). Ladbroke Grove tube. **Open** *10am-6pm Mon-Sat; 11am-5pm Sun.* **Map** *p297 A6* ❸ *Music*

Honest Jon's found its way to Notting Hill in 1979, where it is as much a cultural edifice – the shop's owner helped James Lavelle to set up Mo'Wax records – as a music shop. Here you'll find jazz, hip hop, soul, broken beat, reggae and Brazilian music, as well as the label's own brilliant compilations – the first volumes of the *London is the Place for Me* series, detailing calypso, Afro-jazz and highlife in the post-war years, were a revelation.

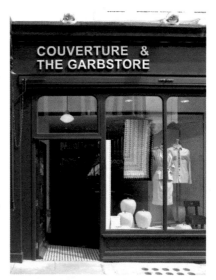

Lutyens & Rubinstein

21 Kensington Park Road, W11 2EU (7229 1010, www.lutyensrubinstein.co.uk). Ladbroke Grove tube. **Open** *10am-6pm Mon, Sat; 10am-6.30pm Tue-Fri; 11am-5pm Sun.* **Map** *p297 A7* ❹ *Books*

Lutyens & Rubinstein sells a beautifully arranged selection of literary fiction and general non-fiction. The core stock was put together by the owners canvassing hundreds of readers on the books they'd most like to find in a bookshop; thus every book stocked is sold because somebody has recommended it. The result is an appealing alternative to the homogeneous chain bookshops, with some unusual titles available. As well as books, the shop stocks a small range of stationery, greetings cards, paperweights, local honey and literary-inspired scents from CB I Hate Perfume.

♥ Merchant Archive

19 Kensington Park Road, W11 2EU (7229 9006, www.merchantarchive.com). Ladboke Grove or Notting Hill Gate tube. **Open** *10am-6pm Mon-Sat.* **Map** *p297 A5* ❺ *Fashion/homewares*

Carrying an edited selection of its own label, new designer outfits, homewares and fine vintage, Merchant Archive is a Notting Hill treasure. On the main floor brands such as Mother of Pearl and Studio Nicholson are shown against a backdrop of glass tables and artwork, with the odd 1920s feathered headpiece tossed atop a rack. Head downstairs to discover most of the vintage stuff.

♥ Portobello Road Market

Portobello Road, W10 (www.portobelloroad. co.uk). Ladbroke Grove or Notting Hill Gate tube. **Open** *General 9am-6pm Mon-Wed; 9am-1pm Thur; 9am-7pm Fri, Sat.* **No cards.** **Map** *p297 B7* ❻ *Market*

Best known for antiques and collectibles, this is actually several markets rolled into one: antiques start at the Notting Hill end; further up are food stalls; under the Westway and along the walkway to Ladbroke Grove are emerging designer and vintage clothes on Fridays (usually marginally less busy) and Saturdays (invariably manic).

There are more than 2,000 specialist antiques dealers squeezed tightly into any

---

available space along Portobello Road, with bargain-hunters jostling with camera-laden tourists to the soundtrack of live jazz. Pickings around Elgin Crescent are meagre, so push on to explore the fashion market under the Westway flyover. Best visited on a less-frantic Friday morning, it's here you'll find fashionistas and trendy teens delving through troves of prized vintage, boutique fashion and retro memorabilia. And don't stop there: continue up to Golborne Road for bargains away from the masses, helped by the presence of eccentric second-hand interiors stalls.

Wolf & Badger

46 Ledbury Road, W11 2AB (7229 5698, www. wolfandbadger.com). Notting Hill Gate tube. **Open** *10am-6pm Mon-Fri; 10am-6.30pm Sat; 11am-5pm Sun.* **Map** *p297 B7* ❼ *Fashion/homewares*

A hotbed of emerging design talent, this innovative boutique champions the work of up-and-coming (mostly) British fashion and homewares designers by offering them retail space and a sizeable return (over 75 %) on anything they sell. New designers are introduced every three months, giving the space a constantly evolving, one-step-ahead vibe that makes it a first port of call for show-stopping dresses, edgy T-shirts and statement accessories.

KENSINGTON & HOLLAND PARK

▶ *High Street Kensington or Holland Park tube.*

Just off **Kensington High Street**, a smart but rarely exhilarating shopping drag, an array of handsome squares are lined with grand 19th-century houses, many of which still serve as single-family homes for the wealthy. Linking with Notting Hill to the north, **Kensington Church Street** has many antiques shops selling furniture so fine you would probably never dare use it. **St Mary Abbots** (smanews.weebly.com), at the junction of Church Street and High Street, is a Victorian neo-Gothic church. It was built – on the site of the 12th-century original – by Sir George Gilbert Scott between 1869 and 1872. Past worshippers have included Isaac Newton and William Wilberforce. As well as beautiful stained-glass windows, it has London's tallest spire (278 feet).

Across the road, in a striking art deco building, is organic-food superstore **Whole Foods Market**. South down Derry Street, past the entrance to the **Roof Gardens** – a restaurant, event space and private members' club with flamingos and a stream, 100 feet above central London – is **Kensington Square**, which has a mighty concentration of blue plaques. The writer William Thackeray lived at no.16 and the painter Edward Burne-Jones at no.41; at no.18, John Stuart Mill's maid made her bid for 'person from Porlock' status by using Carlyle's sole manuscript of *The French Revolution* to light the fire. The houses, though much altered, date from the development of the square in 1685, and were surrounded by fields until 1840.

Further west is one of London's finest green spaces: **Holland Park**, which now has one of London's finest museums at its southern edge: this is the location of the fabulous new **Design Museum**. Also to the south of the park are a couple of historic houses: **18 Stafford Terrace** and, extensively refurbished **Leighton House**.

Sights & museums

18 Stafford Terrace

18 Stafford Terrace, W8 7BH (tours 7602 3316 Mon-Fri, 7938 1295 Sat, Sun, www. rbkc.gov.uk). High Street Kensington tube. **Open** *2-5.30pm Wed, Sat, Sun. Tours (pre-booked only) 11am Wed, Sat, Sun. Closed end June-Sep.* **Admission** *£7; £5 reductions; free under-5s. Tours £10; £8 reductions.* **Map** *p297 B10.*

The home of cartoonist Edward Linley Sambourne was built in the 1870s and has almost all of its original fittings and furniture. On Saturdays, tours are led by an actor in period costume.

❤ Holland Park

Ilchester Place, W8 6LU (7361 3003, www. rbkc.gov.uk/leisure-and-culture/parks/ holland-park). Holland Park/Kensington High Street tube. **Open** *7.30am-30mins before dusk daily.* **Map** *p297 B10.*

Holland Park, whose 55 acres add up to one of London's finest green spaces, was formerly the grounds of Jacobean mansion Holland House, named after its second owner, the Earl of Holland, whose wife was the first person in England to successfully grow dahlias. In the 19th century, Holland House was a hub of political and literary activity, visited by Disraeli and Lord Byron among others, but it was largely destroyed by the Blitz during World War II – enough of it remains to have been Grade I-listed and for a fancy-pants youth hostel, Safestay Holland Park (7870 9629, www.safestay.com/ss-london-holland-park.html), to move in. These days, dahlias are still grown, but there are also the Japanese-style Kyoto Gardens with their koi carp and bridge at the foot of a waterfall. Holland Walk, along the park's eastern edge, is one of the most pleasant paths in central London, and there's a fine café. In summer, open-air theatre and opera are staged.

❤ Leighton House

12 Holland Park Road, W14 8LZ (7602 3316, www.rbkc.gov.uk). High Street Kensington tube. **Open** *10am-5.30pm Mon, Wed-Sun. Tours 3pm Wed, Sat.* **Admission** *£12; £5-£10 reductions. Tours free.* **Map** *p297 B10.*

In the 1860s, artist Frederic Leighton commissioned a showpiece house. He ensured that, behind the sternly Victorian red-brick façade, it was full of treasures from all over the world, as well as his own works and those of his contemporaries. The house is decorated in high style: magnificent downstairs reception rooms designed for lavish entertaining; a dramatic staircase leading to a light-filled studio that takes up most of the first floor; and, above all, the Arab Hall, which showcases Leighton's huge collection of 16th-century Middle Eastern tiles. The only private space in the whole house is a tiny single bedroom – there are even theatrically Moorish-style screens allowing you to observe the downstairs without being seen.

Leighton House Museum

In the know
Play time

The playground at **Holland Park** (see above) is a don't miss for families. It has extensive climbing equipment, a zip wire, a giant see-saw and a tyre swing, as well as a separate fenced-in play area for younger children.

❤ Design Museum

*224-238 Kensington High Street, W8 6AG
(3862 5900, designmuseum.org). High
Street Kensington tube. **Open** 10am-6pm
(last admission 5pm) daily. **Admission** free;
temporary exhibitions vary. **Map** p297 B10.*

It's a fitting destination for a rather itinerant museum. Terence Conran's seed notion of a collection that would introduce the public to the wonders of contemporary design started life as the Boilerhouse Project series of exhibitions at the V&A (*see p126*) between 1982 and 1986, before setting up as a museum in a converted 1950s Thameside banana warehouse in 1989. Nearly three decades later, it finally has the grand space its ambition deserves. Dating to 1962, the Grade II*-listed former Commonwealth Institute building on Kensington High Street is not only itself a classic piece of modern architecture, with a pioneering hyperboloid roof (effectively a series of vertical arches) made of copper-clad concrete, but moving here has given the museum three times as much floorspace. That's plenty of room for temporary exhibitions (three at a time, plus a showcase for designers in residence), the archive, a library, two shops, a ground-floor café and impressive mezzanine restaurant, and, for the first time in its history, a permanent collection.

So much for how it fits together. How does it work? Brilliantly, as it happens. It's rare that a museum generates its own buzz – not noise, as when kids rampage around or events are in full swing, but the buzz of interested conversation – but that's exactly what happens in the generous atrium, with its tumbling staircase/seating area. The main collection is small but crammed with 1,000 interesting things. Called 'Designer Maker User', the exhibition traces the development of 20th- and 21st-century design, starting with a supremely detailed timeline at the entrance. Thereafter there are plenty of artefacts to satisfy visitors who are just looking for a bit of fuzzy hey-wow tech nostalgia – Sony Walkmans, Xbox controllers and early iPhones – but the tale of design is told, from major urban infrastructure and industrial design to crowdfunding and 3D printing, with interactives and old-fashioned captions.

All this – and the designers-in-residence gallery, where you get to meet the people behind all sorts of contemporary work – is free, but the ticketed temporary exhibitions that were the lifeblood of the museum's previous incarnation remain, and they remain excellent. Some take a look at particular designers, including Cartier and Camper; some explore broader themes, such as cycling or recycling; and some do a bit of both, as at the necessarily loose but always compelling annual Designs of the Year awards exhibition.

❤ More design destinations

Barbican Gallery *p228*
Exhibitions on the likes of Le Corbusier and the Japanese house in a building that's a 20th-century classic.

Geffrye Museum *p264*
A charming room-by-room journey through the history of domestic interiors.

London Transport Museum *p183*
Public transport design is fundamental to the city: check out the London by Design and Transport Futures galleries.

Museum of Brands *p296*
The urchin cousin to the Design Museum – this is where the disposable stuff lives: packaging, posters and all sorts of tat.

V&A *p126*
Art deco and modernism, fashion and furniture – if the Design Museum's no.1, the V&A is a close no.2.

Restaurants

For gourmet grazing, try **Whole Foods Market** (63-97 Kensington High Street, W8 5SE, 7368 4500, www.wholefoodmarket. com, 8am-10pm Mon-Sat), London flagship of the US health-food supermarket chain, which occupies the handsome building that was once Barkers department store.

Shed £££

122 Palace Gardens Terrace, W8 4RT (7229 4024, www.theshed-restaurant.com). Notting Hill Gate tube. **Open** *6-11pm Mon; noon-3pm, 6-11pm Tue-Fri; noon-4.40pm, 6-11pm Sat.* **Map** *p297 C8* **7** *British*

From a distance, with its white wooden cladding and high pitched roof, this restaurant does look suspiciously like a shed. Add some piggy portraits, bits of tractor, and charming staff in check shirts and it's a fitting setting for the food, which goes beyond the usual hackneyed take on British. Plates are small and meant for sharing, with delights such as hake with samphire, capers and a slick of red pepper sauce or spatchcock quail with cucumber, poppy seed and barbecue sauce. It's a menu of delicious things that are inventive without becoming tricksy.

❤ Yashin £££

1A Argyll Road, W8 7DB (7938 1536, www. yashinsushi.com). High Street Kensington tube. **Open** *noon-3pm, 6-11pm daily; last order 1hr before closing.* **Map** *p297 C10* **9** *Sushi*

The centrepiece sushi counter gives the game away: set on the dark green tiles behind the team of *itamae* (sushi chefs), a neon sign reads 'without soy sauce'. This is how the chefs ask you to eat your artfully crafted sushi. In place of a dunking, each piece is finished with its own flavourings or even a quick blast from a blowtorch.

In the know
Muffin like it

Just around the corner from Kensington High Street tube, **Muffin Man Tea Room** (12 Wrights Lane, W8 6TA, themuffinmankensington.co.uk) is an old-school English tearoom where you can relax with a cuppa and a cake or pastry.

EARL'S COURT & FULHAM

▶ *Earl's Court, Fulham Broadway or West Brompton tube.*

Earl's Court sells itself short, grammatically speaking, since it was once the site of the courthouse of two earls: both the Earl of Warwick and Earl of Holland. The 1860s saw the area move from rural hamlet to investment opportunity as the Metropolitan Railway arrived. Some 20 years later it was already much as we see it today, bar the fast food joints. The terraces of grand old houses are mostly subdivided into bedsits and cheap hotels.

In 1937, the **Earl's Court Exhibition Centre** was built. At the time it was the largest reinforced concrete building in Europe (a phrase that truly makes the heart sing), but it became a legend due to rock gigs – this was where Pink Floyd built and tore down *The Wall* – although trade shows were its bread and butter. It has all been swept away for an extremely divisive housing development. Nowadays, for music (and poetry) you'll need to head two minutes south down Warwick Road to the atmospheric **Troubadour** (263-267 Old Brompton Road, 7341 6333, www. troubadourlondon.com), a tiny venue but with an impressive pedigree – a young Bob Dylan, in his Greenwich Village folk phase, played in the basement when this was a coffeehouse, as did Hendrix and Joni Mitchell.

West along Warwick Road are the gates of Brompton Cemetery, whose peace and quiet are regularly disturbed at its southern end by neighbouring **Stamford Bridge** (*see p134*), ground of Chelsea FC. **Craven Cottage,** home to Championship side Fulham FC, is a more historic ground, however: the red-brick entrance and ticket gates (built in 1905) are a lovely example of the work of prime football stadium designer Archibald Leitch, who had to incorporate the Cottage into his design – it's grand for a Cottage, but a wonderfully eccentric part of the fabric of the club. Craven Cottage is at the northern end of the park that contains **Fulham Palace**.

Sights & museums

Brompton Cemetery
Fulham Road, Fulham, SW10 9UG (brompton-cemetery.org.uk). Earl's Court or Fulham Broadway tube. **Open** *dusk-dawn daily.*

One of the 'magnificent seven' Victorian cemeteries that ring the capital, Brompton is full of magnificent monuments (28 of them sufficiently impressive as to gain heritage listing status), including suffragette Emmeline Pankhurst and, his grave marked by a lion, 'Gentleman' John Jackson, who taught Lord Byron to box. It's a truly beautiful place.

Fulham Palace

Bishop's Avenue, off Fulham Palace Road, Fulham, SW6 6EA (7736 3233, www. fulhampalace.org). Putney Bridge tube. **Open** *Summer 12.30-4.30pm Mon-Thur; noon-5pm Sun. Winter 12.30-3.30pm Mon-Thur; noon-4pm Sun. Walled garden Summer 10.15am-4.15pm daily. Winter 10.15am-3.45pm daily. Botanical gardens dawn-dusk daily. Tours £6; free under 12s.* **Admission** *free.*

Fulham Palace was the episcopal retreat of the Bishops of London. The present building was built in Tudor times, with later significant Georgian and Victorian additions. It would be more accurate to call it a manor house than a palace, but it gives a fine glimpse into the changing lifestyles and architecture of nearly 500 years, from the Tudor hall to the Victorian chapel; try out the echo in the courtyard. There are regular guided tours of the palace and grounds, and of the gardens. The grounds offer some lovely spots to take a picnic, or indulge in a classy cake from the Drawing Room café; the walled garden is a particular delight. There's also access to a glorious stretch of riverside.

CHISWICK

▶ *Turnham Green tube or Chiswick rail.*

Once a sleepy, semi-rural suburb, Chiswick is now one of London's swankiest postcodes, its residents including broadcasters, actors, advertising bods and a smattering of rock 'n' roll royalty. In recent years, Chiswick High Road, its busy main thoroughfare, has developed a bit of a gastronomic reputation, with several high-end eateries. But come here rather for the surprising concentration of sightseeing attractions. Chiswick Mall is a beautiful residential road that runs along the river from Hammersmith, and includes **Kelmscott House** (26 Upper Mall, 8741 3735, williammorrissociety.org), once home to pioneering socialist William Morris but now a private house, with a small museum in the coach house and basement; it opens to the public 2-5pm on Thursdays and Saturdays. Further west along the riverbank, you'll find **Emery Walker's House** (7 Hammersmith Terrace, W6 9TS, 8741 4104, www. emerywalker.org.uk; tours only), another Arts and Crafts pioneer, whose house has been beautifully restored. Nearby, at no.3,

note the blue plaque for Edward Johnston: he devised the font that bears his name and was used across London's public transport from 1916 until it was reworked in 1979 – in a nice touch, the plaque uses his font rather than the standard English Heritage one. From here, it's a short walk to London's last industrial-scale brewery, **Fuller's** (Griffin Brewery, Chiswick Lane South, W4 2QB, www.fullers.co.uk; tasting tours £20), and **Hogarth's House**, while the **London Museum of Water & Steam** and **Musical Museum** are only a bus ride away. It's possible to return to the river path after Chiswick House; the wonderful **Royal Botanic Gardens** *(see p292)* are just over the bridge.

In the know
More Morris

If Kelmscott House has piqued your interest, visit the **William Morris Gallery** (see *p274*) – right over the other side of town, though, in Walthamstow – and, a train ride out of London, his Arts and Crafts home **Red House** (Red House Lane, Bexleyheath, DA6 8JF, 8304 9878, www.nationaltrust.org.uk/ red-house).

Sights & museums
Chiswick House & Gardens

Burlington Lane, W4 2RP (3141 3352, www.chgt.org.uk). Turnham Green tube or Chiswick rail. **Open** *House 10am-6pm Mon-Wed, Sun. Gardens 7am-dusk daily. Conservatory 10am-4pm Tue-Sun.* **Admission** *House £7.20, £4.30-£6.50 reductions. Gardens & Conservatory free.*

Richard Boyle, the third Earl of Burlington, designed this romantic Palladian villa in 1725. The house was a showpiece, in which the Earl could display his fine collection of paintings (many of which remain), for the entertainment of the artistic and philosophical luminaries of his day. The house is lovely – and nowadays enhanced by a startlingly modern but thoroughly appropriate café – but the gardens are absolutely gorgeous, a place to stroll in regal tranquillity.

Hogarth's House

Hogarth Lane, Great West Road, W4 2QN (8994 6757, www.hounslow.info). Turnham Green tube or Chiswick rail. **Open** *noon-5pm Tue-Sun.* **Admission** *free.*

Hogarth's House was, from 1749 until his death, the country retreat of 18th-century artist and social commentator William Hogarth (1697-1764). Craving somewhere to escape the noise of central London (his previous home was in what is now Leicester Square), he bought the house when this was still very much a rural area. The house has been superbly restored and is now a museum dedicated to Hogarth's life, displaying works such as *Gin Lane*, *Marriage A-la-Mode* and a copy of *The Four Stages of Cruelty*. Hogarth is buried in the nearby church of St Nicholas, past the horrible roundabout to the river.

London Museum of Water & Steam

Green Dragon Lane, Brentford, TW8 0EN (8568 4757, waterandsteam.org.uk). Kew Bridge rail. **Open** *11am-4pm daily.* **Admission** *£11.50, £5-£10 reductions.*

This Grade I-listed pumping station was built in 1838, the first to drive clean water into people's homes, 24 hours a day – at an affordable price. The museum it now houses combines the remarkable working remains of the building's Victorian industrial heyday – nine machines (five still in their original locations), including the 90-inch steam-powered Cornish Engine – with the story of how London's water has been cleaned up since the 17th century. You can also see the waterwheel and the James Kay rotative engine in use – now powered by that new-fangled electricity stuff.

In the know
Steam-powered fun

For the museum's prime attraction, visit at the weekend (or on bank holidays), when the ancient engines are fired up and whir into action, along with a puttering narrow-gauge railway and steam-powered fire engine.

Musical Museum

399 High Street, Brentford, TW8 0DU (8560 8108, www.musicalmuseum.co.uk). Gunnersbury tube or Kew Bridge Overground. **Open** *11am-5pm (last admission 4pm) Fri-Sun. Tours & musical demonstrations 11.30am, 1.30pm, 3.30pm Fri-Sun.* **Admission** *£10, £4-£7.50 reductions. Tickets allow unlimited entry for 12 months; under-16s must be accompanied by an adult.*

A converted church contains one of the world's foremost collections of automatic musical instruments, the legacy of the desire to record and reproduce music before the invention of the microphone. Here you'll find tiny clockwork music boxes, reproducing pianos and spooky orchestrions, as well as 30,000 historic musical rolls. There are sophisticated pianolas, cranky barrel organs, violin players and the self-playing Mighty Wurlitzer, as well as a 230-seat concert hall and orchestra pit from which

In the know
Graves of the famous

It isn't just Hogarth who now sleeps in **St Nicholas's graveyard** (Church Street, W4 2PH, www.stnicholaschiswick.org): the American painter Whistler has his fine bronze tomb here, while Frederick Hitch, who won a Victoria Cross against the Zulus at Rorke's Drift, is under a large rock with a pith helmet on top.

a Wurlitzer console rises as they used to in 1930s cinemas. The museum coffee shop overlooks the river, and there are fun dance, film and music events, as well as temporary exhibitions.

OTHER ATTRACTIONS

As London extends westwards, attractions necessarily become more widely spread. Footie fans will want to make the pilgrimage to England's home of football, **Wembley Stadium**, with the **Wembley Arena** music venue (*see p350*) beside it.

Wembley Stadium

Empire Way, Wembley, HA9 0WS (0844 980 8001, www.wembleystadium.com). Wembley Park tube. **Open** *Tours 10am-4pm daily, except public holidays & during major events at the stadium.* **Admission** *Tours £17-£19, £10-£11 reductions.*

Wembley has been hosting the nation's biggest sporting spectacles since 1923, but it was as the home of England's World Cup Final win over West Germany in 1966 that its legendary status was secured. The old twin towers have long gone, with today's 90,000-seat stadium completely rebuilt before reopening in 2007. The arch that now spans the width of the stadium can be seen from as far away as Richmond Park. If you're not coming to see a sports event or a big concert, you can take the 75-minute Wembley Tour. Knowledgeable and impressively enthusiastic guides allow you to pause and soak up the stadium magic, take a few selfies and imagine yourself caught up in Cup Final fever. The tour includes the England changing rooms, the players' tunnel and the chance to sit in the England manager's hot-seat used during press conferences. You can also climb the 107 steps up to where the winners collect their medals and get your hands on a replica of the FA Cup. There are also exhibits, like the Jules Rimet Trophy and a flag used in the London 1948 Olympic Games.

Experience

XOYO

Events

Your guide to what's happening when

Forget about British reserve. Festivals and events play increasingly elaborate variations on the age-old themes of parading and dancing, nowadays with ever-larger sprinklings of arts and culture. Some are traditional, some innovative, from the splendid ritual of Changing the Guard to the outdoor spectacle of the Greenwich & Docklands International Festival. Weather plays a part in the timing, with a concentration of things to do in the warmer – and sometimes drier – months of summer, but the city's calendar is busy for most of the year.

► *For a sense of seasonal London and advice on when to visit, see p28.*

Bonfire Night fireworks over Albert Bridge

All year round

For London's glorious military pageantry, *see p311* Changing the Guard.

Ceremony of the Keys

Tower of London, Tower Hill, the City, EC3N 4AB (3166 6000, www.hrp.org.uk/tower-of-london/whats-on/ceremony-of-the-keys). Tower Hill tube or Tower Gateway DLR. **Date** *9.30pm daily (advance bookings only).*

Join the Yeoman Warders after-hours at the Tower of London as they ritually lock the fortress's entrances in this 700-year-old ceremony. You enter the Tower at 9.30pm and it's all over just after 10pm, but places are hotly sought after – apply at least two months in advance; full details are available on the website.

Gun Salutes

Green Park, Mayfair & St James's, W1; Tower of London, the City, EC3. **Dates** *6 Feb (Accession Day); 21 Apr & a Sat in June (Queen's birthdays); 2 June (Coronation Day); 10 June (Duke of Edinburgh's birthday); a Sat in June (Trooping the Colour, see p311); State Opening of Parliament (see p313) Lord Mayor's Show (see p317) Remembrance Sunday (see p318); also for state visits.*

There are gun salutes on many state occasions – see the list of dates given above for a complete breakdown of when the cannons roar. A cavalry charge features in the 41-gun salutes mounted by the King's Troop Royal Horse Artillery in Hyde Park at noon (opposite the Dorchester Hotel), whereas, on the other side of town, the Honourable Artillery Company ditches the ponies and piles on the firepower with 62-gun salutes (1pm at the Tower of London). If the dates happen to fall on a Sunday, the salute is held on the following Monday.

Spring

League (EFL) Cup Final

Wembley Stadium, Stadium Way, Middlesex, HA9 0WS (cup.efl.com). Wembley Park tube. **Date** *early Mar.*

Less prestigious than the FA Cup, the League Cup is a knockout football competition with a 50-year history – but widely regarded as the annual trophy that's 'better than nothing'. Still, the winners do get to play in the UEFA Europa League.

London Beer Week

drinkup.london/beerweek. **Date** *Mar.*

A city-wide celebration of all things hop. Along with the bevy of participating bars and pubs, there's also a host of beer-pairing dinners, brewery tours – with a rickshaw service laid on to zip between them – and meet-the-maker talks.

WoW: Women of the World

Southbank Centre, Belvedere Road, South Bank, SE1 8XX (7960 4200, www.southbankcentre.co.uk/whats-on/festivals-series/women-of-the-world). **Date** *Mar.*

A festival championing everything that is great about women and girls. Through discussion, debate, performances and activism, female achievements are celebrated and the obstacles that prevent women from achieving their full potential are explored.

Kew at Springtime

Kew Gardens, Surrey, TW9 3AB (8332 5655, www.kew.org). Kew Gardens tube/ Overground, Kew Bridge Overground/rail or riverboat to Kew Pier. **Admission** *£15/50; £14 reductions; £2.50 under 17s.* **Date** *early Mar-May.*

💗 Best events

Changing the Guard
p311
Pomp and ceremony.

Greenwich & Docklands International Festival
p313
Dramatic outdoor arts.

Pride London *p314*
Out and about.

BBC Proms *p314*
Classical music bonanza.

Notting Hill Carnival
p315
Europe's biggest street party.

Totally Thames Festival
p316
Celebrations on the river.

London Frieze Art Fair
p317
Arty parky happenings.

Lord Mayor's Show *p317*
The City on parade.

Greenwich & Docklands
International Festival

Changing the Guard

London is a past master when it comes to military pomp

On alternate days from 10.45am – or daily from 10.15am April-July – one of the five Foot Guards regiments lines up in scarlet coats and tall bearskin hats in the forecourt of Wellington Barracks; at exactly 11.27am (10.57am April-July),the soldiers start to march to **Buckingham Palace**, joined by their regimental band, to relieve the sentries there in a 45-minute ceremony for **Changing the Guard**. The Guards regiments are the Grenadier, Coldstream, Scots, Irish and Welsh. (For details, visit www.royal.gov.uk/RoyalEventsandCeremonies/ChangingtheGuard/Overview.aspx: do check in advance for weather cancellations or last-minute changes of schedule.)

Not far away, at **Horse Guards Parade** in Whitehall, the Household Cavalry regiments – the Life Guards and Blues and Royals – mount the guard daily at 11am (10am on Sunday). Although this ceremony isn't as famous as the one at Buckingham Palace, it's more visitor-friendly: the crowds aren't as thick as they are at the palace. After the old and new guard have stared each other out in the centre of the parade ground, you can nip through to the Whitehall side to catch the departing old guard perform their dismount choreography: a synchronised, firm slap of approbation to the neck of each horse before the gloved troopers swing off.

As well as these near-daily ceremonies, London sees other, less frequent parades on a far grander scale. The most famous is **Trooping the Colour**, which is staged to mark the Queen's official birthday on the Saturday closest to 13 June (her real birthday is in April). At 10.45am, the Queen rides in a carriage from Buckingham Palace to Horse Guards Parade to watch the soldiers, before heading back to Buckingham Palace for a midday RAF flypast and the impressive gun salute from Green Park.

Also at Horse Guards, for two successive evenings in June, a pageant of military music and precision marching begins at 8pm when the Queen (or another royal) takes the salute of the 300-strong drummers, pipers and musicians of the Massed Bands of the Household Division. This is known as **Beating Retreat** (www.householddivision.org.uk/beating-retreat, tickets 7839 5323).

Changing the Guard

Aphex Twin plays Field Day

Kew Gardens is at its most beautiful in spring, with five million flowers carpeting the grounds.

British Science Week
7019 4937, www.britishscienceweek.org. Date mid Mar.

From the weird to the profound, this annual week of events engages the public in celebrating science, engineering and technology.

St Patrick's Day Parade & Festival
7983 4000, www.london.gov.uk/events. Date mid Mar.

Join the London Irish out in force for this annual parade through central London, which is followed by toe-tapping tunes in Trafalgar Square. Held on the Sunday closest to 17 March.

BFI Flare: London LGBT Film Festival
7928 3232, www.bfi.org.uk/flare. Date late Mar.

Highlighting the importance of the city's LGBT communities, the rebranded Lesbian & Gay Film Festival is the UK's third-largest film festival, cramming in a superb range of international films over the best part of a fortnight.

Oxford & Cambridge Boat Race
River Thames, from Putney to Mortlake (www.theboatrace.org). Putney Bridge tube, or Barnes Bridge, Mortlake or Putney rail. Date Apr.

Blue-clad Oxbridge students (dark blue for Oxford, light blue for Cambridge) race each other in a pair of rowing eights, as they have done since 1829, but now watched by tens of millions worldwide. Experience the excitement from the riverbank – along with 250,000 other fans.

La Linea
www.comono.co.uk. Date early Apr.

A contemporary Latin-music festival, featuring everything from brass bands to flamenco guitar, held over a fortnight in April.

London Marathon
Greenwich Park to the Mall via the Isle of Dogs, Victoria Embankment & St James's Park (7902 0200, www.virginlondonmarathon.com). Blackheath & Maze Hill rail (start), or Charing Cross tube/rail (end). Date mid Apr.

One of the world's elite long-distance races, the London Marathon is also one of the world's largest fundraising events – nearly 80% of participants run for charity, so zany costumes abound among the 36,000 starters. Held on a Sunday.

Breakin' Convention
Sadler's Wells, Rosebery Avenue, Clerkenwell, EC1R 4TN (7863 8214, www.breakinconvention.com/events/festival). Angel tube. Date Early May bank holiday.

Hip hop and dance festival.

FA Cup Final
Wembley Stadium, Stadium Way, Middlesex, HA9 0WS (0800 169 2007 Wembley Stadium, www.thefa.com/thefacup). Wembley Park tube or Wembley Stadium rail. Date mid May.

The oldest domestic knockout tournament is an annual highlight for many international football fans. For all that the competition – which began in 1871 – has lost a little lustre for the top teams, who all fear being defeated by lowly opposition, it retains the capacity to surprise.

Museums at Night
01273 523982, museumsatnight.org.uk. Date May.

Part of a UK-wide biannual festival, Museums at Night sees doors kept open after-hours at cultural venues across London. It returns in October.

Covent Garden May Fayre & Puppet Festival

Garden of St Paul's Covent Garden, Bedford Street, WC2E 9ED (7375 0441, www. punchandjudy.com/coventgarden.htm). Covent Garden tube. **Date** *2nd Sun in May.*

All-day puppet mayhem (12.30-5.30pm) devoted to celebrating Mr Punch at the scene of his first recorded sighting in England in 1662. Mr P takes to the church's pulpit at noon. Held on a Sunday.

Chelsea Flower Show

Royal Hospital, Royal Hospital Road, Chelsea, SW3 4SR (0844 995 9664, www.rhs. org.uk shows-events). Sloane Square tube. **Date** *mid May.*

Elbow through the huge crowds to admire perfect blooms, or get ideas for your own plot, with entire gardens laid out for the show, as well as tents with their walls packed with endless varietals. The first two days are reserved for Royal Horticultural Society members and tickets for the open days can be hard to come by.

▶ *The show closes at 5.30pm on the final day, but the display plants are sold off from around 4pm.*

State Opening of Parliament

Palace of Westminster, SW1A 0PW (7219 4272, www.parliament.uk). Westminster tube. **Date** *May/June.*

Pomp and ceremony attend the Queen's official reopening of Parliament after its recess, an event that marks the formal beginning of the parliamentary year. She arrives (at about 11.15am) and departs in the state coach, accompanied by troopers of the Household Cavalry.

Summer

Field Day

Victoria Park, Victoria Park Road, Hackney, E3 5SN (www.fielddayfestivals.com). **Date** *June.*

One of the best music festivals in London, with a leftfield booking policy. Acts range from weird pop and indie rock to underground dance producers and folk musicians.

London Festival of Architecture

www.londonfestivalofarchitecture.org. **Date** *June.*

An entertaining mix of talks, discussions, walks, screenings and other events, always gathered under a punchy theme.

LIFT (London International Festival of Theatre)

7968 6800, www.liftfestival.com. **Date** *June.*

Biennial festival that sees hundreds of artists sharing performances from across the globe in a month-long celebration. The next instalment is in 2018.

Camden Rocks Festival

camdenrocksfestival.com. **Date** *June.*

This one-day festival brings a slavering horde of rock and metal bands to venues all over Camden.

Bushstock

Shepherd's Bush (www.bushstock.co.uk). **Date** *June.*

A multi-venue music festival run by independent record label Communion Presents, focusing on new and emerging talent.

Opera Holland Park

Holland Park (3846 6222, www. operahollandpark.com). **Date** *June-Aug.*

A canopied outdoor theatre hosts a season of opera, including works aimed at children.

Open Garden Squares Weekend

7839 3969, www.opensquares.org. **Date** *mid June.*

Secret – and merely exclusive – gardens are thrown open to the public for this horticultural shindig. You can visit roof gardens, children-only gardens and prison gardens, as well as a changing selection of those tempting oases railed off in the middle of the city's finest squares. Some charge an entrance fee and must be booked in advance. Tickets available online.

Aegon Tennis Championships

Queens Club, Palliser Road, West Kensington, W14 9EQ (7386 3400, www. queensclub.co.uk). Barons Court tube. **Date** *mid June.*

The pros tend to treat this week-long grass-court tournament as a summer warm-up session for the world-famous Wimbledon Tennis Championships.

♥ Greenwich & Docklands International Festival

8305 1818, www.festival.org. **Date** *late June/ early July.*

This annual week of outdoor arts, theatre, dance and family entertainment is spectacular. Events take place at the Old Royal Naval College and other sites, including Canary Wharf and Mile End Park.

❤ Pride London
0844 344 5428, www.prideinlondon.org.
***Date** late June/early July.*

This historic celebration of the LGBT community (taking place since 1972, initially in support of the Stonewall rioters) now welcomes some 800,000 revellers to a week of events, culminating in a celebratory parade held on Saturday.

Wimbledon Tennis Championships
All England Lawn Tennis Club, Church Road, Wimbledon, SW19 5AE (8944 1066, www.wimbledon.com). Southfields tube or Wimbledon tube/rail. ***Date** late June-mid July.*

Getting into Wimbledon requires considerable forethought, as well as luck. Seats on the show courts are distributed by a ballot, which closes the previous year; enthusiasts who queue on the day may gain entry to the outer courts – and even get rare tickets for Centre Court. You can also turn up later in the day and pay reduced rates for seats vacated by spectators who've left the ground early.

Wireless Festival
Finsbury Park, N4 2DW (0333 321 9999, www.wirelessfestival.co.uk). Manor House tube or Finsbury Park tube/rail. ***Date** early July.*

Three nights of rock and dance acts, with headliners including the likes of The Weeknd and Skepta.

Hampton Court Palace Flower Show
Hampton Court Palace, East Molesey, KT8 9AU (0844 995 9664, www.rhs.org.uk/shows-events/rhs-hampton-court-palace-flower-show). ***Date** early July.*

A spectacular setting featuring world-class gardens, as well as marquees showcasing work by some of the country's leading designers and nurseries.

Summer Streets
Regent Street (www.regentstreetonline.com/campaigns/summerstreets). Oxford Circus or Picadilly Circus tube. ***Date** every Sun in July.*

Enjoy the rare spectacle of traffic-free road in Zone 1 as Regent Street's classy curve is pedestrianised for a street party. The festivities take on a different theme each week, with free entry, installations, demonstrations and activities to get stuck into. A highlight is the Garden Party: the street is lined with grass and a bandstand hosts a live brass band.

Lovebox Weekender
Victoria Park, Bow, E3 5TB (0333 321 9999, www.loveboxfestival.com). Mile End tube or Cambridge Heath Overground. ***Date** mid July.*

Expect some of the best names that the London nightlife scene has to offer – plus some international big-hitters (Blondie, Sly Stone) – over two days in myriad themed stages, tents and arenas.

Somerset House Summer Series
Somerset House, Strand, WC2R 1LA (7845 4600, www.somersethouse.org.uk/whats-on/summer-series-somerset-house). Temple tube. ***Date** mid July.*

Somerset House welcomes an array of big and generally pretty mainstream acts for roughly ten days of open-air gigs, as well as movie screenings.

Citadel Festival
Victoria Park, Bow, E3 5TB (citadelfestival.com). Mile End tube or Cambridge Heath Overground. ***Date** July.*

A civilised Sunday festival with a top musical line-up and sundry arts-driven distractions.

British Summer Time Festival
Parade Ground, Hyde Park, W2 2UH (www.bst-hydepark.com). Marble Arch, Lancaster Gate, Hyde Park Corner, Knightsbridge tube. ***Date** 2 weekends in July.*

Hyde Park plays host to some of the planet's biggest musical stars, with an upmarket festival vibe that takes in small stages, theatre and comedy, food and drink.

❤ BBC Proms
Royal Albert Hall, Kensington Gore, South Kensington, SW7 2AP (0845 401 5040, www.bbc.co.uk/proms, tickets www.royalalberthall.com). South Kensington tube. ***Date** mid July-mid Sept.*

The Proms overshadows all other classical-music festivals in the city, with around 70 concerts, covering everything from early-music recitals to orchestral world premières, and from boundary-pushing debut performances to reverent career retrospectives. BBC Radio 3 plays recordings of the concerts.

RideLondon
7902 0212, www.prudentialridelondon.co.uk. ***Date** early Aug.*

This cycling festival encourages around 100,000 people to don branded fluorescent vests and ride an eight-mile traffic-free circuit from Buckingham Palace to the Tower.

Competitive races also form part of the weekend's festivities.

Carnaval del Pueblo

Burgess Park, Southwark, SE5 7QH (www. carnavaldelpueblo.com). Elephant & Castle tube/rail. **Date** *early Aug.*

This vibrant outdoor parade and festival is more than just a loud-and-proud day out for Latin American Londoners: with a procession from Elephant Road to Burgess Park, it attracts people from all walks of life (as many as 60,000, most years) looking to inject a little Latin spirit into the weekend.

Camden Fringe

www.camdenfringe.org. **Date** *Aug.*

An eclectic bunch of new, experimental and short shows, staged by everyone from experienced performers to newcomers.

Sunfall

Brockwell Park, Herne Hill, SE24 9BJ (www. sunfall.co.uk). Herne Hill rail. **Date** *Aug.*

Catch big names and cult heroes at this new day-and-night dance festival in south London. A day of raving in Brockwell Park is followed by after-parties featuring jazz, electronica, house, hip hop, dubstep, techno, soul, drum & bass and disco.

Great British Beer Festival

Olympia London, Hammersmith Road, Kensington, W14 8UX (01727 867201, www. gbbf.org.uk). Kensington (Olympia) tube/ Overground. **Date** *mid Aug.*

A great chance to enjoy London's extraordinary beer renaissance in one place. Hiccup.

Meltdown

Southbank Centre, Belvedere Road, South Bank, SE1 8XX (7960 4200, www. southbankcentre.co.uk). **Date** *mid Aug.*

The Southbank Centre invites a guest artist – in 2017, English-Tamil rapper M.I.A. followed the likes of David Bowie, Patti Smith and Ornette Coleman – to curate a fortnight of gigs, films and whatever other events appeal to them.

Carnaval del Pueblo

London Mela

Wembley Park, 5 Exhibition Way, Wembley, HA9 0FA (www.londonmela.org). Wembley Park tube. **Date** *late Aug.*

Thousands flock to this exuberant celebration of Asian culture, dubbed the Asian Glastonbury. You'll find urban, classical and experimental music, circus, dance, comedy, children's events and food.

❤ Notting Hill Carnival

Notting Hill, W10 & W11 (www. thelondonnottinghillcarnival.com). Ladbroke Grove, Notting Hill Gate or Westbourne Park tube. **Date** *late Aug.*

Two million people stream into Notting Hill for Europe's largest street party. Massive mobile sound systems dominate the streets with whatever bass-heavy party music is currently hip, but there's plenty of tradition from the West Indies too: calypso music and a spectacular costumed parade.

South West Four

Clapham Common, Clapham, SW4 (www. southwestfour.com). Clapham Common or Clapham South tube, or Clapham High Street Overground. **Date** *late Aug.*

London's key dance-music festival, held over the August bank holiday weekend.

Autumn

Tour of Britain

www.tourofbritain.co.uk. **Date** *early Sept.*

Join spectators on the streets of the capital for a stage of British cycling's biggest outdoor event.

London African Music Festival

7328 9613, www.joyfulnoise.co.uk. **Date** *Sept.*

A wonderfully eclectic affair, held over a fortnight in September. Recent performers have included Osibisa (from Ghana), Modou Toure (Senegal) and Hanisha Solomon (Ethiopia).

❤ Totally Thames Festival
*Between Westminster Bridge & Tower Bridge (7928 8998, www.totallythames.org). Blackfriars or Waterloo tube/rail. **Date** Sept.*

A giant party along the Thames, this month of events is London's largest free arts festival. It's a family-friendly mix of carnival, pyrotechnics, art installations and live music alongside craft and food stalls. Events include the Great River Race – a 22-mile marathon for all manner of traditional rowed and paddled boats. The festival is brought to an end with a lantern procession and fireworks.

Horseman's Sunday
*St John's Hyde Park, Hyde Park Crescent (www.stjohns-hydepark.com). Marble Arch or Lancaster Gate tube. **Date** Sun in Sept.*

Reverend Stephen Mason leads a cavalcade of over 100 horses and riders in celebration of riding in the capital. A service at St John's Church (from 10am) is followed by a blessing of the horses (around noon), together with an alfresco fair.

Open-House London
*3006 7008, www.open-city.org.uk. **Date** mid Sept.*

An opportunity to snoop around other people's property, for one weekend only. Taking part are more than 500 palaces, private homes, corporate skyscrapers, pumping stations and bomb-proof bunkers, many of which are normally closed to the public.

Kings Place Festival
*Kings Place, 90 York Way, King's Cross, N1 9AG (7520 1490, www.kingsplace.co.uk/ festival). King's Cross St Pancras tube/rail. **Date** mid Sept.*

Cramming in more than 100 events over three days – classical, jazz and experimental music, as well as spoken word and other events – this is a great little arts festival in a superb venue.

London Fashion Week
*Somerset House, Strand, WC2R 1LA (www.londonfashionweek.co.uk). Temple tube. **Date** mid Sept.*

Extraordinary biannual outbreak of fashionable happenings across London (it returns each February). Although mainly focused on Somerset House, events see gaggles of paparazzi and informal catwalks in the most unlikely places.

OnBlackheath
*Blackheath, SE3 (www.onblackheath.com). Blackheath or Lewisham Overground. **Date** mid Sept.*

While the John Lewis sponsorship doesn't imply wild times for the OnBlackheath weekend music and food festival, the line-up is less dad-rock than you might expect, with Primal Scream, Hot Chip, Belle & Sebastian and James among the 2017 headliners.

London Literature Festival
*Southbank Centre, Belvedere Road, South Bank, SE1 8XX (7960 4200, www. southbankcentre.co.uk /whats-on/festivals-series/london-literature-festival). Waterloo tube/rail. **Date** mid Sept-mid Oct.*

The London Literature Festival combines superstar writers with stars from other fields: architects, comedians, sculptors and cultural theorists, examining anything from queer literature to migration.

Great River Race
*River Thames, from Millwall Docks, Docklands, E14, to Ham House, Richmond, Surrey, TW10 (8398 8141, www. greatriverrace.co.uk). **Date** mid Sept.*

Much more interesting than the Boat Race (*see p312*), the Great River Race sees an exotic array of around 300 traditional rowing boats (including skiffs, canoes, dragon boats and Cornish gigs) from around the globe racing in the 'river marathon'. Hungerford Bridge, the Millennium Bridge and Tower Bridge are all good viewpoints.

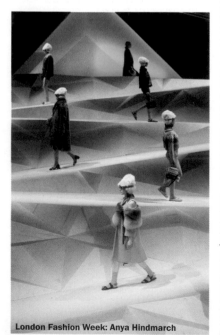

London Fashion Week: Anya Hindmarch

Pearly Kings and Queens Harvest Festival

Guildhall Yard, The City, EC2V (www. pearlysociety.co.uk). Bank tube. **Date** *Sept.*

A proper Cockney knees-up with Pearly Kings and Queens, decked in their pearl-button 'smother suits', leading a parade to St Mary-le-Bow church. Expect traditional English entertainment, including maypole dancing, Morris dancers and a marching band.

American Football: NFL

Wembley Stadium, Stadium Way, Middlesex, HA9 0WS (www.nfluk.com). Wembley Park tube or Wembley Stadium rail. **Date** *late Sept-early Nov.*

The NFL took a regular-season match out of North America for the first time in 2007 – it was a huge success, and immediately became an annual fixture.

October Plenty and Apple Day

Southwark, SE1 9DT (www.thelionspart. co.uk/octoberplenty). **Date** *Oct.*

An autumn harvest festival mixing ancient seasonal customs with contemporary celebrations. Starting with dancing outside Shakespeare's Globe (*see p360*), a procession heads across to Borough Market (*see p92*) for Apple Day activities.

Museums at Night

01273 523982, museumsatnight.org.uk. **Date** *Oct.*

See p312 Museums at Night.

The Big Draw

3758 4118, www.campaignfordrawing.org. **Date** *Oct.*

Engage with your inner artist at the month-long Big Draw, using anything from pencils to vapour trails.

Dance Umbrella

7407 9380, www.danceumbrella.co.uk. **Date** *Oct.*

A leading international dance festival, featuring a range of events (many free) in unusual spaces.

London Film Festival

www.bfi.org.uk/lff. **Date** *mid Oct.*

The most prestigious of the capital's film fests – in fact, the key film festival in the country. Over 200 new British and international features are screened each year, mainly at the BFI Southbank and Leicester Square's Vue West End, and there's always a smattering of red-carpet events for the celebrity-crazed.

❤ London Frieze Art Fair

Regent's Park, NW1 (3372 6111, friezelondon. com). Regent's Park tube. **Date** *mid Oct.*

The biggest contemporary carnival in London's art calendar occupies a purpose-built venue at the south end of Regent's Park, where some 1,000 artists are displayed over the four-day festival. Highlights include the daily-changing Projects; debates and discussions as part of the Talks strand; and Live, showing performance-based installations.

Diwali

Trafalgar Square, WC2N 5DN (7983 4000, www.london.gov.uk). Charing Cross tube/rail. **Date** *Oct/Nov.*

A celebration of the annual Festival of Light by Hindu, Jain and Sikh communities.

London to Brighton Veteran Car Run

Departs Serpentine Road, Hyde Park, W2 2UH (01483 524433, www.veterancarrun. com). Hyde Park Corner tube. **Date** *early Nov.*

The London to Brighton Veteran Car Run is not so much a race as a sedate procession southwards by around 500 pre-1905 cars. The first pair trundles off at sunrise (around 7-8.30am), but you can catch them a little later crossing Westminster Bridge, or view them on a closed-off Regent's Street the day before the event (11am-3pm).

Bonfire Night

Date *5 Nov & around.*

Britain's best-loved excuse for setting off fireworks: the celebration of Guy Fawkes's failure to blow up the Houses of Parliament in 1605. Check the dedicated page at www. timeout.com for a list of public displays right across town – several are put on for free, and many charge only a nominal entry fee.

❤ Lord Mayor's Show

7606 3030, www.lordmayorsshow.org. **Date** *early Nov.*

This big show marks the traditional presentation of the new Lord Mayor for approval by the monarch's justices. The Lord Mayor leaves Mansion House in a fabulous gold coach at 11am, along with a colourful

> **In the know**
> **Pair of mayors**
>
> The Lord Mayor is a City officer, elected each year by the livery companies and with no real power outside the City of London; don't confuse him with the Mayor of London, currently Sadiq Khan (*see p32*).

procession of floats and marchers. At 5.15pm, there's a fireworks display on the river.

Remembrance Sunday Ceremony
Cenotaph, Whitehall, Westminster, SW1. Charing Cross tube/rail. **Date** *early Nov.*

Held on the second Sunday in November, the Sunday nearest to 11 November – the day World War I ended – this solemn commemoration honours those who died fighting in the World Wars and later conflicts. The Queen, the prime minister and other dignitaries lay poppy wreaths at the Cenotaph. A two-minute silence at 11am is followed by a service of remembrance.

London Jazz Festival
efglondonjazzfestival.org.uk. **Date** *mid Nov.*

Covering most bases, from trad to free improv, this is the biggest London jazz festival of the year, lasting the best part of a fortnight.

Winter

Christmas Celebrations
Covent Garden (www.coventgardenlondonuk. com); Bond Street (www. bondstreetassociation.com); St Christopher's Place (www.stchristophersplace. com); Marylebone High Street (www. marylebonevillage.com); Trafalgar Square (www.london.gov.uk). **Date** *Nov-Dec.*

Of the big stores, Fortnum & Mason (*see p98*) still creates enchantingly old-fashioned Christmas windows. Otherwise, though, skip the commercialised lights on Oxford and Regent streets and head, instead, for smaller shopping areas such as St Christopher's Place, Bond Street, Marylebone High Street and Covent Garden. It's traditional to sing carols beneath a giant Christmas tree in Trafalgar Square – an annual gift from Norway in gratitude for Britain's support during World War II – but you can also join in a mammoth singalong at the Royal Albert Hall, enjoy the starry choral Christmas Festival at St John Smith Square or an evocative carol service at one of London's historic churches. London's major cathedrals all, naturally, celebrate Christmas with splendid liturgies and music.

Spitalfields Music Festival
7377 1362, www.spitalfieldsmusic.org. uk. **Date** *Dec.*

A series of multi-genre music events, featuring world-class artists, in some of the most extraordinary venues and spaces in East London, ranging from resplendent churches to urban warehouses and vibrant outdoor markets. Also runs one-off events throughout the year.

Great Christmas Pudding Race
Covent Garden (www.xmaspuddingrace.org. uk). Covent Garden tube.

This fancy-dress race – during which contestants attempt to keep a pud balanced on a plate while negotiating foam slaloms and other inflatable hazards – is a fundraiser for Cancer Research UK.

New Year's Eve celebrations
Date *31 Dec.*

The focus of London's public celebrations has officially moved from overcrowded Trafalgar Square to the full-on fireworks display launched from the London Eye and rafts on the Thames. You have to get there early for a good view. Those with stamina can take in the New Year's Day Parade in central London the next day (www.lnydp.com).

London International Mime Festival
www.mimelondon.com/festival. **Date** *Jan/Feb.*

Theatrical magic in many forms, from haunting visual theatre to puppetry for adults.

Great Spitalfields Pancake Race
Old Truman Brewery, 91 Brick Lane, Spitalfields, E1 6QL (8800 6665, www. alternativearts.co.uk). **Date** *Shrove Tuesday.*

This very silly fundraiser for the London Air Ambulance sees teams of four in fancy dress grab their crêpes and run through the cobbled streets of Spitalfields in the hope of winning a specially engraved frying pan.

Chinese New Year Festival
Around Gerrard Street, Chinatown, W1, Leicester Square, WC2 (7333 8118, www. lccauk.com). Leicester Square or Piccadilly Circus tube. **Date** *Feb.*

Celebrate the Chinese New Year (Year of the Dog on 16 Feb 2018) in style with festivities that engulf Chinatown and Leicester Square. Lion dancers gyrate alongside a host of acts in the grand parade to Trafalgar Square.

London Fashion Week
Date *mid/late Feb.*

See p316 London Fashion Week.

Six Nations Tournament
Twickenham Stadium, 200 Whitton Road, Middlesex, TW2 7BA (8892 2000,www. rbs6nations.com). **Date**s *Feb-Mar.*

This major rugby union tournament for the northern hemisphere teams sees England take on Wales, Scotland, Ireland, France and Italy, with England's home fixtures played at the club's headquarters at Twickenham. Book a long way ahead.

BAG YOURSELF
A BARGAIN

Whether it's food, drink, theatre or
events, we've got exclusive offers
and the best tickets in town.

Film

Plug yourself into London's non-stop film scene

Londoners still have a feel for the romance of film that out-of-town multiplexes will never satisfy. Perhaps that's why there's such a lively and varied range of screenings in the capital. Giant picture palaces hosting red-carpet premières attended by A-list actors? Check out the Odeon Leicester Square. Cheap-as-chips repertory cinema? The Prince Charles is right around the corner. Refurbished art deco gems? Try the gorgeous, historic Phoenix or the Rio in Dalston. A world-class film festival? Happens every autumn. Outdoor screenings in remarkable settings, ciné clubs, film seasons devoted to every genre and national cinema under the sun? Yes, yes and yes. So get some popcorn and sit yourself down.

Where to go

Leicester Square has the biggest first-run cinemas and stages most of the big-budget premières – but it also has the biggest prices. By contrast, the independents provide a cheaper night out and they often show films that wouldn't come within a million miles of a red carpet.

Outside the mainstream, the British Film Institute's flagship venue gets top billing. **BFI Southbank** screens seasons exploring and celebrating various genres of cinema and TV. It also has a brilliant bar. After the BFI, the **Curzon** group is the favoured choice for most cineastes, but London has a growing number of arthouse cinemas – and in increasingly unlikely places, such as Kensal Green (**Lexi**) and Crouch End (**ArtHouse**).

There's a vogue for hosting screenings in unusual venues. These include dedicated spaces like the Tanks, a multimedia space in the basement of **Tate Modern** extension (*see p87*), and ad hoc ones in places that are attractions in their own right – even St Paul's Cathedral has got in on the act.

Several luxury hotels have excellent screening facilities: most of the Firmdale mini-chain have screening rooms – the **Covent Garden Hotel** (*see p398*) is a long-term industry favourite – and the Curzon at the **Mondrian** (*see p399*) is a great little cinema, inexpensive for its South Bank location.

Outdoor screenings pop up right across the capital in summer: these are listed on *p326*. And film lovers have two key options when it comes to exhibitions: the **London Film Museum** (*see p184*) is the one for fans of memorabilia, with its display of cars from

---

the Bond movies, but serious film buffs should book a tour of the **Cinema Museum** (The Master's House, 2 Dugard Way, SE11 4TH, 7840 2200, www.cinemamuseum.org. uk, £7, £5 reductions), where cinema seats and signs, stills and posters, projectors and other machinery tell cinema's history from the 1890s.

Giant screens & multiplex cinemas

♥ BFI IMAX

1 Charlie Chaplin Walk, South Bank, SE1 8XR (0330 333 7878, www.bfi.org.uk/imax). Waterloo tube/rail. **Tickets** *£16.60-£20.80; £11.20-£16.40 reductions.* **Screens** *1.* **Map** *p78 N9.*

London's – indeed, the UK's – biggest cinema screen at 5800sq ft, the BFI IMAX is in the centre of a busy roundabout next to Waterloo station. As well as the massive screen, you get superlative sound quality here is spectacular and seats arranged at such a vertiginous angle there's no chance of a head blocking your view. It's not cheap – just over £20 for a premium seat – but if you like your blockbusters vast and noisy, there's really nothing else like it in town.

Cineworld at the O2

The O2, Peninsula Square, Greenwich, SE10 0DX (0871 200 2000, www.cineworld. co.uk). North Greenwich tube. **Tickets** *£11; £8 -£8.50 reductions. Extra for 3D, D-BOX, IMAX.* **Screens** *11.*

People don't just come to the O2 Arena (*see p344*) for gigs: this 11-screen multiplex from the Cineworld chain supersizes everything, from the jaw-dropping dimensions of the Sky Superscreen – the widest in Europe – down to the jam-packed programme.

Cineworld Leicester Square

5-6 Leicester Square, WC2H 7NA (0871 200 2000, www.cineworld.co.uk). Leicester Square tube. **Tickets** *£9.95-£12.95 adult; £9.95 reductions. Impact £15.50-£18; £9.95-£12.50 reductions. IMAX £16-£18; £9.95-£12.95 reductions.* **Screens** *9.* **Map** *p181 K7.*

♥ Best cinemas

BFI IMAX *p322*
An eye-bogglingly big screen makes this the best for blockbusters.

Everyman Belsize Park *p325*
A lovely little luxury cinema.

Rio Cinema *p327*
London's best independent cinema.

PeckhamPlex *p327*
Rough-and-ready bargain.

Picturehouse Central *p323*
Central and simply gorgeous.

Prince Charles *p323*
For celluloid silliness, see a singalong screening here.

One of London's oldest cinemas (formerly known as the Empire, it opened as a theatre in 1884, then as a cinema after World War II), it was until recently home to London's biggest non-IMAX cinema screen (that's now at the O2 Cineworld). Its massive main auditorium is these days separated into a full IMAX screen and the smaller (but still impressive) 400-seat Impact theatre, with seven smaller screens tucked away elsewhere in the building. The programme is mainstream and prices reflect the central location.

Odeon Leicester Square
Leicester Square, WC2H 7LQ (0333 006 7777, www.odeon.co.uk). Leicester Square tube. **Tickets** *£14-£22; £7-£19.50 reductions.* **Screens** *5.* **Map** *p181 K7.*

London's number-one destination for red carpet premières. Not only do you get blockbuster bangs in the huge 1,683-seat auditorium, you get them in splendour: the Odeon Leicester Square has gorgeous 1930s art-deco nymph motifs on the walls and is one of the few remaining cinemas to retain its circle – from which the view (at extra cost) is pretty spectacular.

♥ Picturehouse Central
Trocadero, Shaftesbury Avenue, Piccadilly, W1D 7DH (0871 902 5755, www. picturehouses.com). Piccadilly Circus tube. **Tickets** *£13.50-£16.50; £7.50-£11.50 reductions.* **Screens** *7.* **Map** *p163 L8.*

On the corner of Shaftesbury Avenue, this central London cinema is an absolute gem. It's the antidote to Piccadilly Circus's rage-inducing pavements, with three floors of beautifully designed space. Before you even get anywhere near the plush screening rooms, a hundred hanging lightbulbs lead you up a grand terracotta-tiled staircase past a mural inspired by a century of cinema. A climb up another level will take you to a members-only bar with a roof terrace that looks out over the busy streets of central London.

♥ Prince Charles
7 Leicester Place, off Leicester Square, WC2H 7BY (7494 3654, www.princecharlescinema. com). Leicester Square tube. **Tickets** *£8-£11.50.* **Screens** *2.* **Map** *p181 K7.*

This is the only time you'll spend in a cinema when no one's going to shush you. Singalong

In the know
Get your bearings

At the **BFI IMAX** (see *p322*) it's worth locating your nearest loo before the film starts if you're prone to a mid-film pee – they're all but impossible to find.

In the know
Music to your ears

The **Odeon Leicester Square** (see *below*) still has a fully operational 1937 pipe organ. If you can, hear it in action providing the soundtrack for a silent film.

screenings at the Prince Charles are all about audience participation: whether your movie is *Frozen*, *Rocky Horror* or *The Sound of Music*. You can even settle in for a marathon all-night pyjama party. Having started life screening porn, the Prince Charles is central London's wildcard cinema, providing a fantastic blend of new-ish blockbusters and arthouse titles, with heaps of horror, sci-fi and teen-flick all-nighters, double bills and short seasons. It's comfy, cheap and cheerful.

Arthouse & neighbourhood cinemas
There are plenty of central London arthouses, but several of the most atmospheric are in the suburbs.

ArtHouse Crouch End
159A Tottenham Lane, Crouch End, N8 9BT (8245 3099, www.arthousecrouchend.co.uk). Bus 41, 91, N41, N91,W3. **Tickets** *£7-£11; £4 reductions.* **Screens** *2.*

Voted London's best cinema by *Time Out* readers, this two-screen independent in a former Salvation Army Hall opened its doors in 2014 and quickly became a favourite with locals. The ArtHouse prides itself on being not just a cinema but also a venue offering music, comedy and theatre. Its programme leans towards independent and foreign movies, and there's a welcoming foyer bar and café.

Barbican
Silk Street, the City, EC2Y 8DS (7638 8891, www.barbican.org.uk). Barbican tube or Moorgate tube/rail. **Tickets** *£11.50; £6 Mon; £6-£10.50 reductions.* **Screens** *3.* **Map** *p212 Q6.*

After a top-to-toe refurb, the Barbican Centre cinemas – perhaps the key rival to BFI Southbank – are better than ever. Screen One, inside the main Barbican complex, is a 280-seat auditorium screening the best new blockbusters and high-end arthouse films, while the two smaller screens around the corner on Beech Street have been kitted out with plush, comfy chairs and a friendly, welcoming café-bar serving coffee, cakes, beer, wine and pizza. The programme also includes plenty of festival screenings and classics, many of which

FILM

are chosen specifically to tie in with art and music events happening elsewhere in the Barbican complex.

BFI Southbank

South Bank, SE1 8XT (7928 3232 tickets, www.bfi.org.uk). Embankment tube or Waterloo tube/rail. **Tickets** *£8.25-£12.10; £8.25-£9.35 reductions.* **Screens** *4.* **Map** *p78 N9.*

A fraction to the east of the Royal Festival Hall complex (*see p80* and alongside the National Theatre (*see p362*), the BFI's success is still built on its core function: thought-provoking seasons giving film fans the chance to enjoy rare and significant British and foreign films. It's a terrific place to enjoy movies of all stripes and nations, enhanced by excellent director and actor Q&A events. The two bar-cafés are also of good quality, with the riverside one especially popular – and not only with cinema-goers.

Ciné Lumière

Institut Français, 17 Queensberry Place, South Kensington, SW7 2DT (7871 3515, www.institut-francais.org.uk). South Kensington tube. **Tickets** *£7-£9; £5-£7 reductions.* **Screens** *1.* **Map** *p122 E11.*

The Ciné Lumière in South Kensington is the cinema of the French Cultural Institute and offers a good mix of new releases (focusing on foreign, independent and, of course, French films) and retrospective seasons. It regularly hosts French filmmakers too. The venue itself is welcoming and well equipped, up a marble staircase from a grand lobby area and café-restaurant.

Curzon

Chelsea *206 King's Road, SW3 5XP. Sloane Square tube then bus 11, 19, 22, 319.* **Screens** *1.* **Map** *p122 F12.*

Mayfair *38 Curzon Street, W1J 7TY. Green Park or Hyde Park Corner tube.* **Screens** *2.* **Map** *p140 J9.*

Bloomsbury *The Brunswick Centre, WC1N 1AW. Russell Square tube.* **Screens** *6.* **Map** *p194 M5.*

Soho *99 Shaftesbury Avenue, W1D 5DY. Leicester Square tube.* **Screens** *3.* **Map** *p163 L7.*

Victoria *58 Victoria Street, SW1E 6QW. Victoria tube/rail.* **Screens** *5.* **Map** *p100 K10.*

Tickets *0330 500 1331, www. curzoncinemas.com. £8.50-£18.50; £6.50-£11.50 reductions.*

It's starting to feel like Curzon knows something about the supposedly defunct notion of 'cinema' that other arthouses don't. The group's key venues are well established, but recent years have seen vigorous expansion. The perennially hip Soho outpost is the coolest, with its buzzing café and decent basement bar, but there's 70s splendour at the Grade II-listed Mayfair, location of occasional premières and a venue so classy it's the only cinema where we've been told off by a fellow movie-goer for eating popcorn too loudly. Chelsea has always been perfect for a Sunday screening after a King's Road brunch. In 2015, we were delighted to welcome back the Renoir as the Curzon Bloomsbury, its two screens having become six, one of which is – winningly – dedicated to documentaries. By then Curzon had opened the purpose-built Victoria in 2014, as well as taking on the programming for the Ham Yard hotel (1 Ham Yard, W1D 7DT), just off Piccadilly, and Mondrian at Sea Containers (*see p399*).

Electric

Portobello *191 Portobello Road, Notting Hill, W11 2ED (7908 9696, www. electriccinema.co.uk). Ladbroke Grove or Notting Hill Gate tube.* **Tickets** *£15.50-£18 adult; £10 children.* **Screens** *1.* **Map** *p297 A7.*

Shoreditch *64-66 Redchurch Street, E2 7DP (3350 3490, www.electriccinema. co.uk/shoreditch). Shoreditch High Street Overground or Old Street tube/rail.* **Tickets** *£18; £8.* **Screens** *1.* **Map** *p256 S4.*

Once a past-it fleapit, the Electric Portobello was a pioneer of the 'boutique' cinema trend: a luscious destination with leather seats and sofas, footstools and a bar inside the auditorium, a place where you can sip fine wines with your celluloid pleasures. There are even six date-perfect luxurious, velvet-lined double beds in the venue. The Electric has also taken over a snug little screen in the East End. Formerly the Aubin, the Electric Shoreditch also exudes class: again, there are leather armchairs and footstools, but we like the cosy cashmere blankets and chic little tables to hold your drinks.

♥ Everyman & Screen Cinemas

Everyman Belsize Park *203 Haverstock Hill, NW3 4QC.* **Tickets** *£12.50-£26.50; £10.50-£13.50 reductions.* **Screens** *1.*

Everyman Hampstead *5 Hollybush Vale, NW3 6TX. Hampstead tube.* **Tickets** *£13-£19.50; £11-£17.50 reductions.* **Screens** *2.*

Screen on the Green *83 Upper Street, Islington, N1 0NP. Angel tube.* **Tickets** *£15.40-£25.50; £10.60-£12.80 reductions.* **Screens** *1.*

Tickets *0871 906 9060, www. everymancinema.com.*

Do you like the smell of expensive leather? Everyman has half a dozen venues across London, each with plush seats, posh food and carpets you could lick without getting a stomach bug. It all started with the Everyman Hampstead, which has a glamorous bar and two-seaters (£39) in its 'screening lounges', complete with foot stools and wine coolers, but the Belsize Park is our favourite – a flagship for the luxe-ing of the chain, it has good food and drink, and seats so comfy you might find yourself nodding off. It was one of three former Screen cinemas, of which Screen on the Green retains its name. It's another beauty, having lost seats to make space for the more comfortable kind, gained a bar and a stage for gigs, but kept its classic neon sign.

Genesis Cinema Whitechapel

93-95 Mile End Road, Stepney, E1 4UJ (7780 2000, www.genesiscinema.co.uk). Whitechapel tube/Overground or Stepney Green tube. **Tickets** *£7-£8.50; £4 Mon, Wed; £3.50-£6 reductions. Studio 5 £11-£13; £8.* **Screens** *6.* **Map** *p256 W6.*

Not only is the Genesis cheap, it's also beautifully renovated – by guys who design film sets for a living (try knocking on the bricks on the mezzanine). The end result is a perfect local cinema, with proper old East End ladies drinking coffee in the café next to cool kids on their laptops. There's a bar upstairs, where snacks include crodoughs from 100-year-old Rinkoffs bakery. For a date, book seats in the Studio 5 boutique screening room, which has armchairs.

Hackney Picturehouse

270 Mare Street, Hackney, E8 1HE (0871 902 5734, www.picturehouses.com). Hackney Central or London Fields Overground. **Tickets** *£7-£11.60; £4-£10.60 reductions.* **Screens** *4.*

This branch of the Picturehouse chain only opened in 2011, but it's impossible to remember Hackney without it. The buzzy ground-floor bar/café serves good burgers, and bang-on programming mixes top-of-the-range mainstream with articr films – for the former, book Screen 1, with its beast of a screen, big sound and steep incline for uninterrupted viewing. On the top floor, the Hackney Attic is home to music quizzes, open-mic nights and other live events.

Lexi

Pinkham Lighthouse, 194B Chamberlayne Road, Kensal Rise, NW10 3JU (0871 704 2069, thelexicinema.co.uk). Kensal Green tube or Kensal Rise Overground. **Tickets** *£7.50-£11; £7-£7.50 reductions.* **Screens** *1.*

One of London's friendliest cinemas, the Lexi is run mostly by enthusiastic local volunteers, with every penny of profits going to charity.

Electric Portobello

Festivals & Summer Screenings

Let's take it outside – in summer, London goes crazy for alfresco cinema

The best-known open-air screenings are those in the lovely neoclassical courtyard of **Somerset House** (www.somersethouse.org.uk/film; *see p191*). Book well ahead – and bring your own picnic and cushions. There are plenty of other alfresco opportunities, however. **Free Film Festivals** (www.freefilmfestivals.org) puts on free outdoor screenings in interesting public spaces mainly in south-east London, while **Pop Up Screens** (www.popupscreens.co.uk) shows popular films in parks in west London. From May to September, the **Rooftop Film Club** (7635 6655, www.rooftopfilmclub.com) offers a different spin on outdoor films, screening movies in the rooftop garden of the **Queen of Hoxton** (1-5 Curtain Road, EC2A 3JX) or on top of the Bussey Building (*see p338*) and **Roof East** (Roof East, floors 7-8, Stratford multistorey carpark, Great Eastern Way, Stratford, E15 1XE).

There's also a film festival in the capital on pretty much any given week during the year, but the **London Film Festival** in October (www.bfi.org.uk/lff) is far and away the most prestigious. Nearly 200 new British and international features are screened, mainly at the BFI Southbank and Leicester Square's Vue West End. It's preceded by the leftfield **Raindance Festival** (www.raindance.org), with a terrific shorts programme. The other highlight of autumn is the **Portobello Film Festival** (www.portobellofilmfestival.com) in early September. It offers an eclectic programme of free screenings. Short films hog the limelight each January at the **London Short Film Festival** (www.shortfilms.org.uk). In September, check out the **Open City London Documentary Festival** (www.opencitylondon.com).

March is a busy month. There's the **Human Rights Watch International Film Festival** (www.hrw.org/iff) and the **London International Animation Festival** (www.liaf.org.uk), screening 300 or more animated shorts. Towards the end of the month are the lesbian, gay and transgender screenings of **BFI Flare** (www.bfi.org.uk/llgff), the UK's third largest film festival. June or July sees the **East End Film Festival** (www.eastendfilmfestival.com) explore its fondness for films starring London. But by now you're way back into the alfresco season...

In a category all of its own is the hugely popular **Secret Cinema** (www.secretcinema.org). Its 'we're not going to tell you what the film is' schtick is a bit tired (everybody works it out in advance, of course), but their events are the apotheosis of event cinema. Effectively building a huge film set and hiring a raft of bit-part actors for each costumed screening – an entire town square was built for *Back to the Future*, but they normally 'just' take over a hotel or warehouse – viewers are invited to dress appropriately and learn songs or bits of dialogue, so that they become participants in the film. Secret Cinema is an expensive night out, but boy is it good fun.

Somerset House

FILM

You might see anything from recent
blockbusters to arthouse and foreign films,
with the programme filled out by special
events, Q&As and classic-movie seasons (a
run of Truffaut oldies was accompanied by
cheese and wine tastings). The chairs are
comfy, the sound system is great and the
bar is cosy. The Lexi team is also responsible
for the peripatetic outdoor cinema screen
Nomad (www.whereisthenomad.com).

♥ PeckhamPlex
*95A Rye Lane, Peckham, SE15 4ST (0844 567
2742, www.peckhamplex.london). Peckham
Rye rail. **Tickets** £4.99-£5.99. **Screens** 6.*

South London film fans talk of the
PeckhamPlex with misty-eyed fondness.
Opening in a former supermarket in 1994,
it ain't fancy, and you'd struggle to describe
the decor in entirely favourable terms, but
this rough-around-the-edges institution

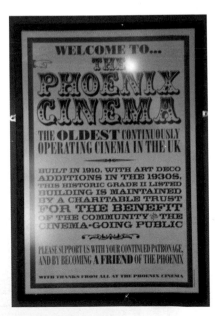

has character and charm. However, the only
thing you really need to know it is that tickets
are just £4.99 – or £5.99 if you want to see a
film in 3D – all day, every day of the week.
That's it: no nonsense, no frills, no faff. The
programme focuses on the latest big releases,
as well as the odd smaller film too.

Phoenix
*52 High Road, East Finchley, N2 9PJ (8444
6789, www.phoenixcinema.co.uk). East
Finchley tube. **Tickets** £7-£9.50; £5-£7
reductions. **Screens** 1.*

This gorgeous single-screen venue can fairly
claim to be London's oldest continuously
operating cinema: it was completed in 1910
and opened in 1912. Since 1985, it has been
run as a charitable trust. The programme
mixes independent and foreign films, and the
auditorium is one of the most beautiful places
to watch a film in London. This is also a great
place to catch directors introducing their
work, late-night films and special events.

Regent Street Cinema
*University of Westminster, 309 Regent
Street, W1B 2UW (7911 5050, www.
regentstreetcinema.com). Oxford Circus
tube. **Tickets** £12; £7-£11 reductions.
Screens 1. **Map** p140 J6.*

Reopened in 2015, this historic beauty is
barely a minute's walk north of Oxford Circus.
The hall dates to 1848, but the cinema's real
claim to fame is that the Lumière brothers
demonstrated their pioneering moving-film
camera and what they'd shot with it here in
1896 – effectively the first movie screening
in Britain. The reborn cinema is state-of-
the-art, but can also show work on original
16mm and 35mm formats. The programme
covers classics, director retrospectives,
double bills, documentaries, world cinema
and even kids' films.

♥ Rio Cinema
*107 Kingsland High Street, Dalston, E8 2PB
(7241 9410, www.riocinema.org.uk). Dalston
Kingsland Overground. **Tickets** £6-£10;
£4-£8 reductions. **Screens** 1.*

Another great deco survivor, restored
to its original sleek lines, the Rio is east
London's finest independent. Alongside
mainstream releases, the Rio is well known
for its programme of Turkish and Kurdish
films and documentaries.

LGBT

The inside scoop on where to be out

Acceptance of gay lifestyles in London feels broader than ever. In fact, many clubs – in Dalston, particularly – no longer bother much about sexual orientation. The attitude is that gay, bi-, polysexual, even hetero- if you must... whatever, just so long as everyone gets to have a good time. There's anxiety, however, about the health of the gay scene in central London. The closure of key venues has caused plenty of soul-searching. Has Grindr killed the gay bar? Is it rising rents? Noise complaints from intolerant neighbours? Still, some things you can count on: London's headline homo event remains Pride (*see p314*), but it is now surrounded throughout the year by smaller, more DIY goings-on and a major gay and lesbian film festival.

The lay of the land

Roughly speaking, London's gay scene is split into three key zones: **Soho**, **Vauxhall** and **east London**. Each of these has its own character, with Soho the most mainstream; Vauxhall is the most decadent, and east London the most outré.

Centred on **Old Compton Street**, the Soho scene continues to attract the crowds, with pretty boys sipping espresso martinis at pavement café tables as unfeasibly tanned chaps in muscle vests stroll past. But all is not well in London's historic gay heartland: a few years back, the cabaret community – ever imaginative – was moved to parade coffins through the streets to protest the death of the area's nightlife. Gay Soho has been caught between the rising rents that now stalk central London and a council that, while friendly to the pink pound, is intolerant of nightlife that might upset affluent residents. At least the party continues down the road at the legendary **Heaven**, home to **G-A-Y**. If your dream has always been to see Madonna or Kylie in a club, here's your chance – the list of singers who've done PAs here is a *Who's Who* of squeal-tastic gay pop icons.

Down south, Vauxhall is also looking fearfully at the major redevelopment of the area, led by the approaching arrival of the US Embassy. It remains vital for three reasons: long-standing alt-cabaret venue **RVT**; utterly enjoyable club night **Horse Meat Disco**, and, for now, the fact that purist hedonists can arrive in London on a Friday evening and dance non-stop here for an entire weekend before flying out of town again. Though you need a high tolerance for throngs of shirtless, sweaty chaps to do so.

The most alternative, creative and vibrant of the capital's queer scenes is in east London, although even here there are regular closures. Still, in **Dalston**

Superstore and the **Glory**, you'll rub shoulders with fashion and music movers and shakers (plus assorted straight folk), to soundtracks built by ferociously underground DJs. With so much coolness, it can get a little snooty, but a lot of the bars and clubs round Shoreditch and Dalston are also properly mixed, which makes the area ideal for a night out with straight mates.

Gals-only events are still under-represented, but a welcome addition is **SHE Soho** – the city's only full-time drinking den for lesbians. Also worthwhile are Monday and Wednesday nights at **Retro**; the monthly R&B night **R&She** at East Bloc; and basement bar **Tipsy** (20 Stoke Newington Road, N16 7XN, www.tipsybar.co.uk). **Glass Bar** (www.theglassbar.org.uk) runs various events, while the **Bijou Cocktail Social** (www.elysionevents.co.uk) runs glam pop-up events at various locations.

Stand-alone nights and one-off events pop up all the time (check out timeout. com for the latest), but **Ruby Tuesdays at Ku Bar** (www.rubytuesdays.co.uk) and queer performance nights **Duckie** (hosted by Amy Lamé) and **Bar Wotever** at RVT are popular with girls and boys. Lastly, special mention should go to the **NYC Downlow** (thedownlowradio.com/the-downlow), a travelling homo disco straight out of 1970s New York that you can catch at festivals such as Lovebox (loveboxfestival. com; *see p314*).

Each spring, in **BFI Flare** (www.bfi.org. uk/flare), London also has its own LGBT film festival – the third largest film festival in the country, gay or straight. But the daddy on the queer calendar is **Pride** (*see p314*), which now attracts around 800,000 LGBT people and their straight friends. No longer billed as a protest, but a celebration, it's one day in June every year when LGBT people from all over the country descend on London for a massive street party.

❤ Best clubs & venues

Dalston Superstore *p334*
Fashionable fun in London's gay party zone.

RVT *p334*
Key alt-cabaret venue in Vauxhall.

Horse Meat Disco *p334*
Not exactly disco but pure dancing joy.

Friendly Society *p331*
Best gay bar in Soho.

SHE Soho *p333*
London's only dedicated lesbian venue.

Pride

Restaurants & cafés

More or less every café and restaurant in London welcomes gay custom. Certainly nowhere in or around Soho will so much as bat an eyelid at you and your other half having a romantic dinner. Thanks to its prime location, **Balans** (60-62 Old Compton Street, Soho, W1D 4UG, 7439 2183, www. balans.co.uk) has long been the gay café-restaurant of choice and opens almost all night for those seeking a post-club bite. .

▶ *For other drinking and dining options in Soho, see p165.*

Pubs & bars

Unless otherwise stated, the pubs and bars listed here are open to both gay men and lesbians. If you're in east London, it's worth visiting **Dalston Superstore** (*see p334*) during the day for café grub: the food's good (with breakfast quite a trendy scene) and there are Wi-Fi and art displays.

Circa
62 Frith Street, Soho, W1D 3JN (7734 6826, www.circasoho.com). Tottenham Court Road or Leicester Square tube. **Open** *1pm-1am daily.* **Map** *p163 L7.*

Circa is one of Soho's more versatile LGBT spaces. Swing by in the afternoon and you'll find large leather sofas perfect for sinking into over a catch-up with mates. But later on, the dancefloor area at the back fills up as DJs spin club hits and pop remixes until 1am. It's worth noting that Circa attracts a more image-conscious crowd than many Soho drinking spots. This isn't a place where anyone goes in for 'geek chic' or 'normcore': think tight T-shirts and skinny jeans instead.

Comptons of Soho
51-53 Old Compton Street, Soho, W1D 6HN (3238 0163, www.faucetinn.com/comptons/ co.uk). Picadilly Circus or Leicester Square tube. **Open** *noon-11.30pm Mon-Thur; noon-midnight Fri, Sat; noon-10.30pm Sun.* **Map** *p163 L7.*

Long before Soho became known as London's gay village, long before the likes of Ku Bar and G-A-Y, there was Compton's. Once an old-fashioned gay club with blacked-out windows and sawdust on the floor, the venue now has two floors, clear-glass windows and far nicer toilets. Compton's is still popular with a crowd of beer-drinking, blokey gay men and remains kinda cruisey. But don't let the throng of punters spilling on to the street put you off. The upstairs lounge is a good place for a date or conversation, and the ground floor is a surprisingly inviting bar space.

Duke of Wellington
77 Wardour Street, Soho, W1D 6QB (7439 1274, thedukeofwellington.london). Leicester Square or Piccadilly Circus tube. **Open** *noon-midnight daily.* **Map** *p163 L7.*

This traditional two-floor pub attracts a similar (though less cruisey) crowd to Comptons. Downstairs is a decent-sized drinking space with more standing room than seats; upstairs is a cosier lounge bar that can be hired for private events. The ambience is more chilled than many Soho venues, but it fills up quickly on Friday nights and weekends. There's '80s music on Sundays and a '90s night on Tuesdays, but the Duke of Wellington is most inviting on Mondays, when many drinks cost £2. Even Soho's Tardis-like Wetherspoon's, the Cross Keys, can't beat those prices.

Freedom Bar
66 Wardour Street, Soho, W1F 0TA (7734 0071, freedombarsoho.com). Leicester Square or Piccadilly Circus tube. **Open** *4pm-3am Mon-Thur; 2pm-3am Fri, Sat; 2-10.30pm Sun.* **Admission** *free; £5 after 10pm Fri, Sat.* **Map** *p163 L7.*

This glitzy cocktail lounge and DJ bar, spread over two floors, isn't a designated LGBT venue, but because of its location and laissez-faire ambience, anyone on the LGBT spectrum should feel right at home. The glam ground-floor bar attracts a fashion-conscious crowd, who sip cocktails among chandeliers, zebra-print banquettes and Venetian mirrors. A few 'strays' and dolled-up gal pals add colour. The large basement club and performance space hosts weekday cabaret and gets busy with the gay party crowd over the weekend.

❤ Friendly Society
79 Wardour Street, Soho, W1D 6QB (7434 3804). Leicester Square tube. **Open** *5-11.30pm Mon-Thur; 5pm-midnight Fri, Sat; 4-10.30pm Sun.* **Map** *p163 L7.*

Friendly Society benefits from the power of surprise: after entering through a bland back-alley doorway, you're greeted at the bottom of the stairs by Soho's most idiosyncratic drinking den. Barbie dolls hang from the ceiling, there's a big fishbowl in the middle and old movies are projected on to a back wall. Although the short cocktail menu has been the same for ever, the staff always seem perplexed when you order one, though that's definitely part of the charm. The crowd here is gay in the broadest sense – anyone with a sense of fun will feel at home, whatever their gender and sexuality. Come here when you fancy dancing to Donna Summer while sipping (relatively) inexpensive prosecco.

G-A-Y Bar

*30 Old Compton Street, Soho, W1D 4UR (7494 2756, www.g-a-y.co.uk). Leicester Square or Tottenham Court Road tube. **Open** noon-midnight daily. **Map** p163 L7.*

Soho's world-famous G-A-Y Bar has everything you'd expect: cheap drink offers, a young crowd and plenty of Britney. The G-A-Y night at Heaven (*see p330*) gets the celebrity cameos, but this popular bar is still a shrine to queer pop idols, with nightly drinks promos every time they play a video from the current diva du jour. There's also a women's bar in the basement, called (delightfully) Girls Go Down – popular with flirty, studenty lesbians, loathed by most older women. G-A-Y bar's plush late-night sibling, **G-A-Y Late**, is round the corner at 5 Goslett Yard.

Halfway to Heaven

*7 Duncannon Street, off Trafalgar Square, WC2N 4JF (7484 0736, www. halfway2heaven.net). Charing Cross tube/rail. **Open** noon-midnight Mon-Thur; noon-3am Fri, Sat; noon-10pm Sun. **Map** p100 M8.*

A traditional gay boozer, situated halfway between Soho and Heaven, hence the name. For a change from the usual central London scene, give those lungs an airing at Kevin Walsh's karaoke nights every Monday and Thursday. The main floor is cosy and traditional, while the basement is clubbier and cruisier.

Her Upstairs

*18 Kentish Town Road, Camden Town, NW1 9NX (herupstairs.co.uk). Camden Town tube. **Open** 5pm-2am Mon-Thur; 5pm-3am Fri, Sat; 5pm-1am Sun. **Map** p241 K2.*

Her Upstairs is co-owned by Meth, one of London's best alternative drag queens, so the performances are fierce and forward-thinking: they aim to give a platform to female drag queens, drag kings and queer performers of colour. On Fridays and Saturdays, the space downstairs opens as a gay club called Them Downstairs, so you can make a real night of it.

King's Arms

*23 Poland Street, Soho, W1F 8QJ (7734 5907, www.kingsarms-soho.co.uk). Tottenham Court Road tube. **Open** noon-11pm Mon, Tue; noon-midnight Wed-Sat; 1-11.30pm Sun. **Map** p163 K7.*

This busy bears' pub has been around for ever, and attracts a loyal crowd of stocky, hairy, beardy guys who like a pint, although anyone's welcome. The aesthetic is old-school and cosy: you could be in a country pub, except it's crammed with gay men. There's

a DJ on Saturdays and karaoke on Sundays, but the King's Arms often shows live sport too. Located a five-minute stroll from Old Compton Street, it's worth trying if you fancy seeing a different side to Soho.

Ku Bar & Club

*30 Lisle Street, Chinatown, WC2H 7BA (7437 4303, www.ku-bar.co.uk). Leicester Square or Piccadilly Circus tube. **Open** noon-3am Mon-Sat; noon-midnight Sun. **Map** p163 L8.*

Occupying a prominent spot on Soho's fringes, this large LGBT venue is regularly voted London's best. Ku is a little classier than local rival G-A-Y, but it attracts a broadly similar crowd and the young, up-for-it vibe is just as much fun. The ground floor offers a bright and modern bar space with video screens playing chart hits; downstairs is a clubbier room where fresh-faced types of all genders cut a rug to pop and dance remixes. A second **Ku Bar**, on nearby Frith Street, offers a more sedate spin on the same experience.

New Bloomsbury Set

*The Basement, 76 Marchmont Street, Bloomsbury, WC1N 1AG (7383 3084, www. newbloomsburyset.net). Russell Square tube. **Open** 4-11.30pm Mon-Sat; 4-10.30pm Sun. **Map** p194 M5.*

Because it's a brisk 15-minute walk from Soho's gay village, this small but charming basement bar often gets forgotten about. That's a shame, because New Bloomsbury Set has smart decor that nods to the artistic and literary clique it's named after and a fabulous happy hour where you can get two cocktails or a bottle of wine for a tenner. As befits its Bloomsbury surroundings, NBS is a little more distinguished than most London LGBT bars and operates an over-21s door policy. It's open from 4pm daily, so it makes sense to pair it with a visit to Gay's the Word, London's legendary LGBT bookshop, which is right around the corner (*see p335*).

Retro Bar

*2 George Court, off Strand, Covent Garden, WC2N 6HH (7839 8760, www. retrobarlondon.co.uk). Charing Cross tube/rail or Embankment tube. **Open** 2-11pm Mon-Sat; 2-10.30pm Sun. **Map** p181 M8.*

Iggy Pop and Kate Bush are on the walls of this bar, where nights are dedicated to punk, glam, slutty pop and electronica (Let it Rock and Lucky Dip on Thursdays). The crowd is mixed in every sense: gay/straight, gay/lesbian and scene queen/true eccentric. Quiz nights (Tuesday) are popular, too, and the bar on occasion even relinquishes control of the music and lets punters be the DJ – bring your iPod.

Rupert Street Bar

*50 Rupert Street, Soho, W1D 6DR (7494 3059, www.rupert-street.com). Leicester Square or Piccadilly Circus tube. **Open** noon-11pm Mon-Wed; noon-11.15pm Thur; noon-11.45pm Fri, Sat; noon-10.30pm Sun. **Map** p163 L7x.*

If your idea of gay life was shaped by TV's *Queer as Folk*, Rupert Street is the bar for you. It's a little bit of Manchester's Canal Street in the heart of Soho. Trapped in the '90s, the decor is all industrial, boiler-room chic, with glass wraparound windows and a large mirror at the back. The staff are beefy and brisk and the clientele is more smartly dressed than average. Popular with the after-work crowd, it gets even busier later on – and also very cruisey.

❤ SHE Soho

*23A Old Compton Street, Soho, W1D 5JL (7437 4303, http://she-soho.com). Leciester Square tube. **Open** 4-11.30pm Mon-Thur; noon-midnight Fri, Sat; noon-10.30pm Sun. **Map** p163 L7.*

Shockingly, this Soho basement bar is London's only exclusively lesbian venue, and takes this responsibility seriously. Run by the team behind Ku Bar, SHE has a comparable flair for laying on entertainment: as well as club nights, it regularly offers comedy, cabaret, karaoke and quiz evenings. BOi BOX, a monthly drag king talent contest hosted by scene heroes Adam All and Apple Derrières, is definitely worth popping in your Google Calendar.

Village Soho

*81 Wardour Street, Soho, W1D 6QD (7478 0530, www.village-soho.co.uk). Piccadilly Circus or Leicester Square tube. **Open** 5pm-1am Mon, Tue; 5pm-2am Wed-Sat; 5pm-11.30pm Sun. **Map** p163 L7.*

This large bar overlooking Old Compton Street is nearly always busy. Decent drink deals help, but Village also succeeds because of its appealing ambience. Downstairs is a louche L-shaped space with cute corner seating; upstairs is a calmer room that's great for people watching if you can bag a window seat. Though there are often go-go dancers at weekends – a rarity in London – Village doesn't just attract gay men; it's a sexy yet welcoming venue for all members of the LGBT community.

Yard

*57 Rupert Street, Soho, W1D 7PL (7437 2652, www.yardbar.co.uk). Leicester Square or Piccadilly Circus tube. **Open** 2-11.30pm Mon, Tue; noon-11.30pm Wed, Thur; noon-1am Fri, Sat; noon-midnight Sun. **Map** p163 L7.*

One of the most reliable gay bars in Soho. The downstairs al fresco courtyard boasts sedate lighting, wooden banquettes and a fair bit of flora, giving things an almost bucolic feel. The upstairs loft bar offers views down to all this, with leather sofas offering spots in which to recline. The Yard hosts a variety of visitors, but mostly it's home to a mature gay crowd.

Clubbing

London's club scene is particularly subject to change: venues close, nights end and new soirées start. Check timeout.com for details of what's on when you're here. If you want to stay up all night and next day as well, head to Vauxhall. Popular nights at **Fire** (South Lambeth Road, SW8 1RT, www.fireclub. co.uk) include Orange, a Sunday staple, or there's **Union** (no.66, www.clubunion.co.uk) on the Albert Embankment.

Dalston Superstore *p334*

♥ Dalston Superstore

117 Kingland High Street, Dalston, E8 2PB (7254 2273, dalstonsuperstore.com). Dalston Kingsland Overground. **Open** *noon-midnight Mon; noon-2.30am Tue-Thur; noon-3am Fri; 10am-3am Sat; 10am-2.30am Sun.* **Admission** *varies.*

This Kingsland High Street hangout is a bit of a face on the east London party scene. In true Dalston style it's home to all sorts: popular with a large and diverse LGBT crowd, but welcoming to everyone. A café during the day, at night you can expect queues for a hugely impressive roster of guest DJs spinning a typically east London mix of of pop and dance tunes to a floor that's pitch-black and intense. Regular dates, such as Sunday's Disco Brunch (soul, disco and funk with all-day breakfast and cocktails), are well worth putting in the diary. Upstairs, alt-cabaret drag stars whip revellers into shape with sharp one-liners.

East Bloc

217 City Road, Hoxton, EC1V 1JN (eastbloc. co.uk). Old Street tube. **Open** *10.30pm-4am Thur; 10.30pm-6am Fri, Sat.* **Admission** *varies.* **No cards.** **Map** *pull-out Q4.*

Tucked away under a Turkish supermarket near Old Street, you'll find this deliciously dingy disco basement. East Bloc is compact yet filled with intrigue as you slink from one grotto-like room to the next. The music varies from night to night, but it generally attracts a varied crowd including beardy homo hipsters, edgy East End drag queens and trendy gay girls with asymmetric haircuts.

Glory

281 Kingsland Road, Dalston, E2 8AS (7684 0794, www.theglory.co). Haggerston Overground. **Open** *5pm-midnight Mon-Thur; 5pm-2am Fri, Sat; 1-11pm Sun.* **Admission** *varies.* **Map** *p256 S3.*

Just 'a clutch bag's throw away from Haggerston station... and one-and-a-half-songs-on-an-iPod's stroll from Shoreditch High Street', this bar and venue was co-opened by drag legend Jonny Woo. On the one hand it's a place you can nip into for a quick after-work drink: the bar staff offer proper cocktails as well as the usual beers, wines and spirits. But on the other, it's a platform for forward-thinking queer entertainment, hosting everything from cabaret to performance to DJ nights. It's a genuinely mixed space where the vibe is less 'anything goes', more 'everything encouraged' and it is perfect for what Woo clearly regards as something of a crusade: to keep gender-ambiguous and adventurous alternative cabaret thriving. Prepare to be glorious.

Heaven

Under the Arches, Villiers Street, Covent Garden, WC2N 6NG (7930 2020, heavennightclub-london.com). Embankment tube or Charing Cross tube/rail. **Open** *hours vary.* **Admission** *varies. No cards.* **Map** *p181 M8.*

When it opened in 1979, Heaven was revolutionary. London's first gay superclub, it was the birthplace of Hi-NRG and an early adopter of acid house, as well as being a magnet for queer celebrities. Nearly four decades later, Heaven is far from the cutting edge, but still offers the UK's most famous gay night out. On Thursdays it hosts the G-A-Y Porn Idol amateur strip contest, Fridays is filled with '80s and '90s cheese at G-A-Y Camp Attack, and Saturdays are reserved for the main G-A-Y club night, featuring pop star PAs. Tourists and the younger crowd love it, and just about every LGBT Londoner has danced the night away here at least once.

♥ Horse Meat Disco

Eagle London, 349 Kennington Lane, Vauxhall, SE11 5QY (7793 0903, www. eaglelondon.com). Vauxhall tube/rail. **Open** *8pm-late Tue-Thur; 9pm-4am Fri, Sat; 8pm-3am Sun.* **Admission** *£6 before 10pm, £8 after. No cards.*

Not your average gay club. Skinny Soho boys and fashionistas rub shoulders with scally lads and bears in a traditional old boozer. The hip soundtrack is an inspired mix of Studio 54, New York punk and new wave. As one *Time Out* critic put it: 'If you ever wished you could hang out in a club like the one in *Beyond the Valley of the Dolls* or *Scarface*, you'll love Horse Meat Disco.' One of London's very best club nights: a must.

> **In the know**
> **Post-Meat market**
>
> When Horse Meat isn't in residence, the **Eagle** is a hub for those wishing to try a bit of leather.

♥ RVT

Royal Vauxhall Tavern, 372 Kennington Lane, Vauxhall, SE11 5HY (7820 1222, www.rvt.org. uk). Vauxhall tube/rail. **Open** *7pm-midnight Mon-Thur; 6.30pm-3am Fri; 9pm-2am Sat; 3pm-1am Sun.* **Admission** *free-£8.*

This pub turned legendary gay cabaret venue, a much-loved stalwart on the scene for years, operates an anything-goes booking policy. The most famous fixture is Saturday's queer performance night Duckie (www. duckie.co.uk), with Amy Lamé hosting acts at midnight that range from strip cabaret to porn puppets. Other events include the

Sunday Socials with house spun by DJ Simon Le Vans at 3pm, followed by a cabaret act at 5.30pm and guest DJs from 9.30pm. The aim is to please the crowd of regulars. Punters verge on the bear, but the main dress code is 'no attitude'.

Savage

Metropolis, 234 Cambridge Heath Road, Bethnal Green, E2 2NN (www.savagedisco. com). Cambridge Heath Overground. **Open** *10pm-5am Sat.* **Admission** *£6. No cards.* **Map** *p256 V3.*

The restless polysexual party animals Sink The Pink (sinkthepink.co.uk) helm this weekly disco bash at strip club-cum-club space Metropolis, where you can roam around three floors of filthy fun for only a fiver. If you've never been before, prepare for pure Vegas decor, a dancing pole running through two floors, a wet room and top London DJs (including Horse Meat Disco's Severino and The 2 Bears' Raf Daddy) on rotation, playing deliciously dirty disco, house and party bangers until 5am. Savage stuff indeed.

VFD

66 Stoke Newington Road, Dalston, N16 7XB (7682 0408, vfdalston.com). Dalston Junction or Dalston Kingsland Overground. **Open** *10pm-3am Fri.* **Admission** *£5-£6. No cards.*

Formerly (and still commonly) known as Vogue Fabrics, this bijou Dalston basement hosts drag and spoken word events, as well as genre-spanning club nights and parties. Attracting a creative and fashion-conscious LGBT crowd who love to dress up (though no one will really care if you rock up in sneakers and a polo top), VFD has the chutzpah to host club nights with names like Cuntmafia and Sassitude, but never takes itself too seriously. After all, the venue's most famous feature is the massive penis mural in the loos.

WayOut Club

The Minories, 64-73 Minories, EC3N 1JL (07778 157290, www.thewayoutclub.com). Tower Hill tube. **Open** *9pm-3am Sat.* **Admission** *£12.* **Map** *p219 S8.*

London's best-known trans night has changed venues a few times, but it now takes place every Saturday under a railway arch on the fringe of the City. It's open to everyone at the T end of the LGBT spectrum, plus their friends and admirers, and attracts a loyal crowd of friendly regulars. The capital's nightlife has more options for the trans community now than when WayOut began in 1993, but the night endures because it's so warm and inclusive; there's even a changing area for punters who don't want to travel in drag.

RVT

XXL

1 Invicta Plaza, South Bank, SE1 9UF (www. xxl-london.com). Southwark tube. **Open** *9pm-3am Wed; 10pm-7am Sat.* **Admission** *£5-15. No cards.* **Map** *p78 P9.*

Held every Saturday in a cavernous space near London Bridge, XXL is the UK's biggest bear night. It's a men-only affair, but you don't have to be hench 'n' hairy to have fun: the crowd is friendly and anyone who enjoys whipping his top off on the dancefloor will feel at home. XXL regularly attracts up to 2,000 punters, most of whom will be found dancing to house remixes in the main area; others slope off to explore the dark room.

In the know
Gay's the Word

Established in 1979, **Gay's the Word** (66 Marchmont Street, Bloomsbury, WC1N 1AB, 7278 7654, www.gaystheword.co.uk) is a pioneering independent bookshop, the only dedicated LGBT bookshop in the UK and still flushed from its leading role in the superb gays-and-miners movie *Pride*. The stock covers fiction, history and biography, as well as more specialist subjects such as queer studies, sex and relationships, children and parenting. In addition to regular author readings and book signings, there are weekly lesbian and monthly trans discussion groups.

Nightlife

*Head out of central London to discover the best of the city
after dark*

To say London has brilliant and diverse nightlife is an
understatement, whether it's clubbing, gigs, cabaret or comedy.
These days, though, big is rarely best. Yes, we have one of the
world's largest and most influential nightclubs, Fabric, and high
hopes for huge new venue the Printworks, but it's the smaller
spaces that really buzz. In particular, the Bussey Building defines
the revival of Peckham, while good clubbing remains easy to find
among the party bars along the Kingsland Road strip in Dalston.
There's more new music from the edge at places such as XOYO
and the Shacklewell Arms, the latter proving that the London
cliché of indie bands in sticky dives endures. London also has
more than 250 comedy gigs a week and plenty of alt-cabaret.

The O2 Arena

CLUBS

In this era of boutique clubbing, London has all the variety you could possibly wish for – you don't even always have to go to a club to have the club experience. Try bowling and boogieing at **Bloomsbury Bowling Lanes**, for example, or dress up for one of the city's burgeoning number of 'vintage'-themed parties. And these days, some of the best events happen in warehouse locations, usually in east or south London – **The Hydra** (the-hydra.net) and **London Warehouse Events** (www.lwe.events), the guys behind fantastic new venue the **Printworks**, are worth checking out for a fix of big-name electronica. But the days of epoch-defining megaraves is gone, shattered into a thousand microscenes and sound systems that are fleet of foot and quick to respond to the passions of their audience. Upstairs rooms in pubs and the basements of abandoned shops – still especially in east London – are the birthing ground for DJs and promoters who might graduate to more permanent venues, or might vanish without a trace. It's a bewildering scene, but thrilling too.

Where it's at

Shoreditch was the hub of the capital's nightlife scene for a long time. It has, however, become increasingly commercialised in recent years (witness the weekend trails of hen and office parties between Old Street and Spitalfields), despite the groovy work still being done at live space and club **XOYO** – the closure of Plastic People in 2015, after 20 years at the cutting edge, felt like the end of an era. Nights at **Book Club**, which range from disco to science drink-and-thinks, show a newer kind of Shoreditch nightlife. The city's cool kids now routinely take the bus north up the Kingsland Road from Shoreditch into **Dalston** and beyond into Stoke Newington. When you're there, it can be difficult to find the clubs (though do check out the **Nest**) – even more so what's happening in them. Spend a few moments checking *Time Out* magazine (www.timeout.com/clubs) or hunting on Facebook and you'll unearth fabulous happenings at the likes of **Dalston Superstore** (*see p334*) and in any number of shop basements and other informal spaces.

There's more of interest to the south. **Peckham** has put itself at the heart of London nightlife with the superb **Bussey Building** (*see p341*), while the arrival of the **Printworks** has been justly lauded. **Brixton** has a multitude of venues, not least sleek **Phonox**. The gay village in **Vauxhall** is just

♥ Best music venues

Café Oto *p349*
For esoteric musical happenings.

Corsica Studios *p340*
Inventive, anything-goes gigging.

02 Arena *p344*
The place to catch big-ticket, blockbusting legends.

02 Academy Brixton *p344*
Classic rock venue with great atmosphere.

Pickle Factory *p345*
Industrial setting for arty bands and underground DJs.

♥ Best clubs

Bussey Building *p341*
Crazily diverse programming and all-round good fun.

Dalston Superstore *p334*
Polysexual party at the heart of Dalston.

Fabric *p339*
The superclub that defies the haters.

Printworks *p340*
New, big and brilliant.

XOYO *p343*
Keeping Shoreditch clubbing alive.

as welcoming to open-minded, straight-rolling types, with some big line-ups at **Fire** (39 Parry Street, South Lambeth Road, SW8 1RT, 3242 0040, www.firelondon.net) and **Hidden** (100 Tinworth Street, SE11 5EQ, 7820 1171), while the calendar is even fuller at **Corsica Studios** (*see p340*).

To the north, up in **King's Cross**, little remains of the former clubbing nexus that was redeveloped into King's Cross Central. There are some good nights at **Egg**, the **Big Chill House** (257-259 Pentonville Road, N1 9NL, 7427 2540, wearebigchill.com/house) and, with its late weekend licence and killer sound system, the **Star of Kings** pub-club (126 York Way, N1 0AX, 7458 4218, www.starofkings.co.uk). On the way into Islington, the upstairs room at the **Lexington** is known for casual nights with a studenty feel. Further north, **Camden** is still very popular – especially with tourists – but there are credible nights at indie student hangout **Proud**, teeny pub-rave spot **Lock Tavern** and bourbon-soaked gig haunt

Corsica Studios

the **Blues Kitchen**. **Koko** runs some of the biggest student nights around.

In central London, though, there's little to detain clubbers: the **West End** offers bars, pubs and Soho's lively but not especially adventurous gay scene. The best remaining option is the excellent **Blow Up** (www. blowupclub.com) on Friday nights, which celebrated its 21st birthday with a new residency in the club under the St Moritz fondue restaurant (159 Wardour Street, Soho, W1F 8WJ, 7734 3324, www.stmoritz-restaurant.co.uk).

Major venues

Electric Brixton

Town Hall Parade, Brixton, SW2 1RJ (7274 2290, www.electricbrixton.uk.com). Brixton tube/rail. **Open** *Thur-Sun; times vary.* **Admission** *£15-£35.*

The Fridge was a legendary rave paradise in the early '90s, a stomping ground for the rare groove scene, funky jazz-house and, later, hard dance and psy-trance beats. In 2011, however, the converted cinema underwent a £1m refit, with new management in place, and was reborn as Electric Brixton, with a mix of club nights – the likes of Skreamizm with Skream, featuring dubstep with forays into jungle, drum 'n' bass and disco – and live music.

♥ Fabric

77A Charterhouse Street, Clerkenwell, EC1M 6HJ (7336 8898, www.fabriclondon.com). Farringdon tube/rail. **Open** *11pm-6am Fri, Sun; 11pm-8am Sat.* **Admission** *£21-£27.* **Map** *p212 P6.*

Fabric is the club that most party people come to see in London – no wonder there was a major campaign to keep it open when two drug-related deaths led to Fabric being temporarily shut down in autumn 2016. Located in a former meatpacking warehouse, it has a well-deserved reputation as the capital's biggest and best club. Line-ups across the three rooms are legendary, with the world's most famous DJs bringing the finest low-frequencies and the deepest grooves, as the hip crowds that pack out the dancefloors testify.

Ministry of Sound

103 Gaunt Street, off Newington Causeway, Elephant & Castle, SE1 6DP (7740 8600, www.ministryofsound.com). Elephant & Castle tube/rail. **Open** *10pm-4am Tue; 10.30pm-6am Fri; 11pm-6am Sat.* **Admission** *£7-£26.* **Map** *p78 P11.*

In the know
Getting in

The queues for **Fabric** (see *above*) are also legendary, so blag on to the guestlist or buy tickets in advance to avoid a two-hour wait.

Ministry of Sound was once the epitome of warehouse cool and is still the UK's best-known clubbing venue. Laid out across four bars, five rooms and three dancefloors, there's lots to explore. Trance night the Gallery has made its home here on Fridays, while Saturday nights are for big-name DJ takeovers from the likes of Roger Sanchez and Erick Morillo.

Oval Space

29-32 The Oval, Bethnal Green, E2 9DT (7183 4422, www.ovalspace.co.uk). Bethnal Green tube/Overgound or Cambridge Heath overground. Open varies. Admission varies. Map p256 U3.

Located at the base of a disused gasworks off Hackney Road, this hangar-style space is 6,000sq ft of fun, and one of the most impressive and exciting recent additions to London nightlife. A mix of ace one-off parties and regular events mark Oval Space out as one of the most innovative venues around: DJs regularly play spacey techno, twisted electronica, alt hip hop and glitchy house, while on-point events such as Secretsundaze are regulars.

❤ Printworks

Surrey Quays Road, Rotherhithe, SE16 7PJ (printworkslondon.co.uk). Rotherhithe Overground or Canada Water tube/Overground. Open/admission check website for events.

This huge new 6,000-capacity cultural venue with a DJ focus opened in February 2017. The team now in charge of this massive industrial complex, where newspapers including the *Daily Mail* used to be printed, deliberately left it as raw as possible. Printworks Issue 001 ran amazing daytime dance events (techno originator Derrick May and house DJ Seth Troxler were among the acts) through spring 2017 in the Press Halls – an intense laserdome of almost sci-fi proportions, adorned with original bits of print machinery; Issue 002 is due for the autumn. In the meantime, five other event spaces host all manner of cross-cultural activity from art shows, classical concerts, dining events and gigs.

In the know
Fresh air

Oval Space (*see above*) has one of the best terrace spaces in town, put to full use for parties during the summer.

Club & pub venues

If you're clubbing in Camden, the gig venues **Koko** and **Camden Assembly** also host feisty club nights. In addition to the east London venues below, check out gay hangout the **Dalston Superstore** (*see p334*), and the excellent **Village Underground** and **Shacklewell Arms**.

Book Club

100-106 Leonard Street, Shoreditch, EC2A 4RH (7684 8618, www.wearetbc.com). Old Street tube/rail. Open 8am-midnight Mon-Wed; 8am-2am Thur, Fri; 10am-2am Sat; 10am-midnight Sun. Admission free-£20. Map p256 S5.

The Book Club aims to fuse lively creative events, table tennis (there's a ping pong table and regular tournaments) and late-night drinking. You could visit for the drinks alone – cocktails that come with names like Don't Go To Dalston – but the venue crams in a young and laid-back crowd with a packed timetable of events, ranging from Electro-Swing, the night that started a huge trend in mashing up vintage sounds with electro, to arty think-and-drink workshops and classic video-game nights, via the always brilliant Crap Film Club (www.crapfilmclub.org.uk).

❤ Corsica Studios

4-5 Elephant Road, Elephant & Castle, SE17 1LB (7703 4760, www.corsicastudios.com). Elephant & Castle tube/rail. Open 8pm-6am Fri, Sat; 8pm-3am Sun-Thur. Admission free-£15. Map p78 P11.

An independent, not-for-profit arts complex, Corsica Studios seeks to breed a culture of creativity. The flexible warehouse space is one of London's most adventurous, supplementing the DJs that play here with bands, poets, painters and lunatic projectionists. Sure, it's rough around the edges, with makeshift bars and toilets, but the events are second to none. The live-music roster has included gigs from Silver Apples, Acoustic Ladyland and Lydia Lunch.

Lock Tavern

35 Chalk Farm Road, Camden, NW1 8AJ (7482 7163, www.lock-tavern.com). Chalk Farm tube. Open noon-midnight Mon-Thur; noon-1am Fri, Sat; noon-11pm Sun. Admission free. Map p241 J1.

A favourite of artfully distressed rock urchins, it teems with aesthetic niceties inside (cosy black couches and warm wood panels downstairs; open-air terrace on the first floor), but it's the unpredictable after-party vibe that packs in the punters, with big-name DJs regularly providing the tunes.

💔 Bussey Building (CLF Art Cafe)

133 Rye Lane, Peckham, SE15 4ST (7732 5275, www.clfartcafe.org). Peckham Rye Overground.

A four-storey warehouse overlooking a railway, the CLF Art Cafe (known by pretty much everyone as the Bussey Building) is a multi-discipline arts space that hosts London's finest club nights. Top promoters consistently bring in the best names on the underground and alternative dance scenes, across most genres, but leaning towards house, deep techno, garage and disco. The Bussey also hosts regular nights that offer more accessible sounds: the likes of **Zonk Disco** and the twice-monthly **South London Soul Train** make it one of London's best spaces for funk and soul club nights as well. And in the summer, the roof is used for alfresco parties.

The Bussey has helped spark something of a cultural renaissance in Peckham. The area is now one of London's best destinations for exciting night-time entertainment from music and theatre to film. Almost every day of the week, the streets are buzzing, with the area described by *Vogue* as 'the Williamsburg of London'. Don't let that put you off. Peckham is cool but it's open, fun and friendly, with something for everybody out looking for a good time.

In a strange way, it all began with trams. The threatened demolition of a Victorian warehouse near Peckham Rye to make space for a tram depot kickstarted a campaign to bring creativity to this shabby but lively corner of south-east London.

Locals felt Peckham deserved more than a gigantic transport interchange, and did something about it.

Chronic Love Foundation, a collective dedicated to fostering positive global change through the implementation of creative projects, was given the challenge of putting Peckham on the map, and set about the task with relish and imagination.

Using the 120-year-old Bussey Building as its canvas, CLF organised a rolling programme of cultural events that took in all areas of the arts but had a focus on fun rather than education. Within the gargantuan Bussey, a vibe developed that helped save the warehouse from demolition and it has remained the base of CLF's activities ever since.

Once used to manufacture cricket bats, the Bussey now contains arts studios as well as spaces for clubbing, gigs, theatre and cinema; there's a record shop in the basement. Events are often rooted in the area's Afro-Caribbean community, but even the Royal Court Theatre (*see p361*) has held events in the space.

The Bussey's success goes hand-in-glove with that of **Bold Tendencies**, a multistorey car park on the other side of the railway line which transforms each summer into a vibrant arts space complete with rooftop bar, Frank's Café, arguably the most fashionable spot in London. On the ground in between and around these two complexes are a selection of smaller avant-garde galleries, music venues and bars and restaurants, from the informal to the relatively refined.

Nest

*36 Stoke Newington Road, Dalston, N16 7XJ
(7354 9993, www.ilovethenest.com). Dalston
Kingsland or Dalston Junction Overground.
Open 9pm-3am Thur; 10pm-4am Fri;
9pm-4am Sat. **Admission** £5-£10.*

Formerly the hipster institution Bardens
Boudoir, the 350-person capacity Nest
retains much of its predecessor's eclectic,
forward-looking booking policy, but with the
benefit of a big money 'distressed industrial'
refurbishment and, absolutely crucially
for those who suffered here before, much-
improved toilets. It's a bit like a corridor, but
the line-ups are usually great, with music that
hangs out at the dancefloor-focused disco,
electro and house end of the spectrum. One of
Dalston's finest.

Notting Hill Arts Club

*21 Notting Hill Gate, Notting Hill, W11 3JQ
(7460 4459, www.nottinghillartsclub.com).
Notting Hill Gate tube. **Admission** free-£8. **Map** pull-out C8.*

It's not easy these days to go for a big night
out in west London, which is what makes the
scruffily chic basement bar at NHAC such
a draw. Regular hip hop nights, indie band
showcases and events run by local heroes
Communion Records are all part of the
venue's busy schedule.

Old Queen's Head

*44 Essex Road, Islington, N1 8LN (7354
9993, www.theoldqueenshead.com). Angel
tube. **Open** noon-midnight Mon-Wed,
Sun; noon-1am Thur; noon-2am Fri, Sat.
Admission free; £5 Fri after 9pm, £6 Sat
after 8pm; other events vary.*

The Old Queen's Head is another place with
long queues at the weekends. There are two
floors and outside seating front and back, and
during the week you can lounge on battered
sofas. Weekends are for dancing, minor-
league celeb-spotting and chatting up the bar
staff, or trying out the private karaoke room.

In the know
Hooked on classics

The Old Queen's Head (*see above*) is one
of several regular hosts for the Night
Shift (*see p355*).

Phonox

*418 Brixton Road, Brixton, SW9 7AY (7095
9411, phonox.co.uk). Brixton tube/rail. **Open**
Fri-Sun; times vary. **Admission** £5-£20.*

Phonox has a similar feel to XOYO and the
Nest – no wonder: the team behind those
venues took over what was Plan B to create

In the know
Listen up

Nightlife in London is a strange hybrid: at
some clubs, you'll dance all night, but at
others you're expected just to sit down and
open your ears. Run by DJ Cosmo, **Classic
Album Sundays** (www.classicalbumsundays.
com) was the first 'listening party' we came
across: Cosmo selects a classic album (Kate
Bush, Talking Heads, Jimi Hendrix), which
you are invited to listen to, in full and without
disturbances, played on heavy vinyl through
the best audiophile sound system you're
ever likely to experience. The same sound
system puts on its party hat at psychedelic
discos **Journey Through the Light** (www.
loftparty.org) and **Beauty and the Beat**
(www.houseparty.org.uk). Further interesting
variations on the theme include Played Twice
at Dalston's audiophile café bar **Brilliant
Corners** (www.brilliantcornerslondon.co.uk):
first a classic jazz LP is played (Ornette,
Monk, Alice Coltrane) in its entirety, then
a high-calibre contemporary jazz band
reinterprets the record.

a sleek, dark dance cavern where there's
plenty of space for a boogie. Programming
leans very much towards the leftfield side
of dance music – don't expect cheesy '80s
nights, resident DJ HAAI ensures it's quality,
underground house, techno, disco and bass
all the way.

Proud Camden

*Horse Hospital, Stables Market, Chalk
Farm Road, Camden, NW1 8AH (7482 3867,
www.proudcamden.com). Chalk Farm
tube. **Open** Terrace Bar 11am-2.30am
Thur-Sat; 11am-midnight Sun-Wed. Club
9pm-2.10am Thur-Sat. **Admission** free-£15.
Map p241 J1.*

The cobbled floors remain from Proud's
former incarnation as a horse hospital, as
do stables that have been spruced up and
turned into booths. The main space – which
has a stage for live bands – is usually decked
with artwork, while the roof terrace has
been revamped with bright colours and twee
bunting. Club nights usually feature indie-
electro, synth-pop, R&B, hip hop and funk.
There's also a cabaret room on the far side of
the venue.

In the know
Early doors

Entry is free to **Phonox** (*see left*) before 9pm
on Fridays and before 10pm every Saturday.

♥ XOYO

*32-37 Cowper Street, Shoreditch, EC2A 4AP (7608 2878, www.xoyo.co.uk). Old Street tube/rail. **Open/admission** varies.* **Map** *p256 R5.*

There's live music during the week at this 800-capacity venue, but XOYO is first and foremost a club. The former printworks is a bare concrete shell, defiantly taking the 'chic' out of 'shabby chic', but the open space means the atmosphere is always buzzing, as the only place to escape immersion in the music is the small smoking courtyard outside. The Victorian loft-style space provides effortlessly cool programming and high-profile DJs, while the longer residencies – a 12-week stint for Erol Alkan in summer 2017, for instance – is the best kind of old-school.

ROCK & POP MUSIC

The rest of the country might not like it, but every musician is going to have to come to London: you might find yourself watching a US country star in a tiny basement, an African group under a railway arch or a torch singer in a church – all in one night, if you've got the stamina. While corporations have invested in venues, resulting in positives (improved facilities and sound systems) and negatives (overpriced bars and ugly branded names), there's still rough and ready individuality to be found – as well as the newest sounds – in venues such as **XOYO** (*see left*) and the **Shacklewell Arms** (*see p347*). There's often a huge disparity between door times and stage times; doors may open at 7pm, for instance, but the gigs often don't start until after 9pm. Some venues run club nights after the gigs, which means the show has to be wrapped up by 10.30pm; but at other venues, the main act won't even start until 11pm. If in doubt, call ahead.

Major venues

In addition to the venues listed below, the **Barbican Centre** (*see p354*), the **Southbank Centre** (*see p357*) and the **Royal Albert Hall** (*see p355*) also stage regular non-classical gigs.

Alexandra Palace

Alexandra Palace Way, N22 7AY (8365 2121, www.alexandrapalace.com). Alexandra Palace rail or W3 bus. **Tickets** *vary; check the promoter's website.*

This hilltop landmark, adorned with sculptures and frescoes, opened in 1873 as the People's Palace and was devastated by

fire twice – once only 16 days after opening, and the second time in 1980. The layout means bar and toilet provision can be an irritation, but the sound system is beloved of audiophiles: no wonder the Pixies chose it for their first London shows when they reformed, and James Murphy for the last UK appearances of LCD Soundsystem.

Eventim Apollo

45 Queen Caroline Street, Hammersmith, W6 9QH (information 8563 3800, tickets 0844 249 4300, www.eventimapollo.com). Hammersmith tube. **Box office** *In person from 4pm on performance days. By phone 8am-10pm daily.* **Tickets** *£10-£150.*

This 1930s cinema doubles as a 3,600-capacity all-seater theatre (popular with big comedy acts and children's shows) and a 5,000-capacity standing-room-only gig space, hosting shows by major rock bands and others not quite ready for the O2. The venue scored a sensational coup at the end of 2014 when Kate Bush's 'Before the Dawn' was performed here – her first gig since 1979.

Koko

1A Camden High Street, Camden, NW1 7JE (information 7388 3222, tickets 0844 477 1000, www.koko.uk.com). Mornington Crescent tube. **Box office** *In person noon-5pm Mon-Fri (performance days only). By phone 24hrs daily.* **Tickets** *£10-£40.* **Map** *p241 K3.*

Koko has had a hand in the gestation of numerous styles over the decades. As the Music Machine, it hosted a four-night residency with the Clash in 1978; the venue changed its name to Camden Palace in the '80s, whereupon it became home to the

Koko

emergent New Romantic movement and saw Madonna's UK debut. Later, it was one of the first 'official' venues to host acid-house events. Since a spruce-up in the early noughties, it has hosted acts as diametrically opposed as Joss Stone and Queens of the Stone Age, not to mention one of Prince's electrifying 'secret' gigs in 2014. Nonetheless, the 1,500-capacity hall majors on weekend club nights – Annie Mac Presents and Club NME – and gigs by indie rockers, from the small and cultish to those on the up.

♥ O2 Academy Brixton
*211 Stockwell Road, Brixton, SW9 9SL (information 7771 3000, tickets 0844 477 2000, www.academymusicgroup.com/o2academybrixton). Brixton tube/rail. **Box office** In person 2hrs before doors on performance days. By phone 24hrs daily. **Tickets** £10-£40.*

Brixton is still the preferred venue for metal, indie and alt-rock bands looking to play their triumphant 'Look, ma, we've made it!' headline show. Built in the 1920s, this ex-cinema is the city's most atmospheric big venue. The 5,000-capacity art deco gem straddles the chasm between the pomp and volume of a stadium show and the intimate (read: sweaty) atmosphere of a club. Since

becoming a full-time music venue in the '80s, it's hosted names from James Brown to the Stones to Springsteen, Dylan, Prince and Madonna, via the Red Hot Chili Peppers and Run DMC with the Beastie Boys. And with its raked dancefloor, everyone's guaranteed a decent view.

♥ O2 Arena & IndigO2
*Peninsula Square, North Greenwich, SE10 0DX (information 8463 2000, tickets 0844 856 0202, www.theo2.co.uk). North Greenwich tube. **Box office** In person noon-7pm daily. By phone 8am-8pm daily. **Tickets** £15-£70.*

The national embarrassment that was the Millennium Dome has been transformed into the city's de facto home of the mega-gig. This 20,000-seater has outstanding sound, unobstructed sightlines and the potential for artists to perform 'in the round'. Shows from even the world's biggest acts (U2, Beyoncé, the reformed Led Zep, the mostly reformed Monty Python) don't feel too far away, and the venue seems to handle music, comedy and even sport (international tennis, boxing, basketball) with equal aplomb.

On the same site, IndigO2 is the Arena's little sister – but 'little' only by comparison. It has an impressive capacity of 2,350, arranged as part-standing room, part-amphitheatre seating and, sometimes, part-table seating. IndigO2's niche roster of MOR acts is dominated by soul, funk, pop-jazz and old pop acts, but it does also host after-show parties for headliners from the Arena.

O2 Forum Kentish Town

9-17 Highgate Road, Kentish Town, NW5 1JY (information 7428 4080, tickets 0844 877 2000, www.academymusicgroup.com/o2forumkentishtown). Kentish Town tube/rail. **Box office** *In person 90mins before doors open on show days. By phone 24hrs daily.* **Tickets** *£10-£40.*

Originally constructed as part of a chain of art deco cinemas with a spurious Roman theme (hence the name, the incongruous bas relief battle scenes and imperial eagles flanking the stage), the 2,000-capacity Forum became a music venue back in the early 1980s. Since then, it's been vital to generations of gig-goers, whether they cut their teeth on Ian Dury & the Blockheads, The Pogues, Duran Duran, Killing Joke or the Wu-Tang Clan, all of whom have played memorable shows here.

O2 Shepherd's Bush Empire

Shepherd's Bush Green, Shepherd's Bush, W12 8TT (information 8354 3300, tickets 0844 477 2000, www.academymusicgroup.com/o2shepherdsbushempire). Shepherd's Bush Market tube or Shepherd's Bush tube/Overground/rail. **Box office** *from 4pm on performance days. By phone 24hrs daily.* **Tickets** *£10-£40.*

Once a BBC television theatre, the Empire's baroque interior exudes a grown-up glamour few venues can match. The environment lends a gravitas to the chirpiest of performance, as Lily Allen demonstrated in the flush of her fame, so you can imagine the sensation of seeing the likes of David Bowie or Bob Dylan here. It holds 2,000 standing or 1,300 seated, sightlines are good, the sound is decent (with the exception of the alcove behind the stalls bar and the scarily vertiginous top floor), and the roster of shows is quite varied.

♥ Pickle Factory

13-14 The Oval, Bethnal Green, E2 9DU (www.thepicklefactory.co.uk). Bethnal Green tube/Overground or Cambridge Heath Overground. **Open***/admission check website.* **Map** *p256 V3.*

This former industrial building is owned by the team that runs Oval Space (*see p340*), which is directly opposite. It actually was a pickle factory, but – having been used for foodie pop-ups and exhibitions – was fully revamped as an intimate live music and club space. The programme is an alternative and

esoteric mix of mind-bendingly arty bands and leftfield but thoroughly banging DJ sets from underground heroes.

Roundhouse

Chalk Farm Road, Camden, NW1 8EH (tickets 0300 678 9222, www.roundhouse.org.uk). Chalk Farm tube. **Box office** *In person 9.30am-5pm Mon, Sat, Sun; 9.30am-9pm Tue-Fri. By phone 9am-7pm Mon-Fri; 9am-4pm Sat; 9.30am-4pm Sun.* **Tickets** *£5-£25.* **Map** *p241 H1.*

The main auditorium's supporting pillars mean there are some poor sightlines at the Roundhouse, but this one-time railway turntable shed (hence the name), which was used for hippie happenings in the 1960s before becoming a famous rock (and punk) venue in the '70s, has been a fine addition to London's music venues since its reopening in 2006. Expect a mix of arty rock gigs (the briefly re-formed Led Zeppelin played here), dance performances, theatre and multimedia events.

Scala

275 Pentonville Road, King's Cross, N1 9NL (information 7833 2022, tickets 0844 477 1000, scala.co.uk). King's Cross tube/rail. **Box office** *10am-6pm Mon-Fri.* **Tickets** *free-£25.* **Map** *p194 M4.*

Although the venue has vacillated between use as a picturehouse and concert hall, the Scala's one consistent trait has been its lack of respect for authority: its stint as a cinema was ended after Stanley Kubrick sued it into bankruptcy for showing *A Clockwork Orange.* Nowadays, it's one of the most rewarding venues which to push your way at the front for those cusp-of-greatness shows by big names in waiting – names as varied as the Chemical Brothers and Joss Stone.

SSE Arena, Wembley

Arena Square, Engineers Way, Wembley, Middlesex, HA9 0DH (information 8782 5500, tickets 0844 815 0815, www.ssearena.co.uk). Wembley Park tube or Wembley Stadium rail. **Box office** *In person (performance days only) 10.30am-4.30pm Mon-Fri; from noon Sat on performance days; from 2pm Sun on performance days. By phone 24hrs daily.* **Tickets** *£20-£230.*

Although it has carved out something of a niche for soul music, Wembley Arena has probably seen its commercial heyday end with the ongoing success of the O2 Arena (see p344). While the food and drink could be better, most Londoners have warm memories of at least one megagig at the 12,500-capacity Arena, be it rock or stand-up comedy.

Club & pub venues

In addition to the venues listed below, several London nightclubs multitask, staging regular gigs: **Corsica Studios**, the **Notting Hill Arts Club**, **Proud Camden** and **Nest** are notable. **Borderline** is known for country and folk gigs, but does also host indie bands.

100 Club

*100 Oxford Street, Soho, W1D 1LL (7636 0933, www.the100club.co.uk). Oxford Circus or Tottenham Court Road tube. **Shows** times vary. **Tickets** £10-£25. **Map** p163 K7.*

The 100 Club began life in 1942 hosting the Feldman Club, but over the decades jazz would give way to punk: one historic show, in September 1976, featured the Sex Pistols, the Clash and the Damned. These days the famous, 350-capacity basement room is more of a hub for pub rockers, blues rockers and, in a return to its roots, trad jazzers. The space comes into its own for the odd secret gig by A-list bands such as Primal Scream and Oasis.

Bloomsbury Bowling Lanes

*Basement, Tavistock Hotel, Bedford Way, Bloomsbury, WC1H 9EU (7183 1979, 07508 266983 after 6pm, www.bloomsburylive. com). Russell Square tube. **Open** noon-midnight Mon, Tue, Sun; noon-late Wed, Thur; noon-3am Fri, Sat. **Admission** varies. **Map** p194 L5.*

Offering a late-night drink away from Soho (but not too far away), BBL has been putting on bands and DJs for ages – and the range of activities make it a playground for grown-ups. As well as the eight lanes for bowling, there's pool by the hour, table football, karaoke booths and, beside the entrance, a small cinema.

Bush Hall

*310 Uxbridge Road, Shepherd's Bush, W12 7LJ (8222 6955, www.bushhallmusic.co.uk). Shepherd's Bush Market tube. **Open** varies. **Shows** from 7.30pm. **Tickets** £6-£40.*

This handsome room has been a dance hall, soup kitchen and snooker club. Now, with original fittings intact, it plays host to major bands performing stripped-down shows and to rising indie rockers, as well as top folk acts.

Camden Assembly

*49 Chalk Farm Road, Camden, NW1 8AN (information 7424 0800, tickets 0844 847 2424, camdenassembly.com). Chalk Farm tube. **Open** 5pm-2am Mon, Thur; 3pm-1am Tue, Wed; 5pm-3am Fri; noon-3am Sat; noon-midnight Sun. Shows from 7pm. **Admission** free-£15. **Map** p241 H1.*

Formerly the Barfly, this 200-capacity corner venue is a Camden institution, with Coldplay, Franz Ferdinand and Bombay Bicycle Club among the many bands who played early London gigs here. It was a popular hangout during the Britpop and grunge years – no doubt due to the loud post-band DJ sets and late licence – and a key player in the fusion of indie guitars and electro into an unholy, danceable row.

Garage

*20-22 Highbury Corner, Highbury, N5 1RD (information 7619 6721, tickets 0844 847 1678, www.mamacolive.com/thegarage). Highbury & Islington tube/Overground/rail. **Box office** In person 5pm-close. By phone 24hrs daily. **Tickets** free-£20.*

This 650-capacity alt-rock venue books an exciting and surprisingly wide-ranging calendar of indie and art-rock gigs, from ancient punk survivors such as the Pop Group and Sham 69 to the poppier end of the indie singer-songwriter scale (Fran Healy in the smaller Upstairs, for example).

Hoxton Square Bar & Kitchen

*2-4 Hoxton Square, Shoreditch, N1 6NU (7613 0709, www.hoxtonsquarebar.com). Old Street tube/rail or Shoreditch High Street Overground. **Open** 5pm-midnight Mon, Tue Wed; 5pm-1am Thur; 4pm-2am Fri, Sat; 4pm-midnight Sun. **Tickets** free-£14.50 after 10pm Fri, Sat. **Map** p256 S4.*

This 450-capacity venue is more than just a place to be seen: the line-ups are always cutting-edge and fun, frequently offering a band's first London outing. Get there early or be prepared to queue.

Jazz Café

*5 Parkway, Camden, NW1 7PG (7485 6834, thejazzcafelondon.com. Camden Town tube. Shows from 7pm. **Restaurant** 7pm-11pm daily. Club nights Fri, Sat 10pm-3am. **Tickets** £5-£30. **Map** p241 J2.*

In 2015 the Jazz Café celebrated 25 years in business, having brought some of the most respected names in the jazz and soul world – D'Angelo, Roy Ayers, Bobby Womack – as well as Amy Winehouse and Adele to Camden Town. Then, in 2016, it was relaunched with a new look, a technical upgrade and revamped food and drink. The programming still focuses on funk, soul, R&B and electronic music, but there are more new and rising acts. With a capacity of 440, it's an intimate space, but the two-level layout offers you a choice: get sweaty in the downstairs standing area, or book an upstairs table for a bit of luxury and guaranteed good view.

Lexington
*96-98 Pentonville Road, Islington, N1 9JB (7837 5371, www.thelexington.co.uk). Angel tube. **Open** noon-2am Mon-Wed, Sun; noon-3am Thur; noon-4am Fri, Sat. **Tickets** free-£15. **Map** pull-out O3.*

Effectively the common room for the music industry's perennial sixth form, this 200-capacity venue has a superb sound system in place for the leftfield indie bands that dominate the programme. It's where the hottest US exports often make their London debut: indie greats such as the Drums and Sleigh Bells have cut their teeth here in front of London's most receptive crowds. Downstairs, there's a lounge bar with a vast array of US beers and bourbons, above-par bar food and a Rough Trade music quiz (every Monday).

Oslo
*1A Amhurst Road, Hackney, E8 1LL (3553 4831, www.oslohackney.com). Hackney Central Overground. **Open** varies. **Admission** varies.*

Young and trendy Hackney folk are blended with older live music fans more smoothly than one of the salted caramel martinis they serve in this Victorian railway station. Oslo is a busy, glowingly lit and rather fancy Scandinavian restaurant downstairs, with a more relaxed area for bar food, but head upstairs and you'll find all sorts of musical happenings, including of-the-moment buzz bands and some club nights. The decent-sized stage and proper sound system and lighting rig ensure a roster of good acts – among them Temples.

Shacklewell Arms
*71 Shacklewell Lane, Dalston, E8 2EB (7249 0810, www.shacklewellarms.com). Dalston Kingsland or Dalston Junction Overground. **Open** 5pm-midnight Mon-Thur; 5pm-3am Fri; noon-3am Sat; noon-midnight Sun. **Admission** free-£15.*

The Shacklewell Arms is a magnet for leftfield music. While the bands who have played here include the Horrors, Toy and Haim, DJs tend to come from the electronic, lo-fi, chillwave and post-dubstep arenas, all of which genres contrast brilliantly with the quirkily decorated interior – this former Afro-Caribbean hotspot has had its array of tropical-themed murals and signs pointing to 'the dancehall' updated. Thank goodness.

Underworld
*174 Camden High Street, Camden, NW1 0NE (7482 1932, www.theunderworldcamden. co.uk). Camden Town tube. Shows times vary. **Admission** £5-£17.50. **Map** p241 K2.*

A dingy maze of pillars and bars below Camden, this subterranean oddity is an essential for metal and hardcore fans who want their ears bludgeoned by bands with names such as Bitchwax, Skeletonwitch and Decrepit Birth. Tickets are purchased from the World's End pub upstairs.

Union Chapel
*Compton Terrace, off Upper Street, Islington, N1 2UN (7226 1686 , www.unionchapel.org. uk). Highbury & Islington tube/Overground/ rail. **Open** varies. **Tickets** free-£40.*

Readers of *Time Out* magazine have three times voted Union Chapel their top music venue – and it's easy to see why. The Grade I-listed Victorian Gothic church, which still holds services and also runs a homeless centre, is a wonderfully atmospheric gig venue. It made its name hosting acoustic events and occasional jazz shows, becoming a magnet for thinking bands and their fans. These days, you'll also find classy intimate shows from bigger artists such as Paloma Faith. Watch out for the Daylight Music free afternoon concerts.

❤ Village Underground
*54 Holywell Lane, Shoreditch, EC2A 3PQ (7422 7505, www.villageunderground.co.uk). Shoreditch High Street Overground. **Open** varies. **Admission** varies. **Map** p256 S5.*

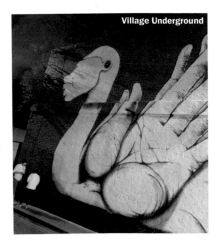

Village Underground

You can't miss Village Underground: four graffiti-covered tube carriages are perched on its roof. These and a series of shipping containers accommodate artists, writers, designers, filmmakers and musicians, while a Victorian warehouse space hosts exhibitions, concerts, plays, live art and club nights.

Windmill

22 Blenheim Gardens, Brixton, SW2 5BZ (8671 0700, windmillbrixton.co.uk). Brixton tube/rail. Open 5-11pm Mon-Thur, Sun; 5.30pm-1am Fri, Sat. Shows vary. Admission free-£12.

There's a barbecue every Sunday afternoon in summer; a somewhat scary dog lives on the roof, frightening unsuspecting smokers; and an actual windmill stands in the adjacent park. The Windmill is certainly not your average music venue, but it's been revelling in its rough-around-the-edges eccentricity for years, its unprepossessing exterior a cloak for its dedication to new leftfield music. The programming is biased towards alt country, alt folk and alt punk. It's worth a visit just to pick up an 'I Believe in Roof Dog' T-shirt.

JAZZ, COUNTRY, FOLK & BLUES

The international big hitters keep on visiting London, but there's a lively homegrown jazz scene too, inspired by freewheeling attractions at the **Vortex**, **Café Oto** and the unhinged monthly **Boat-Ting Club** nights (www.boat-ting.co.uk); Portico Quartet, Led Bib and Kit Downes Trio each won Mercury Prize nominations at the turn of the decade. In addition to the venues below, the **100**

♥ Best all-rounders

Corsica Studios *p340*
Gigs, club nights and freaky deaky light shows.

Pickle Factory *p345*
Music of all stripes, new from the Oval Space crew.

Printworks *p340*
New industrial venue with six event spaces.

Soho Theatre *p350*
Not just plays, but cabaret and comedy.

Village Underground *p347*
Arty happenings, musical and otherwise.

Club hosts blues rock and trad groups, **Bush Hall** is a great setting for leading folk groups, and the **Spice of Life** (6 Moor Street, Soho, W1D 5NA, 7437 7013, www. spiceoflifesoho.com) has solid mainstream jazz. In Hoxton, **Charlie Wright's International Bar** (Courtyard Theatre, 40 Pitfield Street, N1 6EU, www.charliewrights. co.uk) usually has a fine jazz programme. The **Jazz Café** lives up to its name from time to time; there's a lot of very good jazz at the excellent **Kings Place** (*see p354*); and both the **Barbican** (*see p354*) and the **Southbank Centre** (see p357) host dozens of big names. For the admirable **London Jazz Festival**, *see p318*.

606 Club

90 Lots Road, Chelsea, SW10 0QD (7352 5953, www.606club.co.uk). Imperial Wharf Overground or bus 11, 211. Shows 8.30-11.15pm Mon, Thur; 8-9.30pm, 9.45-11.15pm Tue, Wed; 9.30pm-12.45am Fri, Sat; 1.30-3.30pm, 8.30-11.15pm Sun. Admission (non-members) £10-£14.

Since 1976 Steve Rubie has run this club, which relocated to this 150-capacity space in 1987. Alongside its Brit-dominated bills, expect informal jams featuring musos who've come here to wind down from gigs elsewhere. There's no entrance fee as such; bands are funded from a music charge added to your bill at the end of the night.

Blues Kitchen

111-113 Camden High Street, Camden, NW1 7JN (7387 5277, theblueskitchen.com). Camden Town or Mornington Crescent tube. Open noon-midnight Mon, Tue; noon-1am Wed, Thur; noon-3am Fri; 10am-3.30am Sat; 10am-1am Sun. Admission varies. Map p241 K2.

The Blues Kitchen combines credible live music of the earthier variety (roots, blues, rockabilly) with a rather smart interior. The food is spicy New Orleans fare and there's a huge range of American bourbon for sippin'. It's a pleasant Sunday afternoon hangout as well as a late-opening gig venue. Outposts in Shoreditch (134-146 Curtain Road, EC2A 3AR, 7729 7216) and Brixton (40 Acre Lane, SW2 5SP, 7274 0591) have a similar vibe.

Borderline

Orange Yard, off Manette Street, Soho, W1D 4JB (information 3871 7777, tickets 0870 060 3777, borderline.london). Tottenham Court Road tube. Open gigs daily; club nights until 4am Wed-Sat. Admission £3-£20. Map p163 L7.

The best venue in the West End? Surely. Reopening after a revamp in spring 2017, the

Ronnie Scott's Jazz Club p350

Borderline is a 300-capacity dive bar and juke joint, perfectly placed on the fringe of Soho. It has long been a favoured stop-off for touring American bands of the country and blues varieties, though you'll also find a range of indie acts and singer-songwriters going through their repertoire. Be warned: it can get very cramped, but that's all to the good for intimacy and atmosphere.

♥ Café Oto
18-22 Ashwin Street, Dalston, E8 3DL (7923 1231, www.cafeoto.co.uk). Dalston Kingsland or Dalston Junction Overground. **Open** *Café 8.30am-5pm Mon-Fri; 9.30am-5pm Sat; 10.30am-5pm Sun. Shows 8pm.* **Admission** *free-£20.*

Opened in 2008, this 150-capacity café and music venue can't easily be categorised, though its website offers the tidy definition that it specialises in 'creative new music that exists outside of the mainstream'. That means Japanese noise rockers ('Oto' is Japanese for 'sound'), electronica pioneers, improvisors (the Sun Ra Arkestra has had a couple of residencies), noiseniks and artists from the stranger ends of the rock, folk and classical spectrums.

Cecil Sharp House
2 Regent's Park Road, Camden, NW1 7AY (7485 2206, www.cecilsharphouse.org). Camden Town tube. **Open/admission** *varies.* **Map** *p241 J2.*

Headquarters of the British Folk Dance and Song Society, Cecil Sharp House is a great place to visit, even when there isn't any music playing: there's a folk-arts education centre and archive open during the day. Perhaps that sounds a bit worthy? In fact, the Kennedy Hall performance space – with its comfortably sprung floor – is blessed with a well-informed and enthusiastic team of bookers who ensure all angles of trad music are well represented without being preserved in aspic. Events range from Scottish ceilidhs to alt folk.

Forge
3-7 Delancey Street, Camden, NW1 7NL (7383 7808, www.forgevenue.org). Camden Town or Mornington Crescent tube. **Open** *noon-midnight Tue-Thur; noon-1am Fri, Sat; noon-10.30pm Sun. Shows from 7.30pm.* **Admission** *free-£20.* **Map** *p241 K2.*

Run by a non-profit community organisation, this innovative music/restaurant space incorporates a stunning atrium, and hosts concerts of various sizes and formalities. The programme is skewed heavily to jazz, but also features a carefully curated selection of roots and classical shows. There's an on-site restaurant, the Foundry; you can dine while you listen on a Friday, and there's an interesting weekend brunch programme.

Green Note
106 Parkway, Camden, NW1 7AN (7485 9899, www.greennote.co.uk). Camden Town tube. **Open** *7-11pm Mon-Thur, Sun; 7pm-midnight Fri, Sat. Shows 8.30-11pm daily.* **Admission** *£5-£15.* **Map** *p241 J2.*

A stone's throw from Regent's Park, this cosy little venue and vegetarian café-bar hosts singer-songwriters, folkies and blues musicians, with a handful of big names in among the listings.

Pizza Express Jazz Club

10 Dean Street, Soho, W1D 3RW (7439 4962, www.pizzaexpresslive.com). Tottenham Court Road tube. Open 7-10.30pm Mon-Thur; 7.30-9pm, 10pm-midnight Fri, Sat; 6.30-10pm Sun. Lunchtime shows 1.30-3.30pm. Admission £15-£25. Map p163 L7.

The upstairs restaurant (7437 9595) is jazz-free, but the 120-capacity basement is one of the best mainstream jazz venues in town. Singers such as Kurt Elling and Lea DeLaria join instrumentalists from home and abroad on the nightly bills.

Ronnie Scott's

47 Frith Street, Soho, W1D 4HT (7439 0747, www.ronniescotts.co.uk). Leicester Square or Tottenham Court Road tube. Shows 6pm-3am Mon-Sat; noon-4pm, 6.30pm-midnight Sun. Admission free-£50. Map p163 L7.

Opened (on a different site) by the British saxophonist Ronnie Scott in 1959, this jazz institution – the setting for Jimi Hendrix's final UK performance, among many other distinctions – was completely refurbished in 2006. The capacity was expanded to 250, the food got better and the bookings became drearier. Happily, though, Ronnie's has got back on track, with jazz heavyweights dominating once more – from well-established talents such as Chick Corea to hotly tipped purists such as Kurt Elling to futuristic mavericks such as Robert Glasper. Perch by the rear bar, or get table service at the crammed side-seating or at the more spacious (but noisier) central tables in front of the stage.

Vortex Jazz Club

11 Gillett Square, Dalston, N16 8AZ (7254 4097, www.vortexjazz.co.uk). Dalston Kingsland or Dalston Junction Overground. Open 8pm-midnight daily. Admission £5-£18.

In the know
Booze and tunes

Also at Gillett Square, the **Servant Jazz Quarters** cocktail dive (10A Bradbury Street, N16 8JN, 7684 8411, servantjazzquarters.com) serves cocktails and programmes gigs – even, sometimes, jazz.

One of the few venues in the city you could visit on spec and be guaranteed to hear something interesting. Along with the nearby Café Oto, the Vortex is one of London's most lovingly curated venues. Jazz is the order of the day, but the Vortex serves it up in kaleidoscopic variety. For the less daring, there's a regular calendar of big band, piano trio, vocal, free improv, world music and folk-oriented sounds, as well as some poetry gigs. The Vortex hosts its own strand of the London Jazz Festival (*seep318*) and various other forward-thinking events.

COMEDY & CABARET

While the big stadiums – especially the **O2 Arena** and **SSE Arena, Wembley** – host the massive shows (TV star stand-ups and the 2014 Monty Python 'alimony-payment' reunion), it's the circuit of pubs and smaller clubs that defines London's comedy scene. In addition to its stellar programme of plays and cabaret, the **Soho Theatre** (*see p366*) has become one of the best places to see comics breaking free from abbreviated club-circuit sets to present more substantial solo gigs. Usually programming hour-long shows rather than the multi-act bills common elsewhere, it's currently the best venue in London for interesting, innovative and downright funny comedy. Another multi-tasking venue is the **Union Chapel**, whose monthly Live at the Chapel night provides line-ups of big guns (Noel Fielding and Stewart Lee, for example) supported by comics who are headliners in their own right, plus a terrific live band.

To see the best cabaret, head to the always interesting **Bethnal Green Working Men's Club** or the even more alternative **RVT** (*seep334*) and the **Glory** (*see p330*). Many of the best nights, however, are one-off parties in a range of formal and informal venues.

For the week's best line-ups – whether comedy or cabaret – have a look at the free *Time Out* magazine on Tuesday; for comprehensive listings, see www.timeout.com.

99 Club Leicester Square

Ruby Blue, 1 Leicester Place, Leicester Square, WC2H 7BP (07760 488119, www.99clubcomedy.com). Leicester Square tube. Shows 7.30pm Tue-Sat. Admission £7-£17. Map p163 L8.

The general rule when you get a flyer as you walk through Leicester Square is to stick it in the nearest recycling bin – but make an exception for this one. The 99 Club offers quality line-ups five nights a week and tickets are remarkably good value (but expect a hike in prices around Christmas).

Angel Comedy

Camden Head, 2 Camden Walk, Islington, N1 8DY (www.angelcomedy.co.uk). Angel tube. Shows 8pm daily. Admission free; donations appreciated. Map pull-out P3.

One of the best comedy nights in London – and certainly the best free night. That means long queues tend to form outside, with the promoters having to turn folk away every weekend. On Fridays and Saturdays, you can catch rising stars and a few professional comics performing their funniest sets, and weekdays feature either new material spots, improv troupes or solo shows. But the night's biggest sell is the inclusive, welcoming atmosphere – despite being free, punters come for the comedy rather than a cheap night out. Donations are encouraged at the end of the night.

Bethnal Green Working Men's Club

42-44 Pollard Row, Bethnal Green, E2 6NB (7739 7170, www.workersplaytime. net). Bethnal Green tube. Open varies. Admission free-£10. Map p256 U4.

Sticky red carpet and broken lampshades perfectly suit the programme of quirky lounge, retro rock 'n' roll and fancy-dress burlesque parties here. You might get to watch a spandex-lovin' dance duo or get hip with burlesque starlets on a 1960s dancefloor. The mood is friendly, the playlist upbeat and the air full of artful, playful mischief.

CellarDoor

Zero Aldwych, Aldwych, Covent Garden, WC2D 7DN (7240 8848, www.cellardoor. biz). Covent Garden tube. Open varies. Admission varies. Map p181 N8.

Some staggeringly clever design means that although there's room for just 60 in this subterranean converted Victorian loo, CellarDoor never feels claustrophobic. Musical-theatre cabaret crooners and drag queens are the order of the day, giving this sleek establishment a vintage feel. Nearly all shows are free and often great fun – EastEnd Cabaret regularly appears and Champagne Charlie's Trash Tuesday open-mic night is an institution.

Comedy Store

1A Oxendon Street, Soho, SW1Y 4EE (0844 871 7699, www.thecomedystore.co.uk/ london). Leicester Square or Piccadilly Circus tube. Shows times vary. Admission £5-£23.50. Map p163 L8.

In the know
Laughs in the museum

The people behind **Leicester Square Theatre** (*see below*) also run the **Museum of Comedy** (*see p197*), which has its own performance space for stand-up and comedy-themed plays.

The Comedy Store is still the daddy of all the laff clubs. Seemingly as old as London itself (it actually started in 1979, above a strip club), the Store has been instrumental in the growth of alternative comedy, and still to this day hosts stunning shows most nights of the week. The live room was created specifically for stand-up and it shows, with 400 chairs hugging the stage to keep each show intimate. Veteran improvisers the Comedy Store Players perform every Wednesday and Sunday. Don't miss the raucous King Gong new-act night on the last Monday of the month.

Leicester Square Theatre

6 Leicester Place, Leicester Square, WC2H 7BX (7734 2222, www. leicestersquaretheatre.com). Leicester Square tube. Shows times vary. Admission £5-£50. Map p163 L8.

Not strictly a comedy venue (it hosts music and theatre too), the Leicester Square Theatre's basement space is nonetheless home to enjoyable regular comedy nights and Edinburgh Fringe previews, while the 400-seat main house is a favourite room for big names (Stewart Lee, Jerry Sadowitz and Doug Stanhope often play long runs).

Up the Creek

302 Creek Road, Greenwich, SE10 9SW (8858 4581, www.up-the-creek.com). Cutty Sark DLR. Open 7.30-11pm Thur, Sun; 8-11pm Fri; 7-11pm Sat. After-party 11pm-2am Fri, Sat. Admission £8-10 Fri; £12-£14 Sat; £4-£7 Sun. After-party £5. Map p281 Aa14.

Set up by the late and legendary alt-comedian Malcolm Hardee in the 1990s, this purpose-built comedy club is still one of the capital's best. The atmosphere is lively: it's less of a bearpit than it used to be, but the locals aren't afraid to torment comics – if a punter thinks of something funnier than what's being said on stage, they will shout it out. The Sunday Special (www.sundayspecial.co.uk) has a more relaxed vibe, cheap tickets and often features arena-filling names testing new material.

Performing Arts

Crave the food of love? Love the smell of the greasepaint? London's the place for you

London's classical musicians seem unusually open-minded, with classical nights in pubs and jazz strands at august classical auditoriums. But as well as this mix-and-match aesthetic, passionate purists remain – the Barbican and Royal Festival Hall still deliver a big orchestral punch with the traditional repertoire. Music of a different stripe dominates the West End theatres too, where musicals remain the biggest attraction.

That's not to say there's no 'proper' drama: a string of recent successes began life in the National Theatre, the city's flagship publicly funded theatre, as well as at smaller venues such as the Donmar and the Young Vic. What's more, Shakespeare's Globe offers a very different theatrical experience.

Although there are some concerns about a lack of home-grown talent in the ranks of stellar performers in London, the city remains a hub for dance in a way few other cities can match. Even the 85-year-old Royal Ballet produces groundbreaking new work.

Circa's Depart in LIFT 2016

CLASSICAL MUSIC & OPERA

London's classical scene has never looked or sounded more current, with the **Southbank Centre**, the **Barbican Centre** and **Kings Place** all working with strong programmes – although, arguably, less impressive acoustics (*see p356*). Even the once-stuffy **Royal Opera House** (*see p368*) now leavens its programme with occasional commissions, such as Mark-Anthony Turnage's daring opera *Anna Nicole* (2011), the tragic tale of a *Playboy* model and her ancient sugar-daddy. And despite recent troubled times at **English National Opera** (*see p357*), the company has still commissioned and produced top-class work from British composers, such as Ryan Wigglesworth's *The Winter's Tale* (2017) and Tansy Davies' *Between Worlds*, an opera about the events of 9/11 that saw its debut at the Barbican in 2015.

Tickets and information

Tickets for most classical and opera events are available direct from the venues, online or by phone. It's always advisable to book ahead. Several venues, such as the Barbican Centre and Southbank Centre, operate standby schemes, offering unsold tickets at cut-rate prices just before the show. They also have reduced-price tickets for under-26s.

Classical venues

In addition to the major venues below, you can hear what tomorrow's classical music might sound like at the city's music schools, which stage regular concerts by pupils and visiting professionals. Check the websites of the **Royal College of Music** (7591 4314, www.rcm.ac.uk) – which is spending £25 million on two new performance spaces – the **Royal Academy of Music** (7873 7373, www.ram.ac.uk), the **Guildhall School of Music & Drama** (7628 2571, www.gsmd.

In the know
Milton Court

The most recent addition to London's larger concert venues opened in 2013 barely 100 yards from the main external entrance to the Barbican. **Milton Court** (1 Milton Street, EC2Y 9BH, 7628 2571, www.gsmd.ac.uk) is run by the Guildhall School of Music & Drama and includes a 608-seat concert hall and two smaller theatres.

ac.uk) and **Trinity Laban Conservatoire of Music & Dance** (8305 4444, www.trinitylaban.ac.uk). There's also a trend for top-class classical and contemporary classical music in relaxed – for which read 'alcohol friendly' – settings (*see right*).

Barbican Centre
Silk Street, the City, EC2Y 8DS (information 7638 4141, tickets 7638 8891, www.barbican.org.uk). Barbican tube or Moorgate tube/rail. **Box office** *10am-8pm Mon-Sat; 11am-8pm Sun.* **Tickets** *£10-£70.* **Map** *p212 Q6.*

Europe's largest multi-arts centre is easier to navigate after a renovation – although 'easier' still isn't quite the same as 'with ease', so allow a little extra time to get to your seat. The programming remains as rich as ever, and the London Symphony Orchestra, with Sir Simon Rattle its new music director from September 2017, remains in residence. The BBC Symphony Orchestra also performs an annual series of concerts, including the weekend composer portrait Total Immersion, and there's a laudable amount of contemporary classical music, not least an ambitious ENO production in 2015 covering the events of 9/11. Beyond classical, programming falls into a wide range of genres from Sufi music to New York rock legends.

Cadogan Hall
5 Sloane Terrace, off Sloane Street, Chelsea, SW1X 9DQ (7730 4500, www.cadoganhall.com). Sloane Square tube. **Box office** *Non-performance days 10am-6pm Mon-Sat. Performance days 10am-8pm Mon-Sat; noon-6pm Sun.* **Tickets** *£15-£50.* **Map** *p122 H11.*

Jazz groups and rock bands have been attracted by the acoustics in this renovated former Christian Science church, but the programming at the austere yet comfortable 950-seat hall is dominated by classical. The Royal Philharmonic is resident; other orchestras also perform, and there's regular chamber music.

Kings Place
90 York Way, King's Cross, N1 9AG (7520 1490, www.kingsplace.co.uk). King's Cross-St Pancras tube/rail. **Box office** *noon-8pm Mon, Wed-Sat; noon-5pm Tue; noon-7pm Sun.* **Tickets** *free-£50.* **Map** *p194 M3.*

Once a lone pioneer in the revival of King's Cross, Kings Place suddenly finds itself part of the King's Cross Central cultural hub. Beneath seven office floors and a ground-floor restaurant-bar (with prized seats on the canal basin outside), the 415-seat main hall is a beauty, dominated by wood carved from a single, 500-year-old oak tree and ringed by

Pub Classical

Classical music, but without the frosty penguin suits

The vibrancy of London's classical music scene can hardly be doubted, but when you find yourself among reverent octogenarians at some London venues, you may feel you have to be on your best behaviour. Not so at the Orchestra of the Age of Enlightenment's popular series of **Night Shift** concerts (www. oae.co.uk/thenightshift), at which you'll see a far younger audience, perhaps belting out drinking songs by Purcell – with lyrics not fit for publication in a family guidebook. The idea is to gather a small group of performers in the relaxed setting of a pub – the **Old Queen's Head** (see p342) and **George Tavern** (373 Commercial Road, Stepney, E1 0LA, 7790 7335, www.thegeorgetavern.co.uk) are regular hosts – to perform canonical composers such as Mozart, Haydn and Handel. There's no shying away from difficult pieces: the professional and seriously talented performers trust that the combination of

their skill and enthusiasm with the familiar setting will win new audiences to the classical music they love.

Arguably the pioneer of this informal classical scene is one Gabriel Prokofiev, grandson of the Russian composer. He founded **Nonclassical** (www.nonclassical. co.uk), which mixes contemporary classical music and DJs in a combination of 'proper' classical venues (**Kings Place**, see p346), clubs (**XOYO**, see p343; **Hoxton Square Bar & Kitchen**, see p346) and, yes, pubs (**Shacklewell Arms**, see p347).

If you like it urban, check out contemporary music venue **Café Oto** (see p349), where Kammer Klang hosts a monthly cutting-edge classical night. Keep an eye out too for the annual summer series from **Multi-Story Orchestra** (www.multi-story.org.uk), keeping it real with performances in a high-rise car park in Peckham.

invisible rubber pads that kill unwanted noise that might interfere with the immaculate acoustics. There's also a versatile second hall and a number of smaller rooms for workshops and lectures. The programming is tremendous and includes curated weeks featuring composers as wide-ranging as atonalist Arnold Schoenberg and jazzer Kit Downes. Other strands include chamber music and experimental classical, and there are spoken-word events too.

LSO St Luke's

*UBS & LSO Music Education Centre, 161 Old Street, the City, EC1V 9NG (information 7490 3939, tickets 7638 8891, www.lso. co.uk/lsostlukes). Old Street tube/rail. **Box office** (at the Barbican Centre) 10am-8pm Mon-Sat; 11am-8pm Sun. **Tickets** free-£40. **Map** p212 Q5.*

Built by Nicholas Hawksmoor in the 18th century, this Grade I-listed church was beautifully converted into a performance and rehearsal space by the LSO several years ago. The orchestra occasionally welcomes the public for open rehearsals (book ahead); the more formal side of the programme takes in global sounds alongside classical music, including lunchtime concerts every Thursday that are broadcast on BBC Radio 3.

▶ *Intrigued by St Luke's obelisk spire? Hawksmoor also designed the brutal spike of Christ Church Spitalfields (see p258) and the mini-ziggurat atop St George's Bloomsbury (see p199).*

Royal Albert Hall

*Kensington Gore, South Kensington, SW7 2AP (7589 8212, www.royalalberthall.com). South Kensington tube or bus 9, 10, 52, 360, 452. **Box office** 9am-9pm daily. **Tickets** £15-£275. **Map** p122 E10.*

In constant use since opening in 1871, with boxing matches, motor shows and Allen Ginsberg's 1965 International Poetry Incarnation among the headline events, the Royal Albert Hall continues to host a very broad programme. The classical side is dominated by the superb BBC Proms (see p314), which runs every night for two months in summer and sees a huge array of orchestras and other ensembles battling the difficult acoustics. It's well worth catching a concert that features the thunderous Grand Organ.

In the know
Pipe up

If the 9,999 pipes of the Royal Albert Hall's Grand Organ were laid end to end they would reach nine miles. The largest pipe is 2ft 6 wide and weighs nearly a tonne; the smallest is as wide as a drinking straw.

St James's Piccadilly

*197 Piccadilly, Piccadilly, W1J 9LL (7381 0441, www.sjp.org.uk). Piccadilly Circus tube. **Box office** 10am-5pm Mon-Sat; 10am-6pm performance days. **Tickets** free-£28. **Map** p140 K8.*

Hear, here

Where in London will you find classical music performed at its best?

Ever since Sir Simon Rattle signed on the dotted line for the London Symphony Orchestra, one has wondered if the superstar conductor will sheepishly try to avoid eye contact with Barbican management in the lift following his comments that the acoustic of the complex's concert hall (and LSO base) is merely 'serviceable' and, due to size constraints and want of an organ, its stage cannot accommodate 20 per cent of the orchestral repertoire. A few years ago, this looked a minor issue, with the then Chancellor of the Exchequer, George Osborne, promising London a new world-class symphony hall. Then came Brexit, a new prime minister, a new chancellor and the withdrawal of the Tories' £5m budget for a business plan. Even Rattle, still optimistic, concedes that a new symphony hall is now more an 'if' than a 'when'.

His appointment generated the sort of media excitement that once surrounded the activities of his illustrious conducting forebears. The news of Rattle's homecoming in September 2017 came at the end of his long-ago sold-out Berlin Philharmonic concerts at the **Barbican** (see p354) and **Royal Festival Hall** (see p357). The series made front-page news and created a buzz of the rare kind that spreads even beyond classical music circles. He is, therefore, exactly what the sector needs to re-establish classical music as a prestigious cultural force.

But is he right? Are London's concert halls just serviceable? Well, yes. Barbican Hall owns the best, albeit flat, orchestral acoustic, followed by the RFH's uneven one, but neither are a match for Berlin's Philharmonie or even Birmingham's Symphony Hall (built to accommodate Rattle and his sharply honed CBSO in 1991). The BBC Proms, for instance, take place at the **Royal Albert Hall** (see p355), which is suitable for large orchestras and solo pianists, but not for medium-sized bands or Baroque music. Other colossi include **St Paul's Cathedral** (see p224), which hosts LSO concerts: a gorgeous venue, but – with a delay of over nine seconds and a transept rather than an auditorium – far from ideal.

The city is much better served at the smaller end of the scale. **Wigmore Hall** (see p357) is the pre-eminent chamber venue and the only one (along with the **Royal Opera House**, see p358) to hold its own internationally; although, since 2008, a runner-up can be found in Hall One at **Kings Place** (see p354). Meanwhile, **Cadogan Hall** (see p354), a former church, is the right size for Baroque music, though is curiously home to the mighty Royal Philharmonic Orchestra. Mercifully, the Southbank Centre's **Queen Elizabeth Hall** and **Purcell Room** (for both, p357), currently closed for refurbishment, will reopen in April 2018 and should re-emerge with warmer acoustics, while the most recent addition to the performance circuit, **Milton Court Concert Hall** at the Barbican, is a 600-seat auditorium with a bright response.

This community-spirited Wren church holds free 50-minute lunchtime recitals (1.10pm Mon, Wed, Fri; suggested donation £3.50) and offers regular evening concerts covering a variety of musical styles.

St John's Smith Square

Smith Square, Westminster, SW1P 3HA (7222 1061, www.sjss.org.uk). Westminster tube. **Box office** *Non-performance days 10am-5pm Mon-Sat. Performance days 10am-6pm Mon-Sat.* **Tickets** *free-£28.* **Map** *p100 L11.*

St John's is a curiously shaped 18th-century church – it is said that the four-turret design was the result of Queen Anne's demand

In the know
Time Out

Check the free *Time Out* magazine for the performing arts highlights of the week, or visit www.timeout.com for comprehensive cultural listings.

that architect Thomas Archer make it look like a footstool that she had kicked over – which hosts concerts most nights, as well as Thursday lunchtime recitals. Everything from symphony orchestras to solo recitals make the most of its good acoustics. Down in the crypt are two bars for interval drinks and the Footstool Restaurant.

St Martin-in-the-Fields

Trafalgar Square, Westminster, WC2N 4JH (7766 1100, www.stmartin-in-the-fields. org). Charing Cross tube/rail. **Box office** *In person 8am-5pm Mon, Tue; 8am-9.15pm Wed; 8am-8.45pm Thur, Fri; 8am-8.30pm Sat. By phone 10am-5pm Mon-Sat.* **Tickets** *free-£30.* **Map** *p100 M8.*

One of the capital's most amiable venues, St Martin's hosts populist performances of the likes of Bach, Mozart and Vivaldi by candlelight, jazz in the crypt's improved café and lunchtime recitals (1pm Mon, Tue, Fri) from young musicians. There's a fine atmosphere in the beautifully restored interior.

▶ *For more on the church, see p103.*

Southbank Centre
Belvedere Road, South Bank, SE1 8XX (7960 4200, www.southbankcentre.co.uk). Embankment tube or Waterloo tube/rail. **Box office** *In person 10am-8pm daily. By phone 9am-8pm daily.* **Tickets** *£7-£75.* **Map** *p78 N9.*

The centrepiece of the cluster of cultural venues collectively known as the Southbank Centre is the 2,500-seat **Royal Festival Hall**, which was renovated acoustically and externally to the tune of £90m back in 2007; now the neighbouring 900-seat **Queen Elizabeth Hall** and attached 365-seat **Purcell Room** are getting a little TLC and will reopen after refurbishment in early 2018. All three programme a wide variety of events – spoken word, jazz, rock and pop gigs – but classical is very well represented. The RFH has four resident orchestras (the London Philharmonic and Philharmonia Orchestras, the London Sinfonietta and the Orchestra of the Age of Enlightenment), and hosts music from medieval motets to Messiaen via Beethoven and Elgar. Beneath this main hall, facing the foyer bar, a stage puts on hundreds of free concerts each year.

Wigmore Hall
36 Wigmore Street, Marylebone, W1U 2BP (information 7258 8200; tickets 7935 2141, www.wigmore-hall.org.uk). Bond Street tube. **Box office** *Non-performance days 10am-7pm Mon-Sat; 10am-2pm Sun. Performance days 10am-7pm daily.* **Tickets** *free-£35.* **Map** *p140 J6.*

Built in 1901 as the display hall for Bechstein pianos, this world-renowned, 550-seat concert venue has perfect acoustics for the 460 concerts that take place each year. Music from the classical and romantic periods are mainstays, usually performed by major classical stars to an intense audience, but under artistic director John Gilhooly there has been a broadening in the remit: more baroque and jazz (with heavyweights like Brad Mehldau), including late-night gigs. Monday lunchtime recitals are broadcast live on BBC Radio 3.

▶ *The nearby Steinway showroom (44 Marylebone Lane, Marylebone, W1U 2DB, 7487 3391, http://steinway.co.uk/latest-news/concert-schedule) hosts regular recitals.*

Coliseum

Opera venues
In addition to the two big venues listed below, look out for performances at **Cadogan Hall** (*see p354*); summer's **Opera Holland Park** (*see p313*); sporadic appearances by **English Touring Opera** (www.englishtouringopera.org.uk); and much promising work, often directed by big names, at the city's music schools. When it opens in September 2018, the Linbury Studio, downstairs at the Royal Opera House, will be good for more experimental work. A small but lively fringe opera scene has sprung up, with **Hampstead Garden Opera** (www.hgo.org.uk) now operating from Jackson's Lane theatre (8341 4421, 269a Archway Road, N6 5AA); **Pop-Up Opera** (www.popupopera.co.uk) tours taking in weird and wonderful venues; **OperaUpClose** (www.operaupclose.com) occasionally caught up west at the Soho Theatre; **Charles Court Opera** (www.charlescourtopera.com) doing fine operetta in various small theatres; and the annual **Tête à Tête** (www.tete-a-tete.org.uk), which claims to be 'the world's largest festival of new opera', (it programmes 80 performances over three weeks), now settled in King's Cross.

English National Opera, Coliseum
St Martin's Lane, Covent Garden, WC2N 4ES (7845 9300, www.eno.org). Leicester Square tube or Charing Cross tube/rail. **Box office** *10am-6pm Mon-Sat.* **Tickets** *£12-£155.* **Map** *p181 M8.*

Built as a music hall in 1904, the home of the English National Opera (ENO) is in a rocky patch. It was put under 'special funding arrangements' in early 2015; then new music director Mark Wigglesworth, taking over from respected predecessor Edward Gardner, resigned after just six months. He has, in turn, been replaced by eminent conductor Martin Brabbins – at least the announcement that prices had been reduced to £20 and under on 60,000 seats made more positive headlines. The ENO has offered some fascinating collaborations over the last few years: physical theatre troupe Complicité and former Python Terry Gilliam directing Berlioz's *Benvenuto Cellini*, for instance, and Bryn Terfel with Emma Thompson in Sondheim's *Sweeney Todd*. There have also been stagings of rare contemporary works (Ligeti's *Le Grand Macabre*, Glass's *Akhnaten*). But 2012 scheme 'Opera Undressed', encouraging new, younger audience members to attend some classic operas in their everyday clothes, have a drink and enjoy a pre-performance talk, may yet prove to be ENO's most important initiative. All works are in English, and prices are cheaper than at the Royal Opera.

▶ *The £20 Secret Seat offer allows you to book an unallocated seat online – the secret lies in its location in the auditorium. Wherever it turns out to be, your seat will always be worth at least £30.*

Royal Opera, Royal Opera House

Bow Street, Covent Garden, WC2E 9DD (7304 4000, www.roh.org.uk). Covent Garden tube. Box office 10am-8pm Mon-Sat. Tickets £4-£200. Map p181 M7.

Thanks to a refurbishment at the start of the century, the Royal Opera House has once again taken its place among the ranks of the world's great opera houses – but it isn't enough: the £27m 'Open Up' redevelopment is making further infrastructural changes. Critics suggest that the programming at the Opera House can be a little spotty – especially so given the famously elevated ticket prices – but there is a solid spine to the programme: fine productions of the classics, often taking place under the assured baton of Sir Antonio Pappano. Productions take in favourite traditional operatic composers (Donizetti, Mozart, Verdi) and some modern (Mark-Anthony Turnage, Harrison Birtwistle), while the annual month-long Deloitte Ignite festival has filled the opera house with a wide range of free and ticketed events.

▶ *It's not just singing at the Opera House: the Royal Ballet is also based here; see p367.*

THEATRE

For the 13th consecutive year, 2016 saw London's major theatres make more money than they had the year before. The secret of this success is pretty much the same as it's always been – big-production musicals. The most ancient of these (**Les Misérables** and **The Phantom of the Opera**) have been hoofing it on the London stage since the mid 1980s. Of late, homegrown musicals have been rather overtaken by Broadway imports: **The Book of Mormon**, **Aladdin** and **Kinky Boots** are packing them in, and even Andrew Lloyd Webber's latest smash **School of Rock** did Broadway first. It's a trend that's set to continue with Broadway mega-smash **Hamilton** ready to wipe out the dinosaurs when it hits the West End in November 2017. But drama is booming at the moment too, in large part thanks to the efforts of super-producer Sonia Friedman, responsible for a host of pioneering transfers from London's peerless subsidised sector, and for a little play by the name of **Harry Potter and the Cursed Child**.

The **Donmar Warehouse** (*see p181*) traditionally lures high-profile film stars to perform at its tiny Earlham Street home. And while Kevin Spacey may no longer be in charge at the **Old Vic** (*see p361*), heavyweight director Matthew Warchus has proved an inspired replacement, with an eclectic and busy programme that finds room for plenty of big names.

On a smaller scale, Off-West End houses such as the **Young Vic** (*see p367*) and the **Almeida** (*see p364*) continue to produce some of London's most exciting, best-value theatre – much of which moves on to the West End – while the **Barbican Centre** (*see p354*) programmes visually exciting and physically expressive work from around the world.

Theatre districts

In strictly geographical terms, the **West End** refers to London's traditional theatre district, a busy area bounded by Shaftesbury Avenue, Drury Lane, the Strand and the Haymarket. Most major musicals and big-money dramas run here, alongside transfers of successful smaller-scale shows. However, the 'West End' appellation is now routinely applied to major theatres elsewhere in town, including a couple of big commercial theatres next to Victoria, the Old Vic (near Waterloo), plus subsidised venues such as the Barbican (in the City), the National Theatre (on the South Bank), the Royal Court (Sloane Square) and Shakespeare's Globe (Bankside).

Off-West End denotes theatres with smaller budgets and smaller capacities. These venues, many of them sponsored or subsidised, push the creative envelope with new writing, often brought to life by the best young acting and directing talent. The Almeida and Donmar Warehouse offer elegantly produced shows with the odd big star, while the likes of the Bush and Theatre Royal Stratford East bring bold new writing to less central boroughs.

The fringe

The best places to catch next-generation talent include Battersea's **Theatre 503** (503 Battersea Park Road, SW11 3BW, 7978 7040, http//:theatre503.com), above the Latchmere pub. The theatre above the **Finborough** (118 Finborough Road, SW10 9ED, 0844 847 1652, www.finboroughtheatre.co.uk), a pub in Earl's Court, attracts national critics with its small but perfectly formed revivals of forgotten classics. Other venues worth investigating include the **Yard** (*see p366*), a 130-seat venue near the Olympic Park, made from recycled materials and playing to a house of local hipsters; the **Southwark Playhouse** (77-85 Newington Causeway, Southwark, SE1 6BD, 7407 0234, www.southwarkplayhouse.co.uk); and the **Menier Chocolate Factory** (53 Southwark Street, Southwark, SE1 1RU, 7378 1713, www.menierchocolatefactory.com), which, like the **Union Theatre** (229 Union Street, Southwark, SE1 0LR, 7261 9876, www.uniontheatre.biz), has a knack for programming musicals that thrive up-close.

Buying tickets

If there's a specific show you want to see, aim to book ahead, especially if there's a risk of it selling out. If possible, always try to use the theatre or show's own website, which should minimise the sorts of booking fees that come with agents such as **Ticketmaster** (0333 321 9999, www.ticketmaster.co.uk). Shop around: different agencies offer different prices and discounts.

If you're more flexible about your choice of show or are happy to queue, consider buying from the **tkts** booth (The Lodge, Leicester Square, Soho, WC2H 7NA, www.tkts.co.uk), which sells tickets for big shows at much-reduced rates, either on the day or up to a week in advance. It opens at 10am (11am on Sundays); you can check which shows are available on the website. Before buying, be sure you're at the correct booth, in a stand-alone building on the south side of Leicester Square – the square is ringed with other ticket brokers, where the seats are worse and the prices higher.

Many West End theatres hold back a selection of day-seats for each performance, available at a knock-down price to the first customers there in person when the box office opens (usually 10am – but get there much earlier for anything sold out or popular).

Some theatres elect to distribute their day-seats by other means: the phone app **TodayTix** is growing in popularity as a means of dissemination, while **The Book of Mormon** (*see p361*) allocates seats by daily lottery.

Watch out, too, for cut-price Travelex tickets and the Friday Rush at the **National** (*see p363*), for 'groundling' tickets (standing) at the **Globe** (*see p360*) and for 'Secret Seats' at the **Coliseum** (*see p357*).

Major West End theatres

The **Barbican Centre** (*see p354*) continues to cherry-pick exciting and eclectic theatre companies from around the globe. Watch out, too, for imaginatively leftfield family-friendly theatre and installations during the school holidays.

♥ Shakespeare's Globe

21 New Globe Walk, Bankside, SE1 9DT (information 7902 1400, tickets 7401 9919, www.shakespearesglobe.com). Southwark tube or London Bridge tube/rail. **Box office** *10am-6pm daily & before events.* **Tickets** *£15-£100.* **Map** *p78 P8.*

Back in the 1990s, Sam Wanamaker – an American actor and director – dreamt a big dream: why not recreate the theatre where Shakespeare first staged many of his plays, using the original methods and materials? The amazing thing is that in 1997 this flight of fancy became, with a great deal of hard work and determination, a fabulously entertaining reality. Concessions were made along the way – the theatre is some 750 feet from the site of the original – but Wanamaker's conception resulted in an extraordinarily historically accurate facsimile, perched on the bank of the Thames, where Shakespeare is still performed in a theatre as close to the original Globe as could be imagined. After successful tenures as artistic director by Mark Rylance and Dominic Dromgoole, the Globe has had a weird time of late: Emma Rice's time in the post has been marked by popular success but clashes with a tradition-loving board who hated her extensive use of electric light and sound.

In the know
The real deal

The site of the original Globe is marked by a partial ring of stones in the ground on the south side of Park Street, should hardcore Shakespeare fans wish to seek it out. For guided tours of the Globe, *see p86.*

She duly departs in 2018 after just two years at the top, and it'll be fascinating to see who replaces her – the board isn't enjoying a huge amount of sympathy across the industry. Still, the job will surely be filled, because this is one of the greatest theatres in the country. It can also be the most affordable, with the open-air, standing-room pit sensational value at £5 a pop. Open April to October, the open-air main space is stunning, but the Globe's indoor Jacobean theatre, the **Sam Wanamaker Playhouse** (completed in 2014), is arguably even more atmospheric. The 340-seat space is made entirely out of wood, exquisitely decorated and lit by candles, just as the Blackfriars theatre that Shakespeare and his King's Men troupe moved to in 1609 would have been. It has a more eclectic programme than the outdoor space.

The Tempest

Old Vic

The Cut, Waterloo, SE1 8NB (0844 871 7628, www.oldvictheatre.com). Southwark tube or Waterloo tube/rail. Box office In person 10am-6pm Mon-Sat. By phone 9am-7.30pm Mon-Fri; 9am-4pm Sat; 9.30am-4pm Sun. Tickets £10-£90. Map p78 O10.

London's most famous artistic director, Kevin Spacey, moved out in 2015, but don't be fooled into thinking his less famous successor Matthew Warchus is some sort of step down. A seriously heavyweight director (he has been pencilled in to direct the Broadway adaptation of *Frozen*), Warchus has all of Spacey's celebrity pulling power, topped with a bolder, more eclectic approach to programming. His USP is heavyweight new musical work: his brilliant *Groundhog Day* had its tryout run at the Vic in 2016 before heading off to conquer Broadway, and an adaptation of Warchus' hit film *Pride* (2014) is said to be in the works.

Open Air Theatre

Regent's Park, Inner Circle, Marylebone, NW1 4NR (0844 826 4242, www. openairtheatre.com). Baker Street tube. Box office Non-performance days 11am-6pm daily. Performance days 11am-8pm daily. By phone 9am-9pm daily. Tickets £18-£60. Map pull out map H4.

This stunning alfresco theatre made its name as a house of Shakespeare, but under current artistic director Timothy Sheader musicals are much more the thing – its gritty revival of *Jesus Christ Superstar* was a big hit – combined with the odd bleak American drama and, yes, occasional Shakespeare still.

▶ *If you don't want to bring a picnic, book one at the venue, which can be pre-ordered with reserved seating (£49.50 for two people). Alternatively, good-value, tasty food can be bought at the Garden Café.*

Royal Court Theatre

Sloane Square, Chelsea, SW1W 8AS (7565 5000, www.royalcourttheatre.com). Sloane Square tube. Box office 10am-6pm Mon-Sat. Tickets £12-£40. Map p122 H12.

From John Osborne's *Look Back in Anger*, staged in the theatre's opening year of 1956, to the more recent likes of Jez Butterworth, Simon Stephens and debbie tucker green, the emphasis at the Royal Court has always been on new voices in British and international theatre. Since Vicky Featherstone took over as artistic director (the first woman in the role) in 2013, the shows have got artier, though there's still room for established names, including the legendary Caryl Churchill. Expect to find punchy, socially engaged new work by first-time and international

playwrights upstairs, and bigger, state-of-the-nation works by household names downstairs.

Royal Shakespeare Company

01789 403493, www.rsc.org.uk. Box office By phone 10am-6pm Mon-Sat. Tickets £12-£70.

Britain's most famous theatre company hasn't had an official London base since it quit the Barbican in 2002 and it doesn't seem to be in a hurry to find itself one, with its temporary venue of choice being... the Barbican. Its only permanent London showing is the musical *Matilda* (*see p364*), still packing 'em in the best part of a decade after it opened, but each year there's a season of stellar Shakespeare in the capital: the likes of Simon Russell Beale in *The Tempest* or a tetralogy of the Roman plays.

Long-runners & musicals

It's a perilous task predicting which West End shows will run and which will close: homegrown musicals, in particular, have not performed well since *Matilda*. And then there are wild cards like *The Play that Goes Wrong*, a lo-fi fringe comedy that's now been resident in the West End for years. We reckon the following will hang around – though probably none as long as the weary but never bowed *Mousetrap* (St Martin's Theatre, West Street, Cambridge Circus, WC2H 9NZ, 7836 1443, www.the-mousetrap. co.uk), the Agatha Christie drawing-room whodunnit that has been running continuously in the West End since 1952. For a quick tour round other shows, *see p365*.

Aladdin

Prince Edward Theatre, 28 Old Compton Street, Soho, W1D 4HS (0871 716 7960, www. aladdinthemucical.co.uk). Victoria tube/rail. Box office 10am-7.45pm Mon-Sat. Tickets £25-£97.50. Map p163 L7.

Disney's second big-hit London musical (after the undying *Lion King*) is a panto-like affair greatly enlivened by a couple of jaw-dropping set pieces and the presence of US star Trevor Dion Nicholas, who is sensational as the Genie, and shows no sign of leaving as the show enters its second year.

The Book of Mormon

Prince of Wales Theatre, Coventry Street, Soho, W1D 6AS (0844 482 5110, www. bookofmormonlondon.com). Piccadilly Circus tube. Box office 10am-8pm Mon-Sat. Tickets £20-£150. Map p163 L8.

South Park creators Trey Parker and Matt Stone's smash musical about the absurdities

❤ National Theatre

South Bank, SE1 9PX (7452 3000, www. nationaltheatre.org.uk). Embankment or Southwark tube, or Waterloo tube/ rail. **Box office** *9.30am-8pm Mon-Sat.* **Tickets** *£15-£52.* **Map** *p78 N9.*

A still-startling jewel of brutalist design, the National is surely the world's greatest theatre. Nobody would say it gets everything right, but it is worthy of a pilgrimage for anybody remotely interested in the arts. Having passed its 50th anniversary in 2013, the National first completed a major programme of expansion and upgrades, then waved goodbye to its hugely appreciated artistic director, Nicholas Hytner, who had been in the post since 2003 (watch out for his new venue, the Bridge Theatre, due to open in late 2017). It was the end of a certain sort of golden age: Hytner rescued the NT from the doldrums, launching endless hit transfers to the West End, got Travelex to sponsor tickets to bring down the prices, and adroitly balanced the programme to mix big, crowd-pleasing stuff by Shakespeare and household names like Alan Bennett with some startling new work and some properly obscure rediscoveries. His landmark successes – Alan Bennett's *The History Boys* and *War Horse*, both of which went on to become successful movies – showed that the state-subsidised home of British theatre could turn out quality drama at a profit, furnishing an array of West End hits.

Successor Rufus Norris has had a slightly more difficult time of it. His high-powered Chief Executive Tessa Ross departed after a few months, citing the NT's power structure as an issue. Big West End money-spinner *War Horse* finally closed, and *The Curious Incident of the Dog in the Night-Time* followed suit, with no obvious sign of replacements. Meanwhile, the theatre's Arts Council subsidy is on the wane as the government's austerity programme continues. The press has been occasionally unkind, criticising Norris for everything from staging work that's too weird to putting on too much new writing. He has taken the theatre slightly to the left, but the change has perhaps been overstated: productions range from top-notch Shakespeare and new plays to reworked foreign classics and British revivals. Truth be told, the programming doesn't look drastically different to the Hytner era, even if the names of the directors are a little avant-garde these days (think international stars like Ivo van Hove and Yael Farber) and the audiences are perhaps a splash younger. If a new West End hit remains elusive, that's not for want of popular, agenda-setting productions, with a starry revival of Tony Kushner's epic *Angels in America* and van Hove's take on the

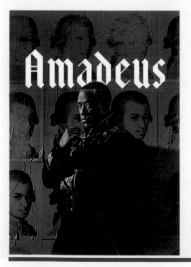

classic '70s film *Network*, starring *Breaking Bad*'s Bryan Cranston, keeping the returns queue busy throughout 2017. The Travelex seasons continue, widening audiences by offering tickets for £15, as does the free outdoor performing arts River Stage, held outside the NT during the summer.

Despite the substantial revamps to the building – new restaurants, a new bar, a new main entrance on the riverside (at long last), the old Cottesloe Theatre revamped into the larger, more high-tech Dorfman – in many ways the real story of the theatre over the last decade has taken place off-site. Its NT Live programme of live screenings of plays to cinemas has brought the National's repertoire into every town in the country. It's an astonishing, game-changing achievement that we're probably still digesting. There are concerns about what it means for regional and touring theatre, but at the moment the NT is 'national' in a way it never truly was before.

In the know
Friday Rush

The NT launched a new initiative in 2015: Friday Rush. At 1pm each Friday, a small number of £20 tickets for the next week's performances in the Olivier, Lyttelton and Dorfman are released for purchase online.

War Horse

---

of Mormonism is not as shocking as you might expect. There's lots of swearing and close-to-the-bone jokes, but beneath it all, this is a big-hearted affair that pays note-perfect homage to the spirit and sounds of Broadway's golden age. And it's very, very funny.

The Girls
Phoenix Theatre, 104-110 Charing Cross Road, Soho, WC2H 0JP (0207 639 1733, www.thegirlsmusical.com). Leicester Square tube. **Box office** *In person 10am-8pm Mon.* **Tickets** *£29.50-£69.50.* **Map** *p181 L7.*

This year's biggest new Brit musical marks the West End debut of Take That's Gary Barlow, who co-writes with his old friend Tim Firth. It's an adaptation of the film *Calendar Girls*, which was also written by Firth, as was a previous non-musical West End stage version. This story of a Yorkshire Women's Institute baring all for a charity calendar is pretty cheesy, but Barlow's name is quite the USP.

Hamilton
Victoria Palace Theatre, Victoria Street, Victoria, SW1E 5EA (0844 248 5138, www. hamiltonthemusical.co.uk). Victoria tube. **Box office** *10am-7.45pm Mon-Sat.* **Tickets** *£37.50-£190.* **Map** *p100 J11.*

From the moment it opens in November 2017, the expectation is that Lin-Manuel Miranda's Broadway-devouring rap musical will be equally unstoppable here. Certainly it has little competition: rival producers are so scared of *Hamilton's* success that barely any new musicals were launched in the months prior to its arrival in the West End.

Harry Potter and the Cursed Child
Palace Theatre, Shaftesbury Avenue, Soho, W1D 5AY (0844 412 4656, www. harrypottertheplaylondon.com). Leicester Square tube. **Box office** *In person 10am-6pm Mon-Sat.* **Tickets** *£15-£65 (1 part); £30-£130 (both parts).* **Map** *p163 L7.*

The final adventure in JK Rowling's Harry Potter series isn't a book or a film, but a monumentally ambitious two-part London stage play, written by Jack Thorne in collaboration with Rowling. John Tiffany's production is phenomenal, as close as you'll ever get to physically stepping into Harry's magical world – small wonder it won a record *nine* Olivier Awards in 2017. Of course, it's sold out till the last trump blows, but you don't need magic to get in – there's a weekly online sale at 1pm on Fridays (the Friday Forty) and the returns queue is worth a shot.

Harry Potter and the Cursed Child *p363*

Matilda the Musical

*Cambridge Theatre, 32-34 Earlham Street, Covent Garden, WC2H 9HU (0844 412 4652, www.matildathemusical.com). Covent Garden tube or Charing Cross tube/rail. **Box office** In person from 10am Mon-Sat. By phone 10am-6pm Mon-Sat. **Tickets** £20-£122.50. **Map** p181 M7.*

Adapted from Roald Dahl's riotous children's novel, with songs by superstar Aussie comedian Tim Minchin, this RSC transfer received rapturous reviews on its first outing in Stratford-upon-Avon and has been going strong ever since, winning multiple Olivier awards.

Les Misérables

*Queen's Theatre, 51 Shaftesbury Avenue, Soho, W1D 6BA (0844 482 5160, www. lesmis.com). Leicester Square or Piccadilly Circus tube. **Box office** In person 10am-8pm Mon-Sat. By phone 24hrs daily. **Tickets** £12.50-£97.25. **Map** p163 L8.*

The RSC's version of Boublil and Schönberg's musical first came to the London stage in 1985. Having recently had its score reworked and gently nudged out of the '80s – plus a massive commercial shot in the arm from the successful 2012 film version – it looks like it's going to stick around for a good while longer. It's not the freshest show in town, but the voices remain lush, the revolutionary sets are film-fabulous, and the lyrics and score (based on Victor Hugo's novel) will be considerably less trivial than whatever's on next door.

The Play that Goes Wrong

*Duchess Theatre, 3-5 Catherine Street, Covent Garden, WC2B 5LA (0844 482 9672, www.theplaythatgoeswrong. com). Charing Cross tube/rail. **Tickets** £20-£65. **Map** p181 N7.*

Is it a classic British comedy in the lineage of *Fawlty Towers*? Or a low-budget rip-off of Michael Frayn's immortal backstage farce *Noises Off*? Maybe a little of both, but, whatever the case, it's impossible not to be delighted by the success of this play, which began life at the tiny Old Red Lion theatre pub and has now been sitting pretty in the West End since 2014. It even has its own seasonal spin-off, *Peter Pan Goes Wrong*.

Off-West End theatres

Almeida

*Almeida Street, Islington, N1 1TA (information 7288 4900, tickets 7359 4404, www.almeida.co.uk). Angel tube. **Box office** 10am-7pm Mon-Sat. **Tickets** £10-£38.*

Since Rupert Goold took over as artistic director in 2013, the Almeida has been reinvented from something rather chintzy to London's hippest theatre, the leftfield programming doing nothing to staunch a seemingly endless stream of acclaimed shows that headed into the West End: *Chimerica*, *1984*, *King Charles III*, *Oresteia* and *Hamlet* are all recent transfer hits. The secrets of the Almeida's success are many: Goold's sheer audacity ranks up there, while associate director Robert Icke is probably the most exciting director of his generation. A dud is incredibly rare here: if you can bag a ticket, you should go.

Battersea Arts Centre (BAC)

*Lavender Hill, Battersea, SW11 5TN (7223 2223, www.bac.org.uk). Clapham Common tube, Clapham Junction rail/Overground or bus 77, 77A, 345. **Box office** 10am-6pm Mon-Sat. **Tickets** £5-£25; pay what you can.*

Housed in the old Battersea Town Hall, the forward-thinking BAC hit the headlines for the wrong reasons in 2015, when it suffered a major fire. Fund-raising efforts showed the esteem felt for the theatre, which has been able to continue its programme of quirky, fun and physical theatre from young companies and from more-established names pursuing new directions. Repairs are going well (fortunately it had insurance).

Donmar Warehouse

*41 Earlham Street, Covent Garden, WC2H 9LX (0844 871 7624, www. donmarwarehouse.com). Covent Garden or Leicester Square tube. **Box office** 10am-6pm Mon-Fri. **Tickets** £7.50-£35. **Map** p181 M7.*

It may be central London's smallest major theatre, but the Donmar's influence outstrips its size many times over. Run by Sam Mendes

The Best of the West End

A selection of shows from London's theatreland

Seen the film?
We could fill this list with the names of homegrown film adaptations that didn't go the distance: not *Ghost*, not *Dirty Dancing*, not *The Full Monty*, not Tim Rice's huge-budget *From Here to Eternity*, not *Bend It Like Beckham*, not even *Made in Dagenham* with the winsome Gemma Arterton. Even *Billy Elliot* finally danced off the stage in 2016. Tim Minchin's adaptation of *Groundhog Day* was excellent – it won the Olivier Awards for Best New Musical and Best Musical Actor in 2017 – but it played only a limited season before heading to Broadway. It seems you have to have been a hit on Broadway first: *Kinky Boots* is set in a Northampton shoe factory, but is somehow an American show (songs by Cyndi Lauper), and Andrew Lloyd Webber's *School of Rock* received his best reviews since the '80s but only after cracking Broadway first. Also worthy of your time are the high-camp *Mamma Mia!* and Disney's two shows, *Aladdin* and *The Lion King* – slightly patchy affairs buoyed by the odd jaw-dropping visual sequence.

Read the book?
Two very different tales of oppressed but gifted children (*Matilda* and *Harry Potter and the Cursed Child*; for both, see p364) pretty much represent the pinnacle of British commercial theatre in their own way: the former a sassy, inventive musical take on Dahl from comic Tim Minchin and the RSC; the latter the visually stunning, two-part, eighth adventure for JK Rowling's wizard Harry Potter – he's all grown up, but his son Albus is having a torrid time at Hogwarts.

Queen Sonia
The big, heartening West End success story of the last few years is Sonia Friedman. Formerly of the Royal Court (see p361), the superproducer is now a sort of living link between London's vibrant new writing theatres and the grand old West End. Her great early success was two seasons at the Apollo for Jez Butterworth's epochal *Jerusalem* – a transfer from the Royal Court. Since then she's established a firm reputation for daring transfers and staging original commercial work with hot off-West End talent. Recent hits include a *Hamlet* starring Andrew Scott, *The Ferryman* by Butterworth and, of course, *Harry Potter and the Cursed Child*. She's not above the odd musical, giving the iconic *Dreamgirls* a UK première a mere 35 years after its debut on Broadway.

Old faithfuls and revivals
Les Misérables (see p364) continues its indefatigable run, unbroken since the 1980s, with *Phantom of the Opera* not far behind it, and the creaky but genuinely unsettling *The Woman in Black* is only a couple of years younger. But you'd have to set the time-machine dial 30 years further into history to catch the première of the *Mousetrap*. Recently, some oldies have enjoyed renewed success (perhaps because any newbies have been frightened off by *Hamilton*, see p363), with lavish revivals of *42nd Street* and *An American in Paris* illuminating the West End with their old-fashioned Broadway glow in 2017.

then Michael Grandage, current boss Josie Rourke has made it her mission to steer the Donmar away from boutique productions of classics with big-name celebrities – though those are still here – and aim for a livelier, younger programme that is orientated more towards new writing.

Gate Theatre
Prince Albert, 11 Pembridge Road, Notting Hill Gate, W11 3HQ (7229 0706, www. gatetheatre.co.uk). Notting Hill Gate tube. **Box office** *By phone 10am-6pm Mon-Fri.* **Tickets** *£10-£20.*

A doll's house of a theatre (it has only 70 seats), with rickety wooden chairs, the Gate is the only producing theatre in London dedicated to international work.

Lyric Hammersmith
Lyric Square, King Street, Hammersmith, W6 0QL (8741 6850, www.lyric.co.uk). Hammersmith tube. **Box office** *9am-6pm Mon-Sat.* **Tickets** *£10-£40.*

Reopening in 2015 after a major facelift and the creation of an entirely new wing, the Lyric decided to launch with a new all-child-cast production of Alan Parker's *Bugsy Malone*, directed by artistic director Sean Holmes. It was revived again the following year, but the real heart of the Lyric lies with experimental and avant-garde work, as epitomised by associate artist Simon Stephens. The new two-storey extension to the hybrid modern/ Victorian theatre adds drama, dance and recording studios, a new café and bar, and even a cinema. Holmes had pledged to bring writers back into the building when he took over in 2009, and has already brought neglected modern classics and new plays to the stage – alongside the cutting-edge physical and devised work for which the Lyric had become known.

Park Theatre

Clifton Terrace, Finsbury Park, N4 3JP (7870 6876, www.parktheatre.co.uk). Finsbury Park tube/rail. Box office 10am-6pm Mon-Sat. In person 4-8pm Tue-Fri; 1-8pm Thur, Sat; also from the café. Tickets £12.50-£26.50.

Opened in 2013 in a former office building, this non-subsidised venue offers a busy off-West End programme across two spaces (a 200-seat main house and 90-seat studio), with a pleasant bar-café on the ground floor in which to chew over what you've seen. The shows are a mixed bag, but the theatre has certainly won some influential followers – Ian McKellen is due to perform a special one-man fundraiser show for the theatre in the summer of 2017.

Soho Theatre

21 Dean Street, Soho, W1D 3NE (7478 0100, www.sohotheatre.com). Tottenham Court Road tube. Box office 9am-9pm Mon-Fri; 1 hr before performance Sat . Tickets £9-£35. Map p163 L7.

Since it opened in 2000, the Soho Theatre has built a terrific reputation – with excellence across three inter-related genres: cabaret, comedy and, yes, theatre. It attracts a younger, hipper crowd than most London spaces, and brings on aspiring writers and youth theatre companies. After a few years finding its feet, it has settled in as a

producer of some of the best work to go to the Edinburgh Fringe, and has scored a notable success by launching the career of *Fleabag* creator Phoebe Waller-Bridge. In many ways the biggest draw is comedy: British and international talent has included Russell Brand, Michael McIntyre, Kristen Schaal and Doug Stanhope. The hard lines, low stage and packed table seating favour comedy over cabaret in the theatre's basement space, but the Soho consistently books outstanding talent from the international cabaret circuit for the room, from Meow Meow and Caroline Nin to London's own David Hoyle, Bourgeois & Maurice and the Tiger Lillies.

Theatre Royal Stratford East

Gerry Raffles Square, Stratford, E15 1BN (8534 0310, www.stratfordeast. com). Stratford tube/rail/DLR. Box office In person & by phone 10am-6pm Mon-Sat. Tickets £8-£26.

This is a community theatre, with many shows written, directed and performed by black or Asian artists. Musicals are big here – *The Harder They Come* went on to West End success a few years ago and, fittingly, the theatre restaged *Oh What a Lovely War* in early 2014 to mark the triple anniversary of the birth of the play (in this theatre), of its creator (iconoclastic director Joan Littlewood) and of the war it satirises – but there is also a fine annual Christmas pantomime and harder-hitting fare.

Tricycle

269 Kilburn High Road, Kilburn, NW6 7JR (information 7372 6611, tickets 7328 1000, www.tricycle.co.uk). Kilburn tube. Box office 10am-6pm Mon-Fri; 1hr before performance or until 6pm Sun. Tickets £9-£29.

Passionate and political, the Tricycle consistently finds original ways into difficult subjects. The theatre space is currently receiving a multimillion pound upgrade, but its cinema space will host the occasional show throughout 2017 before the grand reopening in 2018.

Wilton's Music Hall

Graces Alley, off Ensign Street, Whitechapel, E1 8JB (7702 2789, www.wiltons.org.uk). Aldgate East or Tower Hill tube. Box office 11am-6pm Mon-Fri. Tickets £6-£25.

One of London's last surviving examples of the giant music halls that flourished in the mid 19th century, Wilton's once entertained the masses with acts ranging from Chinese performing monkeys to acrobats, and from contortionists to opera singers. It was here that the can-can first scandalised London. Roughly 150 years later, Wilton's is Grade

II*-listed but again operating as a theatre, offering an atmospheric stage for everything from immersive theatre to situation-specific performances of Bach, cinema screenings and magic shows. There's major ongoing restoration, but the programme remains as packed as ever – and the bar is lively.

Young Vic

66 The Cut, Waterloo, SE1 8LZ (7922 2922, www.youngvic.org). Waterloo tube/ rail. **Box office** *10am-6pm Mon-Sat.* **Tickets** *£10-£57.* **Map** *p78 O9.*

As the name suggests, this Vic has more youthful bravura than its older sister up the road, and draws a younger crowd, who pack out the open-air balcony and its restaurant and bar on the weekends. They come to see European classics with a modern edge, new writing with an international flavour and collaborations with leading companies. Recent winners have included *Yerma*, an update of Lorca's play from Aussie director Simon Stone that included a paintstripper-intense turn from Billie Piper, while summer 2017 sees Sienna Miller star in Benedict Andrews' take on *Cat On a Hot Tin Roof*, which is going straight into the West End.

Puppet & children's theatres

Little Angel Theatre

14 Dagmar Passage, Cross Street, Islington, N1 2DN (7226 1787, littleangeltheatre. com). **Open Box office** *10am-6pm Mon-Fri; 10am-4pm Sat, Sun (from 9am when there is a morning performance).* **Tickets** *£8-£10.*

Tucked away in the back streets of Islington, Little Angel Theatre is a hub of passionate puppeteering activity. Established by South African John Wright in 1961, the Little Angel is London's only permanent puppet theatre and stages diverse productions devised here or by visiting companies. In a quaint twist that reveals the artifice behind the magic, the compact 100-seat theatre shares its space with the workshop where the marionettes are carved and developed. There's a Saturday Puppet Club and workshops and events to inspire the next generation of puppeteers. The shows are very much geared up for audiences of children, so expect to share the auditorium with chatty young'uns.

Puppet Theatre Barge

Opposite 35 Blomfield Road, Little Venice, W9 2PF (7249 6876, www.puppetbarge. com). Warwick Avenue tube. **Box office** *10am-6pm daily (later during evening performances).* **Tickets** *£12; £8.50-£10 reductions.* **Map** *pull-out D5.*

This intimate waterborne stage is the setting for quality puppet shows that put a modern twist on traditional tales, such as *Mr Rabbit Meets Brer Santa Claus* and *The Flight of Babuscha Baboon*. The barge is moored here between October and July; shows themselves are held at 3pm on Saturday and Sunday, and daily during school holidays, plus some matinées. During the summer (Aug-Sept), the barge also holds performances in Richmond.

Unicorn Theatre

147 Tooley Street, Bankside, SE1 2IIZ (7645 0560, www.unicorntheatre.com). London Bridge tube/rail. **Box office** *9.30am-6pm Mon-Sat.* **Tickets** *£9-£22; £7-£13 reductions.* **Map** *p78 S9.*

This light, bright building, with a huge white unicorn in the foyer, has two performance spaces. Its small ensemble company performs in all shows and focuses on an outreach programme for local children.

DANCE

London is the home of two long-established classical dance companies. The **Royal Ballet**, resident at the Royal Opera House, is a company of global stature, which managed to lure star Russian ballerina Natalia Osipova into its ranks. Contemporary premières have included Christopher Wheeldon's *The Winter's Tale* and Liam Scarlett's *Frankenstein*, while Wayne McGregor continues to choreograph extraordinary contemporary ballet. The Royal's (friendly) rival is **English National Ballet**, a touring company that performs most often at the Coliseum (*see p357*) and, for the regular *Swan Lake* 'in the round', at the **Royal Albert Hall** (*see p355*), but has recently expanded into venues more suitable to contemporary dance such as the **Barbican** (*see p354*) and **Sadler's Wells**. The ENB's busy artistic director, Tamara Rojo – also a principal dancer with the company – has breathed real vigour into the ENB, but caused controversy a few years back when bemoaning the lack of a work ethic among local dancers. On the contemporary side, choreographers Akram Khan, Hofesh Shechter and Lloyd Newson of DV8 Physical Theatre went further, suggesting that British ballet schools were failing to produce suitably rigorous dancers, creating a paucity of performers for their challenging work, a claim the schools naturally denied.

Major venues

The **Coliseum** (see *p357*) is home to the English National Ballet, but you'll also see performances there from the likes of the Peter Schaufuss Ballet and visiting Russian companies. The **Barbican** (*see p354*) attracts and nurtures experimental dance, especially in its perfectly intimate Pit Theatre, while London's other major multi-arts centre, the **Southbank Centre** (*see p357*) programmes everything from international contemporary dance and hip hop to South Asian dance at its cluster of venues.

Royal Opera House

For listings, see p358.

For the full ballet experience, nothing beats the Royal Opera House, home of the Royal Ballet. The current incarnation of the building is an appropriately grand space in which to see dreamy ballerinas including Marianela Nuñez and Lauren Cuthbertson. There's edgier fare in the Linbury Studio Theatre. Royal Ballet in Rehearsal sessions offer a rare – and thrillingly close-up – glimpse behind the scenes. The 90-minute sessions are held in the Clore Studio Upstairs, with a capacity of 175. This is ballet at its most stripped-down: no sets, no exquisite costumes and no grand stage. Instead, there's just the piano, the squeak of shoes on the scuffed grey floor, and the intense concentration of the dancers.

Sadler's Wells

Rosebery Avenue, Finsbury, EC1R 4TN (7863 8000, www.sadlerswells.com). Angel tube. **Box office** *10am-8pm Mon-Sat.* **Tickets** *£10-£65.* **Map** *pull-out O4.*

Built in 1998 on the site of a 17th-century theatre of the same name, this dazzling complex is home to impressive local and international performances of contemporary dance in all its guises. The Lilian Baylis Studio offers smaller-scale new works and works-in-progress; the Peacock Theatre (on Portugal Street in Holborn) operates as a satellite venue.

Smaller venues

Greenwich Dance

Borough Hall, Royal Hill, Greenwich, SE10 8RE (8293 9741, www. greenwichdance.org.uk). Greenwich DLR/ rail. **Box office** *9am-9pm Mon-Thur; 9am-5.30pm Fri; 9am-3pm Sat.* **Tickets** *free-£15.* **Map** *p281 Ab14.*

This art deco venue in Greenwich hosts classes and workshops and a regular tea dance, as well as unique cabaret nights, which deliver entertaining dance performances in short bursts. It has a partnership with Trinity Laban (*see right*).

The Place

17 Duke's Road, Bloomsbury, WC1H 9PY (7121 1100, www.theplace.org. uk). Euston tube/Overground/rail. **Box office** *10.30am-5.30pm Mon-Sat. Performance days 10.30am-7pm.* **Tickets** *£11-£14.* **Map** *p194 L4.*

For genuinely emerging dance, look to the Place, which is home to the London Contemporary Dance School and the Richard Alston Dance Company. The theatre is behind the biennial Place Prize for choreography (next in 2018), which rewards the best in British contemporary dance, as well as regular seasons showcasing new work, among them Resolution! (Jan/Feb) and Spring Loaded (Apr/May).

Trinity Laban Conservatoire

Laban Theatre, Creekside, Deptford, SE8 3DZ (8305 9400, tickets 8463 0100, www. trinitylaban. ac.uk). Deptford DLR or Greenwich DLR/rail. **Open** *10am-5.30pm Mon-Fri.* **Tickets** *free-£15.*

Founded in Manchester by innovative and influential movement theoretician Rudolf Laban (1879-1958), the Laban Centre joined forces in 2005 with Trinity College of Music to create the first ever UK conservatoire for music and dance. The centre was designed by Herzog & de Meuron of Tate Modern fame and features an impressive curving, multicoloured glass frontage. The striking premises include a 300-seat auditorium and are home to Transitions Dance Company.

▶ *Also in Deptford, the Albany (Douglas Way, SE8 4AG, 8692 4446, www.thealbany. org.uk) specialises in hip-hop theatre.*

Covent Garden

IT'S SHOWTIME

Book the best of the West End, from big-hitting musicals to brand new shows and all of our critics' top picks.

 TIMEOUT.COM/
LONDON/THEATRE

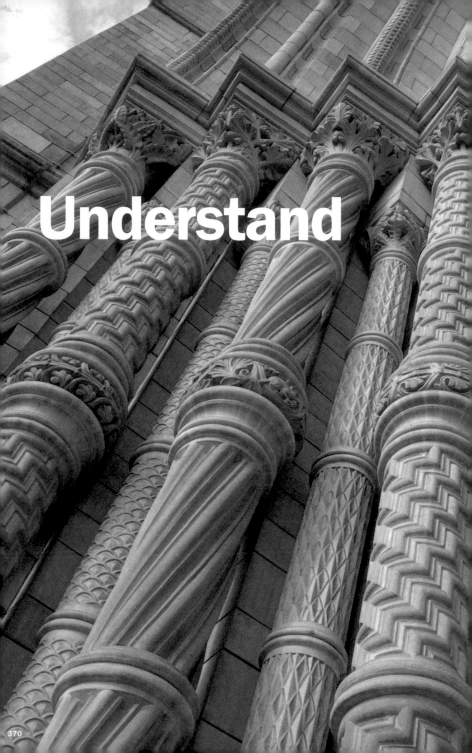

Understand

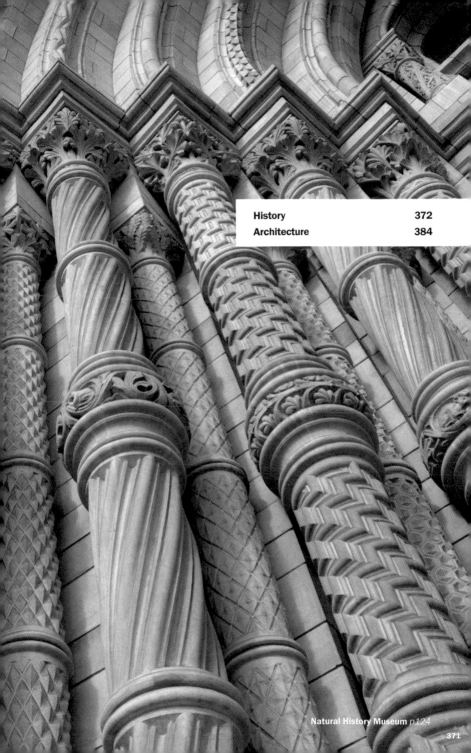

Natural History Museum *p124*

History

The making of modern London

Over the 2,000 years since London began life as a small trading station by a marshy river, the city has faced plague and invasion, fire and war, religious turbulence and financial turmoil, all borne by Londoners with a characteristic upbeat pessimism until the frenzy of commerce can begin again. In the City, Wren churches – built from the ruins of the Great Fire – have walls still blackened by the German incendiary bombs dropped during the Blitz, and shrapnel scars around Cleopatra's Needle remain from a World War I biplane raid. A fragment of glass, embedded in a wall at the Old Bailey, tells of a 1973 IRA terrorist attack, while 52 austere steel columns in Hyde Park commemorate those killed by suicide bombers in 2005. Then, in 2017, London was reminded of its vulnerabilities yet again by further terrorist attacks and by a towerblock fire in west London that killed many dozens of residents. Evidence of strife is everywhere in this city, yet the true Londoner will cheerfully insist there's worse to come. Just don't bet against them handling it with aplomb.

Latin lessons

The city's origins are hardly grand. Celtic tribes lived in scattered communities along the banks of the Thames before the Romans arrived in Britain – creating what archaeologists describe as a 'ritual landscape': a dispersed region of sacred monuments – but there's no evidence of a settlement that we might recognise as the seed of the future metropolis before the invasion of the Emperor Claudius in AD 43. During his conquest, the Romans forded the Thames at its shallowest point (probably near today's London Bridge) and, later, built a timber bridge there. A settlement developed on the north side of this crossing.

Over the next two centuries, the Romans built roads, towns and forts in the area. Progress was halted in AD 61 when Boudicca, the widow of an East Anglian chieftain, rebelled against the imperial forces who had seized her land, flogged her and raped her daughters. She led the Iceni in a revolt, destroying the Roman colony at Colchester before marching on London. The Romans were massacred and their settlement razed.

After order was restored, London was rebuilt; around AD 200, a two-mile-long, 18-foot-high wall was put up around it. Chunks of the wall survive today; the early names of the original gates – Ludgate, Bishopsgate, Newgate and Aldgate – are preserved on the map of the modern city, with the street known as London Wall tracing part of its original course. But by the fourth century, racked by invasions and internal strife, the Roman Empire was in decline. In 410, the troops were withdrawn, and London became a ghost town.

Into the dark

During the fifth and sixth centuries, history gives way to legend. The Saxons crossed the North Sea; apparently avoiding the ruins of London, they built farmsteads and trading posts outside the city walls. Pope Gregory sent Augustine to convert the English to Christianity in 596; Mellitus, one of his missionaries, was appointed the first Bishop of London, founding a cathedral dedicated to St Paul inside the old city walls in 604.

From this period, the history of London is one of expansion. Writing in 731, monk and writer the Venerable Bede described 'Lundenwic' as 'the mart of many nations resorting to it by land and sea'. Only recently have archaeologists found traces of this Anglo-Saxon market around Covent Garden and the Strand. Yet the city faced a new danger during the ninth century: the Vikings. The city was ransacked in 841 and again in 851, when Danish raiders returned with 350 ships. It was not until 886 that King Alfred of Wessex – Alfred the Great – regained the city, re-establishing London as a major trading centre, and refounding it within its old walls.

Throughout the tenth century the city prospered. Churches were built, parishes established and markets set up. However, the 11th century brought more harassment from the Vikings, and the English were forced to accept a Danish king, Cnut (Canute, 1016-35), during whose reign London replaced Winchester as the capital of England.

The country reverted to English control in 1042 under Edward the Confessor, who devoted himself to building England's grandest church two miles west of the

Astronomical clock Hampton Court Palace *p291*

City on an island in the river marshes at Thorney: 'the West Minster' (Westminster Abbey). Just a week after the consecration, he died. London now had two hubs: Westminster, centre of the royal court, government and law; and the City of London, centre of commerce. On Edward's death, foreigners took over. Duke William of Normandy was crowned king on Christmas Day 1066, having defeated Edward's brother-in-law Harold at the Battle of Hastings. The pragmatic Norman resolved to win over the City merchants by negotiation rather than force, and in 1067 granted the burgesses and the Bishop of London a charter – still available to researchers in the London Metropolitan Archives – that acknowledged their rights and independence in return for taxes. He also ordered strongholds to be built at the city wall 'against the fickleness of the vast and fierce population', including the White Tower (the tallest building in the Tower of London) and the now-lost Baynard's Castle.

Parliament and rights

In 1295, the Model Parliament, held at Westminster Hall by Edward I and attended by barons, clergy and representatives of knights and burgesses, agreed the principles of English government. The first step towards establishing personal rights and political liberty, not to mention curbing the power of the king, had already been taken in 1215 when King John put his seal to Magna Carta. Then, in the 14th century, subsequent assemblies gave rise to the House of Lords and the House of Commons. During the 12th and 13th centuries, the king and his court travelled the kingdom, but the Palace of Westminster was now the permanent seat of law and government; noblemen and bishops began to build palatial houses along the Strand from the City to Westminster, with gardens stretching down to the river.

Relations between the monarch and the City were never easy. Londoners guarded their privileges, and resisted attempts by kings to squeeze money out of them to finance wars and construction projects. Subsequent kings were forced to turn to Jewish and Lombard moneylenders, but the City merchants were intolerant of foreigners too.

The self-regulation privileges granted to the City merchants under Norman kings were extended by the monarchs who followed – in return for finance. In 1191, the City of London was recognised by Richard I as a self-governing community; six years later, it won control of the Thames. In 1215 King John confirmed the city's right 'to elect every year a mayor', a position of authority with power over the sheriff and the Bishop of London. A month later, the mayor's seal joined those of the rebel barons on Magna Carta.

Over the next two centuries, the power and influence of the trade and craft guilds (later known as the City Livery Companies) increased as dealings with Europe grew. The City's markets drew produce from miles around: livestock at Smithfield, fish at Billingsgate, poultry at Leadenhall. The street markets ('cheaps') around Westcheap (now Cheapside) and Eastcheap were crammed with a variety of goods. The population within the city walls grew from about 18,000 in 1100 to well over 50,000 in the 1340s.

Wake up and smell the issue

Lack of hygiene became a serious problem. Water was provided in cisterns, but the supply, more or less direct from the Thames, was limited and polluted. The street of Houndsditch was so named because Londoners threw their dead animals into the furrow there; in the streets around Smithfield (the Shambles), butchers dumped entrails into the gutters. These conditions helped to foster the greatest catastrophe of the Middle Ages: the Black Death of 1348 and 1349, which killed about 30 per cent of England's population. The plague came to London from Europe – probably carried by rats on ships, although research in 2015 suggested gerbils may have been to blame – and the plague was to recur in London several times during the next three centuries.

Disease left the harvest short-handed, causing unrest among the peasants whose labour was in such demand. Then a poll tax of a shilling a head was imposed. It was all too much: the Peasants' Revolt began in 1381. Thousands marched to Blackheath, south-east London, led by Jack Straw from Essex and Wat Tyler from Kent; the Archbishop of Canterbury was murdered and hundreds of prisoners were set free. After meeting the Essexmen near Mile End, the 14-year-old Richard II rode out to the rioters at Smithfield and spoke with Tyler. During their discussion, Tyler was fatally stabbed by the Lord Mayor; the revolt collapsed and the ringleaders were hanged. But no more poll taxes were imposed.

Roses, wives and Royal Docks

Its growth spurred by the discovery of America and the opening of ocean routes to Africa and the Orient, London became one of Europe's largest cities under the Tudors (1485-1603). The first Tudor monarch, Henry

Pelican Portrait of Elizabeth I
(Nicholas Hillard, circa 1573-1575)

sailed to the New World. As trade grew, so did London: it was home to 200,000 people in 1600, many living in overcrowded conditions. The most complete picture of Tudor London is given in John Stow's *Survey of London* (1598), a fascinating first-hand account by a Londoner whose monument stands in the church of St Andrew Undershaft.

These were the glory days of English drama. The Rose (1587) and the Globe (1599, now recreated; *see p360*) theatres were erected at Bankside, providing homes for the works of popular playwrights William Shakespeare and Christopher Marlowe. Deemed 'a naughty place' by royal proclamation, 16th-century Bankside was a vibrant mix of entertainment and 'sport' (bear-baiting, cock-fighting), drinking and whoring – all within easy reach of the City, which had outlawed theatres in 1575.

In 1605, two years after the Tudor dynasty ended with Elizabeth's death, her Stuart successor, James I, narrowly escaped assassination on 5 November. Guy Fawkes had been found underneath the Palace of Westminster, at midnight on 4 November, with 36 barrels of gunpowder. Commemorated with fireworks each year as Bonfire Night, the Gunpowder Plot had been hatched in protest at the failure to improve conditions for the persecuted Catholics, but only resulted in an intensification of anti-papist sentiment. James I is more positively remembered for hiring Inigo Jones to design court masques (musical dramas) and London's first influential examples of the classical Renaissance architectural style: the Queen's House (1616; *see p284*), the Banqueting House (1619; *see p105*) and St Paul's Covent Garden (1631; *see p184*).

Royalists and Roundheads

Charles I succeeded his father in 1625, but gradually fell out of favour with the City of London and an increasingly independent-minded Parliament over taxation. The country slid into civil war (1642-49), the supporters of Parliament (the Roundheads, led by Puritan Oliver Cromwell) opposing the supporters of the king (the Royalists).

Both sides knew that control of the country's major city and port was vital for victory, and London's sympathies were with the Parliamentarians. In 1642, 24,000 citizens assembled at Turnham Green to face Charles's army, but the king withdrew. The move proved fatal: Charles never threatened the capital again, and was eventually found guilty of treason. Taken to the Banqueting House in Whitehall on 30 January 1649, he declared himself a 'martyr of the people' and was beheaded.

VII, had ended the Wars of the Roses by might, defeating Richard III at the Battle of Bosworth and, by policy, marrying Elizabeth of York, a daughter of his rivals. By the time his son took the throne, the Tudor dynasty was firmly established. But progress under Henry VIII was not without its hiccups. His first marriage, to Catherine of Aragon, failed to produce an heir, so in 1527 he determined the union should be annulled. When the Pope refused to co-operate, Henry defied the Catholic Church, demanding to be recognised as Supreme Head of the Church in England and ordering the execution of anyone who opposed the plan (including Sir Thomas More, his otherwise loyal chancellor). The subsequent dissolution of the monasteries transformed the face of the medieval city.

When not transforming the politico-religious landscape, Henry found time to develop a professional navy, founding the Royal Dockyards at Woolwich in 1512. He also established palaces at Hampton Court and Whitehall, and built a residence at St James's Palace. Much of the land he annexed for hunting became today's Royal Parks, among them Greenwich, Hyde and Regent's parks.

Renaissance means rebirth

Elizabeth I's reign (1558-1603) saw the founding of the Royal Exchange in 1566, which enabled London to emerge as Europe's commercial hub. Merchant venturers and the first joint-stock companies established new trading enterprises, as pioneering seafarers Francis Drake, Walter Raleigh and Richard Hawkins

A commemorative wreath is still laid at the site of the execution on the last Sunday in January each year.

For the next decade, the country was ruled as a Commonwealth by Cromwell. But his son Richard's subsequent rule was brief: due to the Puritans closing theatres and banning Christmas (a Catholic superstition), the Restoration of the exiled Charles II in 1660 was greeted with great rejoicing. The Stuart king had Cromwell exhumed from Westminster Abbey, and his body was hung in chains at Tyburn (near modern-day Marble Arch). His severed head was displayed on a pole outside the abbey until 1685.

Plague, fire and revolution

The year 1665 saw the most serious outbreak of plague since the Black Death, killing nearly 100,000. Then, on 2 September 1666, a further disaster. The fire that spread from a carelessly tended oven in Thomas Farriner's baking shop on Pudding Lane raged for three days and consumed four-fifths of the City.

The Great Fire at least allowed planners the chance to rebuild London as a modern city. Many blueprints were considered, but Londoners were so impatient to get on with business that the City was reconstructed largely on its medieval street plan (albeit in brick and stone rather than wood). The prolific Sir Christopher Wren oversaw work on 51 of the 54 rebuilt churches. Among them was his masterpiece: the new St Paul's, completed in 1710 and effectively the world's first Protestant cathedral.

In the wake of the Great Fire, many well-to-do City dwellers moved to new residential developments west of the old quarters: the West End. In the City, the Royal Exchange was rebuilt, but merchants increasingly used the new coffee houses to exchange news. With the expansion of the joint-stock companies and the chance to invest capital, the City emerged as a centre not of manufacturing but of finance. Economic instability was common: the 1720 financial disaster known as the South Sea Bubble ruined Sir Isaac Newton.

Anti-Catholic feeling still ran high. The accession in 1685 of Catholic James II aroused such fears of a return to papistry that a Dutch Protestant, William of Orange, was invited to take the throne with his wife, Mary Stuart (James's daughter). James fled to France in 1688 in what became known (by its beneficiaries) as the 'Glorious Revolution'. It was during William's reign that the Bank of England was founded, initially to finance the king's religious wars with France.

GIN LANE.

Gin Lane (William Hogarth, 1751)

Creation of the prime minister

In 1714, the throne passed to George, the Hanover-born great-grandson of James I. The German-speaking king (he never learned English) became the first of four Georges in the Hanoverian line.

During George I's reign (1714-27), and for several years after, Sir Robert Walpole's Whig party monopolised Parliament. Their opponents, the Tories, supported the Stuarts and had opposed the exclusion of the Catholic James II. On the king's behalf, Walpole chaired a group of ministers (the forerunner of today's Cabinet), becoming, in effect, Britain's first prime minister. Walpole was presented with 10 Downing Street (built by Sir George Downing) as a residence; it remains the official prime ministerial home.

During the 18th century, London grew with astonishing speed. New squares and terraced streets spread across Soho, Bloomsbury, Mayfair and Marylebone, as wealthy landowners and speculative developers cashed in on the new demand for leasehold properties. South London also became more accessible with the opening of the first new bridges for centuries: Westminster Bridge (opened 1750) and Blackfriars Bridge (completed 1769) joined London Bridge, previously the only Thames crossing.

Gin-soaked poor, nasty rich

In London's older districts, people were living in terrible squalor. Some of the most notorious slums were located around Fleet Street and St Giles's (north of Covent Garden), only a short distance from fashionable residences. To make matters worse, gin ('mother's ruin') was readily available at low prices; many poor Londoners drank excessive amounts in an attempt to escape the horrors of daily life. The well-off seemed complacent, amusing themselves at the popular Ranelagh and Vauxhall pleasure gardens or with trips to mock the patients at the Bedlam lunatic asylum. Public executions at Tyburn were popular events in the social calendar; it's said that 200,000 people gathered to see the execution (after he had escaped from prison four times) of the folk-hero thief Jack Sheppard in 1724.

The outrageous imbalance in the distribution of wealth encouraged crime, and there were daring daytime robberies in the West End. Reformers were few, though there were exceptions. Henry Fielding, author of the picaresque novel *Tom Jones*, was also an enlightened magistrate at Bow Street Court (now destined to become a hotel). In 1751, he and his blind half-brother John set up a volunteer force of 'thief-takers' to back up the ineffective efforts of the parish constables and watchmen who were, until then, the city's only law-keepers. This crime-busting group of proto-cops, known as the Bow Street Runners, were the earliest incarnation of today's Metropolitan Police (established in 1829).

Meanwhile, five major new hospitals were founded by private philanthropists. St Thomas's and St Bartholomew's were long-established monastic institutions for the care of the sick, but Westminster (1720), Guy's (1725), St George's (1734), London (1740) and the Middlesex (1745) went on to become world-famous teaching hospitals. Thomas Coram's Foundling Hospital (see p197) was another remarkable achievement.

Industry and capital growth

It wasn't just the indigenous population of London that was on the rise. Country folk, whose common land had been replaced by sheep enclosures, were faced with a choice between starvation wages or unemployment, and so drifted into the towns. Just outside the old city walls, the East End drew many poor immigrant labourers to build the docks towards the end of the 18th century. London's total population had grown to one million by 1801, the largest of any city in Europe. By 1837, when Queen Victoria came to the throne, five more bridges and the capital's first passenger railway (from Greenwich to London Bridge) gave hints of huge expansion.

As well as being the administrative and financial capital of the British Empire, London was its chief port and the world's largest manufacturing centre. On the one hand, it had splendid buildings, fine shops, theatres and museums; on the other, it was a city of poverty, pollution and disease. Residential areas were polarised into districts of fine terraces maintained by squads of servants, and overcrowded, insanitary slums.

The growth of the metropolis in the century before Victoria came to the throne had been spectacular, but during her reign (1837-1901), thousands more acres were covered with roads, houses and railway lines. If you visit a street within five miles of central London, its houses will be mostly Victorian. By the end of the 19th century, the city's population had swelled to more than six million, an incredible growth of five million in just 100 years.

Great Exhibition of 1851

The Archaeology of Crossrail

Huge tunnels under London have revolutionised our understanding of its history

One of the biggest infrastructure policies seen in Europe for decades, Crossrail has not only provided London with a new high-speed underground rail line, but also became one of the largest archaeological digs ever seen in an urban centre. When completed, the line will connect Heathrow and Canary Wharf, with branches that drift into the suburbs, but the bulk of the engineering challenge has been in central London, where new tunnels connecting east and west London have been driven beneath the city at depths to up to 130 feet. For an archaeologist – more than 100 of them have worked on Crossrail sites – that scale of excavation is paradise. Since work began in 2009, they've found more than 10,000 items on 40 different sites, with objects spanning 55 million years of London's history. These include everything from prehistoric animal bones to plague pits.

The Crossrail project – which will be called the Elizabeth Line when it fully opens in 2019, although Londoners have shown few signs of adopting the official name – has given archaeologists an unprecedented opportunity to slice down and across London, allowing them to make numerous points of comparison at different excavations. While most ordinary people are fascinated by the magnificent ephemera that turned has up – a Tudor bowling ball, medieval ice skates – for the archaeologists the discoveries work together to provide important historical information. The remains of a woolly mammoth jawbone found under Canary Wharf have helped determine the date of their extinction in northern Europe, while DNA testing on teeth taken from skeletons found in a mass grave in the 17th-century Bedlam cemetery near Liverpool Street station confirmed the identity of the bacteria behind London's Great Plague. Human remains have particular value as they allow osteologists to determine things like the diet, life expectancy and lifestyle of everyday Londoners.

Liverpool Street was a particularly rich area. As well as bronze medallions, archaeologists also discovered a graveyard and three Roman-era skeletons that had been decapitated, with the heads laid between their legs – nobody can explain why. Less grisly have been the finds at Tottenham Court Road, where excavations at an old Crosse & Blackwell factory uncovered a treasure trove of 13,000 jam jars. For almost 100 years these had lain undiscovered beneath what became the Astoria theatre.

And Crossrail will leave its own archaeological legacy beneath London. Two of the tunnel boring machines used on the project, Phyllis and Ada, were too large to be extracted from the ground. They've been left buried beneath Farringdon for future archaeologists to discover.

Despite the social problems of the Victorian era, memorably described by Dickens, by the turn of the century steps were being taken to improve conditions for the majority of Londoners. The Metropolitan Board of Works installed an efficient sewerage system, street lighting and better roads. The worst slums were replaced by low-cost housing schemes funded by philanthropists such as the American George Peabody, whose Peabody Donation Fund continues to provide subsidised housing. The London County Council (created in 1888) also helped to house the poor.

The Victorian expansion would not have been possible without an efficient public-transport network with which to speed workers into and out of the city from the new suburbs. The horse-drawn bus appeared on London's streets in 1829, but it was the opening of the first passenger railway seven years later that heralded the commuters of the future. The first underground line between Paddington and Farringdon was an instant success, attracting 30,000 travellers on its opening day in 1863. The world's first electric track in a deep tunnel – the 'tube' – opened in 1890 between the City and Stockwell, later becoming part of the Northern line.

The Crystal Palace

If any single event symbolised this period of industry, science, discovery and invention, it was the Great Exhibition of 1851. Prince Albert, the Queen's Consort, helped to organise the triumphant showcase, for which the Crystal Palace, a vast building of iron and glass, was erected in Hyde Park. It looked like a giant greenhouse; hardly surprising as it was designed not by a professional architect but by the Duke of Devonshire's gardener, Joseph Paxton. Condemned by art critic John Ruskin as the model of dehumanisation in design, the Palace came to be presented as the prototype of modern architecture. During the five months it was open, the Exhibition drew six million visitors. The profits were used by the Prince Consort to establish a permanent centre for the study of the applied arts and sciences; the enterprise survives today in the South Kensington museums of natural history (*see p124*), science (*see p125*), and decorative and applied arts (*see p126*), and in three colleges (of art, music and science). After the Exhibition closed, the Crystal Palace was moved to Sydenham and was used as an exhibition centre until it burned down in 1936.

Zeppelins attack from the skies

London entered the 20th century as the capital of the largest empire in history. Its wealth and power were there for all to see in grandstanding monuments such as Tower Bridge (*see 236*) and the Midland Grand Hotel at St Pancras Station (*see 204*), both of which married the retro stylings of High Gothic with modern iron and steel technology. During the brief reign of Edward VII (1901-10), London regained some of the gaiety and glamour it had lacked in the later years of Victoria's reign. Parisian chic came to London with the opening of the Ritz; Regent Street's Café Royal hit the heights as a meeting place for artists and writers; gentlemen's clubs proliferated; and 'luxury catering for the little man' was provided at the new Lyons Corner Houses (the Coventry Street branch held 4,500 people).

Road transport, too, was revolutionised in this period. By 1911, horse-drawn buses were abandoned, replaced by motor cars, which put-putted around the city's streets, and the motor bus, introduced in 1904. Disruption came in the form of devastating air raids during World War I (1914-18). Around 650

people lost their lives in Zeppelin raids, but the greater impact was psychological – the mighty city and its populace had experienced helplessness.

Change, crisis and sheer entertainment

Political change happened quickly after the war. The suffragettes had fiercely pressed the case for women's rights before hostilities began, and David Lloyd George's government averted revolution in 1918-19 by promising 'homes for heroes' (the returning soldiers). It didn't deliver, and in 1924 the Labour Party, led by Ramsay MacDonald, formed its first government.

A live-for-today attitude prevailed in the Roaring '20s among the young upper classes, who flitted from parties in Mayfair to dances at the Ritz. But this meant little to the mass of Londoners, who were suffering in the post-war slump. Civil disturbances, brought on by the high cost of living and rising unemployment, resulted in the nationwide General Strike of 1926, when the working classes downed tools en masse in support of striking miners. Prime Minister Baldwin encouraged volunteers to take over the public services, and the streets teemed with army-escorted food convoys, aristocrats running soup kitchens and students driving buses. After nine days of chaos, the strike was finally called off.

The economic situation only worsened in the early 1930s following the New York Stock Exchange crash of 1929. By 1931, more than three million Britons were jobless. During

St Paul's Cathedral during the Blitz, 29 December 1940

these years, the London County Council (LCC) began to have a greater impact on the city, clearing slums and building new houses, creating parks and taking control of public services. All the while, London's population increased, peaking at nearly 8.7 million in 1939 – it would be spring 2015 before the city's population exceeded that number. To accommodate the influx, the suburbs expanded, particularly to the north-west with the extension of the Metropolitan line to an area that became known as 'Metroland'. Gabled houses sprang up in their thousands.

At least Londoners were able to entertain themselves with film and radio. Not long after London's first radio broadcast was beamed from the roof of Marconi House in the Strand in 1922, families were gathering around huge Bakelite wireless sets to hear the BBC (the British Broadcasting Company; from 1927, the British Broadcasting Corporation). TV broadcasts started on 26 August 1936, when the first telecast went out from Alexandra Palace, but few Londoners could afford televisions until the 1950s.

Blitzkrieg

Abroad, events had taken on a frightening impetus. Neville Chamberlain's policy of appeasement towards Hitler's Germany collapsed when the Germans invaded Poland. Britain duly declared war on 3 September 1939. The government implemented precautionary measures against air raids, including the evacuation of 600,000 children and pregnant mothers, but the expected bombing raids didn't happen during the autumn and winter of 1939-40 (the so-called 'Phoney War'). Then, in September 1940, hundreds of German bombers dumped explosives on east London and the docks, destroying entire streets and killing or injuring more than 2,000 in what was merely an opening salvo. The Blitz had begun. Raids on London continued for 57 consecutive nights, then intermittently for a further six months. Londoners reacted with stoicism, famously asserting 'business as usual'. After a final raid on 10 May 1941, the Nazis had left a third of the City and the East End in ruins.

From 1942 onwards, the tide began to turn, but Londoners had a new terror to face: the V1 or 'doodlebug'. Dozens of these deadly, explosive-packed, pilotless planes descended on the city in 1944, causing widespread destruction. Later in the year, the more powerful V2 rocket was launched. The last fell on 27 March 1945 in Orpington, Kent, around six weeks before Victory in Europe was declared on 8 May 1945.

'Never had it so good'

World War II left Britain almost as shattered as Germany. Soon after VE Day, a general election was held and Winston Churchill was defeated by the Labour Party under Clement Attlee. The new government established the National Health Service in 1948, and began a massive nationalisation programme that included public transport, electricity, gas, postal and telephone services. For most people, however, life remained regimented and austere. In war-ravaged London, local authorities struggled with a critical shortage of housing. Prefabricated bungalows provided a temporary solution for some (60 years later, six prefabs on the Excalibur estate in Catford, south-east London, were given protection as buildings of historic interest), but the huge new high-rise housing estates proved unpopular with their residents.

There were bright spots. London hosted the Olympic Games in 1948; three years later came the Festival of Britain, resulting in the full redevelopment of the riverside site into the South Bank (now Southbank) Centre. As the 1950s progressed, prosperity returned, leading Prime Minister Harold Macmillan in 1957 to proclaim that 'most of our people have never had it so good'. However, Londoners were leaving. The population dropped by half a million in the late 1950s, causing a labour shortage that prompted huge recruitment drives in Britain's former colonies. London Transport and the National Health Service were both particularly active in encouraging West Indians to emigrate to Britain. Unfortunately, as the Notting Hill race riots of 1958 illustrated, the welcome these new immigrants received was rarely friendly. Still, there were several areas of tolerance: Soho, for instance, which became famous for its mix of cultures and the café and club life they brought with them.

The swinging '60s

By the mid 1960s, London had started to swing. The innovative fashions of Mary Quant and others broke the stranglehold Paris had on couture: boutiques blossomed along the King's Road, while Biba set the pace in Kensington. Carnaby Street became a byword for hipness as the city basked in its new-found reputation as music and fashion capital of the world – made official, it seemed, when *Time* magazine devoted its front cover to 'swinging London' in 1966. The year of student unrest in Europe, 1968, saw the first issue of *Time Out* hit the streets in August; it was a fold-up sheet, sold for 5d. The decade ended with the Rolling Stones playing a free gig in Hyde Park that drew around 500,000 people.

Then the bubble burst. Many Londoners remember the 1970s as a decade of economic strife and the decade in which the IRA began its bombing campaign on mainland Britain. After the Conservatives won the general election in 1979, Margaret Thatcher instituted an economic policy that cut public services and widened the gap between rich and poor. Riots in Brixton (1981) and Tottenham (1985) were linked to unemployment and heavy-handed policing, keenly felt in London's black communities. The Greater London Council (GLC), led by Ken Livingstone, mounted vigorous opposition to the government with a series of populist measures, but it was abolished in 1986.

Things can only get better?

In May 1997, the British electorate ousted the Tories and gave Tony Blair's Labour Party the first of three election victories. Blair left London with two significant legacies. First, the government commissioned the Millennium Dome, whose turn-of-the-century celebrations it hoped would be a 21st-century rival to the Great Exhibition of 1851. Instead, the Dome ate £1 billion and became a national joke. However, as Labour's fortunes declined, the Dome's saw an upturn. As the O2 Arena, it has hosted gigs by the likes of Prince, Lady Gaga and the reformed Led Zeppelin. Second, following a referendum, Labour instituted the Greater London Authority (GLA), the 25-member London Assembly and the London mayoralty. Thus 2000 saw Ken Livingstone return to power as London's first directly elected mayor. He was re-elected in 2004, a thumbs-up for policies that included a traffic congestion charge. Summer 2005 brought elation, as London won the bid to host the 2012 Olympic Games, and devastation the very next day, as bombs on tube trains and a bus killed 52 people and injured 700.

Aided by support from the suburbs, which felt neglected by Livingstone, thatch-haired Tory Boris Johnson became mayor in 2008 with a healthy majority, and again in 2012 by a slimmer margin – again against Livingstone. His early policies, such as banning alcohol on London transport, scrapping the western extension of the Congestion Charge, as well as introducing a bike-rental scheme and developing an updated Routemaster bus, were popular. The latter was launched as self-financing

through revenue and private sponsorship but was instead regularly topped up with money from Transport for London's already stretched public transport budget (see p74 Routemasters).

The riots and looting of August 2011, whose flashpoint was again in Tottenham, brought issues of youth unemployment, alienation and policing to the fore; how to build enough affordable housing for Londoners is another major problem. The 2012 Olympics and Paralympics were an unbridled success, yet the promised 'legacy' of improvements at a local level in some of London's poorest areas remains frustratingly elusive – a problem underlined in 2017 by the terrifying fire at Grenfell Tower, a council block in the borough of Kensington & Chelsea where at least 80 residents perished.

After a brief interregnum, during which Johnson served both as mayor and MP, a toxic campaign was run for the new mayor. Labour's Sadiq Khan, a civil rights lawyer and bus driver's son from Tooting, prevailed over the millionaire ecologist, Zac Goldsmith (see p32), and on 6 May 2016, Khan was sworn in as Mayor of London – only the third person to hold the position since it was instituted. In June he suddenly became the anti-Brexit mayor of a broadly anti-Brexit city in a country that voted to leave the European Union (see p34).

He faces many challenges. London's population continues to grow – it is believed to have reached the highest level ever, 8.7 million, in 2015 and hasn't stopped – which is placing huge pressure on already limited housing. The banking industry is nervous about the UK's exit from the EU. And, in March and June 2017, terrorism returned to London, with fatal car and knife attacks on Westminster Bridge, at Borough Market and at Finsbury Park mosque.

Meanwhile, the vast new Crossrail train link (see p379) that has been burrowing its way right under the capital from east to west is due to begin operations in 2018, and another new district is growing up around the redeveloped Battersea Power Station. However, this scheme has been battered by the uncertainties of post-2016 geopolitics, and the social value of such developments is routinely criticised, caricatured as providing homes only for the rich and, in truth, failing to provide enough affordable housing for other Londoners (see p390).

Change, at the largest scale, is part of London's DNA. And it looks as though the city will be getting a bellyful over the coming decade.

Key Events

London's history in brief

43 The Romans invade; the settlement of Londinium is founded on the remains of an ancient ritual landscape.

61 Boudicca burns Londinium; the city is rebuilt and made provincial capital.

200 A city wall is built.

410 Roman troops evacuate Britain.

c600 Saxon London is built to the west.

604 Mellitus is consecrated bishop of London.

841 The Norse raid for the first time.

c871 The Danes occupy London.

886 Alfred the Great takes London.

1042 Edward the Confessor builds a palace and 'West Minster' upstream.

1066 William I crowned in Westminster Abbey.

1078 The Tower of London is begun.

1123 St Bart's Hospital is founded.

1197 Henry Fitzalwin is the first mayor.

1215 The mayor signs Magna Carta.

1240 First Parliament at Westminster.

1290 Jews are expelled from London.

1348 The Black Death arrives.

1381 The Peasants' Revolt.

1397 Richard Whittington is Lord Mayor.

1476 William Caxton sets up the first printing press at Westminster.

1534 Henry VIII cuts England off from the Catholic Church.

1555 Martyrs burned at Smithfield.

1565 Sir Thomas Gresham proposes the Royal Exchange.

1572 First known map of London.

1599 The Globe Theatre opens.

1605 Guy Fawkes's plot to blow up James I fails.

1642 The start of the Civil War.

1649 Charles I is executed; Cromwell establishes the Commonwealth.

1665 Outbreak of the Great Plague.

1666 The Great Fire.

1675 Building starts on the new St Paul's Cathedral.

1694 The Bank of England is set up.

1766 The city wall is demolished.

1773 The Stock Exchange is founded.

1824 The National Gallery opens.

1836 The first passenger railway is inaugurated; Charles Dickens publishes *The Pickwick Papers*, his first novel.

1851 The Great Exhibition takes place.

1858 The Great Stink: pollution in the Thames reaches hideous levels.

1863 The Metropolitan line opens as the world's first underground railway.

1866 London's last major cholera outbreak; the Sanitation Act is passed.

1868 The last public execution is held at Newgate prison (now the Old Bailey).

1884 Greenwich Mean Time is established as a global standard.

1888 Jack the Ripper prowls the East End; London County Council is created.

1890 The Housing Act enables the LCC to clear the slums; the first electric underground railway opens.

1897 Motorised buses are introduced.

1908 London hosts the Olympic Games for the first time.

1915 Zeppelins begin three years of bombing raids on London.

1940 The Blitz begins.

1948 London again hosts the Olympics.

1951 The Festival of Britain is held.

1952 The last 'pea-souper' smog.

1953 Queen Elizabeth II is crowned.

1981 Riots in Brixton.

1982 The last London docks close.

1986 The Greater London Council is abolished.

1992 One Canada Square tower opens on Canary Wharf.

2000 Ken Livingstone becomes London's first directly elected mayor; Tate Modern and the London Eye bring tourism to the South Bank.

2005 Suicide bombers kill 52 on public transport.

2008 Boris Johnson becomes mayor.

2010 Hung parliament leads to new Conservative–Lib Dem coalition.

2011 Austerity cuts by the Conservative-Lib Dem coalition lead to riots and looting around the city.

2012 London becomes only the second city to host the Olympic Games for a third time.

2015 The population of Greater London reaches 8.7m, the largest number in its history.

2016 Labour's Sadiq Khan elected mayor; the UK votes for Brexit despite most of London voting to remain.

2017 Civilians are killed by terrorist attacks at Westminster Bridge, Borough Market and Finsbury Park mosque. A huge fire kills at least 80 residents of Grenfell Tower in west London.

Architecture

A wonderful jumble of world-class buildings

For all the derisive newspaper lists of London's worst new buildings, the best modern architecture is swiftly appreciated here: witness the monumental Switch House extension to Tate Modern, for instance. Even hated buildings are liable to become classics eventually: the Brutalist National Theatre and Barbican have been pilloried over the years, but now enjoy huge Instagram followings.

If you swap Insta snaps for hastily printed coffee-house pamphlets, there's not much difference between now and the 17th century, when Wren's magnificent St Paul's Cathedral was objected to because it looked too Roman Catholic for austere Anglican sensibilities.

The truth is that London's defining characteristic is its aesthetically unhappy mix of buildings, a mess of historic bits and modern bobs that gives the city a unique capacity to surprise and delight. Don't come here for grand Renaissance vistas, then, but you can expect snatches of pure inspiration.

British Museum *p198*

Ancient streets, new city

Modern London sprang into being from the ashes left after the Great Fire of 1666, which destroyed four-fifths of the City of London, burning 13,200 houses and 89 churches. The devastation was explicitly commemorated by Sir Christopher Wren's 202-foot **Monument** (*see p233*), but many of the finest buildings in the City stand testament to his talent as the architect of the great remodelling, and to the work of his successors.

London had been a densely populated place built largely of wood, and fire control was primitive. It was only after the three-day inferno that the authorities insisted on a few basic regulations. Brick and stone became the construction materials of choice, and key streets were widened to act as firebreaks. Yet, despite grand, Classical proposals from several architects (Wren among them), London reshaped itself around its old street pattern, and some structures that survived the Fire still stand as reminders of earlier building styles. Chief of these are the City's fragments of **Roman wall** (Tower Hill tube station and the grounds of the Museum of London, *see p228*), have good examples) and the central Norman keep at the **Tower of London** (*see p234*). The Tower was begun soon after William's 1066 conquest and extended over the next 300 years; the Navy saved it from the flames by blowing up surrounding houses before the inferno could reach it.

Another longstanding building, **Westminster Abbey** (*see p109*) was begun in 1245 when the site lay far outside London's walls; it was completed in 1745 by Nicholas Hawksmoor's distinctive west towers. The abbey is the most French of England's Gothic churches, but the chapel – begun by Henry VII – is pure Tudor. Centuries later, the American writer Washington Irving gushed: 'Stone seems, by the winning labour of the chisel, to have been robbed of its weight and density, suspended aloft, as if by magic.'

A late flowering

The European Renaissance came late to Britain, making its London debut with Inigo Jones's 1622 **Banqueting House** (*see p105*). The sumptuously decorated ceiling, added in 1635 by Rubens, celebrated the Stuart monarchy's Divine Right to rule, although 14 years later King Charles I provided a greater spectacle as he was led from the room and beheaded on a stage outside. Tourists also have Jones to thank for **St Paul's Covent Garden** (*see p184*), and the precise little **Queen's House** (*see p284*) in Greenwich, extensively renovated for its 400th anniversary in 2017. Jones mastered the art of piazzas (notably at Covent Garden), porticoes and pilasters, changing British architecture forever. His work influenced succeeding generations of architects, introducing a habit of venerating the past that it would take 300 years to kick.

Nothing cheers a builder like a natural disaster, and one can only guess at the relish with which Wren and co began rebuilding after the Fire. They brandished Classicism like a new broom: the pointed arches of English Gothic were rounded off, Corinthian columns made an appearance and church spires became as complex, frothy and multi-layered as a wedding cake – as the tour guides never tire of explaining as they point up to the lovely spire of **St Bride's** (*see p221*) on Fleet Street.

Wren blazed the trail with his daring plans for **St Paul's Cathedral** (*see p224*), spending an enormous (for the time) £500 on just the oak model of his proposal. But the scheme, incorporating a Catholic dome rather than a Protestant steeple, was too Roman for the establishment and the design was rejected. Wren quickly produced a redesign and gained planning permission by incorporating a spire, only to set about a

St Mary Woolnoth *p230*

series of mischievous U-turns to give us the building, domed and heavily suggestive of an ancient temple, that survives to this day.

Wren's work was continued by Nicholas Hawksmoor and James Gibbs, who benefited from an Act of Parliament that in 1710 decreed 50 extra churches should be built using the money raised by a tax on coal. Gibbs became busy around Trafalgar Square with the steepled Roman temple of **St Martin-in-the-Fields** (*see p103*), as well as the Baroque **St Mary-le-Strand** (*see p190*) and the tower of **St Clement Danes** (*see p190*). His work was well received, but the more experimental Hawksmoor had a rougher ride. Not everyone admired his stylistic innovations; even fewer approved of his financial planning, or lack of it: **St George's Bloomsbury** (*see p199*) cost three times its £10,000 budget and took 15 years to build. Nonetheless, Hawksmoor designed, in whole or in part, eight new places of worship. Like,Wren, Hawksmoor loved the Classical temple, a style at odds with the Act's insistence on spires. **St Mary Woolnoth** (*see p230*) and, in east London, **St George-in-the-East** and **St Anne Limehouse** are all unorthodox resolutions of this contradiction, but the 'spire' of St George's Bloomsbury is barmiest. Aping the Mausoleum of Halicarnassus, Hawksmoor created a peculiar stepped pyramid design, plopped a giant statue of George I in a toga on top and then added unicorns and lions. Hawksmoor's ruinous overspends were one reason why just a dozen of the proposed 50 churches were built.

After action, reaction: one of a large family of Scottish architects, Robert Adam found himself at the forefront of a movement that came to see Italian Baroque as a corruption of the real thing, with architectural exuberance dropped in favour of a simpler interpretation of ancient forms. The best surviving work of Robert and his brothers James, John and William can be found in London's great suburban houses, including **Kenwood House** (*see p249*), but the project for which they're most famous no longer stands: the cripplingly expensive Adelphi housing estate. Almost all of the complex was pulled down in the 1930s and replaced by an office block, apart from the **Royal Society of Arts** building, just off the Strand on John Adam Street.

Soane and Nash

Just as the first residents were moving into the Adelphi in the early 1770s, a young unknown called John Soane was embarking on a domestic commission in Ireland. It was never completed, but Soane eventually returned to London and

went on to build the **Bank of England** and **Dulwich Picture Gallery** (*see p290*). The Bank was demolished between the wars, leaving only the perimeter walls of Soane's masterpiece, but his gracious Stock Office has been reconstructed in the Bank's **museum** (*see p231*). A further glimpse of what the bankers might have enjoyed can be gleaned from his own house, the quirkily marvellous and recently extended **Sir John Soane's Museum** (*see p215*), an exquisite architectural experiment.

A near-contemporary of Soane's, John Nash was a less talented architect, but his contributions – among them the inner courtyard of **Buckingham Palace** (*see p113*), the **Theatre Royal Haymarket** and **Regent Street** (*see p150*) – have comparable influence in the look of contemporary London to those of Wren. Regent Street began as a proposal to link the West End to the planned park further north, as well as a device to separate the toffs of Mayfair from the riff-raff of Soho; in Nash's own words, a 'complete separation between the Streets occupied by the Nobility and Gentry, and the narrow Streets and meaner houses occupied by mechanics and the trading part of the community'.

By the 1830s, the Classical form of building had been established in England for some 200 years, but this didn't prevent a handful of upstarts from pressing for change. In 1834, the **Houses of Parliament** (*see p108*) burned down, leading to the construction of Sir Charles Barry's Gothic masterpiece. Barry sought out Augustus Welby Northmore Pugin. Working alongside Barry, if not always in agreement with him (of Barry's symmetrical layout, Pugin famously remarked, 'All Grecian, sir. Tudor details on a Classic body'), Pugin created a Victorian fantasy that would later be condemned as the Disneyfication of history.

Getting Gothic

This was the beginning of the Gothic Revival, a move to replace what was considered to be foreign and pagan with something that was native and Christian. Architects would often decide that buildings weren't Gothic enough; as with the 15th-century Great Hall at the **Guildhall** (*see p231*), which gained its corner turrets and central spire only in 1862. The argument between Classicists and Goths erupted in 1857, when the government hired Sir George Gilbert Scott, a leading light of the Gothic movement, to design a new home for the **Foreign Office**. Scott's design incensed anti-Goth Lord Palmerston, then prime minister, whose diktats prevailed. But Scott exacted his revenge by building an office in which

Natural History Museum p124

everyone hated working, and by going on to construct wonderful Gothic edifices all over town, among them the **Albert Memorial** (*see p124*) and what is now the **Renaissance St Pancras** hotel, which still forms the front of St Pancras train station.

St Pancras station (*see p204*) was completed in 1873, after the Midland Railway commissioned Scott to build a London terminus that would dwarf that of its rivals next door at King's Cross. Using the project as an opportunity to show his mastery of the Gothic form, Scott built an asymmetrical castle that obliterated views of the train shed behind, itself an engineering marvel completed earlier by William Barlow.

Other charming, imposing neo-Gothic buildings around the city include the **Royal Courts of Justice** (*see p222*), the **Natural History Museum** (*see p124*) and **Tower Bridge** (*see p236*). Under the influence of the Arts and Crafts movement, medievalism morphed into such mock Tudor buildings as the wonderful half-timbered **Liberty** department store (*see p152*).

Being modern

World War I and the coming of modernism led to a spirit of renewal and a starker aesthetic. **Freemasons' Hall** (*see p182*) and the BBC's **Broadcasting House** (*see p144*) are good examples of the pared-down style of the 1920s and '30s, but perhaps the finest example of between-the-wars modernism can be found at **London Zoo** (*see p245*).

Built by Russian émigré Bertold Lubetkin and the Tecton group, the spiral ramps of the former Penguin Pool were a showcase for the possibilities of concrete. The material was also put to good use on the London Underground, enabling the quick, cheap building of cavernous spaces with sleek lines and curves: the collaboration between London Underground supremo Frank Pick and architect Charles Holden created design masterpieces such as **Southgate** and **Arnos Grove** stations at the north end of the Piccadilly line, and **Chiswick Park station** to the west on the District line, as well as the transport headquarters at **55 Broadway** – which featured sculptures by modern masters Jacob Epstein, Eric Gill and Henry Moore. Even local government offices were built with care and skill: see for yourself at the likes of **Hornsey Town Hall** (www.hthartscentre.co.uk), which reopened to the public in 2014. Further innovations were employed on the gorgeous **Daily Express** building (121-128 Fleet Street), built in 1931 using the pioneering 'curtain wall' construction, its radical black Vitrolite and glass façade hung on an internal frame.

The bombs of World War II left large areas of London ruined, providing another opportunity for builders to cash in. Lamentably, the city was little improved by the rebuild; in many cases, it was left worse off. The destruction left the capital with a dire housing shortage, so architects were given a chance to demonstrate the grim efficiency with which they could house

Take a Look at London

Get the inside view on the city's architecture

Both the **Architectural Association** (36 Bedford Square, Bloomsbury, WC1B 3ES, 7887 4000, www.aaschool.ac.uk, closed Sun) and the appropriately handsome **Royal Institute of British Architects** (66 Portland Place, Marylebone, W1B 1AD, 7580 5533, www.architecture.com, closed Sun) have terrific exhibitions on different aspects of architecture, but for a focused look at London's architectural future, get off the tube at Goodge Street and visit **New London Architecture** (26 Store Street, Bloomsbury, WC1E 7BT, 7636 4044, www. newlondonarchitecture.org, closed Sun). It's been hosting inventive temporary exhibitions for a decade now, but the centrepiece exhibit is permanent: a 39-foot-long scale model of the city, with all major developments with planning permission indicated, gives real insight into the city's recent and future architecture. Exhibitions at the new **City Centre** (80 Basinghall Street, the City, EC2V 5AR, 7600 8362, www.thecitycentre.london, closed Sun) are more narrowly focused on the many developments in the City; it has a good model too (open 10am-5pm Fri, Sat).

In addition, Open-City's **Open House London** (*see p316*) festival is a key date in the architecture calendar each year. It does a terrific job of getting locals engaged with their city by giving public access to amazing buildings of all epochs.

large numbers of families in tower blocks. There were post-war successes, however, including the **Royal Festival Hall** (*see p80*) on the South Bank. The sole survivor of the 1951 Festival of Britain, the RFH was built to celebrate the end of the war and the centenary of the Great Exhibition, held in 1851 and responsible for the foundation in South Kensington of the Natural History Museum, the Science Museum and the V&A. Next to the RFH, the **Hayward Gallery** (currently under major renovation) is an exemplar of the 1960s vogue for Brutalist architecture, a style that is more thoroughly explored at the **Barbican** (*see p227*) and is currently all over Instagram in one of the more surprising recent architectural fads.

Here come the Starchitects

The 1970s and '80s offered a pair of alternatives to concrete: postmodernism and high-tech. The former is represented by César Pelli's blandly monumental **One Canada Square** (*see p275*) in Docklands, an oversized obelisk that's perhaps the archetypal expression of late '80s architecture – and whose impact is hard to imagine now it stands in a copse of inferior office blocks. Richard Rogers's high-tech **Lloyd's of London** building (*see p232*) is much more widely admired. A clever combination of commercial and industrial aesthetics that adds up to one of the most significant British buildings since the war, it was mocked on completion in 1986 but, having been thoroughly rehabilitated, is now in danger of being choked by surrounding skyscrapers: Rogers' disappointing 48-storey **122 Leadenhall** ('the Cheesegrater') just opposite, and the City's current tallest building on nearby

Bishopsgate – the 755-foot, 46-storey **Heron Tower**.

Apart from Rogers, the city's most visible contemporary architect has been Norman Foster, whose **City Hall** and **30 St Mary Axe** (universally known as 'the Gherkin', for obvious reasons; *see p233*) caught up with Big Ben and black taxis as movie shorthand for 'Welcome to London!' – only to be overtaken in 2012 by the giant glass spike of Renzo Piano's **Shard** (*see p94*), facing the City across the Thames. Foster's prolific practice set new standards with the exercise in complexity that is the £100-million Great Court at the **British Museum** (*see p198*). The Great Court is the largest covered square in Europe, but each of the 3,300 triangular glass panels that make up its roof is unique.

Much new architecture is to be found cunningly inserted into old buildings. Herzog & de Meuron's fabulous transformation of a Bankside power station into **Tate Modern** (*see p87*) is the most famous example – the firm repeated its success, perhaps even bettered it, with the ambitious new Switch House extension, a vast quasi-pyramid that unfolds itself upwards like self-assembled origami. The views from the top are breathtaking – much to the chagrin of dwellers in the luxury flats opposite, who are taking legal action against the gallery for invasion of privacy.

Zaha Hadid died in spring 2016, but her swooping, sinuous architecture has finally made itself felt in her adopted city: her stunning Aquatics Centre was opened in the Olympic Park in 2011, followed by the **Serpentine Sackler Gallery** (*see p131*) in 2013 and the new Winton Gallery, the dedicated maths section of the **Science Museum** (*see p125*), in 2016.

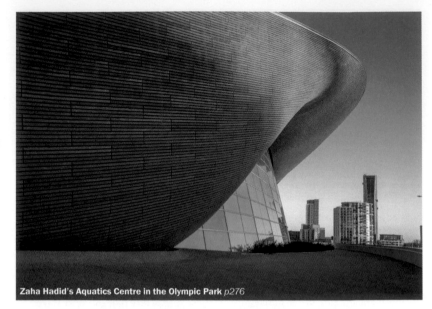

Zaha Hadid's Aquatics Centre in the Olympic Park *p276*

Arts and local colour

Architecture hasn't all been about headline projects and eye-troubling commercial developments. Will Alsop's multicoloured **Peckham Library** (122 Peckham Hill Street) helped to redefine community architecture in 2000, and architects have continued to play a major role in redefining public libraries. David Adjaye subsequently designed the **Idea Stores** (www.ideastore.co.uk) in Poplar (1 Vesey Path, East India Dock Road) and Whitechapel (321 Whitechapel Road), with a crisp, softened industrial aesthetic that is a world away from the familiar Victorian library, while in 2011 Piers Gough's upside-down pyramid, **Canada Water Library** (21 Surrey Quays Road), provided a focus for a rather incoherent district in south-east London. The subtle Robbrecht en Daem expansion of **Whitechapel Gallery** *(see p263)* into the stylistically very different former library next door reversed this process, giving a new democratic openness to a pair of landmark Victorian buildings, while Caruso St John finally won themselves a Stirling Prize in 2016 for a brilliant conversion of early 20th-century scenery-painting warehouses into Damien Hirst's vast **Newport Street Gallery** *(see p83)*.

The end of the megabuilds?

In the north of London, the transformation of King's Cross incorporates the reopened St Pancras International station; a refurbished **King's Cross station** with an arresting new roof; the new-build office/concert venue **Kings Place** *(see p354)*; and Central Saint Martins art college, in a redeveloped Victorian granary on the fine **Granary Square** *(see p204)*, with its restaurants, geometric, choreographed fountains and terracing down to the canal. The 67-acre brownfield redevelopment, King's Cross Central, will eventually also comprise 1,900 new homes, serviced by 20 new streets and another four squares, in a part of London that was given its own new postcode: N1C.

Just as impressive – and also with its own postcode, E20, cannily borrowed from the fictional London borough in long-running BBC TV soap opera *EastEnders* – is the **Olympic Park** *(see p276)*. Having fulfilled its function as the heavily policed major venue for the 2012 Olympics and Paralympics, its slow conversion into a public amenity began (its 'legacy', to use the jargon). Taxpayers had reason to expect rather a lot from a project for which the original £2.4bn budget was increased to an eye-watering £9.3bn. The promised social housing remains controversial, but otherwise the results are pretty impressive: from a superb park, with excellent playgrounds, to the beautiful wood-clad Velodrome, Hadid's Aquatics Centre and the red spirals of the Anish Kapoor-designed **ArcelorMittal Orbit** – whose latest bid for local affection was the installation of a giant slide *(see p276)*. The reopening of the Olympic Stadium as West

Ham's football ground for the 2016/17 season brought the process to a turbulent end, with poor results on the pitch and crowd trouble off it, but it seems to have settled as the Irons inched up the Premier League to midtable safety.

The future of the future

When London's population breached the 8.7m mark in 2015 – it's the city's highest population in history – it seemed clear what architects would be doing for the foreseeable future: housing and planning for housing. Since the country voted for Brexit, despite London mostly voting to remain, things haven't been quite so certain. Will Brexit have a dramatic effect on migration into London if the country rejects the EU's open borders policy? An impressive proportion of newcomers to London are actually from elsewhere in the UK. And will Brexit have a chastening effect on the loathed luxury sector of the housing market, which successive London mayors have used to subsidise affordable housing? A certain chilling has already been noted as a result of changes to stamp duty, which is paid on property purchases above a certain amount.

For now, the megabuilds continue getting the green light: Vauxhall and the benighted **Battersea Power Station** (*see p289*) is one; the regeneration of Tottenham (where the 2011 riots began) focused on Spurs' new football stadium another. Only Boris Johnson's pet Earls Court Project seems to be bogged down. However, battles continue over how the vanishing pot of public money gets distributed.

Where there is regeneration in London, it can feel a lot like gentrification. Witness the new 'town centre' at Stratford, on the eastern flank of the Olympic Park, where the Westfield Stratford City mall has been doing serious business and a recalibration of 'affordable' has put homes out of many people's reach. See also Woolwich, where big business is behind the £30m Siemens sustainability centre on the Royal Docks, linked across the Thames by Mayor Boris Johnson's first vanity project: the underused **Emirates Air Line cable car** (*see p277*) – to the **O2 Arena** (*see p344*) – with its own cluster of new buildings, including a university campus. His second vanity project, the **Garden Bridge**, planned to link the Embankment to the South Bank, seems unlikely to be completed – Mayor Sadiq Khan has refused it any more cash (despite £37million of public funds already having been spent without any construction work taking place).

Planners have been pointing to the eastern docks area of London, the 'Thames Gateway', as the city's future for many years – that possibility is underpinned by the steady progress of the colossally ambitious **Crossrail** project (*see p379* The Archaeology of Crossrail). Due to start operations in 2018, this railway has already wormed its way under key areas of the city, including Oxford Street, to connect the London suburbs and beyond to the east and west with the city centre. It is an extraordinary feat of civil engineering.

Those same planners, however, are also beginning to reach a consensus that London must also be allowed to expand outwards, which would involve the politically suicidal move of building on the sacred Green Belt – a girdle of protected land that is, they argue, less the bucolic fantasy its name conjures than an agglomeration of golf courses, minor industry and low-density suburban dwellings. On his path to being elected mayor in 2016, Khan explicitly – and repeatedly – ruled out any such manoeuvre.

Are we on our way to a better future city? The arguments either way are fierce, but one thing is clear: heading up, out or under – one way or another, we are well on our way to a bigger future London.

Emirates Air Line cable car *p277*

Plan

PICCADIL

LY CIRCUS

Accommodation

Even at the height of the recession, London's hoteliers seemed to think it was boomtime. Whether the country's faltering steps towards Brexit cools their ardour remains to be seen, but so far the pace of deluxe openings has hardly slowed, with the Beaumont and Mondrian at Sea Containers two of the more notable additions over the last few years. They are, of course, overlooked – if not overshadowed – by the lofty Shangri-La at the Shard. By far the splashiest new opening of the last few years was Marylebone's none-more-trendy Chiltern Firehouse, but given that the chances of a mere mortal getting to stay there are close to zero, we've chosen to recommend the restaurant in our Explore chapter and leave the hotel itself to its clientele of celebs and investment bankers.

Z Hotel's unexpected interior courtyard, with open 'corridors' stacked above it.

The price of rooms in London is pretty shocking, but it's not all top-dollar activity. The pioneering Hoxton has opened an even better sister-hotel – the Hoxton Holborn – and the excellent Dutch citizenM chain is expanding its properties over here. Qbic and the Z hotels are other bargain favourites. Erm, perhaps that's relative bargain favourites.

In fact, it might be worth retraining as an artist first if you want a really cheap room: then you could take advantage of one inventive social enterprise that's diversified into the hotel trade (*see p399* Green Dreams).

Staying in London

There are some ridiculously good deals offered online for 'London rooms', sometimes even 'central London rooms' or 'well-connected London rooms'. Always do your research on the location before you part with any money. Greater London is pretty huge and few people have a vision of their holiday that involves

In the know
Price categories

Our price categories are based on hotels' standard prices (not including seasonal offers or discounts) for one night in a double room with en suite shower/bath.

Luxury	£350+
Expensive	£250-£350
Moderate	£130-£250
Budget	up to £130

COME LIE WITH US

From five-star stays to budget beds and
brilliant boutiques, we've hand-picked
the best hotels for you to book online.

Suite Dreams

Fancy an alternative to a conventional hotel?

London Serviced Apartments (8004 0007, www.londonservicedapartments.co.uk) specialises in holiday lets, while **London Holiday Accommodation** (7265 0882, www.londonholiday.co.uk) offers half a dozen decent-priced self-catering options near to Tower Bridge. For serviced apartments, try the South Bank or Earl's Court 'campuses' run by **Allstay Apartments** (3465 9100, www.allstay.co.uk).

Several agencies can arrange for individuals and families to stay in Londoners' homes. They include **At Home in London** (01474 708701, www.athomeinlondon.co.uk), **London Bed & Breakfast Agency** (01474 708701,

www.londonbb.com) and **London Homestead Services** (7286 5115, www.lhslondon.co.uk). There is usually a minimum length of stay.

Of course, they seem a little old-fashioned now: **www.airbnb.co.uk** has made a rapid transition from in-the-know insider funkiness to the mainstream, with its offer of 'unique places to stay from local hosts'. It doesn't offer a curated selection of properties, of course, and that notion of 'hosting' has rather gone since the early days, but you'll get a good range of places to choose from – and plenty of feedback from other clients to keep you from bad decisions.

spending an hour on public transport to get to the heart of things. That said, there's no need to focus exclusively on the West End, fun though a stay bang in the middle of London is – it's a privilege only a tiny percentage of Londoners get to share, after all. Get somewhere to stay on the South Bank and you certainly won't regret it, but the City – the original walled square mile(ish) of London – is a superb concentration of major sights furnished with plenty of business hotels. They may not be the funkiest places, but there are deals to be had, particularly at weekends. East London retains some of its art-and-fashion coolness and is much better served by hotels than it was even a couple of years ago. You'll be delighted you found somewhere thereabout if you're planning on some hard nights of clubbing. Or, if you can afford it, a stay in one of the grand old Mayfair hotels is a holiday without even having to step out of the door.

Antony Gormley-designed ROOM: a striking Cubist-influenced sculpture outside the front entrance to the Beaumont Hotel.

Money matters

In London, the average price of a double room for the night seems to be settling somewhere around £135, which we've used to set our price categories (*see p394*). But these categories are just a guide. A hotel's rates can vary widely, both top to bottom and over the course of the year. As a rule, it's best to book as far ahead as possible, and always try hotels' own websites first: many offer special online deals throughout the year; pretty much every business hotel will offer steep reductions for a Sunday night stay.

Be aware that a few hotels – particularly at the top of the price range – don't include VAT (a 20 per cent sales tax) in the rates they quote. And watch out for added extras. Some hotels charge for Wi-Fi, some do not. If you're bringing a car (which we recommend you don't – London isn't a good city for drivers), always check with the hotel before you arrive: few central hotels offer parking, and those that do charge steeply for it.

It's also worth looking at hotel booking websites: uk.hotels.com is often good. If you're feeling more adventurous – especially if you fancy a stay in one of the thriving neighbourhoods outside central London – www.airbnb.co.uk is worth a look (*see left* Suite Dreams).

Great Northern Hotel, designed by Lewis Cubitt, was the city's first railway hotel opened in 1854, part of the Victorian railway explosion.

ACCOMMODATION

— STRAND PALACE HOTEL —

IN THE HEART OF THE CAPITAL WHERE
THE CITY MEETS THE WEST END

372 STRAND, LONDON WC2E 0JJ
STAY@STRANDPALACEHOTEL.CO.UK • +44 (0)20 7379 4737

372
Strand Palace Hotel
LONDON

Luxury
Beaumont
Brown Hart Gardens, Mayfair, W1K 6TF (7499 1001, www. thebeaumont.com). Bond Street tube. **Map** *p140 H7.*
Oddly, the Grade II-listed façade is the least impressive part of this hotel. The first new Mayfair hotel for a decade is set in the vast 1926 garage where Selfridge's shoppers used to get their jalopies tuned up, but it is in the painstakingly and totally rebuilt interiors – bland hire-car offices in 2011 – that this art deco fantasia sings. There's smooth service and a lovely private bar/drawing room off the foyer. The staff gets the marriage of glamorous formality and approachability just right, and the owners' personal travel bugbears have created some really thoughtful touches, from the sliding screens that isolate beds from bathrooms to the free soft drinks, movies and shoeshines.

Towering over the handsome square in front of the **Beaumont** is the Antony Gormley-designed ROOM: on the outside it's a striking Cubist-influenced sculpture; on the inside it's a two-storey suite in immaculate art deco style, leading through to a low-lit, almost womb-like bedroom right inside the sculpture.

Claridge's
55 Brook Street, Mayfair, W1K 4HR (7629 8860, www.claridges. co.uk). Bond Street tube. **Map** *p140 J7.*
Claridge's is sheer class and pure atmosphere and, with its signature art deco redesign, still simply dazzling. Photographs of past guests, including Churchill and sundry royals, grace the grand foyer, as does an absurdly over-the-top Dale Chihuly chandelier. Without departing too far from the traditional, Claridge's has managed to keep its main restaurant Fera actively fashionable (the excellent Simon Rogan is in charge), and A-listers can gather for champers in the discreet bar. The rooms divide evenly between deco and Victorian style, with period touches such as deco toilet flushes in swanky marble bathrooms. Bedside panels control the mod-con facilities at the touch of a button. If money's no object, opt for a David Linley suite, in duck-egg blue and white, or lilac and silver.

Covent Garden Hotel
10 Monmouth Street, Covent Garden, WC2H 9HB (7806 1000, www.firmdalehotels.com). Covent Garden or Leicester Square tube. **Map** *p181 M7.*

The excellent location – in the heart of London's theatre district – and tucked-away screening room of the always-superb Firmdale hotels ensure that it continues to attract starry customers, with anyone needing a bit of privacy able to retreat upstairs to the lovely panelled private library and drawing room. In the guest-rooms, Kit Kemp's distinctive style mixes pinstriped wallpaper, pristine white quilts and floral upholstery with bold, contemporary elements; each room is unique, but each has the Kemp trademark upholstered mannequin and granite and oak bathroom. On the ground floor, the 1920s Paris-style Brasserie Max and the retro zinc bar retain their buzz – outdoor tables give a perfect viewpoint on Covent Garden boutique life in summer.

Dorchester
53 Park Lane, Mayfair, W1K 1QA (7629 8888, www.thedorchester. com). Hyde Park Corner tube. **Map** *p140 H9.*
A Park Lane fixture since 1931, the Dorchester's interior may be thoroughly, opulently classical, but the hotel is cutting-edge in attitude, providing an unrivalled level of personal service. With the grandest lobby in town, amazing

Mondrian at Sea Containers

Green Dream

A new hotel is looking to make Wood Green an artistic heartland

Scruffy Wood Green – way up in north London – isn't an area you'd associate with the world's cultural elite, but Somerset House, the Royal Court theatre and the British Council have all encouraged their artists to stay at a new hotel there when they're in town and use its spaces for rehearsals.

Opening in a converted 1930s art deco building near the Piccadilly line station in 2016, the **Green Rooms** has rooms starting at £18 a night in one of two dorms, £45 for one of 22 doubles or £80 for either of the studio apartments. These prices are wildly cheap for London, which the not-for-profit organisation behind the hotel hopes will attract artists, actors, musicians and other visiting creative types (normal punters wanting to stay here will pay a little more). That the Night Tube (see p406) stops here at weekends doesn't hurt, either.

On the ground floor, the rather handsome lobby, bar and restaurant have become a bit of a workspace for laptop-crackers, and the restaurant also offers six-month residencies to chefs mentored by Johnny Smith, of Shoreditch's Michelin-starred Clove Club. Upstairs is a large gallery space where guests are encouraged to engage with a diverse programme of exhibitions, and performance and arts-related events.

The notion is that offering a place for creative people to stay is the way to create a place that inspires creativity. Even in Wood Green.

views of Hyde Park, state-of-the-art mod cons and a magnificent spa, it's small wonder the hotel continues to welcome movie stars (the lineage stretches from Elizabeth Taylor to Tom Cruise) and political leaders (Eisenhower planned the D-Day landings here). It's said to have the deepest baths in London. You're not likely to be eating out, either: the Dorchester employs 90 full-time chefs at the The Grill, Alain Ducasse and the wonderfully atmospheric China Tang. There's even an angelic tearoom in the spa: the Spatisserie.

A few years ago, the Dorchester opened an entirely new hotel, **45 Park Lane** (7493 4545, www. dorchestercollection.com/en/london/45-park-lane), in the former Playboy Club premises, almost opposite the entrance to its predecessor.

Mondrian at Sea Containers

20 Upper Ground, South Bank, SE1 9PD (3747 1000, www. morganshotelgroup.com/mondrian/mondrian-london). Blackfriars tube. **Map** *p78 O8.* Location's everything here: this Mondrian is right on the Thames, with the views on the bank side of the building among the best in London – low enough to feel part of the city, high enough to feel exclusive. The rooms are nicely

furnished by Tom Dixon in a kind of postmodern deco style, minimalist without leaving you feeling the sharp edges. Public spaces are terrific and playfully ship-themed (not least the prow that encases the reception desks) and there are plenty of areas for meetings. There's a connoisseurs' bar (Dandylyan, *see p84*) and less accomplished restaurant on the ground floor, as well as a blingier bar in a glass cube on the roof (the Rumpus Room, closed Mon, Sun) and a cosy Curzon cinema.

Shangri-La at the Shard

31 St Thomas Street, Southwark, SE1 9QU (7234 8000, www. shangri-la.com/london). London Bridge tube/rail. **Map** *p78 R9.* The Shangri-La is unusual in many ways. The hotel proper starts on floor 35 with a spacious foyer and restaurant: the ground floor is just a pre-reception and security bag scanner before the uncannily smooth and swift lift. The building's pyramid shape means every room is different, with most floor space and hence the poshest suites on 36 and 37, not at the top. And the rooms are priced by view: the most expensive look north, offering 180° Thames vistas. Those views are amazing, as you'd expect: absorbing as dusk falls and the city lights come on, especially

from the lobby and restaurant. The Skypool, fitness room and bar feel a bit remote, way up on floor 52. The decor is cosmopolitan Asian neutral, with some unimpressive bits of design offset by imaginative touches (binoculars for you to enjoy the view, torches to ease jetlagged room navigation in bedside drawers). Staff members are multicultural and friendly, cheerfully solving problems and seeming rather pleased to be here.

Expensive
Boundary

2-4 Boundary Street, Shoreditch, E2 7DD (7729 1051, www. theboundary.co.uk). Liverpool Street tube/rail or Shoreditch High Street Overground. **Map** *p256 S5*
Design mogul Sir Terence Conran's Boundary Project warehouse conversion was a labour of love. Its restaurants – which include Albion (*see p264*), Tratra, a French restaurant by best-selling cookery book writer Stéphane Reynaud, and a rooftop bar – are high quality but relaxed places, and all 17 bedrooms are beautifully designed. Each has a handmade bed, but all are otherwise individually furnished with classic furniture and original art. The five studios, lofts and

suites range in style from the bright and sea-salt fresh Beach to modern Chinoiserie by Sir David Tang, while the remaining bedrooms (the slightly larger corner bedrooms have windows along both external walls) are themed by design style: Mies van der Rohe, Eames, Shaker. There's also a charming Heath Robinson room, decorated with the cartoonist's sketches of hilariously complex machines.

Great Northern Hotel

King's Cross St Pancras Station, Pancras Road, King's Cross, N1C 4TB (3388 0800, www.gnhlondon. com). King's Cross tube/rail. **Map** *p194 M3.*
Designed by Lewis Cubitt, the city's first railway hotel opened in 1854, part of the Victorian railway explosion. It has had plenty of rough times since then, not least the 12 years it was dark, but almost £40m of renovation has recreated the place as a classic. The furniture is by artisans and, in many cases, bespoke: witness the Couchette rooms, each with a double bed snugly fitted into the window to playfully echo sleeper carriages; the neatly upholstered bedside cabinets; or the ceiling lights raised and lowered by fabulously steampunk pulleys. You're not expected to suffer the privations of a Victorian traveller, though: fast Wi-Fi, film and music libraries on the large TV, Egyptian cotton sheets and walk-in showers are all standard. There's no room service but each floor has a simply charming pantry, full of jars of vintage sweets, a stand of fresh cakes, tea and coffee, newspapers and books – even a USB printer. There's also Plum + Spilt Milk, a grand restaurant with a quiet bar, on the first floor, while the busy ground-floor GNH Bar has direct access to King's Cross station.

London Edition

10 Berners Street, Fitzrovia, W1T 3NP (7781 0000, www. editionhotels.com/london). Oxford Circus or Tottenham Court Road tube. **Map** *p194 K6.*
The London Edition makes a big impact as you walk into its grand hall of a lobby, complete with double-height rococo ceilings,

floor-to-ceiling windows and marble pillars. And there's more to the space: it's the setting for the lobby bar, with an eclectic mix of comfortable, snazzy seating – sofas with faux-fur throws and wing-backed chairs – plus a snooker table, a blackened steel bar, a real fire and a colossal silver egg-shaped object hanging where you might expect a chandelier. Off on one side is the equally opulent Berners Tavern (*see p207*), where Jason Atherton is executive chef. With banquette seating and many paintings, it has the vibe of a grand café and a brasserie-style menu to match. Hidden away at the back of the public area is the clubby, wood-panelled Punch Room bar, where the speciality is – you've guessed it – punch. Bedrooms are a contrast: akin to lodges or dachas, with matte oak floors, wood-panelled walls and more faux-fur throws tossed on luxurious beds. Larger rooms come with sofas, some have large furnished terraces, and all have rainforest showers, Le Labo toiletries (with the hotel's woody signature scent) and iPod docks.

Portobello Hotel

22 Stanley Gardens, Notting Hill, W11 2NG (7727 2777, www. portobellohotel.com). Holland Park or Notting Hill Gate tube. **Map** *p78 B7.*
The Portobello is a hotel with nearly half a century of celebrity status, having hosted the likes of Johnny Depp, Kate Moss and Alice Cooper, who used his tub to house a boa constrictor. It remains a pleasingly unpretentious place, with a more civilised demeanour than its legend might suggest. There is now a lift to help rockers who are feeling their age up the five floors, but there's still a 24-hour guest-only bar downstairs for those who don't yet feel past it. The rooms are themed – the superb basement Japanese Water Garden, for example, has an elaborate spa bath, its own private grotto and a small private garden – but all are stylishly equipped with a large fan, tall house plants and round-the-clock room service.

Rookery

12 Peter's Lane, Cowcross Street, Clerkenwell, EC1M 6DS (7336 0931, www.rookeryhotel.com). Farringdon tube/rail. **Map** *p212 P6.*
The Rookery has long been something of a celebrity hideaway deep in the heart of Clerkenwell. Its front door is satisfyingly hard to find; when Fabric (*see p339*) devotees are about the front rooms can be noisy, but the place is otherwise as creakily calm as a country manor. Once inside, guests enjoy an atmospheric warren of rooms, each individually decorated in the style of a Georgian townhouse: huge clawfoot baths, elegant four-posters, antique desks, old paintings and brass shower fittings. While the decor is dialled to 18th-century glamour, modernity is definitely not forgotten. There's an honesty bar in the bright and airy drawing room at the back, which opens on to a sweet little patio. The ground-floor suite has its own hallway, a cosy boudoir and a subterranean bathroom with a double-ended cast-iron bath.

W London Leicester Square

10 Wardour Street, Leicester Square, W1D 6QF (7758 1000, www.wlondon.co.uk). Leicester Square tube. **Map** *p163 L8.*
Where the old Swiss Centre used to be in the north-west corner of Leicester Square is the UK's first W Hotel, the entire building veiled in translucent glass that is lit in different colours through the day. (The presence of M&M World downstairs dials the wow-factor down a little, but it's the thought that counts.) The brand made its name with hip hotels around the world that offer glamorous bars, upmarket food and functional but spacious rooms. The London W is no exception: Room 913 is a large nightclub/bar space with possibly the largest glitterball in town; while the W lounge offers classy cocktails and a Sunday brunch party. There's also a branch of the deathlessly popular concept restaurant Burger & Lobster (*see p165*). The rooms – across ten storeys – are well equipped, with their own munchie boxes. FIT (the

hotel's state-of-the-art fitness facility), placed next to the pale and serene Away Spa on the sixth floor, offers fine views over Soho. Oh, and there's a private 3D cinema.

Mid-range
Bermondsey Square Hotel
Bermondsey Square, Tower Bridge Road, Bermondsey, SE1 3UN (7378 2450, www. bermondseysquarehotel.co.uk). Borough tube or London Bridge tube/rail. **Map** *p78 R11.*
This is a deliberately kitsch new-build hotel on a redeveloped square. Loft suites are named after the heroines of psychedelic rock classics (Lucy, Lily, Jude, Ruby and Eleanor); some have private terraces or a hammock, or Japanese baths. Rooms have classic discs on the walls, and you can kick your heels from the suspended Bubble Chair at reception. But, although occupants of the Lucy suite get a multi-person jacuzzi (with a great terrace view), the real draw isn't the gimmicks – it's well-designed rooms for competitive prices. The restaurant-bar has been through a few hit-and-miss incarnations, but the bar's lounge area remains a good spot to relax in and the staff are helpful.

Hoxton Holborn
199-206 High Holborn, Holborn, WC1V 7BD (7661 3000, thehoxton. com). Holborn tube. **Map** *p194 M6.*
Shoebox, Snug, Cosy and Roomy. That's the choice you get when you stay at the Hoxton's trendy Holborn outpost, but who cares about room size when you're just about as close to the centre of London as it's possible to be. In truth, following the template set by the original Hoxton hotel in east London, the rooms are so well designed you barely notice their size. Clever use of mirrors helps to enlarge the space, reflecting the room's dark walls, soft lighting and casually hip vibe. Add to that a snazzy TV and a lovely walk-in shower. The West End's bars and restaurants are right on your doorstep but the hotel bar, decked out in 1970s

furniture, does a mean negroni to get you started.

K West
Richmond Way, Shepherd's Bush, W14 0AX (8008 6600, www.k-west.co.uk). Shepherd's Bush tube/ Overground.
Behind the sleek glass façade of this former BBC building – where Bob Marley once played – is a thoroughly modern hotel with a sense of fun. An in-house DJ spins until the early hours at weekends, there's a super-swish spa and each airy, sizeable room comes with its very own smart tablet and, even more helpfully, smart phones that come with unlimited data browsing so you can go off into London and explore the city. Service is wonderfully attentive, rooms are clean and smart and it's great value for money.

La Suite West
41-51 Inverness Terrace, Bayswater, W2 3JN (7313 8484, www.lasuitewest.com). Bayswater or Queensway tube. **Map** *pull-out map D7.*
A typical row of west London townhouses on the outside, La Suite has been transformed on the inside by designer Anouska Hempel, with sleek lines and a

black and white palette. A discreet side entrance leads into a long, minimalist reception area with an open fire and a zen-like feel. An Asian influence persists in the rooms, with slatted sliding screens for windows, wardrobe and bathrooms helping to make good use of space (which is limited in the cheaper rooms). Thoughtfully designed white marble bathrooms, with rainforest shower and bath, give a feeling of luxury despite not being huge. The large terrace running along the front of the building, with trees planted for an arbour-like effect, is a big summer asset for drinks, lunch or dinner, and the Raw vegetarian restaurant is an unusual take on hotel dining. All in all, clever design, a friendly vibe and – importantly – keen pricing make for a great hotel for this price range. Highly recommended.

Shoreditch Rooms
Ebor Street, Shoreditch House, Shoreditch, E1 6AW (7739 5040, www.shoreditchhouse.com/hotel). Shoreditch High Street Overground. **Map** *p256 U5.*
One of several accommodation offerings from the Soho House members' club, Shoreditch Rooms

Hoxton Holborn

might even be the best, perfectly catching the local atmosphere with its unfussy, slightly retro design. The rooms feel a bit like urban beach huts, with pastel-coloured tongue-and-groove shutters and swing doors to the en suite showers. They feel fresh, bright and comfortable, even though they're furnished with little more than a bed, an old-fashioned phone and DAB radio, and a big, solid dresser (minibar, hairdryer and treats within, flatscreen TV on top). Guests get access to the fine eating, drinking and fitness facilities (yes, there is a gym, but more importantly an excellent rooftop pool) in the members' club next door. Everything's put together with a light touch, from the 'Borrow Me' bookshelf by the lifts (jelly beans, umbrellas, boardgames) to the room grades: Tiny (from just £125), Small or Small+ (with little rooftop balconies from which to survey the grey horizon).

Zetter Hotel
86-88 Clerkenwell Road, EC1M 5RJ (7324 4567, www.thezetter. com). Farringdon tube/rail. **Map** *p212 P5.*
Zetter is a fun, laid-back, modern hotel with some interesting design notes. There's a refreshing lack of attitude and a forward-looking approach, with friendly staff and firm eco-credentials

(such as free Brompton bikes for guests' use). The rooms, stacked up on five galleried storeys around an impressive atrium, look into an intimate and recently refreshed bar area. They are smoothly functional, but cosied up with choice home comforts such as hot-water bottles and old Penguin paperbacks, as well as having walk-in showers with REN smellies. The downstairs is home to Club Zetter, while the fabulous sister-hotel Zetter Townhouse, in a historic building just across the square, has a fantastic cocktail bar with a hip vintage feel.

Budget
citizenM London Bankside
20 Lavington Street, Southwark, SE1 0NZ (3519 1680, www. citizenm.com). Southwark tube. **Map** *p122 O8.*
This casually stylish new build is a superbly well-designed – and well-located – addition to London's affordably chic hotels. The ground floor is a slick yet cosy café-bar and reception area: self-check-in, but with staff on hand to help and, where better rooms are available, offer upgrades. Guests are invited to use this area as their 'living room' and – thanks to the neat design – do so. The rooms themselves are tiny but well thought through: there are blackout blinds, drench showers

with removable sideheads, storage under the bed and free movies. The rooms are also fun: those blinds are automatic, controlled – as are the movies, air-con and funky coloured lighting – from a touch-sensitive tablet. While the Bankside branch gets our nod for its location right behind Tate Modern, the two more recent London citizenMs – one in Shoreditch (6 Holywell Lane, EC2A 3ET), the other near the Tower of London (40 Trinity Square, EC3N 4DJ) – are also very handy for holidaymakers.

Dictionary Hostel
10-20 Kingsland Road, Shoreditch, E2 8DA (7613 2784, thedictionaryhostel.com/en). Old Street tube/rail or Shoreditch High Street Overground. **Map** *p256 S4.*
Club kids, you've found your home: right at the axis of Kingsland Road and Old Street and so walking – or crawling – distance from Hoxton's best dance spots. There's a bar downstairs, Translate, and also a laundrette, a café, a cute, plant-covered interior courtyard and an intimate roof terrace. There are dorm beds and private rooms starting at £17 (with TVs, kettle and coffee). Jam-jar lighting, swings in the dorms and fairy-lit communal areas are quirky touches, which make for an

Qbic London City Hotel

enjoyable stay. Breakfast is free and includes the highly prized bagels from nearby Brick Lane.

Jenkins

45 Cartwright Gardens, Bloomsbury, WC1H 9EH (7383 9210, www.juddhotelbloomsbury. com). Russell Square tube or Euston tube/rail. **Map** *p194 L4.*
This well-to-do Georgian beauty has been a hotel since the 1920s. It still has an atmospheric, antique air, although the rooms have mod cons enough – TVs, mini-fridges, tea and coffee, and free Wi-Fi. Its looks have earned it a role in Agatha Christie's *Poirot*, but it's not chintzy, just floral. The breakfast room is handsome, with snowy cotton tablecloths and Windsor chairs, and the buffet breakfast – which includes hot options – is free.

Luxury Inn

156 Tottenham Road, De Beauvoir, N1 4DY (7683 3056, www.theluxuryinn.com). Dalston Junction rail.
If you're after modern amenities in a contemporary setting, which still retains a certain historical charm, then head to this family-run bed and breakfast, set in a converted factory in the conservation area of De Beauvoir,

between Islington and Dalston. Its four en suite rooms surround a stylish loft space. With a self-service breakfast in a shared dining room-lounge area, free run of the kitchen, and a lush courtyard garden you can really make yourself at home.

Qbic London City Hotel

42 Adler Street, Whitechapel, E1 1EE (3021 2644, www.qbichotels. com). Aldgate East or Whitechapel tube. **Map** *p256 T7.*
The Dutch invasion of stylish budget hotels continues with this Brick Lane offering, created by the incredibly rapid fit-out of a former office building using modular 'Cubi' bedrooms. The hotel also works with local cycling charity Bikeworks and with Food Cycle, which provides free soup every afternoon. The rooms are sold at four levels – starting at £69 a night for no view, and increasing in price if you want to see the Whitechapel Road, the inner courtyard or Altab Ali Park. Prices are pegged by keeping down the numbers of staff, which means self check-in and no cash accepted – even vending machines are card only. Still, the essentials are covered: TVs in each room, Wi-Fi throughout, free snack breakfast (or £13 for a

continental) in the natty social space downstairs. The location is gritty but great: minutes from Brick Lane.

Z Hotel Soho

17 Moor Street, Soho, W1D 5AP (3551 3700, www.thezhotels.com/ soho). Leicester Square tube. **Map** *p163 L7.*
For the money, the Z is an absolute bargain. First, the location is superb: it really means Soho, not a short bus-ride away – the breakfast room/bar exits on to Old Compton Street. Then there's the hotel itself, which is surprisingly chic – especially the unexpected interior courtyard, with open 'corridors' stacked above it, and room to sit and drink or smoke at the bottom – and very cheerfully run, down to free wine and nibbles of an evening. The rooms are quite handsome, and have everything you need, from a little desk to free Wi-Fi, but not much more. Including space: expect beds (perhaps a little short for anyone over 6ft tall) to take up most of the room, a feeble shower, and no wardrobes or phones. A great little hotel – in both senses – and, we're pleased to report, part of a chain that's expanding.

Getting Around

ARRIVING & LEAVING

By air

Gatwick Airport *0844 892 0322, www.gatwickairport.com. About 30 miles south of London, off the M23.*

Of the three rail services that link Gatwick to London, the quickest is the **Gatwick Express** (0345 850 1530, www.gatwickexpress.com) to Victoria; it takes 30mins and runs 4.30am-12.30am daily. Tickets cost £19.90 single or £35.50 for an open return. Under-16s pay £9.95 for a single and £17.45 for returns; under-5s go free. Online prices are cheaper.

Southern (0345 127 2920, www.southernrailway.com) also runs a rail service between Gatwick and Victoria, with trains every 5-10mins (hourly 2-4am and every 15-30mins midnight-2am, 4-6am). It takes about 35mins, and costs from £12 for a single, £15.80 for a day return (after 9.30am) and £31.40 for an open period return. Under-16s get half-price tickets; under-5s go free. Book online and save 10%.

Thameslink Great Northern (www.thameslinkrailway.com) costs from £19.90 single and from £27.20 day return (after 9.30am). A **taxi** to the centre costs from £90 and takes a bit over an hour.

Heathrow Airport *0844 335 1801, www.heathrowairport.com. About 15 miles west of London, off the M4.*

The **Heathrow Express** train (0845 600 1515, www.heathrowexpress.co.uk) runs to Paddington every 15mins (5.10am-11.25pm daily) and takes 15-20mins. Tickets cost £22-£25 single and £37 return (more if you buy on board); under-15s travel at half-price; under-2s free. Many

airlines have check-in desks at Paddington Station.

The journey by tube is longer but cheaper. The 50-60min **Piccadilly line** ride into central London costs £6 one way (half price 11-15s; free under-10s). Trains run every few minutes from about 6am to 12.30am daily (7am-11.30pm Sun). Fares using Oyster cards are cheaper (£3.10-£5.10).

The **Heathrow Connect** (0345 604 1515, www.heathrowconnect.com) rail service offers direct access to Hayes, Southall, Hanwell, West Ealing, Ealing Broadway and Paddington stations in west and north-west London. The trains run every 15-30mins, from 4.42am to 11.05pm, terminating at Heathrow Central (Terminals 2 and 3). From there, take a free shuttle to Terminal 4; between Central and Terminal 5, there's free use of the Heathrow Express. A single from Paddington is £10.30; an open return is £20.70.

National Express (0871 781 8171, www.nationalexpress.com) runs daily coach services to London Victoria (35-60mins, 4.20am-10.05pm daily), leaving Heathrow Central bus terminal every 20-30mins. It's £10 for a single (£5 under-16s) or £16 (£8 under-16s) for a return.

A **taxi** into town will cost £45-£70 and take 30-60mins.

London City Airport *7646 0088, www.londoncityairport.com. About 9 miles east of central London.*

The **Docklands Light Railway** (DLR) includes a stop for London City Airport and runs every 8-15mins. The journey to Bank station in the City takes around 20mins, and trains run 5.36am-12.16am Mon-Sat,

7.06am-11.16pm Sun. Tickets cost £4.90; £2.45 11-15s. A **taxi** costs around £40 to central London.

Luton Airport *01582 405100, www.london-luton.com. About 30 miles north of London, J10 off the M1.*

It's a short shuttle bus ride from the airport to Luton Airport Parkway station. From here, the **Thameslink Great Northern** rail service (*see left*) calls at many stations; journey time is 35-45mins. Trains leave every 15mins or so and cost £14.20 one-way and £22.80 return. Trains between Luton and St Pancras run at least hourly all night.

By coach, the Luton to Victoria journey takes 60-90mins. **Green Line** (0844 801 7261, www.greenline.co.uk) runs a 24hr service. A single is £10 and returns cost £17; under-15s £7.50 single, £12 return; under-5s free.

A **taxi** to London costs from £80.

Stansted Airport *0844 335 1803, www.stanstedairport.com. About 35 miles north-east of London, J8 off the M11.*

The **Stansted Express** train, www.stanstedexpress.com) runs to and from Liverpool Street Station; the journey time is 40-45mins. Trains leave every 15mins, and tickets cost £16.60 single, £28 return; under-16s travel half-price, under-5s free.

Several companies run coaches to central London. The **National Express** service (0871 781 8171, www.nationalexpress.com) from Stansted to Victoria takes 1hr 45mins. Coaches run roughly every 20mins (24hrs daily), more at peak times. A single is £13 (£6.50 for under-16s), an open return is £19 (£9.50 for under-16s).

A **taxi** into the centre of London costs from £60.

By coach

Coaches run by **National Express** (0871 781 8171, www.nationalexpress.com), the biggest coach company in the UK, arrive at **Victoria Coach Station** (164 Buckingham Palace Road, SW1W 9TP, 0343 222 1234, www.tfl.gov.uk), a good 10min walk from Victoria tube station. This is where companies such as **Eurolines** (0871 781 8177, www.eurolines.co.uk) dock their European services.

By rail

Trains from mainland Europe run by Eurostar (0343 218 6186, www.eurostar.com) arrive at **St Pancras International** (Pancras Road, Euston Road, N1C 4QP, 7843 7688, www.stpancras.com).

PUBLIC TRANSPORT

Details on timetables and other travel information are provided by **Transport for London** (0343 222 1234, www.tfl.gov.uk). Complaints or comments on most forms of public transport can also be taken up with **London Travel Watch** (3176 2999, www.londontravelwatch.org.uk).

Travel Information Centres

These offer help with the tube, buses and DLR; they can be found in the locations detailed below. Call 0343 222 1234 for more information.

Euston *opposite Platform 8, 8am-6pm Mon-Sat, 8.30am-6pm Sun.*
Gatwick Airport *North Terminal arrivals hall, 9.15am-4pm daily. South Terminal arrivals hall 9.15am-4pm daily.*
Heathrow Airport *Terminals 1, 2, 3 underground station concourse, 7.30am-8.30pm daily.*
King's Cross *Western Ticket Hall, near St Pancras, 8am-6pm Mon-Sat, 8.30am-6pm Sun.*
Liverpool Street tube/ rail *9am-5pm daily.*
Piccadilly Circus tube *9.30am-4pm daily.*

Victoria (main station) *opposite Platform 8 8am-6pm daily.*

Fares & tickets

Tube and DLR fares are based on a system of six zones, stretching 12 miles out from the centre of London. A flat cash fare of £4.90 per journey applies across zones 1-3 on the tube, and £6 for zones 1-6; customers save up to £2.50 per journey with a pre-pay Oyster card or by paying with a contactless debit or credit card. Anyone caught without a ticket, Oyster or contactless card is subject to an £80 on-the-spot fine (reduced to £40 if you pay within three weeks).

Using the system

It is best to use either your contactless credit/debit card or to get an Oyster card (for both, *see right*). The latter can be obtained from www.tfl.gov.uk/tickets, by calling 0343 222 1234, at tube stations, Travel Information Centres, some rail stations and newsagents.

To enter and exit the tube using an Oyster (or contactless) card, simply touch it to the yellow reader, which will open the gates. Make sure you also touch the card to the reader when you exit the tube, or you'll be charged a higher fare when you next use your card to enter a station. On certain lines, you'll see a pink 'validator' – touch this reader in addition to the yellow entry/exit readers and on some routes it will reduce your fare.

Alternatively, paper single or day tickets can be bought from self-service ticket machines. TfL is in the process of closing all Underground ticket offices; carry a charged-up Oyster card to avoid being stranded. If you are using a paper ticket, enter by placing it in the slot with the black magnetic strip facing down, then pull it out of the top to open the gates. Exiting is done in much the same way; however, if you have a single journey ticket, it will be retained by the gate as you leave.

Oyster cards

A pre-paid smart card, Oyster is a far cheaper way of getting around

on public transport than buying paper tickets. You can charge up standard Oyster cards at tube stations, Information Centres (*see left*), some rail stations and newsagents. There is a £5 refundable deposit payable on each card. You can get your pay-as-you-go credit (up to £10) and your deposit refunded at a tube station ticket machine. Young visitor cards are also available for children.

Visitor Oyster cards are available from Gatwick Express outlets, National Express coaches, Superbreak, www.visitbritainshop.com, Oxford Tube coach service and on Eurostar services. The only difference bemailtween Visitor Oysters and 'normal' Oysters is that they come pre-loaded with money.

A tube journey in zone 1 using Oyster pay-as-you-go costs £2.40, compared to the cash fare of £4.90. A single tube ride within zones 1-3 costs £2.80 (off peak)/£3.30 (peak); a ride in zones 1-6 costs £3.10 (off peak)/£5.10 (peak). Children's fares (11-15 years) are 75p (off peak)/80p (peak). Peak hours are 6.30-9.30am, 4-7pm Mon-Fri. Up to four children under 11 can travel for free when travelling with an adult.

Oyster now has day capping of £6.60 if you're travelling between zones 1-2 off peak, £9.50 between zones 1-4 off peak, and £12 between zones 1-6 off peak – it thus works out cheaper than a Day Travelcard (*see p407*).

Contactless payment

If you have a credit or debit card with the contactless symbol)) you can use it instead of getting an Oyster card – and you will pay the same fare. Just place it on the yellow or pink readers in exactly the same way as you would an Oyster. If you use public transport every day for a week during your stay, it's likely to be marginally cheaper even than Oyster: usage is capped at the level of a weekly – not daily – Travelcard.

GETTING AROUND

Day Travelcards

If you're only using the tube, DLR and buses, using Oyster to pay-as-you-go will always be capped at the same price as or slightly lower than an equivalent Day Travelcard. However, if you're also using certain National Rail services, Oyster may not be accepted: opt, instead, for a Day Travelcard, a standard ticket with a coded stripe that allows travel across all networks.

Anytime Day Travelcards can be used all day. They cost £12.30 for zones 1-2 (£6.10 child), £17.50 for zones 1-6 (£8.70 child). Tickets are valid for journeys begun by 4.30am the next day. The cheaper **Off-Peak Day Travelcard** allows travel after 9.30am Mon-Fri and all day at weekends and public holidays. It costs £12.30 (£6.10 child) for zones 1-6.

Children

Under-5s travel free on buses without the need to provide any proof of identity. Five-to 10-year-olds can also travel free, but need to obtain a 5-10 Zip Oyster photocard. For details, visit www.tfl.gov.uk/tickets or call 0343 222 1234.

An 11-15 Zip Oyster photocard is needed by 11- to 15-year-olds to pay as they go on the tube/DLR and to buy 7-day, monthly or longer period Travelcards.

Photocards

Photocards are not required for 7-Day Travelcards or Bus Passes, adult-rate Travelcards or Bus Passes charged on an Oyster card. For details of how to obtain 5-10, 11-15 or 16+ Oyster photocards, see www.tfl.gov.uk/tickets or call 0343 222 1234. There is a non-refundable £10 administration fee for each ID card.

London Underground

Delays are fairly common, with lines or sections of lines frequently closed at weekends for engineering work. Trains are hot and crowded in rush hour (7.30-9.30am and 4.30-6.30pm Mon-Fri) – avoid the rush by travelling after 9.30am and you'll also pay less for your fare. The 12 colour-coded lines that together

comprise the underground rail system – also known as 'the tube' – remain the quickest way to get around, carrying some 3.5 million passengers every weekday. Comments or complaints are dealt with by **TfL Customer Services** on 0343 222 1234 (8am-8pm daily).

Timetables

Tube trains run daily from around 5.30am (except Sunday, when they start an hour or so later, and Christmas Day, when there's no service). You shouldn't have to wait more than 10mins for a train; during peak times, services should run every 2-3mins. Times of last trains vary; they're usually around 12.30am (11.30pm on Sun). The Night Tube, offering a limited 24hr service, runs Fri/Sat on the Victoria, Jubilee, and most of the Central, Northern and Piccadilly lines. Tubes also run all night on New Year's Eve. Otherwise, you're limited to night buses (*see p407*).

Fares

The single fare for adults across the network is £4.90 for journeys within zones 1-3; £6 for zones 1-6; £7.40 for zones 1-7; £8.50 for zones 1-9. Using Oyster pay-as-you-go or a contactless card, journeys within zone 1 cost £2.40; zones 1-3 costs £2.80 (off peak)/£3.30 (peak); zones 1-6 costs £3.10 (off peak)/ £5.10 (peak). The single fare for children aged 5-15 is 75p (off peak)/85p (peak) for any journey in zones 1-6. Peak hours are 6.30-9.30am, 4-7pm Mon-Fri. Under-5s travel free.

Night Tube

It seems extraordinary that London – the proud city of infrastructure innovations that ran the world's first urban underground railway in 1863 – lacked an all-night tube service until August 2016. Now almost all of the Central, Northern and Piccadilly lines, and the entire Jubilee and Victoria lines, have services through Friday/Saturday and Saturday/Sunday. They are fast, frequent (roughly every 10mins) and, well, pretty much like using the daytime tube. The fares are off-peak and you can continue to use your Day

Travelcard (or capped pay-as-you-go card) until 4.30am in the morning after the day covered by that card (or pay-as-you-go cap). If you're lucky enough to be staying near a Night Tube station, you'll bless it; questions about how efficiently the Night Tube will replace the detailed coverage of the routinely derided night bus (*see p407*) network remain, for now, a subject for nerds, night-workers and transport gurus.

Overground

The Overground (0343 222 1234) is a patchwork of different rail services, some tracing a complex orbital route roughly following the boundary of zones 2 and 3 (the orange-and-white line on the tube map). For those planning to visit areas of London with poor Underground coverage – notably (and perhaps not coincidentally) some of the buzzier bits of east and south London – the Overground is a valuable friend. From December 2017, the **Night Tube** will begin Overground as well as Underground services, with a very useful link between New Cross Gate and Dalston Junction; from 2018 it will head as far north as Highbury & Islington.

Fares

Fares are the same as the tube.

National Rail services

Independently run commuter services co-ordinated by **National Rail** (03457 48 49 50, www.national rail.co.uk) leave from the city's main rail stations. Visitors heading to south London, or to more remote destinations such as Hampton Court Palace, use these services.

Fares

Travelcards are valid on these services within the right zones, but not all routes accept Oyster pay-as-you-go or contactless payments.

Docklands Light Railway

The mostly elevated DLR trains (0343 222 1234, www.tfl. gov.uk/modes/dlr) run from Bank station (where they connect with the Central, Northern and Waterloo & City lines) or Tower Gateway, close to Tower Hill tube (Circle and District lines). At Westferry station, the line splits east and south via Island Gardens to Greenwich and Lewisham; a change at Poplar or Canning Town can take you north to Stratford. The easterly branch forks after Canning Town to either Beckton or Woolwich Arsenal. Trains run 5.30am-12.40am daily, and there are lots of good views of Docklands to be enjoyed.

Fares

Fares are the same as the tube.

Crossrail

Formally known as the Elizabeth Line after our dear queen, the dauntingly massive infrastructure project universally celebrated as Crossrail has been burrowing under the most expensive parts of London since 2009. From 2018, the central sections will be in operation; from 2019, sleeper-town residents will be whisked into London from east and west at great speed. *See p379.*

Buses

Buses are now cash-free, so you must have a ticket, valid pass or, better, an Oyster card or contactless payment card (for both, *see p405*) before boarding any bus. You can buy a ticket from machines in tube and rail stations. Inspectors patrol buses at random; if you don't have a ticket, card or pass, you may be fined £80 (£40 if you pay within 21 days).

All buses are now low-floor vehicles that are accessible to wheelchair-users and passengers with buggies. The only exception is Heritage route 15, which is served by the historic and world-famous open-platform Routemaster buses.

Fares

Using Oyster pay-as-you-go costs £1.50 a trip; your total daily payment, regardless of how many journeys you take, will be capped at £4.50. Under-16s travel for free (using an Under-11 or 11-15 Oyster photocard, as appropriate; *see p405*). You can take a second bus journey for free if you board within an hour of touching in on your first bus. Be aware that you can't pay your fare on London buses in cash. You'll need a charged Oyster card, valid travel card or contactless debit or credit card ready when you board.

Night buses

Many bus routes operate 24hrs a day, seven days a week. There are also some special night buses with an 'N' prefix, which run from about 11pm to 6am – they're used by a sometimes exhilarating combination of nightshift workers and partiers, in different proportions depending on the time of night. Most night services run every 15-30mins, but busier routes run every 10mins or so. Fares are the same as for daytime buses; Bus Passes and Travelcards can be used at no extra fare until 4.30am of the morning after they expire, with Oyster day-capping in effect until then too.

Green Line buses

These serve the suburbs within 40 miles of London (0844 801 7261, www.greenline.co.uk); services run 24hrs a day.

Water transport

Most river services operate every 20-60mins between 10.30am and 5pm, and may run more often and later in summer. For commuters, **Thames Clippers** (www.thamesclippers.com) runs a service between Embankment Pier and Royal Arsenal Woolwich Pier (limited period, otherwise to North Greenwich); stops include Blackfriars, Bankside, London Bridge, Canary Wharf and Greenwich. A standard day roamer ticket (valid 9am-9pm) costs £18.50, £9.25 for a child (5-15s), while a single from Embankment to Greenwich is £8, £4 under-16s, or £6.30 for Oyster cardholders. Book online for reductions.

Westminster Passenger Service Association (7930 2062, www.wpsa.co.uk) runs a daily service from Westminster Pier to Kew, Richmond and Hampton Court from April to October. At around £13 for a single, it's not cheap, but it is a lovely way to see the city, and there are discounts of 33-50% for Travelcard holders.

Thames River Services (7930 4097, www.thamesriverservices. co.uk) operates from the same pier, with trips to Greenwich and Tower Pier, and the Thames Barrier from May to Oct. A trip to Greenwich costs £12.50. Travelcard holders get a third off. Book online for reductions.

TAXIS & MINICABS

Black cabs

The licensed London taxi, aka 'black cab' (although they now come in many colours), is a much-loved feature of London life. Drivers must pass a test called 'the Knowledge' to prove they know every street in central London, and the shortest route to it.

If a taxi's orange 'For Hire' sign is lit, it can be hailed. If a taxi stops, the cabbie must take you to your destination if it's within seven miles. Fares rise after 8pm on weekdays and at weekends.

You can book black cabs using the very handy free Hailo app (for a list of apps visit tfl.gov. uk/modes/taxis-and-minicabs/taxi-and-minicab-apps), or from **Radio Taxis** (7272 0272) and **Dial-a-Cab** (7253 5000; cards only). Complaints about black cabs should be made via Transport for London (0343

222 4000, www.tfl.gov.uk). Note the cab's badge number, which should be displayed in the rear of the cab and on its back bumper.

Minicabs

Minicabs (saloon cars) are generally cheaper than black cabs, but can be less reliable. The police and TfL regularly warn against the use of any but licensed firms (look for a disc in the front and rear windows), so be sure to avoid drivers who illegally tout for business in the street: if they're unlicensed they might well be uninsured and may be dangerous. When you book a cab, ask the price; when your car arrives, confirm the price with the driver before getting in.

If you text **HOME** to 60835 ('60TFL'), Transport for London will reply with the numbers of the two nearest licensed minicab operators and the number for **Radio Taxis**, which provides licensed black taxis in London (it costs 35p plus standard call rate).

You can also use the **Uber** app to hail – and pay for – a minicab. It's extremely unpopular with black cab drivers, who regard use of the app as a kind of metering, but extremely popular as a cheap and efficient way of getting home.

DRIVING

London's roads are often clogged with traffic and roadworks, and parking (*see right*) is a nightmare: walking or using public transport is almost always the better option. If you hire a car, you can use any valid licence from outside the EU for up to a year after arrival. Speed limits in the city are generally 20 or 30mph.

Congestion charge

Drivers coming into central London between 7am and 6pm Monday to Friday have to pay £11.50, a fee known as the congestion charge. The congestion charge zone is bordered by Marylebone, Euston and King's Cross (N), Old Street roundabout (NE), Aldgate (E), Tower Bridge Road (SE), Elephant & Castle (S), Vauxhall, Victoria

(SW), Park Lane and Edgware Road (W). You'll know when you're about to drive into the charging zone from the red 'C' signs on the road. Enter the postcode of your destination at www.tfl.gov.uk/modes/congestioncharging to discover if it's in the charging zone.

Passes can be bought from some newsagents, garages and NCP car parks; you can also pay online at www.tfl.gov.uk/modes/congestion charging, by phone on 0343 222 2222 or by SMS. You can pay any time during the day; payments are also accepted until midnight on the next charging day, although the fee is £14 if you pay then. You only pay once per day, no matter how many times you go in and out of the zone. Expect a fine of £130 for non-payment (reduced to £65 if you pay within 14 days).

Breakdown services

AA *(Automobile Association) 0800 085 2721 information, 0800 887766 breakdown, www. theaa.com.*

ETA *(Environmental Transport Association) 0333 000 1234, www.eta.co.uk.*

RAC *(Royal Automobile Club) 0330 159 1111 information, 0800 197 7815 breakdown, www.rac. co.uk.*

Parking

Central London is scattered with parking meters, but finding an unoccupied one is usually difficult. Meters cost upwards of £1 for 15mins, and in some areas they are limited to 2hrs; if you're going to spend a lot of time driving in particular areas, find out whether there's an app for that location that allows easy payment – sometimes even permitting remote top-up payments. Parking on a single or double yellow line, a red line or in residents' parking areas during the day is illegal, and you may be fined, clamped or towed.

However, in the evening (from 6pm or 7pm in much of central London) and at various times at weekends, parking on single yellow lines is legal and free. If you find a clear spot on a single

yellow line during the evening, look for a sign giving the local regulations. Meters also become free at certain times during evenings and weekends. Parking on double yellow lines and red routes is always illegal.

Use an app like **AppyParking** to help you find the nearest free car parking; otherwise, there are many **NCP** car parks (www.ncp. co.uk), open 24hrs a day.

Clamping & vehicle removal

The immobilising of illegally parked vehicles with a clamp is common in London. You'll have to stump up a release fee (£70) and show a valid licence. The payment centre will de-clamp your car within four hours. If you don't remove your car at once, it may get clamped again, so wait by your vehicle.

If your car has disappeared, it's either been stolen or, if it was parked illegally, towed to a car pound by the local authorities. A release fee of £200 is levied for removal, plus upwards of £40 per day from the first midnight after removal. You'll also probably get a parking ticket, typically £130 (reduced by 50% if paid within 14 days). Contact **Trace**

Information Service (0845 206 8602, trace.london).

CYCLING

There has been a lot of talk about improving provision for cyclists in London and impressive sums of transport budget set aside for the purpose. Certain notorious junctions have been improved and work progresses on the 'superhighways' – segregated north–south and east–west cycling routes through the centre of town – but it will be a good while before their success can be judged. Nonetheless, no one needs to be scared of London's streets – some 180 million journeys are made each year by bike, almost all of them safely. Ride calmly, assertively and obeying the rules of the road, and always avoid getting caught on the inside of a left-turning bus or lorry. TfL's 'Cycle safety tips' are at tfl.gov.uk/modes/cycling. Serious cyclists can contact the **London Cycle Network** (www.

londoncyclenetwork.org.uk) and **London Cycling Campaign** (7234 9310, www.lcc.org.uk).

TfL also runs a handy **cycle hire scheme** Santander Cycles (0343 222 6666, tfl.gov.uk/modes/cycling/santander-cycles), with more than 750 docking stations and 11,000 bikes in operation. Nicknamed 'Boris Bikes' after the former mayor, Boris Johnson, who introduced them, the cycles – distinguished by their red Santander sponsorship branding – are picked up from and returned to a string of 24hr bicycle stations. To hire a bike, go to a docking station, touch the 'Hire a cycle' icon and insert a credit or debit card. The machine will print out a five-digit access code, which you then tap into the docking point of a bike, releasing the cycle, and away you go. A £2 fee buys 24hr access to the bikes; the first 30 minutes are free.

WALKING

By far the best and most enjoyable way to see London is on foot, but

the city's street layout is ancient and therefore complicated. We've included a foldout map of central London at the back of this book, as well as maps in the appropriate Explore chapters ; the standard *Geographers' London A-Z* or Collins' *London Street Atlas* are useful supplements if you don't like to navigate by smartphone. There's route advice at www.tfl.gov.uk/modes/walking (the map of walking times between stations, which can be downloaded from content.tfl.gov.uk/walking-tube-map.pdf, is particularly useful for showing the on-the-ground proximity of various central tube stations). Look out too for the yellow-topped 'Legible London' information posts as you stroll around (www.tfl.gov.uk/microsites/legible-london) – they're basically maps oriented to the direction you're heading, rather than with north at the top. Remember: no matter how well you know our city, going for a walk will reveal further secrets.

Resources A-Z

Travel Advice

For up-to-date information on travel to a specific country – including the latest on safety and security, health issues, local laws and customs – contact your home country government's department of foreign affairs. Most have websites with useful advice for would-be travellers

Australia
www.smartraveller.gov.au

Canada
www.voyage.gc.ca

New Zealand
www.safetravel.govt.nz

Republic of Ireland
www.dfa.ie

UK
www.fco.gov.uk/travel

USA
www.state.gov/travel

ACCIDENT & EMERGENCY

In the event of a serious accident, fire or other incident, call 999 – free from any phone, including payphones – and ask for an ambulance, the fire service or police. If no one is in immediate danger, call 101.

Emergency departments

Listed below are most of the central London hospitals that have Accident & Emergency (A&E) departments which are open 24 hours daily.

Charing Cross Hospital *Fulham Palace Road, Hammersmith, W6 8RF (3311 1234, www.imperial.nhs. uk). Hammersmith tube.*

Chelsea & Westminster Hospital *369 Fulham Road, Chelsea, SW10 9NH (3315 8000, www.chelwest.nhs.uk). South Kensington tube.*

Royal Free Hospital *Pond Street, Hampstead, NW3 2QG (7794 0500, www.royalfree.nhs.uk). Belsize Park tube or Hampstead Heath Overground.*

Royal London Hospital *Whitechapel Road, Whitechapel, E1 1BB (7377 7000, www.bartshealth.nhs.uk). Whitechapel tube/Overground.*

St Mary's Hospital *Praed Street, Paddington, W2 1NY (3312 6666, www.imperial.nhs. uk). Paddington tube/rail.* **Map** *pull-out E6.*

St Thomas' Hospital *Westminster Bridge Road, South Bank, SE1 7EH (7188 7188, www. guysandstthomas.nhs.uk). Westminster tube or Waterloo tube/rail.* **Map** *p78 M10.*

University College Hospital *235 Euston Road, NW1 2BU (3456 7890, www.uclh.nhs.uk). Euston Square or Warren Street tube.* **Map** *p194 K5*

ADDRESSES

London postcodes are less helpful than they could be for locating addresses. The first element starts with a compass point – N, E, SE, SW, W and NW, plus the smaller EC (East Central) and WC (West Central). However, the number that follows relates not to geography (unless it's a 1, which indicates central) but to alphabetical order. So N2 is way out in the boondocks (East Finchley), while W2 covers the very central Bayswater district.

AGE RESTRICTIONS

Buying/drinking alcohol 18
Driving 17
Sex 16
Smoking 18

CUSTOMS

Citizens entering the UK from outside the EU must adhere to duty-free import limits:

• 200 cigarettes or 100 cigarillos or 50 cigars or 250g of tobacco
• 4 litres still table wine plus either 1 litre spirits or strong liqueurs (above 22% abv) or 2 litres fortified wine (under 22% abv), sparkling wine or other liqueurs
• other goods to the value of no more than £390

The import of meat, poultry, fruit, plants, flowers and protected animals is restricted or forbidden; there are no restrictions on the import or export of currency if travelling from another EU country. If you are travelling from outside the EU, amounts over €10,000 must be declared on arrival.

People over the age of 17 arriving from an EU country are able to import unlimited goods for their own personal use, if bought tax-paid (so not duty-free).

Quite what the arrangements will be post-Brexit it seems not even the government yet knows – but the likelihood of any rapid changes is remote. For the current details, see www.gov.uk.

DISABLED

As a city that evolved long before the needs of disabled people were considered, London is difficult for wheelchair users, though access and facilities are slowly improving. All the capital's bus fleet is now low-floor for easier wheelchair access; there are no steps for any of the city's trams, though these are not widespread; and all DLR stations have either lifts or ramp access. However, steps and escalators to the tube and overground trains mean they are often of only limited use to wheelchair users, and even stations with lifts can be a real headache to navigate (King's Cross is but one example). A blue symbol on the tube map (see *pp430-431*) indicates stations with step-free access. The **Step-free Tube Guide** map is free; call 0343 222 1234 or download it from tfl.gov.uk/accessguides.

Most major attractions and hotels offer good accessibility, though provisions for the hearing- and sight-disabled are patchier. Enquire about facilities in advance.

Access in London is an invaluable reference book for disabled travellers. It's available for a £10 donation (sterling cheque, cash US dollars or via PayPal to gordon_couch@yahoo. com) from **Access Project** (39 Bradley Gardens, W13 8HE, www. accessinlondon.org).

Artsline *www.artsline.org.uk*. Information on disabled access to arts and culture.

Can Be Done *Congress House, 14 Lyon Road, Harrow, Middx, HA1 2EN (8907 2400, www.canbedone. co.uk). Harrow on the Hill tube/ rail. Open 9.30am-5pm Mon-Fri.* Disabled-adapted holidays and tours in London, around the UK and worldwide.

Disability Rights UK *Ground floor, CAN Mezzanine, 49-51 East Road, Islington, N1 6AH (0808 800 0082, 0084 textphone, www. disabilityrightsuk.org). Old Street tube/rail. Open 9am-8pm Mon-Fri; 10am-2pm Sat.*
A national organisation for disabled voluntary groups, publishing books and offering advice, links to other organisations for help and courses.

Tourism for All *0845 124 9971, www.tourismforall.org.uk. Open Helpline 9am-5pm Mon-Fri.* Information for older people and people with disabilities in relation to accessible accommodation and other tourism services.

Wheelchair Travel & Access Mini Buses *Unit 44, Martlands Industrial Estate, Smarts Heath Lane, Woking, Surrey, GU22 0RQ (01483 233640, www.wheelchair-travel.co.uk).*

Hires out converted vehicles (a driver is optional), plus cars with hand controls and wheelchair-adapted vehicles.

DRUGS

Illegal drug use remains higher in London than the UK as a whole, though it's becoming less visible on the streets and in clubs. Despite fierce debate, cannabis has been reclassified from Class C to Class B (where it rejoins amphetamines), but possession of a small amount might attract no more than a warning for a first offence. More serious Class B and A drugs (ecstasy, LSD, heroin, cocaine and the like) carry stiffer penalties, with a maximum of seven years in prison for possession plus a fine.

ELECTRICITY

The UK uses the European standard 220-240V, 50-cycle AC voltage. British plugs have three pins, so travellers with two-pin European appliances should bring an adaptor.

Anyone using US appliances, which run off 110-120V, 60-cycle, will need to bring or buy a voltage converter.

American Embassy *24 Grosvenor Square, Mayfair, W1A 2LQ (7499 9000, www.london.usembassy. gov). Bond Street or Marble Arch tube. Open 8.30am-5.30pm Mon-Fri. Map p140 H8.*

Australian High Commission *Australia House, Strand, Holborn, WC2B 4LA (7379 4334, www. uk.embassy.gov.au). Holborn or Temple tube. Open 9am-5pm Mon-Fri. Map p212 N7.*

Canadian High Commission *Canada House, Trafalgar Square, Westminster, SW1Y 5BJ (7004 6000, www.canada.org. uk). Charing Cross tube/rail. Open 9.30am-12.30pm Mon-Fri. Map p100 L8.*

Embassy of Ireland *17 Grosvenor Place, Belgravia, SW1X 7HR (7235 2171, 7373 4339 passports & visas, www.dfa.ie/irish-embassy/great-britain). Hyde Park Corner tube. Open 9.30am-12.30pm, 2.30-4.30pm Mon-Fri. Map p122 H10.*

New Zealand High Commission *New Zealand House, 80 Haymarket, St James's, SW1Y 4TQ (7930 8422, www.mfat.govt. nz/en/embassies). Piccadilly Circus tube. Open 9am-5pm Mon-Fri. Map p163 L8.*

RESOURCES A-Z

Climate

Average temperatures and monthly rainfall in London

	Temp High (°C/°F)	Temp Low (°C/°F)	Rainfall (mm/in)
January	6 / 43	2 / 36	54 / 2.1
February	7 / 44	2 / 36	40 / 1.6
March	10 / 50	3 / 37	37 / 1.5
April	13 / 55	6 / 43	37 / 1.5
May	17 / 63	8 / 46	46 / 1.8
June	20 / 68	12 / 54	45 / 1.8
July	22 / 72	14 / 57	57 / 2.2
August	21 / 70	13 / 55	59 / 2.3
September	19 / 66	11 / 52	49 / 1.9
October	14 / 57	8 / 46	57 / 2.2
November	10 / 50	5 / 41	64 / 2.5
December	7 / 44	4 / 39	48 / 1.9

HEALTH

British citizens or those working in the UK can go to any general practitioner (GP). People ordinarily resident in the UK, including overseas students, are also permitted to register with a National Health Service (NHS) doctor. If you fall outside these categories, you will have to pay to see a GP. Your hotel concierge should be able to recommend one.

A pharmacist may dispense medicines on receipt of a prescription from a GP. NHS prescriptions cost £8.40; under-16s, those on benefits and over-60s are exempt from charges. Contraception is free for all. If you're not eligible to see an NHS doctor, you'll be charged cost price for any medicines prescribed.

Free emergency medical treatment under the NHS is available to:
• EU nationals and those of Iceland, Norway and Liechtenstein; all may also be entitled to state-provided treatment for non-emergency conditions with an EHIC (European Health Insurance Card)
• nationals of New Zealand, Russia, most former USSR states and the former Yugoslavia
• residents (irrespective of their nationality) of Anguilla, Australia, Barbados, the British Virgin Islands, the Falkland Islands, the Isle of Man, Montserrat, Poland, Romania, St Helena and the Turks & Caicos Islands
• anyone who has been in the UK for the previous 12 months, or who has come to the UK to take up permanent residence
• students and trainees whose courses require more than 12 weeks in employment in the first year
• refugees and others who have sought refuge in the UK
• people with HIV/AIDS at a special STD treatment clinic

Again, post-Brexit you can expect these arrangements to change, but this is unlikely to happen soon.

The NHS does not charge for the following services:
• treatment in A&E departments
• emergency ambulance transport to a hospital
• diagnosis and treatment of certain communicable diseases
• family-planning services
• compulsory psychiatric treatment.

Contraception & abortion

Family-planning advice, contraceptive supplies and abortions are free to British citizens on the NHS, and to EU residents and foreign nationals living in Britain. Visit www.fpa.org.uk for your local Family Planning Association. The 'morning after' pill (around £25), effective up to 72 hours after intercourse, is available over the counter at pharmacies.

British Pregnancy Advisory Service *03457 304 030, www.bpas.org. Open Helpline 24hrs daily.*
Callers are referred to their nearest clinic for treatment.

Brook Advisory Centre *0808 802 1234, www.brook.org.uk. Open Helpline 9am-5pm Mon-Fri.* Information on sexual health, contraception and abortion, plus free pregnancy tests for under-25s.

Marie Stopes House *Family Planning Clinic/Well Woman Centre, 108 Whitfield Street, Fitzrovia, W1T 5BE (0345 300 8090, www.mariestopes.org.uk). Warren Street tube. Open Clinic 8am-4pm Mon, Wed; 8am-5pm Tue; 7.30am-4pm Sat. Helpline 24hrs daily. Map p194 K5.*
Contraceptive advice, emergency contraception, pregnancy testing, an abortion service, cervical and health screening, and gynaecological services. Fees may apply.

Dentists

Dental care is free for resident students, under-18s and people on benefits. All others must pay. To find an NHS dentist, contact the local Health Authority or a Citizens' Advice Bureau (*see p413*).

Dental Emergency Care Service *Guy's Hospital, floors 17-28, Tower Wing, Great Maze Pond, SE1 9RT (7188 8006, www.guysandstthomas.nhs.uk/our-services/dental). London Bridge tube/rail. Open 9am-12.30pm, 1.30-3pm Mon-Fri. Map p78 Q9.*
Queues start forming at 8am; arrive by 10am if you're to be seen at all.

Hospitals

For a list of hospitals with Accident & Emergency departments, *see p410*; for other hospitals, check www.yell.com.

Pharmacies

Also called 'chemists' in the UK. Branches of Boots (www.boots.com) and larger supermarkets will have a pharmacy. Most keep shop hours (9am-6pm Mon-Sat) but the Boots store at 44-46 Regent Street, Mayfair, W1B 5RA (7734 6126), opens until 11.30pm (6.30pm Sun).

STDs, HIV & AIDS

NHS Genito-Urinary Clinics (such as the Centre for Sexual Health) are affiliated with major hospitals. They provide free, confidential STD testing and treatment, as well as treating other problems such as thrush and cystitis. They also offer counselling about HIV and other STDs, and can conduct blood tests.

The NHS website (www.nhs.uk) also has information, including clinic locations. For helplines, *see p413*; for abortion and contraception, *see p412*.

Mortimer Market Centre for Sexual Health *Mortimer Market, Capper Street, off Tottenham Court Road, Fitzrovia, WC1E 6JB (3317 5252, www.cnwl.nhs.uk). Goodge Street or Warren Street tube. Open 9am-6pm Mon, Thur; 9am-7pm Tue; 1-6pm Wed; 9am-3pm Fri. Map p194 K5.*

Terrence Higgins Trust *314-320 Gray's Inn Road, King's Cross, WC1X 8DP (0808 802 1221, www.tht.org.uk). King's Cross St Pancras tube/rail.*

Open 9.30am-5.30pm Mon-Fri.
Helpline 10am-8pm Mon-Fri.
Map p212 N4.
Advice for those with HIV/AIDS,
their relatives, lovers and friends.

HELPLINES

Helplines dealing with sexual
health issues are listed above,
under STDs, HIV & AIDS.

Alcoholics Anonymous *0800
917 7650, www.alcoholics-
anonymous.org.uk. Open
10am-10pm daily.*

**Citizens' Advice
Bureaux** *03444 111 444 , www.
citizensadvice.org.uk.*
The council-run Citizens' Advice
Bureaux offer free legal, financial
and personal advice. Check the
phone book or see the website for
the address of your nearest office.

Missing People *116 000
freephone, www.missingpeople.
org.uk. Open 24hrs daily.*
Information on anyone who is
reported missing.

NHS Direct *111, www.nhsdirect.
nhs.uk. Open 24hrs daily.*
A free, first-stop service for
medical advice on all subjects.

Rape Crisis *0808 802 9999,
www.rapecrisis.org.uk. Open
noon-2.30pm, 3-5.30pm, 7-9.30pm
Mon-Fri; noon-2.30pm, 7-9.30pm
Sat, Sun.*
Information and support.

Samaritans *freephone 116 123,
www.samaritans.org. Open
24hrs daily.*
General helpline for those under
emotional stress.

Victim Support *0808 168 9111,
www.victimsupport.org.uk.
Open 8am-8pm Mon-Fri; 24hrs
Sat, Sun.*
Emotional and practical support
for victims of crime.

ID

Passports and photographic
driver's licences are acceptable
forms of ID.

INTERNET

Most hotels have free high-speed
internet (though some of the
more expensive ones still charge
a fee) and establishments all
over town, especially cafés, have
wireless access, usually free.
Even the Tube is now on Wi-Fi
– although you can only use it
while you're in certain stations:
see tfl.gov.uk/campaign/
station-wifi.

LEFT LUGGAGE

Airports

Gatwick Airport *01293 569 900.*

Heathrow Airport *8759 3344.*

London City Airport *7646 0088.*

Luton Airport *01582 405100.*

Stansted Airport *0330 223 0893.*

Rail & bus stations

London stations tend to have
left-luggage desks rather than
lockers. Call 0845 748 4950
for details.

Charing Cross *7930 5444. Open
7am-11pm daily.*

Euston *7387 1499. Open
7am-11pm daily.*

King's Cross *7837 4334. Open
7am-11pm daily.*

Paddington *7262 0344. Open
7am-11pm daily.*

Victoria *7963 0957. Open
7am-midnight daily.*

LEGAL HELP

Those in difficulties can visit
a **Citizens' Advice Bureau**
(*see p413*) or contact the
Law Centres Federation (*see
below*). Try the **Legal Services
Commission** (0845 345 4345,
www.legalservices.gov.uk)
for information. If you're
arrested, you should call your
embassy (*see p411*).

Law Centres Federation *3637
1330, www.lawcentres.org.uk.
Open 11am-5.30pm Mon-Fri.*
Free legal help for people who
can't afford a lawyer and live
or work in the immediate area;
this office connects you with the
nearest centre.

LGBT

For information on gay and
lesbian life in London, *see
pp328-335*. The phone lines
that we list below provide general
help and information for gay and
lesbian people; for HIV and AIDS
services, *see p412*.

London Friend *86 Caledonian
Road, N1 9DN (7833 1674,
londonfriend.org.uk). Open 7.30-
9.30pm Mon-Wed.*

**London Lesbian & Gay
Switchboard** *0300 330
0630, www.llgs.org.uk. Open
10am-11pm daily.*

LOST PROPERTY

Always inform the police if you
lose anything, if only to validate
insurance claims. Only dial 999
if violence has occurred; use 101
for non-emergencies. Report lost
passports both to the police and
to your embassy (*see p411*).

Airports

For items left on the plane,
contact the relevant airline.
Otherwise, phone the following:

Gatwick Airport *01293 223 457.*

Heathrow Airport *0844 824 3115.*

London City Airport *7646 0000.*

Luton Airport *01582 809174.*

Stansted Airport *0844 824 3109.*

Public transport

Transport for London *Lost
Property Office, 200 Baker
Street, Marylebone, NW1 5RZ
(0343 222 1234, www.tfl.gov.uk/
lostproperty). Baker Street tube.
Open 8.30am-4pm Mon-Fri.
Map p140 H5.*
Allow two to ten working days
from the time of loss. If you lose
something on a bus, call 0343
222 1234 and ask for the numbers
of the depots at either end of
the route. For tube losses, pick
up a lost-property form from
any station. There is a fee to
cover costs.

Taxis

The Transport for London office
(*see p405*) deals with property
found in registered black cabs.
Allow two to ten days from the
time of loss. For items lost in
a minicab or Über, contact the
relevant company.

MEDIA

Magazines & newspapers

Time Out remains London's only quality listings magazine – and it's free. If you want to know what's going on and whether it's any good, this is the place to look. It's widely available in central London every Tuesday. Head to the website www.timeout.com/london for regular updates and more comprehensive listings. The capital's main daily paper (also free) is the sensationalist *Evening Standard*, published Monday to Friday. In the mornings, in tube station dispensers and discarded in the carriages, you'll find *Metro*, a free *Standard* spin-off.

Radio

The stations below are broadcast on standard wavebands as well as digital, where they are joined by interesting additional channels (notably the BBC's genre-busting music channel 6 Music).

Absolute *105.8 FM.*
Laddish rock.

BBC London *94.9 FM.*
All things to do with the capital.

BBC Radio 1 *98.8 FM.*
Youth-oriented pop, indie and dance.

BBC Radio 2 *89.1 FM.*
Bland during the day; better after dark.

BBC Radio 3 *91.3 FM.*
Classical music dominates, but there's also discussion, world music and arts.

BBC Radio 4 *93.5 FM, 198 LW.*
The BBC's main speech station is led by news agenda-setter *Today* (6-9am Mon-Fri, 7-9am Sat).

BBC Radio 5 *Live 693, 909 AM.*
Rolling news and sport. Avoid the morning phone-ins, but Test Match Special cricket commentary is a British institution.

BBC World Service *648 AM.*
Some repeats, some new shows, transmitted globally.

Capital *FM 95.8 FM.*
Pop and chat.

Classic *FM 100.9 FM.*
Easy-listening classical.

Heart FM *106.2 FM.*
Capital FM for grown-ups.

Kiss *100 FM.*
Dance music.

LBC *97.3 FM.*
Phone-ins and talk.

Magic *105.4 FM.*
Familiar pop.

Resonance *104.4 FM.*
Arts radio – an inventively oddball mix.

Smooth *102.2 FM.*
Aural wallpaper.

XFM *104.9 FM.*
Alternative-ish rock.

Television

With a multiplicity of formats, there are plenty of pay-TV options, but binge-watching quality drama via on-demand services is the current obsession. The five main free-to-air networks are as follows:

BBC One
The Corporation's mass-market station. Relies too much on soaps, game shows and lifestyle TV, but has high-quality offerings too, not least the excellent news coverage. The BBC runs no commercials.

BBC Two
A reasonably intelligent cultural cross-section, but now upstaged by BBC Four.

ITV
Weekday mass-appeal shows, with ITV2 producing similar fare.

Channel 4
Successful US imports, more or less unwatchable home-grown entertainment, some great documentaries and quality news.

Channel Five
From high culture to lowbrow filth. An unholy mix.

Satellite, digital and cable channels include the following:

BBC Four
Highbrow stuff, including fine documentaries and dramas.

BBC News
Rolling news.

BBC Parliament
Live debates.

CBBC, CBeebies
Children's programmes – the latter for toddlers.

Discovery Channel
Science and nature documentaries.

E4, More4, Film4
Channel 4's entertainment and movie channels.

5USA
US comedy and drama, plus Australian soaps.

ITV2, ITV3, ITV4
US shows on 2, British reruns on 3 and 4.

Sky News
Rolling news.

Sky One
Sky's version of ITV.

Sky Sports
Four channels.

MONEY

Britain's currency is the pound sterling (£). One pound equals 100 pence (p). Coins are copper (1p, 2p), silver (round: 5p, 10p; seven-sided: 20p, 50p), yellowy-gold or silver in the centre with a yellowy-gold edge (£2). From March 2017, the £1 coin is being replaced by a new 12-sided silver coin with gold-coloured edge; the old yellowy-gold £1 coin ceases to be legal tender in October 2017. Paper notes are blue (£5), orange (£10), purple (£20) or red (£50). You can exchange foreign currency at banks, bureaux de change and post offices; there's no commission charge at the last of these (for addresses of the most central, *see p415*). Many large stores also accept euros (€), notwithstanding Brexit.

Western Union *0808 234 9168, www.westernunion.co.uk.*
The old standby for sending and receiving money. Chequepoint (*see p415*) also offers this service.

Banks & ATMs

ATMs can be found inside and outside banks, in some shops and in larger stations. Machines in many commercial premises levy a charge for each withdrawal, usually £1.50. If you're visiting from outside the UK, your card should work via one of the debit networks, but check charges in advance. ATMs also allow you to make withdrawals on your credit card if you know your PIN; you'll be charged interest plus, usually, a currency-exchange fee. Generally, getting cash with a card is the cheapest form of currency exchange but there are hidden charges, so do your research.

Credit cards, especially Visa and MasterCard, are accepted in most shops (except small corner shops) and restaurants (except caffs). However, American Express and Diners Club tend to be accepted only at more expensive outlets. You will usually have to have a PIN number to make a purchase.

No commission is charged for cashing sterling travellers' cheques if you go to one of the banks affiliated with the issuing company. You do have to pay to cash travellers' cheques in foreign currencies, and to change cash. You will always need to produce ID when you want to cash travellers' cheques.

Bureaux de change

You'll be charged for cashing travellers' cheques or buying and selling foreign currency at bureaux de change. Major stations have bureaux, and there are many in tourist areas and on major shopping streets. Most open 8am-10pm.

Chequepoint 550 Oxford Street, W1C 1LY (7724 6127, www. chequepoint.com). Marble Arch tube. **Open** 24hrs daily. **Map** p140 G7. Other locations throughout the city.

Covent Garden FX 30A Jubilee Market Hall, Covent Garden, WC2E 8BE (7240 9921, www. coventgardenfx.com). Covent Garden tube. **Open** 9.30am-6pm Mon-Fri; 10am-4pm Sat; 10am-2pm Sun. **Map** p181 M8.

Thomas Exchange 5 Market Place, W1W 0AE (7637 7336, www. thomasexchange.co.uk). Oxford

Circus tube. **Open** 9am-6pm Mon-Fri; 10am-5pm Sat. **Map** p140 K7.

Lost/stolen credit cards

Report lost or stolen credit cards both to the police and to the 24-hour phone lines listed below.

American Express 01273 696 933, www.americanexpress.com.

Diners Club 0845 862 2935, www. dinersclub.co.uk.

MasterCard 0800 964767, www. mastercard.com.

Visa 0800 891725, www. visa.co.uk.

Tax

With the exception of food, books, newspapers and a few other items, purchases in the UK are subject to Value Added Tax (VAT), aka sales tax. The rate is currently set at 20%. VAT is included in all prices quoted by mainstream shops, although it may not be included in hotel rates.

Foreign visitors may be able to claim back the VAT paid on most goods that are taken out of the EC (European Community) as part of a scheme generally called 'Tax Free Shopping'. To be able to claim a refund, you must be a non-EC visitor to the UK, or a UK resident emigrating from the EC. When you buy the goods, the retailer will ask to see your passport, and will then ask you to fill in a simple refund form. You need to have one of these forms to make your claim; till receipts alone will not do. If you're leaving the UK direct for outside the EC, you must show your goods and refund form to UK customs at the airport/port from which you're leaving. If you're leaving the EC via another EC country, you must show your goods and refund form to customs staff of that country.

After customs have certified your form, get your refund by posting the form to the retailer from which you bought the goods or to a commercial refund company, or by taking your form to a refund booth to get

immediate payment. Customs are not responsible for making the refund: when you buy the goods, ask the retailer how the refund is paid.

OPENING HOURS

Government offices close on bank (public) holidays (see p416), but big shops often remain open, with only Christmas Day sacrosanct. Most attractions remain open on the other public holidays.

Banks 9am-4.30pm (some close at 3.30pm, some 5.30pm) Mon-Fri; some also Sat mornings.

Businesses 9am-5pm Mon-Fri.

Post offices 9am-5.30pm Mon-Fri; 9am-noon Sat.

Pubs & bars 11am-11pm Mon-Sat; noon-10.30pm Sun; many pubs and bars, particularly in central London, stay open later.

Shops 10am-6pm Mon-Sat, some to 8pm. Many also open on Sun, usually 11am-5pm or noon-6pm.

POLICE

For emergencies, call 999. The non-emergency number is 101. London's police are used to helping visitors. If you've been robbed, assaulted or a victim of crime, go to your nearest police station. (We've listed a handful in central London; look under 'Police' in Directory Enquiries, see p415.)

If you have a complaint, ensure that you take the offending officer's identifying number (it should be displayed on his or her epaulette). The Independent Police Complaints Commission website, www.ipcc.gov.uk, has details of how to complain to the relevant police force.

Belgravia Police Station 202-206 Buckingham Palace Road, Pimlico, SW1W 9SX. Victoria tube/rail. **Map** p100 J12.

Charing Cross Police Station Agar Street, Covent Garden, WC2N 4JP. Charing Cross tube/rail. **Map** p181 M8.

Holborn Police Station *10 Lambs Conduit Street, Bloomsbury, WC1N 3NR. Holborn tube.* **Map** *p194 N6.*

Islington Police Station *2 Tolpuddle Street, Islington, N1 0YY. Angel tube.* **Map** *pull-out O3.*

Kensington Police Station *72 Earls Court Road, W8 6EQ. High Street Kensington tube.*

West End Central Police Station *27 Savile Row, Mayfair, W1S 2EX. Oxford Circus tube.* **Map** *p140 K8.*

POSTAL SERVICES

The UK has a reliable postal service. Royal Mail customer services are on 0845 774 0740. For business enquiries, call 0845 795 0950.

Post offices are usually open 9am-5.30pm during the week and 9am-noon on Saturdays, although some post offices shut for lunch and smaller offices may close for one or more afternoons each week. Some central post offices are listed below; for others, check the Royal Mail website www.royalmail.com.

You can buy individual stamps at post offices, and books of six or 12 first- or second-class stamps at newsagents and supermarkets that display the appropriate red sign. A first-class stamp for a regular letter costs 65p; second-class stamps are 56p. It costs 90p to send a postcard abroad. For details of other rates, see the Royal Mail website.

Post offices

Post offices are usually open 9am-5.30pm Mon-Fri and 9am-noon Sat, with the exception of (11 Lower Regent Street, SW1Y 4LR, 0845 611 2970), which opens 8am-6.30pm Mon-Fri; 9am-5.30pm Sat; noon-4pm Sun. Listed below are the other main central London offices. For general enquiries, call 0845 611 2970 or consult www.postoffice.co.uk.

Baker Street *no.111, Marylebone, W1U 6SG. Baker Street tube.* **Map** *p140 H6.*

Great Portland Street *nos.54-56, Fitzrovia, W1W 7NE. Oxford Circus tube.* **Map** *p194 K6.*

High Holborn *no.181, Holborn, WC1V 7RL. Holborn tube.* **Map** *p212 M7.*

Poste restante

If you want to receive mail while you're away, you can have it sent to Lower Regent Street Post Office (*see above*), where it will be kept for a month. Your name and 'Poste Restante' must be clearly marked on the letter. You'll need ID to collect it.

PUBLIC HOLIDAYS

On public holidays (bank holidays), many shops remain open, but public-transport services generally run to a Sunday timetable. On Christmas Day, almost everything, including public transport, closes down.

Good Friday *Fri 30 Mar 2018, Fri 19 Apr 2019*

Easter Monday *Mon 2 Apr 2018, Mon 22 Apr 2019*

May Day Holiday *Mon 1 May 2017, Mon 7 May 2018, Mon 6 May 2019*

Spring Bank Holiday *Mon 29 May 2017, Mon 28 May 2017, Mon 27 May 2019*

Summer Bank Holiday *Mon 28 Aug 2017, Mon 27 Aug 2017, Mon 26 May 2019*

Christmas Day *Mon 25 Dec 2017, Tue 25 Dec 2018, Wed 26 Dec 2019*

Boxing Day *Tue 28 Dec 2017, Wed 26 Dec 2018, Thur 26 Dec 2019*

New Year's Day *Mon 1 Jan 2018, Tue 1 Jan 2019 (bank holiday Mon 2 Jan 2016)*

RELIGION

Times of services may vary, particularly at festivals and holy days; phone to check.

Anglican & Baptist

Bloomsbury Central Baptist Church *235 Shaftesbury Avenue, Covent Garden, WC2H 8EP (7240 0544, www.bloomsbury.org.uk). Tottenham Court Road tube.*

Services & meetings 11am, 6pm Sun. **Map** *p181 M7.*

St Paul's Cathedral *For listings, see p224.* **Services** *7.30am, 8am, 12.30pm, 5pm Mon-Sat; 8am, 10.15am, 11.30am, 3.15pm, 6pm Sun.* **Map** *p212 P7.*

Westminster Abbey *For listings, see p106.* **Services** *7.30am, 8am, 12.30pm, 5pm Mon-Sat; 8am, 10am, 11.15am, 3pm, 5.45pm, 6.30pm Sun.* **Map** *p100 L10.*

Buddhist

Buddhapadipa Thai Temple *14 Calonne Road, Wimbledon, SW19 5HJ (8946 1357, www.watbuddhapadipa.org). Wimbledon tube/rail then bus 93.* **Open** *Temple 9.30am-5.30pm Mon-Fri; 9am-6pm Sat, Sun. Meditation retreat 7-9.30pm Tue, Thur; 4-5.30pm Sat, Sun.*

London Buddhist Centre *51 Roman Road, Bethnal Green, E2 0HU (8981 1225, www.lbc.org.uk). Bethnal Green tube.* **Open** *10am-5pm Mon-Sat.*

Catholic

Brompton Oratory *For listings, see p132.* **Services** *7am, 8am (Latin mass), 10am, 12.30pm, 6pm (Latin mass) Mon-Fri; 7am, 8am (Latin mass), 10am, 6pm Sat; 8am, 9am (Latin mass), 10am, 11am, 12.30pm, 4.30pm, 7pm Sun.* **Map** *p122 F11.*

Westminster Cathedral *For listings, see p112.* **Services** *7am, 8am, 10.30am (Latin mass), 12.30pm, 1.05pm, 5pm (Vespers), 5.30pm Mon-Fri; 8am, 9am, 10.30am, 12.30pm, 6pm Sat; 8am, 9am, 10.30am, noon, 5.30pm, 7pm Sun.* **Map** *p100 K11.*

Islamic

East London Mosque *82-92 Whitechapel Road, Whitechapel, E1 1JQ (7650 3000, www.eastlondonmosque.org.uk). Aldgate East tube.* **Services** *times vary; check website for details.* **Map** *p212 T7.*

Islamic Cultural Centre & London Central Mosque *146 Park Road, Marylebone, NW8 7RG (7724 3363, www.iccuk.org). Baker*

Street tube or bus 13, 113, 274.
Services times vary; check website for details. *Map p140 G4.*

Jewish

Liberal Jewish Synagogue *28 St John's Wood Road, St John's Wood, NW8 7HA (7286 5181, www. ljs.org). St John's Wood tube.* *Services 6.45pm Fri; 11am Sat.* *Map pull-out F4.*

West Central Liberal Synagogue *The Montagu Centre, 21 Maple Street, Fitzrovia, W1T 4BE (7636 7627, www.wcls.org. uk). Warren Street tube.* *Services times vary; check website for details.* *Map p194 K5.*

Methodist & Quaker

Methodist Central Hall *Storey's Gate, Westminster, SW1H 9NH (7654 3809, www.methodist-central-hall.org.uk). St James's Park tube.* *Services 12.45pm Wed; 11am, 5.30pm Sun.* *Map p100 L10.*

Religious Society of Friends (Quakers) *173-177 Euston Road, Bloomsbury, NW1 2BJ (7663 1000, www.quaker.org.uk). Euston tube/Overground/rail.* *Meetings 11am daily; 6.30-9pm Mon; 6.30pm Thur; 11am Sun.* *Map p194 L4.*

SAFETY & SECURITY

Notwithstanding the terrorist outrages of 2017, you're much more likely to get hurt in a car accident than as a result of criminal activity, but pickpockets do haunt busy shopping areas and transport nodes as they do in all cities.

Use common sense and follow some basic rules. Keep wallets and purses out of sight, and handbags securely closed. Never leave bags or coats unattended, beside, under or on the back of a chair – even if they aren't stolen, they could trigger a bomb alert. Don't put bags on the floor near the door of a public toilet. Don't take short cuts through dark alleys and car parks. Keep your passport, cash and credit cards in separate places. Don't carry a wallet in your back pocket. And always be aware of your surroundings.

SMOKING

A ban on smoking in all enclosed public spaces, including pubs, bars, clubs, restaurants, hotel foyers and shops, as well as on public transport, was introduced in 2007. Smokers now face a penalty fee of £50 or a maximum fee of £200 if they are prosecuted for smoking in a smoke-free area. Many bars and clubs offer smoking gardens or terraces for smokers.

TELEPHONES

Dialling & codes

London's dialling code is 020; standard landlines have eight digits after that. You don't need to dial the 020 from within the area, so we have not given it in this book.

If you're calling from outside the UK, dial your international access code, then the UK code, 44, then the full London number, omitting the first 0 from the code. For example, to make a call to 020 7813 3000 from the US, dial 011 44 20 7813 3000. To dial abroad from the UK, first dial 00, then the relevant country code from the list below. For more international dialling codes, check the phone book or see www.kropla.com/dialcode.htm.

Australia *61*

Canada *1*

New Zealand *64*

Republic of Ireland *353*

South Africa *27*

USA *1*

Mobile phones

Mobile phones in the UK operate on the 900 MHz and 1800 MHz GSM frequencies common throughout most of Europe. If you're travelling to the UK from Europe, your phone should be compatible; if you're travelling from the US, it may not be. Either way, check your phone is set for international roaming, and that your service provider at home has a reciprocal arrangement with a UK provider.

The simplest option may be to buy a 'pay-as-you-go' phone (about £10-£200); there's no monthly fee – you top up talk time using a card. Check before buying whether it can make and receive international calls.

Operator services

Call 100 for the operator if you have difficulty in dialling; for an alarm call; to make a credit card call; for information about the cost of a call; and for help with international person-to-person calls. Dial 155 for the international operator if you need to reverse the charges (call collect) or if you can't dial direct; this service is very expensive.

Directory Enquiries

This service is now provided by various six-digit 118 numbers. They're pretty pricey to call: dial (free) 0800 953 0720 for a rundown of options and prices. The best known is 118 118. Calls from a BT landline cost £1.88 + £2.57 per minute thereafter; 118 888 charges 59p per call, then £1.29 per minute; 118 811 charges 75p per call. Calls from other networks or a mobile may cost more. Online, the www. ukphonebook.com offers ten free credits a day to UK residents; overseas users get the same credits if they keep a positive balance in their account.

Yellow Pages This 24-hour service lists phone numbers of businesses in the UK. Dial 118 247 (£2.75 connection charge plus £2.75p/min) and identify the type of business you require, and where in London. Online, try www.yell.com.

Public phones

Public payphones take coins or credit cards (sometimes both). The minimum cost is 60p (including a 40p connection charge); local and national calls are charged at 60p for 30mins then 10p for each subsequent 15mins. Some payphones, such as the counter-top ones found in pubs, require more. International calling cards, offering bargain minutes via a freephone number, are widely available in shops.

TIME

London operates on Greenwich Mean Time (GMT), five hours ahead of the US's Eastern Standard Time. In spring (25 March 2018) the UK puts its clocks forward by one hour to British Summer Time. In autumn (29 October 2017, 28 October 2018), the clocks go back to GMT.

TIPPING

In Britain, it's accepted that you tip in taxis, minicabs, restaurants (some waiting staff rely heavily on tips), hotels, hairdressers and some bars (not pubs). Around 10% is normal, but some restaurants add as much as 15%. Always check whether service has been included in your bill: some restaurants include an automatic service charge, but also give the opportunity for a gratuity when paying with a card.

TOILETS

Pubs and restaurants generally reserve the use of their toilets for customers. However, all mainline rail stations and a few tube stations – Piccadilly Circus, for one – have public toilets (you may be charged a small fee: have some coins handy for the entrance gate). Department stores usually have loos that

you can use free of charge, and museums (most no longer charge an entry fee) generally have good facilities. At night, options are much worse. The coin-operated toilet booths around the city may be your only option.

TOURIST INFORMATION

In addition to the tourist information centres listed below, travel information centres at King's Cross, Euston, Liverpool Street and Victoria stations, and at Piccadilly Circus tube station (*see p405*) sell tickets for travel and London attractions.

City of London Information Centre *St Paul's Churchyard, City, EC4M 8BX (7332 3456, www.cityoflondon.gov.uk).* **Open** *9.30am-5.30pm Mon-Sat; 10am-4pm Sun.* **Map** *p212 P7.*

Greenwich Tourist Information Centre *Old Royal Naval College, 2 Cutty Sark Gardens, Greenwich, SE10 0LW (0870 608 2000, www. visitgreenwich.org.uk). Cutty Sark DLR.* **Open** *10am-5pm daily.*

Holborn Information Kiosk *89-94 Kingsway, outside Holborn tube, WC2B 6AA (no phone).* **Open** *8am-6pm Mon-Fri.* **Map** *p212 M6.*

Twickenham Visitor Information Centre *Civic Centre, 44 York Street, Twickenham, Middx, TW1 3BZ (8891 1441,*

www.visitrichmond.co.uk). Twickenham rail. **Open** *9am-5.15pm Mon-Thur; 9am-5pm Fri.*

WEIGHTS & MEASURES

The UK is moving slowly and reluctantly towards full metrication. Distances are still measured in miles but all goods are officially sold in metric quantities, with no legal requirement for the imperial equivalent to be given. Nonetheless, imperial measurements are still more commonly used, so we use them in this guide.

Below are listed some useful conversions, first into the metric equivalents from the imperial measurements, then from the metric units back to imperial:

1 inch (in) = 2.54 centimetres (cm)
1 yard (yd) = 0.91 metres (m)
1 mile = 1.6 kilometres (km)
1 ounce (oz) = 28.35 grams (g)
1 pound (lb) = 0.45 kilograms (kg)
1 UK pint = 0.57 litres (l)
1 US pint = 0.8 UK pints or 0.46 litres
1 centimetre (cm) = 0.39 inches (in)
1 metre (m) = 1.094 yards (yd)
1 kilometre (km) = 0.62 miles
1 gram (g) = 0.035 ounces (oz)
1 kilogram (kg) = 2.2 pounds (lb)
1 litre (l) = 1.76 UK pints or 2.2 US pints

Further Reference

BOOKS

Fiction

Peter Ackroyd *Hawksmoor* Adventures of an occultist architect modelled on Wren's counterpart.

Martin Amis *London Fields* Darts and drinking way out east.

Ned Beauman *Glow* Bright young novelist takes on the rave scene in noughties south London.

Anthony Burgess *Dead Man in Deptford* Fictionalised biography of Marlowe.

Norman Collins *London Belongs to Me* Witty saga of '30s Kennington.

Sir Arthur Conan *Doyle The Complete Sherlock Holmes* Reassuring sleuthing shenanigans.

Joseph Conrad *The Secret Agent* Anarchism in seedy Soho.

Charles Dickens *Bleak House* The Victorian master's finest London-centric novel.

Anthony Frewin *London Blues* Kubrick assistant explores the 1960s Soho porn-movie industry.

Jeremy Gavron *An Acre of Common Ground* Best of the noughties glut of Brick Lane fiction.

George the Poet *Search Party* Buzzy debut from the council estate-born, Cambridge-educated poet.

Graham Greene *The End of the Affair* A tale of adultery, Catholicism and the Blitz.

Patrick Hamilton *Twenty Thousand Streets Under the Sky* Dashed dreams at the bar of the Midnight Bell in Fitzrovia.

Neil Hanson *The Dreadful Judgement* Embers of the Great Fire.

Melissa Harrison *Clay* East European immigrant and latch-key kid seek redemption amid the urban nature of south London.

Alan Hollinghurst *The Swimming Pool Library* Gay life in the former cruising hotspot Russell Square.

BS Johnson *Christie Malry's Own Double Entry* A London clerk plots revenge on... everybody.

Doris Lessing *The Golden Notebook* Nobel winner's feminist classic, set mainly in London.

Colin MacInnes *City of Spades; Absolute Beginners* Coffee 'n' jazz, Soho 'n' Notting Hill.

Michael Moorcock *Mother London* A roomful of psychiatric patients live a love letter to London.

Alan Moore *From Hell* Dark and epic graphic novel on the Ripper.

Nick Papadimitriou *Scarp* Hallucinatory explorations of the high ground north of London.

Derek Raymond *I Was Dora Suarez* The blackest London noir.

Nicholas Royle *The Matter of the Heart; The Director's Cut* Abandoned buildings and secrets.

Iain Sinclair *White Chappell/Scarlet Tracings* Psychogeographer in chief combines the Ripper and dodgy book dealers.

Sarah Waters *The Night Watch* World War II on the Home Front.

Virginia Woolf *Mrs Dalloway* A kind of London *Ulysses*.

Non-fiction

Peter Ackroyd *London: The Biography* Loving and wilfully idiosyncratic history of the city.

Nicholas Barton *The Lost Rivers of London* A classic study.

David Bownes, Oliver Green & Sam Mullins *Underground* Illustrated celebration of 150 years of the Tube, which opened in 1863.

James Cheshire & Oliver Uberti *The Information Capital* Fabulous infographics about all aspects of London life.

Mark Daly *Unseen London* Fine behind-the-scenes pics of the city.

Paul Du Noyer *In the City* London in song.

Henry Eliot and Mat Lloyd-Rose *Curiocity: In Pursuit of London* Endlessly brilliant compilation of genuinely fascinating trivia.

Sarah Hartley *Mrs P's Journey* Biography of the woman who created the A–Z street atlas.

Leo Hollis *The Stones of London* A superb take on the city's history – through 12 of its key buildings.

Lucy Inglis *Georgian London* Charming history of the period.

Simon Inglis *Played in London* Comprehensive and riveting account of London's sporting heritage.

Lee Jackson *Dirty Old London* Gripping tale of how the Victorians fought to clean up the Big Smoke.

Edward Jones & Christopher Woodward *A Guide to the Architecture of London*

Ben Judah *This is London* Migrants speak in a self-consciously dystopian portrait of the modern city.

Jenny Landreth *The Great Trees of London* Ancient trees in famous and unlikely city locations.

David Lawrence (ed) *Omnibus* Social history of the London bus.

Jenny Linford *London Cookbook* Unsung producers and chefs share their food secrets.

Jack London *The People of the Abyss* Poverty in the East End.

Anna Minton *Ground Control* Important questions about Canary Wharf-style developments – updated to cover the Olympic Park.

HV Morton *In Search of London* A sparky tour of post-Blitz London.

Iain Nairn *Nairn's London* Opinionated architecture critic's bracing take on the city in 1966.

George Orwell *Down and Out in Paris and London* Waitering, begging and starving.

Samuel Pepys *Diaries* Plagues, fires and bordellos.

Cathy Phillips (ed) *London through a Lens; Londoners through a Lens* Captivating photographs of the city from the Getty archive.

Roy Porter *London: A Social History* An all-encompassing work.

Sukhdev Sandhu *Night Haunts* London and Londoners after dark.

Iain Sinclair *Lights Out for the Territory* Time-warp visionary crosses London.

Craig Taylor *Londoners: The Days and Nights of London Now* A superb and revealing collection of interviews with modern Londoners.

Richard Trench & Ellis Hillman *London under London* Tunnels, lost rivers, disused tube stations and military bunkers.

Peter Watts *Up in Smoke: The Failed Dreams of Battersea Power Station* Multiple failings of the redevelopers of a London icon.

Ben Weinreb & Christopher Hibbert (eds) *The London Encyclopaedia* Indispensable brick of a book.

Jerry White *London in the 18th Century; London in the 19th Century; London in the 20th Century* How London became a global city.

FILMS

Blow-Up *dir Michelangelo Antonioni, 1966* Unintentionally hysterical film of Swinging London.

Death Line *dir Gary Sherman, 1972* Lost Victorian cannibal race is discovered in Russell Square tube station.

Dirty Pretty Things *dir Stephen Frears, 2002* Body-organ smuggling.

Fires Were Started *dir Humphrey Jennings, 1943* War propaganda about the London Fire Brigade.

How We Used to Live *dir Paul Kelly, 2013* Rare post-war footage, with Saint Etienne soundtrack.

Hyena *dir Gerard Johnson, 2015* London-set crime flick.

The Krays *dir Peter Medak, 1990* The life and times of the East End gangsters.

The Ladykillers *dir Alexander Mackendrick, 1951* Classic Ealing comedy.

Happy-Go-Lucky *dir Mike Leigh, 2008* Day and night with a north London optimist.

Lock, Stock & Two Smoking Barrels *dir Guy Ritchie, 1998* Cheeky London faux-gangster flick.

London *dir Patrick Keiller, 1994* Arthouse documentary tracing London's lost stories.

London: The Modern Babylon *dir Julien Temple, 2012* Rousing montage portrait, driven by music, of London from the birth of cinema.

The Long Good Friday *dir John MacKenzie, 1989* Classic London gangster flick.

The National Gallery *dir Frederick Wiseman, 2015* Inquisitive documentary on the employees and paintings of the historic gallery.

Oliver! *dir Carol Reed, 1968* Fun musical Dickens adaptation.

Paddington *dir Paul King, 2014* The immigrant Peruvian bear gets his own movie.

Passport to Pimlico *dir Henry Cornelius, 1949* Ealing comedy classic.

Peeping Tom *dir Michael Powell, 1960* Creepy serial-killer flick.

Performance *dir Nicolas Roeg & Donald Cammell, 1970* Cult movie to end all cult movies.

Sex & Drugs & Rock & Roll *dir Mat Whitecross, 2009* Delirious biopic of Ian Dury.

Skyfall *dir Sam Mendes, 2012* See the SIS building blown up and Bond nearly run over by the Tube.

28 Days Later *dir Danny Boyle, 2002* Post-apocalyptic London, with bravura opening sequence.

Withnail & I *dir Bruce Robinson, 1987* Classic Camden lowlife comedy.

Wonderland *dir Michael Winterbottom, 1999* Love, loss and deprivation in Soho.

MUSIC

Billy Bragg *Must I Paint You a Picture? The Essential Billy Bragg* The bard of Barking's greatest hits.

Blur *Parklife* Key Britpop album.

Burial *Untrue* Pioneering dubstep album – still the benchmark.

Chas & Dave *Don't Give a Monkey's* Cockney singalong.

The Clash *London Calling* Era-defining punk classic.

Dizzee Rascal *Boy in Da Corner* Rough-cut sounds and inventive lyrics from a Bow council estate.

Hot Chip *The Warning* Wonky electro-pop.

Ian Dury *New Boots & Panties!!* Cheekily essential listening from the Essex pub maestro.

The Jam *This is the Modern World* Weller at his fiercest and finest.

Kate Tempest *Everybody Down* Young Brockley-born street poet's debut album.

The Kinks *Something Else* 'Waterloo Sunset' and all.

Linton Kwesi Johnson *Dread, Beat an' Blood; Forces of Victory; Bass Culture* Angry reggae from the man Brixton calls 'the Poet'.

Little Simz *Stillness in Wonderland* London-born Nigerian rapper's concept album.

Madness *Ultimate Madness* The Nutty Boys' wonderful best.

Melt Yourself Down *Melt Yourself Down* Wigged-out psych-jazz-funk supergroup.

MIA *Arular* Agit-pop raver's debut album – and still her best.

Public Service Broadcasting *Inform–Educate–Entertain* Narration from documentaries set to music – shouldn't work, but it does.

Saint Etienne *Tales from Turnpike House* Kitchen-sink opera by London-loving indie dance band.

Skepta *Konnichiwa* Tottenham grime star's 2016 Mercury Prize winner.

Squeeze *Greatest Hits* Lovable south London geezer pop.

The Streets *Original Pirate Material* Pirate radio urban meets Madness on Mike Skinner's debut.

WEBSITES

www.bbc.co.uk/london News, travel, weather, sport.

www.britishpathe.com Archive newsreel footage, from spaghetti-eating contests to pre-war Soho.

bugwomanlondon.com North London nature obsessive.

catsmeatshop.blogspot.co.uk Expert on Victorian hygiene explains urine deflectors and the like.

diamondgeezer.blogspot.com One of London's key bloggers.

www.filmlondon.org.uk London's cinema organisation – with mapped location tours.

greatwen.com Engaged, fun and often thought-provoking blog by our 'London Today' author.

www.hidden-london.com Undiscovered gems – and a neat pronunciation guide to place names.

www.london.gov.uk The official website for the Greater London Assembly, the city's government.

londonist.com News, culture and things to do.

londonreconnections.blogspot.com Heaven for transport geeks: everything from rolling stock plans to major infrastructure work.

www.londonremembers.com Definitive site for London memorials.

mappinglondon.co.uk Great-looking site with the best maps – and ways of mapping – the city.

spitalfieldslife.com Lovely London blog: focused, charming, informative and very human.

www.timeout.com/london Eating, drinking, features and events listings – a vital resource.

www.tfl.gov.uk Information, journey planners and maps from Transport for London, the city's central travel organisation.

APPS

Appy Parking *(free)* Extremely helpful: shows you vacant parking spaces across London.

City Mapper *(free)* Simply the greatest London journey planner, smoothly integrating multimodal transport – tube, rail, bus and bike – with estimated times and much more.

Hailo *(free)* Calls a black cab, tells you how long it will be, and deducts the meter fare from your account.

London: A City Through Time *(£13.99)* Expensive for an app – but you get the superb London Encyclopaedia (clumsily typeset, but perfectly legible), plus interactives.

StreetMuseum *(free)* Brilliant Museum of London app – archive shots geolocated to where you're standing, with informative captions.

William Blake's London *(free)* Geolocate your way round the poet-artist's London with this Tate app.

Time Out London *(free)* Our indispensable guide to the week's happenings in the capital.

City Toilet Finder *(free)* Where's the nearest free public loo in the City?

Uber *(free)* Hails a minicab, with fare quotes – the cab is paid for through the app (prices rise, airline-style, with demand), so no cash is needed.

FURTHER REFERENCE

Index

INDEX

Picture credits

Pages 2 (top), 316 SHAUN JAMES COX/BFC; 2 (bottom) Lukasz Pajor/Shutterstock.com; 3, 64, 77, 271, 310 ElenaChaykinaPhotography/Shutterstock.com; 5, 237 Benjamin B/Shutterstock.com; 7, 14 (bottom), 102 Claudio Divizia/Shutterstock.com; 13 (top), 15 (bottom), 23 (bottom), 44, 58 (top), 172, 244, 325 Rob Greig/Time Out; 13 (bottom), 83, 302 Eugene Regis/Shutterstock.com; 14 (bottom), 48, 53, 54 (bottom) Alys Tomlinson/Time Out; 15 (top), 18 (top), 24 (top), 62, 135, 265 Britta Jaschinski/Time Out; 16 (middle), 41, 91 Helen Cathcart/El Pastór; 24 (bottom), 128, 333, 339 Michelle Grant/Time Out ; 16 (top), 193 Andrew Brackenbury/Time Out; 19 (top), 215, 373 Jonathan Perugia/Time Out ; 17 (top), 55, 167 Addie Chinn/Swift; 17 (bottom), 164 ChameleonsEye/Shutterstock. com; 18 (bottom), 315 Pres Panayotov/Shutterstock.com; 18 (middle) Air Images/Shutterstock.com; 19 (bottom), 341, 347, 362, 363 Time Out; 20 (bottom), 80 (top), 131, 261, 344 Ron Ellis/Shutterstock.com; 20 (top), 291, 374 Alexey Fedorenko/Shutterstock.com; 22, 139 Dutourdumonde Photography/Shutterstock.com; 23 (top) holbox/ Shutterstock.com; 16 (bottom), 25 (top), 226, 259, 292 Kiev.Victor/Shutterstock.com; 25 (bottom), 142, 221, 264 chrisdorney/Shutterstock.com ; 26 (bottom), 179 Christian Mueller/SHutterstock.com; 26 (top) Constantin Iosif/ Shutterstock.com; 27 (bottom), 31 Georgethefourth/Shutterstock.com; 27 (top) Scott Wishart/Time Out; 28 (bottom), 80 (bottom), 92, 115, 119, 130, 249, 409 I Wei Huang/Shutterstock.com; 28 (top) anyaivanova/ Shutterstock.com; 28 (middle) godrick/Shutterstock.com; 32 JStone/Shutterstock.com; 33, 330, 364 John Gomez/ Shutterstock.com; 34, 46, 359 Thinglass/Shutterstock.com; 35 Zoltan Gabor/Shutterstock.com; 37 Pat_Hastings/ Shutterstock.com; 38 (top & bottom) PeterMoulton/Shutterstock.com; 42, 54 (top) Andy Parsons/Time Out; 49, 169, 262 Ming Tang-Evans/Time Out; 50 Bao; 56 (top) Sager + Wilde; 56 (bottom) Oliver Dixon/Imagewise; 57 (top & bottom) Sipsmith Distillery; 58 (bottom) Dave Carr-Smith; 61 Kevin Lake/We Built This City; 63 (top) LN-CC; 63 (bottom), 66, 218 Ed Marshall/Time Out; 65 DrimaFilm/Shutterstock.com; 68 GagliardiImages/Shutterstock.com; 71 dade72/Shutterstock.com; 73 PriceM/Shutterstock.com; 81 Southbank Centre/Victor Frankowski ; 82, 198 FotoGraphic/Shutterstock.com; 85 Pajo rPawel/Shutterstock.com; 86 BMCL/Shutterstock.com; 87 A.B.G./ Shutterstock.com; 89 Marius_Comanescu/Shutterstock.com; 90, 111 Philip Bird LRPS CPAGB/Shutterstock.com; 95, 184, 235 Tony Baggett/Shutterstock.com; 97 Matt Hickman/Anspach & Hobday; 99, 201, 408 Bikeworldtravel/ Shutterstock.com; 106 Offcaania/Shutterstock.com; 109, 147, 234 Anton_Ivanov/Shutterstock.com; 114 Evikka/ Shutterstock.com; 117, 159 Anna Moskvina/Shutterstock.com; 121, 132, 182 4kclips/Shutterstock.com; 125, 388 ileana_bt/Shutterstock.com; 127 (bottom) Martin Hesko/Shutterstock.com; 127 (top) Bruno Mameli/Shutterstock. com; 145 Alex7/Shutterstock.com; 151, 279 Zabotnova Inna/Shutterstock.com; 144, 173 Elena Rostunova/ Shutterstock.com; 153 andersphoto/Shutterstock.com; 158 IR Stone/Shutterstock.com; 161 chaloemsak seesaikam/ Shutterstock.com; ; 165 Stephen Morris; 175 Social Eating House; 176 veroxdale/Shutterstock.com; 180 Julie Clopper/Shutterstock.com; 183 Heike Bohnstengel/Time Out ; 189 Alexandra King/Shutterstock.com; 190 Botond Horvath/Shutterstock.com; 200 Ben Gilbert/Wellcome Collection; 201, 301 Ben Rowe/Time Out; 205 pbombaert/ Shutterstock.com; 206 AC Manley/Shutterstock.com; 208 Roka; 211 peresanz/Shutterstock.com; 223 antb/ Shutterstock.com; 224 Kotsovolos Panagiotis/Shutterstock.com; 225 Luciano Mortula - LGM/Shutterstock.com; 239 Pabkov/Shutterstock.com; 243 Jennifer Balcombe; 245 marcela novotna/Shutterstock.com; 246 Brian S/ Shutterstock.com; 251 Alastair Wallace/Shutterstock.com; 255 Phillip Maguire/Shutterstock.com; 268 House of Hackney; 282, 390 BBA Photography/Shutterstock.com; 295 Ms Jane Campbell/Shutterstock.com; 296 csp/ Shutterstock.com; 299 Nathan Willock; 307 lukedyson.photography; 309 BBA Photography/Shutterstock.com; 311 stoyanh/Shutterstock.com; 312 Andrew Whitton/Fanatic 2017; 321 Alastair Philip Wiper; 326 Peter Macdiarmid/ Somerset House; 327 Adam Lee Davies; 329 James Gourley; 335 Heloise Bergman/Time Out ; 337 The O2; 349 Ronnie Sctott's Jazz Club; 353 Tristram Kenton; 357 Cedric Weber/Shutterstock.com; 360 Padmayogini/ Shutterstock.com; 368 a-image/Shutterstock.com; 371 inavanhateren/Shutterstock.com; 376 Attributed to Nicholas Hilliard [Public domain], via Wikimedia Commons; 377 Vincent Brault/Ens de Lyon William Hogarth [Public domain], via Wikimedia Commons; 378, 380 Everett Historical/Shutterstock.com; 385 Luke David Williams/Shutterstock.com; 386 Roman Babakin/Shutterstock.com; 391 Filip Kubala/Shutterstock.com; 394 Tom Sulllam Photography; 396 The Beaumont; 397 Great Northern Hotel; 398 Ed Reeve; 400 Hoxton Holborn; 402 Qbic London City Hotel; 406 mikecphoto/Shutterstock.com.

Credits

Crimson credits
Editor Simon Coppock
Assistant editor Nicola Gibbs
Contributors Miriam Bouteba, Simon
Coppock, Nicola Gibbs, Jonathan
Lennie, Andrzej Lukowski, Laura
Richards, Peter Watts
Proofreader Ros Sales
Layouts Patrick Dawson, Emilie Crabb, Angus
Dawson, Mihaela Botezatu
Cartography John Scott

Series Editor Sophie Blacksell Jones
Production Manager Kate Michell
Design Mytton Williams

Chairman David Lester
Managing Director Andy Riddle

Advertising Media Sales House
Marketing Lyndsey Mayhew-Dehaney
Sales Lyndsey Mayhew-Dehaney

Acknowledgements

The editor thanks: the staff at Time Out
London for their help, especially Tania
Ballantine, Oliver Keens, James Manning and
Ben Rowe for assistance way beyond the call
of duty; Liz Gibbons, Florence and Esther;
and all contributors to previous editions
of Time Out London whose work forms the
basis of this guide.

Photography credits
Front cover Getty Images/iStockphoto
Back cover left FotoGraphic/Shutterstock.
com, centre right Andrew Brackenbury/Time
Out, right Christian Mueller/Shutterstock.com
Interior Photography credits, *see p428.*

Publishing information
London City Guide 24th edition
© TIME OUT ENGLAND LIMITED 2017
August 2017

ISBN 978 1 780592 53 4
CIP DATA: A catalogue record for this book is
available from the British Library

Published by Crimson Publishing
19-21c Charles Street, Bath, BA1 1HX (01225
584 950, www.crimsonpublishing.co.uk) on
behalf of Time Out England.

Distributed by Grantham Book Services
Distributed in the US and Canada by
Publishers Group West (1-510-809-3700)

Printed by Grafostil

While every effort has been made by the
authors and the publishers to ensure that
the information contained in this guide is
accurate and up to date as at the date of
publication, they accept no responsibility
or liability in contract, tort, negligence,
breach of statutory duty or otherwise for
any inconvenience, loss, damage, costs or
expenses of any nature whatsoever incurred
or suffered by anyone as a result of any
advice or information contained in the guide
(except to the extent that such liability may
not be excluded or limited as a matter of law.

LONDON UNDERGROUND MAP

MAYOR OF LONDON

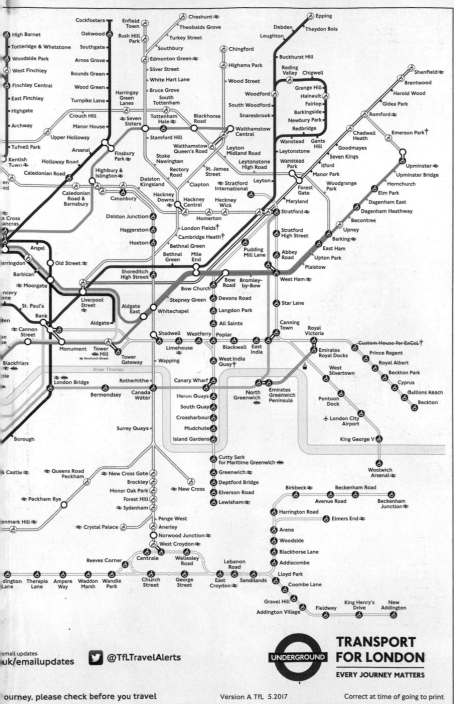

TRANSPORT
FOR LONDON

EVERY JOURNEY MATTERS

UNDERGROUND

@TfLTravelAlerts

email updates
uk/emailupdates

ourney, please check before you travel   Version A TfL 5.2017   Correct at time of going to print

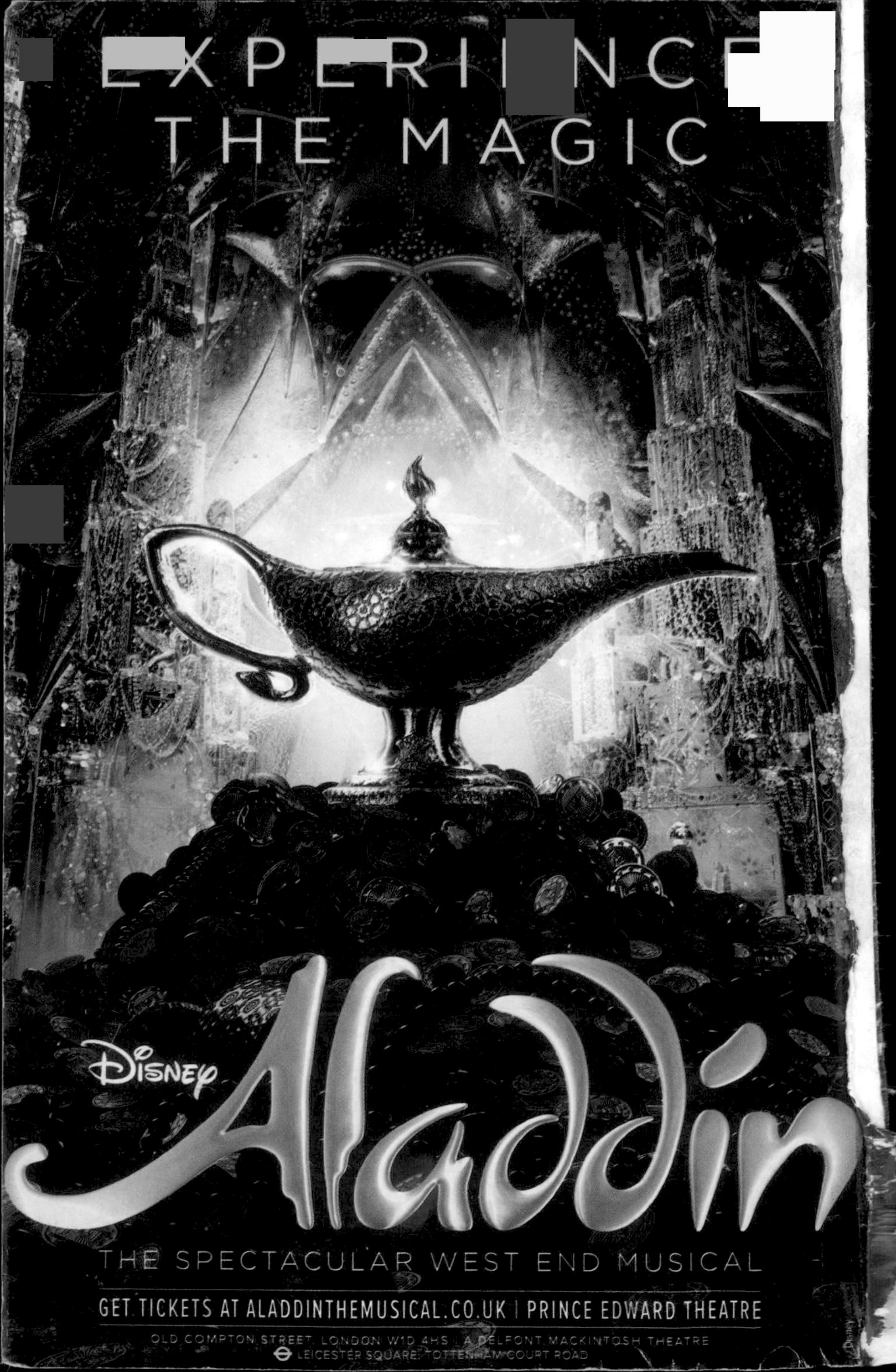

EXPERIENCE
THE MAGIC

Disney Aladdin

THE SPECTACULAR WEST END MUSICAL

GET TICKETS AT ALADDINTHEMUSICAL.CO.UK | PRINCE EDWARD THEATRE

OLD COMPTON STREET, LONDON W1D 4HS | A DELFONT MACKINTOSH THEATRE
LEICESTER SQUARE/TOTTENHAM COURT ROAD